World Bank Accountability – in Theory and in Practice

WORLD BANK ACCOUNTABILITY – IN THEORY AND IN PRACTICE

Andria Naudé Fourie

eleven
international publishing

Published, sold and distributed by Eleven International Publishing
P.O. Box 85576
2508 CG The Hague
The Netherlands
Tel.: +31 70 33 070 33
Fax: +31 70 33 070 30
e-mail: sales@elevenpub.nl
www.elevenpub.com

Sold and distributed in USA and Canada
International Specialized Book Services
920 NE 58th Avenue, Suite 300
Portland, OR 97213-3786, USA
Tel.: 1-800-944-6190 (toll-free)
Fax: +1 503 280-8832
orders@isbs.com
www.isbs.com

Eleven International Publishing is an imprint of Boom uitgevers Den Haag.

ISBN 978-94-6236-599-5
ISBN 978-94-6274-371-7 (E-book)

© 2016 Andria Naudé Fourie | Eleven International Publishing

Cover picture: © Curt Carnemark / World Bank, 'Group reading and writing, India', IN005S05.

Printed in The Netherlands

To Mynie Barwise,

for teaching me about literature and life.

Acknowledgements

To my colleagues at the Erasmus School of Law, Erasmus University Rotterdam, our intellectual interaction over the past decade has expanded my world of ideas beyond anything I would ever have imagined possible, while the friendship I've experienced while being in the austere corridors and overflowing offices of the L-building has filled me with lightness and a deep sense of grace. My sincerest gratitude to all of you.

It almost feels wrong to single out a few individuals, but I would also be remiss if I were not to specifically thank Prof. Dr. Ellen Hey (we can walk, cook, drink wine, appreciate art, music and nature – while also 'solving' many of the world's problems, and unearthing a few more in the process), Dr. Aleksandar Momirov (being able to quote extensively from *The West Wing* should surely qualify as some academic credential), as well as Prof. Dr. Sanne Taekema and Prof. Dr. Elaine Mak for helping me to shape the ideas contained in this book.

Another person that has helped me to shape my ideas – almost entirely through our virtual collaborations – is Prof. Dr. Daniel Bradlow. A heartfelt word of thanks – both to him, and to whomever can truly claim to have created the Internet.

As always, however, the errors and shortcomings are my doing.

Thank you, also, to the previous two Deans of the Erasmus School of Law – Prof. Dr. Maarten Kroeze and Prof. Dr. Susan Stoter – for agreeing to a virtual employment arrangement that (and I feel I can safely generalize here) few academic administrators would even have considered. *De wereld is mijn (t)huis* – indeed.

The research presented in this book would not have seen the light of day without a dedicated team who have worked with me – most of the time, virtually, and in different time zones – over a number of years. Thank you Paulo da Rosa, Jamaal Mohuddy and Emelie Norling. And to Emelie in particular: thank you for supporting me every step of the way and for teaching me that, if all else fails, there are always yoga and tea.

To Selma Hoedt and her team at Eleven Publishing/Boom Juridische Uitgevers – thank you, in particular, for your immense patience. A few deadlines went swooooosh as they flew by while you pretended, politely, not to have heard the noise.

Women continue to fret about whether they can have (or want) 'it all'; and while I still do not know what the 'it' or the 'all' supposedly entails, I am certain that I would not have been able to do 'anything' – including writing this book – without the help of a growing tribe of truly special women who are helping me to raise my daughters: Wilma, Mirelle, Shani, Mindy, Sam, Rhodora, Alejandra, Ann and Darcie – thank you, for 'everything.'

And to Cecile and Amelie, thank you for accepting that this is an important part of who I am. I doubt whether you and the women of your generation will figure 'it all' out either, but I do hope that you will always remember that whatever 'it all' may be for you *is* entirely up to you.

To Jac, finally, thank you for reformatting my footnotes. Fine; thank you for reformatting it three times. Thank you for tolerating my absences and my absentmindedness. But above all, thank you for thinking with me – about *thinking* and about *doing*.

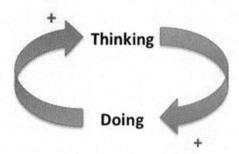

TABLE OF CONTENTS

Conclusion

TABLE OF FIGURES

INTRODUCTION

"As Yogi Berra said: 'In theory there is no difference between theory and practice. In practice there is.'"
– N. Taleb, *Antifragile: Things that Gain from Disorder* (2012) –

1   Towards a Comprehensive Shared Understanding on World Bank Accountability – in Theory and Practice

Why another book about *World Bank accountability*?

Much has certainly been said about the need to strengthen, enhance, expand, measure, assess, ensure or realize the accountability of international financial institutions such as the World Bank,[1] whereas much thought has gone into what such accountability should entail – as reflected in a vast body of literature that cuts across various disciplines and domains of practice.[2]

Much has also been done to translate theory into practice. Over the past few decades, for instance, the World Bank has implemented various reforms to its governance and management structures;[3] the Bank has increased the transparency of its operations by means of a far-reaching policy on Access to Information and has also adopted various measures aimed at ensuring public participation in the decision-making processes concerning Bank-financed development projects.[4] The World Bank has developed and applied an operational policy framework that is aimed at guiding and, in some respects, regulating all aspects of the Bank's development-lending operations, including the management of economic, social and environmental risks.[5] And, finally, the World Bank has established a range of internal 'accountability mechanisms' that are mandated to contribute to the enforcement of the operational policy framework – including mechanisms that are 'citizen-

---

1   Hereinafter, 'World Bank' or 'Bank', referring to the International Bank for Reconstruction and Development (IBRD), and the International Development Association (IDA). On international financial institutions (IFIs) and their operations, as situated in the international legal system, *see* in general Bradlow & Hunter (Eds.) (2010).
2   *See e.g.,* Von Bogdandy et al. (Eds.) (2010); Bradlow & Grossman (1995); Clark (2002); Clark et al. (Eds.) (2003); Coicaud & Heiskanen (Eds.) (2001); Danaher (Ed.) (1999); Darrow (2006); Hernández Uriz (2001); Horta (2002); Kingsbury et al. (2005); Miller-Adams (1999); Nanda (2004-2005); Reinisch (2001); Reinisch (2008); Shihata (1992-1993); Shihata (1988-1989); Shihata (2000); Van Putten (2008); Wellens (2002); Zweifel (2006); ILA (1998); ILA (2004); Head (2003-2004); Fox (1997); Bradlow (1996); Nanwani (2008); Cissé et al. (Eds.) (2012); Wouters et al. (Eds.); Van Putten (2008), pp. 32-65; *and* Raffer (2004).
3   *See e.g.,* Phillips (2009); *and* Bradlow *in* Cissé et al. (Eds.) (2012), e-Book. *Also see* section 3.1.1.
4   *See e.g.,* Miller-Adams (1999); Hunter *in* Bradlow & Hunter (Eds.) (2010); *and see* Independent Accountability Mechanisms Network (2012), pp. 4-5. *See e.g.,* the discussion *in* Ch. 11.
5   *See e.g.,* Bradlow & Chapman (2011); Freestone (2003); Kingsbury (1999); *and* Bradlow & Naudé Fourie (2013). *Also see* section 5.1.

driven' because their procedures can be triggered from outside the institution, by individuals.[6]

Indeed, it is on the basis of such efforts that we have been able to reach consensus that international financial institutions ('IFIs') such as the World Bank have a *duty of accountability*,[7] and it is through the interaction between theory and practice that we have started to draw the contours of this duty, while contemplating the implications thereof.

That being said, we are yet to arrive at the point where we can state that we have reached a comprehensive "shared understanding"[8] on what the accountability of international financial institutions *means* – in theory and in practice.

For some, the World Bank's efforts to address concerns about its accountability have not gone far enough. They question, for instance, the content and scope of operational policies aimed at managing economic, social and environmental risks;[9] or, are critical of the effectiveness of internal accountability mechanisms such as the Inspection Panel.[10] They argue that legal normativity has a distinct and crucial role to play in conceptualizing and operationalizing the World Bank and IFI accountability, but their arguments are influenced by the continued jurisprudential debate about the nature and purpose of international law, and how it operates.[11]

For others, the World Bank's efforts to address these criticisms have gone too far. They argue, for example, that the Bank's prolonged focus on accountability has come at the cost of institutional effectiveness and efficiency; and that the Bank's 'norm-based' approach, which involves the application and enforcement of the Bank's operational policy framework across its development operations, has made it too cumbersome and too expensive to 'do

---

6   *See e.g.*, the discussion *in* section 6.2.

7   As reflected, *e.g.*, in the conceptual work of the International Law Association – *see* ILA (1998) *and* ILA (2004).

8   Conklin (2005), p. 1.

9   *See e.g.*, MacKay (2005) *and* MacKay *in* Bradlow & Hunter (Eds.) (2010) (commenting on the adequacy of the Bank's policy on Indigenous Peoples). For criticism about the World Bank's latest safeguard policy review *see e.g.*, http://www.mintpressnews.com/world-bank-accused-transferring-safeguards-responsibility-borrowers/195453/. *Note*, a safeguard policy review has been initiated in 2012 and was ongoing at the time of writing (October 2015); for more on this review, *see* note 28, Ch. 5.

10 *See e.g.*, Circi (2006); Orakhelashvili (2005); Nurmukhametova (2006); Ananthanarayanan (2004); *and* Carrasco & Guernsey (2008).

11 For an overview of the major arguments in these debates, *see e.g.*, Kingsbury (1997-1998), pp. 348-367; Scobbie *in* Evans (2006), pp. 83-156; *and see* Chinkin *in* Shelton (Ed.) (2000), pp. 21-42. Chinkin notes (at p. 21): "Current debates about the forms and functions of international law-making are a continuation of long-standing tensions between those who assert the paramountcy of state consent and those who urge limitations on state action in favour of international regulation". In this regard, *also see* Higgins (1994), who argues (at p. 17) that the continued jurisprudential debate "is an admission of uncertainty at the heart of the international legal system" – which means that "until the answers to the question of identification, of provenance of norms, are more settled, [...] we do not have the tools for rendering more certain the content of particular norms [...]."

business with the Bank', especially compared with new and newly emerging competitors in the field of international development finance.[12]

The context in which the discourse on World Bank and IFI accountability is situated, moreover, has been undergoing significant change in some respects, while remaining largely static in others.

Since World Bank accountability first became the "catchcry of officials, scholars and activists" during the 1990s,[13] the "international financial and economic system" has been marked by a "growing complexity", which, in combination with a "deepening understanding of the complexities of poverty and development" have "changed the ways in which multi-lateral development banks (MDBs) operate."[14]

Moreover, ongoing shifts in global economic and political power have meant that multilateral development institutions increasingly have to "compete or cooperate with the private sector and other official creditors in funding projects in their member states."[15] "Middle-income countries such as Brazil and India can now borrow cheaply on international capital markets",[16] for instance, whereas China – long a prominent World Bank borrower – has emerged as an influential actor in the field of development finance.[17]

---

12   S. Donnan, 'World Bank: Stress Test', *Financial Times*, April 16, 2015, available at www.ft.com: "Few doubt the bank is in need of change. David Dollar, a former US Treasury official who spent 20 years at the bank, says it has long had a plodding bureaucracy that at times has caused some borrowing nations to shy away. He cites an Indian official who once told him: "Mr Dollar, the combination of our bureaucracy and your bureaucracy is deadly." On new competitors in the field of development finance, *see e.g.*, note 17, Ch. 1; *but also see* note 46, Ch. 3.

13   Woods (2001), p. 83.

14   Bradlow *in* Cissé et al. (Eds.) (2012), e-Book. On the effects of these changes, *also see* the discussion *in* sections 2.1 & 4.1. *Note*, multilateral development banks (MDBs) are a specific category within the broader group of international financial institutions – *see* Bradlow *in* Bradlow & Hunter (Eds.) (2010), pp. 2-5.

15   Bradlow *in* Cissé et al. (Eds.) (2012), e-Book.

16   *Id.*

17   *See e.g.*, G. Parker & A. Beattie, 'EIB Accuses China of Unscrupulous Loans', *Financial Times*, 28 November 2006, available at www.ft.com: "The world's development banks may have to water down the social and environmental conditions they attach to loans in Africa and elsewhere because they are being undercut by less scrupulous Chinese lenders, the European Investment Bank said on Tuesday. Philippe Maystadt, the EIB's president, said banks like his were operating in competition with Chinese lenders anxious to extend Beijing's influence across the world. 'The competition of the Chinese banks is clear,' said Mr Maystadt, whose European Union-backed bank is the world's biggest multilateral lender. 'They don't bother about social or human rights conditions'." *Also see* S. *Lindemann,* 'China's Development Finance to Africa – Risks and Opportunities for DAC Donors', KFW DEVELOPMENT RESEARCH, Focus on Development, No. 7, 16 September 2013, available at: https://www.kfw-entwicklungsbank.de/PDF/Download-Center/PDF-Dokumente-Development-Research/2013_11_15-FE_China_in-Afrika_EN.pdf. *Also see* Miller-Adams (1999), pp. 127-128: "In many ways China, by virtue of its size, is more important to the Bank than the Bank is to China. Nancy Alexander, a long-time observer of the Bank, recounts the story of a junior Bank official on a mission to China who asked his senior colleague whether the Bank was pressuring China to permit greater levels of grassroots participation in development. "The senior official replied, 'We are fortunate that China is allowing the World Bank to participate in its development efforts'." The author references N.C. Alexander (1998), 'The World Bank's New Strategic Alliances', Draft Paper, Development Bank Watchers' Project, Silver Spring Md.: Bread for the World Institute.

As a consequence of these changes, the World Bank's status as the world's 'premier lending institution' has increasingly come under pressure – to the extent, as some commentators have come to argue, that the World Bank is facing "[a] creeping irrelevance", and that the Bank's most recent wave of institutional changes (spearheaded by current World Bank Group President, Jim Yong Kim) is a necessity to counteract the Bank's "journey to the sidelines," or to prevent its "slide into insignificance."[18]

But for all the talk about change, several aspects that form an important part of the discourse on accountability have *not* changed – or, at least, have not changed enough. Development projects such as those (co-)financed by the World Bank and other development-lending institutions continue to involve a wide range of economic, social and environmental risks that require diligent management. And, in instances where these risks do materialize, they continue to result in material adverse effects that might be irreversible or costly to address – and, therefore, impede the realization of *sustainable development*.[19]

In addition, the international legal system remains ill equipped to address accountability issues, in particular from the perspective of 'project-affected people' who are not in a contractual relationship with development-lending institutions. Project-affected people adversely affected by development projects (co-)financed by multilateral development institutions remain without the possibility of legal recourse against these institutions, due to the (qualified) immunity of international organizations before domestic courts[20] and as a result of the limited standing (both of individuals and international institutions) before international judicial courts and tribunals.[21] And while it is generally acknowledged that MDBs, as subjects of the international legal order, have international legal obligations, the content and scope of these obligations remain a matter of debate, particularly since state actors remain the only parties to prominent international treaties governing international environmental and human rights law.[22]

---

18 R. Harding, 'World Bank: Man on a Mission', *Financial Times*, 7 April 2014, available at www.ft.com.
19 On the conceptualization of sustainable development as comprising social, economic and environmental areas ('pillars'), *see e.g.*, Birnie & Boyle (2002), pp. 44-47; Magraw & Hawke *in* Bodansky et al. (Eds.) (2007), pp. 613-638. *Also see* Freestone's remarks *at* note 27, Ch. 5.
20 *See e.g.*, Reinisch (2008); Schermers & Blokker (2003), §§ 1610-1612; Reinisch & Wurm *in* Bradlow & Hunter (Eds.) (2010), pp. 103-136; Herz *in* Bradlow & Hunter (Eds.) (2010), pp. 137-166; *and* Van Putten (2008), pp. 35-36. On the immunity of international organizations as a "structural" impediment to the implementation of an international legal regime on the responsibility of international organizations, *see e.g.*, Crawford (2007), pp. 5-6. *Also see* the World Bank's Articles of Agreement, Article VII.
21 *See e.g.*, Klabbers (2013), pp. 140-154; Schermers & Blokker (2003), §§ 686-482; *and* Crawford (2007), pp. 5-6.
22 *See e.g.*, Bradlow *in* Bradlow & Hunter (Eds.) 2010, pp. 29-30 *and see* pp. 338-389. On the issue of the World Bank's international human rights obligations, *see e.g.*, Darrow (2006); Van Putten (2008), pp. 39-43; McInerney-Lankford *in* Bradlow & Hunter (Eds.) (2010), pp. 239-286; *and* De Schutter *in* Wouters et al. (Eds.) (2010), pp. 51-128. On the 'gaps' in the international legal system and their effects on the accountability of international organizations, *also see* Bradlow & Hunter *at* note 178, Ch. 3. *Also see* the discussion *in* sections 5.1.1 & 5.3.2.

In fact, it is those aspects of the discourse that have remained largely static, which best explain why the accountability of international financial institutions such as the World Bank remains a "normatively desirable" outcome,[23] and why it continues to be a topic of significance – even as the discourse has to address the changes occurring in the underlying context.

1.1   AIM AND CENTRAL ARGUMENTS

With these arguments serving as its point of departure, this book aims to contribute towards the *progressive development of a comprehensive shared understanding* of what the accountability of international financial institutions such as the World Bank means *conceptually* (specifically at lower levels of abstraction that have to incorporate cumulative degrees of detail and complexity) and *operationally* (specifically including the perspective of individuals affected by development-lending operations).

Such a comprehensive shared understanding has to reflect the wide array of diverse *interests, demands, expectations and underlying conceptions* surrounding the multidimensional and interdisciplinary concept of 'accountability'.[24] It also has to address the multiple relationships (some competing or contradictory; others complementary, mutually reinforcing or interdependent) that drive the decisions, actions and behaviours of a wide range of participants.

The analysis presented here therefore aims to expound the *pluralism* and *dynamic complexity* of the particular context in which World Bank development-lending operations are situated – that is: a *transnational regulatory governance context*, which involves various levels of governance, different types of actors (participating in various capacities), different legal systems (international, regional, national, sub-national or local), as well as different forms of normativity (legal and social, or non-legal).[25]

Furthermore, the progressive development of a comprehensive shared understanding on accountability requires the *continuous interaction of the participants to this discourse*, which can be facilitated by the processes of *norm creation, norm application and norm enforcement* underlying the World Bank's development-lending operations.[26]

The analysis employs a conception of social and legal normativity that is based in constructivist and interactional thinking,[27] which can yield insights as to *nature* and *purpose*

---

23   Rubenstein (2007), p. 620. The author sets out various reasons "why accountability might be normatively desirable in a given context." (*Id.*)
24   *See* section 2.2.
25   *See* section 2.1.
26   *See* section 2.3.
27   *See* in general Brunnée & Toope (2010).

of *(social and legal) normativity,* as well as the *mechanism* through which it operates in transnational regulatory governance contexts.

1.2   SCOPE AND APPROACH

While this book focuses on *World Bank* accountability, the analysis presented here is of broader significance for international financial institutions with similar institutional shareholders and comparable development-lending operations.[28] Moreover, the analysis might also be of interest to other types of international organizations. "Given that the IFIs are facing complex and diverse economic, financial, political, social, and environmental issues," as Bradlow comments,

> it can be seen that they are on the cutting edge of difficult and important international law issues. How they respond to these issues will set precedents that have the potential to influence other international actors and to guide their own further responses to these issues.[29]

The scope of the analysis is specifically limited to the World Bank's *development-lending operations,* which, as defined here, are comprised of the *actors, governance* and *management structures,* the core *activities* and *processes,* as well as the intersecting *normative systems*[30] involved in the *design, planning, preparation, appraisal, approval, financing, implementation* and *closure* of *development projects* that are either *financed* or *co-financed* by the *World Bank.*[31]

Finally, the World Bank's development-lending operations are analyzed primarily from the perspective offered by the Bank's citizen-driven accountability mechanism, the

---

28   *See* Bissell & Nanwani (2009), p. 26, commenting that IFIs, despite their differences, "have similar classes of shareholders […] and […] the same donor countries championing accountability mechanisms," notably, "the United States and several European countries including the United Kingdom, Switzerland, Netherlands, and Germany." *Also see* Head (2003-2004), pp. 244-249, who notes that the MDBs finance similar projects, with similar approaches (*e.g.,* they operate on a "reimbursement basis, so that funds are transferred only against expenditures as they are actually incurred"). In addition, "most of the MDBs also engage in some degree in "policy-based" lending by which funds are provided to support (and in return for) the adoption by borrower governments of certain economic and financial policies favoured by the MDBs." (*Id.*) Further-more, MDBs share a number of common criticisms – including their "unaccountability and democracy deficit." (*Id.,* at p. 299.)

29   *See* Bradlow *in* Bradlow & Hunter (Eds.) (2010), pp. 25-30.

30   For a definition of normative systems, *see* section 2.3.

31   *Note:* the scope of this book excludes the project identification, closure and post-implementation stages, in line with the institutional mandate of the Inspection Panel – as discussed *e.g., in* section 4.1.2.

Inspection Panel.[32] Therefore, *Inspection Panel practice*[33] serves as the primary source for the analysis. Academic literature from various disciplinary areas – including public international law and international relations,[34] political science,[35] organization theory[36] and systems dynamics[37] – provide the secondary source.[38]

The remainder of this section will elaborate on the approach underlying the analysis of Inspection Panel practice. But before we proceed, it is important to clarify what has been excluded from the scope of the analysis.

Criticisms concerning the adequacy and/or effectiveness of World Bank measures aimed at addressing accountability concerns – such as commentary related to World Bank governance reforms, the operational policy framework and the Inspection Panel[39] – form an important part of the discourse and are, therefore, part of the analysis presented here. However, the analysis will not be used to formulate a conclusion as to the Panel's 'effectiveness', or, for that matter, about the 'general state' of World Bank accountability – in other words, whether the Bank *is* now more 'accountable' than it used to be, or whether it can now be said that the Bank *has* 'sufficiently' addressed accountability concerns.

There are a number of reasons for this. For one thing, the analytical source material – Inspection Panel practice and academic literature – does not provide enough empirical

---

32   Hereinafter, also 'Panel.'

33   Referring to all material that is generated over the course of the Inspection Panel process, and that pertains to Requests for Inspection (hereinafter, also 'Requests') that have been *registered* at the Panel between 1993 and 2011. All Inspection Panel practice material is publically available at: http://ewebapps.world-bank.org/apps/ip/Pages/Panel_Cases.aspx. *Note*, Requests that had been filed and *registered* at the Inspection Panel (as opposed to filed and *not registered*) have met basic 'admissibility criteria'. On the admissibility and eligibility criteria of the Inspection Panel processes, *see* the Inspection Panel Resolution, §§ 12-14; *and see* the Inspection Panel Operating Procedures (2014), sections 3.1. & 3.2. *Also note*, Inspection Panel practice documents typically contain a mixture of paragraphs and page numbering; thus, citations included throughout this book will specifically indicate whether it refers to a paragraph (§) or page (p./pp.).

34   Notably, international institutional law (*see e.g.*, Von Bogdandy et al. (Eds.) (2010); Alvarez (2005); *and* Bradlow & Hunter (Eds.) (2010)) and international legal theory (*see e.g.*, Brunnée & Toope (2010); *and* Krisch (2010)).

35   Notably, constructivist and interactional approaches – *see e.g.*, Shapiro & Stone Sweet (2002).

36   Notably, the disciplinary area that "is attuned to the internal dynamics of institutions" – *see e.g.*, Miller-Adams (1999), pp. 4-5: "Based in the discipline of sociology, the many variants of organization theory direct attention to the rules, both formal and informal, that guide the operation of an organization, and to the norms, values, and beliefs of its management and staff. An organization's culture, the pattern of norms and attitudes that cuts across the entire social unit, is an embodiment of these rules, norms, and beliefs."

37   Systems dynamics, which is a disciplinary component of systems theory, focuses on "understanding the dynamic behaviour of complex systems" – *see* Sterman, (2000), p. 4. Sterman also notes (*id.*, at pp. 4-5) that systems dynamics "is fundamentally interdisciplinary. Because [it is] concerned with the behaviour of complex systems, systems dynamics is grounded in the theory of nonlinear dynamics and feedback control developed in mathematics, physics, and engineering. Because we apply these tools to the behaviour of human as well as physical and technical systems, system dynamics draws on cognitive and social psychology, economics and other social sciences."

38   For more detail on the interdisciplinary research methodology underlying the analysis, *see* Naudé Fourie (2015) (forthcoming).

39   *See e.g.*, notes 9 & 10, Ch. 1.

data to support such conclusions. More importantly, however, the point of this analysis is to demonstrate why questions concerning 'effectiveness' are so complex to answer definitively; why measuring 'relative improvement' is so challenging. In expounding these issues, however, the analysis can provide some perspectives to those who are specifically engaged with questions concerning the effectiveness and/or adequacy of specific accountability measures.

1.2.1 Inspection Panel practice as a window onto World Bank development-lending operations

Others have commented extensively about the significance of the Inspection Panel's establishment – for instance, that it created a "legally relevant" relationship between the World Bank and project-affected people;[40] or that, as the first citizen-driven independent accountability mechanism ('IAM') of its kind, it provided the impetus for the establishment of similar mechanisms at other multilateral development banks.[41]

Reporting directly to the Board of Executive Directors, the Panel is mandated to investigate claims of alleged *World Bank* failures to comply with its operational policy framework.[42] Such claims of non-compliance must pertain to actual or potential "material adverse effects" – in other words, there has to be a *prima facie* 'causal link' between World Bank "actions or omissions" and actual or potential 'harm'.[43] While the Inspection Panel mechanism can be triggered by an Executive Director,[44] to date, all 'Requests for Inspection' have originated from outside the World Bank – that is, they have been filed by "two or more individuals" residing in the territory of a borrowing member state, and/or their duly authorized representatives (which tend to be local civil society actors).[45]

Once the Inspection Panel deems a Request to be 'admissible' for registration, 'eligible' for investigation and concludes that a full investigation is required, it makes a recommendation to the Board, which subsequently decides whether or not to authorize such an investigation.[46] Once the Board authorizes an investigation, the Inspection Panel verifies

---

40 *See e.g.*, Hey (1997), p. 61; *and* Woods (2001), p. 93.
41 For a comparative overview of IAMs at MDBs, *see e.g.*, Bradlow & Naudé Fourie *in* Hale & Hand (Eds.) (2011), p. 122.
42 International Bank for Reconstruction and Development, International Development Association, Resolution No. IBRD 93-10/Resolution No. IDA 93-6, "The World Bank Inspection Panel" (hereinafter, 'Inspection Panel Resolution', or 'Resolution'), § 12. *Note*, the Inspection Panel Resolution is included in the World Bank's Operations Manual as BP 17.55 (Inspection Panel), Annex A, B & C.
43 Inspection Panel Resolution, § 12.
44 *Id.*
45 *Id.*
46 For the admissibility and eligibility criteria, as well as the Inspection process, *see* the Inspection Panel's Operating Procedures (2014). For statistics on the Panel's findings of eligibility, recommendations of full investigations, and investigations authorized by the Board, *see* Naudé Fourie (2014), pp. 587-591.

the facts at hand and assesses whether or not the Bank's activities constituted compliance with the relevant operational policies. Finally, on completion of an investigation, the Inspection Panel presents its findings to the Board, whereas Bank management is required to present the Board with recommendations in light of the Panel's findings.[47]

Given the limitations of the Panel's mandate, for instance, questions about its effectiveness, different views as to the significance of the number of Requests that had been filed since its establishment,[48] and doubts as to whether the Panel's 'cases' constitute a coherent 'body of practice,' why the focus on Inspection Panel practice?

Clearly, Inspection Panel practice cannot claim to offer a complete overview of World Bank development-lending operations or of World Bank compliance with the operational policies. Nevertheless, as this book argues, the opportunity it presents is unique: its claims, filed by individuals and civil society actors,[49] are investigated by Inspection Panel members that have an adequate degree of functional independence (especially, from Bank management);[50] whereas all its findings are made public.[51] Over the past two decades, moreover, the Inspection Panel has constructed, what can now be called, a body of practice – as reflected, for instance, in its references to previous findings[52] and in its deployment of specific compliance review approaches[53] – while the perspectives offered by this growing body of practice are significant.

As a window onto the Bank's development-lending operations, Inspection Panel practice illustrates "the World Bank's complexity" as reflected, for instance, in "the institution's legal and structural characteristics" and in the complex "nature of its relationship with partners."[54] Indeed, as Boisson De Chazournes argues, Inspection Panel practice serves as "a prism" that "enable[s] one to apprehend the Organization's inner life" while

---

47   Inspection Panel Resolution, §§ 22-23.

48   See e.g., Miller-Adams (1999), pp. 81-82 (commenting that "[o]nly thirteen formal requests were received by the Inspection Panel in its first four years of operation"); and see Ninio in Freestone (2013), p. 69, who notes that the Panel's "[c]ase-load continues to be around 3 new cases per year which cannot be considered excessive given the many new projects the Bank approves every year. However, numbers can be misleading as each new case has the ability to focus the attention of the institution on its fragilities at a considerable cost." For a statistical overview of Inspection Panel cases (including a comparative analysis of the number of cases filed at other IAMs), see Naudé Fourie (2014), pp. 579-604.

49   See Brown Weiss (2010), p. 482; Suzuki & Nanwani (2005-2006), p. 325; and see Independent Accountability Mechanisms Network (2012), p. 1: "IAMs reflect the principle of 'citizen-driven accountability,' which aims to give greater voice and rights of recourse to people with respect to actions that affect them."

50   See section 6.2.4; also see Naudé Fourie (2009), pp. 815-212.

51   See Van Putten (2008), p 232: "The reports, with their findings from the Inspection Panel, are [...] made public exactly as they were written by the Panel members. It is the release of the findings to the public domain that constitutes the strength of the work of such mechanisms". The author (a former Inspection Panel member) adds (id., at p. 233): "Informing the public about the failures of an institution is something rarely executed."

52   See e.g., note 17, Ch. 9.

53   In this regard, see section 6.3.

54   Boisson de Chazournes in Treves et al. (Eds.) (2005), p. 187.

also shedding light on "the difficulties attaching to the setting-up" and operationalization of such "control mechanisms."[55]

Former World Bank Senior Vice President and General Legal Counsel, Ibrahim Shihata, once remarked (in reference to Louis Henkin's argument that "[a]lmost all nations observe almost all principles of international law and almost all of their obligations almost all of the time") that "[a] stronger statement may be safely made about the observance by international organizations, especially international financial institutions, of their rules and procedures."[56] While Shihata's statement might be open for debate, it is clear that Inspection Panel findings typically constitute an intricate mix of 'compliance', 'partial compliance' and 'non-compliance' – a pattern that is also reflected in several formal World Bank Management[57] responses to Requests and responses to Inspection Panel reports.[58]

The analytical approach employed in this book has been to focus on the "negative definition."[59] In other words, the analysis concentrates primarily on instances where the Inspection Panel found the World Bank to be 'partially compliant' and 'non-compliant.' The approach therefore resembles Failure Model and Effects Analysis ('FMEA'), which focuses on data points furthest removed from the mean – or, furthest removed from 'desired or planned outcomes' (whether positive or negative),[60] because such data points are considered to be more 'information rich'.[61]

That being said, it is also important to keep in mind that, as Freestone remarks, the Bank "is almost self destructive in its self analysis."[62] While the reports generated by those internal accountability mechanisms that "report directly to the Board of Executive Directors" – notably, the Inspection Panel and the Independent Evaluation Group[63] – contain

---

55 Boisson de Chazournes *in* Treves et al. (Eds.) (2005), pp. 202-203.
56 Shihata (2000), p. xx. Shihata quotes Louis Henkin, 'How Nations Behave', 47 *Law and Foreign Policy* (1979).
57 Hereinafter, also 'Bank management' or 'Management.'
58 For an overview of Inspection Panel findings and Management responses, *see* in general Naudé Fourie (2014). *Also note,* to date, the Inspection Panel has not concluded any of its investigations without identifying instances of partial compliance and/or non-compliance.
59 Cronin (2014), e-Book, quoting Werner Herzog: "I don't think I could ever put my finger on what constitutes true poetry, depth and illumination in cinema. The sins, on the other hand, are easy to name. The bad films have taught me most about filmmaking. Seek out the negative definition."
60 FMEA is a "qualitative and systematic'" analytical tool employed in a wide range of practice domains to analyze failures (or, the risks of failures), as well as the effects or impacts of such failures. For an example of how FMEA theory is applied in the 'six sigma' context, *see* http://www.isixsigma.com/tools-templates/fmea/quick-guide-failure-mode-and-effects-analysis/. *And see e.g.,* D. White & J. Fortune (2002), 'Current Practice in Project Management – An Empirical Study', 20 *International Journal of Project Management* 1, 1; *and* H. Liu, L. Liu & N. Liu (2013), 'Risk Evaluation Approaches in Failure Mode and Effects Analysis: A literature Review,' 40 *Expert Systems with Applications* 2, 828.
61 This argument is based on Shannon's theory on the 'information content' of specific data points – *see* in general C.E. Shannon (1949), *The Mathematical Theory of Communication*, Chicago: University of Illinois Press.
62 Freestone (2013), pp. 2-3.
63 On the IEG, *see* section 6.2.1.

"very valuable sources of publicly available information", Freestone argues, "they are often far more critical of Bank decision making and operational performance than external critics."[64]

As to how the analysis of Inspection Panel practice is presented in this book, there is a preference for including longer, direct extracts from Inspection Panel practice material. There are three reasons behind this preference.

Firstly, many who are interested in the topic of 'World Bank accountability' are not necessarily familiar with the work of the Inspection Panel – nor, for that matter, with the World Bank's development-lending operations.[65] The inclusion of longer extracts from Inspection Panel practice material provides readers with the opportunity to familiarize themselves with the broader 'transnational development context'.

Secondly, since Inspection Panel cases involve multiple actors, numerous claims relating to various operational policies, and are often concerned with the intricate 'technical' aspects of development projects, longer extracts provide readers with the context necessary to follow the arguments being made in the practice material.[66]

Finally, longer, direct extracts provide a better demonstration of the complexity of the underlying issues addressed in this book. This complexity is also illustrated by the fact that several of the examples from Inspection Panel practice are indicative of more than one issue. While a publication of this nature has to proceed in a linear fashion, this book makes extensive use of cross-references to reflect the complexity – and, non-linearity – of these issues.[67]

1.3   HOW THIS BOOK IS ORGANIZED

Chapter 2 of the Introduction sets out the conceptual models that facilitate the analysis presented in this book – whereas the analysis is organized in two parts.

---

64   *Id. Also see* Wade's comments *at* note 231, Ch. 7. *And see* Miller-Adams (1999), p. xi, who comments that "the complexity of the [World Bank] makes it possible for social scientists to find evidence for every hypothesis and its opposite in their investigations of the World Bank. This note of caution rang true as I plunged into the details of Bank policy and practice. From some vantage points, the extent of change undergone by the World Bank over the past decade appears truly staggering. From others, it seems that the Bank is indeed immutable. In such a complex environment it is difficult to generalize about the nature or extent of change, let alone the processes that underpin it. Yet I believe that generalizations are possible, although they must be informed by the specifics of each case [...]."

65   In this regard, *also see* Bradlow & Hunter (Eds.) (2010), p. xxix: "[...] the developmental work of international organizations has received relatively less attention from international legal scholars. In fact, it is striking how little attention has been paid to the international legal issues relating to the operations of the IMF, the World Bank Group, and the regional development banks [...]."

66   For a 'structured summary' of all the Inspection Panel cases mentioned in this book, *see* Naudé Fourie (2014).

67   In this regard, *also see* Sterman's description of the features of 'dynamic complexity' *in* section 2.1.

Part I (*Chapters 3 to 7*) focuses on how World Bank accountability is *conceptualized* – or, World Bank accountability *in theory*. **Part II** (*Chapters 8 to 15*) concentrates on the manner in which World Bank accountability is *operationalized* – or, World Bank accountability *in practice*. Part II therefore demonstrates, and further problematizes, the issues highlighted in Part I.

Part II is further organized as two segments. **Segment A** (*Chapters 8 to 11*) introduces thematic or structural issues distilled from Inspection Panel practice that cut across policy areas, while **Segment B** (*Chapters 12 to 15*) focuses on prominent compliance issues highlighted during Inspection Panel investigations, concerning specific policy areas. Part II can therefore also serve as a reference work for those interested in specific aspects of World Bank development-lending operations.

Chapter 16 concludes this book by considering a specific implication of the analysis presented here, namely: that it is indicative of a particular type of problem or issue – a 'wicked problem' or a 'complex societal issue' – that needs to be addressed by means of an interactional, collaborative and integrative approach.

2   Conceptual Models Facilitating Interdisciplinary Inquiry and Discourse

"Interdisciplinary learning is a process"

> by which individuals and groups integrate insights and modes of thinking from two or more disciplines or established fields, to advance their fundamental or practical understanding of a subject that stands beyond the scope of a single discipline.[1]

Moreover, as Boix Mansilla adds, "[i]nterdisciplinary learners *integrate* information, data, techniques, tools, perspectives, concepts, and/or theories from" various disciplinary areas so as to "craft products, explain phenomena, or solve problems, in ways that would have been unlikely through single-disciplinary means."[2]

In this book, various conceptual models provide an important mechanism for such integration. These models therefore facilitate the interdisciplinary inquiry presented in this book, but can also serve to facilitate the broader discourse on World Bank and IFI accountability – which, as this book argues, should include participants from multiple disciplines and domains of practice.[3]

Chapter 2 introduces three conceptual models, as well as some of the thinking in which these models are based, that provide the foundation for the interdisciplinary inquiry presented in this book, as well as the discourse which this book aims to facilitate.

The first conceptual model contextualizes World Bank accountability by describing World Bank development-lending operations as a form of *transnational regulatory governance*. The model sets out some of the core characteristics of transnational regulatory governance contexts and elaborates on the implications of these characteristics for the issue of accountability.

---

1   Boix Mansilla *in* Frodeman (Ed.) (2010), p. 289.
2   *Id.* (emphasis in original).
3   Conceptual models can be described as "system[s] of concepts, assumptions, expectations, beliefs, and theories" *(see e.g.,* Maxwell (2009), p. 222, quoted *in* Shields & Rangarajan (2013), at p. 24); or a "collection of ideas about how and why variables are related" *(see e.g.,* A. Graziano & Michael Raulin (2013), Research methods: A Process of Inquiry (8th ed.) Upper Saddle River, NJ: Pearson, p. 405). In legal scholarship, conceptual models have been described as "neutral reference system[s] in the form of concepts", or "abstract models derived in an inductive process from specific instances of real-existing law" *(see e.g.,* Brand (2007), p. 437). Brand also argues that "conceptualization is firmly established in the social sciences" and is "accepted by analytical jurisprudence as crucial to our perception and understanding of law." *(Id.)*

The second model conceptualizes *accountability as an interdisciplinary* and *multifaceted concept*, and sets out four *interdependent dimensions of accountability* that ask: *accountability to whom, for what, how assessed, and how ensured?*

The third model presents a *conception of legal and social normativity* based in constructivist and international thinking that describes the *nature* of normative systems and sets out competing conceptions as to the primary *purpose* of normative systems. The model also describes how normative systems *operate* – by focusing on the *methods* or *approaches* employed by the actors participating in the processes of norm creation, norm application and norm enforcement; and on the '*community of practice*' as mechanism for facilitating such interaction.

2.1 WORLD BANK DEVELOPMENT-LENDING OPERATIONS AS SITUATED IN THE TRANSNATIONAL DEVELOPMENT CONTEXT

Transnational regulatory governance refers to a "concept [that] has become a widely used analytical perspective for describing the conduct of world affairs in many disciplines".[4] As a result, it has different definitions and designations, including 'global governance',[5] 'global regulatory governance'[6] and 'post-national governance'.[7] Generally speaking, however, it concerns governance and regulation "beyond the State"[8] – that is to say, it concerns the "activities, institutions, actors or processes that cross at least one national border," and

---

4   Von Bogdandy *in* Von Bogdandy et al. (Eds.) (2010), p. 7.
5   *Id.*
6   Kingsbury *in* Cissé et al. (Eds.) (2012).
7   *E.g.*, Krisch (2010), pp. 4-6. Krisch traces the use of the term 'postnational' to Habermas (*see e.g.*, J. Habermas (1998), *Die Postnationale Konstellation*, Frankfurt am Main: Suhrkamp Verlag) *as well as* to Zürn (*see e.g.*, M. Zürn (1999), 'The State in the Postnational Constellation – Societal Denationalization and Multi-Level Governance', ARENA Working Papers, WP 99/35). Krisch elaborates (*Id.*, at p. 6): "The national constellation, that is the convergence of resources, recognition and the realization of governance goals in one political organization – the national state –, seems to be a process of transformation into a post-national constellation. The nation state is no longer the only site of authority and the normativity that accompanies it." For a critical view of the term 'postnational', *see e.g.*, Shaffer (2012), p. 582: "Although transnational legal ordering must be subject to contestation, as in Krisch's pluralist vision, the nation state remains central to it. We have yet to arrive at a post-national world. Although the term post-nationalism goes too far, Krisch's pluralist values of 'taking into account', mutual accommodation, conditional recognition, deliberation, and legitimate difference, will be critical for creating legal orders in transnational governance."
8   *See* Hale & Held *in* Hale & Held (Eds.) (2011), p. 5. The authors differentiate (*at id.*) between "international" (which concerns "state-to-state interactions in which one sovereign country deals with another"); "transnational" (which "is used to refer to interactions that cross national boundaries at levels other than sovereign-to-sovereign"); "transborder" (which is considered to be "a more general category to include all boundary-spanning interactions"); and, finally, "global" (which refers to "transborder interactions that include (approximately) the entire world system"). They add, however, (*id.*, at p. 15) that "such a clear distinction is often difficult to maintain in a world of hybrid governance." *Also see* Von Bogdandy *in* Von Bogdandy et al. (Eds.) (2010), p. 7, fn. 8, who notes that the "concept of 'governance' was borrowed from economics."

typically involves "actors other than national governments."[9] Consequently, as depicted by Figure 1 (below), transnational regulatory governance also involves various intersecting normative systems that include different forms of legal and non-legal (social) normativity.

The World Bank's development-lending operations are considered as a form of transnational regulatory governance – or, as described here, World Bank development-lending operations are situated in the *transnational development context* – since it involves a wide range of state and non-state actors, acting in various capacities.[10] The decision-making structures and processes involved in World Bank development-lending operations cut across the international, supranational, regional, national as well as sub-national ('local') levels.[11] In addition, World Bank development-lending operations involve intersecting normative systems that include legal and social norms and which, in turn, operate at the international, national, and sub-national ('local') levels.[12]

World Bank development-lending operations also share the core features of transnational regulatory governance contexts[13] – features, as is argued here, that are indicative of high degrees of pluralism and "dynamic complexity."[14]

For instance, transnational regulatory governance contexts are marked by a shift in emphasis from 'actors' to 'structures' and 'processes' – to the extent that transnational regulatory governance is increasingly "understood as a continuous structure or process, rather", as Von Bogdandy remarks, "than a batch of acts of specific, identifiable actors causing specific, identifiable effects."[15] Furthermore, there tends to be a shift from formal to informal governance and regulatory arrangements, whereas the distinction between what is considered formal and informal is often ambiguous.[16]

Transnational regulatory governance contexts also facilitate functional shifts, for instance, where state actors delegate or transfer public functions (that traditionally belonged solely in the domain of the state) to non-state actors, including international institutions, private sector actors and civil society organizations. Such functional shifts, in turn, have resulted in a situation where "non-state entities have started to compete with states for the

---

9   Hale & Held *in* Hale & Held (Eds.) (2011), p. 15.
10 *See e.g.,* section 3.1.
11 *See e.g.,* sections 3.1.1 & 4.1.2.
12 *See* Ch. 5.
13 For examples of different forms of transnational regulatory governance, *see* in general Hale & Held (Eds.) (2011).
14 *See* Sterman (2000), pp. 21-23. *And see* J.W. Forester (1969), *Urban Dynamics*, Riverside, California: Pegasus Communications, Inc., p. 107: "Like all systems, the complex system is an interlocking structure of feedback loops [...]. This loop structure surrounds all decisions of public or private, conscious or unconscious. The processes of man and nature, of psychology and physics, of medicine and engineering all fall within this structure."
15 Von Bogdandy *in* Von Bogdandy et al. (Eds.) (2010), pp. 7 & 9.
16 Von Bogdandy *in* Von Bogdandy et al. (Eds.) (2010), p. 9. For criticism of the "growing use of non-formal law-ascertainment criteria," *see* D'Aspremont (2011), pp. 221-223.

scarce resource of politico-legal authority (i.e., the power to set authoritative standards)."[17] In other words, as Klabbers explains, these actors "do not merely wish"

> to be involved in monitoring international law, as the traditional role of NGOs was, or wish to receive benefits created under international law by states; instead, they increasingly demand a seat at the table.[18]

An additional feature of transnational regulatory governance contexts concerns the conventional systems of categorization that have long been employed to differentiate between different types of actors and functions ('public' versus 'private' sector), for instance, between levels of governance ('international' versus 'national'), or between different levels and forms of normativity. In transnational regulatory governance contexts, conventional systems of categorization tend to lose their functional value,[19] which means that "a multitude of formal and informal connections [are] taking the place of what once were relatively clear rules and categories."[20]

The "proliferation of actors and institutions at the transnational level," as Hale and Held comment, have "disrupted a common, though often implicit, assumption of the 'traditional' literature on transborder institutions," namely:

> that such institutions can be grouped into cohesive regimes or 'institutions processing norms, decision, rules, and procedures which facilitate a convergence of expectations'. While this canonical definition of an international regime is broad enough to encompass a great degree of complexity, in practice scholars have often discussed regimes as if they were reducible to a single international organization or treaty.[21]

Instead, "the expansion and overlap of international institutions"

> require students of global politics to think in terms of 'regime complexes', defined as 'an array of partially overlapping and nonhierarchical institutions governing a particular issue area'.[22]

---

17 *See* Klabbers *in* Klabbers et al. (Eds.) (2009), p. 12.
18 *Id.*
19 Krisch (2010), p. 4.
20 *Id.*
21 Hale & Held *in* Hale & Held (Eds.) (2011), pp. 11-12.
22 *Id.*

Or, to describe this situation in terms of systems dynamics terminology, transnational regulatory governance contexts involve heterarchical or intersecting systems that are, in turn, comprised of complex "interlocking structure[s] of feedback loops".[23] Social systems marked by such dynamic complexity tend to be, as Sterman comments, "[d]ynamic";[24] whereas the interactions among variables are "[t]ightly coupled",[25] "[g]overned by feedback",[26] "[n]onlinear";[27] "[h]istory-dependent";[28] "[s]elf-organizing";[29] "[a]daptive";[30] "[c]ounterintuitive;[31] "[p]olicy resistant"[32] and "[c]haracterized by trade-offs".[33]

---

23 *See* Sterman (2000), pp. 21-23.

24 *I.e.*, prone to change, albeit varying scales and rates of change. *See* Sterman (2000), p. 22. On examples of changes in the transnational development context, *also see* sections 4.1 & 4.2.

25 *I.e.*, "[t]he actors in the system interact strongly with one another and with the natural world. Everything is connected to everything else." *See* Sterman (2000), p. 22.

26 Due to the "tight couplings among actors, our actions feed back on themselves. Our decisions alter the state of the world, causing changes in nature and triggering others to act, thus giving rise to a new situation which then influences our next decisions. Dynamics arise from these feedbacks." *See* Sterman (2000), p. 22. On the notion of 'feedback', *also see* Anderson & Johnson (1997), p. 4: "Feedback is the transmission and return of information [...]. The most important feature of feedback is that it provides the catalyst for a change in behavior." *And see* Sterman (2000), p. 14-15: "Just as dynamics arise from feedback, so too all learning depends on feedback. We make decisions that alter the real world; we gather information feedback about the real world, and using the new information we revise our understanding of the world and the decisions we make to bring our perception of the state of the system closer to our goals." *Also see* Powers (1973), p. 351: "Feedback is such an all-pervasive and fundamental aspect of behavior that it is as invisible as the air that we breathe. Quite literally it is behavior – we known nothing of our own behavior but the feedback effects of our own outputs."

27 *I.e.*, "[e]ffect is rarely proportional to cause, and what happens locally in a system (near the current operating point) often does not apply in distant regions (other states of the system). [...] Nonlinearity also arises as multiple factors interact in decision making [...]." *See* Sterman (2000), p. 22.

28 *I.e.*, "taking one road often precludes taking other and determines where you end up (path dependence). Many actions are irreversible [...]." *See* Sterman (2000), p. 22.

29 *I.e.*, "[t]he dynamics of systems arise spontaneously from their internal structure" – whereas the underlying structure of a system "consists of the feedback loops, stocks and flows, and nonlinearities created by the interaction of the physical and institutional structure of the system with the decision-making processes of the agents acting within it." *See* Sterman (2000), pp. 22 & 107.

30 *I.e.*, "[t]he capabilities and decision rules of the agents in complex systems change over time. [...] Adaption also occurs as people learn from experience, especially as they learn new ways to achieve their goals in the face of obstacles." Sterman (2000), p. 22. *Note*, on institutional learning as an outcome of accountability processes, *see* section 7.1.5.

31 *I.e.*, "[...] cause and effect are distant in time and space while we tend to look for causes near the events we seek to explain." *See* Sterman (2000), p. 22.

32 *I.e.*, "[t]he complexity of the systems in which we are embedded overwhelms our ability to understand them. The result: Many seemingly obvious solutions to problems fail or actually worsen the situation." *See* Sterman (2000), p. 22.

33 *I.e.*, "[t]ime delays in feedback channels mean the long-run response of a system to an intervention is often different from its short-run response. High leverage policies often cause worse-before-better behavior, while low leverage policies often generate transitory improvements before the problem grows worse." *See* Sterman (2000), p. 22. On the need to enhance the transparency surrounding trade-off decisions, *see e.g.*, Ch. 9.

Figure 1   A Transnational Regulatory Governance 'Space' Marked by Pluralism and Dynamic Complexity

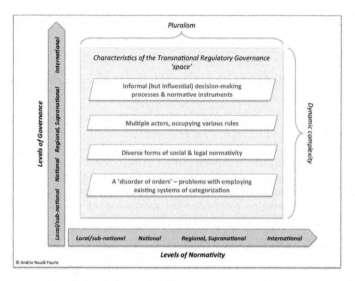

An important consequence of these characteristics concerns the identification of "unilateral" or "non-authoritative acts".[34] The ability to attribute such acts to specific actors is critical because non-state actors – and international institutions in particular – have come to exercise public power or authority, as evidenced, for instance, in activities involving norm creation, norm application and norm enforcement.[35] However, as Kingsbury points out, "[i]ntergovernmental organizations and other institutions engage in this activity beyond the reach of controls imposed by the public law, democratic apparatus, or other review structures of individual states."[36] This further adds to the challenges involved in holding international institutions to account for their exercise of public power, and explains why, as Von Bogdandy observes, "some international institutions are seen as a risk"

> to individual rights, collective self-determination, as well as impediments to, rather than conveyors of, global justice. With respect to individual rights, the striking absence of judicial review and procedural safeguards – even when

---

34 Von Bogdandy *in* Von Bogdandy et al. (Eds.) (2010), p. 4.
35 *Id*. Von Bogdandy adds (*Id.*, at p. 5) that "any kind of governance activity by international institutions," "be it administrative or intergovernmental, should be considered as an exercise of international public authority *if* it determines individuals, private associations, enterprises, states, or other public institutions." (Emphasis in original).
36 Kingsbury *in* Cissé et al. (Eds.) (2012), e-Book.

international institutions have a deep impact upon individuals – meets with harsh critique.[37]

"As a result," Von Bogdandy concludes, "the perception of global governance in scholarship today"

> ranges from endorsement to chastisement. The policies of several institutions
> of global governance are questioned, and often enough, perceived as more or
> less illegitimate.[38]

Subsequently, various international legal scholars argue that is has become paramount "to lay open the legal setting" underlying transnational regulatory governance activities in order "to find out how, and by whom, they are controlled" – and, in particular, "to develop legal standards for ensuring that [international institutions] satisfy contemporary expectations for legitimacy."[39]

The development of such *legal standards*, however, has also proven to be challenging, for several reasons. For instance, because transnational regulatory governance activities are "undertaken by a wide array of actors" that "frequently overlap in their domains of activity," as Kingsbury comments, "the regulatory processes in which any particular actor is engaged" are frequently "influenced by, and perhaps in tension with, activities of other global (extrastate) institutions and national or subnational institutions."[40]

More significantly, there are competing conceptions as to what constitutes 'law' in transnational regulatory governance contexts.[41] Because the exercise of public authority in transnational regulatory governance contexts can "take on all sorts of legal and quasi-legal forms,"[42] it results in norms that are clearly legal or social in nature – but it also generates a third category of norms that comprise a wide array of "concoctions" of "formal and informal instruments".[43] And since these norms have been created in the "contested

---

37 Von Bogdandy *in* Von Bogdandy et al. (Eds.) (2010), p. 9.
38 *Id.* For similar comments, *also see* De Wet *in* Von Bogdandy et al. (Eds.) (2010), pp. 855-856.
39 Von Bogdandy *in* Von Bogdandy et al. (Eds.) (2010), p. 4. Von Bogdandy adds, however, that "constraining effects do not only emanate from binding instruments or legal subjects." (*Id.*, p. 11.)
40 Kingsbury *in* Cissé et al. (Eds.) (2012), e-Book.
41 *Also see* note 11, Ch. 1. *And see e.g.*, Kingsbury (2009); the author notes (at p. 23) that the article aims to clarify "[w]hat justification is there for using the term 'law' in the theory and practice of the emerging field designated 'global administrative law'".
42 Klabbers *in* Klabbers et al. (Eds.) (2009), pp. 12-14.
43 Kingsbury *in* Cissé et al. (Eds.) (2012), e-Book.

terrain in the no-man's land between international law and politics",[44] they present multiple "challenges for traditional international law analysis."[45]

But this "process of 'legal pluralization'" is also "accompanied by a broader normative pluralization: it is no longer immediately evident (presuming it ever was) that legal authority is the sort of authority to strive for."[46] As Orford puts it, "a renewed public interest in cosmopolitan legality" has emerged "at the same moment as a perceived crisis of relevance [of] existing international law and institutions."[47] The "questions to which international law is expected to offer an answer" – including the accountability of international financial institutions – "are some of the most important, vital and intriguing questions of our time;"[48] but there is also a lingering perception that "international law as a discipline has lost its capacity to provide a compelling understanding of what is at stake when these questions arise."[49] Consequently, legal normativity, "as a source of constraints on the abuses of hegemonic power" finds itself at "the limits of modern political organization."[50]

Or, as Kingsbury remarks, "[l]aw contributes appreciably, but generally only in limited ways,"

> alongside political, economic, social, and historical factors [...] in explaining why certain institutions exist in the global administrative space with particular memberships and structures, why these have the mandates and decision rules they do, and why other institutions, mandates, or rules do not exist.[51]

---

44 Toope *in* Bodansky et al. (Eds.) (2007), p. 107. *Also see* Goldmann *in* Von Bogdandy et al. (Eds.) (2010), who observes (at p. 662): "If one were to display this variety of instruments on a scale that ranges from binding international law to non-legal instruments, hardly any thinkable step on this scale would remain empty."
45 *See* Kingsbury *in* Cissé et al. (Eds.) (2012), e-Book. *Also see* Klabbers (2013), p. 139: "[...] it is arguably no coincidence that issues of responsibility and accountability have recently come to occupy a prominent place in international legal discussions. While the law on responsibility is as old as international law itself, discussions on responsibility and accountability have tended to be few and far between. This is no longer the case, and it may well be that accountability has become such a hot topic because there is such a great uncertainty concerning both the sources and subjects of international law and global governance. Where no one can be certain any longer whether norms are 'legal' and whether those from whom the norms emanate have law-making authority, it stands to reason that attention focuses on the output side; at least there may be merit in trying to hold actors to account if their behaviour is questionable."
46 *Id.*
47 Orford (Ed.) (2006), pp. 1-31.
48 *Id.*
49 *Id.*
50 *Id.* Hence, Orford argues that legal scholars, with the help of other disciplinary areas, need to "think about what happens to law at the limits of modern political organization." (*Id.*, p. 2). *Also see* Kingsbury's remarks on the need to clarify the place of 'law' in transnational regulatory governance contexts, *at* notes 51-54, Ch. 2.
51 Kingsbury *in* Cissé et al. (Eds.) (2012), e-Book.

On the other hand, Kingsbury adds, "the roles of law are of rapidly growing importance", especially since "the stakes involved in GRG regimes are high."[52] In fact, "[n]ew understandings of law and its roles are emerging" in part because international institutions "have increasingly sought to shore up their legitimacy, and to enhance the effectiveness of their regulatory activities, by applying to (and between) themselves procedural norms" including "transparency, participation, reasoned decision making, [...] legality," and by establishing "mechanisms of review and accountability."[53] Yet, Kingsbury concludes, "[t]oo little is [...] known about the differences law makes in such regimes."[54]

In other words, as Krisch comments, "[l]aw and politics have been transformed," but "we don't quite know yet how" – which is to say: "we do not have a settled understanding of what structures are currently taking shape, or in what directions the changes go or should go."[55] And as we attempt to make sense of "the increasingly dense and politically significant exercise of power beyond the state",[56] we are "experience[ing] [...] a 'disorder of orders', with countless analytical and normative proposals competing for influence."[57]

Krisch's own normative proposal, which conceptualizes a pluralist "postnational legal order" as a "frame comprised of different [heterarchical] orders and their norms,"[58] provides an important foundation for this discussion.[59] While such a conceptualization would not meet all expectations,[60] it has a few important strengths.

---

52   *Id.*
53   *Id.*
54   *Id.*
55   Krisch (2010), p. 4.
56   Kingsbury *in* Cissé et al. (Eds.) (2012), e-Book.
57   Krisch (2010), p. 4, quoting N. Walker (2008), 'Beyond Boundary Disputes and Basic Grids: Mapping the Global Disorder of Normative Orders', *International Journal of Constitutional Law* 6, 373-396.
58   Krisch (2010), p. 12.
59   Other prominent examples of such competing normative proposals in the area of international legal scholarship include 'global' or 'international constitutionalism' (*see e.g.*, Klabbers et al. (2009); De Wet (2006); Fassbender (1998); Dunoff & Trachtman (Eds.), (2009); *and* Kumm (2004)) *and* 'global administrative law' (GAL) (*see e.g.*, Kingsbury et al. (2005); Kingsbury (2009); Krisch (2006); Chesterman (2008) (b); *and* Kingsbury *in* Cissé et al. (Eds.) (2012)). For criticisms of international constitutionalism and GAL, *see e.g.*, Chimni (2005); Kuo (2008-2009); *and* Kuo (2011-2012). *Also see* Alvarez (2005), who observes (at p. 51): "[...] international lawyers have been and remain leading proponents for the 'constitutionalization' of the UN and other IOs and leading advocates for resolving international disputes through formal institutionalized adjudication. As David Kennedy has put it, the majority of international lawyers tend to see themselves engaged in a common 'international project,' in which all things international (including international organizations and their courts) are good and resorts to notions of 'sovereignty' are seen as parochial or bad."
60   *See e.g.*, Morison & Anthony *in* Anthony et al. (Eds.) (2011), pp. 237-238, commenting that a pluralist model might "not be ideal in terms of democracy" and would certainly "challenge civil society to ensure that it is involved and it will require authority to be open to such involvement. It will be messy and incomplete and the political struggle that will be possible there will be unequal and unfair." For an overview of other shortcomings of a pluralist model, *also see* Krisch (2006), pp. 274-277. *E.g.*, Krisch highlights the "lack of certainty" flowing from the "disappearance of a clearly competent authority and the resulting fluidity of decisions," which means that "the clarity and stabilization of expectations that we usually expect from the law would be severely compromised." (*Id.*, at p. 275). In addition: "Such an order might appear unsatisfactory to those

For instance, as Krisch argues, it has the ability to "overcom[e] the categorical separation between the spheres, without [...] merging them fully or necessarily defining the degree of authority their different norms possess," while specifically allowing for "this frame [to be] filled" – and the assignment of "authority" to the particular "layers and bodies of law" to be determined – through the "mutual challenge" between competing constituencies.[61] Moreover, the "appropriate place" for debates concerning the meaning of abstract concepts such as "public interest", 'legitimacy,' 'sustainable development' or 'accountability', is "within some form of political contestation."[62]

Or, as Morison and Anthony contend, because a pluralist conceptualization of law and politics recognize "the reality of the new global order",[63] it is able to account for the "shifting weights of the different constituencies in the fluid process of constructing global governance."[64] And, importantly, it "respects the fact that people have different views and make different choices."[65]

2.2 WORLD BANK ACCOUNTABILITY CONCEIVED AS AN INTERDISCIPLINARY, MULTI-DIMENSIONAL AND INTERDEPENDENT CONCEPT

'Accountability', as Mulgan observes, has become a "chameleon-like term."[66] "[A] word that a few decades ago was rarely used," came to "crop up everywhere performing all manner of analytical and rhetorical tasks and carrying most of the burdens of democratic 'governance'.[67]

In the area of "health care", for instance, accountability is generally understood to involve "the obligation to answer for a responsibility that has been conferred;"[68] and in the development context, accountability has been defined as "the means by which individuals and organizations report to a recognized authority (or authorities) and are held responsible for their actions;" or, as "the process of holding actors responsible for actions."[69]

---

who have clear views on the single right constituency for particular issues. (*Id.*, p. 274). Despite these shortcomings, Krisch asserts that a "pluralist vision of postnational law" would constitute at least a "normatively adequate response." (*Id.*, p. 248). For a critical view of Krisch's "postnational vision", *see e.g.*, Shaffer (2012), who comments, *e.g.*, (at p. 572) that it "can also be viewed as too radical for the world outside Europe in being grounded in a European 'postnational' experience, as reflected in his three case studies in which Europe is central."

61   Krisch (2010), p. 12.
62   Morison & Anthony *in* Anthony et al. (Eds.) (2011), pp. 237-238.
63   *Id.*
64   Krisch (2006), p. 274.
65   *Id. Also see* Fox's remarks *at* note 77, Ch. 1.
66   Mulgan (2000), p. 555. *Also see* Brown Weiss (2010), p. 479; *and* Curtin & Nollkaemper (2005), p. 4.
67   Curtin & Nollkaemper (2005), p. 4, quoting Mulgan (2000), *at* p. 555. *Also see* Brown Weiss (2010), p. 479.
68   Van Putten (2008), p. 15.
69   Ebrahim (2003), pp. 813-814.

Legal conceptualizations of accountability, as formulated by the International Law Association ('ILA'), for instance, tend to emphasize that international institutions exercise public power or authority, which creates the "duty to account" for the exercise thereof.[70] The ILA further conceptualizes 'the accountability of international organizations' as being comprised of different forms (for instance, "legal, political, administrative or financial" – while arguing that "[a] combination of the four forms provides the best chances of achieving the necessary degree of accountability")[71] and describes three 'levels' of accountability.[72]

But while the core definitions employed by different disciplinary areas contain similar elements, accountability remains "a broad term that reflects a range of understandings rather than a single paradigm"[73] – as becomes evident whenever the discussion proceeds to lower levels as abstraction. This is because the meaning of abstract notions such as accountability or compliance are influenced by underlying theoretical conceptions;[74] and, as Fox argues because accountability is an "inherently relational" concept.[75] Hence, its "meaning varies greatly depending on the actors involved (for example, contractual, corporate, and political accountability are all quite different)."[76] As for "[t]he standards

---

70   *See e.g.*, ILA (2004), p. 5.

71   *Id.*

72   *I.e.*, 1st level: various "forms of internal and external scrutiny and monitoring, irrespective of potential and subsequent liability and/or responsibility"; 2nd level: "tortious liability for injurious consequences arising out of acts or omissions not involving a breach of any rule of international and/or institutional law"; and 3rd level: "responsibility arising out of acts or omissions which do constitute a breach of a rule of international and/or institutional law." (*Id.*) *Note*, Inspection Panel practice constitute an example of 'first level accountability' that combines various forms of accountability. *Also note*, the International Law Commission ('ILC') has adopted 'Draft Articles on the Responsibility of International Organizations', dealing with matters that pertain to the ILA's notion of '2nd' and '3rd' level accountability. Moreover, "[i]n resolution 66/100 of 9 December 2011, the [UN] General Assembly took note of the articles on the responsibility of international organizations, the text of which was annexed to the resolution, and commended them to the attention of Governments and international organizations without prejudice to the question of their future adoption or other appropriate action. It further decided to return to the topic at its sixty-ninth session, in 2014, with a view to examining, inter alia, the question of the form that might be given to the draft articles." *See* http://legal.un.org/avl/ha/ario/ario.html.

73   Mulgan (2000), *at* p. 555.

74   *See* Kingsbury *at* note 3, Part I.

75   Fox *in* Clark et al. (Eds.) (2003), p. xii.

76   *Id. Also see, e.g.*, Ebrahim (2003), pp. 813-814 (arguing that accountability concerns being "held responsible" by others and "taking responsibility" for oneself; accountability therefore has an internal and external dimension); *see* Fox *in* Clark et al. (Ed.), p. xii (arguing that accountability involves *answerability*" and therefore concerns a variety of processes aimed at "holding actors responsible for their actions", including "formal processes in which actions are held up to standards of behaviour or performance"); *and see* Curtin & Nollkaemper (2005), pp. 7-8 (who underline the distinctions between "giving account" and "holding to account" – but also argue that the last-mentioned comprises "a more demanding definition" since it requires "the possibility that the actor will have to face consequences" and also because it "requires a social relationship between the actor and what can be loosely termed an accountability forum of one type or another." Curtin & Nollkaemper add (*at id.*) that this relationship "may require the establishment of a mechanism (*e.g.*, a non-compliance procedure) by which account can be rendered" and that while "[a]ccountability often is

themselves", that is, "what counts as compliance", Fox argues that both "the scope and meaning of *public* accountability more generally, are all contested and shaped through political conflict."[77]

Hence, the interdisciplinary nature of the concept can be problematic. Dowdle argues, for example, that the "growing crisis in public accountability," is aggravated "by the fact that different people seem to have very different and often conflicting ideas as to what constitutes or satisfies a meaningfully 'public' accountability."[78] For instance,

> [e]conomic development agencies [...] often see public accountability in terms of rationalized and transparent systems of bureaucratic control. Human rights activists see it primarily in terms of popular participation in and supervision of political decisionmaking. Legal development agencies see it primarily in terms of judicial enforcement of legal norms.[79]

In other words, Dowdle concludes, "while there is common perception of an accountability problem, there is also deep division about its exact causes and about what our appropriate response to that problem should be."[80]

And because the notion of accountability is "used in many different ways in political discourse and academic writing", it is often, as Kingsbury points out, "underspecified for any operational purpose."[81]

Perhaps these issues do point to the need for a more focused conceptualization of accountability within specific disciplinary contexts. Some international legal scholars, for instance, critical of the ILA's broader approach, argue that we are in need of a conceptualization of the accountability of international institutions that is "unequivocal[ly] legal" – although, as noted earlier, such a conceptualization would also have to deal with the competing conceptions of is meant by 'law'.[82]

---

understood as a retrospective process that involves giving an account of prior conduct", "some objectives of accountability (such as prevention) necessarily connect past and future conduct."

77   *Id.* (emphasis in original). *Also see* Morison & Anthony's comments *at* note 62, Ch. 2.

78   Dowdle (2006), p. 1. *Note*, Dowdle discusses public accountability in the national context and argues that an accountability "crisis" is caused primarily "by the forces of globalization and privatization." (*Id.*)

79   *Id.*

80   *Id.*

81   Kingsbury *in* Cissé et al. (Eds.) (2012), e-Book. For additional conceptualizations of accountability, *see* section 2.2.

82   *See e.g.*, Dekker *in* Wouters et al. (Eds.) (2010), p. 23: "[...] the rather traditional approach to international (institutional) law underlying [the ILA study] makes it difficult to conceptualise an unequivocal *legal* concept of the 'accountability' of international organisations'." Dekker proposes (*id.*, at p. 36) that "insights" derived from "so-called institutional legal theory" can facilitate the conceptualization of "an alternative concept of accountability" that "cover[s] in principle all situations of claims of non-compliance by international organisations with legally valid – but not necessarily also legally binding – rules and principles of international law." *And see* Curtin & Nollkaemper (2005), p. 19: "The approach and outcome of the work undertaken by

To be sure, even when we purposefully engage in interdisciplinary inquiry, the disciplinary area(s) in which we have been schooled continue to influence us – which is also why the approach underlying this analysis might perhaps be better described as *legal-interdisciplinary*.[83]

That said, this book argues that a comprehensive shared understanding on accountability needs to reflect its interdisciplinary nature. Moreover, as the ILA comments, "for the sake of its operationality," accountability is not a "monolithic" concept that requires "uniform and indiscriminate application."[84] Simply put, "such rigidity would not survive the complexities of international reality."[85] Instead, the ILA concludes, our conceptualizations of accountability needs to maintain a "delicate balance between preserving the necessary autonomy in decision-making", required by international institutions, "and responding to the need, both in the sphere of international law and international relations, to have these actors accountable for their acts and omissions."[86]

In other words, the conceptualization and operationalisation of accountability in the "new kaleidoscopic world" of the transnational development context requires, as Brown Weiss puts it, the deployment of "a broader and more encompassing lens."[87]

The remainder of this section provides such a 'lens' by setting out four interdependent facets or dimensions of World Bank accountability, that also form the basis for the structure of Part I (Chapters 3 to 7), as illustrated by Figure 2.

Based on a core normative statement – *the World Bank, as an international financial institution exercising public power, has a duty to account for the exercise thereof*[88] – the conceptual model expounds a series of questions: *to whom* should the Bank be accountable?

---

the ILA with regard to the accountability of international organizations, exemplified the point that even when a specific and focused attempt is made to apply the concept of accountability to international organizations in general, the underlying conceptual approach may still be very limited. In other words, there is some evidence that some of the exploratory work that has been undertaken within the confines of traditional international law is marked by extreme caution and a non-fundamental approach to the changing contours of the exercise of public power."

83 Legal-interdisciplinarity describes a wide variety of approaches that obtain "input" from non-legal disciplines, where such 'input' "serves", in essence, "as a necessary contribution to […] legal arguments." *See* Van Klink & Taekema (Eds.) (2011), pp. 10-13. For a conceptualization of legal-interdisciplinarity, *see e.g.,* Vick (2004), pp. 184-185, conceiving a spectrum where, "[a]t one end is research that attempts to answer what are essentially doctrinal questions about legal rules or proposed law reforms by using, in part, information gained from other disciplines" and "[a]t the opposite end […] would be research that merges the questions asked and assumptions made by different disciplines so completely that potentially an entirely new discipline could emerge." The analytical approach employed in this book can be considered as an example of an "intermediate approach" that "appl[ies] the method or theoretical constructs of a different discipline to legal materials or aspects of a legal system in order to study social phenomena related to or affected by the law." (*Id.*) *Also see* Naudé Fourie (2015).

84 ILA (1998), pp. 15-17. *Also see* Bradlow & Hunter (Eds.) (2010), p. 81.

85 *Id.*

86 ILA (2004), pp. 5-6.

87 Brown Weiss (2010), p. 480.

88 *See* note 70, Ch. 1.

Accountable *for what? How* is such accountability to be *assessed* or *determined?* And *how* is World Bank accountability to be *ensured?*[89]

Figure 2   Interdependent Dimensions of World Bank Accountability

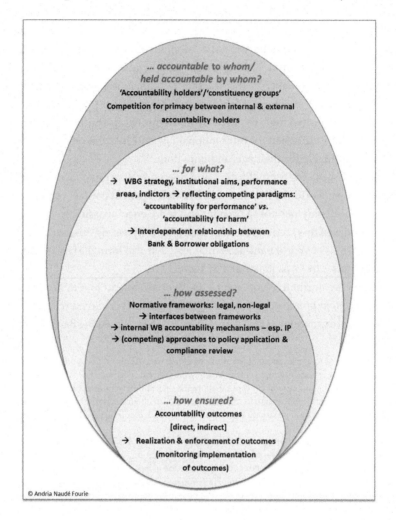

... *accountable to whom/ held accountable by whom?*
'Accountability holders'/'constituency groups'
Competition for primacy between internal & external accountability holders

... *for what?*
→ WBG strategy, institutional aims, performance areas, indictors → reflecting competing paradigms:
'accountability for performance' *vs.*
'accountability for harm'
→ Interdependent relationship between Bank & Borrower obligations

... *how assessed?*
Normative frameworks: legal, non-legal
→ interfaces between frameworks
→ internal WB accountability mechanisms – esp. IP
→ (competing) approaches to policy application & compliance review

... *how ensured?*
Accountability outcomes
[direct, indirect]
→   Realization & enforcement of outcomes
(monitoring implementation of outcomes)

© Andria Naudé Fourie

---

89   For the employment of similar frameworks, *see e.g.,* Brown Weiss (2010), pp. 489-490; Scott, (2000); *and see* P. Barberis, 'The New Public Management and a New Accountability', 76 Administration (1998) pp. 451-470. *Also see* Oleschak-Pillai *in* Wouters et al. Eds.) (2010), pp. 406-429, who analyzes the 'effectiveness' of the Inspection Panel on basis of the following analytical framework: "to whom, for what, through what mechanisms, with what kind of accountability outcomes."

To whom should the World Bank be accountable; or, who should hold the Bank accountable?
The first dimension of the conceptual model is concerned with identifying the "accountability holders" or the constituency groups demanding World Bank accountability.[90] The model also considers the relationship between various accountability holders – notably, the *competition for primacy between internal and external constituency groups*, as well as their relationships with "power wielders", which "refer[s] to the actor whose actions" are "meant to [be] constrain[ed]."[91]

What should the Bank be held accountable *for*; or, what is the content and scope of World Bank obligations?
The second dimension focuses on the factors influencing the content and scope of World Bank obligations. Pointing to the influence of the dual public-commercial nature of the World Bank's development-lending operations and the evolving understanding of (sustainable) development,[92] the dimension presents two competing conceptions representing different arguments as to what the Bank should be held accountable for: *performance* or *harm*?[93] The dimension also analyzes how the *division between Bank and Borrower obligations* influences the demands and expectations concerning what the Bank should be held accountable for.

How should World Bank accountability be *assessed*?
The third dimension of World Bank accountability is specifically concerned with the normative assessment of World Bank activities. It therefore expounds the *intersecting normative frameworks*[94] surrounding the Bank's development-lending operations;[95] the *internal accountability mechanisms* involved in *assessing the compliance* of World Bank activities with specific norms;[96] and the (often competing) *approaches* to norm application and compliance review.[97]

How should World Bank accountability be *ensured*?
The fourth dimension relates to the 'consequences, products, results, sanctions' – here, broadly referred to as *accountability outcomes* – to which internal accountability mecha-

---

90 On the distinction between accountability holders and power wielders, *see e.g.,* Rubenstein (2007), p. 616; *and see* in general Grant & Keohane (2005).
91 *Id. See* the discussion *in* section 3.2.
92 *See* the discussion *in* section 4.1.
93 *See* the discussion *in* section 4.2.
94 For a definition of normative frameworks, *see* section 2.3.
95 *See* the discussion *in* Ch. 5.
96 *See* the discussion *in* section 6.2
97 *See* the discussion *in* section 6.3.

nisms such as the Inspection Panel contribute.[98] The dimension focuses on the *realization* and *enforcement* of specific accountability outcomes that highlight the dynamics driven by various relationships. By expounding the wide range of demands and expectations concerning the role of the Inspection Panel and the value of its contribution with regard to the realization and enforcement of accountability outcomes, this dimension also serves to demonstrate the intricate relationships between all the dimensions of World Bank accountability.[99]

As such, this model incorporates all three elements contained in Grant and Keohane's definition of accountability – namely, "standards", "information" and "sanction."[100] It also encompass the "core accountability processes" underlying, what Rubenstein describes as the "standard accountability" model,[101] which "function as an endless loop" – starting with the "negotiat[ion] and agree[ment] on the *standards* to which a power wielder will be held";[102] the "gather[ing] [of] *information* about whether the power wielder has complied with those standards";[103] the process of "*sanction*[ing] the power wielder if it fails to adhere to the standards without justification or excuse";[104] which, in turn result in changes to the applicable standards that occur "as a result of the back-and-forth discussion typical of most accountability processes."[105]

The weakness of the 'standard accountability model', however, is that "accountability holders are often too weak to (help) sanction power wielders", whether due to their "ill-health, poverty, illiteracy, social or political exclusion, and dangers of organizing collectively."[106] This situation is "exacerbated", Rubenstein adds, "by the absence of domestic and international institutions that make sanctioning powerful actors (especially transnational actors) easier."[107]

While the preferable solution to this problem would be to address the "inequality" or "power imbalances" between accountability holders and power wielders, Rubenstein argues for the employment of a model of "surrogate accountability" in the "short and medium term," which efficacy is not entirely dependent on the ability of accountability holders to sanction power wielders.[108] In a surrogate accountability model, an "actor" (or, a "surro-

---

98   *See* the discussion *in* section 7.1.
99   *See* the discussion *in* section 7.2.
100 *See* Grant & Keohane (2005); *and see* Rubenstein (2007), pp. 618.
101 *See* Grant & Keohane (2005); *and* Rubenstein (2007), pp. 617-620.
102 *E.g.*, *as* discussed *in* section 5.1.
103 *E.g.*, *as* discussed *in* section 6.3.
104 *E.g.*, *as* discussed *in* section 7.1.
105 Rubenstein (2007), p. 620. Shapiro & Stone Sweet describes this outcome as the normative development that occurs within the context of "dispute resolution triads" – *see e.g.* the discussion *in* section 7.1.6.
106 Rubenstein (2007), p. 617. *And see e.g.*, the discussion *in* section 3.1.5.
107 *Id. And see e.g.*, the discussion *in* section 2.1.
108 *Id.*

gate") "substitutes for accountability holders during one of the phases of the accountability process."[109]

This book argues that citizen-driven accountability mechanisms such as the Inspection Panel provide a form of 'surrogate accountability', in particular with regard to the processes of "finding and gathering information."[110]

2.3   INTERACTIONAL NORMATIVE PROCESSES, EMBEDDED IN A RESILIENT AND ADAPTABLE COMMUNITY OF INTEREST

Normative systems[111] consist of multiple components.[112] The conceptual model of social and legal normativity presented in this section focuses specifically on the *actors*[113] participating in the core normative processes of *norm creation*, *norm application*, and *norm enforcement*;[114] the *outcomes* of these processes – notably, the adoption and further devel-

---

109 *Id.* Rubenstein adds that surrogate accountability remains "second-best", but it "can provide some of the benefits of standard accountability, but not others" and that it should therefore be "evaluated according to different normative criteria than standard accountability." (*Id.*)

110 In the regard, *see e.g.*, the discussion *in* sections 6.2.4, 6.3 & 7.2.

111 On the definition of a 'system', *see e.g.*, Anderson & Johnson (1997), pp. 1-2: "[…] a system is a 'group of interacting, interrelated, or interdependent components that form a unified whole," whereas *processes* are often discrete components of systems. On the notion of legal systems, *see e.g.*, Gerber (1998), p. 729 ("In the context of law, the concept of 'system' is typically used in a vague way to refer to the totality of factors involving law in a particular jurisdiction"); *see* Brand (2007), p. 435 (defining law as "a normative system that consists of principles, rules, institutions, and other institutionally defined instruments"); *and see* Higgins (1994), p. 2 (arguing that international law should not be viewed merely as "a body of rules," concerned "only [with] resolving disputes", but that its characteristics are better explained when described as "a normative system" that regulates "normative conduct", referring to "conduct which is regarded by each actor, and by the group as a whole, as being obligatory, and for which violation carries a price.") *Also see* Allott (1999), p. 36: "Law is a system of legal relations. A legal system is an infinite number of interlocking legal relations forming a network of infinite density."

112 *See e.g.*, Reinisch *in* Alston (Ed.) (2005), pp. 38-39 (responding to the question 'what is a legal framework'?): "Are we talking about rule, about norms, laws, treaties, ethical standards, morality? Does it make sense to conceive of a legal framework as different sources of law? Or should we look at procedures and forums wherein we make legal arguments? Are we talking about political or legal processes? Is the framework defined by national or international courts, political bodies in international organizations, special accountability mechanisms, NGOs, the public, and/or the press? Probably, all of these elements constitute a 'legal framework' in a broad sense wherein we have to come to terms with non-state actors and their human rights 'performance'." Reinisch proposes a number of "elements that are generally considered to form, at least part of, a legal framework", namely: "(1) the standards or behavioural rules themselves, substantive rules in an old-fashioned diction; (2) the procedures used in discussing, supervising, and maybe even enforcing compliance with standards; and finally; (3) the institutions, forums, networks, etc. within which procedures are activated to invoke the standards." (*Id.*)

113 *See e.g.*, the discussions *in* sections 3.1 & 6.2.

114 *Note*, the processes of norm creation, norm application and norm enforcement can be compared to the "core accountability processes" described by Rubenstein (*see* the discussion in section 2.2), and the "three phases" outlined by "transnational legal process" theory, which Sarfaty describes as including: "interaction [or, "norm emergence"], interpretation, and internalization." (*See* Sarfaty (2005), pp. 1809-1810.) Sarfaty describes these

opment of *normative frameworks*[115] (referring to distinct configurations of norms, which encompass notions such as 'principles', 'rules', 'standards' and 'best practises'),[116] and the realization of various forms of *sanctions, corrective* and *improvement measures*;[117] as well as the *methods or approaches* actors employ in realizing such outcomes.[118]

The first characteristic of normative systems highlighted here concerns their "horizontal" nature – which is to say, they are "inherently social" and are "constructed through rhetorical activity and social practice, producing increasingly influential mutual expectations or shared understandings of actors."[119] This feature, as Fuller argued, is shared by "*all* systems of legal normativity, even state systems of law.*"[120]

---

three phases as follows (*at id.*): "One or more transnational actors provokes an interaction (or series of interactions) with another, which forces an interpretation or enunciation of the global norm applicable to the situation. By so doing, the moving party seeks not simply to coerce the other party, but to internalize the new interpretation of the international norm into the other party's internal normative system." *Also see* Koh (1996), pp. 183-84, who defines 'transnational legal process' thinking as "the theory and practice of how public and private actors – nation-states, international organizations, multinational enterprises, non-governmental organizations, and private individuals – interact in a variety of public and private, domestic and international fora to make, interpret, enforce, and ultimately, internalize rules of transnational law."

115 On the sources of normativity relevant to World Bank development-lending operations, *see* Ch. 5.

116 *Note*: different disciplines tend to assign different meanings to these terms – *see e.g.*, Brunnée & Toope (2010), p. 15, clarifying (at fn. 46) "that it is common for constructivists to talk of 'norms' when they mean 'institutions', the latter being properly viewed as aggregations of interrelated norms. Institutions, both formal and informal, are simply particular cases of 'social structure'." There are also different understandings as to the 'hierarchical relationships' between such terms in the area of law. *See e.g.*, Beyerlin *in* Bodansky et al. (Eds.) (2007), p. 427, employing "Dworkin's terminology" to differentiate between "legal principles," "legal rules" and "policies" – which are understood to "encompasses a wide range of instruments that lack legally binding force but that nonetheless have normative quality in political-moral terms. This subtype of policies, as well as 'principles' and 'rules', are subsumed under the broad term of 'norms'." However, Beyerlin rejects Dworkin's practice of "speak[ing] of 'standards' instead of 'norms'", arguing that such a description can "give rise to misunderstandings, as it is also used in legal writings to designate those subtypes of norms that are less precise than rules." The definition employed in this book reflects Toope's conception – *see* Toope *in* Bodansky et al. (Eds.) (2007), p. 107: "The category of 'norm' is inclusive and general. A norm may be vague or specific – it may mean a widespread social practice, a social prescription, a legal principle articulated to shape the evolution of a regime, or a precise legal rule. The common core of the concept of 'norm' is that the desideratum contained in the norm is intended to influence human conduct. Note the word 'influence': norms do not necessarily determine human action. They help to shape behaviour, but they rarely if ever dictate it. Since norms operate in many different ways, they relate to the concepts of formality and informality differentially as well. Norms can be formal rules of law, but they can also be informal social guides to proper conduct."

117 For examples of such outcomes, *see* the discussion *in* section 7.1.

118 *See e.g.*, the discussion *in* section 6.3 & 16.2.1.

119 Brunnée & Toope (2010), pp. 33-36 (emphasis in original). *Note*, while Brunnée and Toope has developed a general theory or 'account' of international *law*, their research has been informed by constructivist approaches in international relations theory and by the jurisprudence of Lon Fuller, which, in turn, are informed by broader considerations of normativity – in this regard, *also see* notes 129 & 130, Ch. 2.

120 Brunnée & Toope (2010), pp. 33-36 (emphasis in original).

Normative systems are therefore "best viewed" as involving "continuing challenge rather than as a finished project"[121] since they are "formed and maintained through continuing struggles of social practice."[122] They are, as Brunnée and Toope put it, "the work of [their] everyday participants," who engage in

> a continuous effort to construct and sustain a common institutional framework
> to meet the exigencies of social life in accordance with certain ideals.[123]

But this also means that legal normativity ('law') "is not an all-or-nothing proposition" – it "can exist by degrees".[124] And because "both rules of law and legal systems can and do half exist,"[125] it is "possible to talk about law that is being constructed."[126] Or, as Toope argues, "norms can be informal and precise as well as informal and vague"; which is to say, "'formality' is not an appropriate test for the existence of non-existence of law."[127]

Fuller conceptualized these arguments by means of a "continuum of legality", in which social ('non-legal') norms are situated at one end of a spectrum and 'legal' norms at the other end – as illustrated by Figure 3.[128]

In terms of such a conceptualization of legal and social normativity, it could clearly be challenging "to know exactly" when a particular norm, normative framework or, indeed, an entire normative system has crossed the 'theoretical threshold' from 'non-law' to 'law' – in other words, whether it has "transition[ed] from social to legal normativity."[129]

---

121 Brunnée & Toope (2010), pp. 22-23. *Also see* Sarfaty (2005), pp. 1809-1810, who notes: "[t]he key factor in the transnational legal process is repeated participation, which 'helps to reconstitute national interests, to establish the identity of actors as ones who obey the law, and to develop the norms that become part of the fabric of emerging international society'."

122 Brunnée & Toope (2010), pp. 22-23.

123 *Id.* The authors are referencing K.I. Winston, 'Three Model for the Study of Law', *in* W.J. Witteveen and W. van der Burg (Eds.) (1999), *Rediscovering Fuller: Essays on Implicit Law and Institutional Design,* Amsterdam: Amsterdam University Press 1999, pp. 51 & 63. *Also see* Toope *in* Bodansky et al. (Eds.) (2007), who notes (at pp. 112-113): "This understanding of law is connected to Habermasian discourse theory. However, Habermas's dependence upon a shared 'lifeworld' as a basis for communicative action causes immense problems for those international lawyers who doubt the existence of such a common lifeworld in international society." In this regard, *also see* Hale's comments *at* 188, Ch. 7.

124 Brunnée & Toope (2010), pp. 22-23.

125 *Id.*

126 *Id.*

127 Toope *in* Bodansky et al. (Eds.) (2007), p. 107. Toope is referencing F. Kratochwil (1989), *Rules, Norms, and Decisions: On the Conditions of Practical and Legal Reasoning in International Relations and Domestic Affairs,* Cambridge: Cambridge University Press, pp. 200-201.

128 Brunnée & Toope (2010), pp. 22-23. For other conceptualizations that describe "relative normativity" in the international legal order, *see e.g.,* Shelton *in* Evans (2006), pp. 159-184; *and see* Goldmann *in* Von Bogdandy et al. (Eds.) (2010).

129 *Id.* The authors note (*id.,* at p. 26) that Fuller's disinterest in clearly distinguishing between law and non-law had been fuelled by his "strong pluralism" and "interest in the wide variety of mechanisms of normative social ordering outside law."

Figure 3   The 'Continuum of Legality'

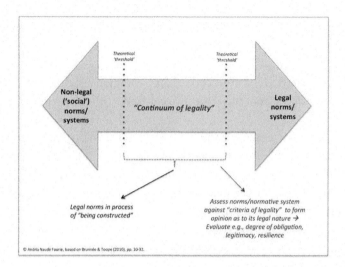

Although Fuller"reject[ed]" the necessity of having "a bright line distinction between law and non-law", he also argued that "legal norms are distinguishable by the explicit responsibilities they impose."[130] Hence, Fuller proposed eight "markers" or "criteria of legality" for the purpose of such an assessment, which, Fuller argued, are "internal to law" – namely: "generality, promulgation, non-retroactivity, clarity, non-contradiction, not asking the impossible, constancy, and congruence between rules and official action."[131]

Elaborating on Fuller's conceptualization, Brunnée and Toope suggest that legal norms, in addition to their degree of 'legality', might also be identified by their degree of 'legitimacy'

---

130 Brunnée & Toope (2010), p. 26.
131 Brunnée & Toope (2010), pp. 6-7. For other conceptual frameworks aimed at achieving similar outcomes, *see e.g.*, Goldstein et al. (Eds.) (2001), pp. 17-34. The authors identify 'three dimensions' that reflect the 'legalization' of norms: "delegation" (the degree to which "third parties have been granted the authority to implement, interpret, and apply the rules; to resolve disputes; and (possibly) to make further rules."); "obligation" (the degree to which actors are "legally bound by a rule or commitment in the sense that their behavior thereunder is subject to scrutiny under the general rules, procedures, and discourse of international law."); and "precision" (that is, the extent to which "the rules unambiguously define the conduct they require, authorize, or proscribe"). *Also see* Goldmann *in* Von Bogdandy et al. (Eds.) (2010), pp. 661-711, describing several "parameters for the definition of standard instruments" – which he defines (at p. 679) as "a combination of a rule of identification for authoritative instruments of a specific type and a specific legal regime that is applicable to all instruments coming under the rule of identification." Proposed identification criteria include: "generic parameters" (such as "author", "procedure", "promulgation"), "textual parameters" (such as "designation" and different levels of "addressees"), and "parameters concerning follow-up" (concerning various forms of "enforcement"). (*Id.*)

– referring to "the specific sense of obligation that they generate," which, in turn, results in compliance with or "fidelity to law."[132]

In other words, Brunnée and Toope conclude, "legal norms can only arise in the context of social norms based on shared understandings."[133] Therefore, "within *all* systems of normativity,"

> social norms are constructed through rhetorical activity and social practice, producing increasingly influential mutual expectations or shared understanding of actions. In turn, if these shared understandings are reinforced through action based upon Fullers' criteria of legality, it becomes possible to generate obligation, or fidelity to law.[134]

One benefit of such a conceptualization is that, while it provides the ability to evaluate a norm, normative framework or normative system so as to form a conclusion as to where it is situated on the spectrum between social and legal normativity, it becomes "less important", as Chinkin notes, to "dra[w] a formal distinction between hard and soft obligations."[135] Instead, our focus of inquiry can be expanded so as to include, for instance,

---

132 Brunnée & Toope (2010), pp. 26 & 34. *Note*, Brunnée & Toope argue (at p. 26) that the identification of legal norms is "crucial in upholding an admittedly weak rule-of-law tradition" within the international legal order. On the notion of the 'international rule of law', *see e.g.*, Chesterman (2008(a)), p. 32, defining it as "the application of rule of law principles to relations between States and other subjects of international law", and distinguishing the international rule of law from the notion of "promoting the rule of law", at the domestic level, "through international forums", "treaties" and "international organizations" (*see* pp. 16-25).

133 Brunnée & Toope (2010), p. 15.

134 Brunnée & Toope (2010), p. 34 (emphasis in original). For a critical view of legal approaches grounded in "constructivism and its 'normative optics'", *see e.g.*, Alvarez (2005), pp. 53-54; *and see* A. Slaughter (2000), 'International Law and International Relations', 285 *Recueil des Cours* 12, p 48: "Many lawyers are norm entrepreneurs; virtually all lawyers engage daily in deliberation and persuasion – a world of discourse. Many lawyers are intuitively uncomfortable with purely Rationalist instrumental accounts, believing deeply and verifying empirically through their practice the ways in which the rules that they shape in turn shape the identity and interests of the actors who operate within those roles. For these lawyers, Constructivism provides a deeply satisfying account of how and why what they do matters." For an opposing theoretical conception of international legal normativity, *see e.g.*, D'Aspremont (2011). The author argues (at pp. 221-222): "[…] international legal scholars have been inclined to deformalize the ascertainment of international legal rules with a view to capturing these new manifestations of public authority in their conceptual 'net'. Such a stretch of international legal scholars' nets – which has materialized in an [sic] growing use of non-formal law-ascertainment criteria – has most of the time been driven by lofty purposes, primarily the domestication of these new exercises of public authority, their subjection to accountability mechanisms, and a better program-mation of the emergence of new rules of international law. Some very serious doubts have nonetheless been cast as to whether deformalization of law-ascertainment actually contributes to the realization of any of these noble objectives." In addition (*id.*, at p. 222): "[…] the deformalization at play in contemporary theory of the sources of international law comes with a disproportionate high price in terms of normativity and authority of international law, meaningfulness of scholarly debate, and the possibility of a critique of inter-national legal rules."

135 Chinkin *in* Shelton (Ed.) 2000, p. 23.

the "processes at work within the law-making environment", the "products that flow from" such processes, as well as their "societal impact."[136] Insights, in other words, that can enhance our understanding of "how norms function in a horizontal normative order."[137]

As to the purpose of normative systems (or, what they "are for"), the model describes two competing paradigms – 'instrumentalism' and 'formalism'[138] – that that are based in very different arguments as to which constituency group's interests, demands and expectations should be served (primarily) through the particular normative system.[139]

The instrumentalist paradigm typically reflects the perspective of "power-wielders"[140] or "dominant decision-makers,"[141] which consider the primary purpose of normative systems as *enabling* the dominant decision-makers to take particular action.[142] Because normative systems are viewed as a means to advance "particular claims and agendas",[143] instrumentalism emphasize the need for differentiation, discretion and flexibility with respect to the methods or approaches employed in the application and enforcement of normative frameworks.[144]

The formalist paradigm, by contrast, usually reflects the perspective of those who seek to hold decision-makers to account – or, who have particular interests associated with the actions undertaking by dominant decision-makers. Viewed from this perspective, the primary purpose of a normative system is to limit or *restrain* the actions of dominant decision-makers.[145] Formalism aims to advance "a relatively autonomous formal technique" as a "standard of criticism and means of controlling those in powerful positions,"[146] and therefore tends to emphasize the need for consistency, certainty, and fairness with respect

---

136 *Id.*

137 Brunnée & Toope (2010), p. 6. *Also see* note 120, Ch. 2.

138 *Note*, this conceptual framework is employed by Koskenniemi (*see* Koskenniemi *in* Koskenniemi *in* Evans (Ed.) (2006), pp. 57-78), with respect to the international legal system. *Also note*: 'formalism' and 'instrumentalism' have attained different meanings in various disciplines. Other terms associated with instrumentalism include, *e.g.*, 'managerialism,' 'pragmatism' and 'functionalism'; whereas terms often associated with formalism include, *e.g.*, 'legalism', 'legalization' and 'judicialization'.

139 *See e.g.*, the discussion *in* section 3.2.3.

140 *See* note 91, Ch. 2.

141 Koskenniemi *in* Evans (Ed.) (2006), p. 57.

142 *Id.*

143 *Id.*

144 *Id.*

145 *Id.*

146 Koskenniemi *in* Evans (Ed.) (2006), pp. 57-59. *And see* Goldmann, *in* von Bogdandy et al. (Eds.) 2010, pp. 665-666, arguing that "[l]egal concepts" can "serve as analytical tools, provide a medium for critique, and have the capacity of transposing imponderable discourses about legitimacy" – and accountability – "into more precise, sustainable, manageable and reliable concepts of legality." Law, Goldmann adds, has the "capacity to rationalize fundamental conflicts about questions of justice through the use of formalistic arguments about rights and obligations." (*Id.*)

to the methods or approaches employed in the application and enforcement of normative frameworks.[147]

The "contrast between instrumentalism and formalism is quite fundamental" as Koskenniemi remarks with respect to the manner in which these competing paradigms unfold in the international legal system.[148] "From the instrumental perspective," for instance, "international law exists"

> to realize objectives of some dominant part of the community; from the formalist perspective, it provides a platform to evaluate behaviour, including the behaviour of those in dominant positions. The instrumental perspective highlights the role of law as social engineering, formalism views it as an interpretative scheme. The instrumental perspective is typically that of an active and powerful actor in possession of alternative choices; formalism is often the perspective of the weak actor relying on the law for protection.[149]

In the international legal system, moreover, the instrumentalist paradigm tends to be dominant, whereas formalism tends to have negative connotations – such as 'narrowness', 'cumbersomeness', 'bureaucracy' or 'ineffectiveness'.[150]

Crucially, however, neither instrumentalist nor formalist "logic is fully constraining."[151] The purpose of the international legal system, therefore, as Koskenniemi concludes, is "to realize the political values, interests, and preferences of various international actors", *while also* "appear[ing] as a standard of criticism and means of controlling those in powerful positions."[152]

---

147 Koskenniemi *in* Evans (Ed.) (2006), p. 57.

148 Koskenniemi *in* Evans (Ed.) (2006), pp. 68-69. *Note*, however, that formalism as described here, are not limited to 'formal norms' as the only possible "standard of critique". In this regard, *also see e.g.,* Toope *in* Bodansky et al. (Eds.) (2007), p. 117: "The great difficulty with the debate between upholders of the formal in the face of self-styled realists is the wide degree of division over what is meant by formalism in law" since "various conceptions" of formalism are "often conflated. What is more, formalism is often simply employed as an accusing epithet in fundamental legal theoretic disputes. To add to the confusion, many particular rules can be cast as formal or informal, depending upon one's underlying theoretical commitments." In this regard, *also see* Toope's comments *at* note 116, Ch. 2; *and compare* these arguments with those of D'Aspremont *at* note 134, Ch. 2.

149 *Id.*

150 *Id.* Koskenniemi adds (at p. 68) that there is an "almost uniformly pejorative use of the term 'formalism' in international law"; whereas instrumentalism, especially when equated with 'pragmatism', is typically regarded in a positive light.

151 Koskenniemi *in* Evans (Ed.) (2006), pp. 63, 57 & 71.

152 *Id. Note*, Koskenniemi also points out (at pp. 63-64) that the recognition of the 'dual purpose' of international law does not serve "to claim political neutrality;" instead, it argues that the question, "'what is international law for?' needs to be removed from the context of legal routines to the political arenas where it can be used to articulate claims by those who are sidelined from formal diplomacy and informal networks and feel that something about the routines of both is responsible for the deprivations they suffer. In other words, there

That being said, normative systems are also characterised by the tension derived from the competition between these paradigms. One "way of thinking about this tension between formalism and instrumentalism", as Toope suggests,

> is to trace out their philosophical roots. Aristotle argued that all human action is to some purpose. Law should not be excluded. Hobbes stressed what we would now call a positivist, self-referential, and self-explaining quality in social systems, including law.[153]

"Drawing these strains of thinking together", however, "results in the *relative* autonomy of international law", which is to say:

> [...] there is no identity between law and power or between law and politics. Might does *not* make right, and law is not merely the infinitely malleable tool of political aspiration. At the same time, neither law and power nor law and politics are opposites. Law embodies both substantive and procedural values that provide it with relative independence from unmediated power and politics.[154]

The dual nature of normativity is illustrated, for instance, by the fact that "[f]ormal and informal norms" often "operate side by side" – while "[e]ach can be influential and each can fail to influence."[155] In fact, Toope adds, it has become uncommon – and certainly in transnational regulatory governance contexts – for actors to "simply choose" whether "to employ either a formal or an informal 'tool'."[156] "Indeed," Toope concludes, "this metaphor is simply wrong" – "[n]either formal rules nor informal norms are mere tools"

> for law is never purely instrumental. Law relates to our deepest hopes and fears. It is rooted in our collective aspirations for a better world. If purported law fails to manifest those values, it will not work as law because it will not command our adherence. Its illegitimacy will destroy our hopes and reinforce our fears. Since law is rooted in both the logics of aspiration and of duty, it will always be necessarily and appropriately both informal and formal.[157]

---

is reason to defend a legal 'formalism' against a 'pragmatism' that views international law only in terms of the immediate objectives it serves."
153 Toope *in* Bodansky et al. (Eds.) (2007), p. 107 & pp. 112-113.
154 *Id.*
155 Toope *in* Bodansky et al. (Eds.) (2007), p. 124.
156 *Id.*
157 *Id.*

This 'dual nature' is also reflected in other conceptualizations of legal normativity. Frank, for instance, in considering the role of 'fairness' in the international legal system, argues that law should promote both "stability" and "change."[158] Whereas Higgins, in reflecting on the relationship between the exercise of (legal) "authority" and (political) "control" within the international legal system, emphasizes that the "authority which characterizes law exists not in a vacuum."[159] Instead, legal authority exists "exactly where it intersects with power."[160] Law should therefore not be understood as "authority battling against power," Higgins concludes, but rather as the "interlocking of authority with power."[161] In other words, we cannot "say [that] law is about authority only, and not about power too; or that power is definitionally to be regarded as hostile to law. It is an integral part of it."[162] Or, as Brunnée and Toope argue, "law *enables* human beings to organize their lives and their relationships with each other," while "limi[ting] the potential abuse of authority by insisting on 'criteria of legality' that *constrain* arbitrary exercises of power."[163]

But while we might observe the instrumentalist and formalist aspects of normative systems readily enough, explaining why this occurs – and how it works – can be more challenging.

Constructivist thinking, for instance, describes the "'duality of structure': structures constrain social action, but they also enable action."[164] In the process of doing so, however, social structures are influenced and potentially changed as a result of the "friction of social action against the parameters of the structure."[165] In other words, as complex 'social structures,' normative systems can enable and restrain social actions because they are "mutually constituting" in nature.[166]

Furthermore, normative systems are able to deal with the tensions arising from competing paradigms or conceptions, as well as the tensions caused by competing interests, demands and expectations, when they are embedded in resilient and adaptable 'communities of practice'.

---

158 Frank (1995), p. 7. Frank argues (at p. 175) that "[f]airness is the rubric under which the tension ["between stability and change"] should be discursively managed."

159 Higgins (1994), p. 4. *Also see* the ILA's remarks *at* note 86, Ch. 1.

160 *Id.*

161 *Id.*

162 *Id.*

163 Brunnée & Toope (2010), p. 21 (emphases added).

164 *See* Brunnée & Toope (2010), p. 21, quoting A. Giddens (1984), *The Constitution of Society: Outline of the Theory of Structuration*, Cambridge: Polity Press.

165 *Id.*

166 Brunnée & Toope (2010), pp. 14-15 & pp. 33-36. *Also see* Allott (1999), pp. 3-8: "Law is a means of continuous self-constitution for a society, embodying the society's possibilities, and transforming behavior so that the society becomes what it imagines it could be. [...] [N]orms have an important constitutive function. The struggle of international constitutionalism is to establish a higher law, constitutive of international society and of the increasingly important global public realm [...]." *And see* note 4, Part I.

Communities of practice have the ability to "'cut across state boundaries and mediate between states, individuals, and human agency, on one hand, and social structures and systems, on the other.'"[167] Furthermore, as communities that "are both 'in, and of, *practice*'", they are "above all, […] 'learning communities'".[168] Yet, as Adler argues, "[t]heir enterprise does not necessarily imply 'a common goal or vision'" – the only requirement is that their "members 'must share collective understandings' of 'what they are doing and why'."[169]

In the context of normative systems, such "share[d] collective understandings" must include, at least initially, a basic recognition and acknowledgement of the "need for normativity" as well as a commitment to the "particular norms intended to shape behaviour."[170] Importantly, however, the norms that form part of these 'initial shared understandings' do not have to be 'thick' (or, including norms that are both procedural and substantive in nature). In fact, because it is often challenging to reach political consensus on 'thick' norms (which are typically more value-laden), the norms adopted as part of initial shared understandings tend to be largely 'thin' or procedural in nature.

While "[n]orm entrepreneurs and epistemic communities" may be "influential in promoting" the adoption of particular norms as part of this 'initial shared understanding', as Brunnée and Toope argue, "the effective creation of norms is not a unidirectional projection of ideas or values."[171] Instead, norms are created "through communities of practice that shape the mutual engagement of various actors in international society".[172]

Moreover, for a normative system to "exist and to endure," it has to "maintain" and, ideally, "expand underlying shared understandings" about the content and scope of specific norms.[173] Through the "mutual engagement" of the community of practice in the processes of norm creation, norm application and norm enforcement, actors representing diverse interests can interact, negotiate, whereas "even adversaries [can] learn from each other."[174]

---

167 *See* Brunnée & Toope (2010), p. 86, quoting E. Adler (2005), *Communitarian International Relations: The Epistemic Foundations of International Relations*, London & New York: Routledge, at p. 13.

168 *Id.* (emphasis in original).

169 *Id.*

170 Brunnée & Toope (2010), p. 350.

171 Brunnée & Toope (2010), p. 86. *Also see* Sarfaty (2005), p. 1810, who employs a conceptualization based in "transnational legal process theory", which argues that the process of norm creation "is catalyzed by 'transnational norm entrepreneurs' (*i.e.*, nongovernmental actors, both individuals and organizations) and transnational issue networks, which advocate for the adoption and diffusion of new norms." *Note*, on 'norm entrepreneurs', *also see* note 134, Ch. 2.

172 Brunnée & Toope (2010), p. 86.

173 Brunnée & Toope (2010), p. 352.

174 Brunnée & Toope (2010), p. 86. *But see* Koskenniemi's argument that "it is international law's formalism" that "provides the shared surface – the *only* such surface – on which political adversaries recognize each other as such and pursue their adversity in terms of something shared, instead of seeking to attain full exclusion – 'outlawry' of the other. In this sense, international law's value and its misery lie in its being the fragile surface of political community among social agents – States, other communities, individuals – who disagree about their preferences but do this within a structure that invites them to argue in terms of an assumed universality. (Koskenniemi *in* Evans (Ed.) (2006), p. 77 (emphasis in original).)

"Over time," Brunnée and Toope conclude, "with increasing interaction, communities of practice can become more interconnected and value-based, allowing for [the development of] richer substantive rules."[175]

This book argues that the processes of norm creation, norm application and norm enforcement pertaining to the World Bank's development-lending operations have become embedded in such an community of practice.

This community of practice is based on the recognition that international financial institutions such as the World Bank have a 'duty of accountability', and that there is a need for normativity to facilitate the process of determining what the content and scope of such a duty should entail – even as the need for *legal* normativity may not have been recognized as explicitly.

Specific (albeit mostly 'thin') norms were adopted as part of this initial shared under-standing, as reflected in the World Bank's development of an operational policy framework over the course of 1980s and early 1990s,[176] and in the establishment of 'internal account-ability mechanisms' mandated to contribute towards the enforcement of these norms across World Bank development-lending operations.[177] These developments, in turn, led to the adoption of similar normative frameworks and the establishment of similar accountability mechanisms at other multilateral development banks.[178]

Spearheaded by the efforts of the World Bank Group, the process of norm creation gradually became more interactional across the transnational development context, as a result of increased levels of participation in the adoption and amendment of operational policies – that is, increased participation by both internal and external constituency groups.[179] Moreover, the establishment of citizen-driven independent accountability mechanisms, starting with the World Bank's establishment of the Inspection Panel in 1993 and closely followed by the establishment of functionally equivalent bodies at the

---

175 *Id.* The authors add (at pp. 42-43) that a major benefit "of working with such a "thin", "procedural" conception as basis", "is its congeniality to pluralistic contexts, while "permit[ing] and encourage[ing] the gradual building up of global interaction." *Note,* for similar arguments about the role of triadic dispute resolution (which is "constructed and maintained by rules") as "a crucial mechanism of social cohesion and change", *see* Shapiro & Stone Sweet (2002), pp. 66 & 70: TDR "constitutes modes of governance" that "facilitat[e] social exchange and the adaptation of rule systems to the exigencies of those who exchange: hence its social utility. Other things being equal, it must be that dyadic governance is inherently less flexible and more brittle than triadic governance. Whereas conflict can destroy dyadic contracts, conflict activates TDR and establishes parameters of a politics that can recast the normative basis of social exchange." In other words, "[t]o put it in constructivist terms, triadic governance coordinates the complex relationship between structures and agents, helping to constitute and reconstitute both over time." *Note,* on the role of TDR in normative development, *also see* the discussion *in* section 7.1.
176 *See e.g.,* the discussion *in* section 5.1.
177 *See e.g.,* the discussion *in* section 6.2.
178 *See e.g.,* Bradlow & Naudé Fourie (2013), pp. 16-27.
179 *See e.g.,* the discussion *in* section 5.1.

remaining WBG institutions and other MDBs,[180] further increased the interactional nature of the processes of norm application and enforcement.[181]

Recent years have also seen the emergence of an informal (but increasingly formalizing) 'Independent Accountability Mechanisms Network' that consists of the members and staff of several citizen-driven accountability mechanisms, institutionally affiliated with multi-lateral development banks.[182]

Indeed, as this network continues to expand its membership and the range of its activities, it is becoming the embodiment of a broader normative community of interest in the transnational development context.

****

The core conceptual models introduced in this chapter, as well those presented throughout this book, are based in theory. It is important to clarify, therefore, that this book views theory as a valuable "tool that organizes inquiry [by] connecting problem and data" – and not, in other words, "as an illusive, sacred Truth".[183] When different theories are integrated in conceptual models such as those presented here, they serve as "heuristics"[184] or "dynamic hypotheses" that "suppor[t] and infor[m]" inquiry[185] – and, in the process, operate as "a special kind of ["intermediate"] theory"[186] that can facilitate discourse.

In this regard, it is also important to keep in mind that what we call 'opposing' or 'competing' conceptions or "schools of thought" can be "misleading to the extent that it suggests hermetically self-contained alternatives."[187] Opposing theories, as Alvarez comments, "do not necessarily represent the views of any single scholar" – "[i]n reality, scholars within these various schools have borrowed from each other, both with respect to methodology as well as substantive conclusions."[188] Therefore, Alvarez concludes, opposing theories are "best regarded as ideal types in the Weberian sense" – meaning, they are "generalized rubrics that might be useful for didactic purposes."[189]

---

180 For an overview of IAMs at MDBs, *See e.g.*, Bradlow & Naudé Fourie *in* Hale, T. & Held, D. (Eds.), (2011).

181 *E.g.*, on the 'dispute resolution triad' formed by Requesters, Bank management and the Inspection Panel, *see* the discussion *in* section 7.1.

182 *See e.g.*, the discussion *in* section 3.1.3.

183 Shields & Rangarajan (2013), pp. 23-24. The authors note that this approach is based on "insights from John Dewey", as reflected *e.g.*, *in* J. Dewey (1938), *Logic: The Theory of Inquiry*. New York, NY: Henry Holt and Company.

184 Taleb (2012), e-Book.

185 Shields & Rangarajan (2013), pp. 1-11. On the role of 'dynamic hypotheses' in guiding conceptual modelling efforts in the area of systems dynamics, *see e.g.*, Sterman (2000), p. 95.

186 Shields & Rangarajan (2013), p. 24.

187 Alvarez (2005), pp. 45-57.

188 *Id.*

189 *Id.*

An important benefit of employing a "theory as tool perspective", as Shields and Rangarajan point out, "is that common theoretical dualisms",

> such as means/ends, fact/value, theory/practice, or administration/policies, function as useful distinctions rather than rigid dichotomies that represent certain truths.[190]

The conceptual models in which different theories are integrated might assist the operationalization of abstract concepts because they can help to "make things simple[r]" and therefore "easy[ier] to implement."[191] It remains important, however, to recognize that neither theory nor the conceptual models we create by integrating theories, methods and observations drawn from practice are "perfect".[192] They are "just expedient."[193] As long as we remember that, we are less likely to be "fooled by their powers;" however, as Taleb cautions, "[t]hey become dangerous when we forget that."[194]

---

190 *Id.*
191 Taleb (2012), e-Book.
192 *Id.*
193 *Id.*
194 *Id.*

Part I
Conceptualizing World Bank Accountability

"There are at least six questions associated with accountability: Who is accountable? To whom? For what? When? How? And with what consequences? The answers to these questions are multifaceted, context-specific, and sometimes culturally dependent."[1]

"Accountability is often viewed as a crucial tool for limiting unconstrained power, and therefore as vital for democratic politics. Yet, standard accountability mechanisms rely on actors being able to sanction one another. When the actor that is supposed to be sanctioned is more powerful than the actors that are supposed to impose the sanction, accountability as it is standardly described breaks down."[2]

"Discussion of compliance [with international law] often proceeds as if the concept of 'compliance' is largely shared; that is, as if there was a shared understanding that compliance is adequately defined as conformity of behavior with legal rules, and the real problems are about such matters as measuring, monitoring and improving compliance, and the simultaneous optimization of levels of compliance and rigor of the relevant standards. [...] [However,] the concept of 'compliance' with law does not have, and cannot have, any meaning except as a function of prior theories of the nature and operation of the law to which it pertains. 'Compliance' is thus not a free-standing concept, but derives meaning and utility from theories, so that different theories lead to significantly different notions of what is meant by 'compliance.'"[3]

"We shape our buildings; thereafter, our buildings shape us."[4]

---

1   Brown Weiss (2010), p. 481.
2   Rubenstein (2007), p. 631.
3   Kingsbury (1998), pp. 345-346.
4   Winston Churchill, as quoted in Sterman (2000), p. 137.

3 'To Whom' Should the World Bank be Accountable? 'Power Wielders' and 'Accountability Holders'

Who should hold the World Bank accountable and are, therefore, accountability holders? And when we talk about World Bank accountability, who are the *power wielders* within the Bank we have in mind, and what is the nature of their relationships with the *accountability holders*? These questions, which relate to the first dimension of World Bank accountability (in terms of the conceptual model introduced in the previous chapter), form the focus of Chapter 3.

The chapter initiates the discussion by setting out the *prominent actors involved in the World Bank's development-lending operations*, and by explaining the (often overlapping) capacities in which they are involved in World Bank (co-)financed development projects. Next, the chapter *introduces two broad constituency categories* functioning in the context of World Bank development-lending operations: *internal* and *external* accountability holders.[1]

This chapter departs from the argument that both categories of accountability holders have legitimate claims to holding the World Bank's power wielders into account, or by demanding such accountability. However, these claims are based in different (complementary and contrasting) theoretical understandings, and the effect of these differences become particularly clear when the matter of 'primacy' is considered – that is, *which constituency group's interests, demands and expectations might claim primacy over those of the other*. The competition for primacy between internal and external accountability holders is illustrated, finally, by the *debate about the reasons for the Inspection Panel's establishment, and the decisive factors that led to its inception*.

3.1 Prominent actors involved in World Bank development-lending operations

Organization theorists such as Philip Selznick and his contemporaries emphasized the importance of understanding "the internal aspects of institutions and their relationship

---

1   *Note*, different theories – based in different disciplines – attach different meanings to these terms. *Thus*, the term 'accountability holders', as used here, concerns those '*to whom*' the World Bank should be accountable, and, as this chapter will illustrate, therefore encompasses other terms such as 'shareholders', 'stakeholders', 'interest groups', and 'constituents' or 'constituency groups'.

to the environments in which they operate."[2] They argued "that organizational behavior is explained"

> not by the formal structure of an organization, but by subterranean processes such as conflicts between informal groups, recruitment policies, dependence upon outside constituencies, and the striving for prestige.[3]

Whereas "open systems" theorists such as Thompson contended that "institutions cannot be analyzed as discrete entities because they depend on exchanges and interaction with other systems,"[4] such as those systems involving their "customers, suppliers, regulators, and competitors."[5]

The scope of this book precludes in-depth analyses of all these aspects; nevertheless, this section outlines the (what is often perceived as a) "bewildering" range of actors involved in World Bank development-lending operations, as well as the different complementary and potentially conflicting capacities in which they operate.[6]

3.1.1   World Bank governance structure, management and staff

When we talk about the 'World Bank', we typically refer to two sister-intergovernmental or international organizations (that is, the IDA and IBRD) that are endowed with international legal personality.[7] Behind the abstract notion of 'the Bank', however, are three distinct groups of actors that play critical roles with respect to the Bank's development-lending operations, namely: the World Bank's governance and management structures, as well as its staff members.

The World Bank's governance structure is set out in its Articles of Agreement and can be described in terms of the hierarchy depicted by Figure 4.[8]

---

2   Miller-Adams (1999), p. 13.
3   *Id.*
4   Miller-Adams (1999), p. 13, quoting J. Thompson (1967), *Organizations in Action*, New York: McGraw Hill.
5   Miller-Adams (1999), p. 13, quoting W.R. Scott (1981), *Organizations: Rational, Natural and Open Systems*, Englewood Cliffs, N.J.: Prentice-Hall, Inc.
6   *See e.g.*, Miller-Adams (1999), p. 16, arguing that there has been a "bewildering growth" both "in the number and variety" of World Bank 'stakeholders'.
7   For a discussion of the 'legal status' of international organizations in international and national legal systems, *see e.g.*, Schermers & Blokker (2003), pp. 1562-1686.
8   Available at: http://go.worldbank.org/BA0GA6O820.

Figure 4   World Bank Governance and Management Structure

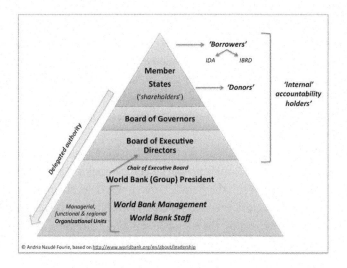

© Andria Naudé Fourie, based on http://www.worldbank.org/en/about/leadership

Member states – 'donors' and 'borrowers'

As an international financial institution, the World Bank's member states are also its 'shareholders'. However, the respective shares held by member states affect their relative voting power within the Bank's governance structure.[9] When considering the Bank's member states, the distinction is often made between 'donors' and 'borrowers'. Generally speaking, a 'donor' "refers to a country that makes contributions specifically to IDA", whereas 'borrower' denotes "a country that borrows from IDA or IBRD or both."[10] For the sake of clarity, it should be noted here that all World Bank member states "pay capital subscriptions, and this payment is distinct from a given country's lending and borrowing."[11]

---

9   *E.g.*, voting power in the IBRD is allocated as follows: "Each member receives votes consisting of share votes (one vote for each share of the Bank's capital stock held by the member) plus basic votes (calculated so that the sum of all basic votes is equal to 5.55 percent of the sum of basic votes and share votes for all members)." *See* http://www.worldbank.org/en/about/leadership/VotingPowers.

10   On the distinction between 'part 1 Donors and part 2 Borrowers – *see e.g.*, L. Nielsen, Classifications of Countries Based on Their Level of Development: How it is Done and How it Could be Done, Available at: http://core.ac.uk/download/pdf/6455187.pdf. Nielsen observes (at pp. 9-10): "With the establishment in 1960 of its concessional financing entity, *The International Development Association* (IDA) the World Bank identified two lists of IDA member countries. Part 1 countries were expected to contribute financially to IDA and Part 2 countries were other countries of which only a subset could be expected to draw on the concessional resources."

11   World Bank (2011), e-Book. *Also note* that some donors borrow from the Bank, albeit much smaller loan amounts, for a lower number of projects. *E.g.*, in July 2013, the Bank was funding one project in France and 31 projects in Japan. *See* http://www.worldbank.org/projects.

The World Bank's borrower member states are broadly segmented, first, in terms of "middle-income and creditworthy poorer countries",[12] which are serviced by loans offered by the IBRD. The IBRD raises its funds primarily "by issuing AAA-rated bonds to institutional and retail investors in global capital markets."[13] Although it "earns a small margin on this lending, the greater proportion of its income comes from investing its own capital."[14] The second client segmentation group consists of "the world's poorest countries", which are funded by the IDA by means of development credits[15] and grants.[16] The IDA's funds are raised "largely by contributions from the governments" of the IDA's donor or "high-income member countries."[17]

All IDA and IBRD member states are represented on the *Board of Governors* (hereinafter the 'Governors'), which is the Bank's primary decision-making body. However, as this body "only meet[s] twice a year", the Bank's Governors "delegate most of their powers" to appointed Executive Directors.[18] Voting powers on the Board of Governors are weighted in terms of relative shares held by the member state[19] – a situation that has often been criticized for its 'asymmetricality' – meaning:

the rich countries are the policy-givers because of the system of weighted voting, and the poor countries, as borrowers, are the policy-takers; and in some cases

---

12 World Bank (2011), e-Book.

13 *Id.*

14 *Id.* The Bank also notes (*at id.*), while the IBRD "is driven by development impact rather than by profit maximization," it "has earned a positive operating income each year since 1948."

15 *Id.* The Bank notes (*at id.*): "Credits are loans at zero or low interest with a 10-year grace period before repayment of principal begins and with maturities of 20 to 40 years. These credits are often referred to as concessional lending."

16 *Id.* The Bank adds (*at id.*): "IDA eligibility is a transitional arrangement that gives the poorest countries access to substantial resources before they are capable of obtaining the financing they need from commercial markets. As their economies grow, countries graduate from IDA eligibility. The repayments, or reflows, that they make on IDA loans are used to help finance new IDA loans to the remaining poor countries."

17 *Id.* The Bank adds (*at id.*): "Representatives of donor countries meet every three years to replenish IDA funds", whereas "[a]dditional funds come from World Bank Group transfers and from borrowers' repayments of earlier IDA credits, including voluntary and contractual acceleration of credit repayments from eligible IDA graduates."

18 Phillips (2009), p. 13. Notable examples of these decision-making powers include the approval of development-lending financing, as well as policy decisions – such as the adoption of the operational policies (*see* section 5.1) and the establishment of internal mechanisms such as the Inspection Panel (*see* section 6.2). *Note*, the Inspection Panel's founding Resolution(s) and subsequent Board clarifications of the Resolution(s) have been incorporated in the World Bank's operational policy framework as BP. 17.55 (Inspection Panel), Annex A, B and C – available at: http://go.worldbank.org/DZDZ9038D0.

19 *E.g.*, regarding the IBRD, the Bank notes that "[e]ach member receives votes consisting of share votes (one vote for each share of the Bank's capital stock held by the member) plus basic votes (calculated so that the sum of all basic votes is equal to 5.55 percent of the sum of basic votes and share votes for all members)." *See* http://www.worldbank.org/en/about/leadership/VotingPowers.

the rich countries do not follow the very policies that they insist the poor countries should follow.[20]

Board of Executive Directors

The Executive Directors "are in permanent residence" at World Bank headquarters in Washington, DC and collectively function as the 'Board of Executive Directors' (hereinafter the 'Executive Board' or 'Board').[21] The Board is chaired by the World Bank Group's President, which, as the institution's 'chief executive officer' also heads World Bank management and staff. The Executive Board's membership and voting arrangements, as well as its overall effectiveness, have been the focus of persistent criticisms – as well as institutional reforms in more recent years.

Although the Executive Board typically "make[s] decisions by consensus", formally speaking, its voting arrangements, as with the Board of Governors, are determined by the "relative voting power of individual executive directors", which, in turn, "is based on the shares held by the countries they represent."[22] Another prominent point of criticism concerns the fact that only a few of the Bank's member states have their 'own', dedicated 'country director'.[23] Hence, "[o]ne of the most persistent complaints about the governance of [...] particularly the World Bank and the IMF" has been "that they were not representing their membership very effectively".[24] Or, as Woods argues (with respect to both the IMF and the Bank), the Executive Board is "the lynchpin of accountability," and "the quality and depth of [its] oversight and control" of the "institution's work is vital."[25] Yet, there are strongly held views that, "in practice, the Board rarely holds the management and staff of the institutions tightly to account" and that the Executive Directors frequently "rubber-stamp decisions coming before them."[26]

In this regard, Woods highlights a number of contributing factors, noting, firstly, that "it is difficult" for Board members"

to prepare positions on all countries, papers and issues brought to Board meetings. Many Executive Directors are in the job only for a short time. Indeed,

---

20   Head (2003-2004), p. 262.
21   Phillips (2009), p. 13. *See:* http://www.worldbank.org/en/about/leadership/directors.
22   World Bank (2011), e-Book. The approval of Inspection Panel investigations constitute a prominent example of the Board's practice with regards to consensus decision-making. For a discussion of the more problematic aspects of this approach, *see e.g.,* Shihata (2000), pp. 37-41.
23   World Bank (2011), e-Book.
24   Bradlow *in* Cissé et al. (Eds.) (2012), e-Book.
25   Woods (2001), pp. 87-88.
26   *Id.*

in some multi-country constituencies there is regular and rapid rotation of the Executive Directorship.[27]

Secondly, "the Executive Board is not assisted in playing an active role by the staff and management",

> who seldom divulge internal disagreements to the Board, tending instead to attach 'considerable importance' to presenting a unified view in Board discussions.[28]

Thirdly, reflecting the organization theory arguments mentioned at the onset of this chapter, "many decisions are taken – or agreement reached on them – prior to Board meetings," and the "real debates over policy and issues are conducted outside of the Board."[29] "For example," Woods elaborates, "a loan that did not meet with US approval"

> would seldom be presented to a Board for discussion. Before getting that far, in most (but not all) cases staff and management would have been in dialogue with those whose agreement was necessary for the loan to go through.[30]

Fourthly, some commentators attribute the Board's ineffectiveness to individual "Directors' protectiveness"

> towards the countries they represent, and their consequent expectation (and reciprocation) of similar deference from their colleagues on the Board.[31]

Moreover, as Bradlow observes, "there are only limited ways for a frustrated state to hold the executive director accountable for [a particular] decision."[32] Consequently, "what is supposed to be 'peer pressure' in fact becomes 'peer protection'."[33]

Others, finally, point to the fact that "executive directors are somehow sandwiched between the governors and the Bank's top management, which can in turn talk directly to

---

27 *Id. Also see* notes 226, 227 & 228, Ch. 3.
28 *Id.*
29 *Id.*
30 *Id.* On the organization theory arguments in question, *see* notes 4-5, Ch. 3.
31 *Id.*
32 Bradlow *in* Cissé et al. (Eds.) (2012), e-Book. In this regard, Bradlow highlights (*at id.*) "recent efforts of the World Bank and the IMF to hold their boards more accountable for their performance" as a "positive development that has the potential to result in more accountable IFIs."
33 Woods (2001), pp. 87-88.

the governors."[34] Such a "multi-polar communications network", as Phillips argues, "compounds the problem" of the World Bank having "multiple objectives and uncertain means to meet those objectives"[35] – an issue that will be discussed in the next chapter.[36]

However, in light of the ongoing shifts in global political and economic power – and, as Bradlow argues, especially "[a]s signs that the global political economy could be running into problems appeared and accelerated after the financial crisis fully erupted in 2008" – "there were significant efforts to reform the governance" of prominent international financial institutions.[37] Crucially, these reform "efforts resulted in changes in voting arrangements, representation on boards of directors, and the selection of top manage-ment."[38] The World Bank agreed, for instance, "to increase the share of its developing and transitional member states in its total vote", which meant that "these countries [at the time of writing] constitute 47.19 percent of the total vote in the Bank."[39] This increase constituted "an increase of 4.59 percent in their share of the total vote since 2008."[40] In addition, the size of the Executive Board was increased "from 24 to 35 members, with the new member being a third African executive director."[41]

Opinions on the effectiveness of these changes, however, remain mixed. "More mixed constituencies" can certainly result in "more representative views", as Phillips argues, for instance, and "the U.S. voting share has fallen steadily" as a result of recent governance reforms; nevertheless, the US has to date maintained "its veto [when] the supermajority for changing the constitution [the Bank's Articles of Agreement] was raised in 1989 to 85%."[42] Or, as Bradlow points out, the "existing powers, primarily the Group of Seven (G7) countries, still control the global agenda and can still block reform efforts that they oppose."[43]

While this "situation may change over time as power shifts more toward newly rising powers", it might also mean that the recent round of reforms to the World Bank's gover-nance structure "are unlikely to produce sustainable and stable governance arrangements in the IFIs until the process of change in the balance of global power plays itself out."[44] In

---

34 Phillips (2009), p. 13.
35 *Id.*
36 *See* in particular section 4.2.
37 Bradlow *in* Cissé et al. (Eds.) (2012), e-Book.
38 *Id.*
39 *Id.* Bradlow also notes (*at id.*): "[…] within these totals, there will be some realignment of voting shares so that the most dynamic emerging markets increase their share of the votes and have a vote in the Bank that is more commensurate with their role in the global economy."
40 *Id.*
41 *Id.*
42 Phillips (2009), pp. 14-16.
43 Bradlow *in* Cissé et al. (Eds.) (2012), e-Book.
44 *Id.*

the mean time, the "current constituency system of representation at the board level" retains many of its problematic aspects.

On the other hand, as Miller-Adams points out, borrowers – especially prominent borrower states such as China, India and Brazil – can also be dominant actors, "although theirs tends to be a "negative" power, the power to say no rather than to place a new issue on the institution's agenda."[45] "This source of influence", Miller-Adams elaborates, "has its roots"

> in the Bank's steady expansion and historical equation of success with higher lending levels. In order for the Bank to grow, and before it can request a capital increase, demand for its loans must rise, and that demand comes from borrowers. Thus, borrowers exert control over the Bank by their willingness or unwillingness to accept the conditions of Bank lending. Those borrowers that have access to other sources of capital (such as middle-income countries that can now borrow on private markets) and large countries in which the Bank needs to do business in order to maintain its loan volume (such as China) are more powerful than the smaller and poorer developing countries.[46]

World Bank president, management and staff

The daily operations of the Bank proceed "under the leadership and direction of the president, management and senior staff, and the vice presidents in charge of regions, sectors, networks and functions."[47] In Inspection Panel practice material, these actors are collectively referred to as *Bank management* (hereinafter also 'Management') *and staff.*[48]

The *President* of the World Bank Group is formally "selected by the Board of Executive Directors for a five-year, renewable term."[49] In practice, however, the appointment of the Bank's President is determined by a 'gentlemen's agreement' dating from the Bretton Woods era, in accordance with which Europe is guaranteed to have its candidate appointed as Managing Editor of the IMF, whereas the US is guaranteed that the candidate it puts

---

45 Miller-Adams (1999), pp. 10-11.

46 *Id.* For evidence of the growing power of prominent borrower states, *see e.g.*, the Bank's recent agreement with China "to establish a $50 million fund to help reduce poverty" as well its announcement to "discuss closer collaboration" with the proposed Multilateral Interim Secretariat for Establishing the Asia Infrastructure Investment Bank (AIIB) – *see* World Bank Press Release, 16 July 2015, available at http://www.worldbank.org/en/news/press-release/2015/07/16/china-launches-first-world-bank-trust-fund-to-end-poverty-and-promote-development. *Also see* note 17, Ch. 1.

47 *See* http://go.worldbank.org/HWEWI4KIO0.

48 For a discussion of criticisms regarding "weaknesses in [MDB] staffing and management" and the relationship with the perceived accountability deficit of MDBs, *See e.g.*, Head (2003-2004), pp. 295-297.

49 *See* http://go.worldbank.org/HWEWI4KIO0.

forward will be elected as World Bank President.[50] While this informal arrangement continues, it has become progressively contentious in recent decades.[51]

Phillips identifies the 1946 resignation of the Bank's first President (Eugene Meyer) – a mere six months after his appointment – as a "signal event for the governance of the institution",[52] as well as the nature of the working relationship between Bank management and the Board of Executive Directors. Meyer's resignation was the result of "what he saw as excessive interference by the U.S. director", and he subsequently "advised John McCloy, the nominee to succeed him, to insist as a condition of taking the job"

> that the board be excluded from close supervision of Bank [management] activity. It was agreed that, from then on, loan proposals would be originated by management and that the Board would be limited to supervision and responding to management initiatives.[53]

This meant, in effect, that from then on, "Management ran the Bank."[54]

Former World Bank President Jim Wolfensohn observed that, at the onset of his term, the Board "had less information and less involvement"

> by a significant margin than it would have liked. [...] The board was a necessary element in the approval process [...] [but] it was much less engaged than it is today. It got much less information. There was considerably less disclosure of problems. And what I believe I have started [...] is to treat the board as a board and say 'management must notify the board of everything it knows so that the board can participate as a board and take responsibility.'[55]

Currently, the "vice presidential unit (VPU) is the main organizational unit" employed by the World Bank, with "each vice presidency" generally "correspond[ing] to a world region, a thematic network, or a central function of the World Bank."[56] Institutional reforms initiated during the Wolfensohn-presidency had identified "decentralization" as a "top priority,

---

50   *See e.g.*, Bradlow *in* Cissé et al. (Eds.) (2012), e-Book.
51   *See e.g.*, A. Beattie, 'World Bank: An exercise of influence, The Tussle for the Presidency Highlights the Complexities Facing Global Institutions', *Financial Times*, 2 April 2012, available at: www.ft.com.
52   Phillips (2009), p. 14. *Also see* Mallaby (2004), pp. 20-21.
53   Phillips (2009), p. 14.
54   Van Putten (2008) p. 345 (quoted from an interview conducted by the author).
55   *Id.* On the relationship between the Inspection Panel and the President, *also see* Van Putten (2008), pp. 241-242. Van Putten notes (*Id.*, at p. 241): "[i]f difficulties arose, it was a matter of [the President], rather than the panel, being placed in a dilemma: he had to decide whether to support management in its resistance to the panel's findings or to accept the findings of an independent panel working on behalf of the board of the bank."
56   For more information about the Bank's organization structure, *see* http://go.worldbank.org/WM8TMERJO0.

with the goal being to bring a higher proportion of Bank Group staff members closer to their clients."[57]

While there remain several challenges to transform the role of the Board of Executive Directors vis-à-vis Bank Management,[58] there is evidence of change in this regard including, for instance, a recent announcement that the World Bank would "establish dual performance reviews of its president by its Board and of the Board by the president and senior management."[59] These performance reviews would be performed with reference to a new "corporate governance scorecard", which will be discussed in more detail later on.[60] That being said, strong perceptions remain that, while "formal authority resides with the Board of Executive Directors,"

> it is the Bank's top managers who set the agenda for the Board and whose proximity to the organization's day-to-day operations gives them substantial de facto power.[61]

Notable aspects of institutional culture

World Bank management and staff "share a common set of values by virtue of their background and academic training," despite "the fact that they come from many different countries."[62] Miller-Adams provides an extensive analysis of World Bank institutional culture and its effect on the institutionalization of different agendas.[63] Two aspects of the

---

57 World Bank (2011), e-Book: "The institutions of the Bank Group together have a full-time staff of close to 15,000 professionals [in 2011] [...] from some 170 countries. Of these individuals, about 40 percent are located in offices in more than 110 developing countries." "Staff members typically have strong academic backgrounds, a broad understanding of development issues, and international work experience." For a critical view of past institutional reforms – including decentralization and the establishment of a 'matrix' organization structure, *see e.g.*, Mallaby (2004), pp. 145-173. *Also note*, current institutional reforms spearheaded by World Bank Group President Jim Yong Kim (ongoing, as of May 2015) have also been met by criticism. *See e.g.*, Financial Times Editorial, 'The World Bank Risks Sliding Into Irrelevance', *Financial Times*, 20 November 2014, available at www.ft.com: "Mr Kim's plan is to move the bank away from its geographic focus with the creation of 14 global practices along sectoral lines, such as health and education. The idea is to make the bank's still considerable technical expertise more efficiently available to its clients. The result so far is more centralisation."

58 One example of a new role fulfilled by the Board relates to the establishment of the Inspection Panel, where the Board has to act as the "final arbiter" in case of conflicting interpretations of the operational policies – in this regard, *see* Bradlow & Naudé Fourie *at* note 232, Ch. 6. On the changing role of the Board in the adoption and amendment of the operational policies, *also see* section 5.1.

59 Bradlow *in* Cissé et al. (Eds.) (2012), e-Book.

60 *Id.* On the Bank's new corporate performance scorecard, *see* section 4.2.2

61 Miller-Adams (1999), pp. 19-20. Indeed, Miller-Adams describes this aspect (*at id.*) as one of the core "normative feature[s]" of the World Bank.

62 *Id.*

63 Notably, with respect to the internalization of private-sector engagement, broadening participation through CSO involvement, and the 'governance' agenda (linking development effectiveness to borrower governance reforms) – *see* in general Miller-Adams (1999).

Bank's institutional culture, briefly outlined here, are of particular relevance for the discussion on World Bank accountability, notably: "the official avoidance of politics" ('apolitical' norm) and the "emphasis on technical analysis based in the disciplines of economics and finance".[64]

While the practicality of the Bank's insistence on its "apolitical" identity have been questioned,[65] it serves several important purposes – notably, it enables "the Bank to work with a diverse group of governments"; makes it possible for staff members, "drawn from many different countries", to "set aside their personal and/or national politics and identify themselves with the institution for which they work;" and enhances the Bank's "legitimacy in the eyes of its borrowers".[66]

On the other hand, "the official avoidance of politics" can influence the content and scope of World Bank accountability – especially how the Bank delineates its own obligations versus those of its borrowers, as will be discussed in the next chapter.[67] It has also been instrumental in the longstanding debate on the nature of the Bank's international human rights obligations – an issue extensively discussed in literature and also reflected in Inspection Panel practice.[68]

With respect to the second aspect, the strongly held belief "that development can be achieved through technical means", Miller-Adams argues that this has meant that the Bank has consistently "relied on well-honed techniques that, whenever possible, involve quantitative measurement and can be applied in a wide range of countries".[69] Consequently, with its initial focus on large-scale infrastructure projects, "Bank staff consisted largely of specialists with expertise in a given technical area, such as agronomy, engineering, or hydrology" – and as the Bank's focus expanded to include development policy lending, the "influence of economists" and other "financial experts" grew over time.[70] In more recent years, the Bank has aimed to broaden its "skills mix" (notably, by appointing higher numbers of social scientists), however, some commentators argue that "the 'mastery of technical knowledge based on objective and rational analysis' remains the order of the day."[71]

---

64 Miller-Adams (1999), pp. 19-20.
65 See e.g., Wolfensohn's comment at note 226, Ch. 7. For arguments with respect to the role played by the Bank's apolitical culture in respect of insufficient norm internalization regarding the policy on Indigenous Peoples, see e.g., general Sarfaty (2005), pp. 1802-1803.
66 Miller-Adams (1999), p. 23.
67 See section 4.3.
68 See e.g., sections 5.1.1 & 5.3.2.
69 Miller-Adams (1999), p. 24.
70 Miller-Adams (1999), p. 24; and see section 4.1.
71 Miller-Adams (1999), p. 24. The author quotes N. Kardam (1990), 'The Adaptability if International Development Agencies: The Response of the World Bank to Women in Development', in K. Staudt (Ed.), Women, International Development and Politics: The Bureaucratic Mire, Philadelphia: Temple University

While there may be several explanations (and, indeed, justifications) for this emphasis, it is particularly significant to note that the "technical norm" is "rooted in conditions of the Bank's establishment".[72] That is, the Bank "has had a triple-A credit rating (the highest possible) since the late 1950s, and its bonds are held by the most cautious of investors."[73] It is the "Bank's substantial skill in maintaining strict financial policies and performing well in purely financial terms", Miller-Adams argues, which "has allowed it to act as an intermediary"

> through which the resources of the world's most conservative investors can be channeled to developing countries for what, under other circumstances, would be considered distinctly risky ventures.[74]

On the other hand, the cultural emphasis on 'technical' and 'commercial' skills forms an important component of criticisms related to development effectiveness (reflected, for instance, in the problematic aspects of the Bank's "approvals culture").[75] It also forms the backdrop of the discussion on the achievement of 'institutional equilibrium' among diverse (and potentially conflicting) institutional aims – an issue that will be dealt with in the next chapter, as well as in Part II of this book.[76]

3.1.2   World Bank clients – borrowers, guarantors, project sponsors and project implementing agencies

The term 'borrower', as used in World Bank development-lending operations, could either refer to "the recipient of an IDA grant, the guarantor of an IBRD loan" – or to a particular "project implementing agency, if it is different from the borrower."[77] Moreover, in instances where a borrower member state acts as the guarantor of a particular project, 'borrower' could also refer to "a private or public project sponsor receiving from another financial institution a loan guaranteed by the Bank."[78]

Press, p. 117; *and* M.M. Cernea (1993), 'Sociological Work within a Development Agency: Experiences in the World Bank', Unpublished Paper.
72 Miller-Adams (1999), p. 25.
73 *Id.*
74 *Id.; also see* Ch. 9.
75 *See* Shihata (2000), pp. 2-3; *and see* section 4.2.1.
76 *See* section 4.2.2 *and* Ch. 9.
77 OP 4.10 (Indigenous Peoples), fn. 2; for explanations/definitions of acronyms, abbreviations and other terminology used in World Bank development-lending operations, *see* the Appendix.
78 OP 4.01 (Environmental Assessment), fn. 1; for explanations/definitions of acronyms, abbreviations and other terminology used in World Bank development-lending operations, *see* the Appendix.

The project sponsor or project implementing agency[79] of a particular Bank-financed development project is ultimately charged with executing the activities associated with the design, preparation and implementation of the specific project.[80] Project sponsors and implementing agencies could be either public or private sector actors and might also act as co-financiers.[81] Private sector actors involved in this capacity could be privately owned or publically listed multinational corporations, whereas public sector actors acting as project sponsors, implementing agencies and/or co-financiers might also involve different levels of government within the relevant member states.

For example, in *Panama: Land Administration*, implementation of the project was described as the "responsibility of the Ministry of Finance (MEF)", which was acting

> in collaboration with the Ministry of Agriculture, the Ministry of Governance and Justice, the Ministry of Public Works, the Ministry of Housing – all of which act through various agencies under their competence – and the Project Coordination Unit (PCU). Two new entities were created specifically for this Project, the Superior Council for Land Administration and the Technical Operational Committee, which are responsible for the policy and technical regulatory frameworks necessary for Project implementation. Temporary decentralization units (UTOs) in each province represent the national agencies.[82]

Whereas the implementing agencies of the different project components in *Cambodia: Forest Concession Management* included

> the former DFW [Department of Forestry and Wildlife], which was reorganized in 2003 and became the Forestry Administration (FA). 'The FA is a semi-autonomous agency of the Ministry of Agriculture, Forestry and Fisheries (MAFF). A Deputy Director serves as Project Director.' Concession plan reviews are the responsibility of a Technical Review Team (TRT) created by the FA. The forest crime monitoring and prevention role was initially carried out under a project financed by the Food and Agriculture Organization (FAO) and the

---

79 A term of art used in the context of World Bank development-lending operations – for explanations/definitions of acronyms, abbreviations and other terminology used in World Bank development-lending operations, *see* the Appendix. *Also note,* 'project implementing agency' as used in this context is not to be confused with scenarios where "the Bank has committed itself to act as trustee or implementing agency for a number of significant trust funds designed to address global environmental and social issues", such as the Global Environment Facility (GEF). In this regard, *see e.g.,* Freestone (2013), p. 8.

80 On the project cycle and formal division between Bank and Borrower obligations in terms of the project cycle, *see* sections 4.1.2 & 4.3.1.

81 *See e.g., Nigeria/Ghana: West African Gas Pipeline* (2006); *Chad: Petroleum Development and Pipeline* (2001); *Uganda: Power Projects* (2001) and (2007).

82 *Panama: Land Administration* (2009), ER, § 10.

United Nations Development Program (UNDP), within which the NGO Global Witness served as "independent monitor." Presently, this function is the responsibility of a commercial firm contracted under the [Bank-financed project].[83]

Some development projects have a cross-border element, such as *Argentina/Paraguay: Yacyretá*,[84] *Lesotho/South Africa: Highlands Water*[85] or *Nigeria/Ghana: West African Gas Pipeline*.

In respect of the *West African Gas Pipeline* project, for instance, the IDA "provided a guarantee, in the amount of US$50 million, for certain obligations of Ghana related to the purchase of natural gas from the West African Gas Pipeline Company Limited (WAPCo)" and MIGA "provided a US$75 million in political risk guarantee to WAPCo in relation to the construction of the pipeline and associated facilities."[86] Moreover, the *West African Gas Pipeline* project was also "implemented by WAPCo" – the project 'Sponsors' – which shareholders at the time "include[d] Shell, Chevron, Nigerian National Petroleum Corporation (NNPC), Volta River Authority (VRA) of Ghana, BenGaz o Benin, and SotoGaz of Togo (the Sponsors)."[87] Whereas the Request for Inspection was filed by "Requesters from Nigeria's Delta Region", as well as by "Requesters from Ghana."[88]

Whatever the nature (and number) of actors involved, it is important to underline that all development projects (co-)financed by the World Bank (thus, IDA and IBRD) involve a World Bank member *state*, which sovereignty has to be respected. Respect for the principle of state sovereignty is reflected, for instance, in the Inspection Panel Resolution, which stipulates that the "borrower and the Executive Director representing the borrowing (or guaranteeing) country"

shall be consulted on the subject matter both before the Panel's recommendation on whether to proceed with the investigation and during the investigation.

---

83   *Cambodia: Forest Concession Management* (2005), ER, § 5.
84   The project concerned a hydroelectric facility on the Paraná River between Argentina and Paraguay, implemented by a bi-national entity, Entidad Binacional Yacyretá, ('EBY') – "the borrower's implementing agency." *See Argentina/Paraguay: Yacyretá Hydroelectric Project* (1996), ER, § 1.
85   The project objectives included the transformation of Lesotho's water resources into export revenues in an environmentally and socially sustainable manner; and providing water "to urban and industrial users in the Gauteng province [South Africa]." *See Lesotho/South Africa: Highlands Water* (1998), ER, p. 4.
86   *Nigeria/Ghana: West African Gas Pipeline* (2006), IR, p. ix.
87   *Id.*
88   *Nigeria/Ghana: West African Gas Pipeline* (2006), IR, p. 10. On diversity among project-affected people, *see e.g.*, section 3.1.5.

Inspection in the territory of such country shall be carried out with its prior
consent.[89]

However, tensions can arise between the requirement to respect state sovereignty and the
manner in which the Bank execute its "regulative capacity", by "set[ting] rules and monitor[ing] and sanction[ing] behaviour" of its borrowers.[90] As Miller-Adams explains, "[w]hen
a country receives a World Bank loan,"

> it becomes bound by a series of requirements embodied in the loan covenants
> and related documentation. These requirements include not only the terms of
> the loan (its repayment schedule, interest rate, and so on), but the conditions
> that are specified by the loan, such as the completion of a given project or the
> enactment of agreed-upon policy reforms. Only if these conditions are met
> will the Bank agree to release future installments of the loan. (Virtually all
> World Bank loans are paid out in tranches over several years.) And only if the
> country continues to service its World Bank debt will future loans be committed
> and disbursed.[91]

In addition, the Bank's relationships with its borrowers are also influenced by borrowers'
respective "interests and power", which typically "differ considerably", and which might
therefore result in differentiated treatment.[92] "[I]n some cases (e.g., Brazil and India)", as
Phillips remarks, "the Bank has been essentially a partner, while in others (e.g., Mozambique
and Nepal) it retains power over the country's economic and political agenda."[93]

That being said, recent reforms to the Bank's governance structure have also affected
the Bank's relationships with its borrowers.[94] Where IFIs such as the World Bank had in
the past been "*de facto* […] actors in the policy-making processes of many of the member
states that rely on their financial services", recent governance reforms have caused the IFIs
to "become more sensitive to the interests of those member states that use their financial
services."[95] And as a result of this 'client-centric' approach, borrower-member states "are

---

89 Inspection Panel Resolution, § 21. To date, Borrower consent to visit borrower territory featured prominently
    as an issue only in *India: NTPC Power* (1997). For a discussion thereof, *see e.g.,* Clark *in* Clark et al. (Eds.)
    (2003), pp. 178-185; *and see* Freestone (2013), pp. 58-59.
90 Miller-Adams (1999), p. 18.
91 *Id.*
92 Phillips (2009), p. 14.
93 *Id.* For similar arguments, *also see* Miller-Adams *at* note 46, Ch 3.
94 Bradlow *in* Cissé et al. (Eds.) (2012), e-Book.
95 *Id.* On 'client satisfaction' as a performance area, *also see* section 4.2.2.

gaining international power and influence while remaining subject to the influence of the IFI's richer and more powerful member states."[96]

In addition, as Miller-Adams underscores, there remain "strong incentives for the Bank to continue to lend,"

> especially to its large borrowers, even if all the terms of a loan are not complied with. One fear is that if lending slows, the Bank will shrink in size and become a less central player in the international economy. Another incentive arises when the Bank is owed a considerable sum by a borrower on the brink of insolvency. In such a case, the Bank's institutional interest lies in ensuring that the borrower is able to service this debt, even if [it] means lending the borrower new money to do so.[97]

3.1.3   Co-financiers and their citizen-driven IAMs

The World Bank "often cofinances its projects" with other institutions within the larger World Bank group and with "governments, commercial banks, export credit agencies, multilateral institutions, and private sector investors."[98] The Bank defines 'co-financing' as "any arrangement under which funds from the Bank are associated with funds provided by sources from outside the recipient country for a specific lending project or program."[99]

In *Nepal: Arun III*, for instance, the project was "cofinanced by the Asian Development Bank, Kreditanstalt fur Wiederaufbau, the Government of France, the Swedish Agency for International Technical and Economic Cooperation, the Finnish International Development Agency and other donors [...]."[100] *Colombia: Cartagena Water & Environmental Management* was financed, "[i]n addition to the IBRD loan," through "US$7.58 million from the Borrower, US$4.6 million from ACUACAR, the implementing agency for the Project, and US$20 million from the Government of Colombia, the guarantor of the Loan."[101] 'ACUACAR', moreover, was a "mixed ownership company with 46% capital participation of private Spanish operator Aguas de Barcelona S.A. (AGBAR), 50% capital participation by the District of Cartagena, and 4% employees and others."[102]

And in *Cambodia: Land Administration* (LMAP), the Bank's co-financed project served as "the major vehicle to date for [generating] donor support to the Government's overar-

---

96   *Id.*
97   Miller-Adams (1999), p. 18; on the enforcement of legal remedies against borrowers, *also see* section 15.1.
98   World Bank (2011), e-Book.
99   *Id.*
100   *Nepal: Arun III* (1994), ER, § 3.
101   *Colombia: Cartagena Water & Environmental Management* (2004), ER § 6.
102   *Colombia: Cartagena Water & Environmental Management* (2004), ER, fn. 6.

ching LAMDP [Land Administration, Management and Distribution Program]."[103] "Three of the Development Partners, Canada, Finland and Germany, provided co-financing or parallel-financing to the [Bank-supported LMAP] Project."[104] Moreover, the 'Development Partners' "coordinate[d] their support for [the government's overarching] LAMDP"

> through the Technical Working Group on Land (TWG-L), which also includes representatives of other development agencies and civil society organizations. Germany, through the Deutsche Gesellschaft für Technische Zusammenarbeit GmbH (GTZ), provides technical assistance to the Project in the areas of policy development, dispute resolution, State land management and titling. Finland supports the development of a modern, multi-purpose cadastre system. Canada, through the Canadian International Development Agency (CIDA), initially supported LAMDP and Project implementation with grant funding managed by the Bank, but in 2008 it began to provide direct support for technical assistance and investments in three additional provinces, thus expanding the Project's geographical scope. The LASED project is also supported with co-financing from Germany. Other Development Partners have also been active in the land sector. The Asian Development Bank (ADB), together with the Bank and GTZ, contributed to the formulation of Cambodia's overarching land policy in 2001, which provided the basis for the 2001 Land Law. More recently, ADB has worked closely with the Ministry of Economy and Finance (MEF) in the development of a draft resettlement policy and related sub-decree. Denmark has taken a lead role in Participatory Land Use Planning and Commune Land Use Planning. Between 2001 and 2005, UN Habitat, GTZ, the United Kingdom's Department for International Development (DfID) and Cities Alliance supported an informal settlements program implemented by the MPP.[105]

Finally, *Kazakhstan: South-West Roads*, a road construction project crossing several state borders, was financed by multiple co-financiers. The European Bank for Reconstruction and Development (EBRD) had agreed to "finance road sections between the Russian Federation border to Martuk in Aktobe oblast (102 km)," whereas the "Asian Development Bank (ADB) jointly with the Japan International Cooperation Agency (JICA)" had agreed to

---

103 *Cambodia: Land Management and Administration* (2009), MR, §§ 17-18.
104 *Id.*
105 *Id.* On the effect of similar or comparable activities alongside activities related to Bank-financed development projects, *see* section 8.2.2.

finance road sections between Taraz and Korday within Zhambyl oblast (about 321 km); the Islamic Development Bank (IDB) will finance 159 km of road sections between the border of South Kazakhstan oblast and Taraz; and IBRD (the 'Bank') finances sections of the Corridor in the South-West regions of Kazakhstan between Shymkent and Aktobe oblast border (approx 1,062 km). Moreover, the Government of Kazakhstan is financing the remaining sections of the Corridor. This in addition to the construction of 273 km of roads in Aktobe oblast (Aktobe - Karabutak – Irgiz) completed in 2006, plus 205 km of the Almaty-Bishkek road completed in 2005 with ADB and EBRD loans, and the ongoing construction of 215 km of roads in Aktobe oblast (Karabutak to the Kyzylorda oblast border) and the road section from Shymkent to the border with Uzbekistan.[106]

Seen from the perspective of project-affected people, however, the involvement of multiple financiers can be confusing, especially when projects are co-financed by various institutions within the World Bank Group. For instance, as the Inspection Panel observed in *Chile: Quilleco Hydropower*, previous, current and planned hydropower projects in Chile "have been supported financially by the IBRD or by the IFC."[107] "[F]or local people", as the Panel explained, "these projects have had the support of the 'Banco Mundial' (World Bank)"

and for them it is difficult to understand how these two institutions that have the same President and Board of Directors are juridically and functionally different and independent between themselves. When the Panel team explained these differences the answer back was, '[Y]es, but both institutions belong to the World Bank.' In this sense, it is easy to understand the range of people that submitted this Request for Inspection and why they expected all institutions that belong to the World Bank Group to be bound by the findings of earlier reviews of these projects, and especially by the – Lessons Learned: Pangue Hydroelectric – that according to them was issued by IFC's Environmental and Social Development Department after a CAO review of that project. This document covers Indirect Impacts, Cumulative Effects, Added Value and Disclosure issues, and seems to contain valuable lessons for future engagements with hydroelectric projects.[108]

---

106 *Kazakhstan: South-West Roads* (2011), ER, § 6, fn. 4.
107 *Chile: Quilleco Hydropower* (2010), ER, §§ 46 & 69.
108 *Chile: Quilleco Hydropower* (2010), ER, §§ 46 & 69. The Requesters refer to the following IFC/MIGA Compliance Advisory Ombudsman (CAO) cases: *Chile/Empresa Electrica Pangue S.A.-01/Upper Bio-Bio Watershed* and *Chile/Empresa Electrica Pangue S.A.-02/Upper Bio-Bio Watershed*, available at: www.cao-ombudsman.org/cases/default.aspx.

Further complexity might occur as a result of the involvement of other (citizen-driven) independent accountability mechanisms (IAM), institutionally affiliated with such co-financiers.[109] Indeed, several of the claims filed at the Inspection Panel have also been filed at the IAMs of co-financiers, such as the EBRD's Project Complaints Mechanism, the AfDB's Independent Review Mechanisms, as well as at the Aarhus Convention's Compliance Committee.[110] In instances where such claims had been filed concurrently or around the same period (thus, at the Inspection Panel and another IAM), the Inspection Panel has consistently cooperated with the relevant IAM (either formally or informally).[111] In other instances where the case at hand had been dealt with by another IAM before a Request for Inspection had been filed – for instance, as in *Albania: Power Sector*, which had previously been considered by the Aarhus Compliance Committee – the Inspection Panel had taken the findings of the Aarhus Compliance Committee into consideration in the course of its own investigation.[112]

Significantly, the growing number of IAMs at multilateral development banks and other transnational investment banks have established an informal (but increasingly formalizing) network through which they share practical experiences – the Independent Accountability Mechanisms Network, which is described as a "network of members and staff of the IAMs,"

> who seek to identify and foster means for cooperation within their respective
> mandates, contribute to the regular exchange of ideas and best practices, and
> assist with institutional capacity-building in accountability as components of
> corporate governance.[113]

---

109 On other IAMs at multilateral development banks, *see e.g.*, Van Putten (2008), pp. 105-162; *and see* Bradlow & Naudé Fourie *in* Hale & Held (Eds.) (2011), pp. 122-137.

110 For Inspection Panel cases also filed at other IAMs, *see* Naudé Fourie (2014) – *e.g.*, *Uganda: Power Projects*, at p. 187; and for comparative IAM case statistics, *see* pp. 602-603.

111 *See e.g., Uganda: Power Projects* (2007), IR, § 29; and *Argentina/Paraguay: Yacyretá Hydroelectric Project* (1996) – *see* Shihata 2000, pp. 123-124; *and* Bradlow & Naudé Fourie *in* Hale & Held (Eds.) (2011), p. 129. *Note*, this aspect has since been formalized in the recent version of the Inspection Panel's Operating Procedures – *see* Inspection Panel Operating Procedures, April 2014, § 62: "If the Panel receives a complaint that is also submitted to the independent accountability mechanism(s) of other international financial institutions, relating to a co-financed project, the Panel will make its best efforts to cooperate with the other accountability mechanism(s) as relevant. At all times, the cooperation must remain within the requirements and constraints of the mechanisms' respective mandates, rules and procedures including requirements of confidentiality and disclosure of information. Building on past practice, and sharing of experience across the Independent Accountability Mechanisms Network, the elements of such cooperation will be set forth in a Memorandum of Understanding agreed between the Panel and the other mechanism(s)."

112 On the manner in which the Panel incorporated the Aarhus Committee's findings, *also see* notes, 127, 128 & 129, Ch. 5.

113 Independent Accountability Mechanisms Network (2012), p. 2.

Such learning networks are facilitated by the fact that the "World Bank and the various regional development banks" "have adopted broadly similar sets of operational policies and supervisory mechanisms."[114] Ultimately, such "cross-institutional normativity might", as Kingsbury argues, "eventually assume qualities of a *droit commun.*"[115]

3.1.4   Civil society organizations ('local' and 'international' NGOs)

"[B]orrower states are obviously privileged partners, as the vast majority of loan operations are made with them or with related entities";[116] however, according to the World Bank, "[m]ost development projects approved by the Bank Group involve the active participation" of 'non-governmental organizations' (NGOs) or 'civil society organizations' (CSOs), which the Bank defines as "the wide array of nongovernmental and not-for-profit organizations"

> that have a presence in public life and that express the interests and values of
> their members, as well as other organizations that are based on ethical, cultural,
> political, scientific, religious, or philanthropic considerations.[117]

The Bank has also established "grant programmes" that enable "the Bank to supply non-state entities, such as foundations or associations, with funds" to facilitate their activities.[118]

In "the context of the preparation and implementation of [World Bank] operational activities," "other actors may" – "even if they are not a party to the transactional operations" – "wish to intervene"

> in order to put forward their point of view or because they advocate interests
> related to the development of Bank-financed operations. Such is often the case
> for non-governmental organizations (NGOs), be they local, national or inter-
> national.[119]

One example of such intervention concerns the filing of claims before the Inspection Panel 'on behalf of' project-affected people. The Inspection Panel Resolution provides for duly

---

114 Kingsbury *in* Cissé et al. (Eds.) (2012), e-Book. *Also see* in general, Bradlow & Chapman (2011); Bradlow & Naudé Fourie *in* Hale & Held (Eds.) (2011), pp. 122-137; *and* Boisson de Chazournes *in* Shelton (Ed.) (2000), pp. 281-302.

115 Kingsbury *in* Cissé et al. (Eds.) (2012), e-Book. On the intersecting normative frameworks surrounding World Bank development-lending operations and the normative development of these frameworks, *see* sections 5.1.1 & 7.1.6.

116 Boisson de Chazournes *in* Treves et al. (Eds.) (2005), p. 188.

117 World Bank (2011), e-Book.

118 Boisson de Chazournes *in* Treves et al. (Eds.) (2005), p. 188.

119 *Id.*

authorized local NGOs to file a Request for Inspection Panel on behalf of "two or more" project-affected people residing in the 'territory of the borrower', whose identities the Inspection Panel must be able to verify.[120] For example, the *Uzbekistan: Energy Loss Reduction* Request was

> submitted by Messrs. Boriy Botirovich Alikhanov and Saydirasul Sanginov and Ms. Dilorom Fayezieva, on their behalf and on behalf of the Ecological Movement of Uzbekistan, representing *"more than 100 NGOs"* (the "Requesters") as downstream affected people of a transboundary Project.[121]

Whereas *West Bank/Gaza: Red Sea-Dead Sea Water Conveyance Study Program* was submitted by "two Palestinian civil society organizations – Stop the Wall Campaign and the Palestinian Farmers Union, and an international human rights nongovernmental organization – the Global Initiative for Economic, Social and Cultural Rights."[122]

International NGOs authorized by project-affected people, which are not based in the territory of the borrower of the project in question could potentially file a Request for Inspection without the involvement of a local NGO, but only with the explicit consent of the Executive Board.[123] To date, only one Inspection Panel Request (*China: Qinghai*) had been filed in accordance with this procedure,[124] and international NGOs tend to be involved more in a 'behind-the-scenes' capacity, for instance, by providing technical and/or financial assistance to local NGOs and/or project-affected people.[125]

Generally speaking, Inspection Panel practice illustrates the influence of civil society actors – whether they are local or international. For instance, the majority of Inspection Panel Requests list a local NGO as one of the Requesters,[126] and it has been argued that the involvement of civil society strengthens the probability that a Request might lead to a full Inspection Panel investigation.[127] For instance, a study of "twenty-eight Inspection

---

120 *See* Inspection Panel Operating Procedures (2014), Section 2.3, Article 18.
121 *Uzbekistan: Energy Loss Reduction* ER, § 1 (emphasis in original). *Also note,* this example demonstrates why the absolute number of 'cases' filed at the Inspection Panel can be misleading as to the significance of the Inspection Panel's 'body of practice' – *see* section 1.2.1. On Shihata's concerns about the filing of Requests by NGOs 'on their own behalf' (in addition to being on behalf of project-affected people in the territory of the Borrower), which Shihata reviewed as a form of '*actiones populuris*' that he considered to be an unauthorized expansion of Inspection Panel's mandate, *see* Shihata (2000), pp. 208-210.
122 *West Bank/Gaza: Red Sea-Dead Sea Water Conveyance Study Program* (2011), ER, § 3.
123 Inspection Panel Resolution, § 12.
124 *See e.g.,* Clark & Treakle *in* Clark et al. (Eds.) (2003), pp. 211-238.
125 For examples of various forms of cooperation between 'local' and 'international' civil society organizations in the context of Inspection Panel cases, *see* in general Clarke et al. (Eds.) (2003). For an example of a US-based NGO aiding local affected people in filing Inspection Panel claims, *see* http://www.accountabilitycounsel.org.
126 For statistics on Requesters being assisted by CSOs, *see* Naudé Fourie (2014), p. 581.
127 *See* in general Clarke et al. (Eds.) (2003).

Panel cases" conducted by Hale and Slaughter in 2006 showed that "Inspection Panel cases that attract more attention from civil society and the media stand a significantly higher chance of leading to [internal World Bank] policy changes."[128]

Hunter argues that, as a result of the enhanced "global civic dialogue between" international financial institutions and "the public", there is a growing "professionalization of advocacy around the IFIs."[129] Consequently, "[o]pposition to IFI-financed projects" is "increasingly expressed in the need for a stronger environmental and social policy framework."[130] However, instead of "(or perhaps in addition to) taking to the streets, civil society opponents to IFI operations sought changes in the policy framework and raised their concerns with bank management, the executive directors, or the media."[131] In other words, it can be argued that "non-state entities" such as NGOs have "started to compete with states"

> for the scarce resource of politico-legal authority (i.e., the power to set authoritative standards. They do not merely wish to be involved in monitoring international law, as the traditional role of NGOs was, or wish to receive benefits created under international law by states; instead, they increasingly demand a seat at the table.[132]

Accompanying these shifts in power, however, are increased criticisms about the accountability and legitimacy of civil society actors, fuelled "in part" by "a series of highly publicized scandals that have eroded public confidence in nonprofit organizations, coupled with a rapid growth in NGOs around the world" – and arguably exacerbated by NGOs' own "exaggerate[ed] claims to legitimacy, which may be based more on a belief in value-

---

128 Hale *in* Hale & Held (Eds.) (2011), pp. 152-153; *and see* Hale & Slaughter (2006).
129 Hunter *in* Bradlow & Hunter (Eds.) (2010), pp. 202-203. For a critical account of the effect of the Bank's engagement with international civil society, *see* Mallaby (2004) pp. 1-10; for criticism of the Inspection Panel's *Chad Pipeline* and *China Qinghai* investigations and the influence of international advocacy groups in these investigations, *also see* Mallaby (2004) pp. 270-285 and pp. 341-356. On the influence of civil society actors in the establishment of the Inspection Panel, *also see* section 3.2.3.
130 Hunter *in* Bradlow & Hunter (Eds.) (2010), pp. 202-203.
131 *Id.*
132 Klabbers *in* Klabbers et al. (Eds. (2009), p. 12. *Also see* Brett (2003), who notes (at p. 2) that "[t]heories of development management have changed dramatically since the 1950s. Over the past 30 years we have placed our faith in state controls, markets, and now in 'bottom-up' systems based on participation and empowerment. Orthodox public administration theory advocated 'hierarchies of authority, divisions of labour, adherence to rules and spans of control', but these are now thought to deny 'the flexibility and responsiveness that provide the necessary conditions for effective management'." On the "increased involvement of non-state actors" in public participation, *also see* Ebbesson *in* Bodansky et al. (Eds.) 2007, pp. 681-703; and on the influence of NGOs on the institutionalization of the Bank's 'participation agenda', *see in general* Miller-Adams (1999).

driven organizations than on actual monitoring and assessment of their accomplish-ments".[133]

Malaby, for instance, typifies what he calls "campaigning" NGOs (as opposed to "those with programs in the field") as an "army of advocates pound[ing] upon the World Bank's doors",

> demanding that Bank projects bend to particular concerns: no damage to
> indigenous peoples, no harm to rain forests, nothing that might hurt human
> rights, or Tibet, or democratic values. These constant NGO offensives tie up
> the World Bank, frequently disabling its efforts to fight poverty; despite their
> diminutive stature, the Lilliputians are wining. Unless we wake up to this danger,
> we will lose the potential for good that big organizations offer: to rise above
> the single-issue advocacy that small groups tend to pursue, and to square off
> against the world's grandest problems in all their hideous complexity.[134]

Some of these NGOs simply "cannot be placated", Mallaby concludes, because "their whole reason for existence is to be implacable."[135] "Campaigning NGOs" "almost have to be radical" because "if they stop denouncing big organizations,"

> nobody will send them cash or quote them in the newspapers. Partly for this
> reason, and partly out of a likable conviction that the status quo is never good
> enough, most NGOs do not have an off switch. You can grant their demand
> that you abandon structural adjustment or call in the Inspection Panel, but
> they will still demonstrate outside your building.[136]

In this respect, Josselin and Wallace argue, for instance, that "[t]here is, without question, a structural imbalance in global civil society." That is,

---

133 Ebrahim (2003), p. 813. *Also see* in general Ebrahim (2007); Keohane (2003); Woods (2001), pp. 95-97; *and see* Kamminga *in* Alston (Ed.) (2005), p. 95, who summarizes the criticisms against NGOs as follows: "[…] the influence of NGOs on the international plane has been growing out of all proportion; that special interest groups cannot be expected to balance all relevant interests; that only States can be relied upon to do so; that while it may be right for pressure groups to exercise their influence within States they should not be allowed to do so on the international plane; and that unlike States (democratic States that is) NGOs are accountable to no one. In sum, the fear expressed by these observers is that NGOs have become so effective that they are beginning to present a threat to the Westphalian inter-State system."

134 Mallaby (2004), pp. 6-7.

135 Mallaby (2004), p. 277.

136 *Id.* For the debate between Mallaby and Jim MacNeill (former Inspection Panel chair), *also see* note 225, Ch. 7.

NGOs and enterprises in the OECD world in general, and in the USA in particular, have access to far greater resources and skills, better communications, and easier access to wielders of public and private influence. In so far as they act as 'enactor and carriers of world culture', the predominant cultural values they carry are those of the liberal, capitalist West.[137]

"While it would be wrong to deny the positive role" of these organizations at the international level, it is important to note that they "are not benign by definition; neither are they necessarily following a universalistic agenda."[138] It is also significant that "[t]he most effective and radical critics of the prevailing culture are also based in the liberal, capitalist West,"

> providing indirect access to authoritative power centres through transnational networks to disadvantaged or excluded groups in less-developed – and less democratic – states. For pluralists, the increasing density of transnational linkages provides evidence of the countervailing influence of global civil society in checking the power of dominant economic and state interests. But the influence of Western actor (both state and non-state), and most of all American ones, on the content and spread of 'global norms' is hard to overlook, even if, as argued by Colonomos, these norms then acquire a 'life' of their own.[139]

On the other hand, as Kamminga cautions, the role assumed by NGOs at the international level "should not be exaggerated."[140] There is arguably "still much more reason for concern"

> about the negative if 'irresponsible' governments than about 'irresponsible' NGOs. The formal and informal checks on the influence of NGOs on the international plane are such that there is no need for a general system of *appellation contrôlée* under international law.[141]

The distinction between "local or 'Southern' NGOs, within borrowing countries" and "transnational or 'Northern' lobbying organizations, usually based in Washington DC or one of the G-7 capitals" remains, nevertheless, a significant one[142] since, as Woods observes,

---

137 Josselin & Wallace (2001), pp. 256-257.
138 *Id.*
139 *Id.*
140 Kamminga *in* Alston (Ed.) (2005), pp. 109-110.
141 *Id.*
142 Woods (2001), pp. 95-97.

"[t]he implications for the accountability of the IFIs of developing relations with [local versus transnational NGOs] are somewhat different."[143]

For example, in the context of World Bank development-lending operations, local NGOs might be "given a more active role in the formulation or implementation of policy" (thus, becoming 'implementing NGOs'), in which case "the accountability of local NGOs ought to be compared to that of local government agencies."[144] "In the 1980s and early 1990s", Woods argues, "it was sometimes too readily assumed"

> that the former were preferable; and in the World Bank's work in Africa this
> led to criticisms of the Bank for undermining the capacity of governments in
> the region. A decade later, it has become more obvious that using NGOs to
> bypass government institutions risks thwarting the desired processes of 'insti-
> tution building' and 'state modernization'.[145]

Indeed, as Miller-Adams argues, the "attitude of developing country governments" towards the involvement of local and transnational NGOs has proven to be a "crucial variable in how far the [Bank's] participation agenda can [be] advance[d]."[146] Simply put, "Bank staff cannot promote a more active role for NGOs without at least the tacit support of the borrower."[147] Many "[o]utside advocates recognize the importance of borrower support" but argue that "the Bank should do more"

> to encourage developing country governments to adopt participatory
> approaches. As one long-time observer of the Bank puts it, "In the long run,
> citizens in borrowing countries are better served by participatory governments
> than by a participatory World Bank."[148]

3.1.5   Project-affected people (beneficiaries, adversely affected people and 'Inspection Panel Requesters')

The final category of actors discussed in this section concerns the individuals who are at the centre of Bank-financed development projects, namely, 'project-affected people' (also

---

143 *Id.*
144 Woods (2001), p. 97. For an example where local NGOs acted as 'implementing NGOs', *see India: Mumbai Urban Transport* (2004). In this regard, *see e.g.* note 131, Ch. 8.
145 Woods (2001), p. 97.
146 Miller-Adams (1999), p. 93.
147 *Id.*
148 Miller-Adams (1999), p. 93, quoting N.C. Alexander (1998), 'The World Bank's New Strategic Alliances', Draft Paper, Development Bank Watchers' Project, Silver Spring Md.: Bread for the World Institute, at p. 5.

referred to as 'PAP' in World Bank operations practice). This broad category includes those individuals and communities who stand to benefit from the realization of specific development objectives ('*project beneficiaries*'), as well as those who are (or who are at risk of being) adversely affected by certain component(s) of a project ('*adversely affected people*').[149]

This category also includes Inspection Panel 'Requesters', which refers to "two or more people" residing in the territory of the Borrower[150] who have a "shared interest" in a Bank (co-) financed project, and who claim to be adversely affected by actual or potential harm following from the Bank's failure to comply with its operational policies.[151]

It is important to note, in other words, Inspection Panel Requesters might be comprised of adversely affected people and/or of project beneficiaries (fully supporting the project in question) claiming that project benefits are not or will not be realized as a result of the World Bank's non-compliance with its operational policies.

Furthermore, project-affected people typically represent a significant degree of diversity, which might be the result of various ethnic, cultural, religious, and socio-economic factors. Such diversity, moreover, often manifests as different interests, which might not be (easily) reconcilable. In *Nigeria/Ghana: West African Gas Pipeline*, for instance, the Nigerian Requesters from the "Delta Region" were "mainly concerned with the Project's impact on gas flaring reduction and with the safety of an existing pipeline to which WAGP is to be linked", whereas the "Requesters and affected communities living near the gas pipeline in Nigeria complain[ed] mainly about low compensation rates for the land they had to give up for the pipeline."[152] On the other hand, Requesters

> living in southwestern Nigeria, where the pipeline goes under the sea, claim
> that the construction process hurt their fishing enterprise. The Requesters from

---

149 On the place of the individual in the international legal order, *see e.g.*, Klabbers (2013), pp. 107-123: "[…] while it is plausible to say that the individual has come to be recognized as a subject of international law, such a claim on its own does not say all that much. A decent international legal order must not only recognize individuals as subjects, but also provide individuals with decent levels of protection and opportunities, regardless of where they live and regardless of whether they are refugees, migrants or internally displaced persons."

150 Inspection Panel Resolution, § 12. For examples of Inspection Panel cases with a 'transboundary element', *see* note 89, Ch. 6.

151 For criticisms of the 'procedural limitations' in the Inspection Panel's mandate (particularly pertaining to Requesters), *see e.g.*, Carrascott & Guernsey (2008), pp. 601-602; Treakle et al. *in* Clark et al. (2003), p. 267; Bissell & Nanwani (2009), p. 31. *Also see* Shihata's analysis of this aspect of the Resolution (Shihata (2000), pp. 207-209). For an overview of the informal steps the Panel has taken to address criticisms concerning the limited place of Requesters therein, *see* Brown Weiss (2010), p. 484. *Also note*, several of these steps, developed in practice, have since been formalized in the latest version of the Panel's Operating Procedures – *see* Inspection Panel Operating Procedures (2014).

152 *Nigeria/Ghana: West African Gas Pipeline* (2006), IR, p. 10.

Ghana are concerned about inadequate consultation regarding the Project's economic viability, the pipeline's safety, and its impacts on coastal fisheries.[153]

Unsurprisingly, Requests for Inspection filed at the Inspection Panel might not be welcomed – neither by Bank management nor by its borrowers. Inspection Panel practice certainly provides examples of interference and intimidation, as well as instances of physical violence. Such incidents typically become public knowledge because the Inspection Panel makes specific note thereof in their reports to the Board, which are subsequently published. For example, in *Brazil: Paraná Biodiversity*, the Panel noted that the Requesters

> felt unduly pressured by Bank staff and others not to file a Request for Inspection and then to withdraw the Request. The Requesters have cited various arguments as having been used to exert pressure. The Panel finds that this practice threatens the integrity of the Panel process, and may have a chilling effect on local people who genuinely feel harmed or potentially harmed by Bank projects. The Panel wants to call the attention of the Board of Executive Directors and Bank Senior Management to this matter, and trusts that these kinds of practices will not occur in the future.[154]

Similarly, in *India: Uttaranchal Watershed Development*, the Panel registered its concern

> as it has been in a previous Request, [i.e. Argentina: Santa Fe (Request no. 42/43)] as to whether knowledge is available in the field that the Bank is financing the Project, and whether locally affected people can effectively bring their concerns about the Project to the Bank. The Panel is concerned about potential intimidation locally affected people might face, considering that even the Country Director faced difficulties in reaching the Project area and affected people during her visit. The Panel would like to emphasize the importance of making information available and accessible to local communities regarding the Project and the means by which they may raise their concerns.[155]

And in *Uganda: Power Projects*, the Panel noted that it had "heard testimony"

> that some resettled people who submitted the letter of complaint have been subjected to pressure to refrain from complaining about the proposed Project.

---

153 *Id.* For other examples of projects affecting income and livelihood, *see* section 12.5.
154 *Brazil: Paraná Biodiversity* (2006), ER (No. 1), § 43.
155 *India: Uttaranchal Watershed Development* (2007), ER, § 52.

Individuals indicated to the Panel that they were, on other occasions, threatened for wanting to speak out about their concerns. Some indicated that while they have not refused the dam, they joined the letter stating their concerns regarding their resettlement and are fearful of the consequences.[156]

Whereas in *Liberia: Development Forestry*, the Panel notified the Board of "a matter of serious concern", that is, the Panel had "information indicating that members of the affected community represented in this Request"

> have been put under pressure and intimidation since bringing their complaint to the Panel. This is a matter of great concern to the Panel, firstly in terms of the implications for the affected people themselves, and secondly for its potentially deterring effect on the ability of people to bring their concerns to the Inspection Panel without fear of reprisal, thus undermining the integrity of the Inspection Panel process and ultimately the Bank's accountability. The Panel notes the importance of ensuring that any such actions are stopped, and appreciates that Management has expressed its commitment to address this issue with the highest authorities of Liberia.[157]

Unfortunately, as Hansungule observes, "[w]here the poor victims" (of harm suffered as a result of the adverse impacts of development projects) "try to turn to their states for redress", they "would most often be viciously met with harassment by state officials and politicians who as a rule do not tolerate such actions from their citizens."[158] "Politicians in development countries", Hansungule elaborates, "very often view such litigants as ungrateful individuals"

> bent on tarnishing the good image of their country to the Bank in particular and to the international community in general. Few politicians in developing countries can understand the importance of an individual or even a community raising complaints against a Bank project that has already received the blessing of the government 'at the highest levels'.[159]

On the other hand, Hansungule adds, being from "a third world African country" himself, he "can testify to the extreme vulnerability of the so-called economies of third world

---

156 *Uganda: Power Projects* (2007), ER, § 82.
157 *Liberia: Development Forestry* (2010), ER, § 116.
158 Hansungule *in* Alfredsson & Ring (Eds.) (2001), p. 145.
159 *Id.*

countries."[160] These borrowers "depend mainly on outside funding to finance their development projects, with the World Bank being among the most important sources of this funding" and "[w]ith this vulnerability in mind," therefore, "it is easy to see why these states tend to over-react to any form of protest directed against such projects as those financed by the Bank."[161]

3.2   World Bank accountability to internal and external accountability holders

This section considers two categories of 'accountability holders' or 'constituency groups', namely: those 'internal' to the organization, notably the World Bank's member states as represented in its governance structure ('shareholders') (*see* Figure 4); and those 'external' to the organization, such as project-affected people and civil society organizations ('stakeholders').[162]

3.2.1   *Internal accountability holders: World Bank member states and governance structure*

From the 'internal perspective', the World Bank's duty of accountability exists exclusively – or, at least, primarily – towards its member states (which are also its institutional shareholders), through the Bank's governance and management structure. This perspective is based in various – related – accountability models, such as the "shareholder model"[163] and "delegation model",[164] and also embodies notions of "vertical"[165] and "top-down"[166] accountability. In terms of these conceptions, 'power wielders' (thus, actors exercising power) – "ought to be accountable to those who have entrusted them with it, and to be held to the authority granted or to refrain from acting in violation of its purposes."[167] Arguments based in these theories question, for example, the accuracy of contentions that

---

160 *Id.*
161 *Id.*
162 For similar conceptualizations, *see e.g.,* Brown Weiss (2010), p. 481; Grant & Keohane (2005), pp. 29-43; *and* Hachez & Wouters (2012), p. 48. On models of accountability employed in "the global sphere", *also see* Harlow *in* Anthony et al. (Eds.), Values in Global Administrative Law, Oxford: Hart Publishing (2011), pp. 185-191. For criticism of these types of 'dichotomies', *see* Rubenstein *at* note 210, Ch. 2.
163 Hachez & Wouters (2012), p. 48.
164 Grant & Keohane (2005), pp. 29-43.
165 Woods (2001), pp. 92-95.
166 Grant & Keohane (2005), pp. 29-43. *Note* that "top-down" accountability also incorporates the notion of management demanding accountability of the institution's staff.
167 Brown Weiss (2010), p. 481, referring to Grant & Keohane (2005), pp. 29-43.

the international financial institutions such as the World Bank are "lawless institution[s]"[168] that 'should *be made* accountable'.[169] If, as Krisch observes, 'accountability' is defined as having

> "to answer for one's action or inaction, and depending on the answer, to be exposed to potential sanctions, both positive and negative", most institutions are accountable.[170]

Therefore, "[t]o speak of an 'accountability deficit' in global governance" is "somewhat misleading" since many (if not the majority of) "regulatory institutions on the global level", and certainly "intergovernmental organizations" such as the World Bank, "are in fact highly accountable – up to the point that they often enjoy little freedom of independent action and are closely tied to the wishes of their constituents."[171]

On the other hand, practice erodes the strength of these arguments. For example, as Bradlow and Hunter contend, the shareholder model is based on the assumption that an IFI's"relationships with its members" are, "in principle", "conducted at the level of the state"; hence, "all interactions between the international organization and non-state actors in its Member States are expected to be indirect and involve the mediation of the state."[172] The organization's member states, therefore, "should be able to hold the organization accountable for its decisions and actions that affect the state and its citizens."[173] However, as noted earlier, various deficiencies in the governance structures of international financial organizations challenge this assumption.[174] While the shareholder model may therefore be an accurate reflection of the "formal legal relationship" between the Bank and its member states, it is "challenged by the functional reality"

> of the active and direct engagement of many international organizations with non-state actors in their Member States, and of their ability to have significant impacts on the lives and activities of these non-state actors.[175]

---

168 *See e.g.*, Clark et al. (Eds.) (2003) who argue (at p. xiii): "Before the contested construction of the World Bank's minimum social and environmental standards and the creation of the Inspection Panel, the World Bank was a 'lawless institution,' insofar as it was insulated from any legal responsibilities to people directly affected by its actions. The Inspection Panel's most important innovation is that it is designed to respond directly to grievances from citizens of developing countries about the environmental and social impacts of World Bank-funded projects."
169 Shihata (2000), pp. 8-9.
170 Krisch (2006), pp. 249-250.
171 Krisch (2006), p. 250.
172 Bradlow & Hunter (Eds.) (2010), p. xxvii.
173 *Id.*
174 *See* section 3.1.1.
175 Bradlow & Hunter (Eds.) (2010), p. xxvii.

Furthermore, because the borrower member state effectively becomes "a partner with the organization in an operation that is of interest to the state" it may "have little incentive to raise the non-state actors' concerns."[176] Given that borrower states typically "occupy a relatively weak position" in the Bank's governance structure, they might also "experience difficulty in having its concerns actually heard in the organization."[177] Consequently, Bradlow and Hunter conclude, "the key decision-makers have power without responsibility."[178]

That being said, it is important to note, as Woods highlights, that dissatisfaction with the World Bank's lending operations and governance structure was increasingly voiced since the 1980s – "[n]ot only [by] radical non-governmental organizations (NGOs) but equally [by] [the IMF and the World Bank's] major shareholders", who demanded "that the institutions become more transparent, more accountable and more participatory."[179]

3.2.2   External constituent groups: project-affected people, civil society and broader public interest

From the 'external perspective', the World Bank's duty of accountability has to be expanded so as to include ' external stakeholders' – or, as some might argue, exists primarily towards 'external stakeholders' – by which is meant, "the wider public, and in particular the people affected by [the organization's] activities",[180] due to the *public* nature of the Bank's mission.[181] The "stakeholder model"[182] or "participation model" of accountability, which also embodies the notions of "horizontal accountability"[183] and "bottom-up accountability",[184] therefore argues that "people with power ought to be accountable to those who are affected by their decisions."[185]

---

176 *Id. Also see* Hansungule's comments in this regard, *at* section 3.1.5.
177 Bradlow & Hunter (Eds.) (2010), p. xxvii; *and see* section 3.1.1.
178 Bradlow & Hunter *in* Bradlow & Hunter (Eds.) (2010), pp. 389-390. The authors (at p. 388) also point to "two gaps" in the international legal regime (concerning the lack of "applicability of international law to IFIs"; and the "extensive immunity under domestic legal regimes"), which "net effect" "is that the IFIs are able to claim the power to decide for themselves what law is applicable to them, and then to act on their view of the applicable law. If, as Philip Allott puts it: 'Law constrains or it is a travesty to call it law', then IFIs are essentially lawless institutions." The authors reference P. Allott, Eunomia: New Order for a New World (New York: Oxford University Press) (1990), at p. xlvii. *Note*, on the formalist and instrumentalist paradigms, *see* section 2.3.
179 Woods (2001), p. 83.
180 Hachez & Wouters (2012), p. 48.
181 On the dual commercial-public nature of the Bank's mandate, *see* section 4.2.2.
182 Hachez & Wouters (2012), p. 48.
183 Woods (2001), pp. 92-95.
184 Brown Weiss (2010), p. 481.
185 Grant & Keohane (2005), pp. 29-43. *Also see* Brown Weiss (2010), p. 481.

The strongest demands for the expansion of World Bank accountability to external stakeholders have arguably come from civil society actors based in prominent donor and borrower member states, supported by various academic commentators. These demands culminated in prominent public protests surrounding the World Bank's 50-year celebrations,[186] which also took place against the backdrop of specific controversial World Bank-financed development projects in Brazil and India,[187] and became increasingly 'professionalized' over time.[188]

It remains a matter of debate whether pressure exerted by external or internal accountability holders or, for that matter, by power wielders within the Bank's management structure, is the decisive factor in affecting institutional change – as demonstrated by competing accounts of the history of the Inspection Panel's establishment, as will be discussed below.[189] Ultimately, however, it can hardly be contested that the Bank *has* changed over the past decades.

At least three aspects of the World Bank's development-lending operations provide strong support for the argument that the World Bank has come to recognize that its duty of accountability has been expanded so as to include external stakeholders – or, at least, that its duty of accountability has extended to include specific constituency groups such as civil society actors and project-affected people.

The first aspect refers to the Bank's efforts to enhance the transparency of its decision-making processes – as prominently demonstrated by the World Bank's adoption of a progressive policy on Access to Information.[190] The second aspect refers to the Bank's continuing efforts to internalize the "participation agenda", as noted earlier.[191] "[W]ith increasing public accountability to, and participation from, civil society in both donor and developing countries," as Bissell and Nanwani argue, both access to information and increased participation have contributed to the "ero[tion] of the "traditional view" that an international financial institution such as the World Bank "is formally accountable only to its member governments."[192]

---

186 *See e.g.*, French (1994); Versi (1994); Danaher (Ed.) (1994).
187 *See* Shihata (2000), p. 5 (on the India Sardar Sarovar "Narmada Lesson"); *and see* in general Berger (1993-1994), about the 'independent review' of the Sardar Sarovar project, conducted by Thomas Berger and Bradford Morse, which served, in many respects, as the 'prototype' for the World Bank's Inspection Panel. *Also see* Independent Accountability Mechanisms Network (2012), pp. 4-5; *and* Miller-Adams (1999), pp. 73-74.
188 *See* Hunter *in* Bradlow & Hunter (Eds.) (2010), pp. 199-238. Hunter presents the participation of civil society actors in the 'policy-making' activities of IFIs as an example of the 'professionalization' of civil society activism.
189 *See* section 3.2.3.
190 On the adoption of the policy on Access to Information, *see* section 5.1.
191 *See* in general Miller-Adams (1999). On the operationalization of access to information and participation at the project level, *see* Ch. 11.
192 Bissell & Nanwani (2009), p. 5.

The third aspect mentioned here refers to the creation of the Inspection Panel in 1993, which changed the nature of the relationship between the World Bank and external stakeholders – specifically, project-affected people and the civil society actors authorized to act on their behalf – by providing them, "for the first time under international law," with "a window of access"

> to file claims [directly] with these institutions on their complaints with [multi-lateral development bank-financed] projects and with the opportunity to influence decision making processes at these institutions.[193]

In other words, for "non-state actors who are not in a contractual relationship with the IFIs, but who are nonetheless directly affected by their actions" – and,

> for whom the combination of limited application of international legal principles and extensive immunity from the application of national law results in the IFIs operating essentially in a lawless vacuum

– the establishment of citizen-driven independent accountability mechanisms at the multilateral development banks has been a development of critical importance.[194] Nevertheless, as Bradlow and Hunter caution, mechanisms such as the Inspection Panel "have created a limited means of accountability for these stakeholders", particularly since "[t]hese mechanisms are not empowered to offer non-state actors compensation for any harm they have suffered, or to order the IFIs to change their operations or conduct."[195]

3.2.3   Constituency groups competing for primacy

This book therefore departs from the argument that the World Bank should be accountable to (or, should be held accountable by) both internal and external accountability holders. What remains contentious, however, is whether the interests of internal or external constituency groups should enjoy 'primacy'. In other words, as Krisch puts it, criticisms about the accountability "deficit" of international organizations are actually concerned with "the problem [...] that these institutions are often accountable in the wrong way: in part, they are accountable to the wrong constituencies."[196] Or, as De Wet argues, "the forum under

---

193 Bissell & Nanawani (2009), p. 10 (emphasis added). *Also see* Hey's comments *at* note 40, Ch. 1.
194 Bradlow & Hunter *in* Bradlow & Hunter (Eds.) (2010), pp. 390-391. *Also see* Woods (2001), p. 90.
195 Bradlow & Hunter *in* Bradlow & Hunter (Eds.) (2010), pp. 390-391. On the issue of 'redress for harm', *see* section 7.1.3
196 Krisch (2006), p. 250. Krisch elaborates (*at id.*): "The World Bank, it is often claimed, should respond to the people affected by its decisions, rather than primarily to the (mostly developed) countries that fund it. The

which accountability arises" continues to be "one of the most controversial issues pertaining to international accountability, as it touches on the issue of *who should control public authority*" – which, as noted before, is grounded in very different underlying conceptions.[197]

For instance, in conceptions that emphasize the "sovereign equality of States", member states are considered the "primary constituency with a vital interest in policing the public authority exercised within the international institution."[198] A "liberal democratic" conception, on the other hand, recognizes the "great disparity in power and population between States" and argues that this "reality would not be reflected in a 'one State on vote' model on accountability."[199] In addition, a 'one State on vote' model might also "not necessarily [be] representative of the electorate in any particular State."[200] Therefore, "the national constituency in the form of the national electorate" should be "the primary one."[201]

In terms of the "internationalist" model, on the other hand, "the international community (of States) as a whole constitutes the main constituency".[202] The "cosmopolitan" perspective, finally, "goes even further in that it insists on a genuinely global constituency for issues of global governance."[203] Consequently, cosmopolitanism "attribute[s] less importance to the role of States as part of the constituency and emphasize[s] the role of civil society in the international legal order."[204] There is, however, disagreement on "how to institutionalize accountability" to "a truly global public", "with proposals ranging from representative options such as a world parliament to more deliberative proposals."[205] Furthermore, key notions such as "public interest" remain an "(ill-defined) term", as Morison and Anthony observe, which

> has traditionally occupied a range of abstract and more practical places in administrative law and which can be invoked by legislative, executive and judicial actors, as well as those drawn from civil society.[206]

[Financial Action Task Force] should be accountable to those states subject to its measures, not just to its members. Or the Security Council should have to answer to the individuals it targets directly with its sanctions, not only to its member governments or the broader membership of the UN."

197 De Wet *in* Von Bogdandy et al. (Eds.) (2010), p. 857 (emphasis added).

198 *Id.*

199 De Wet *in* Von Bogdandy et al. (Eds.) (2010), pp. 857-858. This is reflected, for instance, in deficiencies in the Bank's governance and voting structure – as discussed in section 3.1.1.

200 *Id.*

201 *Id. Also see* Krisch (2006), p. 253, who points out that the "nationalist approach" remains the dominant conception.

202 De Wet *in* Von Bogdandy et al. (Eds.) (2010), p. 858.

203 Krisch (2006), p. 255.

204 De Wet *in* Von Bogdandy et al. (Eds.) (2010), p. 858.

205 Krisch (2006), p. 253.

206 Morison & Anthony *in* Anthony et al. (Eds.) (2011), pp. 215-238. The authors argue (*at id.*) that it might be "accepted that conceptions of public interest have moved on from more wholly State-centric understandings," but they are "essentially sceptical of the project of finding or creating a workable notion of public interest within the emerging global administrative space", arguing, instead, that "we must settle for the sort of plu-

However, the main problem with all of these arguments, as De Wet points out, is that "there is not necessarily one primary constituency for the purpose of accountability or oversight within any particular international institution".[207] Instead, "the constituency entitled to claim accountability from an international institution"

> can consist of a variety of international actors (with or without international legal personality), provided their interests or rights are affected by the conduct of the international institution in question.[208]

The existence of "multiple constituencies can lead to a conflict between different constituencies within the same international institution"[209] – and, as illustrated by the previous section, also to conflict *within*, due to high degrees of diversity in particular constituency groups, and due to the multiplicity of roles fulfilled by certain actors within them, which might blur the distinction between 'accountability holders' and 'power wielders'.[210]

On the other hand, "it is also possible", as De Wet adds, for "the day-to-day relationships between the constituencies" to be "characterized by mutual accommodation" – or, where all constituency groups are seen to be "fulfil[ing] a complementing role for the purpose of accountability of a specific act of public authority."[211] Woods argues, for instance, departing from the conception that "the primary agencies which should hold the [international financial] institutions to account are their member governments, through bolstered and improved forms of vertical accountability", that IFIs

> are now working in a world political system in which groups both within and across countries are becoming more effective at demanding more account of

---

ralist approach advocated by Krisch." On such an approach, *see* in general – Krisch (2006) and (2010), *and see* section 2.1.

207 De Wet *in* Von Bogdandy et al. (Eds.) (2010), p. 858.

208 *Id.*

209 *Id.*

210 On this distinction, *see* 2.2. In this regard, *also see* Rubenstein (2007), who argues (at p. 627) that "efforts to specify subtypes of accountability using categories of "delegate" versus "participation" or "upward" versus "downward" elide the very possibility of surrogate accountability" since "[t]hese dichotomies focus attention on actors' structural relationships to one another—literally, where they stand in relation to one another (*e.g.*, above, below). Surrogate accountability, in contrast, focuses attention on what actors – in particular, what actors capable of acting as surrogates – *do*. The concept of surrogate accountability opens up possibilities for noticing, describing, and normatively evaluating activities that the aforementioned dichotomies conceal. Rather than assume that, for example, all governments that donate to NGOs are automatically involved in upward accountability, while all aid recipients are automatically involved in downward accountability, the concept of surrogate accountability highlights the fact that donor governments can act in dramatically different ways: they can set standards, gather information, and/or sanction NGOs on aid recipients' behalf, or they can pursue an agenda opposed to aid recipients' interests." On 'surrogate accountability', *also see* notes 108 + 109, Ch. 2.

211 De Wet *in* Von Bogdandy et al. (Eds.) (2010), p. 858.

the work of international organizations, both through governments and directly from the organizations concerned.[212]

Consequently, "horizontal accountability has become a large plank in both [the IMF and the World Bank's] responses to those who criticize their unaccountability. A further part of this response has been to engage more directly with their critics, and in particular with non-governmental organizations."[213] Indeed, Woods emphasizes that "horizontal or 'sideways' accountability" can serve to complement and enhance "vertical accountability by contributing agencies and processes which exist to monitor and to enforce the mandate, obligations, rules and promises of institutions."[214]

While it is therefore possible – and, arguably, desirable – for internal and external accountability holders to function in terms of a complementary relationship, the accountability holders in transnational governance contexts are more likely to "function relatively independently" and, frequently, through "mutual challenge", as Krisch argues, "rather than through fulfilling assigned roles in a coherent overall system".[215] In other words, "[i]f we accept the basic normative strength of the claims of the national, international and cosmopolitan groups to be constituencies of global regulatory governance,"

> we should deny any of them formal primacy; they can all make a valid claim to hold global regulatory governance accountable. Their relative strength will then result not from a predetermined hierarchy, but from their influence, their allegiances and support, which will be determined in the political processes of a pluralist order.[216]

Such a "heterarchical" system, in which there are "mutual challenges between different regimes and different levels of global regulatory governance," can "accommodate multiple constituencies" because equilibrium or "stability" "comes not from final decisions based on authority" but is reached as a result of the "processes of negotiation and compromise as well as challenge and concession between the different constituencies involved."[217]

---

212 Woods (2001), p. 95.
213 *Id.*
214 Woods (2001), pp. 92-95.
215 Krisch (2006), p. 248.
216 Krisch (2006), p. 274.
217 Morison & Anthony *in* Anthony et al. (Eds.) (2011), pp. 237-238. The authors are referencing Krisch (2006), p. 278.

Illustrative: The establishment of the Inspection Panel

Various accounts of the Inspection Panel's establishment provide an illustration of the competition for primacy between internal and external accountability holders, but also serve to demonstrate that mutual contestation might result in complementary outcomes.

One of the earliest discussions of the reasons behind the establishment of the Inspection Panel can be found in Ibrahim Shihata's seminal work.[218] Shihata identified two factors as having played a decisive role in its establishment: firstly, demands from internal constituency groups regarding the *enhancement* of World Bank accountability and performance, by means of the Bank's existing governance and management structures; and, secondly, demands from external constituent groups – especially, as mentioned, civil society organizations – related to the *expansion* of World Bank accountability with respect to project-affected people.[219] However, various commentators, at the time, were inclined to emphasize the influence of one factor over the other.

Shihata, for example, emphasized the role played by internal shareholders, who was particularly concerned about the Bank's efficiency and effectiveness, as evidenced by influential internal reports such as the 'Wapenhans-report'.[220] These reports were commissioned by the Bank in the aftermath of a number of controversial projects such as the *India: Narmada* project,[221] which were generally considered as having failed to realize key development objectives.[222] The Wapenhans report in particular "highlighted the Bank's need" to have "access, when necessary,"

> 'to a reliable source of independent judgment about specific operations that may be facing severe implementation problems' and concluded that '*the interests of the Bank* would be best served by the establishment of an independent Inspection Panel.'[223]

While Shihata acknowledged that "[t]hese [internal] concerns"

---

218 Shihata (2000), pp. 1-5. *Also see* Bradlow (1993-1994), pp. 557-571.
219 Shihata (2000), pp. 1-5. For similar arguments made regarding the "success" of the Bank's internalization of the "participation agenda", *see e.g.*, Miller-Adams (1999), p. 95: " [...] working with NGOs has not been presented as an end in itself, but as a means through which the Bank can improve the quality of its projects"; in other words, the "emphasis has been on achieving greater development effectiveness," instead of "strengthening civil society within borrower countries". The author adds (*at id.*): "Coming as it did at a time of management and shareholder concern about the Bank's performance (highlighted by the findings of the [OED] Wapenhans Report in 1992), the participation agenda was seized on by those seeking ways to improve the performance of the Bank's lending program. Participation thus helped fill an institutional need that had arisen quite independently of the other factors that gave birth to the agenda."
220 *See e.g.*, Boisson de Chazournes *in* Alfredsson & Ring (Eds.) (2001), p. 67; *and* Miller-Adams (1999), p. 77.
221 On the *Narmada* case, *see e.g.*, Van Putten (2008), pp. 67-73; *and see* note 187, Ch. 3.
222 Shihata (2000), pp. 5-7.
223 *See* World Bank Report, 'Portfolio Management: Next Steps, A Program of Action', July 22, 1993, referenced by Shihata (2000), pp. 3-4 (emphasis added).

coincided with, and were influenced by sources inside and outside the Bank on what they perceived as the Bank's inadequate attention to the standards reflected in its rules[,]

there was significance in the fact, Shihata argued, that "the initial concern was a managerial one."[224] Shihata, as noted earlier, was also critical of much of the existing literature on World Bank accountability, arguing that many of the Bank's critics "ignore[d]"

the structure of accountability institutionalized in these organizations by their constituent instruments (that is, their internal system of accountability), while focusing only on accountability to the public at large or to the NGOs that assert representation of public interest (that is, external accountability).[225]

Former World Bank President Jim Wolfensohn highlighted the need for "an informed board [of Executive Directors] that was up to date and engaged on the issues" as having played a major role in the Inspection Panel's establishment.[226] The Board, Wolfensohn argued, "needed an arm that would be able to follow through the issues which they were interested in" and "report to them directly on each problem."[227] In other words, the Board needed a body such as the Inspection Panel to

do the thing which board members just couldn't do, which is travel out to the field, talk to NGOs, receive complaints, and ensure that management would do what it had promised to do.[228]

Other commentators identified the public pressure exerted by external stakeholders, notably, civil society organizations based in the United States and Europe, as the decisive factor in the Panel's establishment – as demonstrated, for example, by US-based NGO submissions made before the US Congressional sub-committee on Financial Services in the period surrounding the IDA's 10th replenishing round in 1992.[229] Hansungule, for

---

224 Shihata (2000), pp. 1-2.
225 Shihata (2000), p. 237.
226 Van Putten (2008), p. 346. *Note*, the author quotes from an interview conducted with Jim Wolfensohn.
227 *Id.*
228 *Id. Also see* Bradlow (1993-1994), pp. 557-571.
229 Shihata (2000), p. 20. For similar arguments emphasizing the decisive role of civil society actors during periods of Board review of the Inspection Panel function, *see e.g.*, Bradlow (1999); M.M. Philips, 'Effort Would Curb Watchdog of World Bank – Big Borrower Nations Seek Limit on Probing Harm to People and Ecology', *The Wall Street Journal*, 12 January 1999; *and* Bissell & Nanwani (2009), who note (at p. 36): "In June 2008, Lori Udall testified and provided a statement on behalf of seven NGOs, including BIC, USA and CIEL, before the U.S. House of Representatives Committee on Financial Services in its hearing on the 15th Replenishment of IDA, that although the NGOs did not recommend opening the resolution creating the

instance, objected to Shihata's account as an attempt "to underplay the role of external pressures towards this change,"[230] which "is only grudgingly acknowledged and only in a few lines while attention is lavishly given to the Bank officials' roles."[231] "It would be too much of a coincidence to be true", Hansungule concluded, "that the Bank decided just at the same time the Narmada dam catastrophe broke out to establish the Panel merely as a follow up to the earlier plans."[232]

The importance of the debate on "who may claim to be the 'founding farther' of the Inspection Panel"[233] has subsided over time as most commentators now seem to have accepted the significance of both factors and, in some instances, the mutual dependency between them. As Van Putten comments, it was "obvious" at the time "that the outside world, particularly, the NGOs operating internationally [...] were demanding accountability" and it can hardly be denied "that they had a strong impact and were feeding the discussion at the bank."[234] "Nevertheless," Van Putten adds, "the forces inside the institution"

> clearly came to the same conclusions, with Shihata being the frontrunner. In an institution of the World Bank's magnitude one can find the same commitment to evaluation and positive change that one sees coming from outside the bank.[235]

Ultimately, "[t]he rationale behind the panel's establishment was twofold", as Baimu and Panou point out – that is, "to enhance the efficiency of the Bank's operations and to meet the demand for greater transparency and accountability."[236] Moreover, "[l]inked to these two factors is the question of institutional reputation," which, "although it is an elusive concept in the case of international organizations" "appears to have played no insignificant role in the circumstances leading to the creation of the Inspection Panel."[237] That being said, the competing narratives about the Panel's establishment and its primary 'raison d'être', so to speak, continue to echo in conflicting demands and expectations about the role of the Inspection Panel and the 'real' value of its contribution towards the realization of specific outcomes – a matter that will be addressed later on in Part I of this book.[238]

WBIP at this time given the current political climate among the Board and Management, they would recommend reforms and updates to make the Panel process more accessible and user-friendly to affected people."
230 Hansungule *in* Alfredsson & Ring (Eds.) (2001), pp. 148-149.
231 *Id.*
232 *Id.*; *and see e.g.,* note 187, Ch. 3, on the Narmada case.
233 Van Putten (2008), p. 63.
234 *Id.*; *also see* pp. 65-104.
235 Van Putten (2008), p. 63.
236 Baimu & Panou *in* Cissé et al. (Eds.) (2012), e-Book.
237 *Id.*
238 *See* section 7.2.

****

"The Bank operates within a more complex environment than at any time in its past," as Miller-Adams observes,

> with more member countries, new competitors, and increasingly active NGOs that represent not only concerned populations in donor countries but also groups within borrower countries that are affected by Bank activities.[239]

"Managing this wider range of stakeholders", Miller-Adams adds, "and extracting from them the resources necessary for the maintenance of the institution has become an increasingly difficult task for World Bank leaders."[240] Part of this difficulty arise from the fact that multilateral development institutions (acting as 'agent' for its member states) hold "different obligations to each" of its "multiple users" and that these "users have different amounts of information about and leverage over [the] agenc[y]."[241] This, in addition, "complicates the problem of accountability and the kinds of leverage it can involve" since, as Brett points out, the institution is compelled "to manage three kinds of interaction where leverage is involved" – namely:

> internal relationships between workers and managers; vertical relationships with political masters, donors or shareholders; and external relationships with users.[242]

Bret argues, therefore, that the "strengthening" of accountability "implies a pluralistic approach to development management", because it requires all aspects of the institution involved in the mediation of "internal", "vertical" and "external" relationships to be "strengthened simultaneously."[243]

Moreover, given the wide range of actors involved in World Bank development-lending operations, the diversity of these actors and the complexity of their interactions – including, as noted in this chapter, the fact that they might fulfil multiple roles – answering the question, *to whom should the World Bank be accountable*; or, *who should hold the World Bank accountable?*, is no simple matter. Indeed, as Krisch argues, "[c]laims for stronger accountability of global governance" concern "not only the fairly uncontroversial argument that any public power should be accountable" but involve "much more contested normative

---

239 Miller-Adams (1999), p. 16.
240 *Id.*
241 Brett (2003), pp. 19-20.
242 *Id.*
243 Brett (2003), p. 23.

positions on who should control public power – since, after all, accountability is about control."[244]

Much of the analysis presented in this book reflects the "mutual challenge" for primacy between, what has been described here as, *internal* and *external* accountability holders. Furthermore, in light of the diversity among different actors, challenges for the primacy of interests might also exist within a distinct constituency group.

As the "distribution of power" among accountability holders continues to shift – driven, notably, by economic and political changes in the global landscape, reforms of the World Bank's governance and management structure, enhanced access to information and participation in decision-making processes by external stakeholders, and by the filing of Requests for Inspection at the Inspection Panel – another question that comes to the fore is whether it is inevitable that accountability implies a "zero-sum" game in which "more accountability to one actor" will "necessarily" "mea[n] less to another."[245] As the following chapters will explore in more detail, the existing *interdependencies* between the various *dimensions of accountability* – as well as the *interdependencies* existing between the *interests, demands, expectations and conceptions surrounding these dimensions* – suggest that this does not have to be an inevitable aspect of operational reality.

---

244 Krisch (2006), p. 250.
245 Krisch (2006), pp. 250-251.

4 WHAT SHOULD THE WORLD BANK BE ACCOUNTABLE 'FOR'?

What the World Bank should be (held) accountable *for* might, on the face of it, appear to be a simple question with a straightforward answer. As an international development institution, the Bank should be (held) accountable for 'doing what it supposed to be doing' – which is, in accordance with its Articles of Agreement and accompanying corporate strategy: to execute a mission related to *poverty reduction* by assisting/facilitating/supporting (sustainable) *development* in its member states, by providing *financing, research* and *expertise* (thus: 'money', 'knowledge' and 'know-how').[1]

Of course, decades' worth of debates – about (to name but a few matters) the Bank's interpretation of its Articles of Agreement, its evolving corporate strategy, the effectiveness of sweeping institutional changes spearheaded by various World Bank Presidents over the past few decades, the relationship between poverty reduction and development, what constitutes development and how it can be achieved in a sustainable manner – indicate that this is anything but a simple question. Indeed, conceptualizing this dimension of World Bank accountability, which also initiates the discussion on what the content and scope (extent) of World Bank accountability should be, requires an understanding of the complex dynamics shaping it. Chapter 4 focuses on these matters.

Chapter 4 sets off by providing a brief introduction to *four stages of World Bank development assistance*, as well as the *lending instruments* and *core activities* that characterize the Bank's development-lending operations. Next, the chapter considers two factors that continue to shape the content and scope of World Bank obligations – the first, concerns the Bank's periodic *strategic repositioning* and accompanying *institutional reforms*. These events reflect the diverse interests, demands and expectations of internal and external constituency groups – and have resulted in wide-ranging institutional aims, which in turn, have been translated into broad *performance areas, indicators and targets*. The chapter also points to some of the challenges involved in *achieving institutional equilibrium* among potentially competing institutional aims – in particular, dealing with the tension between two competing conceptions: accountability *for performance* versus accountability *for harm*.

The second factor concerns the *division between World Bank and Borrower obligations* in the context of specific development projects. Chapter 4 analyzes the formal division of obligations and identifies several aspects that suggest that this delineation is far more permeable – and complex – than it may appear at first glance.

---

1   Currently, the World Bank summarizes its mission as "working for a world free of poverty" – *see*: http://www.worldbank.org.

4.1   Four stages of development assistance

"The rationale for a public sector in international financing institutions," as Phillips observes, "remains fundamentally a simple one," namely:

> to meet a social (public goods) necessity that the private sector will not meet
> – that is, it has to address market failures, or market gaps, and it has to address
> them in relation to world development.[2]

At the time of the establishment of the 'International Bank for Reconstruction and Development' in 1944, the 'public goods necessity' was primarily related to the 'reconstruction' of a post-World War Europe.[3] But as "talk of 'development' first emerged" during the 1950s, the World Bank's focus gradually shifted to 'development', as reflected, for instance, in the establishment of the IBRD's sister organization, the International Development Association.[4]

In general terms, the Bank's approach to providing development assistance has been determined primarily by its evolving understanding of how best to address market "failures/gaps".[5] This 'evolving understanding', of course, has been influenced by the interests, demands and expectations of the Bank's constituency groups; and, as noted earlier, more recent changes in the global economic and political landscape have introduced new competitors in the area of international development financing, which are increasingly proving to have a significant impact on the development of this 'understanding'.

The understanding on 'how best to address market failures/gaps' has, arguably, gone through four stages. During the first stage, development assistance was conceptualized "mostly in macro-economic terms," with the emphasis placed on the achievement of "domestic growth" by addressing "a general capital deficiency" – that is, by financing 'bricks and mortar' or "infrastructure projects."[6] The second stage of development assistance underscored the importance of employing "a structural" approach aimed at addressing both "capital deficiency" and "a related skill/know-how deficiency,"[7] whereas the Bank's approach during the third stage reflected the view that market failures/gaps are "largely a problem of"

---

2   Phillips (2009), pp. 6-7.
3   On the history of the World Bank, *see*: http://www.worldbank.org/en/about/history.
4   Boisson de Chazournes *in* Treves et al. (Eds.) (2005), p. 188.
5   Phillips (2009), pp. 6-7.
6   Boisson de Chazournes *in* Treves et al. (Eds.) (2005), p. 188; *and see* Phillips (2009), pp. 6-7.
7   *Id.*

indigenous capacity, know-how, and 'information', with capital scarcity only applicable to the more marginal, poorest economies, within a complex set of resource scarcities.[8]

In other words, "[a]s the rationale for public intervention in imperfect markets, or the provision of public goods, has broadened out," as Phillips explains, "so has the realization that a specifically global development institution should be developing its long-term rationale not in the general category of public goods,"

> but rather in global public goods, that is, in failing global markets. Such goods include vaccines, food security, environmental protection, and global climate initiatives. The category also includes the creation of new worldwide markets such as for carbon trading. These are goods and services whose supply requires collective global action. In the long run, therefore, it might be expected that the Bank would increase its focus on these types of products.[9]

During this time, the Bank's (and other MDBs') expanding agenda was also driven by the emerging "international consensus on 'sustainable development' as a new global paradigm."[10] "[I]n the wake of MDBs' internal post-UNCED ['Rio conference'] reviews of development banking operations," as Handl observes, the MDBs "explicitly endors[ed] much of what the paradigm connotes as significant to their financial role in development activities," although, Handl adds, "[t]his adaptation of policy [...] merely accentuated a trend that had been set in motion well before the 1992 [UNCED] Rio Conference."[11]

The sustainable development paradigm also served to demonstrate the "growing complexity of the problems [IFIs] face," and served as basis for the emergent understanding of the intricate interrelationships between various development goals.[12] As Bradlow and Grossman comment, for example, the continuously increasing "number of internationalized problems has highlighted how intertwined these problems are," and, as a result, has illustrated "that it has become more difficult for the international community to resolve any one of these issues in isolation from other issues."[13] This means, for instance, that "the IFIs cannot address the problem of poverty or the monetary problems of developing countries without"

---

8   *Id.*
9   Phillips (2009), pp. 6-7. *Also see* Miller-Adams (1999), pp. 1-2.
10 Handl (1996), p. 642.
11 *Id.* On the expanding agendas of IFIs, *also see e.g.*, Bradlow *in* Bradlow & Hunter (Eds.) 2011, p. 27-28; *and see* Head (2003-2004). On the operationalization of the 'Rio Declaration' principles of 'access to information' and 'participation in decision-making', *also see* Ch. 11.
12 Bradlow & Grossman (1995), pp. 412-414.
13 *Id.*

considering the issues of refugees, environmental degradation, the capacity of the state to effectively and equitably manage its resources, population policy, and human rights, including the status of women, indigenous people, and minorities. Environmentalists cannot seek resolution of environmental problems without addressing the issues of poverty, refugees, information flows, population, and even security concerns.[14]

While the expanding agendas of international financial institutions may therefore have been inevitable, it also brought about important consequences. For instance, the expansion of IFI agendas is also related to what has been described as an increase in the "direct involvement" of international institutions such as the World Bank "in aspects of global governance through 'quasi' or immediate legislative, administrative, and judicial tasks."[15] Viewed as an expansion of the exercise of 'international public authority', these developments reignited, as Reinisch argues, "the ancient query of *quis custodiet ipsos custodes*? (who guards the guardians)."[16] Moreover, as Handl point out, "the issue of expanding the scope of considerations relevant to development loan activities in concert with the ascendancy of the 'sustainable development' paradigm"

> has always been joined with the controversial question of the outer limits of MDBs' discretion in this matter under their respective constituent agreements. For, unlike the Agreement Establishing the European Bank for Reconstruction and Development (EBRD) [for instance], which specifically directs that Bank to 'promote in the full range of its activities environmentally sound and sustainable development,' the constituent agreements of the MDBs, in general [including the World Bank], do not contain such an explicit mandate. Rather, they are subject to the standard requirement that the MDB concerned refrain from interfering in the 'political affairs' of any member and be guided in its decisions exclusively by 'economic considerations'.[17]

As the "trend toward using the MDBs as instruments of global policy guidance or influence" (or, "global policy regulation") continued, it became "common to find these institutions requiring their borrowing member countries to accept and adhere"

---

14 *Id.*
15 Reinisch (2001), p. 132.
16 *Id.*
17 Handl (1996), p. 643. On the 'apolitical norm' as part of World Bank institutional culture, *see* section 3.1.1.

to prescribed policies on environmental protection, indigenous peoples, involuntary resettlement, governance, corruption, public participation, the role of women in development, and poverty reduction.[18]

However, commentators increasingly argued that multilateral development institutions such as the World Bank had "become far too broad and scattered in their focus, and hence less effective in their operations because they have responded to every policy fad that has come along." "The result of this looseness," as Head summarizes these criticisms,

> ha[d] been both a dilution of the [MDB's] commitment to true economic development and an expansion of [MDB] purposes and operations into areas in which they have no authority and no competence. This adventure into *ultra vires* activity – getting involved, for example, in judicial reform, micro-credit, women's rights, and poverty reduction – ha[d] left the [MDBs] too broad and too shallow. They [had become] gripped by 'policy proliferation' or 'policy paralysis,' so something ha[d] to change to get them back on their proper (narrow) track.[19]

Or, as Miller-Adams points out, there was a growing sentiment "that the [World] Bank is a development finance institution, not a world government," and should therefore "not operate as a self-appointed reformer of its borrower countries.[20] However, since "the Bank ha[d] taken upon itself the mantle of reformer" in several "spheres", which had "far out-stepped the boundaries of its original development finance role", the "question", as Miller-Adams observes, remains: "where the line is drawn"

> between those factors that affect development (legitimate for Bank involvement) and those that do not (off limits to the Bank). Since it is the Bank, with the tacit approval of its members, that draws this line for itself, its protestations of the limits on its activities rings somewhat hollow.[21]

These criticisms (and the Bank's responses to them) have played an important role in heralding what appears to be a fourth stage of development assistance, which has seen a 'contraction' or 'refocusing' of the Bank's development agenda – as depicted in Figure 5.[22]

---

18 Head (2003-2004), pp. 251-252.
19 Head (2003-2004), p. 265. *Also see* Van Putten (2008), p. 33. For an overview of contrasting criticisms about the narrow economic focus of MBDs, *see* Head (2003-2004), p. 264.
20 Miller-Adams (1999), p. 127.
21 *Id.*
22 *See e.g.*, Miller-Adams (1999), p. 128. On comments that the World Bank intends to increase its involvement in projects involving involuntary resettlement, *see* note 1, Ch. 12.

Figure 5   Four Stages of Development Assistance

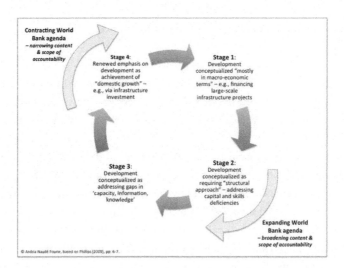

Miller-Adams argues, for instance, that the Bank has progressively, 'reigned in' its development policy lending operations in recent years so as to have them become more "tightly focused on issues of technical capacity and institutional development" – and not simply because

> a broader agenda – one that included factors like pluralism, elections, freedom of association, or protection of human rights – would contravene the Bank's apolitical ethos[,]

but, more importantly, because "[s]uch an agenda would also undercut [the Bank's] ability"

> to incorporate governance criteria into some of its largest lending programs. [...] Strict adherence to a governance agenda with strong political content would impair World Bank lending to large borrowers like Brazil, China, India, Indonesia, and (until recently) Mexico and hurt the Bank's ability to keep lending levels steady.[23]

---

23   Miller-Adams (1999), pp. 127-128.

Indeed, concerns about the impact of the Bank's ever-expanding agenda on member state sovereignty,[24] as well as growing disquiet about the effect of the broadening content and scope of Word Bank obligations on the 'limits of the Bank's accountability' may well have influenced the Bank's renewed emphasis on large-scale infrastructure investment. However, with the influx of new entrants to the international development financing market, as well as these new competitors' focus on large-scale infrastructure (without, as noted, many of the condititionalities required by the Bank and other MDBs), the fourth stage of development assistance appears to have brought us full circle. The question remains, however, whether the contraction of the World Bank's agenda will invariably lead to a lowering of demands and expectations as the content and scope of World Bank obligations – of 'what', in other words, the World Bank should be (held) accountable 'for'.

4.1.1   Development lending instruments

The World Bank's "product menu has broadened considerably" as a result of its evolving mission, but its product menu can nevertheless be distilled to "two basic products" based on "financing and information" – or "money and knowledge."[25] This section (aligned with the scope of this book) focuses on the 'money' – that is, lending instruments that facilitate the core activities of the Bank's development-lending operations – although it should be noted that the distinction "between money and knowledge" is more intricate in practice since, as Phillips observes, "to a degree," "money leverages knowledge by providing it with a transmission vehicle and a high profile in the eyes of the governments that approve projects").[26]

---

24 *See e.g.,* Head (2003-2004), pp. 258-259. Generally speaking, conditionalities attached to the loan/credit agreement "are more commonly used in policy-based lending." *See* Sarfaty (2005), fn. 15; *and see* section 5.1.

25 Phillips (2009), p. 10. As the Bank describes it (*see* World Bank (2011), the World Bank provides "loans, risk management, and other financial services; policy advice; and technical assistance", which "may be packaged together or offered as stand-alone services"; and these products facilitate "a broad range of programs aimed at reducing poverty and improving living standards in the developing world." In this regard, *also see* the World Bank Institute (WBI), which "is a global connector of knowledge, learning and innovation for poverty reduction. We connect practitioners and institutions to help them find suitable solutions to their development challenges. With a focus on the 'how' of reform, we link knowledge from around the world and scale up innovations" – *see*: http://wbi.worldbank.org/wbi/.

26 Phillips (2009), p. 10. Phillips also notes (at pp. 6-7) that the "allocation of the Bank's resources between financing and information or knowledge creating is a key determining factor in the Bank's role as a development assistance organization and is also a potentially critical factor in its financial sustainability because knowledge generation does not generally pay for itself. This has led to some recent reversion from knowledge creation back to large-scale lending." *And see* comments that the Bank intends to increase its involvement in large-scale infrastructure lending, *at* section 4.1.

The World Bank has obtained a strong "structural position as an intermediary in the international economy" since it "stands at the center of a two-part "principal-agent" relationship" – meaning:

> donor countries provide the Bank with funds and delegate to it the power over how and to whom they should go. The Bank then lends these funds to developing countries, requiring them to fulfill certain obligations in exchange for the money. In both relationships, substantial asymmetries of information exist, with the Bank in the privileged position. These asymmetries mean greater influence for the Bank vis-à-vis its member countries, both donor and borrower.[27]

The Bank (co-)finances a wide range of development projects by "offer[ing] two basic types of lending instruments to its client governments: investment loans and development policy loans."[28]

Investment lending instruments (co-)finance projects with a "long term (5–10 years)" focus. These projects, as the World Bank explains, are typically aimed at economic and social development through the construction of "physical and social infrastructure necessary to reduce poverty and create sustainable development" and concern "a broad range of sectors – from agriculture to urban development, rural infrastructure, education, and health."[29] Development projects (co-)financed by investment lending instruments have, "on average, accounted for 75 to 80 percent of the Bank's portfolio," "over the past two decades."[30]

Because the World Bank's initial focus on financing "hardware, engineering services, and bricks and mortar" expanded, as noted, to include "institution building, social development, and the public policy infrastructure needed to facilitate private sector activity,"[31] the Bank developed new lending instruments aimed at financing these types of projects – that is, development policy loans. Development policy lending, which the Bank describes as "quick-dispersing financing to support government policy and institutional reforms,"[32]

---

27 Miller-Adams (1999), p. 12.
28 World Bank (2011), e-Book. *Note*: 'loan' is here used in a generic sense; but technically, the Bank only provides loans to IBRD-clients; IDA clients can obtain credits or grants. *Also note*, 'development policy lending' was formerly known as 'structural adjustment lending'. For an example of a project financed by a 'learning and innovation loan', *see e.g.*, section 10.1
29 World Bank (2011), e-Book.
30 *Id.* For descriptive statistics on the World Bank projects that have been the subjects of Inspection Panel Requests, *see* Naudé Fourie (2014) pp. 583-585.
31 *Id.*
32 *Id.*

has, over the "past two decades," "accounted, on average, for 20 to 25 percent of total Bank lending" portfolio.[33]

Nevertheless, whatever the nature of the lending instrument (or the modality of the project it finances), it is important to recognize that the Bank's development-lending operations are marked by a distinct dichotomy. Bradlow, for instance, describes this as the "dual character" of development lending transactions.[34] As "intergovernmental orga-nizations [...] [that] are created by states for a public purpose," the "authority and man-dates" of international financial institutions are "based on an international agreement to which all their Member States are party."[35] IFIs are therefore "subjects of international law," and their "rights and obligations" "arise from the applicable public international law principles."[36] However, Bradlow adds, IFIs also "engage in financial transaction, which, despite their public purpose, are, by nature," commercial – or,

> similar to market-based financial transaction. Legally the structure of these transactions share many characteristics with the private sector's financial con-tracts. However, unlike these private transactions, the IFIs' transactions, because they involve agreements between international organizations and states, are also subject to those international legal principles applicable to international agreements.[37]

The client offerings of IFIs are therefore specifically "designed to serve a public purpose," which might be "related to either macroeconomic policy or to the general goals of devel-opment and poverty alleviation," but "while the nature of the transaction in which they engage may be similar to market based financial institutions, the purpose of the transactions is different."[38] "Unfortunately," as Bradlow concludes,

> there is not a well-developed public international financial law" that addresses both the public purpose of [international financial institutions'] financial operations and the commercial nature of their transactions.[39]

---

33 *Id.* On issues related to the Bank's application of safeguard policies to development policy lending projects, *see* Ch. 10. For examples of development policy lending objectives, *see* note 101, Ch. 5.
34 Bradlow *in* Bradlow & Hunter (Eds.) (2010), pp. 1-2.
35 *Id.*
36 *Id.*
37 *Id.*
38 Bradlow *in* Bradlow & Hunter (Eds.) (2010), p. 3.
39 Bradlow *in* Bradlow & Hunter (Eds.) (2010), pp. 1-2.

Or, as Miller-Adams explains, as "a government-oriented institution", the World Bank focuses on the "public sector;"[40] in "everyday practice" this means that "Bank staff members interact"

> primarily with government officials and have minimal contact with civil society. At the same time, the World Bank adheres strongly to the notion that its work is apolitical, a provision that is also expressed in its founding charter. The Bank's identity as an institution "above politics" helps preserve its legitimacy with its 180 member countries and forges a degree of unity among its multinational staff.[41]

On the other hand, the Bank is also "a mover of money."[42] "Since the 1970s," Miller-Adams notes, "the Bank's member countries and managers have judged its success in terms of the number and size of the loans it makes" because it is "[o]nly by steadily increasing its lending volume" that the Bank can "make claims on its member countries for capital increases."[43] Moreover, "in the development field where the criteria for success are so long-term and uncertain, lending volume" has always been one "of the few ways in which the Bank could be judged as having had an impact."[44] Consequently, "the Bank's organizational culture puts a premium on concluding loans [...] and staff members have been evaluated and promoted on their success in doing so" – creating what has been called "approval culture".[45]

4.1.2   The development project cycle

The projects (co-)financed by World Bank investment loans and development policy loans "are conceived and supervised according to a well-documented project cycle,"[46] which, as Miller-Adams points out, is "based on an engineering model and divided into stages of identification, preparation, appraisal, negotiation and board approval, implementation and supervision, and evaluation" – as depicted in Figure 6.[47]

---

40   Miller-Adams (1999), p. 5.
41   *Id.* On the 'apolitical norm' as notable component of World Bank institutional culture, *see* section 3.1.1.
42   *Id.*
43   *Id.*
44   Miller-Adams (1999), p. 5.
45   *Id.* On the 'approvals culture', *also see* note 70, Ch. 4.
46   World Bank (2011), e-Book. For information about current and past World Bank-financed development projects, *see*: http://www.worldbank.org/projects/.
47   Miller-Adams (1999), p. 71.

Figure 6   The World Bank Project Cycle

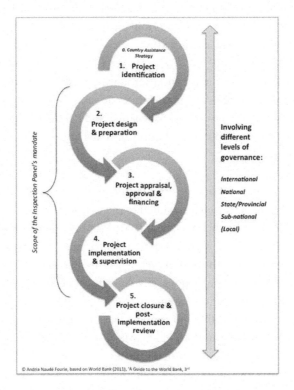

Each stage of the project cycle involves core activities and also generates standard documentation as output (many of which are referenced in the examples of Inspection Panel practice included throughout this book), which are publically accessible in accordance with the Bank's Policy on Access to Information.[48] Hence, project documents "can be valuable sources of information," as the World Bank observes, "for interested stakeholders wanting to keep abreast of the work the Bank is financing and for businesses wishing to participate in Bank-financed projects."[49]

The core activities related to each stage of the project cycle are 'regulated', 'directed' and/or 'informed' by the World Bank's operational policy framework (as will be discussed in the next chapter)[50] and involve the governance and management structures, as well as

---

48   For the Bank's policy on Access to Information, *see*: http://go.worldbank.org/TRCDVYJ440. For an example of standard project documentation – as generated over the course of *Chad: Petroleum Project* – *see*: http://www.worldbank.org/projects/P044305/petroleum-development-pipeline-project?lang=en.

49   World Bank (2011), e-Book.

50   The operational policies reflect varying degrees of detail and specificity, which might affect their degree of obligation – *See e.g.*, Bradlow & Naudé Fourie (2013), pp. 13, 40-62. On the effects of these variations on policy application and compliance assessment approaches, *also see* section 6.3.

the decision-making processes of the World Bank, borrowers, as well as project implementing agencies – and, therefore, cut across the international, national and sub-national levels. This is significant because, as Curtin and Nollkaemper argue, "[m]any of the problems of the current accountability gap are caused"

> by the fact that government and governance operate across different levels (sub-national – national – regional – international; general – functional; public – private). A major question then is whether and how accountability mechanisms at one level can supplement or fill gaps that arise at other levels or even straddle various levels.[51]

The development project cycle also serves as the basis of the institutional scope of the Inspection Panel's mandate, which is limited to stages two, three and four. Therefore, the examples from Inspection Panel practice included throughout this book focus solely on World Bank activities related to project design, preparation, approval, financing, implementation and supervision.[52] The project cycle is also used to explain the formal delineation between Bank and Borrower obligations, as will be discussed later on in this chapter.[53]

However, while the "project cycle remains central to most of the Bank's work,"[54] it has also been criticized for its inability to support participatory approaches that are "more integrated and iterative" in nature and which would "cente[r] on the needs of the borrower and beneficiary, not the requirements of the aid agency."[55] Such flexibility is of increasing importance, as Miller-Adams argues, since the "core technology" of the Bank (that is, the "central tasks around which an organization is built") "has changed along with its task environment"[56] in two important respects, namely, the "addition of new stakeholders and greater openness to outside views."[57] These changes have meant, specifically,

---

51 Curtin & Nollkaemper (2005), p. 13. For characteristics of transnational regulatory governance contexts, *see* section 2.1.

52 At the time of the Inspection Panel's inception, its mandate was also unique in the sense that it specifically included the design and appraisal phase. In this regard, *see e.g.*, Nathan, (1995), p. 137, who argues that "before the Inspection Panel's establishment, there was no mechanism by which the Bank and its staff could be investigated regarding projected and ongoing projects before it was too late to make any adjustments." For more on the Panel's mandate, *see* section 6.2.4.

53 *See* section 4.3.1.

54 Miller-Adams (1999), p. 71. Miller-Adams refers specifically to new Adaptable Program Loans (APLs) and Learning and Innovation Loans (LILs) – *see* pp. 85-86; *and see* section 10.1 for examples of such projects.

55 Miller-Adams (1999), p. 71.

56 Miller-Adams (1999), pp. 16-17. Miller-Adams also argues (at p. 125) that the "project cycle was designed for 'brick and mortar' projects", and is therefore not as suitable for development policy lending projects. Compare this argument with the Inspection Panel's comments about the effect of project 'modality' on the scope of Bank (and Borrower) obligations – *see e.g.*, section 10.1.

57 Miller-Adams (1999), p. 69.

that project-related decisions are less centralized than in the past, and the emphasis on stand-alone investment-oriented projects has given way to policy adjustment lending and a range of programs designed for purposes other than investment.[58]

Furthermore, Miller argues, although the Bank's "top-down, expert stance,"

whereby the Bank develops a lending program in line with its own diagnosis of a borrower's problems and brings to bear the technical skills and financing it believes are needed to address those problems[,]

remains a fundamental part of its 'core technology', the World Bank has also "begun to acknowledge that it does not have all the answers and is increasingly willing to consult with outside groups".[59]

4.2   MULTIPLE INTERESTS, DEMANDS AND EXPECTATIONS, RESULTING IN COMPLEMENTARY AND COMPETING INSTITUTIONAL AIMS

The competition for primacy among (and, occasionally, within) the World Bank's internal and external constituency groups is reflected in the wide range of institutional aims to which the Bank has committed itself over the years. These aims, in turn, are the products of the World Bank's periodic re-articulation of its mission and revision of its corporate strategy, and of the Bank's implementation of far-reaching institutional reforms – which seem to have become a constant feature of the institutional landscape, particularly since the early 1990s.[60]

4.2.1   Strategic repositioning and institutional reforms

In 1992, for instance, the World Bank, as Phillips describes it, "took a hard look at internal problems", as set out by the influential 'Wapenhans Report', and subsequently adopted "five recommendations," namely:

sustainable development impact should be the indicator of performance; success required local ownership; the quality of the project design was critical to the

---

58   *Id.*

59   *Id.* On issues related to the 'balance' between 'technical/commercial' and 'non-technical/non-commercial' project components, *also see* Ch. 9.

60   On these institutional reforms, *see* in general Phillips (2009); *and see* Mallaby (2004).

project's outcomes; a country focus was needed beyond project analysis; and portfolio performance must become a central concern of the business.[61]

Implementing these recommendations, moreover, would require the Bank "to change the ways it interacts with borrowers,"

> from a pattern dominated by prescription, imposition, condition-setting, and decision-making to one characterized by explanation, demonstration, facilitation, and advice. Such a perspective will lead to stronger borrower commitment and institutional capacities, better [borrower] accountability for project performance, and ultimately a better Bank loan portfolio.[62]

An additional consequence of the Wapenhans report has been the increased focus on the consistent application and enforcement of the Bank's operational policy framework throughout its development-lending, as reflected, for instance, in the strengthening of existing internal accountability mechanisms and in the establishment of the Inspection Panel.[63]

In early 1997, Jim Wolfensohn, World Bank Group President at the time, announced "a proposal for reforms known as the Strategic Compact," which was positioned as having the ability to "deliver a fundamentally improved institution in the future" – an institution, in other words, that would be

> quicker, less bureaucratic, able to respond continuously to changing client demands and global development opportunities and more effective in achieving its main mission: reducing poverty.[64]

---

61 Phillips (2009), pp. 37-38. The Wapenhans Report (as quoted in Phillips (2009), at p. 37) also emphasized: "the Bank must be no less restrained in diagnosing and seeking to remedy its own shortcomings than it is seeking to help member countries recognize and address theirs." For the text of the 'Wapenhans Report', *see* http://www-wds.worldbank.org/external/default/WDSContentServer/WDSP/IB/1992/09/22/000009265_3961003221227/Rendered/PDF/multi0page.pdf.

62 World Bank (1993), p. 12. Also compare this statement with Freestone's comments *at* note 176, Ch. 5.

63 *Also see* section 3.2.3.

64 Phillips (2009) pp. 38-39. Phillips quotes from p. 1 of the 'Strategic Compact'. On the Board's approval of the Strategic Compact, former Bank President Jim Wolfensohn commented (*Id.*): "What we are seeking to do is to increase the effectiveness of the Bank in what we believe to be a changing world, [...]. We are looking for significant improvements in the effectiveness of the Bank, in the projects rated satisfactory and we will be introducing new products that are tailored to the needs of our clients." *See* http://go.worldbank.org/YOOJ7Y4ZG0.

Subsequent institutional reform efforts were therefore focused on improving "the Bank's investment lending model" so as to "respon[d] better to borrowers' needs and the changing global environment."[65] These reforms were "organized around five pillars," namely:

> [f]ocusing more on results and risk; [m]oving from an emphasis on supervision to one on implementation support; [r]evising the options for investment lending and designing a new way to link disbursements more directly to results; [c]reating tools, training programs, and templates to support the implementation of reforms; [and] [s]implifying the policy framework for investment lending.[66]

Despite the implementation of various initiatives and reforms flowing from the 'Strategic Compact', however, an independent poll involving "2,600 'opinion leaders' from around the world", conducted in 2003 (which, as Phillips points out, came "at the end of a period of major reform involving unprecedented outreach to member countries"), found that "a large number of those surveyed"

> had quite a dim view of the [World Bank]. Less than half of Africa's opinion leaders were happy with its work, and about 60% of South Asians and Middle Easterners. Somewhat better, over 70% of East Asians including Chinese thought it was doing well. But about a third of those interviewed in Nigeria, Mexico, and Pakistan actually thought that the Bank was a negative factor in the world. Most of the respondents thought that the Bank's economic reform proposals hurt more than they helped while only a minority believed that it was doing a good job of reducing poverty.[67]

In 2013, spearheaded by current World Bank Group President Jim Yong Kim, the Bank unveiled yet another major re-articulation of its corporate strategy, which would be "aligning" "all of the institution's work" across the five sister-organizations, in order to realize "the twin goals of eliminating extreme poverty and boosting shared prosperity in a sustainable manner."[68] The World Bank (IBRD and IDA) announced, furthermore, that it would "adop[t] a new country engagement model that is designed to tailor policies and programs to the needs and priorities of individual countries."[69] Echoing earlier reform initiatives, the World Bank also affirmed that its

---

65   World Bank (2011), e-Book.
66   Id.
67   Phillips (2009), pp. 24-25.
68   World Bank (2015), e-Book.
69   Id.

> [e]mphasis will shift from an approvals culture to a results delivery culture
> centered on implementation, real-time citizen feedback, and midcourse evalu-
> ation and correction.[70]

In addition, the Bank announced that a "Group-wide expenditure review" had identified "cost-saving measures of at least $400 million on the annual cost base to be achieved over fiscal 2015-17."[71] These cost-saving measures, the Bank explained, were aimed to realize "increased lending capacity and budget flexibility" and "optimize the cost structure of the Bank Group",[72] but were also "designed to ensure that the Bank Group's operational capacities and its ability to deliver services to clients [would] not be compromised."[73]

The execution of the new corporate strategy would involve, once again, the implemen-tation of "sweeping institutional changes designed to significantly raise the World Bank Group's financial capacity as well as its operational efficiency."[74] As with previous initiatives, the recent wave of institutional reforms has proven to be highly controversial among Bank staff members.[75]

Such controversies are not without consequence. The World Bank, as Miller-Adams points out, "is an extremely complex organization."[76] Therefore, although "[s]weeping plans to revise and streamline its bureaucratic structure have become regular features of Bank life" – typically "occurring when a new president assumes control" – the institutional changes following from these major 'strategic repositionings' "have resulted in a high degree of organizational turmoil and often a loss of staff morale."[77] Yet, Miller-Adams adds, it is highly debatable whether these changes "have achieved either greater simplifica-tion or enhanced efficiency."[78]

'Institutional turbulence' may have become a regular feature at the Bank; however, as a recent *Financial Times* editorial argues, this time around, "turmoil at the world's main development bank" (which included "fallout from the first employee "work stoppage" in

---

70 *Id. Note*, these issues were also highlighted in the Wapenhans Report – as Shihata elaborated (*see* Shihata (2000), pp. 2-3): "[…] the Bank staff were often concerned about getting as many projects as possible approved under the Bank's lending project. In such an 'approval culture,' less attention had been given to the commit-ment of borrowers and their implementing agencies, or to the degree of 'ownership' assumed by borrowers of the projects financed by the Bank and the policies underlying them. At the project level, the leading design problem identified was that projects had become too complex." On the impact of project design complexity on compliance, *see e.g., Cambodia: Land Management and Administration* (2009), *e.g.,* as discussed *at* section 8.2.2.

71 World Bank (2015), e-Book.

72 *Id.*

73 *Id.*

74 *Id.*

75 *Also see e.g.,* note 79, Ch. 4.

76 Miller-Adams (1999), p. 5.

77 Miller-Adams (1999), p. 5. *And see* in general Phillips (2009).

78 *Id.*

[the Bank's] history [...] and the threat of more to come") "barely causes a ripple."[79] The "rest of the world is moving on" – for the simple reason that, "[b]oth in terms of the cost of development loans and the conditions attached, the bank is increasingly undercut by others, most notably China."[80]

On the other hand, to paraphrase Mark Twain, reports of the World Bank's demise may be premature. For instance, as Miller-Adams argues with regard to the internalization of "new agendas" and their "incorporat[ion] into the fabric of the organization," "externally driven explanations reveal themselves to be overly mechanistic and capable of providing only a partial picture" of what actually occurs within the institution.[81] "One shortcoming of this kind of explanation", Miller-Adams argues, "is that it undervalues"

> the substantial resources, financial and otherwise, amassed by the Bank over the years. Instead of relying directly on member contributions (like the United Nations), the IBRD has its own access to worldwide capital markets on extremely favorable terms. With net income of over $1 billion annually since 1985, the Bank has accumulated substantial financial assets, amounting to $18 billion at the end of 1997. A staff of more than 10,000, recruited from every part of the world (and especially its top universities) and an extensive research operation have contributed to making the Bank Group the world's largest single repository of technical expertise about development issues and a major contributor to development thinking. A sprawling (and spreading) physical complex in Washington, DC, and regional offices around the globe provide a physical counterpart to these financial and intellectual resources. Its assets make the World Bank a powerful force in its own right. Even when external pressure is applied, an institution with the size and strength of the Bank may not respond in ways that are expected. The metaphor used most often in regard to efforts to change the World Bank is that of trying to reverse the course of an ocean liner. Both processes are slow, unwieldy, and hard to control.[82]

While some might consider these attributes to be evidence of the Bank's inability to compete in a changing development financing market, they might also, in the longer run, prove to be instrumental in the Bank's survival.

---

79 Financial Times (Editorial), 'The World Bank risks sliding into irrelevance: Kim's continuous upheaval is no substitute for strategic vision', *Financial Times*, 20 November 2014, available at: www.ft.com.
80 *Id.*
81 Miller-Adams (1999), p. 12.
82 *Id.*

4.2.2 Achieving 'institutional equilibrium': reconciling and prioritizing competing institutional aims

Ultimately, factors such as the public/commercial duality inherent to the World Bank's mission, the evolving understanding on development assistance, as well as the diverse interests, demands and expectations of internal and external constituents have resulted in a complex context in which the Bank has to achieve 'institutional equilibrium' or balance. Achieving institutional equilibrium requires the realization of the wide range of institutional aims to which the Bank has committed itself, the reconciliation of competing institutional aims – and, where such 'reconciliation' is not possible, the achievement of institutional equilibrium requires decisions involving prioritization between interests and the making of various trade-off decisions.

In practice, however, this is far more challenging than what it sounds like in theory. One potential issue concerns the assumptions underlying the Bank's institutional aims – notably, the assumption that particular aims are complementary when they might potentially be contradictory. Consider, for instance, the Bank's description of an earlier round of institutional reforms as aiming to "promote inclusiveness, innovation, effectiveness, accountability, *and* results."[83] Such a statement might hit all the right notes with the Bank's multiple constituency groups, but it does not explain that, while 'innovation' might arguably be closely associated with 'effectiveness' and 'results', efforts to enhance 'inclusiveness' and 'accountability' tend to affect 'effectiveness' and could also alter 'results'.

The most recent World Bank Group-wide "Corporate Scorecard" (hereinafter, 'scorecard'), which had been adopted towards the end of 2014, serves as another illustration of this point.[84] The scorecard sets out the Bank's revised performance areas, indicators and targets, in alignment with its 2013 corporate strategy, and is organized along three tiers. Tier 1 concerns the "long term development outcomes that member state countries are achieving" and "[r]eflects the broader context in which the World Bank Group is operating;" whereas Tier 2 "[r]eflects the results reported by World Bank Group clients with the support of World Bank Group-financed operations that promote growth, inclusiveness, and sustainability/resilience."[85] In other words, the World Bank only *contributes* to the realization of performance targets in Tiers 1 and 2. This discussion, therefore, focuses on Performance Tier 3, which measures World Bank "operational and organizational effectiveness" and therefore contains only *World Bank* performance areas, indicators and targets.[86]

---

83 World Bank (2011), e-Book (emphasis added).
84 World Bank Group and World Bank Corporate Scorecard, October 2014. Available at: http://documents.world-bank.org/curated/en/2014/10/20275677/world-bank-group-world-bank-corporate-scorecard-october-2014.
85 World Bank (2014), p. 5.
86 *Id.*

Figure 7   World Bank Development-lending Operations: Performance Areas and Indicators

Development Impact			
Development outcomes [IEG] ratings	Satisfactory outcomes for IBRD/IDA operations	(as share of operations; as share of commitments)	Performance indicator
Client feedback	Client feedback	On WB effectiveness & impact on results	On WB responsiveness & staff accessibility
Strategic Context			
Incorporating citizen & beneficiary feedback	Projects with beneficiary feedback during implementation	Resolved registered grievances	
Mainstreaming of priorities	Projects with gender-informed analysis, actions & monitoring	Projects with climate change co-benefits implementing agreed climate actions	
Operational Delivery for Clients			
Financing for clients	IBRD/IDA commitments	Private capital mobilized	IBRD/IDA disbursements
Quality & timeliness of lending operations	Satisfactory Bank performance [IEG rating]: at entry; during project supervision	Time: from concept note to 1st disbursement	Disbursement ratio
Knowledge & science of delivery for results	Measure of knowledge flow	Operations design drawing lessons from evaluative approaches	
Financial Sustainability & Efficiency			
Total revenue			
Average annual growth of IBRD business revenue			
Support Cost ratio			
Managing Talent			
Employee engagement			
Managerial effectiveness			
Staff diversity			

Performance area

Source: World Bank Group Corporate Scorecard, Oct. 2014, p. 13.

Tier 3, as illustrated in Figure 7, is organized by way of five performance areas: "development impact", "strategic context", "operational delivery for clients", "financial sustainability and efficiency" and "managing talent", while each of these performance areas is further divided into sub-categories.[87]

Used "as an accountability and management tool", it can be argued that a performance scorecard such as this simplifies the matter of 'what the Bank should be held accountable for' – assuming, of course, that it indeed enjoys "sound institutional ownership" and, crucially, are also sufficiently supported by the Bank's external constituency groups.[88] However, it does not clarify how Management and staff will deal with the underlying tensions between (and within) performance areas in order to achieve institutional equilibrium in practice. For example, the resolution of "registered grievances" through mechanisms such as the Inspection Panel might affect the achievement of "[borrower] client satisfaction",[89] or, might be in a contradictory or competitive relationship. The same could be said of performance areas aimed at achieving both "quality *and* timeliness" or "quality *and* efficiency"[90]

As Mallaby observes with respect to previous institutional reform efforts, the Bank was "mulling over the client surveys that painted the Bank as slow and unresponsive," which were juxtaposed against "numerous reports on the declining quality of projects".[91] Hence, Mallaby concludes, the World Bank "faced a dual and in some ways contradictory problem" – that is, "[i]t needed to move faster, to deliver to its clients", but could also "not allow haste to compromise its already dubious quality."[92] Or, as Sarfaty argues with respect to the Bank's approach to applying its policy on Indigenous Peoples, "[i]n projects affecting indigenous peoples," World Bank management and staff "must balance competing interests"

> in deciding whether and when to apply the indigenous peoples policy and how to implement the policy once it is applied. […] As a result, actions are continuously contested and renegotiated within the institution itself. These internal contestations often correspond to divisions between competing interest groups and are most pronounced in regard to countries where domestic legal systems do not recognize indigenous peoples or sufficiently address indigenous-peoples-

---

87 World Bank (2014), p. 7. The Bank notes (*Id.* at p. 5) that the scorecard is a "living document[t] to be adapted and improved based on experience with their implementation and evolving external and internal priorities."

88 World Bank (2014), p. 5. *Note*, the reference to 'management' and 'accountability' here probably refers to the fact that the scorecard is to be employed for the purposes of 'vertical' and 'horizontal' accountability – on this distinction *see e.g.*, section 3.2.3.

89 On negative borrower responses to claims filed at the Inspection Panel, *see e.g.*, section 3.1.5; *and see* Naudé Fourie (2009), pp. 186-192. *Also see* section 4.3.2.

90 World Bank (2014), p. 7.

91 Mallaby (2004) p. 153.

92 *Id.*

related issues. For example, economists may disagree with environmentalists and anthropologists over whether to apply the indigenous peoples policy in a borrower country where there are no legal provisions that recognize special rights for indigenous peoples.[93]

Consequently, Sarfaty adds, the "Bank's approach to indigenous rights" is "a useful lens"

> for understanding the institution's role in the transnational legal process, where international norms seep into domestic law, often in the face of competing national self-interest. The dynamics of this process shed light on how the Bank balances its mandate of poverty reduction with human-rights-related concerns. They also have implications for the role of international institutions in the transnational legal process.[94]

As Phillips concludes, the "multiple objectives" of the Bank's "many principles," in combination with the Bank's "undefined product, and its heterogeneous member-clients"

> create a complicated and indeterminate decision-making environment that it has to solve through negotiation, and it is thus particularly vulnerable to political interference even though it claims to be apolitical.[95]

Viewed from a pluralistic perspective, on the other hand, this mutual contestation between institutional aims is a reality of the transnational development context – and, as some commentators argue, might be normatively desirable.[96] That being said, Inspection Panel practice also demonstrates that it is often unclear *how* the Bank deals with underlying tensions between institutional aims.[97]

Accountability for performance and harm

The remainder of this section describes two conceptions that compete for primacy with respect to 'what the Bank should be (held) accountability for' – that is: *accountability for*

---

93   Sarfaty (2005), pp. 1794-1795. On the Bank's application of its policy on Indigenous Peoples, *see* Ch. 13.
94   Sarfaty (2005), pp. 1794-1795.
95   Phillips (2009), p. 14. On the requirement of 'political neutrality', *see* the IBRD's Articles of Agreement, Art. IV, Section 10: "The Bank and its officers shall not interfere in the political affairs of any member; nor shall they be influenced in their decisions by the political character of the member or members concerned. Only economic considerations shall be relevant to their decisions, and these considerations shall be weighed impartially in order to achieve the purposes stated in Article I." On the comments of China's Executive Director in the aftermath of the Panel's China: Qinghai investigation, *see* note, 104, Ch. 4. On the apolitical value as key aspect of institutional culture, *see* section 3.1.1.
96   *See* Krisch (2010); as discussed *in* section 2.1.
97   *See* in particular Ch. 9; *and see* section 14.3 on the consideration of design alternatives.

performance and *accountability for harm*. Each of these conceptions tend to emphasize different institutional aims and typically hold contrasting views about 'risk' and 'cost' – but, as illustrated in Figure 8, also have several interdependencies.

Figure 8   Accountability for Performance and Harm

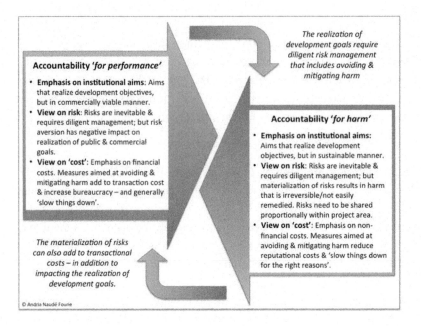

The *accountability for performance* perspective tends to emphasize institutional aims geared primarily towards the realization of public (development) and commercial (financial) objectives. In terms of the Bank's corporate performance scorecard, for instance, this perspective underscores the importance of performance areas such as client satisfaction, institutional effectiveness and efficiency, financial stability and growth of the Bank's development-lending portfolio. This emphasis is often demonstrated in scenarios where the achievement of 'institutional equilibrium' requires 'prioritization' and 'trade-off' decisions – and where institutional aims related to public (but especially) commercial goals are 'prioritized' or 'chosen' over those aimed at mitigating and/or offsetting harm.

Environmental, social and economic risks, moreover, are viewed as an inevitable part of development, which requires diligent management – but not to the extent that the institution becomes risk averse, since risk aversion affects the realization of public and commercial goals. In addition, measures aimed at mitigating and/or offsetting harm are typically viewed as having the effect of increasing transaction cost – because it 'makes the project more expensive to implement' *and* 'makes it more cumbersome to do business with the Bank'.[98]

By contrast, the *accountability for harm* perspective tends to emphasize institutional aims geared primarily towards the realization of public (development) objectives, while underscoring the importance of the 'sustainability' thereof.[99] In terms of the Bank's corporate performance scorecard, for instance, this perspective underscores the importance of performance areas such as development effectiveness, mainstreaming of gender and environmental priorities, the quality of the Bank's development-lending portfolio, and the satisfactory resolution of project-affected peoples' grievances. This emphasis is often demonstrated in criticisms of project scenarios where 'institutional equilibrium' was achieved by 'prioritizing' institutional aims related to commercial aims over public ones.

While the *accountability for harm* perspective typically recognizes environmental, social and economic risks as an inevitable part of development that requires diligent management – it emphasizes the adverse effects ('harm') caused by the materialization of risks, as well as the fact that such harm is often irreversible.[100] In addition, the materialization of environmental, social and economic risks can add to transactional costs, especially when costs are not viewed only from a 'net present value perspective' and also include other types of 'cost', such as reputational costs to the Bank and to its borrowers.[101]

Different responses to the Inspection Panel's investigation report of the *China: Western Poverty Reduction (Qinghai) Project* provide a striking demonstration of the differences between these competing conceptions. For instance, from the perspective of external constituency groups (notably, of various civil society actors), the Inspection Panel's findings served as vindication of their intense public advocacy campaign, while China's subsequent withdrawal of its request for financing was generally viewed as a 'victory'.[102] Internal constituency groups, on the other hand, criticized the "cost of the extra work that the panel report calls for" (which Bank management "estimated at around $4 million, or 10 per cent of the total loan"); they argued that these costs, in combination with "the fear of an inquisitorial process", had caused Bank staff to become risk averse – to the extent that they

---

98 *See e.g.*, Rubenstein (2007), p. 621: "[...] accountability mechanisms [...] impose costs. The costs of accountability in a given context might include the time and resources necessary for deliberation, monitoring and enforcement, constraints on creative problem solving, and/or slower response times in emergencies." *And see e.g.*, Woods (2001), p. 94: "[t]he warning about the abuse of inspections or horizontal accountability agencies is an important one" since such "inspections cost money and take time." *Also see* David Dollar's comment *in* note 12, Ch. 1. On internal World Bank accountability mechanisms, *see* section 6.2.

99 *See e.g.*, Bradlow & Naudé Fourie (2013), pp. 3 & 33.

100 *See e.g.*, Independent Accountability Mechanisms Network (2012), pp. 4-5.

101 *See e.g.*, *Cameroon: Petroleum Development & Pipeline Project* (2002), IR, § 123.

102 *See e.g.*, Clark & Treakle *in* Clark et al. (Eds.) (2003), pp. 211-246.

are now refusing to contemplate projects involving either involuntary resettlement or indigenous peoples, because they cannot compete with other sources
which do not have to take into account such high additional costs.[103]

In a public statement released at the time when the Inspection Panel and Bank management
presented their respective findings and recommendations regarding the *Qinghai* project
to the Board, the Chinese Executive Director was emphatic in his assertion that "China
accepts no conditions beyond Management's original recommendations that had been
agreed between Management and my authorities."[104] "It is unacceptable to my authorities,"
the Executive Director added,

> that other Bank shareholders would insist on imposing additional conditions
> on Management's recommendations – namely coming back to the Board for
> approval again for a project that was already approved last year. If that is the
> case, China will therefore turn to its own resources to implement the Qinghai
> Component of the project, and in its own way. Our efforts in fighting poverty
> will not be interrupted because of this development. We regret that because of
> political opposition from some shareholders the World Bank has lost a good
> opportunity to assist some of the poorest people in China, probably in the
> world, after so much effort by World Bank management and staff. Mr. Chair-
> man, we are greatly concerned about what has become clear in this process –
> and which constitutes a great challenge facing this institution. Namely the fact
> that compliance policies have been interpreted by some to an extreme and used
> for political purposes. By such action the Bank's mission – particularly its
> development effectiveness – has been jeopardized. We call for discussion on
> this as soon as possible. From the very start, the whole process has been under
> enormous political pressure. We believe therefore it is once again necessary to
> bring to our shareholders attention the importance in this institution of sepa-
> rating economic considerations from politics.[105]

The differences between the competing conceptions of *accountability for performance*
versus *accountability for harm* might be clear – just as, the differences between the

---

103 *See* R. Wade, 'A Defeat for Development and Multilateralism: the World Bank has been Unfairly Criticised
over the Qinghai Resettlement Project', *Financial Times*, 4 July 2000, available at www.ft.com. *And see* Bottelier's comments, *at* note 218, Ch. 7.

104 Statement read to the World Bank Board of Executive Directors by the Chinese Executive Director, Zhu
Xian on behalf of the Chinese government, on presentation of the Inspection Panel's Investigation Report
concerning the *China Western Poverty Reduction (Qinghai) Project. See* World Bank Press Release, 7 July
2000, available at: http://go.worldbank.org/TX5D7PGU80.

105 *Id.*

instrumentalist and formalist paradigms are clear, to which these conceptions are, respectively, related.[106] However, there are also distinct causal relationships between these conceptions. From the *accountability for performance* perspective, for example, it can be argued that what constitutes 'diligent risk management' will always include measures aimed at mitigating and/or offsetting harm; whereas *the accountability for harm* perspective highlights the argument that harm has a negative impact on the realization of public (development) goals (foremost), but also affects the realization of commercial aims.

Such arguments, in turn, explain why it can be concluded that the World Bank should be (held) accountable for *both* 'performance and harm'.[107] However, recognizing the validity of this argument in conceptual terms is one thing; translating it into clear operational terms, another. Significantly, it is often internal accountability mechanisms such as the Inspection Panel, which mandate spans across the wide range of institutional aims, performance areas, indicators and targets, that have to make sense of the underlying tensions between these conceptions, as many of the examples from Inspection Panel practice included throughout Part II of this book, demonstrate.[108]

For instance, Brown Weiss, a former Inspection Panel chair, underscores that "*effective development entails taking risks*", but adds that "[h]aving a process for holding management and staff accountable minimizes the chance that those harmed will be overlooked" while also enhancing the possibility of a "broader acceptance for risky but necessary activities."[109] Furthermore, on the criticism that the existence of the Inspection Panel has resulted in a practice of "Panel-proofing" (in which "important but risky elements" are "omitted" in order to circumvent a potential Inspection Panel investigation), Brown Weiss argues that this "critique" tends to say more about "the quality of the project", and can therefore "be a convenient cover for other things that are wrong with the project."[110]

Moreover, in recent publications, the Inspection Panel explicitly emphasizes that "risk-taking is an essential part of development work," which means that it is critical that Bank management and staff are "able to take the risks that go along with innovation," and that they "venture into challenging circumstances where risks and potential rewards may be high."[111] However, the Panel adds, "[e]ffective safeguard policies"

---

106 On instrumentalism (which describes the primary purpose of normative systems as *enabling* social action) and formalism (which describes the primary of normative systems as *restraining* social action), *see* section 2.3.
107 On arguments that neither the logic of instrumentalism nor of formalism is "mutually conclusive", *see* section 2.3.
108 In this regard, *see* in particular Ch. 9.
109 Brown Weiss (2010), pp. 488-489 (emphasis in original).
110 *Id.*
111 Inspection Panel (2012), p. 2 (emphasis added).

provide means to identify and manage risks, and citizen-driven accountability *helps to enable risk-taking* by providing a safety net for affected people in the event that risks materialize.[112]

"For an institution whose vision is a world free of poverty," the Panel asserts,

> it is important to consider the question of risk to whom. The need for risk-taking in development work does not mean that risk should be transferred disproportionately to local people or the environment in which they live.[113]

Hence, the Panel concludes, "[a]n important contribution of the Panel over many years" has been "exactly to identify risks"

> that may have been underestimated or not addressed. And, importantly, a main purpose of the Panel process is to lead to a proper organizational response with results for the affected people, especially those who are vulnerable and often marginalized in development processes. This also protects the reputation of the Bank.[114]

4.3   WORLD BANK AND BORROWER OBLIGATIONS

The distinction between Bank and Borrower obligations is of significance since the topic of this book is concerned with *World Bank* accountability.[115] This section therefore provides an overview of the 'formal delineation' of Bank and Borrower obligations. However, as the subsequent analysis of this delineation illustrates, Bank and Borrower obligations involve intricate relationships, which ultimately means that what the World Bank is to be (held) accountable for, is also shaped by the content and scope of Borrower obligations.

---

112 *Id.* (emphasis added). For a similar argument, *see* Independent Accountability Mechanisms Network (2012), pp. 26-27.
113 Inspection Panel (2013), p. 1. For similar remarks, *also see* MacNeill's comments *at* note 225, Ch. 7.
114 Inspection Panel (2013), p. 1.
115 *Note*, in this book, as in the context of World Bank development-lending operations, 'obligations' and 'responsibilities' are used interchangeably; whereas 'responsibility' does not typically refer to the international *legal* responsibility of international organizations for an 'international wrongful act' – as defined, *e.g.*, in ILA (2004).

4.3.1   *The formal division between Bank and Borrower obligations*

The World Bank's descriptions of the formal division between Bank and Borrower obligations typically depict a fairly straightforward picture. In *Honduras: Land Administration*, for example, Management underlined that "[Borrower] Governments are responsible"

> for preparing projects, which includes preparation of background documents (e.g., Social Assessment, EA), policy and operational manuals (e.g., IPDP, Process Framework, Project Operational Manual), and consultations. The Bank's role is to appraise these documents and processes and, if they are in accordance with Bank policies, including safeguard policies, endorse them as the basis for Bank financing. After Project Effectiveness,[116] the role of the Government is to implement the project whereas the Bank supervises project implementation.[117]

Or, as the World Bank explains the division between Bank and Borrower obligations in relation to the project cycle, "the Bank *helps governments take the lead*"

> in preparing and implementing development strategies, in the belief that if the country owns the program and it has widespread stakeholder support, the program has a greater chance of success.[118]

Thereafter, "borrower government[s]" and their "implementing agency or agencies are responsible for the project preparation phase, which can take several years."[119] Borrower governments usually "contrac[t] with [private sector] consultants and other public sector companies for goods, works, and services," during the project design and preparation and subsequent implementation stages in order to assist the Borrower with executing the relevant project tasks.[120] Furthermore, the Bank adds, project "[b]eneficiaries and stakeholders are also consulted" during the design and preparation stage in order "to obtain their feedback and enlist their support for the project."[121] "Because of the time, effort, and resources involved," the Bank emphasizes,

---

116 That is, the moment when the loan/credit agreement becomes 'effective' – *see* OP/BP 13.00 (Signing of Legal Documents and Effectiveness of Loans and Credits).
117 *Honduras: Land Administration* (2006), MR, § 29.
118 World Bank (2011), e-Book (emphasis added).
119 *Id.*
120 *Id.*
121 *Id.*

the full commitment of the government to the project is vital. The World Bank generally takes an *advisory role* and *offers analysis and advice, when requested,* during this phase.[122]

The Borrower is also "*responsible* for any studies required by the safeguard policies, with *general assistance provided* by Bank staff members."[123] However, "the *Bank itself assesses* the relevant capacity of the implementing agencies at this point" in order "to reach agreement with the borrower"

> about arrangements for overall project management, such as the systems required for financial management, procurement, reporting, and monitoring and evaluation.[124]

The Borrower is responsible for implementing the project, albeit "with technical *assistance and support* from the Bank's team."[125] The World Bank also assigns "[f]inancial management and procurement specialists" to the project to "ensure that adequate fiduciary controls on the use of project funds are in place."[126] During the project implementation stage, the Borrower's contracted project implementing agency (or agencies) have to "repor[t] regularly on the project's activities."[127] The Borrower and Bank also "*join forces* and prepare a midterm review of the project's progress," whereas "the [Borrower] government and the Bank" are charged with monitoring, "throughout the implementation phase," "the project's progress, outcomes, and effects on beneficiaries," which includes the obligation of obtaining "data for evaluating and measuring the ultimate effectiveness of the operation and the project in terms of results."[128]

The World Bank's obligations during the project implementation stage are focused in specifically on providing 'supervision', which includes identifying (potential) issues, taking corrective actions and/or facilitating remedial actions to be undertaken by the Borrower.[129] Such actions, in turn, could include the exercise of legal remedies against the Borrower (as provided for in the loan/credit agreement) and/or overseeing that the Borrower takes

---

122 *Id.* (emphasis added).
123 *Id.*
124 *Id.* (emphasis added).
125 *Id.*
126 *Id.*
127 *Id.*
128 *Id.* (emphasis added). *See* OP/BP 13.60 (Monitoring and Evaluation) – *e.g.*, Article (OP 13.60): "Monitoring and evaluation provides information to verify progress toward and achievement of results, supports learning from experience, and promotes accountability for results. The Bank relies on a combination of monitoring and self-evaluation and independent evaluation. Staff take into account the findings of relevant monitoring and evaluation reports in designing the Bank's operational activities."
129 On the distinction between Bank corrective actions, and Borrower remedial actions, *also see* section 7.1.2.

the necessary steps to address the issues in question.[130] Finally, as the Bank explains, once a project is "completed and closed at the end of the loan disbursement period"

> – a process that can take anywhere from 1 to 10 years – the Bank and the borrowing government document the results, the problems, and the lessons learned from the project in a report. The knowledge gained from this results-measurement process is intended to benefit similar projects in the future.[131]

Reflecting on the original motivations for the 'formal division' between Bank and Borrower obligations, Boisson de Chazournes observes that the Bank originally "required that borrower countries submit loan or credit requires, accompanied by a description of the projects ready to be undertaken."[132] "However," the Bank "soon realized that borrower countries often lack the means and human resources necessary to elaborate such documents."[133] Consequently, Bank management and staff became increasingly involved "in the design and preparation of the projects it was to finance,"[134] followed by "the negotiation of a loan or credit agreement between the borrower and the Bank," which would typically contain "a description of the project and the conditions in which it is to take place" – that is:

> loans or credits may be subject to conditions to be implemented either upon entry into force of the loan or credit agreement or upon disbursement of the funds allocated for the project. During the implementation phase of the project, the institution is under an obligation of oversight and of 'due diligence' to ensure that the funds intended for a loan are used by the borrower exclusively for the purposes for which they were disbursed.[135]

The division between Bank and Borrower obligations is an issue that invariably comes up in Inspection Panel practice since the Panel's mandate is explicitly limited to *World Bank actions and omissions*, taken or occurring in respect of *World Bank obligations*, as set out in the Bank's operational policy framework.[136] An important question, therefore, would

---

130 *See e.g.*, section 15.1.
131 World Bank (2011), e-Book. *Note*, post-implementation review falls under the purview of the IEG (formerly OED), *see* section 6.2.1.
132 Boisson de Chazournes *in* Treves et al. (Eds.) (2005), pp. 193-194. *Note*, between 1995 and 1999, the author worked as Senior Counsel in the World Bank's Legal Department (Environment and International Law Unit).
133 Boisson de Chazournes *in* Treves et al. (Eds.) (2005), pp. 193-194. On issues of borrower capacity, *see e.g.*, section 8.3.
134 Boisson de Chazournes *in* Treves et al. (Eds.) (2005), pp. 193-194.
135 *Id.*
136 *Also see e.g.*, Inspection Panel Resolution, § 21: "The borrower and the Executive Director representing the borrowing (or guaranteeing) country shall be consulted on the subject matter both before the Panel's recom-

be *what actions or omissions* would constitute a "failure" on the part of the Bank, which would be able to trigger the Inspection Panel process.[137] Ibrahim Shihata argued that World Bank failures "would occur in such cases when [the Bank] fails to reflect its operational policies in the actions required from the borrower"

> or when, after reflecting them as required, it fails to properly supervise project implementation to ensure that the borrower abides by its contractual obligations.[138]

However, Shihata emphasized, "harm to affected parties resulting from project implementation would, in the first instance, be attributed"

> to those who implemented the project, even though there could be instances where the Bank had contributed to the harm by not strictly following its policies in the design or appraisal of the project, in the actions it requires from the borrower, or in the supervision of their implementation.[139]

Nevertheless, Shihata added, "if the Bank's binding policies or procedures relate exclusively to measures to be taken by Bank staff,"

> a failure would take place if the staff fail to take such measures as envisaged, unless, of course there were exceptions allowed under the policies and procedures that were properly followed. If, on the other hand, the policies related to potential measures to be taken by the borrower, as is often the case under Bank operational policies (for example, the preparation and implementation of environmental assessment reports or resettlement plans), the staff responsibility would be limited to seeing to it that the borrower's obligations were clearly

---

mendation on whether to proceed with the investigation and during the investigation. Inspection in the territory of such country shall be carried out with its prior consent." In its 1999 review of the Inspection Panel, the Board also specified: "The profile of Panel activities, in-country, during the course of an investigation, should be kept as low as possible in keeping with its role as a fact-finding body on behalf of the Board. The Panel's methods of investigation should not create the impression that it is investigating the borrower's performance. However, the Board, acknowledging the important role of the Panel in contacting the requesters and in fact-finding on behalf of the Board, welcomes the Panel's efforts to gather information through consultations with affected people. Given the need to conduct such work in an independent and low-profile manner, the Panel – and Management – should decline media contacts while an investigation is pending or underway. Under those circumstances in which, in the judgement of the Panel or Management, it is necessary to respond to the media, comments should be limited to the process. They will make it clear that the Panel's role is to investigate the Bank and not the borrower." *See* BP 17.55 (Inspection Panel), Annex C, § 12.

137 Shihata (2000), pp. 47-48.
138 *Id.*
139 *Id.*

provided for, the plans expected from the borrower were drawn up in time (as defined in Bank policies, and such obligations and plans were then carried out by the borrower as agreed.[140]

"Clearly," Shihata concluded, "the obligation of the staff with respect to actions to be taken by the borrower"

is not to guarantee that the intended outcome will materialize in each case, but to make their best effort, with the due diligence required under the Staff Rules, to ensure that the borrower will indeed carry out its obligations. To quote a French legal expression, this is an '*obligation de moyens*' and not an '*obligation de résultat*'.[141]

4.3.2   Analysing a complex delineation

As the preceding examples already hinted, the division between Bank and Borrower obligations involves a much higher degree of complexity and permeability than formal descriptions would suggest. In fact, it might be decidedly challenging to discern Bank from Borrower obligations – especially from the perspective of project-affected people. This section analyzes specific aspects of the division between Bank and Borrower obligations that shape the content and scope of World Bank accountability. As depicted in Figure 9, the discussion is limited to the project design, preparation, appraisal, approval and implementation stages, aligned with the Inspection Panel mandate.[142]

---

140 *Id.*
141 *Id.* (emphasis added). On the distinction between obligations '*de moyens*' and '*de résultat*', *see e.g.,* R. Schulze (Ed.), *New Features in Contract Law*, Sellier: European law Publishers, (2007), p. 185. "The basic aim of this distinction is to draw a line between duties which include an undertaking to achieve a specific result [obligation de résultat] and those duties which may be directed to such a result [obligation de moyens'] but which only force the debtor to deploy certain methods [such as "the duty of care" – *see* Alessi, below] and thereby meet the required standards of behaviour." Schulze adds (*at id.*) that this distinction is "nowadays part of several legal systems including the UNIDROIT Principles on International Legal Contracts", which are available at: http://www.unidroit.org/publications/513-unidroit-principles-of-international-commercial-contracts. *Also see* D. Alessi, 'The Distinction between Obligations de Résultat and Obligations de Moyens and the Enforceability of Promises', (2005) 13 *European Review of Private Law* 5, pp. 657-692.
142 On the Panel's mandate, *see* Inspection Panel Resolution, § 12; *and see* section 6.2.4. On the scope of the analysis contained in this book, *see* section 1.2.

Figure 9 Expounding World Bank and Borrower Obligations

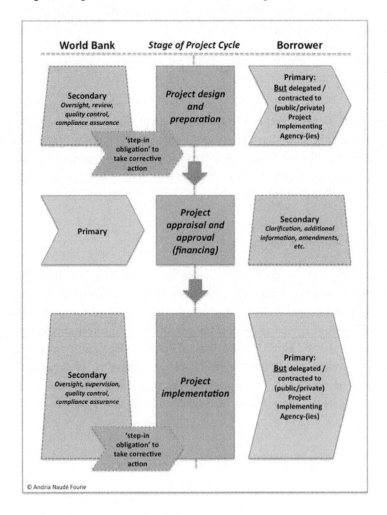

© Andria Naudé Fourie

Primary and secondary obligations

A first aspect of the analysis points to the distinction between different types of obligations, here described as 'primary' and 'secondary' obligations. Primary obligations resemble *obligations de résultat* because they are based on a duty to realize a particular result or output and therefore require obligated actors to undertake specific concrete actions, such as conducting an environmental assessment (EA) in accordance with certain specifications.[143]

---

143 On the distinction between obligations '*de moyens*' and '*de résultat*', *see* note 141, Ch. 4.

Secondary obligations are a derivative of primary obligations and are related to the notion of *'obligations de moyens'* since they are based on the duty "to deploy certain methods", such as 'due diligence standards' in order to ensure that "the required standards of behaviour" are met.[144] For instance, where the primary obligation for completing the EA falls on the Borrower, the Bank's secondary obligation entails ensuring that the EA process meets the Bank's quality requirements, as specified in the Bank's policy on Environmental Assessment. However, the secondary obligation is dependent upon the initiation of the activities related to the primary obligation. For example, BP 4.01 (Environmental Assessment) demonstrates what this distinction looks like in practice:

> Environmental assessment (EA) for a proposed Bank-financed operation is the responsibility of the borrower. Bank staff *assist* the borrower, *as appropriate*. The Region coordinates Bank review of EA in consultation with its Regional environment sector unit (RESU) and, as necessary, with the support of the Environment Department (ENV).[145]

At this point, it is worth noting that, during each particular stage of the project cycle, only one of the parties to the loan/credit agreement (Bank or Borrower) has the primary obligation for completing the core tasks of that stage.[146] Moreover, the primary responsibility shifts between Bank and Borrower throughout the stages of the project cycle, although the Bank's obligations are mostly secondary in nature. The distinction between primary and secondary obligations, as well as the shifts in the type of obligation held by Bank and Borrower might result in ambiguity as to who is responsible for what – an uncertainty that might not only be experienced by project-affected people, but also by borrowers and project implementing agencies. In *Nepal: Arun III*, for example, the Inspection Panel commented that it had found "[i]n too many instances," that

> progress has been stalled by the need to complete another, prior step. NEA's [the project implementing agency] 1993 "Environmental Assessment and Management Executive Summary" could not be updated to reflect the changes in road alignment, as recommended by the PoE [Panel of Experts], since the additional KMTNC [local 'implementing NGO' carrying out studies related to the Project] studies were not available until February 1995. As a result, the

---

144 *Id.*

145 BP 4.01 (Environmental Assessment), § 1 (emphasis added).

146 *Note,* the Borrower typically delegates and/or contract specific tasks to public or private sector project implementing agency(ies), but the primary responsibility remains with the Borrower, as signatory of the loan/credit agreement. On project implementing agencies, *see* section 3.1.2; on capacity issues of project implementing agencies, *see* section 8.3.

project went through appraisal and negotiation without fulfilling this suggestion from the PoE.[147]

And, concerning the primary "[r]esponsibility for resettlement," the Inspection Panel affirmed that it "rest[ed] with the borrower", "according to paragraph 6 of OD 4.30."[148] "Nevertheless," the Panel added, "it is also clear that [the Bank] is responsible for assuring compliance with OD 4.30."[149] In practice, assuring compliance would specifically mean that "the Staff Appraisal Report and the Memorandum and Recommendation of the [Bank] President have to certify that the borrower's [resettlement] plan" is in compliance with the Bank's policy on Involuntary Resettlement.[150] However, the Panel concluded, "[b]etween those two kinds of responsibility,"

> the reality is that "ownership" of the resettlement issue is hard to find. According to a Bank review in 1993, "few countries have demonstrated their commitment to the principles and objectives of resettlement articulated in OD 4.30. Equally few Task Managers are convinced about its importance, necessity, and viability." Against that background, it is necessary to be careful in assessing the real progress made in the Arun III project. With regard to supervising the Credit 2029-NEP, for instance, the borrower indicates that it filed three reports on the ACRP issues between 1988 and 1990, and yet there is no record yet found of those reports being scrutinized by IDA.[151]

The Bank's 'step-in obligation'

A second aspect concerns what is described here as the supposed 'shift' that occurs during the design/preparation and implementation stages of the project cycle – when, in other words, the primary obligation for completing the core design, preparation and implementation tasks lies with the Borrower. This 'shift' occurs when the Borrower is not (sufficiently) meeting its primary obligations – when, for instance, the Borrower is not undertaking certain actions, or when its actions do not meet the relevant requirements as specified in the loan/credit agreement.

Under such circumstances, arguably, the nature of the Bank's secondary obligation changes as it becomes an obligation to intervene, to take decisive actions – a 'step-in obligation', if you will[152] – aimed at ensuring that the Borrower undertakes the necessary

---

147 *Nepal: Arun III* (1994), IR, § 81.
148 *Nepal: Arun III* (1994), IR, § 22.
149 *Id.*
150 *Id.*
151 *Id.*
152 Based on the notion of 'step-in rights', which is a familiar notion in project finance. *See e.g.*, Winter & Price (2006), p. 263: "A project has step-in rights: '[...] if a person who provides finance in connection with the

actions in order to bring those aspects of the project 'into compliance'. However, the Bank needs to execute this 'step-in obligation' in a manner that preserves its long-term relationship with the Borrower, respects the principle of state sovereignty, fosters Borrower ownership for development – while, simultaneously accounting for any institutional and/or professional capacity deficiencies of the Borrower and/or its project implementing agencies.

Adding to this complexity, moreover, are questions about the fitting 'moment' when this 'shift' should occur in particular project scenarios and what the appropriate content and scope of this 'step-in obligation' should be. Since the normative yardsticks to be employed in addressing such questions typically involve considerable degrees of managerial discretion – and, therefore, subjectivity (such as 'due diligence' standards) – these matters often involve significant controversy.

Indeed, many of the contentious matters in Inspection Panel practice concern, for example, whether or not the Bank has done 'enough' in executing its secondary obligations; whether or not the Bank should have 'stepped in' sooner to ensure that the Borrower meets its primary obligations; what should the Bank have done differently as part of executing its 'step-in obligation'; and, crucially, how far the Bank's secondary obligations (including its 'step-in obligation') stretched – and, indeed, if there should be a limit to the Bank's obligations.

For example, as Bank management argued during the 2002 investigation of *Paraguay/Argentina: Yacyretá Hydroelectric Project*, "the Bank as well as EBY [project implementing agency] worked under the assumption that Paraguayan labor laws would be applied effectively" and that "employers would proceed according to the law and properly compensate their employees."[153] Although "this assumption was optimistic," Management acknowledged, "*there are limits to how far EBY (and thus indirectly the Bank) can and should be required to monitor* the ultimate use of the compensation paid."[154] Or, as Woods argues, "there are limits to how accountable the IMF and World Bank can be to the governments and peoples most affected by their lending and policies.[155] This reality, in turn, "raises a more profound issue"

> as to how far-reaching the activities of relatively unaccountable agencies should be. [...] [For instance,] Robert Dahl warns that we should be 'wary of ceding the legitimacy of democracy to non-democratic systems'. His point is that domestic political systems have a potential to be democratically accountable

---

project has a conditional entitlement under an agreement to – (a) assume sole or principal responsibility under an agreement for carrying out all or part of the project, or (b) make arrangements for carrying out all or part of the project.'"

153 *Paraguay/Argentina: Yacyretá Hydroelectric Project* (2002), IR, §§ 299-300.
154 *Id.* (emphasis added). On issues of compensation in involuntary resettlement scenarios, *see* section 12.3.
155 Woods (2001), p. 100.

in a way that international organizations cannot. The implication is that the IMF and the World Bank should be reined in from far-reaching policy conditionality. Their activities should be limited to those for which they can claim to be effectively accountable.[156]

Intricate interdependencies between Bank and Borrower obligations

The final aspect analyzed here concerns the intricate interdependencies between Bank and Borrower obligations, and the consequences thereof. In short, much of what internal and external constituency groups demand and expect the Bank to be accountable 'for', concerns secondary obligations. In *Uganda: Power Projects*, for instance, the Inspection Panel was critical of what it called "an unduly optimistic assessment of the costs, benefits and risks of the Project, including"

> (i) an under-estimation of capital costs in the PAD; (ii) an under-estimation of the likely impact of the Project on tariffs; (iii) a non-recognition of the likely shortfall in UETCL revenue against the capacity charge up to 2002; and (iv) non-recognition of some key risks, notably in collection rates and exchange rates.[157]

However, with respect to "all of these, and especially the third category," the Inspection Panel noted, "Bank management *was substantially dependent on the work of others.*[158]

Or, as Boisson de Chazournes argues, the very "notion of the 'project cycle' highlights" the "very close relationship, not to say dependency, between these actors in the conduct of operational activities".[159] Indeed, with "the acts of both the Bank and the borrower being so closely connected," "it is difficult to conceive that one of them would not be tempted to offload its responsibility onto the other,"[160] which, in turn, could make it difficult – both for Requesters and the Inspection Panel – to discern Bank from Borrower obligations. In such situations, Boisson de Chazournes adds, the "Bank's Board would have to fulfil the function"

---

156 *Id.* (2001), p. 100. Woods is referencing R. Dahl (1999), 'Can International Organizations be Democratic?', *in* I. Shapiro & C. Hacker-Cordon (Eds.), *Democracy's Edges*, Cambridge: Cambridge University Press, pp. 19-36, at p. 33. On the contraction of the content and scope of World Bank obligations during a supposed fourth stage of development assistance, *see* section 4.1.

157 *Uganda: Power Projects* (2007), IR, § 633 (emphasis added).

158 *Id.*

159 Boisson de Chazournes *in* Treves et al. (Eds.) (2005), pp. 193-194.

160 Boisson de Chazournes *in* Treves et al. (Eds.) (2005), p. 195. For examples in the context of project supervision activities, *see e.g.*, section 15.3.

conferred upon it by the Resolution establishing the Inspection Panel; namely, to make a final decision, at the stage when the Panel recommendations are being discussed and approved, about the attribution of responsibilities.[161]

However, this argument points to another consequence of the 'permeability' between Bank and Borrower obligations: the political sensitivities among Board members that measures aimed at ensuring World Bank accountability – such as the Inspection Panel, which mandate explicitly excludes Borrower obligations – are actually a smokescreen for achieving other goals. Boisson de Chazournes observes, for instance, that the close relationship between Bank and Borrower obligations "had provoked ferocious discussions within the Board" – in particularly during the first five years since Panel's inception – because borrowers "saw, under the cover of the Inspection Panel procedure,"

> a means of circumventing respect for their sovereignty, enabling interference in their domestic affairs. They particularly opposed the use of the Panel as a tribune by non-state actors apparently without any legitimacy to do so.[162]

Or, as Suzuki argues, while the exclusion of Borrower obligations from the Inspection Panel mandate is "consistent with the principle of non-interference with the domestic affairs of other states," the Panel's "competence to investigate the [Bank's] failure to follow up on the borrower's obligations under the loan agreement" brings up the matter "what constitutes such failure."[163] This, in turn, "is an essentially relative question" – that is, "it depends on the relations between the [Bank] and the borrower concerned, and it may necessarily address the performance of the borrower, at least to some extent."[164]

In this regard, Hansungule's comments are also of significance. Hansungule points out that "Bank resources" provide 'third world country'-borrowers' with "the psychological security they otherwise do not have."[165] "[I]t is this aspect" in particular, "which makes governments in developing countries react negatively"

> to such ideas as the introduction of an Inspection Panel. They fear that an inspection of the World Bank project which may be the only major project in the country may lead to the withdrawal of the Bank, which does not add well to the political chances of the ruling politicians.[166]

---

161 Boisson de Chazournes *in* Treves et al. (Eds.) (2005), p. 195.
162 Boisson de Chazournes *in* Treves et al. (Eds.) (2005), p. 193. *Also see* note 89, Ch. 4.
163 Suzuki *in* Bradlow & Hunter (Eds.) (2010), p. 84. *Also see* Shihata's comments in this regard, *at* notes 137-138, Ch. 4.
164 Suzuki *in* Bradlow & Hunter (Eds.) (2010), p. 84.
165 Hansungule *in* Alfredsson & Ring (Eds.) (2001), p. 155.
166 *Id.*

Furthermore, as Miller-Adams argues, "[t]here is an evaluative component to the Bank-borrower relationship as well," namely: "Bank staff makes on-going judgments as to whether a borrower is managing its economy successfully by following policies the Bank has deemed appropriate."[167] "In addition to monitoring a country's economic performance,"

> Bank staff and management routinely engage in a dialogue with policymakers in borrowing countries. Informal and off the record, this policy dialogue is none the less influential in shaping the Bank's perception of a given borrower's economic policies. The evaluative function has broader ramifications: Bank approval of a country's economic policy – signalled, for example, by the conclusion of a large adjustment loan – is a key factor in establishing that country's creditworthiness in the eyes of private investors.[168]

Consequently, while "[t]he Inspection Panel was conceived as an instrument to improve transparency and accountability in Bank operations," as Suzuki and Nanwani contend, "[i]n practice," "some Executive Directors and government officials have seen the Panel more as an instrument"

> for pressuring Bank Management into insisting on borrower compliance with legal covenants related to the projects in question. The Resolution envisaged that the Panel would focus primarily on the *Bank's adherence* to its own policies and procedures. The Resolution is clear on this. In every case in which the Panel has proposed an investigation, it has stressed that it is the Bank alone, *not the government or borrower,* that is to be the subject of any investigation. Whatever the original intent, however, the practical result is that borrowing countries themselves feel under threat of an 'investigation' and, given the perceived political implications of this, they have acted accordingly to block or avoid any further Panel involvement in the review of World Bank-financed projects. The terms 'investigation' and 'inspection' are difficult for borrowing countries to accept because of the negative connotations inevitably associated with them. The result often has been a sharp division among the Executive Directors, usually, for obvious reasons, along Part I [Donor] and II [Borrower] lines.[169]

---

167 Miller-Adams (1999), p. 19.
168 *Id.*
169 Suzuki & Nanwani (2005-2006), pp. 325-326 (emphasis in original). *Note,* on the distinction between 'part 1 Donors and part 2 Borrowers', *see* section 3.1.1; for more comments as to the 'real' purpose of the Inspection Panel, *see* section 7.2; and for the contrasting paradigms of instrumentalism and formalism, *see* section 2.3.

Several examples from Inspection Panel practice might indeed be interpreted as implicit criticisms of Borrower performance – or, at least draw public attention to adverse conditions within borrower countries, which might not always be welcome attention from the perspective of borrower states. In *Papua New Guinea: Smallholder Agriculture*, for example, the Inspection Panel observed that the "sustainability" of a specific Road Maintenance Trust Fund (RMTF) was dependent "on contributions from [a] Provincial government that have a poor track record in supporting provincial road infrastructure."[170] The Panel subsequently found that Bank management failed to "carry out the necessary due diligence"

> to assess how provincial governments had spent tax revenues derived from export grants in the past, nor did it examine whether provincial governments would be committed to apply these tax payments to their proposed RMTF contributions in the future. [...] Virtually everyone the Panel met with was concerned about the Oro provincial government's ability to contribute funds to an RMTF – especially after the Project ended – as the Government of Papua New Guinea would no longer underwrite those costs. Many felt that the WNB [West New Britain] provincial government might be able to make payments, but that the Oro provincial government would not. Most informants felt that counterpart funds could possibly be counted on to flow to the provincial government from Government of Papua New Guinea during the life of the Project, but not once the Project ends. During the Panel's meeting with the Provincial Administrator in Oro, he confirmed to the Panel that they simply had no resources to pay into the RMTF even if they wanted to.[171]

Bank management, on its part, might on occasion have added to this tension through its insistence on the lack of a 'causal link' between alleged harm and World Bank actions or omissions, when responding to Requests filed at the Inspection Panel.[172] For instance, in its response to the Inspection Panel Request filed with respect to *Papua New Guinea: Governance Promotion* (GPAL), Bank management argued that there was "no cause and effect"

> between the impacts described and actions or omissions on the part of the Bank. [...] The Requesters' claims of adverse effects are entirely related to the

---

170 *Papua New Guinea: Smallholder Agriculture* (2009), IR, §§ 483-484.

171 *Id.* (emphasis added). For additional examples, *also see Brazil: Itaparica Resettlement and Irrigation* (1997), ER, § 27(4); *Ghana: Second Urban Environment Sanitation* (2007), IR, § 291; and *Albania: Integrated Coastal Zone Management* (2007), IR, p. xxiii and IR, §§ 241-242.

172 One of the 'technical eligibility criteria' – *see* Inspection Panel Resolution, § 12. On the issue of the 'causal link' between harm and World Bank actions, *also see* section 6.2.4

Kiunga-Aiambak road project. The Bank does not have any role in the construction, operation or maintenance of the Kiunga-Aiambak Road, and the activities that caused the adverse effects described by the Requesters were not financed under the GPAL, were not among the policy objectives of the GPAL and were not included among the GPAL conditions. For the most part they were the result of purportedly illegal actions by private entities, and they began prior to preparation of the GPAL. In Management's view, to hold the Bank responsible for unlawful practices carried out by private entities that have no relationship with the Bank's assistance program in Papua New Guinea and to recommend a full investigation would be contrary to the letter and spirit of the Resolution and Clarifications related to the Inspection Panel.[173]

****

The content and scope of World Bank obligations – which ultimately influence what the World Bank should be (held) accountable *for* – are continuously shaped by various factors, including: the evolving understanding about development assistance and its complex relationships with sustainability; new entrants to the development financing market; and the intricate relationship with Borrower obligations.

In commercial contexts, as Phillips points out, "the objectives are clear – produce with the least-cost technology, sell, and make a profit."[174] World Bank development-lending operations, however, are surrounded by "multiple interests" that are expressed in terms of multiple institutional aims.[175] For instance, "borrower shareholders" "might pursue the objective of reducing interest rates, loan conditions, and lender interference," whereas "donor member shareholders" "might be trying to increase loan conditions and interference in order to satisfy their political constituencies back home."[176] Moreover, as illustrated in the previous chapter, there are also "a number of groups, beyond government and financiers, that have an interest in the Bank as their 'agent'".[177] This "spectrum of interested parties consists of lenders, shareholders, and informal activist groups," which, in turn, "can be divided into different interest subgroups."[178] Therefore, although each of these groups

---

173 *Papua New Guinea: Governance Promotion* (2001) MR, §§ 69-70. *Note*, in his case, the Inspection Panel agreed with Management's argument (*see* ER, § 55). For additional examples where the matter of the 'causal link' was at stake, *also see Brazil: Itaparica Resettlement and Irrigation* (1997), ER, § 7; *India: Madhya Pradesh Water Sector Restructuring* (2010/2011), MR, p. vi; *and see* ER, § 27; and *Paraguay/Argentina: Yacyretá Hydroelectric Project* (2002), ER, § 40.
174 Phillips (2009), pp. 12-13.
175 *Id.*
176 *Id.*
177 *Id.*
178 *Id.*

"subscribes to the objective of economic development and poverty reduction" (or, at least "in theory"), they "might have different objectives" "in practice"[179] – which ultimately translate to very different ideas as to what the World Bank should be (held) accountable for. As a result, different constituency groups tend to emphasize one of two competing conceptions – accountability for harm; or accountability for performance – which, in turn, also echo the tensions between instrumentalism and formalism.[180]

Over time, this complex reality has wrought a wide range of institutional aims, which operationalization can be far more challenging than it appears in theory – in particular because there are significant underlying tensions between some of these aims. Achieving institutional equilibrium or balance between these aims, in other words, often requires efforts to reconcile conflicting aims, and, where this does not prove to be possible, to make decisions involving prioritization and trade-offs.

The second dimension of World Bank accountability – what the Bank should be accountable for – concerns, to a large degree, the Bank's challenges regarding the achievement of institutional equilibrium among multiple, diverse institutional aims, and the challenges involved in managing a complex relationship with borrowers while also meeting its own obligations in a matter that is aligned with the demands and expectations of internal and external constituency groups. And, as the following chapters illustrate, these challenges are often brought to the fore by the practice of internal accountability mechanisms such as the Inspection Panel.

---

179 *Id.*
180 *See* section 2.3.

5 ASSESSING ACCOUNTABILITY: COMPLIANCE WITH NORMATIVE FRAMEWORKS

How should World Bank accountability be assessed, determined or measured? The answer to this question depends, in part, on *what* the Bank should be (held) accountable *for* and *to whom* should the Bank be accountable. And, as the previous chapters demonstrated, different conceptions might emphasize World Bank accountability to internal accountability holders, for performance; whereas other conceptions might highlight World Bank accountable to external accountability holders, for harm.

It could therefore be argued, for instance, that World Bank accountability should be assessed by means of a performance scorecard setting out performance areas, indicators and targets (as introduced in the previous chapter).[1] However, there are several reasons why this chapter excludes such an approach (that is, aside from any arguments against the adequacy of a 'scorecard' tool for such purposes).[2] For instance, because (at least some) of the Bank's activities are characterized as being normative in nature (specifically those involving norm creation, norm application and norm enforcement), their assessment require a form of normative evaluation.[3] Moreover, as noted earlier, this book focuses on the place of normativity in the conceptualization and operationalization of accountability.[4]

Chapter 5 is therefore concerned specifically with the assessment of World Bank accountability against various intersecting normative frameworks. The chapter considers various sources of normativity surrounding the World Bank's development-lending operations, which can be used to evaluate or assess World Bank actions and omissions in order to determine whether or not these constitute compliance with the procedural and substantive norms contained in the relevant normative frameworks.

The chapter sets out five normative frameworks, illustrated in Figure 10, that vary in terms of their levels of formality, specificity, legality and obligation,[5] namely: the *credit/loan agreement* between the Bank and Borrower; the Bank's *operational policy framework*; *national law* (referring to the borrower state's domestic legal and regulatory system); *international law* (referring to the international legal obligations of both the Bank and

---

1   *See* sections 4.2.2.
2   One such objection might be that performance scorecards, at least on their own, do not contain sufficient degrees of specificity and obligation in order to influence and direct behaviour.
3   *See* section 2.1.
4   *See* sections 1.1 & 2.3.
5   On these distinctions, *see* the discussion *in* section 2.3.

borrower states); and *international industry and/or professional standards* and *best practice.*[6] In discussing each of these normative frameworks, the chapter also expounds the relationships between them and points to some of the implications of these – notably, for the content and scope of World Bank accountability, and for the delineation between Bank and Borrower obligations.

5.1 THE CREDIT/LOAN AGREEMENT AND THE WORLD BANK'S OPERATIONAL POLICY FRAMEWORK

The credit/loan agreement entered into by the World Bank and the Borrower with respect to a specific development project is an international agreement between an international organization and a state actor, and is therefore governed by the international legal system.[7] However, as Bradlow notes, these agreements "contain unusual governing law clauses" – notably, the specification "that the rights and obligations of the Bank"

> under such agreements shall be valid and enforceable in accordance with their terms notwithstanding the law of any state or political subdivision thereof to the contrary.[8]

In other words, the credit/loan agreement sets out the Bank and Borrower's respective rights and obligations with regard to the specific project and supersedes national law – although, as will be discussed below, there are also specific interfaces between the credit/loan

---

6   For another example of a normative framework that can be used to asses accountability, *see e.g.,* ILA (2004), pp. 8-15, which sets out 'recommended rules and practices' that had been "derived from principles, objectives, and concepts common to all IO-s", including the principles of: "good governance" (encompassing "participatory decision-making process", "access to information", a "well-functioning international civil service", "sound financial management", and "reporting and evaluation"), "good faith", "constitutionality and institutional balance", "principle of supervision and control", stating the reasons for decisions or a particular course of action", "procedural integrity", "objectivity and impartiality", and "due diligence".

7   On the rules of international institutional law governing the area of international agreements between international organizations and states, *see e.g.,* Schermers & Blokker (2003) pp. 1742-1800.

8   For a discussion of the legal nature of loan/credit agreements between the Bank and borrowers, *see e.g.,* Bradlow *in* Bradlow & Hunter (Eds.) 2010, p. 11; *and see* Wirth *in* Shelton (Ed.) (2000), p. 334. For the regulation of aspects concerning the establishment and cancellation of legal agreements between the Bank and its borrowers, *see e.g.,* OP/BP 3.10 Financial Terms and Conditions of IBRD Loans, IBRD Hedging Products, and IDA Credits; OP/BP 13.00 Signing of Legal Documents and Effectiveness of Loans and Credits; OP/BP 12.00 Disbursement; *and* OP/BP 13.40 Suspension of Disbursements; OP/BP 13.50 Cancellations. *Also note*: projects co-financed by other lenders will involve additional loan/credit agreements between the Borrower and such lenders, which are not discussed in this section – in this regard, *see* OP/BP 14.20 Cofinancing.

agreement, the Bank's operational policy framework, the Borrower's national legal system and the international legal system.[9]

Figure 10   World Bank Development-Lending Operations and Intersecting Normative Frameworks

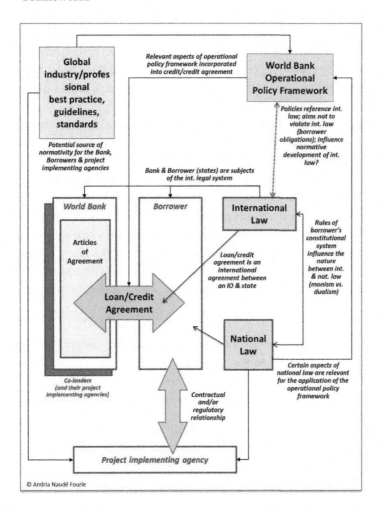

© Andria Naudé Fourie

---

9   *See* section 5.2; *and see* section 8.2. *Note:* "When making a loan, the Bank uses a variety of documents to define its contractual relationships with the borrower, guarantor, and other entities that are responsible for the project or that have a direct interest in the project or in the achievement of its objectives" – such as loan and guarantee agreements, security arrangements, and covenants, which aim to "set out the parties' obligations with clarity and specificity" whereas "covenants are tailored to the specific responsibilities of the contracting party (*i.e.*, borrower, guarantor, or implementing entity)." (*See* OP 7.00 Lending Operations: Choice of Borrower and Contractual Agreements, §§ 8-17.)

During the initial stages of the project cycle, the Bank, in consultation with the Borrower, determines which of the Bank's operational policies would be applicable to the specific project. Although these operational policies do not constitute, as Freestone explains, "instructions to borrowing counties," they are, in effect, 'incorporated' into the loan/credit agreement as conditionalities since the Borrower has to agree that the project would "be in compliance with Bank policy and procedural requirements" in order "to qualify for World Bank financing."[10] Furthermore, should the Bank subsequently find that the Borrower is not meeting its obligations in terms of the loan/credit agreement, which includes complying with the relevant operational policies, the World Bank "may enforce the contractual duties of the recipient State through actions in the shape of the suspension or even termination of the financing of projects."[11]

Or, as Boisson de Chazournes explains, "[b]y entering into [the loan/credit] agreement, the borrower state is under the obligation to take necessary measures to comply with its contractual obligations which may include policy issues," whereas the World Bank, "[w]ithin the framework of its responsibilities," "should exercise all due diligence required to make sure that all borrower's obligations are fully complied with."[12] This practice, Boisson de Chazournes adds, "progressively has gained acceptance with respect to environmental and social policy requirements," and ensures that the relevant "policy requirements thus become enforceable under international law like any other provision of a loan or credit agreement."[13]

On the other hand, the inclusion of such conditionalities is also criticized. Sarfaty notes, for instance, that conditionalities "are sometimes considered intrusions on a country's sovereignty,"

> especially when the borrower country is under great financial pressure to accept a loan. In its 1992 Wapenhans Report, the Bank's Operations Evaluation Department acknowledged the one-sidedness of negotiations between the Bank and borrower countries. According to the report, borrowers complained that

---

10 *See* Freestone (2003), note 49, Ch. 5. *Also note*: "Compliance with the Bank's policy on involuntary resettlement would thus be [an example of a] policy conditionality attached to the loan – *see* Sarfaty (2005), fn. 25.

11 Röben *in* Von Bogdandy et al. (Eds.) (2010), p. 830. The author considers these examples "to form part of [the exercise of] public authority [because] the World Bank may impose [sanctions] unilaterally", even though these sanctions are "based on a contract." (*Id.*)

12 Boisson de Chazournes *in* Alfredsson & Ring (Eds.) (2001), p. 77. *Note*, this comment also demonstrates the distinction between 'primary' and 'secondary' obligations' as discussed *in* section 4.3.2.

13 Boisson de Chazournes *in* Shelton (Ed.) (2000), pp. 289-290. Boisson de Chazournes provides examples (also at pp. 289-290) of "various contractual techniques used for integrating such [policy] measures and commitments into loan and credit agreements", *for instance*: "drafting a stipulated prior condition, meaning that the loan or credit agreement only comes into force when the condition has been met, or including a stipulated condition with respect to the disbursement of the loan or credit. Another technique is to include a covenant committing the borrower to execute specific measures by a certain date." For additional examples of such techniques, *also see* Sarfaty (2005), pp. 1797-1787.

"[d]uring negotiations, the Bank overpowers borrowers – and the country negotiating team often doesn't have the strength to resist."[14]

Other criticisms concern the argument "that conditionalities"

> may not directly relate to the success of the project or the repayment of the loan. Instead, they may be extensions of the Bank's development ideology and its vision of the country's long-term economic future.[15]

The operational policies have been formulated, as the Bank explains, to ensure that its development-lending operations "are economically, financially, socially, and environmentally sound."[16] Therefore, "[e]ach operation must follow these policies and procedures to ensure quality, integrity, and adherence to the Bank Group's mission, corporate priorities, and strategic goals."[17] The operational policy framework, as described here, includes the policy on Access to Information, which enjoys a place of prominence within the World Bank Group;[18] Operational Policies (OP); Business Procedures (BP); as well as Guidelines and Operational Memos (Op Memos). The OPs, BPs and Op Memos are currently combined in the Bank's 'Operations Manual'.[19]

The current version of Bank's policy on Access to Information, which has been in effect since 2010 (further updated in 2013), marked "a fundamental shift in the Bank's approach to disclosure of information," that is, whereas the previous versions of the policy were based on "an approach that spells out what information it can disclose," the current version is based on an approach "under which the Bank will disclose any information in its possession that is not on a list of exceptions."[20] Importantly, it "also includes a clear process"

---

14   Sarfaty (2005), pp. 1797-1798. *Also see* Freestone's comment *at* note 176, Ch. 5.
15   Sarfaty (2005), pp. 1797-1798. *Note*, where such criticisms have, in the past, focused more on conditionalities associated with 'Structural Adjustment Lending' (now, 'Development Policy Lending'), criticism have since been extended to those conditionalities associated with safeguard policies.
16   World Bank (2011), e-Book.
17   *Id.*
18   Available at: http://www.worldbank.org/en/access-to-information.
19   Available at: http://www.worldbank.org/opmanual/. For a discussion of the internal process to convert the policies into the OP/BP structure, *see e.g.*, Shihata (2000), pp. 41-46. For criticism of the conversion process, *see e.g.*, Clark (2002), p. 206. *Note*, updated versions of policies are not applied retrospectively – therefore, when the Inspection Panel reviews policy compliance, it considers the policy versions that were applicable to the project at the time. *Also see* Miller-Adams (1999), p. 22, who comments that the operational policies are "[m]ore relevant than the Articles [of Agreement] for determining Bank practice" since that is "what Bank staff refer to when they seek guidance for their work." The operational policy framework therefore "provide[s] an important intermediate level of authority and advice between the formal rules of the Articles of Agreement and the informal norms that shape the Bank's organizational culture." (*Id.*)
20   World Bank (2011), e-Book.

for making information publicly available and gives information seekers a right to appeal if they believe that they were improperly or unreasonably denied access to information or that a public interest case may override an exception that restricts certain information.[21]

The World Bank describes the Operational Policies as "short, focused statements that follow from the Bank's Articles of Agreement, the general conditions, and policies approved by the Board," whereas the Business Procedures "explain," in more detail and with a higher degree of specificity, "how Bank staff carry out the policies set out in the OPs."[22]

Both OPs and BPs contain 'binding' obligations, which means that they are "mandatory upon staff and [...] constitute a basic 'do no harm' code."[23] Op Memos and GPs, on the other hand, are "interim instructions intended to elaborate" on the OPs and BPs.[24] OP Memos and GPs are therefore 'not binding' on Bank management and staff, although they are, as the Bank explains, "hortatory aiming at 'doing good'" and "la[y] out the parameters for a lexicon of good practice."[25] While both the OPs and BPs may reflect external industry and/or professional standards and best practice guidelines, OP Memos and GPs would typically have stronger links with this source of normativity.[26]

---

21 *Id.* For more information about this appeals procedure, *see* http://www.worldbank.org/en/access-to-information/appealsprocess. *Also note*, this process includes the functioning of an "AI Appeals Board", which is described as "an impartial body that considers second-stage appeals under the World Bank Policy on Access to Information", and which "consists of three independent, outside experts nominated by the World Bank's President and endorsed by the World Bank's Board of Executive Directors." *See* http://www.worldbank.org/en/access-to-information/ai-appealsboard.

22 Bradlow & Naudé Fourie (2013), p. 3. *And see*, Shihata (2000), p. 45: "A question may be raised with regard to Bank rules that are not reflected in the specific instruments in the textual definition of *operational policies and procedures* [as defined in the Inspection Panel Resolution, at § 12, *see* note 25, Ch. 5]. Practically, all operational rules are reiterated in these instruments, however. If an operational rule incorporated in the Bank's Articles of Agreement or in the decisions of its Board is not mentioned in this list of documents, its violation would still be subject to the Panel's review, if the other applicable eligibility conditions are met." (Emphasis in original.)

23 Bradlow & Naudé Fourie (2013), p. 3. *Note*, questions about the mandatory nature of some Operational Directives (the previous format of the operational policies) were cited as the main reason for the conversion to OP/BP format – *see e.g.*, Naudé Fourie (2009), pp. 170-172.

24 Bradlow & Naudé Fourie (2013), p. 19.

25 Freestone (2003), p. 143. *Also note*, only OPs and BPs fall within the institutional scope of the Inspection Panel's mandate – *see* Inspection Panel Resolution, § 12: "For purposes of this Resolution, 'operational policies and procedures' consist of the Bank's Operational Policies, Bank Procedures and Operational Directives, and similar documents issued before these series were started, and does not include Guidelines and Best Practices and similar documents or statements." *But see* Shihata's comment *at* note 22, Ch. 5.

26 *See* Freestone (2003), p. 143. The author adds (*at id.*) that "experience has shown that it is difficult to collect good practice" in the GP/Op memo; therefore, for "key policies, such as the safeguard policies, a more systematic treatment of the issues involved has been developed through separate sourcebooks which are available, and continually updated online." *And see* World Bank (2011), e-Book: "Good practices are statements that contain advice and guidance on policy implementation, such as the history of an issue, the sectoral context, and the analytical framework, along with examples of good practice. Although they may be included in the

A number of OPs and BPs form a special category within the operational policy framework, namely, the "environmental and social safeguard policies," which the World Bank describes as "a cornerstone of its support to sustainable poverty reduction," because the "objective of these policies is to prevent and mitigate undue harm to people and their environment in the development process."[27] The safeguard policies, which, at the time of writing were still undergoing a lengthy internal 'review' process' (involving external 'consultations',[28] cover the policy areas of "environmental assessment, natural habitats, pest management, involuntary resettlement, indigenous peoples, forests, cultural resources, dam safety, international waterways, and projects in disputed areas."[29] Another operational policy "govern[s] the use of borrower systems" in the place of the Bank's "environmental and social safeguards."[30] The safeguard policies "require screening of each proposed project," as the Bank explains in order "to determine"

> the potential environmental and social risks and opportunities and how to address those issues. The Bank classifies the proposed project into risk categories depending on the type, location, sensitivity, and scale of the project and the nature and magnitude of its potential environmental and social impact. This categorization influences the required risk management and mitigation measures for the proposed project.[31]

The Bank argues that the significance of its operational policy framework, and the safeguard policies in particular, lies therein that they contribute to the "thorough evaluation" of "environmental and social issues" by "Bank and borrower staff in the identification, preparation, and implementation of Bank-financed programs and projects" and therefore

---

manual, good practices are generally maintained and made available by the Bank units responsible for specific policies."

27   World Bank (2015), e-Book. For a discussion of the "evolution" of the World Bank's "environmental and socially sustainable mandate", *see* Freestone (2013), pp. 9-16, *and see* pp. 63-71 (authored by Alberto Ninio). Freestone concludes (at p. 36): "The concept of sustainable development has been said to rest on a three-cornered stool of social, economic and ecological sustainability. [...] [I]n the 1980s the Bank accepted that environmental issues had important economic impacts, so now the Bank is beginning to appreciate the way that human rights concerns can also have economic consequences."

28   As of August 2015. On the consultation process surrounding the safeguards review, *see* http://consulta-tions.worldbank.org/consultation/review-and-update-world-bank-safeguard-policies. *Also see* the Inspection Panel's comments in this regard: "While a review and update of [the safeguard] policy framework is warranted, in view of changes in Bank operations and among the clients which it serves, the updates to be introduced must carefully reflect the standards of accountability with which the institution wants to be associated." *See* Inspection Panel, (2012), p. 1.

29   World Bank (2011), e-Book.

30   *Id. See* OP/BP 4.0; *and see e.g., South Africa: Eskom Investment Support* (2010).

31   World Bank (2011), e-Book. On issues related to environmental risk categorization, *see* section 14.1.

enhance the "effectiveness and development impact of projects and programs supported by the Bank."[32] In addition, the Bank notes, the "[s]afeguard policies"

> have often provided a platform for the participation of stakeholders in project design and have been an important instrument for building ownership among local populations.[33]

And, as the Inspection Panel commented in *China: Western Poverty Reduction (Qinghai)*, "[t]hroughout the 1990s, the World Bank has played a leading international role"

> in promoting sound procedures for project assessment. With ODs 4.01 on Environmental Assessment in place, and later 4.30 on Involuntary Resettlement and 4.20 on Indigenous Peoples, the Bank is widely regarded as being in the forefront of international attempts to use environmental and social policies to ensure the sustainability of development projects. It has gained an enviable reputation for sound environmental assessment procedures among environmental professionals. Its performance in overseeing environmental assessments for Bank funded projects, to ensure that they meet the standards it has set and promoted, is watched closely by both environmental scientists and organizations interested in sustainability.[34]

It is also important to note that "the Bank requires that its policies be complied with even in operations where it is not the only, or indeed the major, financier"; this means that "all the components of a project must comply" – "not only those actually financed by the Bank."[35] This principle also "applies" whether additional "financing is from the public or private sector or even from the borrowing country's own money."[36] In other words, the "'leveraging' effect" of the operational policies is, as Freestone observes, "substantial."[37]

In addition, the World Bank's operational policy framework has become a crucial "assessment criterion for the Bank's projects by a civil society avid for international actors' accountability."[38] Moreover, the fact that the Bank's operational framework has become

---

32 *Id.*
33 *Id.*
34 *China: Western Poverty Reduction (Qinghai)* (1999), IR, § 33.
35 Freestone (2013), p. 14. On the co-financing of development projects, *see* section 3.1.3.
36 *Id.*
37 *Id.*
38 Boisson de Chazournes *in* Treves et al. (Eds.) (2005), p. 191. *Also take note of* the Legal Harmonization Initiative (LHI), which is "is a joint undertaking of several international financial institutions (IFI), including the World Bank, bilateral aid agencies and United Nations agencies in support of the implementation of commitments expressed in the Paris Declaration to improve aid effectiveness through harmonization and alignment. The LHI is aimed at harmonizing and streamlining legal tools among donors and partner countries,

a "parameter[r] for good conduct" becomes "all the more important," as Boisson de Cha-zournes observes, "if one keeps in mind"

> that the World Bank acts increasingly as a facilitating body in projects uniting public and private financial actors: its operational policies can then influence the behaviour of other creditors who may be implicated in the process.[39]

On the other hand, as noted earlier, there is also the awareness (and mounting concern for some) that the Bank's growing number of competitors does not insist on compliance with similar operational policies or, at least, not to the same extent. For example, in 2007, "Philippe Maystadt, [at the time] head of the European Investment Bank," "caused a stir" by suggesting that "the EIB and the World Bank lower their standards to avoid being undercut by Chinese banks" – pointing to the fact that comparable social and environmental safeguards

> at present do not apply to the China Development Bank (CDB), whose assets are bigger than the World Bank and Asian Development Bank combined, nor to the China Export-Import (ExIm) Bank, the official government export credit agency. Both have few qualms about backing controversial projects.[40]

Finally, concerning the adoption and amendment of the operational policies, Freestone observes that the policies were initially developed, adopted and amended only by involving the Bank's management structure – thus, without involving the Board – because the policies were initially considered to be "internal documents of no interest to anyone other than" World Bank management and staff.[41] Towards the end of the 1980s, Freestone notes, a few exceptions were made with respect to policies with high degrees of "sensitivity or complex-ity," which "were *discussed with* the Board prior to being issued."[42] Consequently, it can be said that the World Bank's operational policy framework "emerged in the interstices in the Bank's institutional structure", as Alvarez argues, and was therefore not "the product of any explicit provision in the Bank's charter governing what its loan policies ought to be."[43]

---

including the removal of key legal impediments to harmonized approaches, towards aid effective operations at the country level." *See* http://go.worldbank.org/YUJ6W5UE50.

39   Boisson de Chazournes *in* Treves et al. (Eds.) (2005), p. 191.

40   A. Beattie & A. Yeh, 'China Treads on Western Toes in Africa', *Financial Times*, 12 January 2007, available at: www.ft.com.

41   Freestone (2003), p. 142.

42   *Id.* (emphasis added). *Also see* Shihata (2000), p. 42.

43   Alvarez (2005), p. 235. *Also see* Toope's comment *at* note 44, Ch. 2.

Over time, however, the Board's role with respect to the adoption and amendment of operational policies expanded, whereas the policies were increasingly made "publicly available."[44] Subsequently, the Bank's operational policy framework, "particularly those dealing with the controversial social and environmental aspects" of the Bank's development-lending operations, has "become the subject of great public interest and public debate" – a situation which was compounded by the fact the safeguard policies "have also tended to be the ones most often invoked in the requests for inspection to [...] independent accountability mechanisms" such as the Inspection Panel.[45] Therefore, as Bradlow argues, international financial institutions, with the World Bank Group at the forefront, came to appreciate "that their policies"

> have significance and relevance outside the institutions and that their external stakeholders have the capacity to influence the content of these policies.[46]

As a result, IFIs "have begun to develop informal, transparent, and participatory procedures for making these policies," whereas "[t]he World Bank Group, in particular"

> has used such informal procedures with sufficient frequency that it is developing an implicit rule-making procedure that involves disclosure of policy drafts, opportunities for public comment on these drafts, and explanations of how the public comments have been addressed by the institution in formulating the final versions of the policy.[47]

That being said, these informal "rule-making processes" still needs to be "fully institutionalized," as Hunter points out.[48]

---

44 Bradlow *in* Cissé et al. (Eds.) (2012), e-Book.
45 *Id. Note*, however, in more recent years, claims concerning the policy on Project Supervision have exceeded claims related to the safeguard policies. For an overview of the policies most often raised in Inspection Panel Requests, *see* Naudé Fourie (2014), p. 579.
46 Bradlow *in* Cissé et al. (Eds.) (2012), e-Book.
47 Bradlow *in* Cissé et al. (Eds.) (2012), e-Book. In this regard, *also see* Ebbesson *in* Bodansky et al. (Eds.) (2007), who argues (at p. 682) that "[t]he development of international norms concerning public participation in environmental decision-making reflects the general moves in international governance, as well as in numerous states, towards expanding the involvement of non-state actors in decision-making procedures. Governments have lost the exclusive mandate, if they ever had it, to represent the public and to speak and act on behalf of public interests."
48 Hunter *in* Bradlow & Hunter (Eds.) (2010), pp. 223-232; *and* Bradlow & Naudé Fourie (2013), pp. 25-27; *and see* Rubenstein (2007), pp. 618-619, who argues that for accountability mechanisms to be effective, both "the power wielder and accountability holders" have to "recognize" or "endorse" the normative standards employed in measuring accountability, as well as accept their legitimacy – at least to the extent that there can be "deliberation and mutual persuasion about how they should be interpreted and applied in a particular case."

5.1.1   The 'legal nature' of the operational policy framework

The question about the 'legal nature' of the World Bank's operational policy framework continues to elicit contrasting responses. Freestone, for example, argues that the "Bank's policies do not purport to set objective international standards, nor are they instructions to borrowing counties."[49] Simply put, "[t]he responsibility for designing and implementing a project"

> rests on the shoulders of the borrower. However, for a project to qualify for World Bank financing it must be in compliance with Bank policy and procedural requirements. If a borrower or grant recipient country *refuses to allow a Bank requirement to be met* – for example, the public release in a country of an environmental assessment report for an IDA investment project – *then* Bank staff *are required* to discontinue the operation.[50]

Former World Bank General Legal Counsel Ibrahim Shihata repeatedly emphasized the non-legal nature of the operational policies. Shihata argued, for instance, that "a violation by the Bank of its policy, even if established by the [Inspection] Panel"

> is not necessarily a violation of applicable law that entails liability for ensuing damages; and (ii) since the Panel is not a court of law, its findings on Bank violations cannot be taken ipso facto as a conclusive evidence against the Bank in judicial proceedings.[51]

Around the same time, Schlemmer-Schulte asserted that the "implementation of the Bank's policy standards in projects"

> does not result in substantive rights that individuals in borrowing countries may claim against the Bank, nor does the Inspection Panel represent a legal

---

49 Freestone (2003), p. 144. *Also see* Bradlow & Naudé Fourie (2013), pp. 25-27; *and* Hunter *in* Bradlow & Hunter (Eds.) (2010), pp. 223-232.

50 Freestone (2013), p. 14. *Note*: the example mentioned by Freestone refers to a requirement "in OP 4.01 [Environmental Assessment], para. 19 for projects classified as A." *Also note*, the example demonstrates the relationship between the credit/loan agreement and the operational policy framework.

51 Shihata (2000), p. 234. For criticism of this argument, *see e.g.*, Suzuki *in* Bradlow & Hunter (Eds.) (2010), p. 82, calling Shihata's argument "unsettling, in that the ILC Commentary provides that 'an obligation arising from the rules of the organization has to be regarded as an obligation under international law'. The question is whether the rules of the organization may preclude or limit the applicability of the responsibility regime." For a discussion of the classification of IAMs in general and of the Inspection Panel specifically, *see* sections 6.1 & 6.2.4.

remedy mechanism through which positions described in the Bank's policies or rights referred to in the Resolution could be enforced against the Bank.[52]

"The Bank's policies are internal instructions, which Bank managers issue to staff members for their guidance," and while they are "binding on staff, and the standards embodied in the policies create a duty for staff to exert their best efforts to achieve them," "their actual achievement," Schlemmer-Schulte added, "depends primarily"

> on the action of other parties, most notably the borrower. The policies become binding on the Bank's borrowing member countries when they are incorporated in loan documentation that binds borrowers. They do not give enforceable rights against the Bank to the people potentially affected by Bank-financed projects, as the Bank does not enter into a contractual relationship with these people. People are included in a project's design and implementation through the actions of the borrower, who assumes the obligation of implementing Bank standards contained in the loan agreement.[53]

Likewise, Boisson de Chazournes departs from the argument that the operational policies are "internal documents," which "present certain characteristics of an administrative character within the organization in which they are to be implemented;" and are, therefore, "not by themselves binding under international law" since they "only become binding when they are reflected in loan agreements."[54] However, Boisson de Chazournes adds, the Bank's operational policy framework "ha[s] external effects," since it "shape[s] both the Bank's and its partners' behaviour within the context of their mutual relationship during design, appraisal and implementation phases of a project."[55] "In so doing," Boisson de Chazournes concludes, "some of them"

---

52 Schlemmer-Schulte (1999), p. 1. The author was, respectively, Senior Counsel/Associate General Counsel/Special Advisor to the Senior Vice President and General Counsel of the World Bank, between 1995 and 2002. *Also note*, the example demonstrates the distinction between primary and secondary obligations – *see* section 4.3.2.

53 Schlemmer-Schulte (1999), p. 1.

54 Boisson de Chazournes *in* Alfredsson & Ring (Eds.) (2001), p. 77.

55 Boisson de Chazournes *in* Treves et al. (Eds.) (2005), p. 191. *Also see* Boisson de Chazournes *in* Shelton (Ed.) (2000), p. 289: "[...] Operational Standards create normative and procedural expectations for the staff and partners of the Bank and contribute in many ways to forging and developing accepted practices under international law. [...] The Operational Standards also may play a crucial role in fostering the emergence of new international practices that seek to promote sustainable development and in facilitating respect for international legal instruments negotiated and adopted in other arenas. Finally, they play an important role in assessing the quality of the World Bank's activities."

contribute to the creation of norms of general international law or codify existing norms of general international law. They may also acquire the status of conventional law when their stipulations are re-used in loan and credit agreements bonding both the borrower and the Bank.[56]

Similarly, Alvarez argues that while the operational policies may not originally have been "promulgated with general normative intent,"[57] they have, over time, become a "form of particularly potent institutional law."[58] The Inspection Panel's establishment, in particular, has "judicialized" the Bank's policies and "by empowering private guardians to ensure compliance with their terms," Alvarez concludes, the Inspection Panel mechanism has "transformed the Bank's Guidelines effectively into law, at least in terms of general perception."[59] Whereas Bradlow and Hunter contend that the operational policies of international financial institutions, constitute, at the very least, "a soft 'lex specialis' to govern [IFIs'] own operations in regard to their Member States."[60] Since the IFIs "implement this soft law," Bradlow and Hunter conclude, "it has the potential"

> to raise expectations among the stakeholders in these operations who begin to expect the [IFIs] to comply with this soft law in their operation[s] and to anticipate that they can hold the [IFIs] to account if they fail to comply with them. In addition, the standards set by one [IFI] have the potential to influence the standards of other [IFIs]. In these ways, these soft law standards have the potential to 'harden' at least within the limited sphere of [IFIs].[61]

To be sure, however, this process also "create[s] expectations in the intended beneficiaries of these policies," which, "in turn has implications for both lawmaking and accountability in the IFIs.[62] Concerning the process of "lawmaking,"

> the fact that the intended beneficiaries begin to develop an expectation of certain standards of treatment from the IFIs has the potential to create expectations about the policy-making process in the IFIs. In particular, it leads these beneficiaries and other stakeholders to expect that the drafting of the policies and procedures will not be a closed process and that they will have opportunities to participate in their formulation. This in turn means that the [IFIs] will have

---

56 Boisson de Chazournes *in* Treves et al. (Eds.) (2005), pp. 191-192.
57 Alvarez (2005), p. 236. For similar arguments, *also see* Wirth *in* Shelton (Ed.) (2000), pp. 333-337.
58 Alvarez (2005), p. 235.
59 *Id.* For similar arguments, *also see* Bradlow & Naudé Fourie (2013).
60 Bradlow *in* Bradlow & Hunter (Eds.) (2010), p. 26.
61 *Id.*
62 *Id.*

to establish certain procedures for drafting and adopting these policies and procedures. In other words, a form of international administrative law relating to rulemaking is beginning to emerge in regard to these policies and procedures.[63]

Several international legal scholars have pointed to the linkages between some operational policy provisions and international law, as well as with national law. The consultation standards in the Bank's Indigenous Peoples policy, for instance, which are based on the recognition that any "strategy for addressing the issues pertaining to indigenous peoples must be based on the *informed participation* of the indigenous people themselves" are, as Kingsbury observes, "consistent with an emerging understanding in many national law systems that consultation with indigenous peoples is required or ordinarily expected in such circumstances," whereas "ILO Convention 169 of 1989 makes such consultation obligatory by Article 6,"

> which links consultation with rights to participation, and further requires that states parties undertake consultations in good faith with the objective of achieving agreement or consent. This provision was applied by the Colombian Constitutional Court in finding that members of U'Wa groups had been insufficiently consulted prior to issue by the government to a large oil company of an oil exploration licence covering their traditional areas.[64]

Indeed, Kingsbury concludes, "[p]ractice and expectations are now such"

> that there would be grave doubts about the legitimacy of a major Bank policy in this area, had the Bank chosen not to engage in consultation with indigenous peoples where consultation was possible and practicable.[65]

With regard to international environmental law, Di Leva points to the distinct "relationship" between "key IFI safeguard policies" and "the 1992 Rio Declaration on Environment and Development" – which, although "not a binding legal instrument," "it is widely regarded"

---

63 *Id. Also see* Hunter's comments *at* note 48, Ch. 5.

64 Kingsbury (1999), p. 325 (emphasis in original). On ILO Convention 169 of 1989, that is, the Convention concerning Indigenous and Tribal Peoples in Independent Countries, *see* http://www.ilo.org/dyn/normlex/en/f?p=NORMLEXPUB:12100:0::NO::P12100_INSTRUMENT_ID:312314.

65 Kingsbury (1999), p. 325; *also see* pp. 323, 326 & 327. On the meaning of 'prior informed consultation', *see* section 13.3.

as reflecting a political consensus surrounding the foundational principles of sustainable development, some of which reflect emerging principles of customary international environmental law.[66]

Social and environmental safeguard policies such as those of the World Bank, Di Leva concludes, "support the principles and objectives of international environmental law as set forth in the [UNCED] Rio Declaration."[67]

Sarfaty, furthermore, observes that the Bank's policy on Access to Information "follows international standards on access to information, public awareness, and participation in decisionmaking", while the policy on Physical Cultural Resources "makes explicit reference to country obligations under international treaties, such as the 1972 Convention Concerning the Protection of the World Cultural and Natural Heritage".[68]

However, "[e]ven when not explicitly referred to" in specific policy provisions, Sarfaty contends, "international instruments are often considered for interpretive purposes in implementing best practices."[69] It can therefore be argued that the Bank's operational policy framework might eventually "acquire the status of customary norms by serving as models for national legislation and for the policies of other multilateral development banks."[70] Or as Boisson de Chazournes puts it, the operational policies "contribute to the development of new international practices" in the sense that "[t]hey create normative expectations"

and pave the way for the consolidation of patterns of behaviour. In addition, they lead to the emergence of principle and rules and may contribute to their recognition as *lex lata* under international law.[71]

The linkages between the operational policy framework and international law also surface in Inspection Panel practice, as in the *Chad: Petroleum* case, for instance. In Bank management's response to the Request (which included, among other things, claims about human rights violations), it underlined that the World Bank was "concerned by human rights in

---

66 Di Leva *in* Bradlow & Hunter (Eds.) (2010), p. 351; *also see* note 11, Ch. 4. On the 'Rio Declaration on Environment and Development' ('Rio Declaration'), adopted in 1992 during the United Nations Conference on Environment and Development, *see* http://www.unep.org/Documents.multilingual/Default.asp?DocumentID=78&ArticleID=1163. On the operationalization of the Rio Declaration Principles of 'access to information' and 'participation in decision-making', *see* Ch. 11; the operationalization of the principle of 'access to justice' is reflected in the discussions contained *in* sections 7.1.1 (recourse for PAP), 7.1.3 (redress for PAP) & 12.6 (project-level grievance mechanisms).
67 Di Leva *in* Bradlow & Hunter (Eds.) (2010), p. 351.
68 Sarfaty (2005), p. 1800.
69 *Id.*
70 Sarfaty (2005), pp. 1800- 1801.
71 Boisson de Chazournes *in* Shelton (Ed.) (2000), pp. 300-301.

Chad as elsewhere," but that the Bank's "mandate does not extend to political human rights."[72] Human rights considerations were also not formally part of its own mandate, the Inspection Panel countered, especially not insofar as it pertained to borrower obligations; nevertheless, in this instance, the Panel emphasized that it had "felt obliged"

> to examine whether the issues of proper governance or human rights violations in Chad were such as *to impede the implementation of the Project in a manner compatible with the Bank's policies.*[73]

This approach, "which finds *human rights implicitly embedded in various policies* of the Bank," the Panel affirmed, "is within the boundaries of the Panel's jurisdiction."[74] Similarly, in *Honduras: Land Administration*, the Inspection Panel underlined that the Bank's operational policy framework

> [has] been designed and are frequently reviewed so that the Bank, in executing its projects respects the international rules and standards designed to safeguard the rights of indigenous peoples.[75]

In this instance, the Panel concluded that "OD 4.20 [Indigenous Peoples] broadly reflects the spirit and provisions of ILO Convention No. 169" on Indigenous and Tribal Peoples.[76]

In terms of the 'interactional account of international law' introduced earlier – by which "law can exist by degrees" and normative frameworks or normative systems are conceptualized in terms of their relative positioning on a "continuum of legality"[77] – it can be argued that the World Bank's operational policy framework has originally been positioned towards the non-legal ('social') end of the spectrum but has been moving towards the 'legal' end of the spectrum, when assessed against Fuller's "criteria of legality" (including "generality, promulgation, non-retroactivity, clarity, non-contradiction, not asking the impossible, constancy, and congruence between rules and official action").[78] This movement has been the result of enhanced Board and public participation in the rule-making and amendment processes surrounding the operational policies; the continuous application of the policies across the Bank's development-lending operations over the past

---

72 *Chad: Petroleum* (2001), MR, § 16. *Also see* Request, § 4.
73 *Chad: Petroleum* (2001), IR (ES), §§ 34-35 (emphasis added).
74 *Chad: Petroleum* (2001), Inspection Panel Chair's Address to the Board, § 8 (emphasis added).
75 *Honduras Land Administration* (2006) Request, p. 2; *and* IR, § 256.
76 *Id.*
77 *See* section 2.3.
78 *See* note 131, Ch. 2.

few decades; and, in particular, as a result of various functions performed by the Bank's accountability mechanisms.[79]

On other hand, questions about 'congruence' between the operational policies and 'official World Bank actions' (as typically arise in the context of the realization and enforcement of accountability outcomes)[80] and the degree of discretion provided for in many policy provisions, or the need for 'flexible application' of the policies across the Bank's development-lending operations,[81] are arguably standing in the way of the operational policy framework from crossing the 'theoretical threshold' between 'non-law' and 'law'.[82]

5.2   National law (the Borrower's constitutional system)

As noted, the credit/loan agreement, as an international agreement between an international organization and a state (as well as those aspects of the operational policy framework incorporated in the agreement)[83] supersedes a Borrower's domestic constitutional system (referring to legislative, executive and legal functions). In several respects, however, it would present a more comprehensive picture to state that national law functions 'in concert with' the credit/loan agreement and the Bank's operational policy framework – or, at least, that national law remains a relevant source of (legal) normativity within the context of World Bank-financed development projects.

For instance, some of the operational policies (notably, on Environment Assessment, Indigenous Peoples and Involuntary Resettlement) specifically require *compliance* with relevant aspects of national law.[84] The policy on Environmental Assessment stipulates, for example, that the environmental assessment process should

> tak[e] into account the variations in project and country conditions; the findings of country environmental studies; national environmental action plans; the country's overall policy framework, national legislation, and institutional capabilities related to the environment and social aspects [...].[85]

Hence, national law also features in Inspection Panel practice.

---

79   On the functions of internal accountability mechanisms, *see* section 6.2.
80   *See e.g.,* section 7.1.
81   *See* section 6.3.
82   *See* section 2.3.
83   As explained *in* section 5.1.
84   *See* Boisson de Chazournes *in* Alfredsson & Ring (Eds.) (2001), p. 78.
85   OP 4.01 (Environmental Assessment), Article, 3. For arguments regarding the need for differentiation when applying the operational policy framework across the Bank's development-lending portfolio, *see e.g.,* section 6.3.1.

In *Colombia: Cartagena Water & Environmental Management*, for example, where the location of a planned marine outfall formed a core concern for the Requesters, World Bank management asserted that "marine outfalls" were "permissible provided that appropriate studies are conducted" in terms of Colombian "laws and regulations," as had been done in this instance.[86] Furthermore, Management argued, "the Requesters have previously raised these legal arguments [as reflected in the Request] with the Colombia administrative adjudication process, which has already adjudicated each of them."[87]

And in *Albania: Power Sector*, the Requesters claimed "that the selection of the Vlora site [for a new Thermal Power Plant] contradicts" Albania's 2003 "Act on Cultural Heritage," which stipulates "that any investor or constructor"

> that builds a project in an area with archaeological remains should use expert archaeologists to verify that the construction will not cause harm to local cultural heritage.[88]

In terms of the Act, "investors in any industrial construction project" should also "'consult with the experts of the Albanian Institute of Archaeology and the Institute of Cultural Monuments' during the preparation and implementation of their projects."[89] The Panel noted that it "was not able to find in the project files any indication that either the borrower or the Bank itself has consulted with these Institutes."[90]

Some operational policies also require the Bank to conduct an analysis of certain aspects of national law in order to ascertain whether borrowers' domestic legal systems have to be supplemented or supported by means of specific project activities.

For example, as the Inspection Panel explained in *Panama: Land Administration*, "[a]s part of its preparation, appraisal, and later on, supervision activities, the Bank analyzes local laws to ensure"

> that the local legal framework is appropriate for the project or program to be financed and to enable attainment of its objectives. The same internal analysis is made with regard to legislation and regulations issued in relation to certain conditions of tranche release, effectiveness, or disbursement to ensure that such legislation is consistent with the objectives of the project or program in question.[91]

---

86   *Colombia: Cartagena Water & Environmental Management* (2004), IR, § 24.
87   *Id.*
88   *Albania: Power Sector* (2007), IR §§ 222-223 (emphasis in original).
89   *Id.*
90   *Albania: Power Sector* (2007), IR §§ 222-223 (emphasis in original).
91   *Panama: Land Administration* (2009) IR, § 173.

"The attainment of the objectives of the Bank's operational policies related to indigenous peoples" in particular,

> requires a full and thorough understanding of the local legal framework when the implementation of a given project may affect those peoples' legitimate rights and aspirations.[92]

Or, in *Ghana: Second Urban Environment Sanitation*, the Inspection Panel found that "the RPF gave insufficient attention to the needs of vulnerable groups including women and other displaced persons who are not protected through national land compensation legislation."[93] Notably, the "section on national legal, regulatory and administrative framework"

> does not refer to issues and risks relating to the borrower's capacity and commitment to implement the resettlement instrument, notwithstanding well-known concerns affecting past land acquisition efforts.[94]

Whereas in *Cambodia: Land Management and Administration*, the Inspection Panel commented "that the degree of security provided by traditional, customary or other non-formal land tenure systems, especially in urban areas,"

> has declined substantially since the early 1990s. This situation was well known before the Project was designed, and the Panel notes that the PAD clearly recognizes this problem and the challenges involved. However, as further elaborated below, the Panel found critical weaknesses in both Project design and implementation with respect to measures to protect poor and vulnerable groups relying on customary or other non-formalized tenure rights.[95]

Furthermore, in projects to which the Bank's policy on the Use of Borrower Systems might be applicable,[96] the Bank has to conduct a 'safeguards diagnostic review' (SDR) in order to determine whether the "borrower's environmental and social safeguard system," as reflected in the Borrower's "laws, policies, and institutions,"[97] is "equivalent to the Bank's," that is: "if the borrower's system is designed to achieve the objectives and adhere to the

---

92   *Id.*
93   *Ghana: Second Urban Environment Sanitation* (2007), IR, § 260.
94   *Id.*
95   *Cambodia: Land Management and Administration* (2009), IR, § 256.
96   OP/BP 4.00 Piloting the Use of Borrower Systems to Address Environmental and Social Safeguard Issues in Bank-Supported Projects.
97   *South Africa: Eskom Investment Support* (2010), ER, § 15(xiii).

applicable operational principles" specifically set out in the policy.[98] In *South Africa: Eskom Investment Support*, for example, the Inspection Panel found that the project's safeguards diagnostic review did "not adequately assess"

> the lack of provision in South African law to use an independent advisory panel during preparation and implementation of projects that are 'highly risky or contentious or that involve serious and multi-dimensional environmental and/or social concerns', which is an operational principle set forth in Table A1 of OP 4.00 (para A.8).[99]

Moreover, as noted earlier, although the World Bank enjoys qualified immunity before domestic courts, the Borrower's national judicial system constitutes a relevant consideration in the context of Bank-financed development projects since it forms a part of the broader project-level 'grievance mechanism', as illustrated by scenarios involving involuntary resettlement.[100]

In addition, the realization of specific project aims might require borrowers to amend or enact new domestic legislation or implement other forms of institutional and regulatory reform, as is often the case in development policy lending projects.[101] Inspection Panel practice also provides several examples where the enactment of national legislation, not directly required by or related to the Bank-financed development project, has affected project implementation or holds the potential to do so.[102]

Finally, the broader constitutional context might also play a role in the application of the particular operational policies, for instance, in the definition of 'indigenous people', which is a critical aspect of the Policy on Indigenous People because it determines the policy's applicability to the specific project.[103] In *Cambodia: Forest Concession Management*,

---

98 OP/BP 4.00, § 2.
99 *South Africa: Eskom Investment Support* (2010), IR, § 193.
100 On issues related to project-level grievance mechanisms, *see* section 12.6.
101 *See e.g., Bangladesh: Jute Sector* (1996), MR § 7: "The objective of the JSAC [project] is to support the Government of Bangladesh in carrying out its program of reforms in the jute sector, the ultimate goal of which reform program is to create a viable, privately-owned jute industry operating on a normal commercial basis in a reformed policy environment [...]." *See Pakistan: Tax Administration Reform* (2010), MR § 18: "The project development objective is "to fundamentally reform the Federal Board of Revenue for a more efficient and effective revenue administration system." The "overriding objective is to raise revenues through improved compliance with tax laws and broadening the tax base, improving the effectiveness, responsiveness and efficiency of tax administration through institutional and procedural reforms, improving collection through transparent and high quality tax services, and strengthening audit and enforcement procedures." *And see Honduras: Land Administration* (2006), MR § 13, where one project component "supports increased transparency and improved governance of the country's main land administration institutions. The component's main outputs include the establishment of the National Property Administration System (SINAP), through strengthened legal, regulatory, and institutional frameworks."
102 *See e.g.*, section 8.2.1.
103 *See* section 13.1. For additional examples where definitions impact project scope, *see e.g.*, section 10.4.

for example, the Panel acknowledged that the Borrower's "present Constitution" did not recognise "indigenous peoples as a special category"; however, the Panel argued, there was "ample recognition in past and present Cambodian Government practice and legislation"

> for the status of some ethnic populations as having a "social and cultural identity distinct from the dominant society that makes them vulnerable to being disadvantaged in the development process" which is the definition used in the Bank policy on indigenous peoples, OD 4.20. The highland minority populations of northern and northeastern Cambodia especially (including Kouy, Kreung, and others), whose indigenous status has been emphasized in the Request for Inspection, have long been recognized as indigenous peoples.[104]

5.3   INTERNATIONAL LAW: BORROWER AND WORLD BANK OBLIGATIONS

When international law is considered as a source of normativity in the context of World Bank-financed development projects, it is important to distinguish between the international legal obligations of borrower states and those of the Bank. As subjects of the international legal system, both the Bank and its borrowers have international legal rights and obligations.

5.3.1   *International legal obligations of borrower states*

The relationship between World Bank development-lending operations and international law – insofar as the international legal obligations of *borrowers* are concerned – is articulated in several operational policies which, "as a general requirement," stipulate that the Bank will not finance projects that would, in any way, lead to a contravention of borrowers' international legal obligations.[105] For example, OP 4.01 (Environmental Assessment) stipulates that the EA process "takes into account"

> [...] obligations of the country, pertaining to project activities under relevant international environmental treaties and agreements. The Bank does not finance project activities that would contravene such country obligations, as identified during the EA.[106]

---

104 *Cambodia: Forest Concession Management* (2005), IR, § 78.
105 *See e.g.*, Boisson de Chazournes *in* Alfredsson & Ring (Eds.) (2001), p. 78. The author notes (*at id.*): "through a [World Bank operational] policy adopted in 1984," "the Bank ha[d] committed itself not to finance projects" "that contravene any international environmental agreements to which a member country concerned is a party."
106 OP 4.01 (Environmental Assessment), Article 3. *Also see e.g.*, OP 4.36 (Forests), § 6: "The Bank does not finance projects that contravene applicable international environmental agreements." *Also see* Boisson de

Inspection Panel practice also provides examples of instances where the matter of a borrower's international legal obligations becomes a relevant matter due to the Bank's obligation not to finance projects that would result in a violation of international law. In *Honduras: Land Administration*, for example, the Inspection Panel considered whether the provisions of OD 4.20 (Indigenous Peoples) constituted an obligation for the Bank to ensure that the project did not cause the Borrower to violate ILO Convention No. 169, as per OMS 2.20 (Project Appraisal), which stipulates that the Bank is under an obligation "not to finance projects" that are "not consistent with the Borrower's international obligations."[107]

The Bank's General Legal Counsel, on being consulted by the Panel on this matter (as required by the Inspection Panel Resolution),[108] advised that OMS 2.20 referred "only to agreements that are 'essentially of an environmental nature'."[109] However, the Inspection Panel disagreed with this interpretation, arguing that it "seems to limit, and even amend, existing Bank policies."[110] The "text of OMS 2.20," the Panel concluded,

> does not refer only to environmental agreements. Rather it requires more broadly that a 'project's possible effects on the country's environment and on the health and well-being of its people must be considered at an early stage.[111]

Whereas in *Papua New Guinea: Smallholder Agriculture*, the "Requesters also raised OMS 2.20 on Project Appraisal, [but] in the context of the International Covenant on Economic, Social, and Cultural Rights (ICESCR), to which Papua New Guinea is a signatory."[112] The Inspection Panel concluded that "OP/BP 4.10 [Indigenous People] covers, and is consistent with, the Treaty's main objectives related to social and cultural rights (insofar as those

---

Chazournes *in* Alfredsson & Ring (Eds.) (2001), p. 78, who notes that there are "[v]arious means" through which borrowers can "integrate their international commitments in their legal order", which would subsequently "become part of the domestic legal order of the borrower and should be taken into consideration when implementing the relevant policies and procedures." On the relationships between borrowers' domestic legal systems and World Bank-financed development projects, *see* section 5.2.

107 *Honduras: Land Administration* (2006), IR, §§ 254-258. *Also see* notes 75-76, Ch. 5.

108 *See* Inspection Panel Resolution, § 15: "The Panel shall seek the advice of the Bank's Legal Department on matters related to the Bank's rights and obligations with respect to the request under consideration."

109 *Honduras: Land Administration* (2006), IR, §§ 254-258. The Bank's Legal Counsel added (*at id.*): "considering that the 1999 Operational Policy 4.01 on Environmental Assessment states in paragraph 3 that 'The Bank does not finance project activities that would contravene [...] country obligations, as identified during the EIA' under environmental treaties and agreements, paragraph 24 of OMS 2.20 has been superseded by OP 4.01 of 1999." (*Id.*)

110 *Honduras: Land Administration* (2006), IR, §§ 254-258.

111 *Id.* For more examples from Inspection Panel practice pointing to similar issues, *see e.g.*, Ch. 10.

112 *Papua New Guinea: Smallholder Agriculture* (2009), IR, § 155.

objectives pertain to indigenous peoples)," and the "Panel's analysis of compliance" would therefore be "focused solely within parameters of OP/BP 4.10."[113]

References to 'the borrower's international legal obligations' are generally understood to be referring to 'legally binding' international law ('hard law') – thus, excluding obligations flowing from non-legally binding instruments that might, nevertheless, be 'legally relevant' ('soft law').[114] In *South Africa: Eskom Investment Support*, for example, the Inspection Panel acknowledged that "the commitments indicated in relation to the Copenhagen Accord [on climate change]"[115] were "assumed voluntarily and not as a matter of international legal obligation"

> and that the [Government of South Africa] (a non-Annex I party to UN Framework Convention on Climate Change) does not have a target and timetable obligation under the Kyoto Protocol to reduce GHG emissions. The Panel notes that South Africa does not have a specific obligation to reduce GHG emissions under an international environmental agreement within the meaning of the relevant operational principle of OP 4.00. In this context, an issue of policy compliance by Management on this point does not arise.[116]

However, the Panel added, this situation did "not mean that Bank financing"

> should make it difficult for the country to meet the commitments it has made, even if not legally binding. The Panel observes, in this regard, that a key element of the Project objective is to support both economic growth objectives and the long-term carbon mitigation strategy of the Guarantor.[117]

As Alvarez argues, the Bank's operational policies incorporate "by reference" international legal instruments adopted by various UN organs.[118] And, to the extent that these instruments "are incorporated" in credit/loan agreements, the World Bank as well as its borrowers have to "comply with such instruments."[119] Hence, Alvarez concludes, the World Bank "strengthens compliance with both soft and hard [international] law produced by it and

---

113 *Id.*
114 *See e.g.*, Shelton *in* Shelton (Ed.) (2000), p. 6, reflecting the general view that "[…] international law is created through treaty and custom, and thus 'soft law' is not legally binding *per se*." On the jurisprudential debate about the nature of international law, in particular with regard to the law-making process, *see* section 2.3.
115 Adopted under the auspice of the UN Framework Convention on Climate Change, *see* http://unfccc.int/meetings/copenhagen_dec_2009/items/5262.php.
116 *South Africa: Eskom Investment Support* (2010), IR, §§ 427-428.
117 *Id.* On the definition of 'Guarantor, *see* the Appendix.
118 Alvarez (2005), p. 237.
119 *Id.*

other [international organizations]."[120] Indeed, the Bank's operational policy framework, "no less than some treaties," becomes "a mechanism to 'harden' a dense network of otherwise 'soft law' norms or treaties whose terms are vague or that have drawn few parties."[121]

Or, as Swepston observes, "there are aspects of the policies and procedures of the World Bank, and of those of the regional Banks, that bear a close resemblance to the more 'conventional' standards" contained in ILO instruments.[122] However, the "Bank's policies are considerably more constraining" than ILO instruments, "because they can be imposed on borrowing countries by contract and enforced by financial penalties".[123] Moreover, although the Bank's policies "are of narrower application than ILO standards which apply to the entire country and not only to a given project", Swepston adds, "Bank policies influence government behaviour" as a result of the "'1,500-lb. Gorilla' syndrome" – in other words, "while the ILO and the UN must rely on persuasion, publicity and leverage for their policies to prevail,"

> the World Bank does not have to bargain for its views to be taken into account, for reasons we all know. Yes, we are all aware that the World Bank's share of international investment in development has diminished, but it remains an immensely powerful voice, often able to fix conditionalities of which the rest of the international system remains innocent.[124]

The Inspection Panel's investigation of *Albania: Power Sector* provides an illuminating example of the close relationships between Bank and Borrower international legal obligations. In the *Albania: Power Sector* case, as Baimu and Panou argue, the Inspection Panel dealt with "issues of concurrent responsibility between the Bank and the borrowing state"[125] – that is, it concerned the Bank's obligations in terms of its policy on Environmental Assessment and the Borrower's obligation in terms of the Aarhus Convention.[126]

Prior to "submitting a request to the panel," the Requesters had filed a claim at "the Compliance Committee of the Aarhus Convention," alleging

> that Albania was not complying with its obligations concerning public access to information and participation in the construction of a Bank-financed thermal

---

120 *Id.*
121 *Id.*
122 Swepston *in* Alfredsson & Ring (Eds.) (2001), p. 250.
123 *Id.*
124 *Id.*
125 Baimu & Panou *in* Cissé et al. (Eds.) (2012), e-Book.
126 That is, the Convention on Access to Information, Public Participation in Decision-Making and Access to Justice in Environmental Matters. On the Aarhus Convention Compliance Committee, *see* http://www.unece.org/env/pp/cc.html.

power plant project and an energy park. The committee accepted the request and found the allegation to be justified.[127]

The Panel took note of the fact that the Aarhus compliance committee's "review focused [only] on the actions of Albania [as a Party to the Aarhus Convention]," and "not on the Bank," but it nevertheless concluded that the findings of "the Committee are relevant" for its own investigation "because Bank policy gives the main responsibility for consultation to the borrower and requires the Bank to ensure that the borrower fulfills this requirement."[128] On completion of its investigation, the Inspection Panel

> concluded that the Bank did not ensure that the project preparation activities complied with the consultation and public participation requirements of the Aarhus Convention, and thus did not comply with OP 4.01 – Environmental Assessment.[129]

5.3.2   International legal obligations of the World Bank

As a subject of the international legal system, international law constitutes a source of (international legal) obligation for international financial institutions such as the World Bank.[130] While this statement are hardly contested anymore, what remains contentious, is the matter of the substantive and procedural content, as well as the extent of international financial institutions' international legal obligations, in particular in areas such as international environmental law and international human rights law.[131] This contention is caused "in large part, because IFIs," as noted earlier,

> are not signatories of prominent international covenants and because their Articles of Agreement (or, their interpretations thereof) provide them with a great deal of flexibility in determining the content of their international legal obligations for themselves.[132]

---

127 Baimu & Panou *in* Cissé et al. (Eds.) (2012), e-Book. On the cooperation between IAMs, *see* section 3.1.3.
128 Baimu & Panou *in* Cissé et al. (Eds.) (2012), e-Book.
129 *Id.*
130 For an analysis of key "general principles of international law applicable to IFIs", *see* Bradlow *in* Bradlow & Hunter (Eds.) (2010), pp. 11-30.
131 For a summary of the human rights criticisms aimed at the Bank, *see e.g.*, Head (2003-2004), p. 257. For an example from Inspection Panel practice where the human rights obligations of the World Bank became a central point of contention, *see e.g.*, *Chad: Petroleum Development and Pipeline* (2001); *and see* notes 72-74, Ch. 5.
132 *Note*, in this regard, that there is a lack of clarity in international law whether international financial institutions – beyond what is specified in their operational policies – "have any specific international legal obligations with which they must comply in the structuring and drafting of their financial transactions" or with regards

At a high level of abstraction, as Bradlow observes, it is typically acceptable to suggest that international financial institutions' "governance structures and decision-making principles should conform to universally applicable customary and treaty-based international legal principles," such as 'respect for state sovereignty' and 'non-discrimination'.[133] By becoming an IFI-member state, for instance, "a state agrees to surrender some decision-making autonomy in return for the benefits of participation in the IFI," but "the principle of national sovereignty" nevertheless "imposes some constraint on the demands that an IFI can place"

> on a particular member state and should help each member state preserve as much independence and policy space as is practicable in its relation with each IFI and consistent with the demands of overall effective global financial governance.[134]

The "principle of nondiscrimination," moreover, would be applicable "to both the member states of the IFIs and all those nonstate actors with which the IFIs interact or which are directly affected by their operations."[135] Therefore, "all similarly situated states and nonstate actors" can expect to "receive similar treatment in their dealings with the IFIs," whereas "those who are differently situated"

> should receive differential treatment that reflects the differences in their situations. The key question thus becomes what standards can be used for ensuring that all stakeholders receive treatment that is fair and reasonable.[136]

In addition, Bradlow notes, "IFIs should base their treatment of all states on the same principles," which means that "they should apply these principles"

> in a way that is responsive to the similarities and differences in the situations of each member state and of the affected nonstate actors. Recognition should be given to the fact that weaker and poorer states are significantly different in capacities from rich and powerful nations.[137]

---

to "planning, evaluating, and implementing the projects, activities, or policies they fund." *See* Bradlow, *in* Bradlow & Hunter (Eds.) 2010, p. 2. *Also see* in general Wouters et al. (Eds.) (2010).

133 *Id.* Other international legal principles highlighted by Bradlow in his analysis include 'state responsibility' and various 'principles derived from international environmental law'.

134 Bradlow *in* Cissé et al. (Eds.) (2012), e-Book. *Also see* the ILA's remarks, *at* notes 84, 85 & 86, Ch. 2.

135 Bradlow *in* Cissé et al. (Eds.) (2012), e-Book.

136 *Id. Also see* section 6.3.

137 Bradlow *in* Cissé et al. (Eds.) (2012), e-Book. On issues related to borrower capacity, *see* section 8.3.

That said, while international financial institutions, with the World Bank at the vanguard, generally express their willingness to "work to comply fully" with the "requirements of their constituent treaties and with the customary international law and general principles of law applicable to them as international organizations," it is, as Bradlow points out, "easier for the IFIs to enunciate these principles than to apply them in the day-to-day management of their operations and in their governance."[138] In this regard, Bradlow argues, contrary to arguments emphasizing the close relationships of the operational policy framework and international law, that it is "noteworthy how few of the [multilateral development banks'] operational policies mention relevant international legal principles," in particular outside the context of borrower obligations, "or explain how management and staff are expected to ensure that operations comply with applicable international law," which could perhaps be

> explained by the fact that the applicable international legal principles, standards, and norms are not easy to implement, particularly within the contexts of complex development projects.[139]

Moreover, this situation is exacerbated by "the "exquisite ambiguity" within the Articles of Agreement of IFIs, as well as "the relative lack of precision in the applicable international legal principles".[140]

On the other hand, international financial institutions can hardly "avoid dealing with the issues addressed by these international legal principles in their operations, particularly those that raise safeguard issues."[141] And because many of the international legal principles applicable to IFIs' development-lending operations "relate to important, complex, and often unresolved international legal issues" – including the international legal responsibility of IFIs such as the World Bank – their efforts to conceptualize and operationalize notions such as accountability (efforts that are "further enhanced by the work of the independent accountability mechanisms"), have "become relevant and active creators of international law."[142]

---

138 Bradlow *in* Cissé et al. (Eds.) (2012), e-Book.
139 *Id.*
140 Bradlow *in* Cissé et al. (Eds.) (2012), e-Book; *and see* Bradlow *in* Bradlow & Hunter (Eds.) 2010, pp. 29-30.
141 Bradlow *in* Cissé et al. (Eds.) (2012), e-Book.
142 Bradlow *in* Cissé et al. (Eds.) (2012), e-Book; *and* Bradlow *in* Bradlow & Hunter (Eds.) 2010, pp. 29-30. *Also see* Miller-Adams (1999), who notes (at p. 135) that "the Bank's charter has proven flexible enough to accommodate significant changes in its activities. In part this is because the charter is a minimal document that focuses on issues of process rather than purpose. In larger part it is because responsibility for interpreting the charter falls to the Bank itself, giving its leaders the freedom to pursue any number of paths provided the Bank's fundamental rules are left intact." On normative development as an outcome of accountability processes, *see* section 7.1.6.

In other words, arguments in favour of the legal nature of the Bank's operational policy framework, noted earlier,[143] gain particular significance because in applying and enforcing the operational policies, the Bank effectively draws the contours of its international legal obligations in key areas such as international human rights and international environmental law.[144]

However, consider Swepston's comment that international legal instruments "are carefully negotiated and different interests taken into account, and then are subject to ratification before becoming binding on States," whereas the World Bank's operational policy framework is, as noted earlier, essentially "the fruit of staff work" that "are submitted to the political bodies of the Bank only for approval", although this process has become more participatory over time. While it may well be that the increasingly interactional nature of the processes of norm-creation, norm application and norm enforcement surrounding the Bank's development-lending operations "make the World Bank the most effective implementation agency for human rights in the United Nations system"

> because it extracts from human rights standards what is useful and is able to work for the implementation of these principles with a certain force that other parts of the system lack[;][145]

it also "has its drawbacks."[146] For instance, Swepston notes, "[i]t is a matter of [legitimate] concern if the staff of any agency"

> rewrites international human rights standards to its own specifications, and then applies them in that form rather than in the form in which they were adopted. It is a matter of even more concern if that agency then examines the implementation of those standards through its own projects, as it understands them and without reference either to the original standards themselves or to the way they have been supervised by the international bodies established for that purpose.[147]

---

143 *See* section 5.1.1.
144 *E.g., see* in general Bradlow & Naudé Fourie (2013).
145 Swepston *in* Alfredsson & Ring (Eds.) (2001), pp. 255-256.
146 *Id.*
147 *Id.*

5.4   INTERNATIONAL INDUSTRY AND/OR PROFESSIONAL STANDARDS AND 'BEST PRACTICE'

The final normative framework discussed in this chapter concerns the standards and best practices specific to particular industries and professions, developed at a global level. As defined here, industry/professional standards are typically the products of formal "standard setting" processes "carried out by private or quasi-private entities;"[148] whereas industry/professional 'best practices' typically evolve by means of informal processes.[149] While industry and/or professional standards and best practice "are not primarily (or at least initially) regulatory," as Morrixon and Roth-Arriaza observe, they do "seek to change behaviour through a complex mix of incentives and do not rely primarily on external deterrence-based enforcement."[150]

These standards and best practices are a significant source of normativity in the context of World Bank development-lending operations because they guide the behaviours necessary to ensure sufficient levels of quality and, crucially, safety. For example, the Bank's policy on Safety of Dams specifies that in instances where "the Bank finances a project that includes the construction of a new dam," "the dam be designed and its construction supervised by experienced and competent professionals."[151] "For small dams," the policy notes, "generic dam safety measures designed by qualified engineers are usually adequate,"[152] whereas in the case of "large dams," the policy "requires reviews by an independent panel of experts [PoE] (the Panel) of the investigation, design, and construction of the dam and the start of operations."[153] "The number, professional breadth, technical expertise, and experience of Panel [oE] members," the policy adds, should be "appropriate to the size, complexity, and hazard potential of the dam under consideration. For high-hazard dams, in particular, the Panel members should be internationally known experts in their field."[154]

---

148 Morrixon & Roth-Arriaza *in* Bodansky et al. (Eds.) (2007), p. 499. Examples of such entities include: the International Organization for Standardization (ISO) and its "sister organizations" (*see* pp. 501-504); "non-state environmental and social certification and labelling programmes" (*see* pp. 504); "OECD guidelines" (*see* p. 506); and the UN Global Compact (*see* p. 506).

149 The World Bank, as mentioned earlier, captures its own (emerging) 'best practice' standards in 'Operational Memo' or 'Guideline'-format – *see* section 5.1.

150 Morrixon & Roth-Arriaza *in* Bodansky et al. (Eds.) (2007), p. 506. The authors add (at pp. 506-507) that these standards are typically "not aimed at states", but aimed "directly at organizations – mostly business organizations but also in some cases non-profit or public-sector organizations." There are, moreover, different kinds of standards (including, for instance, "technical specifications and performance standards; process and management system standards; measurement and reporting standards" that "are market-oriented instruments that act directly on producers, and do not originate from intergovernmental agreements or instruments that apply to producers through the intermediation of national law." *See* Morrixon & Roth-Arriaza *in* Bodansky et al. (Eds.) (2007), pp. 507-510.

151 OP 4.37 (Safety of Dams), § 2.

152 OP 4.37 (Safety of Dams), § 4.

153 OP 4.37 (Safety of Dams), § 4(a).

154 OP 4.37 (Safety of Dams), fn. 8.

Or as Wirth explains, "the Bank makes use of a number of non-binding normative instruments of external origin,"

> such as the FAO Code of Conduct on the Distribution and Use of Pesticides, in its operations. The good practice standards contained in such instruments may inform or be incorporated by reference in international policies, such as the Bank's Policy on Pest Management, which expressly cites the FAO Code.[155]

Such references to external standards, Wirth argues, "may perform a useful legitimating function within the Bank,"

> while legally, through a process similar to that characteristic of the Bank's internal [operational] standards, these instruments may be transformed into binding loan covenants.[156]

Inspection Panel practice also provides examples of compliance issues concerning the involvement of independent industry or professional experts throughout the project cycle, which apply applicable industry and/or professional standards or best practices to the particular project context. In *Uzbekistan: Energy Loss Reduction*, for example, World Bank management affirmed that "two international Panels of Experts" would be "established to provide oversight and quality assurance"

> for both assessment studies, consistent with OPs 4.01 and 4.37: the Environment/Social Panel and the Engineering/Dam Safety Panel. To build confidence in the objectivity of the Panels' advice, members will be selected, managed and funded by the Bank ['Under normal procedures, Panels of Experts are contracted directly by the project proponent/Borrower']. Members will be internationally recognized experts in their fields with experience in similarly large and complex hydropower projects.[157]

Or, in *Papua New Guinea: Smallholder Agriculture*, Bank management acknowledged that "there was insufficient detail in the EA on the matter of effluents".[158] To correct this shortcoming, Management confirmed that it would conduct "a thorough analysis of the impact of increased effluents due to Project activities", as well as monitor the milling

---

155 Wirth *in* Shelton (Ed.) (2000), p. 335.
156 *Id.*
157 *Uzbekistan: Energy Loss Reduction* (2010), MR, § 29.
158 *Papua New Guinea: Smallholder Agriculture* (2009), ER, § 42.

company's "ISO14001 and RPSO certification".[159] The "ISO14001", Management elaborated, "is an international standard for environmental management and a framework for lessening a company's footprint on the environment" whereas "the Roundtable on Sustainable Palm Oil (RSPO)"

> is a global coalition of industry, NGO s, financial institutions, environmental and conservation groups, retailers and consumer product companies that have come together since 2004 to develop a structured way forward for the production and use of sustainable oil palm.[160]

The Inspection Panel also makes extensive use of independent industry/professional experts in fulfilling its fact-finding and compliance review functions.[161] In *South Africa: Eskom Investment Support*, for instance, the Inspection Panel's chair addressed "the question posed" by Board members "regarding the Panel's ability to deal with issues raised in the Request and covered by operational policies and procedures."[162] "In each investigation to date," the chair noted,

> the Panel has retained internationally recognized experts to analyze technical matters and issue findings on policy compliance. I would like to assure the Board that the Panel is equipped to engage experts of the highest quality to assist it with investigations, and this particular case will be no exception.[163]

Moreover, instances where the Inspection Panel makes specific comments about the 'quality' or 'substance' of specific project activities, in addition to 'process' or 'procedural' elements, as will be discussed in the next chapter, also reflect the influence of industry and/or professional standards and best practices in the context of World Bank-financed development projects.[164]

Finally, industry and/or professional standards and practices are also a source of normativity for borrowers and their project implementing agencies. In *Chad: Petroleum*, for example, the Inspection Panel concluded that the project's "[v]aluation and compensation

---

159 *Id.*
160 *Id.*
161 On the Panel's fact-finding function, *see* section 6.2.4.
162 *South Africa: Eskom Investment Support* (2010), ER (IP Chairperson's Statement), pp. 3-4. *Also see Colombia Cartagena Water Supply, Sewerage and Environmental Management Project* (on the 'risk of mud volcanism' and regarding 'the proposed design for the submarine outfall'); *and India: Mumbai Urban Transport* Project, IR (ES), at 34 (on "exposure to [potential] radioactive emissions" at the "resettlement sites").
163 *South Africa: Eskom Investment Support* (2010), ER (IP Chairperson's Statement), pp. 3-4. On the role of subject matter experts in supporting the Panel in their fact-finding role, *also see* Naudé Fourie (2009), p. 260.
164 *See* section 6.3.4.

of lost land was adequate."[165] As an example, the Panel highlighted Esso's practice (a member of the 'Consortium' involved in the financing and implementation of the project's pipeline development component) "of compensating the community rather than the individual for fallow land" as "a sensible one."[166]

****

The intersecting normative frameworks introduced in Chapter 5 serve as yardsticks used to assess World Bank accountability. The application and enforcement of these frameworks – notably, of the operational policy framework – further clarify the content and the scope of World Bank accountability, as the next chapter will illustrate. Reflecting the high degree of pluralism marking the transnational development context in which the Bank's development-lending operations are situated, the normative frameworks surrounding the Bank's development-lending operations are of a diverse nature. The normative yardsticks used to measure World Bank accountability operate at the international, national and sub-national (local) levels; they can be legal or non-legal ('social') in nature – or, when expressed in terms of an interactional conception of (legal) normativity, can be something 'in-between'.[167] They also "reveal the composite nature of the law-making process in the international legal system."[168] "Policy instruments and the attention given to their compliance", Boisson de Chazournes argues,

> contribute in many ways to this process. They reveal that porosity and interactions are core aspects of the contemporary legal system, where a plurality of actors is engaged in activities at the local, national and international levels. Although states retain a pre-eminent role in the making and implementation of international law, international organizations, NGOs, and individuals play an increasingly important role in shaping new practices and ensuring their respect.[169]

In addition, the World Bank's operational policy framework have come to serve as

---

165 *Chad: Petroleum* (2001), IR, § 159.

166 *Id.* For supportive comments about Exxon's best practices employed in the *Chad* project, *also see* Mallaby (2004), pp. 343-347. *Note*, on the influence of previous experience in borrower countries as a basis for project decisions, *also see* the discussion *in* section 6.3.1.

167 *See e.g.*, Shelton *in* Shelton (Ed.) 2000, pp. 17-18: "The lack of a binding form may reduce the options for enforcement in the short term (*i.e.* no litigation), but this does not deny that there can exist sincere and deeply held expectations of compliance with the norms contained in the non-binding form." *Also see* section 2.1.

168 Boisson de Chazournes *in* Shelton (Ed.) (2000), p. 282.

169 *Id.*

guidelines for other investors, including both bilateral aid agencies and private sector lenders, some of whom are anxious to reduce risk and secure an imprimatur from a high-status body with expert project personnel such as the World Bank[170]

with the Bank's policy on Environmental Assessment being "a notable example" since it "inspired similar guidelines at the Asian Development Bank, the European Bank for Reconstruction and Development, the Inter-American Development Bank, several bilateral donors, and various private-sector firms," and came to be reflected in the 1992 Rio Declaration, which "mandates that an environmental impact assessment requirement be incorporated into national legislation and regulations."[171] "This cross-fertilization of international and Bank standards", Sarfaty concludes, "highlights the prominent role that Bank operational policies play in the development of customary international law norms."[172] The operational policies may therefore not "purport to set international standards," as Freestone argues,[173] but they "expressly refer to international standards as a means for identifying the good and best practices to be followed,"[174] which, as Boisson de Chazournes contends, is arguably a further illustration of "the close relationship of the operational policies and procedure with international law principles and standards in areas which fall within the scope of application of the policies."[175]

This being said, Freestone makes the important point that, "[i]n the longer term," "there will be a need to look beyond safeguards and the 'command and control' model upon which they are built"[176] – in particular as concerns grow about the perceived lack of borrower ownership in implementing the safeguard policies, in a changing transnational development context in which a growing number of competitors do not employ the same safeguards, nor insist upon incorporating such standards in loan/credit agreements. Furthermore, a reconsideration of the 'command and control model' might indeed be necessitated by the requirement embodied in the notion of "[s]ustainable development", which compels "the internationalization of environmental and social sustainability principles, not only within the lending and grant-making institutions, but also in the borrowers and host countries."[177]

---

170 Kingsbury (1999), p. 339.
171 Sarfaty (2005), pp. 1800-1801. On issues related to the process of Environmental Assessment, *see* Ch. 14.
172 Sarfaty (2005), pp. 1800-1801.
173 Freestone (2003), *at* note 49, Ch. 5.
174 Boisson de Chazournes *in* Alfredsson & Ring (Eds.) (2001), p. 78. The author adds (at p. 78): "As an example, the OP on management of cultural property [...] makes explicit reference to country obligations under international treaties for defining cultural property under the policy." In this regard, *see* OP 4.11 (Physical Cultural Resources), § 3.
175 Boisson de Chazournes *in* Alfredsson & Ring (Eds.) (2001), p. 79. *Also see* section 4.3.2.
176 Freestone (2013), p. 62.
177 *Id.*

6 ASSESSING ACCOUNTABILITY: ACCOUNTABILITY MECHANISMS AND COMPETING APPROACHES TO COMPLIANCE

Chapter 6 places the spotlight on the internal accountability mechanisms involved in assessing or measuring World Bank accountability. The focus on internal mechanisms is determined, foremost, by the scope of this book, which employs Inspection Panel practice as the primary basis for the analysis presented here. It should nevertheless be noted that the discourse on World Bank accountability also concerns the need for the involvement of external accountability mechanisms – notably, of international courts and tribunals and/or domestic judicial systems. This matter is excluded from the discussion in this chapter since it is dependent upon the adoption of structural changes to the international legal system in order to address issues concerning standing and immunity – which, in turn, requires a sufficient degree of political will among relevant decision-makers, notably, state actors.[1] While such political will remains in short supply – at least in the foreseeable future – it might be cultivated, in the mean time, through the progressive development of a comprehensive shared understanding on the meaning of the accountability of international (financial) institutions, such as the World Bank, to which this book aims to contribute.

The chapter sets off by considering a few systems of classification used for describing or *categorizing internal accountability mechanisms*. This aspect of the discourse on World Bank accountability demonstrates the problem of employing existing systems of categorization to transnational regulatory governance contexts, since all of the classification systems discussed here experience some difficulty in making sense of what bodies such as the Inspection Panel *are*.[2] Next, the chapter provides an overview of *prominent* World Bank *internal accountability mechanisms*, with the focus falling on the Inspection Panel.[3] Finally, with Inspection Panel practice serving as the basis for the discussion, Chapter 6 considers *competing approaches* employed to determine *what constitutes compliance* with the operational policy framework – approaches that have significant implications for the content and scope of World Bank accountability.

---

1   *See* the discussion *in* Ch. 1.
2   *See* section 2.1.
3   In this regard, it is significant to note that the World Bank's latest articulation of its strategy highlights the need for greater cooperation across all the institutions of the World Bank group, including its accountability mechanisms – *see* World Bank (2014), p. 7, on the strategic priority of "working as one World Bank Group".

6.1   CATEGORIZING INTERNAL ACCOUNTABILITY MECHANISMS

On the notion of accountability *mechanism* Ebrahim observes that "it is helpful to differentiate between those [mechanisms] that are "tools" and those that are "processes."[4] "In basic terms," Ebrahim argues, "accountability tools refer"

> to discrete devices or techniques used to achieve accountability. They are often applied over a limited period of time, can be tangibly documented, and can be repeated. For example, financial reports and disclosures are tools that are applied and repeated quarterly or annually, and are documented as financial statements, ledgers, or reports. Performance evaluations are also often carried out at specific points in time, usually at the end of a specific project, and result in an evaluation report.[5]

"[P]rocess mechanisms such as participation and self-regulation", on the other hand, "are generally more broad and multifaceted than tools,"

> while also being less tangible and time-bound, although each may utilize a set of tools (such as participatory rural appraisal) for achieving accountability. Process mechanisms thus emphasize a course of action rather than a distinct end-result, in which the means are important in and of themselves.[6]

As Baimu and Panou point out, World Bank accountability is "pursued not only through oversight mechanisms but also through the promotion of transparency,"[7] as embodied, for example, in the Bank's policy on Access to Information[8] or in initiatives such as the 'Voluntary Disclosure Program (VDP)', which "aims to encourage disclosure to the Bank of corrupt or fraudulent practices."[9]

In terms of this distinction, most of the internal accountability mechanisms introduced in this section can be best described as 'process-mechanisms', although some (typically,

---

4   Ebrahim (2003), pp. 815-816. *Note,* Ebrahim employs this distinction in discussing the enhancement of NGO accountability.

5   *Id.*

6   *Id.*

7   Baimu & Panou *in* Cissé et al. (Eds.) (2012), e-Book.

8   On this policy, *also see* note 18, Ch. 5.

9   Kingsbury *in* Cissé et al. (Eds.) (2012), e-Book. On the VDP, the World Bank notes: "Any entity or individual involved in contracts or projects financed by the World Bank Group (excluding World Bank Group staff) that is not already under active investigation by the Bank may request entry into the VDP by providing preliminary background details. Once the Bank confirms the entity's eligibility, the entity commits to cease all corrupt and fraudulent practices and to disclose all details of impropriety to the Bank." *See* http://go.worldbank.org/3JOFMN95S0.

mechanisms involved in auditing functions) might come close to "straddle[ing] the tool-process boundary."[10]

De Wet employs a classification that is based on some of the accountability models, introduced earlier.[11] Most of the internal accountability introduced here could be described as forms of "intermediary oversight," which, as De Wet explains, are related both to the "internationalist" and "cosmopolitan" accountability models.[12] While there are different "forms of intermediate supervision", these mechanisms typically share a few core characteristics.[13] For instance, their mandates usually "have a formal basis in [...] a constitutive document of the international institution" or in "resolutions adopted in accordance with the constitutive document."[14] Moreover, the oversight or "supervision as such is exercised by an independent body" that "does not have a direct hierarchical relationship with the body that is being supervised," but oversight nevertheless "takes place in the shadow of hierarchy, as the supervising body acts on the authority of a higher body and also reports to it."[15]

A few of the internal accountability mechanisms discussed in this section could be further categorized as a particular form of 'intermediate supervision', namely, mechanisms that provide "individual(ized) oversight."[16] These mechanisms, which include the Inspection Panel, are of particular interest for the purposes of the discourse on World Bank accountability because they are the only ones mechanisms that are 'citizen-driven' – that is, their procedures can be triggered from outside the institution, by external constituent groups.

Internal accountability mechanisms might also be described in terms of their underlying approach and the type of outcomes they produce.[17] In this regard, Romano has devised a "taxonomy" that categorizes the wide range of supposed "international rule of law bodies and procedures," associated with "international governmental organizations," that con-

---

10   Ebrahim (2003), pp. 815-816.
11   De Wet *in* Von Bogdandy et al. (Eds.) (2010), p. 866; *and see* section 3.2.3.
12   De Wet *in* Von Bogdandy et al. (Eds.) (2010), p. 866.
13   *Id*. De Wet also identifies (*at id.*) mechanisms of "[v]ertical oversight", which reflect the "internationalist model", because they emphasize the prominent role of the international institution's "parent organs exercise[ing] formal supervision over a subsidiary organ" – such as the Board of Executive Directors overseeing the activities of Bank management and staff. Horizontal oversight, moreover, (which "resembles the cosmopolitan accountability model", "involves scrutiny of normative activity by NGOs or other members of civil society." Such scrutiny is often facilitated by policies aimed at promoting transparency and public participation in decision-making.
14   De Wet *in* Von Bogdandy et al. (Eds.) (2010), p. 866.
15   *Id.*
16   *Id.*
17   On 'accountability outcomes', *see* Ch. 7.

tribute to the accountability of these institutions – either by "adjudicative" or "non-adjudicative means."[18]

Most of the internal accountability mechanisms discussed in the next section fall within the "class of non-adjudicative means,"[19] that is, they produce "outcomes that are not binding" (which are therefore "called 'reports' or 'recommendations'") since they "do not create a legal obligation on their recipients, who remain free to adopt or ignore them."[20] Moreover, while some of these mechanisms "might be composed of independent members," "not all [of them] [are]."[21] Romano further categorizes the 'rule of law bodies' that resort under the 'non-adjudicative means class' as "human rights bodies" and "international review, accountability, oversight, and audit mechanisms." The Bank's internal accountability mechanisms typically fall in the last-mentioned sub-category.[22]

Moreover, 'individualized oversight' or 'citizen-driven' accountability mechanisms such as the Inspection Panel might be described as a form of "surrogate accountability", which, as Rubenstein argues "occurs when a third party" gathers information and/or "sanctions a power wielder on behalf of accountability holders because accountability holders cannot" effectively fulfill these aspects due to power imbalances.[23] Such "surrogates should, if possible, deliberate with accountability holders and seek their authorization to act on their behalf'; they should also be independent in the sense that neither "accountability holders", nor for that matter, power wielders, should be able to "sanction them."[24]

A final consideration to be mentioned here concerns the question of the 'legal', 'non-legal' or 'quasi-legal' nature of internal accountability mechanisms. In the context of World Bank development-lending operations, this question typically arises with respect to the Inspection Panel – and is a matter that will be discussed in more detail below.[25]

---

18 Romano (2011), p. 251. The author adds (*at id.*): "All bodies within this Kingdom share the fundamental traits of the Domain of International Governmental Organizations, but what characterizes bodies within this Kingdom and separates them from other kingdoms are three further criteria: (iv) They apply international legal standards; (v) act on the basis of pre-determined rules of procedure; (vi) at least one of the parties to the cases they decide, or situation they consider, is a State or an international organization."
19 Romano (2011), pp. 254-255.
20 Romano (2011), pp. 254-255. By contrast, "[a]djudicative means", Romano notes (at p. 253) "produce binding outcomes" and are "composed of independent members". The only internal accountability mechanism discussed here that could be typified as 'adjudicative' is the World Bank's Administrative Tribunal – *see* section 6.2.3.
21 Romano (2011), pp. 254-255.
22 *Id.* For additional examples of bodies/mechanisms belonging to these categories, *see* pp. 258-259.
23 Rubenstein (2007), p. 624.
24 *Id.*
25 *See* section 6.2.4.

6.2   Internal accountability mechanisms involved in the normative assessment of World Bank activities

This section provides an overview of the mandates, institutional scope and functions of prominent internal (World Bank) accountability mechanisms, with an emphasis placed on the Inspection Panel. Most of the mechanisms presented here are, as the descriptor indicates, of particular importance for *internal* accountability holders. However, because their mandates and functions typically measure both accountability 'for performance' and 'for harm', and as the outcomes they generate have become increasingly publically accessible, internal accountability are also of significance to external accountability holders, in assessing World Bank accountability.

6.2.1   *Operations impact evaluation and quality assurance: IEG and OPCS Vice Presidency*

The Bank describes the '*Independent Evaluation Group*' (formerly, the Operations Evaluation Department)[26] as an "independent unit" within the World Bank Group that "reports directly to the Board of Executive Directors."[27] By focusing their efforts primarily at the concluding stage of the project cycle, the IEG "assesses the performance of roughly [one] project out of [four] (about 70 projects a year)," with the primary aim of "measure[ing] [project] outcomes against the original objectives, sustainability of results, and institutional development effects."[28] The IEG also "produces impact evaluation reports" at regular intervals that "assess the economic worth of projects and the long-term effects on people and the environment against an explicit counterfactual."[29] In addition, the IEG "assesses the performance of Bank Group policies, programs, projects, and processes"[30] in order to facilitate institutional learning "about what works in what contexts" and therefore "contributes to improving the Bank Group's operations and impact."[31] These perspectives, in

---

26   *See* http://ieg.worldbankgroup.org.

27   World Bank (2015), e-Book. For criticism of OED (now IEG) institutional independence, *see e.g.*, Nathan (1995), at p. 137: "The Operations Evaluation Department [...] is independent largely in name only. Staff within the Department is interchangeable with staff elsewhere in the Bank, and the Bank's culture prevents the Department from focusing adequately on the shortcomings of the Bank and its staff."

28   World Bank (2011), e-Book. The Bank adds (*at id.*): "IEG impact evaluations have increased as the unit has collaborated more with other international development evaluation units and networks, such as the Evaluation Cooperation Group, the Network of Networks for Impact Evaluation, the United Nations Evaluation Group, the International Initiative for Impact Evaluation, and the OECD Development Assistance Committee Evaluation Network." On the project cycle, *see* section 4.1.2.

29   World Bank (2011), e-Book.

30   *Id.*

31   World Bank (2015), e-Book.

turn, (which form part of what the Bank describes as an "evidence-based policy making" process) "feed into new policies and Bank strategies as they are being developed."[32]

The IEG's "findings", which includes a wide range of reports, as well as individual project's performance ratings "are made public to the Member States and the broader public."[33] In this regard, Woods points out that "not all of the [IEG's] publications" have been "publically available", however, since 1993, this situation has progressively improved "in the context" of World Bank-reviews of its policy on Access to Information.[34] This development is significant, Woods adds, because "the outside scrutiny of such documents"

> not only adds to the external accountability of the organizations, but also ensures that such reviews are taken seriously within the institutions themselves.[35]

The 'Operations Policy and Country Services' (OPCS) Vice Presidency, in conjunction with the "Environmental and International Law Practice Group of the Legal Vice Presidency," "provides support to Bank teams that are dealing with environmental and social risks in Bank-supported operations."[36] Emphasizing that the "Bank's credibility rests on effective implementation of its policies," the OPCS describes its primary function as "enhance[ing] the Bank's operational effectiveness" by means of the 'support and advise' it provides to World Bank management and staff.[37]

The 'Quality Assurance and Compliance Unit' (formerly, the Quality Assurance Group),[38] is "an independent body" situated "within the OPCS Vice Presidency."[39] The Bank has also appointed "a Regional Safeguard Director and a Co-ordinator" "[w]ithin each of the Bank's Regional Vice Presidencies.[40] Each of these 'Co-ordinators', in turn, "provides specialist advice"

---

32 *Id.* The Bank adds (*at id.*): "This type of evaluation seeks to identify the extent to which changes can be attributed specifically to the interventions being evaluated", whereas the "unit also supports the development of evaluation capacity in partner countries." For a discussion of the OED/IEG's mandate, *also see* Boisson de Chazournes *in* Shelton (Ed.) (2000), pp. 291-292.

33 De Wet *in* Von Bogdandy et al. (Eds.) (2010), p. 867. For aggregated IEG evaluation reports (of various types), *see*: http://ieg.worldbankgroup.org/webpage/evaluations; for the IEG's performance rating data on individual projects', *see*: http://ieg.worldbankgroup.org/ratings. *Note*, IEG ratings are also used in the Bank's performance scorecard – *see* Figure 7.

34 Woods (2001), pp. 91-92.

35 *Id.*

36 World Bank (2011), e-Book.

37 *Id.*

38 *See* Bradlow & Naudé Fourie (2013), pp. 38-39.

39 *Note*, 'independent' as used in this context means: 'a sufficient degree of functional institutional independence, or refers to 'impartiality'. It should be noted that the internal accountability mechanisms discussed in this section, (with the exception of the Staff Tribunal, the IEG and the Inspection Panel) "operat[e] under the leadership and direction of the president and organizational units responsible for regions, sectors, and general management." *See* http://www.worldbank.org/en/about/unit.

40 Freestone (2013), pp. 61-62.

to the environmental and social specialist teams in each region (in some regions through a Quality Assessment Team) and liaises with the centrally located Quality Assurance and Compliance Unit.[41]

The Quality Assurance and Compliance Unit is specifically mandated to "monito[r] the quality of the Bank's activities," particularly during the project implementation stage, in order "to improve management."[42] The Unit executes its mandate by "examine[ning] project quality" of the Bank's development-lending operations ("shortly after project approval by the Board"),[43] as well as the Bank's "advisory services (after delivery to country clients)."[44] It also "monitors the quality of project supervision" and "reports to the Board of Executive Directors", at regular intervals "on the overall health of the portfolio of ongoing projects" by means of an "Annual Report on Portfolio Performance."[45]

Freestone observes that the Quality Assurance and Compliance Unit "has been significantly strengthened" in recent years

> and has developed an electronic safeguard screening system which the task managers of all Bank projects are required to complete at project concept stage. As projects develop to appraisal stage, the electronic Project Appraisal Document standard forms require specific standardized safeguard questions to be answered. This approach has also recently been extended to Bank documentation at the implementation phase of projects.[46]

6.2.2   Internal audit, institutional integrity and business ethics: IAD Vice Presidency, INT Vice Presidency

The 'Internal Audit' (IAD) Vice Presidency is "an independent and objective assurance and advisory function."[47] The IAD has been "designed to add value" across the World Bank Group, as the Bank remarks, "by improving the operations of the WBG organizations."[48] The IAD is specifically tasked with "evaluating and improving the effectiveness"

---

41   Freestone (2013), pp. 61-62.
42   World Bank (2011), e-Book.
43   For the project cycle, *see* section 4.1.2.
44   World Bank (2011), e-Book.
45   *Id.* For examples of issues related to project supervision, *see* Ch. 15.
46   Freestone (2013), pp. 61-62. For an example of an 'integrated safeguards data sheet' completed at the project appraisal stage, *see*: http://www-wds.worldbank.org/external/default/WDSContentServer/WDSP/LCR/2013/06/21/090224b081c953e2/1_0/Rendered/PDF/Integrated0Saf0nt0Project000P143996.pdf.
47   World Bank (2015), e-Book. On the meaning of 'independent' in this context, *see* note 39, Ch. 6.
48   *Id.*

of "risk management, control, and governance processes."[49] Moreover, the IAD's "Quarterly Activity Report" is "publicly disclosed, under the Bank's Access to Information Policy."[50]

The 'Integrity' Vice Presidency (INT)[51] is mandated to "investigat[e] allegations of fraud, corruption, coercion, collusion, and obstructive behavior related to Bank-financed projects and Bank Group operations," as well as "allegations of serious staff misconduct."[52] Other INT functions include activities aimed at "improv[ing] corporate compliance with World Bank procurement policies," usually through staff training programmes.[53]

Typically, "38 percent of the total [INT] allegations received" are filed by "Bank Group staff"; however, "33 percent" of the total allegations are filed by "non-Bank staff" (typically including "contractors, government officials and employees of NGOs"), whereas "28 percent" are "reported to INT anonymously."[54] In other words, much like the Inspection Panel, the INT is, at least partly, a 'citizen-driven' accountability mechanism or an 'individual(ized) oversight' body.[55]

Finally, the INT "publishes an annual integrity report with aggregate data, outcomes, and generic descriptions of significant cases," as well as "redacted reports by summarizing the findings of its investigations for which entities have been debarred."[56]

6.2.3   Internal justice and conflict resolution: CRS

As a result of its qualified immunity before domestic courts, the Bank "cannot be sued in national courts by staff members with employment claims;" hence, the Bank has established an internal 'Conflict Resolution System' (CRS) to address these matters.[57] The CRS consists of "a group of independent offices," situated within the World Bank Group, that is mandated

---

49 *Id.*

50 World Bank (2015), e-Book. Access IAD Annual Reports at: http://go.worldbank.org/UFMLY4H1D0.

51 *See* http://go.worldbank.org/036LY1EJJ0.

52 World Bank (2011), e-Book. For more information on the 'World Bank's sanctions system' employed by the INT, *see*: http://go.worldbank.org/WICZWZY0E0. The Bank notes (*at id.*) that the sanctions system consists of "a two-tier adjudicative process, with a first level of review carried out by the Bank's Suspension and Debarment Officer (SDO) and, for contested cases, a second level of review by the World Bank Group Sanctions Board, an independent body with a majority of external members." *Also note*: information about any "sanctions imposed by the Bank Group" are publically accessible at: www.worldbank.org/debarr.

53 World Bank (2011), e-Book. *Also note*, the VDP reports into the Integrity VP; on the VDP, *see* note 9, Ch. 6.

54 *See* http://go.worldbank.org/P1T6RY5UB0. For more detail on the electronic and telephonic procedures to 'report suspected fraud or corruption', *see*: http://web.worldbank.org/WBSITE/EXTERNAL/EXTABOUTUS/ORGANIZATION/ORGUNITS/EXTDOII/0,,contentMDK:20659616~menuPK:1702202~pagePK:64168445~piPK:64168309~theSitePK:588921,00.html. *Note*: the Inspection Panel does not register anonymous Requests, although it protects the identity of Requesters, on request – *see* Inspection Panel Operating Procedures, April 2014, §§ 14, 18 & 25(a).

55 *See* De Wet's comments *at* note 16, Ch. 6.

56 World Bank (2011), e-Book. For an overview of redacted INT investigation reports, *see* http://go.worldbank.org/Y43I9YDP10.

57 World Bank (2011), e-Book.

"to addres[s] workplace problems such as disputes regarding staff rules, pay, career advancement, performance evaluation, and benefits."[58]

For instance, the CRS is comprised of the 'Office of Business Ethics' (EBC), which is tasked with ensuring "that staff members understand their ethical obligations to the World Bank Group as embodied in its core values and the various rules, policies, and guidelines under which they operate."[59] The EBC executes its mandate primarily by providing staff with training and communication programmes and by delivering a range of reports to "senior management."[60] The CRS also includes the 'Respectful Workplace Advisors Program', the 'Ombuds Services Office', the 'Office of Mediation Services', 'Peer Review Services',[61] as well as the 'Administrative Tribunal' (AT).

The Administrative Tribunal is the only World Bank accountability mechanism that executes its mandate by (what Romano calls) 'adjudicative means', since it "handles formal claims [filed "by members of the staff of the Bank Group alleging non-observance of their contracts of employment or terms of appointment"] and is an independent judicial forum of last resort staffed by seven external judges."[62] The AT also publishes its decisions, which are, unlike those of the other mechanisms discussed here, "final and binding."[63]

6.2.4   The Inspection Panel

Several aspects of the Inspection Panel's mandate have already been dealt with in other chapters;[64] hence, this section focuses specifically on the Inspection Panel's institutional independence, the institutional scope and complementary nature of the Panel's mandate and functions, as well as the issue of the Panel's 'non-legal' versus 'quasi-legal' nature.

Institutional independence
As with several of the accountability mechanisms mentioned in this section, the Inspection Panel, although described as an 'independent' body, exercises its mandate "in the shadow

---

58 *Id.* On the meaning of 'independent' in this context, *see* note 39, Ch. 6.
59 World Bank (2011), e-Book.
60 *Id.*
61 The Bank notes that the "Office of Mediation Services (MEF)" "report[s] directly to the [WBG] President's office and offer[s] impartial conflict resolution services to WBG staff" – *see:* http://go.world-bank.org/GUK5CUB9M1. On the World Bank Group's Ombuds Services office, which aims include: "[t]o help staff and managers resolve workplace problems"; and "[t]o alert management to trends and issues that should be addressed to improve the working environment and make recommendations for change", *see* http://go.worldbank.org/21EI772HD0.
62 World Bank (2011), e-Book.
63 For more information about the Administrative Tribunal, as well as its published cases, *see* http://web.worldbank.org/external/default/main?pagePK=7333373&contentMDK=22956391. *Also see* Romano's remarks *at* note 20, Ch. 6.
64 *See e.g.,* sections 1.2.1, 3.2.3, 4.1.2 & 4.3.2.

of hierarchy."[65] In case of the Panel, this 'independence' means that the Panel reports directly to the Board of Executive Directors and not to World Bank management, whose 'actions and omissions' it investigates.[66] Moreover, the Board has to authorize the Panel's investigations, whereas the Panel's (non-binding) findings and recommendations have to be approved by the Board – points of longstanding criticism.[67]

That being said, the Inspection's founding Resolution includes several provisions that are specifically aimed at ensuring that the Panel has a sufficient degree of functional or *de facto* independence – notably from Bank management. For example, individual Panel members can only be removed from office "for cause"; the Panel "shall be given such budgetary resources as shall be sufficient to carry out its activities"; and Inspection Panel staff is prohibited to work for the Bank, in any capacity, after concluding their term.[68]

Furthermore, as I have argued elsewhere, the Inspection Panel has consistently asserted its independence from Bank management and, on occasion, vis-à-vis the Board.[69] For example, as the Inspection Panel chair recently affirmed in his address to the Board on occasion of the Panel's presentation of its investigation report in *South Africa: Eskom Investment Support*:

> the Panel is an instrument of the Board and as such, subject to its oversight and guidance. To effectively perform its functions, however, it needs a degree of independence and credibility that up to now has been assured by this Board.

---

65 *See* De Wet's comments *at* note 14, Ch. 6.

66 *Also see* the Inspection Panel Operating Procedures, April 2014, § 6: "The Panel reports to the Board. The Board's Committee on Development Effectiveness (CODE) is designated as the main interlocutor for the Panel." *Note*, by contrast, that the Compliance Advisory Ombudsman of the IFC/MIGA reports directly to the World Bank Group President – *see*: http://www.cao-ombudsman.org/about/.

67 *See e.g.*, Roos (2001), p. 482 (arguing that "[...] the Panel is not a truly independent body despite these safeguards for independence. The Panel's independence is primarily 'counterbalanced by the fact that it only has advisory powers'."); Ananthanarayanan (2004) ("Despite the claim that the Panel is an autonomous arm of the Bank, it really is hindered by the fact that it can only recommend and not carry out remedial measures, as well as be on quite a tight leash from the Bank Board."); Wahi (2005-2006), p. 356 (describing IAMs as "semi-independent"; *and see* Bissell *in* Alfredsson & Ring (Eds.) (2001), p. 124 (arguing that the Inspection Panel's independence is "partial at best, with the Board often divided in supporting the statutory independence of the Panel from Management."). For similar comments, *also see* Circi (2006), pp. 4-5; Abouchar (1997); Carrascott & Guernsey (2008), pp. 600-601; Suzuki & Nanwani (2005-2006), pp. 215-216.

68 In this regard *see* Inspection Panel Resolution, §§ 5, 8 & 21. *But see* Dunkerton (1995), p. 240, who argues that the "authority and validity of the Panel" are brought into question since, in addition to the limitations in the Panel's mandate, "[...] the Panel's independence is further inhibited by the Bank President's control over the Panel's salaries, travel expense reimbursement, and selection of the Panel's executive secretary."

69 *See* Naudé Fourie (2009), pp. 193-210; *and* Naudé Fourie (2012), pp. 203-206. On the Panel's functional independence, *also see* Van Putten (2008), pp. 232-233 & 239-242. *Also see* Hunter (2003), pp. 207-208, noting that the initial three Inspection Panel members and its supporting staff "grasped quickly the need to elevate the Panel in the Bank hierarchy and to establish and defend its independence from Bank Management who tried to assert control over the process. Mr. Bröder led the panel deftly through delicate times, in the end leaving the Panel strong, independent, and credible to the communities affected by Bank projects."

If the Panel is to properly assess compliance with operational policies, the scope
of its investigations would include all the specific operational policies and
procedures currently in effect.[70]

In addition, as mentioned earlier, the Inspection Panel also formally notifies the Board
(and, since Inspection Panel practice material is published, also the broader public) of any
evidence of potential interference (whether originating from Management or borrowers),
both with respect to the filing of Requests for Inspection and the process of conducting
investigations.[71] In *Albania: Integrated Coastal Zone Management*, for instance, the
Inspection Panel referenced the provision in its Resolution, which stipulates: "[w]hen
requested by the Panel, Bank staff cooperate fully with the Panel in the discharge of its
functions."[72] In this instance, however, the Panel highlighted, it "has been confronted"

> with an array of difficulties in its access to relevant information, at times having
> to sort through misrepresentations, and in obtaining the requisite level of staff
> cooperation.[73]

On the other hand, examples such as these might also underscore the Panel's vulnerability
to political interference, as well as the "ambiguous relationship between the privileged
political decision-making body" and the Inspection Panel, "whose role," as Boisson de
Chazournes observes, "is to investigate dysfunctions within the Organization's activities"
and which are consequently "singled out within the institution."[74] In this regard, Boisson
de Chazournes adds that "[i]t is difficult" for the Board "to accept"

> that the very investigating body it has established – the Panel – should invoke
> its independence to ask its creator to make decisions that risk neglecting the
> sacrosanct harmony within its walls, established, notably, by the generalized
> recourse to consensus.[75]

---

70   *South Africa: Eskom Investment Support*, ER (IP Chairperson's Statement), p. 4.
71   *See* section 3.1.5.
72   Inspection Panel Resolution § 21.
73   *Albania: Integrated Coastal Zone Management* (2007) IR, p. xxvi.
74   Boisson de Chazournes *in* Treves et al. (Eds.) (2005), pp. 202-203.
75   *Id.*

Institutional scope and complementary nature of the Panel's mandate

The Inspection Panel is mandated to register 'Requests for Inspection' concerning all 'projects' (co-)financed by the IDA or IBRD[76] – but only projects that are in the design, appraisal or implementation stages of the project cycle.[77] 'Projects', furthermore, refers to all IDA/IBRD (co-)financed development projects, irrespective of the specific lending instrument or the modality of the project. This matter has been addressed over the course of several Inspection Panel investigations and appears to have been settled.[78]

However, concerning the more recent *Uzbekistan: Energy Loss Reduction* project (which was, at the time, "to be restructured to include an additional component for financing Assessment Studies and technical assistance"),[79] Bank management, in an emphatically worded statement, noted that it "takes issues with and views with extreme concern"

> any suggestion that Bank support for assessments or studies could make it liable to claims regarding actions or omissions under a future project concerning which it has made no decision regarding financial commitment. Such early assessment or studies are an important part of the Bank's role in increasing transparency and capacity in the decision-making process, ensuring the collection and dissemination of information, consideration of stakeholder concerns and issues and the incorporation of international technical expertise into project design. Management views as entirely inappropriate any attempt to allege that a violation of Bank policy and procedures has taken place, when the Bank is proposing to finance the very policy tools that are designed to avoid harm.[80]

Management added "that an Inspection Panel investigation at this stage"

> would undermine the Bank's policy by replacing the independent and integrated environmental and social assessment mandated by OP 4.01 with a limited review of the concerns and issues expressed by one stakeholder group. This practice could seriously undermine the Bank's ability to provide technical support and impartial advice to client countries, and to act as a knowledge bank.[81]

---

76 *Note*, claims concerning projects involving the IFC and/or MIGA fall within the mandate of the CAO – *see*: http://www.cao-ombudsman.org/about/. For the procedure followed when a Request concerns a project that is co-financed by the IFC, *see* the Inspection Panel Operating Procedures, April 2014, § 62.

77 On the project cycle, *see* section 4.1.2.

78 For a discussion of the debate between the Panel and Bank management about the definition of 'project' in the context of the Inspection Panel Resolution, *see* Naudé Fourie (2009), pp. 335-336.

79 *Uzbekistan: Energy Loss Reduction* (2010), MR, p. iv.

80 *Uzbekistan: Energy Loss Reduction* (2010), MR, §§ 53, 84.

81 *Id.*

Similarly, in *West Bank/Gaza: Red Sea-Dead Sea Water Conveyance Study Program* (RSDS), Bank management contested the eligibility of the Request, arguing that:

> (a) [...] the Study Program cannot be considered a 'project' as per Bank practice and falls outside the mandate of the Panel; (b) [...] the Study Program cannot be considered project preparation under Bank policy and practice; and (c) the harm alleged by the Requesters 'does not relate to the Study Program managed by the Bank, but rather focuses on potential harm that could derive from the construction, operation and/or failure of a possible Red Sea – Dead Sea Water Conveyance investment'. Hence, the Study Program, 'by its very nature', cannot result in direct harm.[82]

Management also noted that "[t]he World Bank Group produces and releases on average more than 5,000 studies [...] annually"

> that are purely knowledge products which are independent of a specific lending operation, or geared towards a potential project approach but insufficient to serve as part of the project appraisal or preparation.[83]

The Inspection Panel, on its part, rejected Management's contention that a study program of this nature could not "result in direct harm."[84] "[G]iven that the Study Program is part and parcel of the project preparation process, triggered by the proposed RSDS Project," the Panel argued, "shortcomings in the Study Program,"

> if not corrected, can potentially lead to shortcomings in the design of the RSDS Project. Therefore, in principle, potential harms that may result from the RSDS Project may plausibly be linked back to non-compliance in the Study Program.[85]

It should be noted, however, that the Requesters in the *RSDS* case highlighted what they perceived as a 'hesitancy' on the part of the Panel to register the Request, which the Requesters attributed to "the narrowing of the scope of the mandate of the Inspection Panel in the last year."[86] On submitting additional proof of prior communication with Bank management (as requested by the Panel), the Requesters registered their concern about the Panel Secretariat's insistence upon "additional actions on the part of the

---

82   *West Bank/Gaza: Red Sea-Dead Sea Water Conveyance Study Program* (2011), ER, § 26.
83   *West Bank/Gaza: Red Sea-Dead Sea Water Conveyance Study Program*, MR, § 12.
84   *West Bank/Gaza: Red Sea-Dead Sea Water Conveyance Study Program*, ER, § 69.
85   *Id.*
86   *West Bank/Gaza: Red Sea-Dead Sea Water Conveyance Study Program*, Request, §§ 8 & 10.

Requesters", which they considered to be evidence of Bank "management raising and advancing the burden of proof of a violation and making the mechanism as a whole more discouraging to affected parties."[87]

On the question whether Requests related to projects with a 'transboundary' element meet the eligibility criterion that requires Requesters to be "in the Borrower's territory",[88] the Inspection Panel has consistently supported the affirmative argument (often, countering the Management position in this regard). For example, as the Panel observed in *Uzbekistan: Energy Loss Reduction*, "this is not the first Project with transboundary effects"

> about which the Panel has received complaints. In this particular case, before registering the Request [...], the Panel considered the literal and legalistic reading of the eligibility criterion [...], and also took into account the relevant [Inspection Panel practice] precedents. These precedents adopted an interpretation which calls for a focus on *where* the material adverse effect of the Bank-financed Project occurs, even if it is in a territory that happens not to be that of the Borrower. This interpretation by Management and the Panel was previously accepted by the Board.[89]

Furthermore, as to the requirement that Requests for Inspection can only be considered 'eligible for Inspection' if there is a 'demonstrable causal link' between World Bank actions or omissions and actual or potential "material adverse effect" or 'harm',[90] this "technical eligibility" criterion has been a consistent point of contention between the Inspection Panel and Bank management.[91] For example, as Bank management argued in *Bangladesh: Jute Sector*, "[a]ll relevant IDA policies and procedures have been followed in the design and implementation of the JSAC [project],"

> and the Requesters have failed to demonstrate that any of the harms allegedly suffered by them are the result of the violation by IDA of its own policies and procedures in either the design or implementation of the JSAC. *The delays in*

---

87 *Id.*
88 *See* BP 17.55 (Inspection Panel), Appendix C, § 9(a).
89 *Uzbekistan: Energy Loss Reduction* (2010), IP Chair's Statement to the Board, 3 February 2011, pp. 1-2 (emphasis in original). For additional examples of projects with a 'transboundary element' or 'effect', *see Argentina/Paraguay: Yacyretá Hydroelectric Project* (1996); *Lesotho/South Africa: Highlands Water* (1999); and *Nigeria/Ghana: West African Gas Pipeline* (2006). For additional examples, *see* Naudé Fourie (2009), p. 233.
90 *See* Inspection Panel Resolution, § 12.
91 For descriptive statistics on the eligibility objections of Bank management, *see* Naudé Fourie (2014), pp. 592-593.

JSAC implementation of which the Requesters complain are the result of Government of Bangladesh inaction, and are not within the Inspection Panel's purview.[92]

"Since all projects and programmes financed by the Bank/IDA are carried out by the borrower or executing entity and *never* by the Bank/IDA itself," the Inspection Panel countered (thus, demonstrating that its mandate extends to the review of World Bank 'secondary obligations'),[93]

> if Management's allegation is to be accepted, then the Panel would lack jurisdiction in all cases where delays in the execution of a project or program has caused material and adverse effects to third parties.[94]

The Board's 1999 review of the Inspection Panel mechanism also reflected this conflict between Management and the Panel. In this regard, the Board specifically instructed the Inspection Panel that "the without-project situation should be used as the base case for comparison, taking into account what baseline information may be available", when reviewing the existence of the 'causal link'.[95] In particular, the Board added, "[n]on-accomplishments and unfulfilled expectations that do not generate a material deterioration compared to the without-project situation will not be considered as material adverse for this purpose."[96]

On this point, Shihata made the emphatic argument that, in order for any "existing or potential harm associated with a project" to be "attribute[d] to the Bank", "it is not enough to prove that the project is being or will be financed by the Bank."[97] Rather, the harm in question "must result, in whole or in part, from the Bank's own failure – either in accepting the project design, in appraising the project, or in the supervision of its implementation."[98] "Without this clear distinction and the causality related to it," Shihata emphasized,

---

92   *Bangladesh: Jute Sector (1996)*, MR, § 32 (emphasis added). *Note*, this example also illustrates how Management's comments can be viewed as indirect criticism of the Borrower – and also, how closely related Bank and Borrower obligations can be. On these matters, *see* section 4.3.2.

93   On the distinction between primary and secondary obligations, *see* section 4.3.2.

94   *Bangladesh: Jute Sector (1996)*, ER p. 4 – Box 1 (emphasis in original). For additional examples, *see Brazil: Itaparica Resettlement and Irrigation* (1997), ER, § 7; *Paraguay / Argentina: Yacyretá Hydroelectric Project* (2002), ER, § 18; *India: Madhya Pradesh Water Sector Restructuring* (2010/2011), MR, p. vi and ER, § 27.

95   *See* BP 17.55 (Inspection Panel), Appendix C, § 14. *Note*, this point also demonstrates the importance of collecting accurate baseline data – as discussed *in* section 14.2.

96   *Id.*

97   Shihata (2000), p. 49.

98   *Id.*

a confusion between the Bank's failure and the borrower's failure would always lead to divisive and possibly counterproductive discussions on the inspection function as perceived in the Resolution.[99]

The Inspection Panel's recently updated Operating Procedures seem to reflect a renewed emphasis on the necessity of proving a 'demonstrable causal link' between World Bank actions or omissions and harm. For instance, the Panel has expanded its 'admissibility criteria' – used to determine whether or not a filed Request will be 'registered' (which, in turn, is a prerequisite for further processing of the Request) – so as to include the requirement that "[a]t least one component of the project/program, which is the subject of the Request, can be *plausibly linked to the alleged harm*."[100] The Panel's updated Operating Procedures also stipulate that Investigation Reports should contain, among other things, "[a]n analysis"

> of relevant facts and information, and findings on issues of harm and compliance. If the Panel finds that an issue of alleged harm is not related to the Project or does not relate to a Bank policy or procedure, this will be stated in the report and the issue will not be further analyzed. [...] For each alleged issue of harm the report will provide basic factual information on the link to the project, document the Panel's findings with respect to the Bank's action or omission and its compliance with relevant policies and procedures, and assess the causal link between the Bank's non-compliance and the alleged harm.[101]

But the potential challenges involved in determining the existence of such a 'causal link' are illustrated very prominently in a case such as *Albania: Integrated Coastal Zone Management*. For example, in its initial response to this Request, Bank management challenged the Request's eligibility by arguing that "the demolition of the houses in the Request 'were not limited to the Project area, not caused by or linked to the Project, and were not done in anticipation of the Project or to achieve the Project objectives'."[102] Moreover, Management added, "[t]he demolitions could not have been carried out as part of, or as a result of, the Bank-financed SCDP, because the SCDP has not been prepared yet," and was, in fact, delayed.[103] Management also argued that "[t]he legal issues raised by the Requesters"

---

99 Shihata (2000), p. 49.
100 Inspection Panel Operating Procedures, April 2014, § 25 (emphasis added). This requirement is repeated in the guidelines followed by the Panel when (on finding a Request had met the 'technical eligibility criteria) deciding whether or not to recommend an investigation – *see* 43(a) (*Id.*).
101 Inspection Panel Operating Procedures, April 2014, § 63(c) & (d).
102 *Albania: Integrated Coastal Zone Management* (2007), ER, § 34.
103 *Albania: Integrated Coastal Zone Management* (2007), MR, §§ 29-31.

do not pertain to the application of the Bank's policies and the Bank cannot comment on the Government's application of its national laws outside the scope of the Project.[104]

Therefore, Management concluded, since the demolitions were not linked to the Project, the Requesters were "not entitled to benefits and rights under the Bank Policy on Involuntary Resettlement."[105] However, as various examples from the *Albania* case included throughout this book illustrate, the Inspection Panel's subsequent investigation convincingly refuted these arguments.[106]

With regard to the complementary nature of the Panel's mandate, Ibrahim Shihata argued that "[t]he Bank is an international organization [that is] is accountable to its members," which was demonstrated by the fact that it already had an extensive "internal system of accountability" (as reflected in the accountability mechanisms introduced earlier in this section) when the Panel was established in 1993.[107] The Bank had always operated, Shihata affirmed, based on the ('vertical') governance principle that "staff be accountable to the President, the President to the Executive Directors and the Executive Directors to the Board of Governors."[108] Therefore, "[t]he creation of the Inspection Panel," Shihata concluded, had merely *"complemented this internal system of accountability* by giving a direct access to affected parties before the Panel (which is a facility of the Bank)."[109]

The Inspection Panel mechanism therefore enhances World Bank management's accountability to the Board of Executive Directors, since, Shihata concluded, the Inspection Panel Resolution requires "Management to present to the Board recommendations for corrective action in case the Panel finds a serious violation of Bank policies and procedures" due to the actions of World Bank management and staff – not of borrowers – which has resulted (or has the potential to result in) material adverse effects ('harm') for project-affected people.[110] In other words, as Shihata put it: "The Panel's substantive jurisdiction is limited no doubt to matters that are attributed to the Bank and for which the Bank can take corrective measures."[111]

---

104 *Albania: Integrated Coastal Zone Management* (2007), MR, Annex 1, § 4. *Note*, Management had determined that the policy on Involuntary Resettlement was not applicable to the project – a decision the Panel questioned, as discussed *in* section 12.1.

105 *Albania: Integrated Coastal Zone Management* (2007), IR, p. xii. *Note*, this example also illustrates the ambiguity with which the phrase 'rights and interests' are used; *compare e.g.,* Schlemmer-Schulte' argument *in* note 52, Ch. 5, with the Inspection Panel's statement *in* note 115, Ch. 13.

106 *See e.g.,* sections 8.2.2 & 12.1. *Also see* WBG President Zoellick's comments *at* note 116, Ch. 6.

107 Shihata *in* Alfredsson & Ring (Eds.) (2001), pp. 43-44.

108 *Id.*

109 *Id.* (emphasis added).

110 *Id.*

111 Shihata (2000), p. 210. *Also see* the discussion in sections 7.1.2 & 7.1.3.

The complementary nature of the Panel's mandate is further illustrated by requirements contained in the Resolution specifying, for instance, that the Panel "shall have access to all staff who may contribute information and to all pertinent Bank records," as discussed earlier.[112] The Panel is also instructed to "consult as needed" with the IEG and IAD – as reflected in Inspection Panel practice.[113] For example, "[d]uring the course of [its] investigation" in *Albania: Integrated Coastal Zone Management*, the Inspection Panel noted that it had

> received allegations of corruption from the interviewed people in Albania, consistent with the news report mentioned above that certain people are using the Project and its resources to clear the area around Jale for a tourist resort.[114]

Although "the Panel only informs about, but does not evaluate the allegations of corruption," the Panel nevertheless highlighted "the selective nature of the demolitions carried out by the Construction Police" and noted that this "seems to support the desire to clear a certain area."[115] Significantly, on the basis of the Panel's investigation report, (then) World Bank Group President, Robert Zoellick instructed "the Bank's Acting General Counsel [to] investigate matters," who, in turn, "referred matters to the Bank's Department of Institutional Integrity (INT)."[116] And in *Brazil: Rondônia Natural Resources*, the Inspection Panel noted that "[a] basic recommendation of the OED Report" on the predecessor project "was that much better and more extensive data gathering had to occur"

> before launching follow-on efforts, with particular criticism leveled at the state of knowledge about agro-ecological and socio-economic realities in Rondonia.[117]

The Resolution also instructs the Panel to consult the Bank's General Legal Counsel when a compliance matter is "related to the Bank's rights and obligations."[118] However, as Freestone points out, "the Panel has only rarely sought such advice – indeed, on only two occasions since 1993, even though", Freestone argues, "a number of its Reports"

---

112 Inspection Panel Resolution, § 21.
113 *Id.*
114 *Albania: Integrated Coastal Zone Management* (2007), IR, p. xxii.
115 *Id.*
116 *Albania: Integrated Coastal Zone Management* (2007), WB Press Release, 17 February 2009.
117 *Brazil: Rondônia Natural Resources Management* (1995), Additional Review, § 46. On issue related to baseline data collection, *see* section 14.2.
118 Inspection Panel Resolution, § 15.

inevitably rely heavily on interpretations of the policies under consideration. In at least two situations the Panel seems to have interpreted a policy.[119]

However, as Nathan comments, "[t]o be seen to be independent of the Bank,"

> the Panel must necessarily distance itself from other departments of the Bank, including the Legal Department. Because of a requirement that the Panel 'must seek the advice of the Bank's Legal Department on matters related to the Bank's rights and obligations', constant contact with the Legal Department may be unavoidable. Therefore, the Panel's eventual authority and independence will depend very much on how it handles its relationship with the Bank's Legal Department.[120]

'Formal' and 'informal' functions

The Inspection Panel executes its mandate through a wide range of formal and informal functions, supported by a standardized process.[121] 'Formal' functions, as described here, refer to those functions that have been specifically set out in the Inspection Panel Resolution, whereas 'informal' functions have been developed through Inspection Panel practice and have subsequently been approved by the Board – whether explicitly or implicitly, as a result of the Board's 'no comment' decision-making procedure.[122]

By this distinction, the Inspection Panel has only two formal functions, namely: 'fact-finding' and 'compliance review'.[123] "In response to complaints from project-affected communities," as the Panel describes these two functions, it "independently investigates"

---

119 Freestone (2013), p. 59. *Note*, the author refers to *China: Western Poverty Reduction (Qinghai)* (1999) (on the matter of developing separate or 'standalone' IPDPs – as discussed *in* section 13.2.1); and *Uganda: Power Projects* (2001) (on whether regional EAs are a policy requirement – as discussed *in* section 14.2.2).

120 Nathan (1995), p. 139. *Also see* the Panel's exchange with the Bank's Legal Department in the *Honduras: Land Administration* case, discussed *in* section 5.3.1.

121 For a schematic overview of the Inspection Panel process, *see* the Inspection Panel Operating Procedures, April (2014), p. 8.

122 *See* Shihata (2000), pp. 37-41; *and* Bradlow & Naude Fourie (2013), pp. 41-42. *Note*, on the adoption of new 'informal' functions as expansion of the Inspection Panel's institutional influence by means of this procedure, *see* Bradlow & Naude Fourie (2013), p. 58; *and* Naude Fourie (2009), pp. 222-225. And on the distinction between 'formal and 'informal' norms, *also see* Toope's comments *in* section 2.3.

123 On the value of Panel's the fact-finding function, *see e.g.*, Brown Weiss (2010), p. 487: "Affected people may have important information to convey, both before, during, and after the accountability mechanism acts. During field visits, one can verify the authenticity of those who complain, and ensure that one does not play into a local political agenda. Going to the field makes it possible to see what is really happening. For example, we were assured by the official monitor appointed as part of a forest concession reform project in Cambodia that no illegal logging was taking place, that the largest illegal log would be one carried on a motorcycle. But the next day or so, when we were upcountry, we encountered a large logging truck carrying big logs (a photo appears in the Investigation Report)." For a critical view of the value of the compliance review function, *see e.g.*, Umaña (1998), p. 326, who argues that compliance review "can be described as a 'policing' function,

whether Bank Management has complied with its operational policies and procedures in projects financed by IBRD/IDA, and whether harm has resulted from noncompliance.[124]

Furthermore, the Inspection Panel notes that it "provides an independent, technically based check and balance for the Board on situation(s) relating to compliance and harm in project operations,"[125] which is also why the Inspection Panel contracts independent subject matter experts to assist them over the course of its investigations, as noted earlier.[126]

Over time, the Inspection Panel adopted a few 'informal' functions (which are not reflected in the Inspection Panel's founding Resolution), notably: 'problem-solving'; contributing towards 'institutional learning' and 'policy advice'; and 'monitoring' the implementation of 'Action Plans' adopted in the aftermath of Inspection Panel investigations. The Inspection Panel's functions will be discussed in more detail in the context of the realization and enforcement of accountability outcomes.[127] Suffice it to note at this point that the Panel's 'informal functions', in particular, underscore the complementary nature of the Panel's role, as reflected in the language used by the Panel to describe its functions.

For example, when describing the formal functions of fact-finding and compliance, the Panel states that it "independently *investigates*" and "*provides* a check and balance;" whereas, with respect to problem-solving, the Panel explains:

> *the Panel process as a whole plays a critical role in helping to resolve* problems facing project-affected people. Problem-solving may occur at various stages: preregistration (affected people must approach Management first); eligibility; investigation; and follow-up. The Panel process *places responsibility and creates opportunities* for Management to take effective responsive actions to address problems.[128]

On institutional learning, the Inspection Panel states that the "Investigation Reports and Management Responses," produced over the course of the Inspection Panel process, "include observations and lessons learned, which *promote* corporate learning and trans-

---

[which] has proven to be less useful to the Board since the Panel's 'verdict' does not lead – nor should it lead – to any action beyond correcting failures in project design or execution." On the discussion of the 'value' of the Panel's contribution towards the realization of specific outcomes, *also see* section 7.2.

124 Inspection Panel Annual Report 2011/2012, p. xiv (emphasis added).
125 *Id.*
126 *See e.g.*, Naudé Fourie (2009), p. 260. *And see* section 5.4.
127 *See* sections 7.1 & 7.2.
128 Inspection Panel Annual Report 2011/2012, p. xiv (emphasis added).

parency through their publication,"[129] and the "availability of the Panel *creates incentives for the institution to comply*"

> with policies and procedures, including social and environmental safeguards; *supports* overall Bank mission to fight poverty; and *helps the Bank avoid* actions causing reputational risk.[130]

And, concerning monitoring, the Panel notes that it "*promotes* transparency in Bank operations"

> through publication of reports and findings, and by serving as the independent venue for affected people to raise concerns to the highest decision-making levels of the Bank.[131]

Finally, it is important to note that the World Bank's operational policy framework forms the only basis for the Inspection Panel's fact-finding and compliance review functions – an aspect of its mandate which "creates potential challenges", since, as the Independent Accountability Mechanisms Network argues, "[p]eople can be harmed by IFI-funded projects"

> even when all relevant policies have been followed or the type of harm alleged is not covered by an existing IFI policy. This may leave project-affected people without a redress mechanism, unless other avenues are available at local, national, or international levels.[132]

As the Inspection Panel emphasized in *India: NTPC Power* (in response to an invitation that was extended to the Panel, during their site visit, "to visit villages of unaffected people as to compare conditions in the colonies with them"):

> There are certainly conditions far worse in India and elsewhere in the world than those in the colonies and there is no doubt that there are villages in the area where people are worse off. However, *the yardstick the Panel is asked to use* is whether people involuntary displaced appear at first instance, and without

---

129 Inspection Panel Annual Report 2011/2012, p. xv.
130 *Id.*
131 Inspection Panel Annual Report 2011/2012, p. xiv (emphasis added).
132 Independent Accountability Mechanisms Network (2012), p. 26.

further investigation, to be adversely affected, or harmed by the Project *as measured by the standards of the Bank's resettlement policy.*[133]

On the other hand, as the previous chapter illustrated, the Panel has also developed approaches in which it incorporates references to the norms contained in other normative frameworks – particularly, international legal norms.[134]

A non-legal mechanism or one with 'quasi-legal' characteristics?

"There was much debate at the bank about the 'judicial' character of the Inspection Panel," especially in the years following its establishment.[135] "I was often told that the panel is 'not a court'," as Van Putten, a former Inspection Panel member, observes.[136] "Once, in a lunch meeting," for instance,

> the panel discussed its work and procedures and experiences with a large group of senior management. In response, one manager asked, 'So you guys are a sort of United States Supreme Court?' Sometimes, the word 'semi-judicial' was used.[137]

As a non-lawyer, Van Putten notes that this debate "[n]evertheless, [...] highlighted" that the Inspection Panel procedure "indeed" has a "judicial structure."[138] Moreover, Van Putten adds, "my experience with the working methods of the panel" suggests that they "are definitely based on judicial systems," for example,

> [t]he structure of the panel's reporting is clearly of a legal nature, as is the system of hearings held during investigations (or 'interrogations,' as some have said) inside the bank or during field visits.[139]

Indeed, the influence of legal concepts and processes is certainly visible in the Inspection Panel Resolution, the Panel's eligibility and investigation reports, as well as in formal

---

133 *India: NTPC Power* (1997), ER, § 45 (emphasis added). *But see* Shihata's comments *at* note 22, Ch. 5.
134 *See* sections 5.1.1 & 5.3.
135 Van Putten (2008), p. 85.
136 *Id.*
137 *Id.*
138 Van Putten (2008), p. 85. *But also see* Van Putten (2008), p. xxiii: "That most studies about accountability mechanisms, compliance mechanisms, and review panels – and more specifically the Inspection Panel – have been done by lawyers [is] a hindrance and challenge. So far, accountability mechanisms have been structured mostly within a rather legalistic framework." On the negative connotations of the formalist paradigm, *see* note 150, Ch. 2.
139 *Id.*

Management responses.[140] In *West Bank/Gaza: Red Sea-Dead Sea Water Conveyance Study Program*, for instance, Bank management argued that the Request "fails to comply with the fundamental *jurisdictional* considerations required under the Resolution" on several grounds (noted earlier).[141] As the Inspection Panel's body of practice grew, furthermore, the Panel has increasingly referenced its findings in previous investigations. For example, the Panel noted in *Peru: Lima Urban Transport* that "[s]everal other findings from this investigation resonate[d] with Panel findings in other investigations."[142] For example,

> the Panel's finding in this Project that supervision related to the District of Barranco was not consistently up to speed with events until Barranco residents started to raise their complaints, is similar to the Panel's findings in its investigation of the Ghana UESP II and other Projects relating to Bank failures to identify and adequately respond to issues and problems as they emerged. Also, the Panel's findings relating to dissemination of information and consultation with the affected people in Barranco, especially in the early phases of the Project, is consistent with a recurrent set of findings in Panel investigations related to noncompliance with Bank policy requirements on consultation and disclosure of information.[143]

The Inspection Panel also protects the integrity of its procedure (as well as its institutional independence), much like a judicial institution would.[144] In *Lesotho/South Africa: Highlands Water*, for example, the Panel notified the Board of an "unauthorized use of the contents of the Request."[145] "Under the Resolution," the Panel noted, Management is "invite[d]"

> to deliver a formal Response to a Request for Inspection. In this case, Bank Management discussed and dismissed the allegations in the Request in presentations to the Executive Directors, and it did so on three separate occasions. These occasions were: (i) on April 30, 1998 in the text of the PAD circulated

---

140 *See e.g.*, Inspection Panel Resolution, § 12: "[...] affected party must demonstrate that its *rights or interests* have been or are likely to be directly affected by an action or omission of the Bank as a result of a failure of the Bank to follow its operational policies and procedures with respect to the design, appraisal and/or implementation of a project financed by the Bank (including situations where the Bank is alleged to have failed in its follow-up on the borrower's obligations under loan agreements with respect to such policies and procedures) provided in all cases that such failure has had, or threatens to have, a *material adverse effect* (emphasis added). In this regard, *also see* Shihata's analysis of the Inspection Resolution, especially of the eligibility criteria – *see* Shihata (2000), pp. 55-70.
141 *West Bank/Gaza: Red Sea-Dead Sea Water Conveyance Study Program* (2011), ER, § 26 (emphasis added).
142 *Peru: Lima Urban Transport* (2009), IR, § 216.
143 *Id.* In this regard, *also see* section 1.2.1, *and see* sections 11.1 & 15.2.
144 *Also see* note 69, Ch. 6.
145 *Lesotho/South Africa: Highlands Water* (1998), ER, p. 7.

to the Executive Directors; (ii) at a Board meeting on May 21, 1998 – the date initially scheduled for approval of the loan; and (iii) at the meeting on June 4, 1998 when the Executive Directors approved financing for Phase 1B.[146]

"Such serious disregard of the Panel process threatens its integrity," the Panel emphasized, and while "[t]he Panel is not a judicial entity," the Bank's actions in this instance, "apart from ignoring the Panel's procedures,"

> would also appear to amount to a serious abuse of reasonable due process in any context. It must be recalled that there are two parties involved in the Panel process – the Requesters and the Bank Management. The Requesters do not have any direct access to those who were to vote on the loan they questioned. The Board did not have the benefit of the Panel's independent assessment of the eligibility of the Request.[147]

That said, several features of the Inspection Panel's mandate and process point to its 'pragmatic', 'flexible' – and thus, as some would argue, its 'non-legal' – nature. For instance, Bissell and Nanwani note that, "[a]s a first step" towards "implementing the legalese of the WBIP Resolution," shortly after its establishment, "the Panel condensed the requirements for filing a request for inspection into a half-page set of questions, subsequently translated into multiple languages."[148] Whereas in *Tanzania: Emergency Power,* the Inspection Panel expressed its concern about the "formalistic approach of the [Management] reply," in which Management argued, at length, against the eligibility of the Request.[149] "This approach," the Panel argued, "appears to introduce additional eligibility requirements"

> that would modify the Resolution which is the sole prerogative of the Executive Directors. The Resolution was designed to establish a non-juridical forum with nonlegalistic requirements and procedures to help direct access by adversely affected people on the ground. Experience to date suggests that existing requirements, if strictly interpreted and applied, could become far too complex to enable adversely affected people themselves – often poor and illiterate – to file a legitimate claim.[150]

---

146 *Id.*

147 *Id.* In this regard, *also see* section 3.1.5.

148 Bissell & Nanwani (2009), p. 28. *Note,* this example also demonstrates the negative connotations of the formalist paradigm, as discussed *e.g., at* note 150, Ch. 2.

149 *Tanzania: Emergency Power* (1995), ER, § 8. For Management's arguments against the eligibility of this Request, *see* MR, § 11.

150 *Tanzania: Emergency Power* (1995), ER, § 8. *Also see Bangladesh: Jute Sector* (1996), ER, p. 4 – Box 1; and *Brazil: Itaparica Resettlement and Irrigation* (1997), ER, §§ 12-25, on the debate between the Panel and

Some commentators argue, on the other hand, that citizen-driven, independent accountability mechanisms such as the Inspection Panel, while non-judicial in nature, can be more effective in fulfilling their functions if they were to adopt certain judicial characteristics.

Boisson de Chazournes argues, for instance, that the Inspection Panel's ability to "contribut[e] to fairness and accountability" "would in fact be strengthened with an increased formalization" of its process and methods.[151] Such 'formalization' could include, for example, a "[r]esort to comparative jurisprudence" and to "legal interpretative methods" that could support the Panel in deciding "on the eligibility of a complaint," in "interpreting the operational policies and procedures," as well as in facilitating the drafting of "recommendations to the Executive Directors."[152] "Such processes," Boisson de Chazournes adds, could furthermore "facilitate the building-up of the decision-making process onto decisions and recommendations of the various [World Bank] organs" while also "favour consistency and predictability."[153]

Other commentators (including this author)[154] have argued that the Inspection Panel has indeed, over time, come to display many of the characteristics of judicial institutions, notably as a result of the interpretative methods they employ – a matter that will also be addressed in the next section.[155] Hence, descriptors such as 'quasi-judicial' or "judicial-style accountability" have come to be used with respect to the Inspection Panel.[156] Kingsbury, for instance, ascribes the fact that accountability mechanisms such as the Inspection Panel are becoming 'more like courts' to the "general tendency toward 'judicialization', which often appears"

> where a triangle is formed between complainant, respondent, and institutional adjudicator, [because it] sets up a natural dynamic for the panel to enhance its jurisprudence and its own role, supported by legally oriented NGOs and potentially by some sections of Bank staff whose work such an approach vindicates.[157]

Hence, it is perhaps more accurate to argue that citizen-driven accountability mechanisms such as the Inspection Panel have a hybrid non-judicial/quasi-judicial nature. As Nathan

---

Management about the eligibility criterion that the Panel cannot investigate closed projects, or projects for which '95 % of the loan amount has been disbursed'. On the negative connotations of the formalist paradigm, *see* note 150, Ch. 2.

151 Boisson de Chazournes *in* Alfredsson & Ring (Eds.) (2001), pp. 83-84.

152 *Id.*

153 *Id.*

154 *See* Naudé Fourie (2009), pp. 226-250.

155 *See* section 6.3.

156 *See e.g.*, United Nations (2002), n. 1 *at* p. 116.

157 Kingsbury (1999), p. 332; on normative development as an outcome of compliance review processes, *see* section 7.1.6.

observes, for instance, the Panel's non-judicial nature is reflected in the fact that it is "described as an Inspection *Panel* rather than a *Tribunal*", that it "is very much left to itself in the adoption of its own procedures, rules of evidence and standards of proof",[158] that its "subject-matter could involve highly technical issues",[159] and, finally, that it "is required to submit a *report* rather than an *award*".[160] Hence, it can be argued that "the Panel is a team of 'inspectors' conducting a plain enquiry which ends in the filing of a technical report and, therefore, is not intended to be a judicial or quasi-judicial body."[161]

On the other hand, Nathan adds, the Panel's quasi-judicial nature is reflected in the fact that an Inspection Panel Request, "in effect," concerns "a dispute between an affected party and the Bank" and that "Bank management has to respond to the charges within a specified period."[162] It is also demonstrated by the fact that "the Panel conducts the investigations within the Bank as well as in the country in which the project is located, including hearing testimonies from both sides", and in the fact that "the findings of the Panel have some binding character."[163] Moreover, while "[t]he fact that the [Inspection] members initially [and subsequently] appointed to the Panel are not lawyers would signify, at least from the point of view" of the Board, "that the Panel is not to be regarded as a quasi-judicial body,"

> but as a kind of team to prepare technical reports for their information, following an enquiry which is conducted in a fair and just manner in layman's terms[,]

there is also "nothing to stop the Panel from hiring lawyers"

> to help the Panel in its work and to conduct its enquiries in a judicial manner if it so chooses, in the interests of all concerned, in order to ensure that people's rights and interests are not injured by Bank operations. Because the subject-matter is about the rights and interests of people, any inspection conducted by the Panel must necessarily include examination of witnesses, and cross-examination where necessary, to exonerate Bank staff and managers from charges of infraction of their duties.[164]

---

158 In this regard, *see* section 6.3.
159 As illustrated by many of the examples included throughout Part II of this book.
160 Nathan (1995), pp. 137-138 (emphasis added).
161 *Id.*
162 *Id.*
163 *Id.*
164 Nathan (1995), p. 146. For a statistical overview of the professional qualifications of Inspection Panel members, *see* Naudé Fourie (2014), p. 567.

Hence, it can also be argued that the establishment of the Inspection Panel, as the first citizen-driven international accountability mechanism of its kind, "signify the creation of a new international quasi-judicial organ, albeit unconventional one, with severe limitations."[165]

Hansungule observes that the Panel is clearly "not a court of law and not even like a court of law;" however, it is nevertheless significant that the Panel as well as "Bank officials frequently like to stress this point as if to prove"

> that it is in fact a kind of a court of law. The fact that it is not a court of law or like a court is sometimes denied so often by Bank staff as to suggest that this was in fact the idea behind its establishment.[166]

More important, perhaps, is the likelihood that the Inspection Panel mechanism is "confused with being a court of law in the minds of ordinary members of the public in various countries who will reflect upon it"[167] and that this 'confusion' will result in unrealistic expectations among Requesters. "[I]n the real everyday life of an average citizen," Hansungule elaborates, "the mechanism that immediately springs to mind"

> in connection with a facility for complaints is a court. Few people will envisage a different concept than a court when thinking of a complaint resolving machinery. The same occurs with international and national human rights protection bodies set up to protect human rights. Most people have time and again confused them with courts and therefore criticise their failure to deliver in the discharge of their objectives from this point of view. Court are what are known best for resolving conflicts between subject and national and international persons.[168]

Indeed, Inspection Panel practice also reflects the effects of such expectations. In *Democratic Republic of Congo: Private Sector Development*, for example, the Panel noted that it had "observed" during one of its field visits "that the Requesters generally were not aware of the Panel's role, and were hoping"

> for some sort of "court ruling" which would be binding upon key actors, the World Bank in particular. The Panel, therefore, in every meeting with the

---

165 *Id.*
166 Hansungule *in* Alfredsson & Ring (Eds.) (2001), p. 150.
167 *Id.*
168 *Id.*

Requesters, carefully explained its role in an attempt to forestall further prolif-eration of unrealistic expectations.[169]

Ultimately, as Hansungule concludes, "the Panel should be regarded not so much for what it was intended at the time of its establishment than for what it can do in the current cir-cumstances."[170] "It is understood that it was not [intended] to be a court of law," but this does not mean it "cannot develop into a court of law which it should if this is how it can best realise its objectives."[171] "On the other hand," Hansungule adds, "we should fight the temptation"

> to view it solely as a court of law. It should be regarded for what it is because it is only if we do this that it would be possible to prevent being tempted to entertain inflated expectations from the Panel which it can simply not render.[172]

6.3 WHAT CONSTITUTES 'COMPLIANCE' WITH THE BANK'S OPERATIONAL POLICY FRAMEWORK? COMPETING APPROACHES TO POLICY APPLICATION AND COMPLIANCE ASSESSMENT

The World Bank's operational policy framework does not necessarily provide clear-cut answers on how the policies should be applied in development practice – nor, for that matter, on how compliance with these policies should be assessed. It is clear, however, that the policies continue to vary in terms of the level of detail they contain, as well as their degree of specificity – and, arguably, also the level of obligation they invoke. While some of the policies would seem to substantiate Shihata's original contention that the policies were not meant to be strict "marching orders" issued at the beginning of a project, others appear to be more clearly aimed at regulating a particular policy area.[173]

However, it is important to note that, as 'normative text' (that is, text containing obli-gation, albeit in different forms and degrees, intended to influence behaviour) the opera-tional policies invariably require *interpretation* – firstly, by those tasked to apply the text in practice (Bank management and staff), and, secondly, by those mandated to assess the

---

169 *Democratic Republic of Congo: Private Sector Development* (2009), ER (No. 2), § 110.
170 Hansungule *in* Alfredsson & Ring (Eds.) (2001), p. 151.
171 *Id.* In this regard, *also see* Naudé Fourie (2009) who comments (at p. 13) that several "(now, powerful) national courts started off having no or very limited formal powers of [judicial] oversight" – including "[h]ighly respected institutions such as the Dutch *Raad van State*, the French *Conseil d'État*, and *Conseil Constitutionnel*".
172 Hansungule *in* Alfredsson & Ring (Eds.) (2001), p. 151.
173 Shihata (2000), pp. 41-49. *Compare e.g.*, the level of detail in OP 4.01 (Environmental Assessment) with OP. 13.05 (Project Supervision).

application of the policies (internal accountability mechanisms) in order to determine compliance with the normative text contained in them.[174]

The Inspection Panel Resolution does not provide much guidance in this regard either. The Resolution merely stipulates that the Panel's investigation report "shall consider all relevant facts, and shall conclude with the Panel's findings on whether the Bank has complied with all relevant Bank policies and procedures."[175] Whereas in its 1996 review of the Inspection Panel, the Board affirmed that the Panel's mandate "does not extend to reviewing the consistency of the Bank's practice with *any* of its policies and procedures, but, as stated in the Resolution," the Panel's investigation has to be

> limited to cases of alleged *failure by the Bank to follow its operational policies and procedures* with respect to the design, appraisal and/or implementation of projects, including cases of alleged failure by the bank to follow-up on the borrowers' obligations under loan agreements, with respect to such policies and procedures.[176]

As for the matter of assessing whether there is causal link between 'harm' and World Bank non-compliance, noted earlier,[177] the Board emphasized that conducting such an assessment "in the context of the complex reality of a specific project can be difficult"; it therefore cautioned that "the Panel will have to exercise carefully its judgment on these matters, and be guided by Bank policies and procedures where relevant."[178]

The Inspection Panel's recently updated Operating Procedures provide a bit more detail in describing the "methods used by the Investigation Team to support its fact-finding and analysis", which include:

a. Reviewing and researching Bank project documents and files. Management makes available to the Panel all available project documentation.
b. Visiting the borrowing country, project sites and project areas of impact.
c. Requesting or receiving information from the Requesters, affected people, government officials, project authorities, and others likely to have relevant information. The latter may include representatives of other development and UN organizations, non- governmental organizations and experts.

---

174 Indeed, this principle forms the basis of all legal doctrinal scholarship. *See e.g.*, 'S. Taekema, Relative Autonomy: A Characterisation of the Discipline of Law', *in* Taekema & Van Klink (Eds.), Law and Method: Interdisciplinary Research into Law, Mohr Siebeck (2011), who notes (at p. 45): "All standard sources for lawyers are texts [...]."
175 Inspection Panel Resolution, § 22.
176 Inspection Panel Resolution, § 12 (emphasis added).
177 *See* section 6.2.4.
178 BP 17.55 (Inspection Panel), Annex C, §. 14.

    d. Interviews with individual Bank staff. Management enables the Panel to talk to staff involved with the project, both past and present.

    e. Consulting scientific literature and publications relevant to the issues of harm raised in the Request.

    f. Any other relevant methods the Team considers appropriate to the specific investigation.[179]

It would therefore appear that the "actual course that the Panel will take in its investigations will depend on how the Panel members view their role and on the procedures they adopt in their enquiries."[180] In other words, in forming conclusions as to the approaches to compliance review employed by the Inspection Panel it would be best to analyze Inspection Panel practice. It can be more challenging, however, to find "sufficient empirical information" as to the approaches employed by World Bank management and staff when applying the operational policy framework.[181] For instance, as Bradlow and Naudé Fourie observe, it can be "difficult to know," whether operational issues "are more likely to be attributable to non-compliance with the operational policies", "to shortcomings in the policies themselves," or whether such issues have been specifically caused by the manner in which the relevant policies had been applied.[182] Arguably, "[t]he most direct evidence of non-compliance" – and of the Bank's approach to applying its operational policy framework – "comes from the cases that reach the Inspection Panel,"[183] although, as noted in the Introduction to this book, Inspection Panel practice cannot claim to offer a complete window thereto.[184]

    With this caveat in mind, this section identifies four competing approaches to policy application and compliance assessment, as illustrated in Figure 11, namely: (1) *flexibility* versus *consistency* in the application of the operational policy framework across different projects, and among different borrowers; (2) *broader* versus *narrower* 'margins of discretion' in the application of specific policy provisions; (3) the employment of *expansive* versus *restrictive* interpretation techniques in the application of specific policy provisions; and

---

179 *See* Inspection Panel Operating Procedures, April (2014), § 54. For an example of how the Inspection Panel combines such methods in fulfilling its fact-finding and compliance review functions, *see e.g., Argentina: Santa Fe Road Infrastructure* (2007), IR, § 169: "In the same discussion with the Works Manager, the Panel sought to determine whether he was following the RAP guidelines related to the rights of those whose land has been expropriated. The Works Manager confirmed that before any construction work is started, he is required to confirm with the PIU that compensation for the land in question has been paid or a legal process is in place and the cash compensation deposited in an escrow account. This information indicates that the Bank has ensured that the Borrower is acting in conformity with the provisions of the legal agreements signed with the Bank with regard to one of the main provisions of OP 4.12, namely paragraph 10, which states that "taking of land and related assets may take place only after compensation has been paid."

180 Nathan (1995), p. 146.

181 Bradlow & Naudé Fourie (2013), pp. 27-28.

182 *Id.*

183 *Id.*

184 *See* section 1.2.1.

(4) the conception of compliance as meeting *procedural* and *substantive* requirements. The employment of these approaches can result in competing conceptions as to 'what constitutes compliance' in particular circumstances and, consequently, have a significant effect on the manner in which demands and expectations about the content and scope of the World Bank obligations unfold in development practice.

Figure 11   Competing Approaches to Operational Policy Application and Compliance Assessment

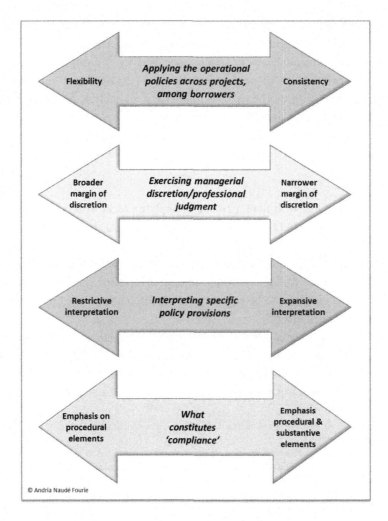

6.3.1   Flexible versus consistent application – across projects and among borrowers

An approach to policy application that emphasizes the need for flexibility is based on the argument that development needs can differ vastly across various national and sub-national levels, within project-affected communities, and also among borrowers. A flexible approach, furthermore, can be necessitated by the complex reality in which World Bank-financed development projects are designed, planned, prepared, assessed, financed and implemented, which invariably requires difficult 'trade-off' decisions to be made.[185] Whereas significant variations in the degree of institutional and/or professional capacity of different borrowers and/or their project implementing agencies could also require a flexible approach, especially in light of the Bank's commitment to develop such capacity.[186] A differentiated approach, moreover, fosters borrower "ownership for sustainable development" and improves the Bank's relationships with its clients – also because it arguably makes it more effective and/or efficient for clients 'to do business with the Bank'.[187]

This approach is reflected, for instance, in Bank management's argument in *China: Western Poverty Reduction (Qinghai)* that the "level and quality of preparation and analysis for this Project were"

> very much in line with Bank practice in applying social and environmental policies to projects *in China* in the context of its political and social systems.[188]

Therefore, a flexible approach to policy application and compliance assessment would allow for appropriate levels of differentiation among borrowers and across different projects, although it would also have to be cognizant of the international legal principle of non-discrimination, for instance.[189]

Viewed from the other end of the spectrum, however, while it may be acknowledged that there is a need for flexibility, as the Inspection Panel argued in *China: Western Poverty Reduction (Qinghai)*, it would be "an entirely different matter to suggest that experience and [country] precedent can *determine what is required by the policies*."[190] And although

---

185 For examples of project scenarios involving trade-offs, *see* in particular Ch. 9.

186 *See* sections 4.2.2 and 8.3.

187 *See e.g., China: Western Poverty Reduction (Qinghai)* (1999), IR, § 40. *Also see* the emphasis placed on country 'ownership' in the OECD's Paris Declaration on Aid Effectiveness, available at: http://www.oecd. org/dac/effectiveness/45827300.pdf. *Also see* David Dollar's comment *in* note 12, Ch. 1.

188 *China: Western Poverty Reduction (Qinghai)* (1999), IR, § 14 (emphasis added).

189 *See e.g.,* Bradlow *in* note 133, Ch. 5.

190 *China: Western Poverty Reduction Project* (1999), IR, § 13 (emphasis added). *Note*, Management defended the decision to assign a lower risk category to the project by arguing, amongst other things, that the decision was based on experience "with [...] a large number of similar integrated agricultural development projects financed by the Bank in China over the last 10 years." *See* IR, pp. xv and § 43; *also see* IR, § 33. In its official

the policies clearly allowed "room for some flexibility and interpretation," as the Panel concluded in the *Qinghai* case, they "cannot possibly be taken"

> to authorize a level of 'interpretation' and 'flexibility' that would permit those who must follow these directives to simply override the portions of the directives that are clearly binding.[191]

Furthermore, it can be argued that the consistent application of the operational policy framework – especially of the safeguard policies – is important to ensure consistent quality across the Bank's development-lending portfolio, which, in turn, is critical to ensure World Bank accountability 'for harm' and 'for performance'.[192] A differentiated approach, more-over, might not necessarily be what the Bank's clients prefer, especially not if there is a perception that 'differentiation' is a smokescreen for the preferential treatment of some borrowers, which would contravene the principle of non-discrimination.[193] In fact, consis-tency of application might be in the interest of the Bank's borrower-clients since it can facilitate a clearer understanding of what their specific obligations involve.[194] In addition, from the perspective of project-affected people and (prospective) Inspection Panel Requesters, consistent application of the Bank's operational policy framework across projects – as well as consistency in the manner in which the Inspection Panel assesses compliance of particular policies – can serve to clarify their 'rights and interests' in terms of the policies.[195] This, in turn, can enable potential Requesters to make an informed decision on, firstly, whether they have a potential 'Request' that could be filed at the Inspection Panel, and, secondly, on the likelihood of them succeeding in having their concerns addressed by filing a Request for Inspection.

Generally speaking, Bank management, in its formal responses to Requests and Inspection Panel investigations, tends to employ a flexible approach, as described here; whereas the Inspection Panel more often emphasizes the need for (at least) a meaningful degree of consistency in the application of the operational policy framework – across projects and among borrowers. It should be noted, however, that these positions are typically

---

response to the investigation report, Management commented: "Many of the Panel's findings appear [...] to be based on an application of elements of each policy as legally binding rules, allowing for little or no flexibility or room for judgment." *Also see* MR to IR, § 20. On the negative connotations of the formalist paradigm, *see* note 150, Ch. 2. On best practice as a source of normativity, *see* section 5.4.

191 *China: Western Poverty Reduction (Qinghai)* (1999), IR, § 37.

192 For a discussion of the reasons behind the Bank's 'uneven' application of its policy on Indigenous Peoples across various geographic regions, *see* Sarfaty (2005), p. 1808.

193 *See e.g.*, Bradlow *in* note 133, Ch. 5.

194 For examples of disagreements between Bank and Borrowers about the content and/or scope of their respective obligations, *see* section 8.1.

195 For an example illustrating the ambiguity with which the phrase 'rights and interests' are used, *compare* Schlemmer-Schulte' argument *in* note 52, Ch. 5, with the Inspection Panel's statement *in* note 115, Ch. 13.

reversed when it comes to interpreting the Inspection Panel Resolution – particularly, the eligibility criteria.[196]

6.3.2   Broader versus narrower 'margins of discretion'

Several of the operational policies contain provisions that provide for 'professional judgment' or 'management discretion', which would indeed facilitate the flexible application of the policy in question. For example, the policy on Environmental Assessment states that "[t]he Bank favors preventive measures over mitigatory or compensatory measures, *whenever feasible*";[197] the policy on Forests stipulates that "[t]he Bank does not finance projects that, *in its opinion*, would involve *significant* conversion or degradation of critical forest areas or related critical natural habitats";[198] and the policy on Involuntary Resettlement requires that "the Bank *satisfies itself* that the borrower has explored all *viable alternative project designs* to avoid physical displacement of these groups. When it is not feasible to avoid such displacement, preference is given to land-based resettlement strategies [...]."[199]

The contentious point, therefore, is typically not whether the policies allow for the exercise of 'professional judgment' or 'managerial discretion' but rather, firstly, whether such discretion is boundless or whether there *is* a limit – or 'margin' wherein such discretion has to be exercised; secondly, accepting that the exercise of discretion is not boundless, *where* the 'margin of discretion' should be drawn; and, thirdly, *who* should determine where the margin should be drawn, in particular instances – management, or internal accountability mechanisms such as the Panel.

Generally speaking, a broader margin of discretion would allow for higher degrees of flexibility and differentiation, whereas a narrower margin of discretion would facilitate higher degrees of consistency in application. Arguments in favour of broader margins of discretion, therefore, would be similar to those made in favour of differentiated policy application between projects and among borrowers, whereas arguments in favour of narrower margins of discretion (as well as the argument that there are limits to such discretion) would be comparable to those made in favour of consistent application.[200]

Several Management responses to Requests or to Inspection Panel investigation reports seem to suggest either that the exercise of discretion does not have to occur within any 'margin', or that it is up to Management (and not the Panel) to draw the boundaries of

---

196 *E.g.*, compare the Panel and Management's positions in *Tanzania: Emergency Power* (1995), as discussed *in* section 6.2.4
197 OP 4.01 (Environmental Assessment), § 2 (emphasis added).
198 OP 4.36 (Forests), § 5 (emphasis added).
199 OP 4.12 (Involuntary Resettlement), § 9 (emphasis added). *Also see* OP 4.10 (Indigenous Peoples), § 20.
200 On these arguments, *see* section 6.3.1.

this 'margin of discretion' in specific circumstances. For instance, concerning the matter of the designated risk categorization in *China: Western Poverty Reduction (Qinghai)*, Management argued that it was "in full compliance with OD 4.01 on environmental assessment," since the decision-making process involved in "[s]creening a project into either Category A or B"

> requires judgement about the overall risks (type of project, location, environmental sensitivity) of the project as well as the nature and magnitude of potential impacts. How the risks and impacts are judged depends on the specific project involved.[201]

In *Nepal: Arun III*, in responding to the Requesters' claim that "the Bank violated its operational policies and procedures by not ensuring that the Plan B project proposals were investigated to the prefeasibility stage,"[202] Management argued that this was

> an area where there are no hard-and-fast rules; professional judgment – about the likely costs and benefits of further study, and of the associated delay – is the determining factor.[203]

On the other hand, Inspection Panel practice provides several examples where the Panel specifically reviewed the 'margin of discretion' – after which the Panel would either agree with Management's exercise of judgment (and therefore conclude that the Bank was 'compliant'), or disagree with the particular margin of discretion (thus, concluding that 'compliance' in the particular instance would have required a narrower margin of discretion).[204]

Importantly, the Inspection Panel generally argues that there *are* limits to the exercise of managerial discretion, for example, as the Panel contended in its 2002 investigation of *Paraguay/Argentina: Yacyretá Hydroelectric Project*. In support of its argument, the Panel employed Ibrahim Shihata's argument that "the 'limits of flexibility' in application is 'not always clear either'."[205] Moreover, as several of the examples from Inspection Panel practice included in Part II of this book demonstrate, the Panel clearly considers the assessment

---

201 *China: Western Poverty Reduction (Qinghai)* (1999), ER, § 17 *and see* MR, p. 18.

202 *Nepal: Arun III* (1994), MR, § 4. *And see* MR, § 22, where Management argued that 'land-for-land' compensation was merely preferable, and not compulsory in terms of policy. On issues related to compensation in involuntary resettlement scenarios, *see* section 12.3.

203 *Nepal: Arun III* (1994), MR, § 4.

204 On the Inspection Panel limiting the exercise of managerial discretion, *also see* Naudé Fourie (2009), pp. 226-230.

205 *Paraguay/Argentina: Yacyretá Hydroelectric Project* (2002), Inspection Panel Review & Assessment, § 247.

of such 'margins of discretion' as falling within the purview of its compliance review mandate.

6.3.3   Restrictive versus expansive interpretation schemes

The use of restrictive versus expansive interpretation schemes – as employed by Bank management and staff when applying the operational policies to particular projects, and by internal accountability mechanisms such as the Inspection Panel when assessing policy compliance – can have a marked impact on the content and scope of the Bank's obligations, as well as on the delineation of obligations between the Bank and its borrowers. In general terms, 'restrictive' interpretation techniques (which typically emphasize the 'ordinary meaning' of words[206] or the original intent of the actors involved in the norm-making process) tend to limit the content and scope of World Bank obligations and emphasize the distinction between Bank and Borrower obligations. On the other hand, the employment of 'expansive' interpretation techniques (such as teleological or purposive interpretation, which emphasizes the underling policy objective),[207] typically has the opposite effect.

Inspection Panel practice demonstrates a general preference on the part of Bank management to follow an approach that would narrow the scope and/or content of the Bank's obligations – whether by allowing for a broad margin of appreciation or by employing restrictive interpretations of specific policy provisions,[208] whereas the Inspection Panel, in conducting its compliance review, tends to follow an approach that would broaden the scope and/or content of the Bank's obligations, typically by allowing for a narrower margin of appreciation or by employing expansive interpretations of specific policy provisions. For example, in *Argentina: Special Structural Adjustment Loan*, the Panel conceded that, based on a "strict interpretation of BP 17.50 on Disclosure of Operational Information,"

---

206 Interpretation of the loan/credit agreement between the Bank and the Borrower state would in principle be governed by Vienna Convention on the Law of Treaties between States and International Organizations or between International Organizations, March 1986 – available at: http://legal.un.org/ilc/texts/instruments/english/conventions/1_2_1986.pdf.

207 *See e.g.*, Naudé Fourie (2009), pp. 236-237.

208 *See* in particular Ch. 10. *But note*, Inspection Panel practice also provides examples where the Panel found that the Bank went 'further' than what was required in the policies. *See e.g.*, *Uzbekistan: Energy Loss Reduction* (2010), ER, § 49: "[...] by financing and managing the Panel of Experts the Bank has gone beyond the requirements of the Policy on Environmental Assessment, OP 4.01, which requires that this be done by the beneficiary or borrowing country." *And see*, *Cambodia: Land Management and Administration* (2009), IR, § 192, where the Inspection Panel's "review of the Project preparation documents" indicated that the Resettlement Policy Framework ('RPF') "was originally prepared to be applicable only in the event of resettlement of people living on land where office buildings would be constructed or other civil works financed by the Project would take place". However, "an internal discussion among Bank staff regarding the applicability of the involuntary resettlement policy in land administration projects led the Project team to expand the scope of the RPF to cover people who occupy public land and who would be evicted as a result of titling that land to the State."

Management's actions were likely compliant; however, the Panel added, a "more open dialogue"

> between Management and CELS [the Center for Legal and Social Studies] as representatives of the then potential Requesters (within the boundaries of the Bank's stated policies, which favor disclosure) could have perhaps avoided the need for a Request for Inspection.[209]

The difference between restrictive and expansive approaches also manifests with respect to the deployment of subjective standards such as 'due diligence', 'meaningfulness' or involving activities that require a certain degree of 'rigour' or 'thoroughness'.[210] For instance, as in *Papua New Guinea: Smallholder Agriculture* when Management commented with regard to the Inspection Panel's finding that "the Social Assessment identified potential adverse and positive effects of [the Project] in accordance with OP 4.10" but "*may* have been more thorough."[211] Management noted that it was "not aware"

> of such qualifications of compliance in the Policy and hence is unable to respond as it considers the matter to be compliant with Bank Policy, as stated by the Panel.[212]

6.3.4   'Process' versus 'substance' – 'compliance' as comprising procedural and substantive elements

The Panel's investigation of *China: Western Poverty Reduction (Qinghai)* (in addition to all the controversy surrounding filing of the Request,[213] the institutional ramifications flowing from the Panel's investigation report,[214] and the renewed significance of this case in light of the changing global political and economic landscape),[215] also marks a defining moment with respect to the evolution of the Inspection Panel's compliance review approach.

In its review of the project's environmental assessment process, the Panel observed that the Bank's policy on "Environmental Assessment mandate[d] a process through which an assessment should move from inception to final appraisal and sign-off"; however, the

---

209 *Argentina: Special Structural Adjustment Loan* (1999), ER, § 27.
210 For examples from Inspection Panel practice, *see* in particular sections 11.1, 11.2, 13.3, 14.3 & 15.3.
211 *Papua New Guinea: Smallholder Agriculture* (2009), MRIR, p. ix (emphasis, in bold, as in original).
212 *Id.*
213 *See e.g.*, Clark & Treakle *in* Clark et al. (Eds.) (2003), pp. 235-238.
214 As discussed, *e.g., in* section 4.2.2.
215 As noted, *e.g., in* Ch. 1.

Panel noted, "some staff" seemed to suggest "that even a one-page environmental assessment of a major project"

> could be in compliance if it passed the desks of, and was checked off by, the appropriate persons at the appropriate times in the decision process. While it might be desirable to ensure professionally acceptable standards of quality, it is not required for compliance. This 'check-list' or 'process' approach to compliance represents a minority view but, in the Panel's view, it is of concern when it is held by senior persons in the project decision-chain.[216]

Such an approach, which the Inspection Panel described as "formalistic," would not only result in a narrowing of the content and scope of the Bank's obligations but would also result in unacceptable quality, which, in the development context, may well lead to the materialization of (potentially irreversible) harm and to inadequate performance.[217]

Therefore, in reviewing the "environmental screening process" that determined the project's risk categorization,[218] the Panel emphasized that it "consider[ed] the screening decision that was made from the perspective of *both the process and the substance requirements of OD 4.01*."[219] Moreover, "in appraising [borrower] compliance," the Panel elaborated, "Management had an obligation to satisfy itself"

> *not only that the process and procedures* mandated by the policies had been followed, but also that the work under review met *professionally acceptable standards of quality*. A senior official put it clearly when he told the Panel that the Management has a duty to ensure that our minimum standards are adhered to, and it has a duty to ensure that the quality of the project meets the standard that the Bank expects.[220]

"In other words," the Panel concluded, "both process and [substantive] quality were essential components of compliance."[221]

---

216 *China: Western Poverty Reduction (Qinghai)* (1999), IR, § 39.

217 *China: Western Poverty Reduction (Qinghai)* (1999), IR, § 39. *Note*, this example also demonstrates the negative connotations of the formalist paradigm – here made with respect to Bank management – *see* note 150, Ch. 2.

218 On issues related to environmental screening or risk categorization, *see* section. 14.1.

219 *China: Western Poverty Reduction (Qinghai)* (1999), IR, 140 (emphasis added).

220 *China: Western Poverty Reduction (Qinghai)* (1999), IR, § 38 (emphasis added). On the complexity involving this division between Bank and Borrower obligations, *see* 4.3.2; on global professional and/or industry standards as a source of normativity, *see* section 5.4.

221 *China: Western Poverty Reduction (Qinghai)* (1999), IR, § 38.

Put differently, when Bank management and staff apply the Bank's policies and when bodies like the Inspection Panel review such application in order to determine 'compliance', it is critical to attend to both the procedural and substantive elements contained within the policies – for the reasons mentioned above, but also because procedural and substantive elements are intrinsically indivisible. Or, as the Inspection Panel emphasizes in a more recent publication, "[t]he Panel's experience illustrates the importance of safeguards that both substantively and procedurally"

> confirm key principles underpinning Bank operations. In line with the commit-ment of no dilution, it is important to identify and acknowledge key principles in the current policy framework that have proven to be critically important to recognize and avoid/address social and environmental harms, manage risks, and protect peoples' legitimate rights and hopes in the context of development work.[222]

****

The Inspection Panel is not often considered in the context of the World Bank's other accountability mechanisms, but the analysis presented in this chapter suggests that there is value in doing so. While criticisms remain about the Panel's institutional independence and the limitations of its mandate, it is also clear that the Inspection Panel "stands out" from other internal forms of "intermediate supervision" in important respects.[223] "The Panel's function," as Shihata explained, "is different from" internal "review and evaluation mechanisms that were meant to provide [the Bank] with the feedback necessary to enhance its knowledge and technical capabilities".[224] Moreover, "[i]t differs from staff supervision of project execution"

> in that it provides an opportunity for in-depth inspection, after an actual complaint has been received, by three independent experts. Unlike the Bank's operational staff, Panel members have not been involved in the project's design, appraisal, or supervision and thus have no interest in the staff's prior action. It is also different from the post-implementation review by the Operations Evaluation Department [now, IEG], in that it allows for independent inspection

---

222 Inspection Panel (2012), p. 1. For an additional example of this approach, *see Nepal: Arun III* (1994), IR, § 22, *at* note 151, Ch. 4.
223 Baimu & Panou *in* Cissé et al. (Eds.) (2012), e-Book.
224 Shihata (2000) pp. 235-236.

from the beginning of the project cycle and, therefore, for possible remedial action before project completion.[225]

Or, as Baimu and Panou observe, the Panel's "subject matter extends to almost all aspects of the principal activity of the institution" and covers most stages of the project cycle.[226] The Panel can investigate all Bank-financed projects, irrespective of the project's modality or the lending vehicle by which the project has been financed and also "provide *the possibility* of a remedial action, not just an *ex post* evaluation."[227] The Inspection Panel is one of only a few internal accountably mechanisms – which are typically all described by the World Bank as being 'independent' – that report to the Board of Executive Directors, and not to Bank management. Furthermore, it remains the only form of "individual(ized) oversight" within the Bank, which body of practice is (to date) *entirely* citizen-driven.[228]

All of these factors considered, it may well be concluded that "the Inspection Panel offers" the most comprehensive and relatively "binding" review of the Bank's activities,"[229] although this argument also has to be considered in light of accountability outcomes to which the Inspection Panel contributes, as will be discussed in the next chapter.

Chapter 6 also introduced opposing approaches to policy application and compliance review and observed that the Inspection Panel and Bank management often find themselves at opposite ends of arguments about the flexible versus differentiated application of the policies, broader versus narrower margins of discretion, restrictive versus expansive interpretations of specific provisions and about the exclusion versus inclusion of substantive considerations when determining *what constitutes compliance* in specific instances.

In this regard, World Bank management, in its response to the Panel's investigation report of *China: Western Poverty Reduction (Qinghai)*, highlighted that "[t]he disconnect between Management and the Panel warrants careful analysis."[230] "How could this situation arise," Management elaborated, "whereby the professional staff and management of the Bank conclude that the Project is in compliance with policies,"

> while the Panel concludes that it is not? In answering the question, the starting point is a recognition that, what it means to be 'in compliance', depends on the interpretation of keywords and phrases. Phrases such as 'meaningful consultation' (OD 4.20), 'significant, irreversible and sector-wide impacts' (OD 4.01) and 'illustrative only' (OD 4.01), which are fundamental to choices made in

---

225 *Id.*
226 *Id.*
227 *Id.* (emphasis added).
228 *Note*, the INT is only partially citizen-driven – *see* section 6.2.2.
229 Baimu & Panou *in* Cissé et al. (Eds.) (2012), e-Book.
230 *China: Western Poverty Reduction (Qinghai)* (1999), MRIR, §§ 9-13.

the implementation of the safeguard policies, are obviously open to interpretation. [...] In several parts of the Panel Report, the authors express the view that
not enough rigor entered the decision-making process of the Bank or the Borrower in the design of the Project. These concerns are expressed in the context
of the analysis of alternatives and in the Panel's view that the Project came to
the Bank for financing after much of its design had been completed. These
concerns raise fundamental questions for the way the Bank does business, and
for our growing emphasis on country ownership and project preparation.
Management believes that where there is a strong track record of achievement
at the program level, and where there is demonstrable analysis and profession-
alism in design at the project level, we should encourage the strong degree of
national and provincial ownership, as embedded in this Project.[231]

In terms of the Inspection Panel Resolution, the Board should be the "final arbiter" of such
conflicts by clearly selecting Bank management's approach over those of the Inspection
Panel, or vice versa.[232] However, as Bradlow and Naudé Fourie note, "the situation is not
usually so easily resolved, because the World Bank Board's practice is to accept the
Inspection Panel's Investigations Reports," as well as Bank management's response and
recommendations for corrective/remedial action "without specific [public] comment."[233]
This practice, in turn, seems to suggest "that the Board has not yet fully accepted that one
consequence of the establishment of the Inspection Panel is to create" such a "new function
for the Board of Directors," but perhaps it also signifies that the Board does "not want to
be seen to be endorsing the Inspection Panel's interpretation of a particular policy provision"[234] or, for that matter, to be seen as supporting Bank management's approach to
applying the operational policy framework.

Whatever the opinion of the Bank's internal constituency groups, however, it is likely
that the Inspection Panel's approaches would typically be viewed with a higher degree of

---

231 Id. For criticism of inconsistencies in the Panel's compliance assessment approach, see e.g., Management's
comments in Uganda: Power Projects (2007) in MRIR, § 54: "[...] the two policies address physical assets or
resources that may be affected by a project and thus, if triggered, require that these be assessed for environmental impact in the EA process. Management expected that the areas of compliance noted by the first
Inspection Panel report of May 2002 would be reviewed by the second Inspection Panel investigation team
using the same methodology. However, there appears to be a divergence of opinions and some inconsistencies,
which also reflect the diversity of views on these issues among local leaders and followers, as demonstrated
in each of the Inspection Panel analyses pertaining to Busoga spirituality and culture. In fact, the first
Inspection Panel investigation report, citing findings from professional studies, found no fault with the
approach of appeasing the spirits."
232 Bradlow & Naudé Fourie (2013), p. 42.
233 Id. Also see Shihata (2000), p. 216. For an overview of Board press releases published in the aftermath of the
Board's adoption of Inspection Panel reports and Management recommendations that illustrate this point,
see in general Naudé Fourie (2014).
234 Bradlow & Naudé Fourie (2013). Also see Bradlow (1996), p. 259.

credibility among external constituency groups, especially since there appears to be a strong perception that World Bank management and staff tend to apply (and enforce) the operational policy framework "flexibly rather than 'legalistically'."[235] Consequently, the Inspection Panel's compliance review approaches and its interpretation of individual policy provisions are more likely to become "the benchmarks that shape project affected people and their representative's expectations concerning their rights vis-à-vis the [...] World Bank."[236]

Ultimately, the discussion about *how* World Bank accountability should be assessed and what it means to be *in compliance* with the operational policies, reflect the underlying tension between instrumentalism and formalism. However, just as the "logic" of neither instrumentalism nor formalism is "fully constraining," neither are the arguments made in favour of or against the competing approaches introduced in this chapter.[237]

Therefore, perhaps the most significant aspect of Inspection Panel practice is not the "disconnect" between the Panel and Bank management, although Inspection Panel indeed offers ample examples of this, but the Inspection Panel's attempts to reconcile competing conceptions of compliance in order to achieve balance or equilibrium between the instrumentalist need for 'pragmatism', 'effectiveness' and 'performance', and the formalist need for 'the rule of law',[238] 'equity' and 'justice'. "Effective safeguard policies provide means to identify and manage risk," as the Inspection Panel argues in a recent opinion piece, "which at times may slow down speed and rightly so.[239] *At the same time*," the Panel adds, "citizen-driven accountability helps"

> to enable risk-taking by providing a safety net for affected people in the event that risks materialize. For an institution whose vision is a world free of poverty, it is important to consider the question of risk to whom. The need for risk-taking in development work does not mean that risk should be transferred disproportionately to local people or the environment in which they live.[240]

---

235 *See* Kingsbury (1999), p. 329: "Episodes of non-compliance with policies relating to indigenous peoples and involuntary resettlement seem often to have been dealt with flexibly by superiors as part of the overall structure of management, with the focus usually on ameliorating project failures and learning for the future. The Operational Directives have thus been understood to be 'binding' on Bank staff within the Bank management structure, but applied and enforced flexibly rather than 'legalistically'."

236 Bradlow & Naudé Fourie (2013), p. 43.

237 On the instrumentalist and formalist paradigms, *see* section 2.3.

238 *Note*, 'rule of law' is here employed in the functional sense of the word – *see e.g.*, Chesterman (2008) (a), p. 36, who argues that a "[f]unctionalist understanding of how and why the rule of law is *used* – as distinct from the formal understanding of what it *means* – matches more closely the manner in which the rule of law is articulated at the international level." *Also see* Bradlow & Naudé Fourie (2013), pp. 15-16.

239 Inspection Panel (2013), p. 1 (emphasis added).

240 *Id.*

"When it comes to interpreting and making judgments about information that has been gathered," as Rubenstein observes, "it can be difficult for everyone – accountability holders, third parties and even power wielders themselves – to judge power wielders' culpability for failing to comply with relevant standards."[241] This is particularly true in contexts marked by dynamic complexity, pluralism and unequal power distribution since "it is often unclear whether power wielders operating in these situations could reasonably be expected to have complied with relevant standards more fully than they did."[242] Hence, internal accountability mechanisms such as the Inspection Panel can serve to supplement the "processes of procuring and interpreting information about power wielders' compliance with [relevant] standards."[243]

---

241 Rubenstein (2007), p. 623.
242 *Id.*
243 *Id.* On the 'surrogate' model of accountability, *see* section 2.2.

7 ENSURING ACCOUNTABILITY: REALIZING AND ENFORCING SPECIFIC OUTCOMES, ALIGNING VARIOUS ACCOUNTABILITY DIMENSIONS

Much of the criticism surrounding World Bank accountability concerns arguments that the World Bank has to 'do more' – or has not 'done enough' – in order *to ensure* it is accountable to its internal and external constituency groups; or, in related arguments, that an internal accountability mechanism such as the Inspection Panel is not *effective* in ensuring World Bank accountability.

Underlying such arguments are strongly held conceptions about concrete outcomes, and what it takes to realize and enforce such outcomes.

To place it in context of the preceding chapters: when the World Bank's internal accountability mechanisms identify certain deficiencies, shortcomings or compliance gaps by measuring or assessing World Bank activities (actions and omissions) against the applicable normative framework(s) – what should happen next? What types of consequences, sanctions, constructive results – *output* or *outcomes* – do we expect to come from these accountability processes? What expectations do we hold about indirect – or unintentional – outcomes? What constructive, corrective or remedial actions are required to bring about concrete outcomes – which actors are charged with the responsibility of realizing corrective or remedial actions? And how, finally, is the realization of specific outcomes enforced?

Chapter 7 concentrates on these questions, which are all related to the final dimension of accountability discussed in this book. The chapter considers six *accountability outcomes that arise in the context of Inspection Panel practice*, namely: *recourse for project-affected people; World Bank 'corrective' and Borrower 'remedial' actions; redress for project-affected people; strengthening of the World Bank governance structure; strengthening of institutional performance*; and, *normative development* of the operational policy framework (which is also the only indirect or derivative outcome considered here in detail).[1]

---

1   Enhanced World Bank legitimacy as a result of accountability processes would be another example of such a 'derivative outcome' – *see* Figure 12. *Also note*, Inspection Panel practice reflects a marked concern for the Bank's 'institutional reputation' – *see e.g., Cameroon: Petroleum Development & Pipeline Project* (2002), IR, § 123: "The Panel considers this issue [the removal of a temporary bridge across the Lom River] to be complex and in need of prompt attention in order to maintain the Bank's reputation and integrity and to comply with the provisions of the Project EMP." On the Panel's concern about 'reputational risks' for the Bank, *also see e.g.*, note 50, Ch. 11. *And see* Baimu & Panou's remarks on the matter of 'institutional reputation' as a reason behind the Panel's establishment *at* note 237, Ch. 3.

While these outcomes have the potential to ensure accountability in a distinct way, in most instances, this potential only becomes material once the outcome is *realized* – which, in turn, typically requires concrete actions – and, ultimately, *enforced* (thus, requiring concrete actions that the aforementioned concrete actions are undertaken). In considering matters of realization and enforcement, however, the chapter also points to the intricate interdependencies between various outcomes – which often hold significant implications for their realization and enforcement; and might also affect the content and scope of World Bank *versus* Borrower obligations.

Finally, Chapter 7 concludes by reflecting on *the Inspection Panel's role in ensuring World Bank accountability*, as well as *the value of its contribution* in this regard. Revisiting the earlier discussion about the reasons for the Panel's establishment, the chapter sets out the wide array of opinions as to what the Panel 'should be doing' (or, *to which 'outcomes' should the Panel be contributing*); and how effective the Panel is in 'doing what it is supposed to be doing' (or, *what is the 'real' value of the Panel's contribution*).

This discussion, in turn, provides a conclusion to Part I of this book, as it serves to illustrate the (primarily) competing interests, demands, expectations and conceptions surrounding the dimensions of World Bank accountability – which often seem to culminate in debates concerning the Inspection Panel and its practice. But what the discussion in this chapter also demonstrates is the complex interdependencies between all the dimensions of accountability. Ensuring World Bank accountability, in other words, requires the constant alignment of all accountability dimensions, as well as the interests, demands, expectations and conceptions surrounding them.

7.1 POTENTIAL ACCOUNTABILITY OUTCOMES ARISING IN THE CONTEXT OF INSPECTION PANEL PRACTICE

When accountability mechanisms employ various forms of normative frameworks to "asses[s] the conduct of an actor," as De Wet argues, it should hold "the possibility of sanctions which can vary from legally enforceable measures to naming and shaming."[2] Or, as Rubenstein argues, for the "standard" accountability model to be effective, there must be a credible "threat of sanction" – which, "not only gives the power wielder an incentive to explain her past activities," but "also gives her an incentive to dissimulate" (that is, "to claim that she has complied with the relevant standards more than she actually has").[3] "For this reason,"

---

2   De Wet *in* Von Bogdandy et al. (Eds.) (2010), pp. 856-857.
3   Rubenstein (2007), p. 619. On the 'standard model of accountability', *see* section 2.2.

there must also be the potential for third parties and/or accountability holders themselves to independently gather information about the power wielder's adherence to the standards.[4]

Indeed, "[i]t is this sanctioning component of the accountability process that gives accountability teeth, and thereby distinguishes it from responsibility, responsiveness, and deliberation [...]."[5] However, Rubenstein adds, "accountability holders" must play a prominent role in the sanctioning process.[6] Generally speaking, "[o]f the three main elements of accountability," ("*standards, information,* and *sanction*"), "the challenges associated with sanction are the most daunting"[7] – or, as Grant and Keohane conclude: "sanctions remain the weak point in global accountability since they can only be implemented by the powerful."[8]

In order for accountability outcomes to be realized and enforced, on the other hand, accountability outcomes (as well as the associated actions required to implement them) have to fit the operational reality of an international financial institution such as the World Bank. Because accountability is a "multifaceted" concept, as the ILA concludes, accountability processes could result in "various degrees of consequences"

> ranging from oversight, monitoring, and evaluation processes to censorship or other forms of sanction to the attribution of legal liability for injuries, resulting in binding remedial action.[9]

The realization and enforcement of accountability outcomes typically arising out of the 'dispute resolution triad' constituted by the Requesters, Bank management and the Inspection Panel (with the Board acting as final 'arbiter') involve considerable challenges, because these are dependent on a number of variables – which include the realization and enforcement of other outcomes, as demonstrated by Figure 12.

---

4   *Id.*
5   Rubenstein (2007), p. 619.
6   Rubenstein (2007), pp. 619-620.
7   Rubenstein (2007), p. 621.
8   Grant & Keohane (2005), p. 41.
9   ILA (1998), pp. 15-17.

Figure 12   Realizing and Enforcing Interdependent Accountability Outcomes

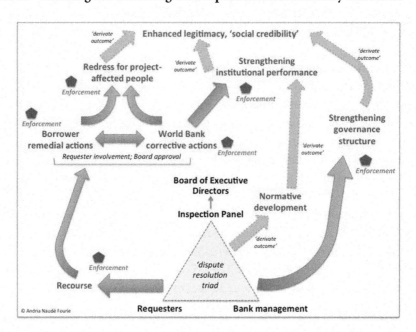

For instance, 'recourse' could result in Bank and/or Borrower 'corrective/remedial actions' – which, in turn, could result in 'redress' – but only if the conditions required to make 'recourse' effective have been met. Bank and/or Borrower 'corrective/remedial actions', moreover, can only result in 'redress' if those actions are enforced – and the same goes for broader institutional outcomes such as 'enhanced performance through learning' and 'strengthened governance and management'. The realization of an 'indirect' outcome such as 'normative development', which is a derivative of the 'dispute resolution triad',[10] could influence the realization of 'institutional learning' and 'policy improvement', but it is also likely to influence the demands and expectations of external accountability holders.

In addition, the enforcement of outcomes – 'redress' for project-affected people' in particular – are likely to affect the other derivate accountability outcome mentioned here, the World Bank's 'legitimacy'.[11] And where such enforcement is seen as deficient – notably,

---

10   On 'triadic governance', *see in general* Shapiro & Stone Sweet (2002); *and see* Stone Sweet (1999) (as quoted in Naudé Fourie (2009) at pp. 50-51), who argues that "triadic dispute resolution" enhances the "capacity of a triadic dispute resolver" (here, the Panel) "to authoritatively determine the content of a community's normative structure." Stone Sweet describes the "'judicialization of dispute resolution' [as] the process through which a TDR mechanism appears, stabilizes, and develops authority over the normative structure governing exchange in a given community."

11   *See e.g.,* Fallon (2004-2005), pp. 1790-1791, who distinguishes between "legal", "moral" and "sociological" legitimacy; where "legal" legitimacy is measured "by legal norms" (and are therefore closely related to the notion of 'legality'), "moral legitimacy" relates to the "moral justification" for the exercise of authority, and

from the perspective of external accountability holders – World Bank legitimacy is likely to be impacted in a negative manner.

The remainder of this section provides a more detailed discussion of these outcomes and the dependencies involving their realization and enforcement.

7.1.1   Recourse for project-affected people ('voice')

In the context of World Bank development-lending operations, where "access to judicial review in the traditional sense is not available," the notion of recourse "necessarily implicates broader, alternative concepts of accountability," such as the establishment of "alternative means of providing affected individuals with access to an impartial review of decisions that affect their lives with a reasonable potential to obtain a remedy."[12] Or, as Wellens argues, in light of the "absence of any kind of legal remedial action at the national or international level for all categories of potential claimants with respect to responsible individual officials," which, as noted earlier, "is a direct consequence of the privileges and immunities granted to officials for all acts undertaken in the course of their official activities,"[13]

> a refusal by an international organisation to investigate complaints about its conduct would be a matter for serious concern, given the evidently pivotal role of such a pre-remedial measure for any subsequent action considered by claimants.[14]

The establishment of project-level grievance systems – a requirement of the Bank's operational policy framework (notably of the policy on Involuntary Resettlement) – would constitute an example of such a "pre-remedial measure";[15] as would the Inspection Panel, which "procedure" "rests on the concept of public participation" and "access to justice, as reflected in Principle 10 of the Rio Declaration on the Environment and Development."[16]

"sociological" legitimacy reflects the notion that "authority is legitimate insofar as it is accepted, as a matter of fact, as deserving of respect or obedience – or, in a weaker usage [...], insofar as it is otherwise acquiesced in." *Note*, the use of the term 'legitimacy' with regard to World Bank accountability typically refers to "moral legitimacy"; whereas comments about the legitimacy of accountability mechanisms such as the Inspection Panel usually refer to "sociological legitimacy".

12   Hunter *in* Bradlow & Hunter (Eds.) (2010), p. 220.
13   Wellens (2002), pp. 266-267.
14   Wellens (2002), pp. 17-18.
15   *See e.g.*, OP 4.12 (Involuntary Resettlement), § 7(d); OP 4.12 Annex A, § 7, *and see* § 17: "*Grievance procedures.* Affordable and accessible procedures for third-party settlement of disputes arising from resettlement; such grievance mechanisms should take into account the availability of judicial recourse and community and traditional dispute settlement mechanisms."
16   Boisson de Chazournes *in* Treves et al. (Eds.) (2005), pp. 190-191.

In addition, Inspection Panel practice might highlight compliance gaps with respect to the effectiveness of project-level grievance mechanisms, which, to the extent that such issues are addressed through Bank (and/or Borrower) actions, would constitute a further example of the realization of recourse for project-affected people.[17]

There are different opinions as to whether recourse is a distinct outcome. For some, for example, recourse is considered to be only a 'means' to another (and more important) 'end' – that is: redress for project-affected people. Others might recognize recourse as a distinct outcome, but argue that its value is considerably diminished should it not result in adequate redress or, at the very least, create conditions that are conducive for the realization of redress. Others point to the intrinsic value of recourse, arguing, for instance, that it gives project-affected people 'voice' and that there is dignity in being able to file a complaint at (and against) a powerful institution such as the World Bank, even if such a complaint does not result in additional desired outcomes.[18]

Inspection Panel practice certainly demonstrates that, by giving project-affected people 'voice' – which provides them the opportunity to make the adverse economic, social and environmental effects ('harm') brought about by a Bank-financed development project concrete, tangible, 'real' – internal and external accountability holders, given the public nature of the Panels proceedings, are given insights into the Bank's development-lending operations that might not otherwise have been available.[19] "The Panel hears the same story all over the world from powerless people who perceive that they are about to be overwhelmed by a World Bank-financed project or program", as Brown Weiss (a former Inspection Panel chair) observes.[20] "In different languages and in different surroundings, the message is the same" –

> we are poor, and what little we have is about to be taken away from us; we are taking our lives in our hands in coming to you, and we do so because we have nothing left to lose and you are our only channel of appeal and our only hope.[21]

---

17 For a discussion of compliance issues related to project-level grievance mechanisms in the context of involuntary resettlement, *see* section 12.6.

18 On the importance of 'voice' in enhancing public accountability, *see e.g.*, Paul (2004).

19 In this regard, *also note* the Panel's comment in *India: Mumbai Urban Transport* (2004), IR (ES), p. 19: "The Bank Project in Mumbai is part of a larger Mumbai effort to build transportation infrastructure in Mumbai and to further develop the city. As part of this effort, many tens of thousands of additional people are being resettled who are not part of the Bank project. People interviewed by the Panel [expressed the hope] that the safeguards built into Bank-financed projects would be extended to other activities not financed by the Bank. In the Project before us, these hopes have not been realized, as newspapers reported early in 2005 the widespread demolition of slum dwellings not included within the Bank Project, which left occupants without any place to live."

20 Brown Weiss (2010), p. 488.

21 *Id.*

"This means," Brown Weiss adds, "that it is essential to ensure that there is no retribution,"

> and when there may be, to take action. Many times, [the Inspection Panel] had
> to make clear to actors at all levels that retribution is, or would be, unacceptable
> and costly.[22]

Therefore, by providing an avenue for recourse, and by "listening to affected people, who are often very poor," Brown Weiss concludes, the Inspection Panel process can become a mechanism "to make those who make decisions affecting [project-affected people] accountable."[23]

In this regard, it should also be noted that the mere filing of a Request for Inspection might affect the power balance among the actors involved in a particular development project (and which is typically skewed against project-affected people). The adjustment of the power balance, in turn, could serve to ensure the realization of redress for project-affected people, as will be discussed later on in this chapter.[24] In *Brazil: Paraná Biodiversity*, for example, shortly "[a]fter the Request for Inspection was submitted to the Panel,"

> Management agreed to carry out a Technical Audit of the Project and the bio-
> diversity conditions in the State, as the Requesters had previously asked in
> order to help address their concerns about the Project. In addition, the Govern-
> ment of Paraná prepared a draft proposal to re-orient strategic directions and
> activities under the Project to respond to concerns of the Requesters.[25]

Importantly, however, the realization of 'recourse for affected people' as a distinct outcome is dependent on a number of different variables. Insofar as project-level grievance mechanisms are concerned, for instance, numerous issues can render them, in essence, ineffective – such as their proper staffing, physical accessibility, and the transparency of their procedures.[26] In order to make effective use of the recourse avenue offered by the Inspection Panel, moreover, several critical factors have to be in place.

For example, project-affected people have to be aware of the World Bank's involvement in the particular development project (which might be particularly challenging in scenarios where multiple financiers are involved);[27] they would have to know about the existence of

---

22   *Id.*
23   Brown Weiss (2010), p. 483.
24   For examples from Inspection Panel practice, *see* section 7.1.3.
25   *Brazil: Paraná Biodiversity* (2007) Final ER, § 3.
26   For a discussion of compliance issues related to project-level grievance mechanisms in the context of invol-
     untary resettlement, *see* section 12.6.
27   *See in general* sections 3.1.2 & 3.1.3 – *and see* in particular the Panel's comments in the *Chile: Quilleco
     Hydropower* case, *at* note 108, Ch. 3.

the Bank's operational policy framework and that the application of specific policies in the project area conveys certain 'rights and interests' on them;[28] they would have to know about the existence of the Inspection Panel (which, in turn, is influenced by financial resources made available by the World Bank for such purposes);[29] potential Requesters would also require a minimum level of resources (both financial and expertise-related);[30] and, finally, project-affected people have to be able to file Requests for Inspection without being prevented to do so – by the Bank and/or the Borrower.[31]

Local and international civil society actors, in particular, make significant contributions to realizing recourse by working towards clearing these obstacles.[32]

7.1.2   World Bank corrective actions and Borrower remedial actions

Recourse to project-level grievance mechanisms or to the Inspection Panel might trigger a variety of actions undertaken by Bank management and/or borrowers, in order to rectify, remedy or address issues related to operational policy non-compliance, with regard to a particular development project. Some of these actions might conceivably constitute 'redress for project-affected people', as will be discussed in the next section.

The distinction between 'corrective' *World Bank* actions and 'remedial' *Borrower* actions has evolved in the context of Inspection Panel practice. It reflects the limitation in the Inspection Panel's mandate that it is only to review *World Bank* "actions and omissions", with regard *World Bank* obligations – as set out in the operational policy framework.[33]

---

28 On the ambiguity surrounding the phrase, 'rights and interests', *see* note 195, Ch. 6.

29 *See e.g.,* BP 17.55 (Inspection Panel), Annex B, p. 2: "Management will make significant efforts to make the Inspection Panel better known in borrowing countries [...]." *Also see* BP 17.55, Annex C, § 17: "The Board underlines the need for Management to make significant efforts to make the Inspection Panel better known in borrowing countries, as specified in the 1996 'Clarifications' [Annex B]." On the Panel's 'outreach' activities, *see e.g.,* Inspection Panel Annual Report (2013/2014), pp. 47-50; *and also see* p. 9 – the Inspection Panel announced that it has "partnered with Management to include information about the Panel in key Bank Project Appraisal Documents (PADs), to better inform project-affected people of the existence of the Panel, and of its mandate."

30 *But see* BP 17.55 (Inspection Panel), Annex B, p. 2: "[Management] [...] will not provide technical assistance or funding to potential requesters."

31 In this regard, *see* section 3.1.5; *and see* Brown Weiss's comment *at* note 22, Ch. 7.

32 *See* section 3.1.4.

33 *Note*, the most recent version of the Inspection Panel's Operating Procedures appears to have done away with using these terms, although the distinction still stands – *see e.g.* IP Operating Procedures (2014), § 68, where the Panel describes "remedial efforts that Management can take on its own to address Bank failure, and a plan of action agreed between the Borrower and the Bank, in consultation with the Requesters, to improve project implementation." *Also note*, this is another example where the employment of legal terminology can be confusing. For the sake of clarity, this book differentiates between 'redress' for project-affected people' (which might also be referred to as 'remedies for PAP') (*e.g.,* as discussed in section 7.1.3); the 'contractual remedies' available in terms of the loan/credit agreement (*e.g.,* as noted in this section, as well as in sections 5.1 & 15.2.2); and the 'remedial actions' undertaken by the Borrower (in terms of the 'Action Plan' agreed in the aftermath of an Inspection Panel investigation) (*e.g.,* discussed in this section).

In terms of the Inspection Panel Resolution, Bank management is required to consider the Inspection Panel's investigation report and provide the Board with a formal "report indicating its recommendations", within a fixed period.[34] Importantly, however, the Resolution does not *oblige* Bank management to accept any of the Panel's findings, nor to make recommendations strictly on the basis of the Inspection Panel's findings (unless, of course, the Board explicitly instructs Bank management to do so).[35] The Resolution stipulates, for instance, that the Requesters should be informed "of the results of the investigation and the action taken in its respect, *if any*";[36] whereas the Inspection Panel's Operating Procedures note that Management's recommendations in light of the Panel's investigation report "*normally* includes proposed actions in response to the Panel's findings", while adding that "Management *may* also include" "a proposal to submit to the Board periodic progress reports on the implementation of the remedial efforts and/or plan of action."[37]

Management's recommendation report would typically include actions which would require *the Bank* to take *specific corrective actions* in light of the Panel's findings.[38] World Bank corrective actions might also include the exercise of legal remedies provided for in the credit/loan agreement, in order to enforce its terms.[39] In this regard, the Bank's policy on Suspension of Disbursements notes: "When an event unrelated to payment constitutes a basis for suspension,"

> the Bank determines case by case whether to suspend disbursements on a loan. The Bank may decide to suspend disbursements as of a specified date, or to warn the borrower that suspension will occur unless the borrower takes certain remedying actions by a specified date. Most, but not all, suspensions that are unrelated to payment occur because a borrower or other contracting party fails to carry out covenants under a Loan, Project, or other relevant Agreement.[40]

---

34   Inspection Panel Resolution, § 23.
35   *Note*, this aspect of Inspection Panel practice has not been as transparent, since the proceedings of Board meetings have only become publically available since the amendment of the Bank's policy on Access to Information in July 2013 – *see* http://web.worldbank.org/WBSITE/EXTERNAL/PROJECTANDOPERA-TIONS/EXTINFODISCLOSURE/0,,contentMDK:22630506~pagePK:64865365~piPK:64864641~the-SitePK:5033734,00.html. *But also see* Edward Ayensu's remarks made to the Board (on occasion of the Board discussion of the Inspection Panel report and Management recommendations on *Chad: Petroleum*, which had been published on the Panel's website shortly thereafter), *at* note 158, Ch. 7.
36   Inspection Panel Resolution, § 23 (emphasis added).
37   Inspection Panel Operating Procedures, (2014), §§ 68-69 (emphases added). *Also see* Brown Weiss (2010), who notes (at p. 484) that, in her "experience" as Inspection Panel member and chair, "the Board has always approved management's Action Plan, but sometimes has asked for significant additional measures" – as the Board had done *e.g.*, in *Paraguay/Argentina: Yacyretá Hydroelectric Project* (2002).
38   On the distinction between primary and secondary obligations, *see* section 4.3.2.
39   *See e.g.*, the discussion *in* section 15.2.2.
40   OP 13.40 (Suspension of Disbursements), § 2.

The realization and enforcement of World Bank correction actions, however, are influenced by several factors, such as cost considerations,[41] internal resource constraints, institutional priorities (which, in turn, might be influenced by ongoing institutional reforms),[42] or the level of institutional credibility enjoyed by the Inspection Panel at that moment.[43]

But the Resolution also instructs Bank management to engage the Borrowers about the adoption of *remedial actions* that "*seek to improve project implementation.*"[44] These remedial actions, in turn, would typically concern the primary obligations of the Borrower. The Resolution adds, however, that Borrower [remedial] Action Plans must be "agreed between the borrower and the Bank, in consultation with the requesters".[45]

While it makes sense to delineate *what the Bank has to do* versus *what the Borrower has to do* in order to address the compliance and performance issues highlighted by an Inspection Panel investigation, the complexities surrounding the realization and enforcement of Bank/Borrower actions are similar to those involving the formal division between Bank and Borrower obligations across the project cycle.[46] Indeed, the interdependencies between Bank and Borrower corrective/remedial actions might have a direct bearing on the realization of 'redress' for project-affected people – and, considering that the Bank's efforts to 'facilitate' the realization of Borrower remedial actions become part of the Bank's secondary obligations, questions regarding the content and scope of World Bank accountability are once again likely to come to the fore.

These questions are particularly challenging to address because, as Baimu and Panou observe, it should not be forgotten that "the Bank, as an international financial *cooperative* institution," has to act, "[t]hroughout the entire project cycle,"

> *in cooperation* with the borrowing state, including designing and carrying out measures to address challenges related to compliance with Bank policies and procedures that the panel may have unearthed in the course of its investigations.[47]

---

41 *See e.g.*, Bank management's overview of the "estimated cost and time required for the [corrective and remedial] actions recommended by Management" in light of the Panel's findings in *China: Western Poverty Reduction (Qinghai)* (1999) – MRIR, p. 6. Management estimated that it would cost an additional $3,070,000 to implement the actions that would "fully respond to the Inspection Panel investigation report". *Also see* the critical remarks *at* notes 218 & 231, Ch. 7.

42 On the influence of institutional reforms on the Bank's institutional aims, *see* section 4.2.

43 On variables influencing the Inspection Panel's degree of internal and external credibility, *see e.g.*, Naudé Fourie (2009), pp. 294-296. *Also see* note 53, Ch. 7.

44 BP 17.55 (Inspection Panel), Annex C, § 15.

45 *Id.*

46 *See* section 4.3.2 – *and also see* Chapter 8.

47 Baimu & Panou *in* Cissé et al. (Eds.) (2012), e-Book (emphases added).

Or, as per Goldmann's classification of enforcement activities, World Bank 'corrective actions' would resort under "compliance control and implementation," whereas the Bank's enforcement of Borrower 'remedial actions' "involve[s] a categorically different exercise of public authority" since it "concerns the interaction with another subject of [international] law."[48]

In other words, the World Bank may be obligated to ensure borrower compliance with those components of the operational policy framework that are applicable to a specific project – an obligation that is typically highlighted by Inspection Panel investigations and subsequently becomes the subject of public scrutiny – but the manner in which the World Bank engages with the Borrower in the formulation and implementation of remedial Action Plans are influenced, for instance, by the Bank's status as 'cooperative' institution, the principle of state sovereignty, and the Bank's emphasis of performance areas such as 'client satisfaction', 'quality and timeliness of lending operations', 'development outcomes ratings' and 'growth of the Bank's lending portfolio'.[49]

As to the 'quality' (or, 'actionability') of Bank and Borrower Action Plans adopted in the aftermath of Inspection Panel investigations, Inspection Panel practice provides limited data in this regard, since the Panel's formal involvement ends with the submission of its investigation report to the Board.

What can be said, however, is that Bank management's formal responses to Inspection Panel investigation reports typically reflect a mixture of 'acceptance', 'partial acceptance' and 'rejections' of Inspection Panel findings – even in an instance such as the *China: Western Poverty Reduction (Qinghai)* case, where Bank management registered a significant "disconnect" between itself and the Panel about 'what constitutes compliance' in certain instances.[50] For example, Management agreed to "reclassify the Qinghai Component as A under OD 4.01," develop "a separate IPDP plan" and make it "publicly available" and conduct "additional consultations" "with a focus on confidentiality of the PAPs."[51] Of course, the Panel's findings and Management's agreement to undertake corrective actions became superfluous when China withdrew its loan proposal shortly thereafter.[52]

On the other hand, the 'acknowledgement' or 'partial acknowledgement' of an Inspection Panel finding does not necessarily translate into detailed actions. In this regard, Management recommendations reflect significant variance, which could be influenced by variables such as the emphasis placed by the Bank's President on the importance of the Inspection Panel, the general level of institutional credibility enjoyed by the Panel (which,

---

48   *See* Goldmann *in* Von Bogdandy et al. (Eds.) (2010), p. 844.
49   For an overview of these performance areas and indicators as reflected in the Bank's corporate performance scorecard, *see* section 4.2.2.
50   *See* note 230, Ch. 6. For an overview of Management responses to Inspection Panel findings, *see in general* Naudé Fourie (2014).
51   *China: Western Poverty Reduction (Qinghai)* (1999), MRIR, § 9.
52   *Also see* note 105, Ch. 4.

in turn, might be significantly affected by individual Panel members and, especially, Panel chairs).[53]

Concerning the Inspection Panel's involvement in the adoption and/or subsequent enforcement of Bank/Borrower corrective/remedial 'Action Plans', the Resolution (and subsequent Board clarifications to the Resolution) sets out the formal position – which significantly limits the Panel's involvement.[54] In practice, however, the Board has formally requested the Inspection Panel's input and/or participation in this regard on a few prominent occasions.[55] Furthermore, in what might be described as a 'formalization' of practice, the Panel's recently updated Operating Procedures also stipulate that "Management *will* communicate to the Panel"

> the nature and the outcomes of the consultations with the affected parties on the action plan agreed between the Borrower and the Bank.[56] The Panel *may* submit to the Board for its consideration a written or verbal report on the adequacy of these consultations. The Panel's reporting *may* be based on information available to the Panel by all sources, and the Panel *may* decide, in consultation with the Executive Director representing the Borrower, that a country visit is needed to be able to prepare its report accurately.[57]

---

53 *See e.g.*, Bradlow & Naudé Fourie (2013), fn. 176, comparing the Management Recommendation in *India: Coal Sector* (2001), MRIR, Annex 1 ("in which Management 'noted' the Panel's findings of non-compliance in many instances, but concluded that there was 'no action to be taken' or that the Bank would 'continue supervision' (*see e.g.*, action numbers 1, 3, 4, 10, 11, 12, 13, 14, 17, 21, 22, 23, 24, 26, 28, 31") with the Management Recommendation in *Pakistan National Drainage Program Project* ("in which Management acknowledged that categorizing the project as a 'category B' for environmental assessment purposes was 'premature' and "that it would have been more appropriate to categorize this as an EA category "A" project' (at para. 41)"). On the other hand, more recent cases also provide examples where Bank management rejected several of the Panel's key findings – *see e.g.*, *Papua New Guinea: Smallholder Agriculture* (2009) (for an overview of the Management Recommendation, *see* Naudé Fourie (2014), pp. 458-459; *and see South Africa: Eskom Investment Support* (2010) (for an overview of the Management Recommendation, *see* Naudé Fourie (2014), pp. 478-479). For a discussion of variables affecting the Panel's behaviour over time – through which the Panel fluctuate between periods of 'activism' versus 'restraint' vis-à-vis Management, *see* Naudé Fourie (2009), pp. 283-315.

54 Inspection Panel § 23; BP 17.55 (Inspection Panel), Annex C, § 15 *and see* § 16: "The Board should not ask the Panel for its view on other aspects of the [Bank management] action plans nor would it ask the Panel to monitor the implementation of the action plans." On the Inspection Panel's involvement in monitoring activities before the 1999-Board review that limited this aspect of the Panel's functions, *see e.g.*, Shihata (2000), pp. 224.

55 *E.g.*, in the aftermath of the *Paraguay/Argentina: (Yacyretá)* (2002) and *India: Mumbai Urban Road Transport* (2003) investigations.

56 *Also see* note 45, Ch. 7.

57 Inspection Panel Operating Procedures (2014), § 70 (emphases added). *Note*, unlike amendments to the Inspection Panel Resolution (which have to be approved by the Board), the Panel's Operating Procedures can be amended by the Panel – although, in practice, the Panel is unlikely to do so without Board involvement.

Furthermore, although the Inspection Panel's mandate does not include a formal monitoring function, it has, as noted earlier, carved out an informal monitoring role for itself in practice[58] by publishing Management progress reports (presented to the Board) concerning the implementation of Bank/Borrower 'Action Plans' adopted in the aftermath of Inspection Panel investigations.[59] This practice has also recently been formalized in the Panel's updated Operating Procedures, which now stipulate that

> [w]hen Management submits to the Board progress reports on the implementation of actions following from a Panel investigation, the Panel prepares a summary of these progress reports and makes the summaries and the reports available on the Panel's website.[60]

The significance of this informal monitoring function, albeit decidedly modest at this point, should not be underestimated since it enhances the transparency surrounding the implementation of corrective/remedial 'Action Plans', which opens up the possibility for external scrutiny in the area of enforcement.[61]

On the other hand, it should also be noted that the implementation of corrective/remedial actions "needed to correct harm and bring the projects into compliance with Bank policy" often requires "considerable time, sometimes several years."[62] However, as Umaña observes, the Inspection Panel "Resolution is based on a scenario in which investigations are either approved or disapproved and are carried out expeditiously, and it certainly did not foresee the Action Plan phenomenon."[63] "In the [1996] Yacyretá case," for example, the "implementation of [Action] Plans A and B,"

> which were scheduled for completion during 2000, have fallen behind schedule, which over time, may make, the work of the Panel irrelevant. In [India:] NTPC, the Independent Monitoring Panel has entered into its second year and problems continue to evolve. The [Brazil] Itaparica case is another example of a solution that may take many years to implement. Whatever the final decision,

---

58 *See* section 6.2.4. *Also note* Van Putten's distinction between "the monitoring of mitigation actions that derive from an earlier [Inspection Panel] investigation" and "post-monitoring, which is monitoring of the effects of projects that have been implemented" – *see* Van Putten (2008), p. 461. In terms of this distinction, the IEG has a 'post-monitoring' function whereas the Panel has a limited 'follow-up monitoring role'.

59 For examples of such 'progress reports' published by the Inspection Panel, *see e.g.*, http://ewebapps.worldbank.org/apps/ip/Pages/ViewCase.aspx?CaseId=2.

60 Inspection Panel Operating Procedures (2014), § 74.

61 *See e.g.*, Hale (2008), p. 14, which describes this as the transparency-effect' of "info-courts; for similar remarks, *also see* Boisson de Chazournes *in* Shelton (Ed.) (2000), p. 296.

62 Umaña (1998), pp. 326-327.

63 *Id.*

> *practice has demonstrated the need for a clearly defined role of the Inspection*
> *Panel during the implementation of Action Plans.*[64]

Or, as the *Independent Accountability Mechanisms Network* comments, "[t]he work of IAMs is essentially for naught if IFI management does not follow through on delivering redress agreed to in the management response or action plan."[65] It should also not be forgotten that, "[i]n the course of problem-solving and compliance investigation, project-affected people incurred high opportunity costs"

> by devoting scarce resources to the IAM process, invest tremendous emotional
> energy, see their hopes and expectations raised, and, in some cases, expose
> themselves to significant personal risk of retribution. For IFI management to
> then fail to implement effective redress when harm has been found is inimical
> to the spirit of citizen-driven accountability. Developing mechanisms that give
> the IAMs a greater role in the follow-up to a case to ensure that remedies are
> effective and properly implemented and are viewed by the complainants as
> adequate is thus critical.[66]

7.1.3 Redress for project-affected people

In the context of Inspection Panel practice, 'redress for project-affected people' could be realized through the implementation of Bank and/or Borrower (corrective/remedial) Action Plans, adopted as a result of the filing of a Request for Inspection – whether at the end of an Inspection Panel investigation or during the early stage of the process, as part of the Panel's 'problem-solving' function.[67] Aside from the challenges involve the realization and enforcement of 'redress' through Bank/Borrower Action Plans (which had been discussed in the previous section), this section considers other aspects – notably, the types of

---

64 *Id.* (emphasis added).
65 Independent Accountability Mechanisms Network (2012), pp. 32-33.
66 *Id.*
67 *Note*, at the time of writing the Panel was "piloting a new approach to enhance opportunities for early solutions to the concerns raised by the Requesters", which would be applied "to certain types of cases that may be amenable to early resolution in the interest of the affected community." *See* Inspection Panel Operating Procedures (2014), fn. 6, p. 13. In accordance with this pilot procedure, the Panel "informs the Requesters of the existence of the Pilot, its nature and conditions. The Requesters then inform the Panel if they support a postponement of the decision on registration to explore this opportunity for early solutions. The Panel informs the Board through a Notice of Receipt of a Request, that it is postponing its decision on registration, attaching Management's proposal of remedial actions." For more detail, *see* Inspection Panel Operating Procedures (2014), Annex 1, "Piloting a new approach to support early solutions in the IP process." On the Panel's 'formal' and 'informal' functions, *see* section 6.2.4.

redress offered and the problem-solving mechanism through which redress might be realized.

"Given the overarching character of accountability as a concept," as Wellens argues, "an exclusively legal approach to the problems and issues involved seems to be prevented"; however, whether we are considering accountability outcomes being generated at the 'first level of accountability' – the category to Inspection Panel practice belongs – or beyond,[68] an important principle remains that "[t]o be adequate, remedies for the implementation of accountability of international organisations should correspond to the kind and nature of the complaints addressed to them."[69]

For example, it has been noted earlier that Bank and/or Borrower corrective/remedial Action Plans, which are primarily aimed at 'bringing a project 'back into compliance', could include activities that might be considered as *redress for project-affected people* – assuming, of course, those activities are realized and enforced. On the other hand, would that be enough? Some argue, for instance, that 'redress' should also include some form of (additional) material compensation. "Civil society," as Bissell and Nanwani note, "is increasingly pursuing the next logical step," which, from their perspective, is: if multilateral development banks are being "held accountable for violating [their] policies and procedures," as determined through the investigations of independent accountability mechanisms such as the Inspection Panel, and if "people have been adversely harmed" as a result of such non-compliance, the MDBs "can, and should, be made financially responsible for the damage caused by violating its policies and procedures" – whereas such

> financial obligations can take on two dimensions: (1) that the bank should provide additional grant financing to the borrower to cover costs to the project resulting from the bank's conduct, or (2) that the bank should compensate individual project affectees for damage that results directly from its noncompliance with its own policies.[70]

MDBs such as the World Bank have not been oblivious to these demands, which might indeed be another reason why the Bank has taken pains to emphasize the non-legal nature of both the Inspection Panel and the operational policies.[71]

In this regard, Inspection Panel practice provides at least one prominent example where the Bank's corrective actions, taken in the aftermath of the Inspection Panel's investigation of *Albania: Coastal Zone Management* (in which the Panel found several instances of

---

68   On the ILA's conceptualization of IO accountability as 'three levels', *see* note 72, Ch. 2.
69   Wellens (2002), p. 8.
70   Bissell & Nanwani (2009), p. 38. For an opposing view, *see e.g.*, Schlemmer-Schulte *at* notes 52 & 53, Ch. 5.
71   *See* sections 5.1.1 (on the legal nature of the operational policies) and 6.2.4 (on the quasi-judicial nature of the Panel).

serious policy non-compliance), included financial compensation, namely: "the Bank agreed to pay legal and court costs of legal actions brought against the government by those found by the Panel to have been harmed by the Bank's actions or omissions."[72]

Nevertheless, "the mechanism of inspection or compliance review" – as embodied by the Inspection Panel's formal mandate – "remains mostly a tool for enhancing internal governance and accountability", as discussed in the next section.[73] "A compliance review panel's substantive jurisdiction," Bissell and Nanwani add, "is limited"

> to the review of compliance by an MDB. It may take remedial action, but its competence does not extend to the making of monetary indemnity or compensation for any material harm. A corollary of the principle of responsibility is the principle of remedy, and the most appropriate mode of settlement for MDBs (for claims that cannot be settled by negotiation) is arbitration. There must be some creative alternative to allow private parties' claims to be settled through arbitration without jeopardizing the organizational effectiveness of MDBs. [...] An important consideration is that an MDB's functions and purposes are delineated by the principle of specialty; member states invest international organizations with certain powers, the limits of which are a function of their common interests. The principle of specialty supports organizational effectiveness, and the need for organizational effectiveness should determine the scope of how an MDB discharges its responsibility and provides remedies in the settlement of private claims.[74]

Indeed, the Inspection Panel has also taken care not to 'over-sell' the ability of its problem-solving function to realize redress for project-affected people. In its recently updated Operating Procedures, for instance, the Panel explains that its process "is part of a wider set of remedies to address grievances stemming from Bank-supported operations" and that "such remedies may be available within a project itself, be part of a borrowing country's own systems, or be part of a wider set of options available within the Bank to respond to grievances at various levels."[75] Ultimately, as the Inspection Panel concludes, its own process "provides an avenue for grievance redress" – that is, 'recourse' –

---

72 *See* A. Ninio *in* Freestone (2013), p. 71. Ninio adds (at *id.*) that the Bank "responded [...] forcefully and with unprecedented measures", including disciplinary actions that were taken with respect to "several senior level staff" (although some of actions were later reversed by the Bank's Administrative Tribunal).

73 Suzuki & Nanwani (2005-2006), pp. 223-225.

74 *Id.*

75 Inspection Panel Operating Procedures (2014), § 4.

as a result of an independent investigation, and also at earlier stages in the process. The Panel does not, however, directly engage in mediation, and does not provide recommendations for remedial actions to be taken by Management or the Borrower.[76]

On the other hand, as noted earlier, Inspection Panel practice provides ample examples where the mere act of filing a Request for Inspection or where the initial processing of such a Request by the Inspection Panel served as a trigger for the realization of corrective/remedial actions, which also included activities that could be considered as 'redress for project-affected people'. In *Argentina: Santa Fe Road Infrastructure*, for example, the Panel found that "information provided to the affected people during the land acquisition process was not always adequate", however, "after initial difficulties,"

> information sharing and related consultations in the land acquisition process improved over time, *especially after the submission of the Request for Inspection.* The Panel finds that with this improvement the Project is now in compliance with OP 4.12.[77]

The Inspection Panel also emphasized that "the submission of a Request for Inspection" "does not prevent Management from engaging in a constructive dialogue with the Requesters to try to address their concerns", as the perception seems to have been among certain Bank and Borrower staff members.[78]

While the Panel's emerging problem-solving function may indeed become more effective than its compliance review function in contributing to the realization of redress for project-affected people (although the current body of practice does not yet contain sufficient empirical data to substantiate such a claim), it should also be noted that redress realized through problem-solving is also not immune to problems of intimidation.[79] In *Cameroon: Petroleum Development and Pipeline*, for example, concerning a dispute about individual compensation for the loss of Okoumé trees, the Panel, on visiting the owner of the trees, confirmed "that the dispute had been resolved and that the amount of compensation was to be set by a third party who was an expert"; however, the Panel also noted that the owner "reiterated that the local government"

---

76 *Id.*

77 *Argentina: Santa Fe Road Infrastructure* (2007), IR, § 160 (emphasis added).

78 *Brazil: Land Reform* (1998), ER, § 15. Panel added (at *id.*): "This was the case, for example, in respect to recent Requests for Inspection submitted on Nigeria: West Africa Gas Pipeline Project and Romania: Mine Closure and Social Mitigation Project."

79 *See* section 3.1.5.

used intimidation to get his consent and that they threatened him with jail for disrupting the Project. The Panel finds that while the process of dealing with this particular case was long and difficult, the compensation was generous, as it was higher than the compensation stipulated for Okoumé trees in the compensation plan. Although, the Panel is very disturbed about the alleged use of threats by local authorities, it notes that this is not related to COTCO's [project implementing agency] or the Bank's behavior or policies. As of mid-April the Panel was informed that this claim is close to resolution, as the owner will be compensated based on the now completed study by the third party expert.[80]

In other words, "[p]roblem-solving is most effective", as the Independent Accountability Mechanisms Network argues, "when it is driven locally"

by the principal parties – those that are closest to, and most likely to be impacted by, the problem – with a focus on solutions that result in better outcomes on the ground. This often means designing a process where both the community and project representatives are the principals in a dialogue or mediation. They have the responsibility to determine who else should be present, and what the ground rules of dialogue will be. [...] The advantage of focusing responsibility back on the parties is that it encourages ownership and control of the process by those people who will ultimately have to live with the outcomes of it.[81]

However, the Independent Accountability Mechanisms Network cautions, "once agreements are reached, this alone"

will not represent a breakthrough in a conflict unless the agreements are implemented and progress is monitored before the IAM exits. Even when local agreements are successfully implemented, they may not overcome more systemic causes of conflict in a locality, region or country that may stand in the way of more sustainable outcomes for the parties involved.[82]

In this regard, as Wellens emphasizes, "[i]nternational organisations should [...] have due regard"

---

80 *Cameroon: Petroleum Development and Pipeline* (2002), IR, § 172.
81 Independent Accountability Mechanisms Network (2012), p. 29.
82 *Id.*

to the unequal position existing between them and the other parties concerned, especially individuals, when they are devising remedial mechanisms to ensure or to enhance their accountability.[83]

7.1.4   Strengthening the World Bank governance structure

Since the Inspection Panel's inception in 1993, expectations regarding its contribution towards the strengthening of the World Bank's governance structure – notably, of the Board – has, arguably, been the least ambiguous (and least controversial) aspect of the debate surrounding the Inspection Panel.

"With the establishment of the Inspection Panel," as Shihata underscored, "the Bank has created an additional accountability mechanism"

> responding to the concerns of third parties affected by Bank Operations. The Inspection Panel thus introduces a possible direct relationship between private affected parties and the Bank. In other words, far from making the Bank accountable for the first time, as some observers have inaccurately stated, the inspection function adds to a system of accountability based on the institutional hierarchy of the organization another system initiated by complaints by affected parties. This new measure of accountability does not substitute for the *upward system of accountability* that exists; it simply assists it to function more efficiently by adding a *downward system of accountability* reaching out to affected parties. Decisions on remedial actions that may result from this new system remain in the hands of the Executive Directors who are responsible for the general operations of the Bank. The Panel simply gives the affected parties a voice in questioning the Bank's actions. It also provides, through its findings, the Executive Directors and the President with *independently ascertained facts* that enable them to perform their duties and to ensure the Bank's compliance with its policies and procedures. In this manner, the additional mechanism neither detracts nor dilutes the existing system of accountability. On the contrary, it is meant to strengthen it and increase its efficiency.[84]

While all the Panel's fact-finding and compliance review activities have the potential to contribute towards the strengthening of the Bank's governance structure, perhaps the most

---

83   Wellens (2002), pp. 25-24.
84   Shihata (2000), pp. 239-240 (emphases added). For the debate about the reason behind the Panel's inception, *see* section 3.2.3. On the complementary nature of 'top-down' and 'bottom-up' accountability, *also see* Wood's comments *at* note 214, Ch. 3. On the complementary nature of the Panel's mandate vis-à-vis other internal accountability mechanisms, *see* section 6.2.4.

vivid examples of the Panel's contribution in this regard are reflected in instances where Inspection Panel practice highlights specific incidents where information presented to the Board (contained, for instance, in documents such as the Project Appraisal Document, which are used by the Board as the basis for its various decision-making processes; or in project status reports, which reflect the project's progress against plans and budgets) have proven to be ambiguous, misleading, or even demonstrably incorrect.

In its 2001 investigation of *Uganda: Power Projects*, for example, the Panel affirmed that "Owen Falls Extension has a potential capacity of 200 MW" and concluded that any "confusion" among various stakeholders about the capacity was the result of "changes in project specifications"

> that were not adequately represented in the documentation. Management has acknowledged that "there was not full and frank disclosure of this situation" to the Board of Executive Directors. In this sense, the Board documents for the Power III Project do not meet the requirements of OD 10.00.[85]

Such input, moreover, might also contribute to the strengthening of institutional performance if it is effectively institutionalized as 'learning', as discussed next; but it could also result in internal corrective measures to address individual managers and staff members' performance – although, it should be added that there tends to be a perception (typically from an external perspective) that there is a "lack of internal sanctions" taken against individuals "who are [so-called] 'repeat non-compliers' with operational policies."[86] While this might be "a valid concern," as Bradlow and Naudé Fourie argue, it must also be considered that "major problems concerning operational policy compliance" could, for instance, "arise from"

> the underlying complexity of the projects being funded by the institutions and the uncertainty of staff as to how properly to apply the policies. This, in turn, is sometimes exacerbated by mixed messages given by management, gaps in the available knowledge, or staff succumbing to time and cost pressures.[87]

That said, the extent to which the Inspection Panel's input actually strengthens the Board's position is not something that that can be conclusively determined on the basis of

---

85 *Uganda: Power Projects* (2001), IR, § 101. *And see, e.g., Albania: Integrated Coastal Zone Management* (2007), as discussed *in* sections 8.2.2 & 12.1; *and India: Mumbai Urban Transport* (2004), as discussed *in* section 10.3.

86 Bradlow & Naudé Fourie (2013), p. 36. *Also see* Ninio's comments *in* note 72, Ch. 7.

87 Bradlow & Naudé Fourie (2013), p. 36.

Inspection Panel practice only.[88] To be an effective 'instrument of the Board', the Inspection Panel has to be accepted as such by the Board; and while the Board generally express its appreciation for the Panel's contribution in official World Bank press releases filed in the aftermath of an Inspection Panel investigation, tensions surrounding the Panel's (implicit) investigation of borrowers could certainly have a negative impact on the realization of this outcome.[89]

7.1.5   Strengthening institutional performance: policy advice and institutional learning

It would appear that World Bank management and staff expect, at the very least, that the Inspection Panel process should not *impede* World Bank performance. And, as noted earlier, Inspection Panel investigations are often perceived as costly and disruptive for the institution. In *Lebanon: Greater Beirut Water Supply*, for instance, the Inspection Panel assured the Board that is was "mindful of the importance and urgency" of the project, as well as

> the need to minimize any disruption in the flow of work in Project implemen-
> tation. In its interactions with Management and the borrower, the Panel would
> emphasize the importance of ensuring that the investigation per se does not
> delay Project implementation. Moreover, the focused nature of the investigation
> as described above would enable the investigation to be carried out in a timely
> manner. [...] The Panel would like to note that the measures outlined above
> with respect to this investigation are in keeping with the Panel's overall efforts
> to increase the efficiency and effectiveness of the Panel's process.[90]

As to what constitutes 'institutional performance', this is likely to be determined by the Bank's institutional aims; however, as discussed earlier, there are complementary but also

---

88 In particular since the proceedings of Board meetings, until fairly recently, been not been published – *see* note 35, Ch. 7.

89 *See e.g.*, section 4.3.2 – *and see* the Chinese Board member's comments *at* note 105, Ch. 4.

90 *Lebanon: Greater Beirut Water Supply* (2010) First ER, p. 5 [Statement of IP's Chairperson to Board]. *Note*, in this case, the Panel postponed its recommendation about the necessity for an investigation, and in its final ER (dated 8 April 2013) the Panel stated (at §§ 56-57) that is was "pleased to note Management's commitment in the course of the Panel process to ensure that the issues raised in the Request and identified by the Panel as warranting further consideration were seriously taken into account to ensure that the Project is in compliance with Bank policies. As a result, important steps are being taken to address potential harm to the Requesters and other Project affected people. [...] [T]he Panel concludes that subsequent investigation of whether the Bank has complied with its operational policies and procedures, with respect to the allegations contained in the Requests for Inspection, is not warranted." On arguments about the perceived costs of internal accountability mechanisms, *see e.g.*, note 98, Ch. 4.

competing relationships among these institutional aims.[91] Subsequently, expectations with respect to the strengthening of institutional performance often reflect these tensions.

Beyond the confines of a particular development project,[92] the strengthening of institutional performance as a discrete outcome of accountability processes typically manifests as contributions towards 'institutional learning' (thus, pointing to recurrent 'structural' or 'thematic' issues)[93] and 'policy advice' (commenting about the adequacy of certain aspects of operational policies).

Institutional strengthening through learning as a distinct outcome of accountability processes is considered particularly significant. From the internal perspective, the Bank's decades of experience with adapting to an evolving understanding of 'what development assistance should entail', combined with the skills and expertise of its highly educated management and staff are often portrayed as the Bank's most valuable asset and – in the context of increased competition – its strongest differentiating factor.[94] Of course, this might also mean that the Bank might experience difficulty to internalize learning emanating from an accountability process such as the Inspection Panel, who are not staffed by Bank 'insiders' (or, at least, not predominantly so).[95]

Indeed, the external perspective often portrays the Bank as an institution that is 'deaf' to its critics and unable to learn from its mistakes – which, in turn, results in a recurrence of social, economic and environmental harm that could arguably have been prevented.[96] Based on this underlying conception, an internal accountability mechanism such as the Inspection Panel is not only expected to contribute to recourse and redress for project-affected people in the context of particular development projects; the institutional learning ensuing from Inspection Panel practice is also expected to strengthen institutional performance – particularly in areas such as environmental and social risk management that can, in turn, be strengthened to become more effective in avoiding and mitigating harm on future projects.[97]

---

91 *See* section 4.2.2.

92 In this regard, the realization and enforcement of Bank and/or Borrower corrective/remedial actions can be seen as strengthening institutional performance particularly in respect to the particular development project which formed the subject of the Inspection Panel Request. *Note*, however, that Bank corrective actions can also include activities aimed at strengthening the broader development-lending portfolio.

93 The examples from Inspection Panel practice collated in Chapters 8 – 11 in particular would resort under this category.

94 In this regard, *see e.g.*, current World Bank President Kim's comments *at* note 263, Ch. 12; *and see* former World Bank President Wolfensohn's comments *at* note 226, Ch. 7.

95 On the measures contained in the Inspection Panel Resolution to ensure its independence form Bank management and staff, *see* section 6.2.4.

96 *See e.g.*, A. Versi, 'Is the World Bank Deaf?', 192 *African Business* 8 (1994); *and* H.F. French, 'The World Bank: Now Fifty, but How Fit?', 7 *World Watch* 4, p. 10 (1994).

97 On the competing conceptions of accountability for 'performance' *versus* 'harm', *see* section 4.2.2.

In the aftermath of the Inspection Panel's first investigation in 1994, Bradlow commented that it was "still too early to determine whether the Bank" would actively "use the findings from the Panel's investigation to improve the Bank's operating policies and procedures";[98] however, Bradlow added, failure to do so "would suggest a remarkable inability of the Bank to learn from experience [...]."[99] That said, similar to the remarks made with regard to other accountability outcomes discussed in this chapter, Inspection Panel practice alone does not provide conclusive evidence as to whether the Bank effectively employs the Panel's findings towards institutional learning and policy improvement. Generally speaking, however, what *can* be discerned from Inspection Panel practice certainly leaves a mixed impression.

On the one hand, Inspection Panel practice provides examples that could be reasonably construed as indicative of (at least) a willingness on the part of the Bank to learn from Inspection Panel investigations. In *Cameroon: Petroleum*, for example, Bank management commented ("[i]n recognition of the importance of independent advice on highly risky and contentious projects with serious and multidimensional environmental concerns") that it would "welcome an opportunity to discuss with the Inspection Panel what constitutes 'independent' advice in the context of" the project.[100] "In conducting [environmental assessments", Management added, "the question of how much data is enough frequently arises,"

> given the need to make case-by-case judgments on the type and amount of data to be collected [...]. In the case of the [oil] pipeline [to be constructed as part of the project], Management considered the trade-offs, because the data collected did provide a sufficient basis for mitigative measures through the EASs and for monitoring. In the context of [this project], Management would welcome an occasion to exchange views with the Inspection Panel on what should constitute adequate data collection.[101]

Whereas in *Ghana: Second Urban Environment Sanitation*, where the Panel highlighted several compliance issues related to the project's "legacy" component, the Panel referenced similar findings made with regard to its *Uganda: Power Projects* investigations.[102] Indeed,

---

98 Bradlow (1996), p. 286.

99 *Id.*

100 *Cameroon: Petroleum Development and Pipeline* (2002), MRIR, § 22.

101 *Cameroon: Petroleum Development and Pipeline* (2002), MRIR, § 28. On compliance issues related to baseline data collection, *see e.g.*, section 14.2. *Note*, this example also demonstrates the approach to policy application and compliance review that emphasise procedural and substantive elements, as discussed *in* section 6.3.4. In this example, however, Management appears to be in agreement with this approach.

102 *I.e.*, related to a predecessor project. For explanations/definitions of acronyms, abbreviations and other terminology used in World Bank development-lending operations, *see* the Appendix.

the Panel noted, "legacy issues are found in many projects, whether or not the initial operation was financed by the Bank."[103] "In response to the Panel's findings included in the [2001 Uganda: Power Projects] Investigation Report," the Panel added, "Management committed"

> 'to develop guidance on how to address environmental and social safeguard issues in legacy projects that suffer significant interruptions in implementation.' The Panel hopes that the issues and findings of the present investigation will also be taken into account in developing this guidance.[104]

Or, as the Inspection Panel noted in a recent publication "there have been a growing number of complaints related to land use and land management projects."[105] These projects, as the Panel concluded in *Panama: Land Administration*, "may constitute an important contribution to social and economic development," but they also "pose significant operational risks" and "are often politically controversial."[106] Hence, it is particularly "important for the Bank to systematically assess,"

> both during design and during project implementation, operational risks and risks of a political economy nature, and devote adequate trained staff and resources to the project. This investigation suggests that the Bank should be given credit for engaging in this extremely important Project in Panama, though it may not have invested sufficient resources to address the risks involved, especially with regard to supervision.[107]

Edith Brown Weiss (a former Inspection Panel member and chair) has shed some light on the Panel's broader institutional impact as a result of key investigations in which she was involved. For example, Brown Weiss notes that after the Panel's investigation of *Democratic Republic of Congo: Transitional Support*,"the region modified its approach for identifying indigenous communities";[108] in response to the Panel's findings in *Cambodia: Forest Concession Management*, "the Bank altered aspects of its forest policy";[109] the Panel's *India: Mumbai Urban Transport* investigation prompted "the Bank [to] revie[w] its risk

---

103 *Ghana: Second Urban Environment Sanitation* (2007), IR, § 331-332.
104 Brown Weiss (2010), pp. 486-487.
105 Inspection Panel (2012), p. 3.
106 *Panama: Land Administration* (2009), IR, § 351.
107 *Panama: Land Administration* (2009), IR, § 351. For issues related to project supervision, *also see* section 15.1.
108 *Id.* For a discussion of these issues (also pertaining to the *DRC: Transitional Support* case), *see e.g.*, sections 10.1 & 13.1.
109 *Id.* As discussed, *e.g.*, in section 10.1.

assessment process";[110] and, "in response to" the Panel's investigation of *Albania: Integrated Coastal Zone Management*, the World Bank's "President called for a review of Project Appraisal Documents and other measures to ensure the quality and accuracy of Bank project documents."[111]

Moreover, as several of the examples from Inspection Panel practice included in Part II of this book demonstrate, the Panel's comments are often not only of relevance for the specific project circumstances. For instance, as the earlier-mentioned *Ghana: Sanitation* example demonstrated, the Panel frequently points to issues it had identified in earlier investigations, highlights certain compliance issues as 'root causes' for issues in other areas,[112] and has also increasingly included 'systemic issues' identified over the course of an investigation in a separate section in its investigation reports.

As to providing input about the adequacy of certain aspects of the operational policy framework, Inspection Panel practice certainly reflects the Panel's willingness to do so when the opportunity presents itself in the context of an investigation.[113] However, there are also different expectations as to whether the Panel should be involved in providing 'policy advice' on a more formal basis, such as being "involved in the [at the time of writing, ongoing] reassessment of safeguard policies".[114] Van Putten notes, for instance, that "[l]egal advisors to the panel consider the involvement of panel members" in a policy advisory capacity "to be a conflict of interest."[115] "Although one can very well understand the more legalistic approach of this view," Van Putten argues, "it is regrettable"

> that the experiences of the members of the panel both at the bank and in the field investigating compliance with the bank and in the field investigating compliance with bank policies are not taken into account when policies are amended by the board. This situation derives from the rule that a judge does not make the law but only enforces it. The discussion in itself is an indication of further steps toward making the accountability mechanisms within the MFIs, such as the Inspection Panel, more judicial.[116]

---

110 *Id.* As discussed, *e.g., in* sections 10.3 & 12.2.

111 *Id.* As discussed, *e.g., in* sections 8.2.2 & 12.1.

112 *E.g., see* note 177, Ch. 11, on shortcomings in the area of information disclosure as a root cause for other compliance issues.

113 *E.g., see* note 100, Ch. 13, on the need for "clearer guidelines" on the development of self-standing/stand-alone IP(D)Ps. *But see* Bank management's response to this recommendation, *at* note 103, Ch. 13

114 Van Putten (2008), p. 235.

115 *Id.*

116 *Id.* On the debate about the judicial nature of the Panel, *see* section 6.2.4; on the negative connotations of the formalist paradigm, *see* note 150, Ch. 2. *Also note*, the Inspection Panel has subsequently provided its input in the safeguards review – *see* Inspection Panel (2012). 'Submission to the World Bank's Safeguard Review and Update Process, The Inspection Panel, Lessons from Panel Cases: Inspection Panel Perspectives', available at: http://go.worldbank.org/QHT9YU3820.

It would appear, however, as if the Panel has come to view contributions to policy advice and institutional learning as part of its 'informal' functions. For instance, the Inspection Panel notes in its recently updated Operating Procedures that the "extensive range of the Panel's investigation and other reports"

> represents an independent assessment of the Bank's application of key operational policies and procedures in challenging circumstances, which may be useful to the Board and Management in establishing good development practice and in identifying and eliminating factors that lead to harm.[117]

The Panel adds that it "presents systemic issues and reflections discerned from its work to the Board, Management, and the public via its Annual Report and other publications as well as through meetings with the Board and Management as and when requested."[118] Furthermore, the "Panel may also present such observations to the Board's Committee on Development Effectiveness in its periodic meetings"[119] and, finally, "hosts meetings and events to discuss outcomes of its investigations and other reports with Management and relevant [external] stakeholders so as to facilitate institutional learning."[120]

On the other hand, Inspection Panel practice also provides examples where Bank management has explicitly rejected such input (and, in the process, revealed a hint of irritation with the Panel), on the basis that it was not part of the Panel's mandate. In its response to the Panel's investigation report in *South Africa: Eskom Investment Support*, for example, Management stated that it took "note of chapter 6 of the Panel's Report on systemic issues,"

> which relate neither to compliance, nor to harm or potential harm in connection with the [Project]. This chapter, as well as other sections of the Report, takes an evaluative rather than compliance approach in reviewing issues at the policy level and discusses unrelated Bank projects. Management respectfully notes that the 1999 Clarification of the Resolution requires that 'the Panel will discuss in its written report only those material adverse effects, alleged in the request, that have totally or partially resulted from serious Bank failure of compliance with its policies and procedures.' Hence, Management offers no comment on issues raised in this chapter.[121]

---

117 Inspection Panel Operating Procedures (2014), § 78.
118 Inspection Panel Operating Procedures (2014), § 79.
119 *Id.*
120 Inspection Panel Operating Procedures (2014), § 80.
121 *South Africa: Eskom Investment Support* (2010), MRIR, § xxxii.

Whereas in its response to the Panel's investigation report in *Papua New Guinea: Small-holder Agriculture*, Bank management highlighted "that many aspects of the harm alleged by the Requesters"

> do not arise from the [Project]. Management notes that the Panel Report discusses a number of issues that relate neither to harm nor to potential harm stemming from the [Project].[122]

These types of Management responses would appear to support Miller-Adams's argument that "participatory approaches", in which the emphasis is placed on "learning from beneficiaries," "violat[e] key tenets of the Bank's organizational culture" in the sense that they "challenge the Bank's expert stance", "fit only awkwardly with the Bank's project cycle," while "the skills needed for working effectively with local groups" – and perhaps also for working with a functionally independent body such as the Inspection Panel – "are not those possessed by the majority of Bank staff."[123]

Be that as it may, the realization and enforcement of activities aimed at institutional strengthening, as an outcome of Inspection Panel practice, are dependent on multiple variables – including, for instance, the level of institutional credibility and 'prestige' enjoyed by the Inspection Panel.[124]

7.1.6   Normative development of the operational policy framework

In other words, the Inspection Panel provides informal 'policy advice' and input towards furthering 'institutional learning' that could also result in the further normative development of the operational policy framework; whereas other internal accountability mechanisms are specifically mandated to do so.[125] The discussion in this section, however, focuses

---

122 *Papua New Guinea: Smallholder Agriculture* (2009), MRIR, §§ 22 & 25. *Also see* MRIR, p. ix: "The Panel Report looks at The World Bank Group Framework and IFC Strategy for Engagement in the Palm Oil Sector and suggests providing input for a follow-up to this Framework on the basis of its investigation of [the Project]. Management feels that a discussion of the Framework, which has been endorsed by the Board, goes well beyond the scope of the compliance review of the [Project]." *But compare* these comments with former World Bank President Jim Wolfensohn's comments *at* note 216, Ch. 7. On the debate between Management and the Panel on the existence of a 'causal relationship' between 'harm' and alleged World Bank policy non-compliance, *see* section 4.3.2.

123 Miller-Adams (1999), p. 98. On notable aspects of the Bank's institutional culture, *also see* section 3.1.1.

124 Indeed, instances where the Inspection Panel affirms its support for underlying project objectives and/or broader World Bank institutional aims – *e.g.*, as illustrated by the examples included in Chapter 9 in particular – could also be construed as the Panel's attempts to strengthen its credibility in the eyes of Bank management and staff. On the importance of the Panel's institutional credibility as a function of maintaining its functional independence, *also see* Naudé Fourie (2009), pp. 186-210.

125 Notably, the IEG; *see e.g.* section 6.2.

on normative development of the operational policy framework as a form of "non-inten-tional" normative development[126] – a 'derivative' accountability outcome that occurs, as argued here, as the (usually, unintended) 'by-product' of the 'dispute resolution triad', or "triangle" that is "formed between" a citizen-driven independent accountability mechanism such as the Panel ("institutional adjudicator"), the Requesters ("complainant") and Bank management ("respondent"), as depicted by Figure 12.[127]

Generally speaking, expectations concerning such normative development are most strongly held by external constituency groups. For instance, from the perspective of (potential) Requesters and the civil society actors assisting them in filing their claims, normative development has the potential to create what lawyers would describe as 'legal certainty' – which, in turn, plays an important role in ensuring that project-affected people can make effective use of the recourse avenue offered by the Inspection Panel mechanism.[128] Triadic dispute resolution, as Shapiro and Stone Sweet posit, "generates a discourse"

> about how people ought to behave. Because rules, reasoning about rules, and the adaption of rules to specific social needs constitute the core of this discourse precedent follows naturally. Precedent helps to legitimize TDR by simultane-ously acknowledging rule-making behavior, while constraining that same behavior with a rule: that like cases shall be settled likewise.[129]

Other external commentators (including this author) have argued that the Panel's normative development of the operational policy framework can serve as a means to assert – and progressively expand – its functional independence and authority vis-à-vis World Bank management.[130] Moreover, as Kingsbury argues, the "system of quasi-independent panel supervision of Bank compliance with its own policies" has "the potential to increase the normative significance of both the [operational] policies and the jurisprudence surrounding their interpretation."[131] The dispute resolution triad formed between Requesters, Bank management and Inspection Panel (with the Board acting as the final 'arbiter') "sets up a natural dynamic for the [Inspection] panel" through which it can "enhance its jurispru-dence" and thereby strengthen "its own role, supported by legally oriented NGOs and potentially by some sections of Bank staff whose work such an approach vindicates."[132]

---

126 Klabbers *in* Von Bogdandy et al. (Eds.) (2010), p. 719.
127 Kingsbury (1999), p. 323.
128 In this regard, *also see* section 7.1.1 on the types of obstacles facing (potential) Requesters in filing a Request at the Inspection Panel.
129 Shapiro & Stone Sweet (2002), pp. 64-65. For arguments concerning the consistent versus flexible application of the operational policy framework, *see e.g.*, section 6.3.
130 *See e.g.*, Naudé Fourie (2009), pp. 213-250; *and see in general* Naudé Fourie (2012).
131 Kingsbury (1999), p. 323. *Also see* Boisson de Chazournes' comments *at* notes 151, 152 & 153, Ch. 6.
132 *Id.*

However, as Kingsbury's remarks indicate, expectations surrounding the Panel's contribution towards the normative development of the operational policy framework are closely related to the debates about the Inspection Panel's 'quasi-judicial' *versus* 'non-judicial' nature, and the 'legal' versus 'non-legal' nature of the policies.[133] Indeed, these issues might help to explain why the Bank often appears reluctant to accept the Panel's 'policy advice' and 'institutional learning' input – and perhaps also why Bank management might be hesitant to accept Inspection Panel findings that manifestly aim to elaborate on the normative content in specific policy provisions (as reflected in numerous examples included in Part II of this book).

By implication, if Bank management accepts such Inspection Panel input, it also accepts the Panel's authority to *interpret* the operational policies; and this, in turn arguably erodes the Bank's authority as the principle entity involved in determining the content and scope of its own obligations – which, as Bradlow points out, IFIs such as the Bank have come to expect due to "the "exquisite ambiguity" in their Articles of Agreement and the prevailing ambiguity regarding their international legal obligations.[134] Moreover, should the Panel's interpretation call for a broadening of the content and scope of World Bank obligation – as is often the case[135] – the Bank might have to deal with the consequences of continuously expanding demands and expectations about 'what it should be (held) accountable for'.[136]

Of course, as noted earlier, Bank management is under no obligation to accept the Inspection Panel's interpretations of particular policy provisions – and, indeed, it frequently does not. In such instances, one might argue that normative development of the operational policy framework has not been realized since the Panel's interpretations have failed to become influential within the institution. However, unlike the other outcomes discussed here (but similar to 'output-legitimacy' mentioned at the onset of this chapter), normative development occurring as a 'by-product' of Inspection Panel investigations retains the potential to influence the demands and expectations of external constituency groups – whether or not the Panel's interpretations are accepted and internalized by the institution.[137]

---

133 *See*, respectively, sections 6.2.4 & 5.1.1.

134 *See* note 140, Ch. 5. *Also see* Freestone's comments *at* note 119, Ch. 6.

135 *See* especially Ch. 10 and Ch. 11.

136 In this regard, *see* Ch. 4.

137 *Also see* Bradlow & Naudé Fourie (2013), pp. 42-43: "In cases in which the IAM and the relevant IFI management follow different interpretations of a particular operational policy provision, the institutional entity responsible for final approval of the IAM's compliance review reports (here, the IFC and World Banks' Board of Executive Directors) becomes, in effect, the final arbiter of how the policies should be interpreted. [...] It is important to note that the situation with respect to external stakeholders is different. Whether or not IFC and World Bank staff and management accept the interpretations of the CAO and Inspection Panel as authoritative, the IAMs' interpretations of the operational policies are the benchmarks that shape project affected people and their representative's expectations concerning their rights vis-à-vis the IFC and World Bank."

Importantly, it also maintains the potential to "influence our understanding of the responsibilities of all international organizations," as Bradlow argues.[138]

Therefore, as Bradlow and Hunter conclude, the "actions and decisions" of IFIs – including the findings of the IAMs affiliated with these institutions – "may not" necessarily "set binding international legal principles", but "they do constitute informative and persuasive examples"

> that other international legal subjects use in formulating their own decisions and positions on these issues. In this way, they are contributing to the accretion of precedents that inform the creation of international customary law and the principles incorporated into international agreements. In some cases, the IFIs' policies and actions create expectations about the type of treatment that stakeholders can expect in certain circumstances, thereby helping to create applicable soft international law that can affect the expectations of these same categories of stakeholders in their dealings with other economic actors.[139]

Furthermore, the findings of citizen-driven accountability mechanisms – in combination with the "sometimes legalistic responses of management" "are creating a dialogue that can contribute to the progressive development of the international law applicable in the context of IFI operations."[140]

Or, as Suzuki and Nanwani argue, "[w]hen the rights and interests of private individuals and groups conflict with those of international organizations" in the context of "claims lodged within an internal accountability mechanism or special tribunal,"

> a reconfiguration of authority and control over decisions of international organizations inevitably occurs. One guide for this reconfiguration is the Universal Declaration of Human Rights of 1948, which is customary international law and has the attributes of *jus cogens*. As such, the human rights provisions in the Universal Declaration are binding not only on states but also on international organizations and "anyone whose choice about an event can have some international significance." Any one of these international actors might be held affirmatively responsible for a particular violation of human rights.

---

138 Bradlow (1996), pp. 287-288. In this regard, *also see* note 187, Ch. 7.
139 Bradlow & Hunter *in* Bradlow & Hunter (Eds.) (2010), p. 395.
140 Bradlow & Hunter *in* Bradlow & Hunter (Eds.) (2010), pp. 395-396. *Note*, this comment also demonstrates the negative connotations of the formalist paradigm – here made with respect to Bank management's narrow interpretation of the operational policies; *see* note 150, Ch. 2.

"Viewed in this light," Suzuki and Nanwani conclude, "the accountability mechanisms of MDBs"

> are at the forefront of the development of the international law of human rights, which "depend[s] in no small measure upon the ability of individuals and private groups to challenge unlawful deprivations."[141]

7.2   DEBATING THE INSPECTION PANEL'S ROLE AND THE VALUE OF ITS CONTRIBUTION TOWARDS ENSURING WORLD BANK ACCOUNTABILITY

The debate about the (primary) reason(s) for the Inspection Panel's establishment and which actors' actions had been 'conclusive' in ensuring the Panel's establishment and survival beyond the first turbulent years of its existence appears, as noted earlier, to have been largely settled.[142] The debate continues, however, about *the Inspection Panel's role* ('what is the Panel supposed to be doing'?) and the 'real' *value of the its contribution* towards ensuring World Bank accountability ('how effective is the Panel in doing what it is supposed to be doing'?)[143] – and continues, moreover, to reflect the competition for primacy between the interests, demands, expectations and conceptions of internal *versus* external constituency groups.

7.2.1   *What is the role of the Inspection Panel?*

Internal and external constituency groups tend to emphasize different aspects of the Inspection Panel's role – as a reflection of their respective interests. Consequently, they also tend to hold different underlying conceptions about the particular outcomes to which the Inspection Panel should contribute *primarily*.

---

141 Suzuki & Nanwani (2005-2006), p. 225; the authors quote M.S McDougal, H.D. Lasswell & L. Chen (1980), *Human rights and World Public Order*, New Haven, Conn.: Yale University Press, at p. 279.

142 *See* section 3.2.3.

143 *Note*, commentators criticizing the 'effectiveness' of the Inspection Panel typically do not define what they mean by it, although their criticisms are generally associated with the (non-) realization of particular outcomes, and therefore usually reflect the "dominant definition of effectiveness in the social science literature", which, as Shany comments, "appears to be based on the 'rational system approach', which offers a rather straight forward formulation: 'an action is effective if it accomplishes its specific objective aim.'" *See* Shany (2010), pp. 10-11. Shany adds (at *id.*): "[T]his performance-standard normally has to be assessed over predefined units of time. Consequently, in order to measure the effectiveness of an organization according to the 'rational system approach', one has to identify the organization's aims or goals – *i.e.*, the desired outcomes it ought to generate, and ascertain the time frame over which some or all of these goals can reasonably be expected to be met."

The external perspective, for example, tends to emphasize (what is described here as) the 'public' facet of the Panel's mandate. "Although the decision to create an independent Panel [was] purely an internal one," as Hansungule argues, for instance, "it is important" "that this [internal decision] is viewed in the context of its public nature."[144] From this viewpoint, the "most important innovation" of the Inspection Panel's mandate, is the fact that is has been "designed," as Clark puts it, "to respond directly to grievances from citizens of developing countries about the environmental and social impacts of World Bank-funded projects";[145] or, as Bissell comments, that citizen-driven accountability mechanisms provide "the interested public with another constructive *channel* through which to maintain a *dialogue* with [multilateral development banks]."[146] A body such as the Inspection Panel, therefore, "combine[s] the possibility of access of individuals and private groups to rights under international law, with the opportunity to question the activities of international organizations."[147] And, given "the difficultly of providing access for individuals and private groups to international adjudication,"[148] Bissell adds, the "extent to which the Inspection Panel"

> is enriching and modifying the Bank's approach to its legal obligations is pro-
> viding an unusual window for members of the public to access quasi-legal
> processes and norms.[149]

"In giving citizens *a right to recourse*, the establishment of IAMs," as the Independent Accountability Mechanisms Network underscores, "was an innovation in both global governance and international law,"

> broadening the concept of accountability and creating a first-ever formal avenue
> for people themselves to challenge the decisions of international institutions
> and seek redress for harm done.[150]

---

144 Hansungule *in* Alfredsson & Ring (Eds.) (2001), p. 153.
145 Clark *in* Clark et al. (Eds.) 2003, p. xiii.
146 Bissell (2002), p. 2 (emphasis added).
147 Bissell (1997), p. 741. *Also see* Boisson de Chazournes *in* Treves et al. (Eds.) (2005), p 187, describing the Inspection Panel as "an unprecedented mechanism in the world of international organizations" since it "provides a direct means of controlling the Bank's operations, thus enabling certain actors to question the legitimacy of Bank activities."
148 Bissell (1997), p. 744.
149 *Id.* For similar comments, *also see* Bissell & Nanwani (2009), p. 10. On arguments about the 'quasi-legal' nature of the Panel, *see* section 6.2.4.
150 Independent Accountability Mechanisms Network (2012), p. 1 (emphasis added). On the ambiguity surrounding the phrase, 'rights and interests', *see e.g.*, note 195, Ch. 6.

The internal perspective, however, typically emphasizes (what is described here as) the 'institutional' facet of the Panel's mandate. Freestone emphasizes, for instance, that the Inspection Panel's role had been set out clearly in its founding Resolution; therefore, "[a]lthough the Panel is authorized to receive requests for inspection from 'an affected party in the territory of a borrower that is not a single individual,'" the Board has mandated the Panel only "to investigate 'failure of the Bank to follow its operational policies and procedures with respect to the design, appraisal and/or implementation of a project.'"[151] In other words, the Panel is, foremost, an instrument of the Board. Therefore, the "objective of the Inspection Panel," as former World Bank President Wolfensohn concludes, should not be to "look for right or wrong" but rather "to look whether management is conducting itself in the way that it has promised."[152] And, as Shihata pointed out, in establishing the Inspection Panel the Bank expected that it would "complement the responsibilities and functions of the [Bank's] existing" accountability mechanisms that aim to "ensur[e] quality control and compliance with the requirements of the Bank's Articles of Agreement."[153]

In other words, while both internal and external accountability holders accept, as their mutual point of departure, that the Inspection Panel mechanism offers project-affected people an avenue for *recourse* that could possibly result in *Bank (and Borrower) actions*, they have very different demands and expectations as to the realization and enforcement of additional outcomes, as illustrated by Figure 13, which further influence their opinions as to the Inspection Panel's 'effectiveness' (as demonstrated in the next section).

Notably, external constituency groups typically hold additional demands and expectations about the realization and enforcement of *redress for project-affected people*, as well as the *normative development* of the operational policy framework (which, in turn, is viewed as significant for the further development of certain areas of international law).

Significantly, both internal and external constituency groups hold demands and expectations about the realization and enforcement of *strengthened World Bank governance* and *enhanced institutional performance*. However, competing conceptions are underlying these demands and expectations.

From the internal point of view, for example, recourse (a form 'horizontal' or 'bottom up' accountability) should strengthen, *principally*, 'vertical' World Bank accountability (that is, staff being accountable to Management; Management being accountable to Executive Board; Executive Board being accountable to Board of Governors).[154] From the external point of view, by contrast, recourse should strengthen *principally*, 'horizontal' or

---

151 Freestone (2013), p. 18.
152 Van Putten (2008), p. 346. *Note*, the author quotes from an interview conducted with former World Bank Group President, Jim Wolfensohn.
153 Shihata (2000), pp. 8-9 (emphasis added).
154 *See* section 3.2.1.

'bottom-up' World Bank accountability (that is, World Bank management and staff being held directly accountable by external constituency groups).[155]

Moreover, internal demands and expectations about the Inspection Panel's role in strengthening institutional performance are typically based in the 'accountability for performance' paradigm; whereas external demands and expectations about the Inspection Panel's role in strengthen institutional performance are typically based in the 'accountability for harm' paradigm.[156]

Figure 13   The Inspection Panel's 'Dual Accountability Mandate' – Reflecting Competing Interests, Demands, Expectations and Conceptions about Accountability Outcomes

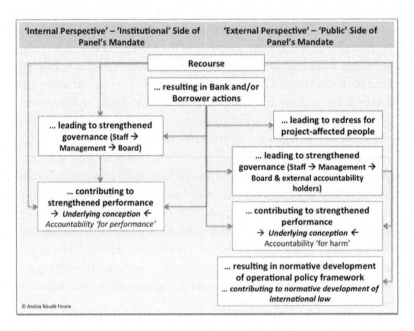

On the other hand, the Inspection Panel's own descriptions of its role reflect both 'public' and 'institutional' facets – or, as explained here, demonstrate the dual nature of the Inspection Panel's accountability mandate – although, to be sure, the Panel also tends to emphasize one facet over the other, depending on its primary audience.

For instance, in his address to the Board, delivered at the time of the Panel's presentation of its investigation report of *Chad: Petroleum*, Edward Ayensu emphasized that "the role of the Management Report", as specified in the Inspection Panel Resolution, "is to inform

---

155 *See* section 3.2.2.
156 *See* section 4.2.2.

the Board about the specific actions Management proposes to address the Panel's findings and not to dispute them."[157] "This is clearly stated in the 1999 Clarification to the Panel's Resolution," Ayensu added,

> where the Inspection Panel is defined as '*a fact-finding body on behalf of the Board.*' This was confirmed recently during Board discussions on the Lake Victoria Environmental Management Project. We, also, carry our duties impartially, and with the assistance of world-renowned experts in their fields.[158]

Whereas in its *India: Mumbai Urban Transport* investigation report, the Inspection Panel described its role as providing "an instrument for groups of two or more private citizens"

> who believe that they or their interests have been or could be harmed by Bank-financed activities to present their concerns through a Request for Inspection. In short, the Panel provides a link between the Bank and the people who are likely to be affected by the projects it finances.[159]

In the Inspection Panel's 2011/2012 Annual Report, on the other hand, the Panel explains that it is "an independent forum," which serves as a "'bottom-up' accountability *and* recourse mechanism"

> that investigates IBRD/IDA-financed projects to determine whether the Bank has complied with its operational policies and procedures (including social and environmental safeguards), *and* to assess related issues of harm.[160]

"The availability of the Panel", moreover, "promotes more inclusive and sustainable development"

> by giving project-affected people, including those who are often poor and most vulnerable, greater voice in Bank-financed projects that affect them.[161]

---

157 *Chad: Petroleum Development and Pipeline* (2001), Inspection Panel Chair Address to the Board, p. 4.
158 *Id.* (emphasis added). For similar comments *see* the Inspection Panel Chair Address to the Board during its discussion of the *South Africa: Eskom Investment Support* case, *at* note 70, Ch. 6.
159 *India Mumbai Urban Transport Project*, IR (ES), p. 2.
160 Inspection Panel Annual Report 2011/2012, p. xiv (emphasis added). *Also see* Inspection Panel Annual Report (1999/2000), p. 7.
161 *Id.* For similar remarks, *also see* Inspection Panel Annual Report (1999/2000), p. 7.

Or, as the Panel described its role in a 2012-publication, the Panel "provides for *accountability and redress* through its process and its assessment of Bank compliance with operational policies".[162] Ultimately, the Panel concluded, the "Panel's work"

> is a testament to the importance of the Bank's safeguard policies in protecting and supporting the rights and interests of people and the environment, *and* improving development outcomes.[163]

Whereas in its recently updated Operating Procedures, the Panel underscores that it has "two important accountability functions".[164] Firstly, the Panel "provides a forum for people, including those who are often poor and vulnerable,"

> to seek *recourse for harm* which they believe result from Bank-supported operations. As such, the Panel is a "bottom-up" or citizen-driven accountability mechanism that responds to grievances and demands for redress. This promotes more inclusive and sustainable development by giving project-affected people a greater voice in Bank- financed projects that impact them.[165]

Secondly, the Panel "provides an independent and impartial assessment *of claims about harm and related non-compliance with Bank policies*"

> as a check-and-balance for the Board and other concerned stakeholders. This contributes towards institutional learning and helps to improve development effectiveness of World Bank operations.[166]

It should also be noted, furthermore, that the Bank often acknowledges the dual aspects of the Inspection Panel's mandate – typically, in formal statements made with regard to the Panel. For example, in a recent edition of the World Bank's official external communications guide, the Bank notes that "[t]he Inspection Panel helps ensure compliance with Bank policies", and that the Panel is

---

162 Inspection Panel (2012), p. 1 (emphasis added).
163 *Id.* (emphasis added). *Note*, this example also demonstrates the Panel's attempts at reconciling (potentially) conflicting institutional aims – as discussed in section 4.2.2. On the ambiguity surrounding the phrase, 'rights and interests', *see e.g.,* note 195, Ch. 6.
164 Inspection Panel Operating Procedures (2014), § 2.
165 *Id.* (emphasis added).
166 *Id.* (emphasis added).

an independent body to which individuals and communities can turn if they believe that their rights or interests have been or could be directly harmed by a Bank-financed project.[167]

In the formal statement released after its adoption of the Inspection Panel's investigation report in the *Albania: Integrated Coastal Zone Management* case, the Executive Board emphasized that the Panel's "investigative process demonstrates the value of an independent Inspection Panel in strengthening the Bank's accountability *and* effectiveness."[168] Whereas current World Bank Group President, Jim Yong Kim, recently affirmed that "[t]he presence of the Inspection Panel in the World Bank"

> is a testament to our basic values. Being accountable *and* delivering results to the people we serve is at the core of our most fundamental commitments.[169]

7.2.2   What is the 'real' value of the Inspection Panel's contribution?

Since the Inspection Panel has to execute a dual accountability mandate, there are significant challenges involved in determining the 'real value' of the Inspection Panel's contribution – or, for that matter, in assessing whether or not the Panel is "really effective."[170] For one thing, as Hale comments, we lack "counterfactual examples (i.e., what would have happened in a specific case had a complaint not been brought before the Panel)."[171]

Nevertheless, when considering the wide range of existing opinions, one conclusion almost seems inevitable: the Inspection Panel does not appear to meet the demands and expectations of either internal or external constituency groups. In this regard, Van Putten recalls "the first warning" she "received after being appointed a member of the World Bank Inspection Panel" – namely: "If you seek to be appreciated and loved, this is the wrong post. Nobody will ever be satisfied by the panel reporting: neither management nor the requesters."[172] "Ever since it began," as Boisson de Chazournes observes, "the [Inspection Panel] procedure has caused tensions,"

> as the different actors involved have not always been satisfied with the process or its results. For instance, Bank Management does not appreciate being questioned, nor do borrower countries appreciate being pinpointed, nor complaining

---

167 World Bank (2015), e-Book.
168 World Bank Press Release, 17 February 2009.
169 Inspection Panel Annual Report 2013/2014, p. 7 (emphasis added).
170 On criticisms about the Panel's lack of effectiveness, *also see* note 10, Ch. 1.
171 Hale *in* Hale & Held (Eds.) (2011), pp. 151-152.
172 Van Putten (2008), p. 217.

private parties not achieving their pursued goals because of blockages or slowness in the course of the procedure.[173]

Indeed, most external and internal views about the Panel seem to fall somewhere between disappointment, disillusionment, indifference or, at best, qualified endorsement.

For instance, external constituency groups (which tend to emphasize the 'public' side of the Inspection Panel's mandate), highlight the negative effects of the limitations within the Panel's mandate – notably: that the Panel is unable to realize and enforce redress for project-affected people. Because the Inspection Panel procedure "does not result in binding decision against the Bank" nor "provide for compensation for affected individuals," as De Wet notes, for example, "the impact of cosmopolitan accountability models within international institutions"

> is still significantly diluted by accountability models directed at the Member states or in some instances the international community of States.[174]

Whereas Oleschak-Pillai, based on an analysis of "the role, reports and outcomes of four cases investigated by the Inspection Panel relating to India," argues that the Inspection Panel might be "an innovative model of accountability in international law," but "it *does not always have positive impacts on outcomes in bank-financed projects.*"[175] Worse, since "[n]on-implementation of any policy of the Bank does not hold any real sanction, either for the borrower or for the Bank," Oleschak-Pillai concludes, "the reports of the Inspection Panel are in some senses creating a source of legitimacy for the operations of the Bank,"

> in that they make pretence of dealing with the issues. In reality, however, implementation remains poor. The Inspection Panel's credibility is at stake mainly because of the Board's refusal to change positions. [...] The World Bank needs to wake up to the fact that merely the existence of the Inspection Panel does not alone create accountability. It also needs to show that the policies reflect international medium standards and that those are actually implemented.[176]

---

173 Boisson de Chazournes *in* Treves et al. (Eds.) (2005), p. 202.
174 De Wet *in* Von Bogdandy et al. (Eds.) (2010), p. 870. On accountability models and their influence on underlying conceptions about the 'primary' constituency of World Bank accountability, *see e.g.*, section 3.2.3.
175 Oleschak-Pillai *in* Wouters et al. (Eds.) (2010), p. 401 (emphasis added).
176 Oleschak-Pillai *in* Wouters et al. (Eds.) (2010), p. 429.

Or, as Clark argues, while "the principles of accountability and rule of law imply that the Bank should be held accountable for development outcomes in projects that it has financed", "claimants to the Inspection Panel are often frustrated"

> by the lack of real change on the ground, the failure to mitigate or adequately compensate for the harm caused by the Bank's role in policy violations, and the Bank's failure to bring projects into compliance despite well-documented problems. In addition, people who have been involuntarily resettled and whose plight has been repeatedly documented do not have an oversight process for determining that their standards of living have been improved or at least restored, the fundamental requirement of the Bank's policy. This is essentially a failure of governance and should be corrected through greater internal responsibility. The Bank's demonstrated weaknesses relating to policy implementation indicates the need for improved capacity. The Bank has adopted a policy framework, but it has not taken ownership of the accomplishment of the objectives of those policies. The Bank has created an accountability mechanism that helps to bridge the information divide between decision-makers and affected communities, but it has not taken responsibility for redress of known problems.[177]

Some commentators have contributed the Panel's lack of effectiveness in this regard to an overly 'narrow' focus on fact-finding and compliance review (often dismissively referred to as the Panel's 'policing function') as opposed to a broader focus on harm and problem-solving approaches that have the potential to remedy the adverse effects of harm. For example, Alvaro Umaña, one of the Inspection Panel's early members, argued that there were "two main functions" provided for in the Inspection Panel Resolution: "to monitor Management's compliance with the Banks operational policies and to assess 'material harm' on affected or potentially affected populations".[178] "Of these two functions," Umaña concluded,

> the first, which can be described as a 'policing' function, has proven to be less useful to the Board since the Panel's 'verdict' does not lead – nor should it lead – to any action beyond correcting failures in project design or execution.[179]

---

177 Clark (2002), p 223.
178 Umaña (1998), p. 326.
179 *Id*. For criticism of Umaña's view as well as the Panel's focus on 'harm' without ascertaining the existence of a 'causal link' between the harm in question and the actions or omissions of the Bank, *see* Shihata (2000), pp. 32-33, and 221-222; on the issue of the 'causal link', *also see* section 4.3.2.

The emphasis on fact-finding and compliance review, Suzuki and Nanwani argue, has meant that "the question of internal compliance or noncompliance has become the focus of the inspection process," while "the real question of accountability toward people who are affected by [Bank] projects has become sidelined."[180] "Once the inspection function accepts the complainants' requests for inspection and authorizes an inspection," Suzuki and Nanwani add,

> the complainants themselves are left outside the system. The affected people who requested 'inspection' will eventually be informed of the outcome of the inspection process only after the process is completed, with the possibility that their problem will remain unresolved.[181]

By contrast, Brown Weiss, a former Inspection Panel chair, argues that the importance of the Inspection Panel's "fact-finding" function should not be underestimated as it "provides an impartial way to determine what is or was happening."[182] Responding to criticisms about the Panel's lack of formal involvement in formulating recommendations for corrective and/or remedial Bank and/or Borrower actions, Brown Weiss argues that "[i]f the Panel, instead of Bank management, were to make recommendations", "it would be all too easy to dismiss them, since management and staff may have spent many more hours on the project or program than the Panel."[183] Furthermore, "[t]he substance of recommendations"

> can be phrased as observations, which others can pick up as appropriate. By finding facts, rather than making recommendations, it ensures that the Panel does not get co-opted into management. In contrast, if management were to adopt a recommendation by the Panel and something were to go awry, leading to a complaint from affected people, management could argue that the Panel cannot impartially review the complaint and hold management accountable, since it had an operational role in the activity. Fact-finding does not directly carry these risks, since those who are responsible for addressing the findings of the Panel remain responsible for how they address them.[184]

---

180 Suzuki & Nanwani (2005-2006), p. 219.
181 *Id. Note*, Inspection Panel practice (as recently formalized in the Panel's updated Operating Procedures) has provided more opportunity for the involvement of project-affected people after the Request had been submitted – as noted *e.g.*, *in* section 7.1.2.
182 Brown Weiss (2010), p. 487.
183 *Id.*
184 *Id.* For examples from Inspection Panel practice supporting this argument, *also see* Naudé Fourie (2009), pp. 216-222.

Brown Weiss also emphasizes the significance of "the pre-emptive effect" of the Inspection Panel mechanism – that is, Bank management and staff pay closer attention to operational policy compliance in the "hope to pre-empt the need for an investigation, or try to ensure that if one occurs, it will validate the actions of the Bank."[185]

For commentators emphasizing the Panel's potential for contributing to normative development, conversely, an emphasis on fact-finding and compliance review (in particular) would not necessarily constitute a cause for concern. In fact, one might argue that problem-solving is less likely to contribute to the normative development of the operational policy framework. It would seem, however, that most of the "high hopes" in this regard, expressed around "the time of [the Panel's] inception", have not materialized – or, at least not in the way international legal scholars would have preferred.[186] While there have been pronounced expectations "that the Inspection Panel along with the progressive development of the safeguard policies," would result in

> 'the upward harmonization of environmental and social standards globally' as
> well as 'influence the development of substantive areas of law applicable to the
> Bank's operations', including human rights law[,]

this "optimism", as Tan argues, "has not been borne out in the decade since [the Inspection Panel's]"

> inception, and although its safeguards have served as a template for other
> development agencies and commercial institutions the Bank's compliance with
> its own safeguard policies has been disappointing.[187]

---

185 Brown Weiss (2010), p. 487. For similar comments, *see* Shihata *at* note 207, Ch. 7. For a negative view on the effect of so-called 'Panel proofing', *see e.g.*, Clark (2002), pp. 221-222; *and see in general* Fox (2000). *But also see* Bradlow & Naudé Fourie (2013) who argue (at p. 37) that the practice of 'Panel proofing' "could be interpreted as Bank management and staff seeking to protect their interpretative prerogatives, or alternatively as the Bank adopting the Panel's interpretations and guidance on the operational policies."

186 C. Tan (2008), 'Mandating Rights and Limiting Mission Creep: Holding the World Bank and the International Monetary Fund Accountable for Human Rights Violations', 2 *Human Rights and International Legal Discourse* 1, p. 97; the author is quoted by Chimni *in* Bradlow & Hunter (Eds.) (2010), p. 50.

187 *Id.* For a different view, *see e.g.*, Naudé Fourie (2012), arguing (at p. 201) "that the Panel has, indeed, been fulfilling its normative potential to a certain degree – and specifically concerning the development of international standards for compliance review processes, human rights and public participation in decision-making. However, [...] the Panel's potential for normative development has to be qualified or, perhaps, restated given its institutional reality within the World Bank." Given this reality, (at p. 233) "the Panel can only generate normative standards in a manner that will preserve its institutional independence and judicial-ization – and its ability to continue future expansion of both. Given the limiting effects of political pressure and limitations inherent in its mandate, the Panel is therefore unlikely to be as explicit about what they are doing as international lawyers would prefer them to be."

For others, the value of the Inspection Panel's fact-finding and compliance review functions lies specifically in the enhanced transparency to which they contribute – which is of significance for internal and external accountability holders. Hale, for instance, argues that fact-finding and compliance review serve an "important editing function", pointing out that "[i]rrelevant information"

> can distract or mislead actors as surely as disingenuous information can. This is especially true in the complicated cases the Panel considers, and in an age where information technology permits a large array of actors to participate in discourse. Modern informational politics suffers from a "paradox of plenty" in which the vast quantities of information available actually make it more difficult to use. By focusing actors' attention on a particular set of facts, the Panel increases the value and force of information.[188]

Hence, Hale describes citizen-driven accountability mechanisms such as the Inspection Panel as "info-courts," which are "quasi-judicial in nature" although they "do not issue legal decisions,"

> but rather create non-binding reports that aim to clarify the facts of compliance or non-compliance in a particular case. The idea is to use transparency to create accountability.[189]

Furthermore, with this conception forming the point of departure of a 2006-study conducted by Hale and Slaughter, the authors found that "the transparency the Panel provides" had "a sizeable effect on Bank behaviour" – much more so than "the level of [external] activism surrounding a case."[190] Therefore, Hale concludes, any assessment of "the Panel's impact on actual practice," should take the 'transparency effect' into account, which would mean, for instance, that "any policy changes" brought about by "Panel investigations (which do nothing more than bring the facts in a certain case to light, that is, they do not have binding force) can be seen as a qualified success."[191]

---

188 Hale (2008), p. 8. On 'information' as a component in the "standard" and "surrogate" accountability models, *also see* section 2.2.

189 Hale *in* Hale & Held (Eds.) (2011), pp. 151-152. On the classification of internal accountability mechanisms, *also see* section 6.1; and on the debate about the 'quasi-judicial' nature of the Inspection Panel, *see* section 6.2.4.

190 *Id. Note*, Hale refers to a study 2000-study conducted by Fox (at *id.*), which found that "once a case [was] being reviewed", the level of external activism had "little effect on Bank behaviour". Hence, Fox concluded, the Panel's impact can, at best, be considered "an ambiguous mix of success and failures."

191 *Id.* For examples of such instances, *see* Brown Weiss's comments in section 7.1.5.

Or, as Boisson de Chazournes comments, although the Inspection Panel does not constitute "a contentious dispute settlement procedure" (nor, for that matter, is it "by any means a mechanism" that can be used to "challeng[e] or asser[t] the international organization's legal responsibility, no more than that of the borrower countries or their decision-making bodies),"[192] "in the event of a dysfunction within the system," the Inspection Panel mechanism nevertheless

> enables problems to be 'objectivized' by way of a control mechanism and may result in a correction of behaviour by the financial organization, for the benefit of the affected populations, through the implementation of corrective actions.[193]

Moreover, by making "the issues at stake [...] known to the public at large," Boisson de Chazournes concludes, 'problem objectivization' also "contributes to fairness and accountability at all stages" of the Inspection Panel process.[194]

Other views, finally, emphasize the complementary nature of the Inspection Panel's mandate, as well as the various interdependencies between accountability outcomes as important input when considering the value of the Panel's contribution. Kingsbury, for example, comments that the Inspection Panel is "clearly a mechanism of review," but it "is not so clearly *on its own* a mechanism of accountability."[195] The Board has to "approve a full inspection of a Bank project," and while the Panel "has powers in relation to management-proposed remedial action plans," "these powers depend on the Board."[196] Moreover, the Inspection Panel "cannot impose remedies or sanctions"

> on the Bank's management other than naming and shaming (although for individual staff, that prospect can operate as a strong and potentially disproportionate sanction).[197]

However, Kingsbury concludes, "[w]hen combined with the Bank's Executive Board," the Inspection Panel "can be viewed"

---

192 Boisson de Chazournes *in* Treves et al. (Eds.) (2005), pp. 199-200.
193 *Id.*
194 Boisson de Chazournes *in* Alfredsson & Ring (Eds.) (2001), p. 83. For examples in support of this argument, *see* the actions taken by the Inspection Panel to protect the integrity of its process – as discussed, *e.g., in* sections 3.1.5 & 6.2.4. In this regard, *also see* Naudé Fourie (2009), pp. 193-196. And *see* Brown Weiss (2010), pp. 488-489: "Ensuring transparency of the claims, process, reports, and findings," therefore, is essential for instilling trust in the system. Transparency allows everyone to identify any mistakes in the findings and to have confidence in them
195 Kingsbury *in* Cissé et al. (Eds.) (2012), e-Book.
196 *Id.*
197 *Id.*

as a composite accountability mechanism vis-à-vis management. The accountor is the Bank's management. The account holders are those persons or groups who trigger the inspection request and are able to participate in the panel's investigation and in any remedial arrangements made.[198]

Whereas Baimu and Panou comment, in similar fashion, that "[t]he panel's process does not provide legal remedies per se," which means that the avenue of recourse provided by the Inspection Panel mechanism "*does not by itself* give affected people rights of redress from the Bank, such as the right to seek financial compensation."[199] That being said, "the panel's process leads to the adoption of an action plan,"

> which seeks to bring the project into compliance with Bank policies and addresses related findings of harm or potential harm. Rather, *the result of the entire process* is to reestablish the situation that would, in all probability, have existed if the violation of the Bank's policies and procedures had not occurred.[200]

Or, as Boisson de Chazournes observes, "[t]he Panel exercises its investigatory and quasi-investigatory powers on a case-by-case basis, not to say on a project-by project basis," and "[i]n so doing, the Panel must decide on the applicability of relevant policies and procedures," after which it "interpret[s] their content with regard to the possible failure of the Bank in complying with them."[201] "Through its interpretative function," Boisson de Chazournes adds,

> it *may* contribute to the promotion of compliance with operational policies and procedures. This process *allows*, in fact, for clarification of the content of operational policies and procedures. It also gives the Inspection Panel the *opportunity* to highlight best practice in applying these instruments, but most importantly, it allows the Inspection Panel to publicize bad practices which have given rise to complaints before the Inspection Panel, and as such reveal possible failures and inconsistencies in complying with operational policies and procedures.[202]

---

198 *Id.*
199 *Id.* (emphasis added).
200 *Id.* (emphasis added).
201 Boisson de Chazournes *in* Alfredsson & Ring (Eds.) (2001), pp. 81-82. *Note*, this example provides a clear description as to what the Panel's mandate entail, in practice; in this regard, the examples included *in* Ch. 10 are particularly illustrative.
202 *Id. But compare* these comments with those of Freestone *at* note 119, Ch. 6.

Therefore, Boisson de Chazournes concludes, Inspection Panel mechanism "provides a new venue for dialogue on compliance issues"

> between a lending institution and the direct beneficiaries of its developmental activities, and in doing so significantly complements initiatives and actions aimed at ensuring compliance with Operational Standards.[203]

From within the World Bank – where the 'institutional' side of the Panel's mandate is typically highlighted – opinions about the value of the Inspection Panel's contribution have been similarly mixed, but have also, at times, appeared to be conflicting. For example, Ibrahim Shihata, generally considered as the principle 'architect' of the Inspection Panel Resolution (even as views presenting Shihata as the 'founding farther' of the Inspection Panel have not been uncontested)[204] underlined that the "efficiency effects of the Panel's work" were "relevant both to the project at hand and to future Bank activities in general".[205] "In fact," Shihata elaborated, "the mere presence of the Panel"

> has contributed to making the Bank's operational staff more diligent in the observation of Bank policies. The usual zeal of presenting projects for Board approval in a manner and pace that meet the lending program's targets has been tempered by Management's greater concern with project implementation and by the zeal of the staff not to put the institution in the embarrassing position of being found in violation of its own policies and procedures. Since these policies are meant to ensure quality in the Bank-financed projects and to serve broader institutional objectives approved by Bank members (through the Executive Directors), the greater attention paid to them is likely to serve the Bank, its members as a whole, and in particular the borrowers concerned.[206]

Furthermore, Shihata added, Inspection Panel Requests "can also raise issues not otherwise known or appreciated"

> and might cause the Bank to adopt more effective or clearer standards in the pursuit of its objectives. In the process, it can enhance the awareness of the borrowers involved of deficiencies in their own processes and attitudes that need to be corrected. The publication of the results of the panel's work should also enable all those concerned with the development process – governments,

---

203 Boisson de Chazournes *in* Shelton (Ed.) (2000), p. 302.
204 *See e.g.,* section 3.2.3.
205 Shihata (2000) pp. 235-236.
206 *Id.*

international financial institutions, NGOs, and others – to draw lessons from this experience and to have them reflected in their subsequent policies and actions. The end result should increase the efficiency of the Bank and of development finance in general.[207]

Shihata cautioned, nevertheless, that such arguments "of course assum[e]"

> that the Panel will always be properly used as envisaged and will carry out its functions with the high degree of competence, integrity, and independence expected from it.[208]

These arguments were also based on the assumption, Shihata conceded, "that the Bank staff will make every effort to facilitate the Panel's work and benefit from its results."[209] However, Shihata did not view this to be a problem – because, he argued, the Inspection Panel process "gives the Bank the opportunity to defend itself before a credible forum"

> against mounting accusations of critics who often lack accurate information but feel free to blame project failures on the Bank. For this reason, the Bank's Management had confidently welcomed the exercise by the Panel of its investigative function. The Bank should have nothing to lose in the process. Whether the facts to be found by the Panel cleared the Bank from the accusations leveled against it or pointed out where the Bank had failed, inspection could be and in fact has been helpful to the institution. In both situations, the Bank demonstrates to all the parties concerned and to the public at large that it is a credible, responsive institution worthy of the broad and continued support it receives from its members.[210]

While the Board and senior Bank officials have always taken pains to affirm their support for the Inspection Panel in formal statements,[211] Inspection Panel practice does, at times, reflect an underlying dissatisfaction with the Panel's process and the nature of its findings.[212] Brown Weiss comments, for instance, that "[a]n accountability mechanism empowers managers and staff who want to get things right and reveals incompetence or lack of critical resources;"[213] yet, "[d]espite the Panel's insistence that it is investigating performance and

---

207 *Id.*
208 *Id.*
209 *Id.*
210 Shihata (2000), p. 240.
211 *E.g.,* as noted *in* section 7.2.1.
212 In this regard, *also see* section 7.1.5.
213 Brown Weiss (2010), p. 488-489 (emphasis omitted).

impacts and not individual responsibility," Brown Weiss adds, "the attitude of Bank staff toward [the Panel's] work"

> has varied from honest and helpful cooperation to frank stonewalling. The cooperation comes from professional staff who welcome the Panel's examination of their work, sometimes because they believe that their performance will be vindicated, and sometimes because they hope it will uncover misjudgments that they themselves opposed during project preparation or implementation.[214]

An interview conducted by Van Putten with former World Bank President, Jim Wolfensohn, reflected much of the institutional ambivalence surrounding the Panel. For instance, in replying to Van Putten's question "whether he still believes in the function of the panel" – especially in the context of the (mostly internal) controversy that surrounded the aftermath of the Panel's *China: Qinghai*-investigation, Wolfensohn affirmed that it was "a very good", albeit "evolving mechanism".[215] "I think the principle" that "interested parties can approach the Panel,"

> have the agreements looked at in a public way, from a group that is independent of management – is an extremely important and commendable tool. Extremely important. *But if you are going to get benefit from [the Inspection Panel process], it shouldn't be just to come up with the verdict guilty or not guilty. It should be something which is a part of the process.*[216]

What these 'benefits' should be, however, seems to be less clear. In fact, demands and expectations originating from within the institution also reflect the underlying tension between the instrumentalist and formalist paradigms.[217]

In the aftermath of the Inspection Panel's investigation of the *China: Qinghai*, for example, some commentators questioned the fact that the Inspection Panel was not expected "to consider trade-offs between the costs and benefits of additional assessments and studies it recommends."[218] This oversight, as Bottelier argued, for instance, would "explain a tendency towards unrealistic perfectionism" reflected "in parts of the [Panel's investigation] report."[219] "Bank staff and borrowers have to make trade-offs continuously in the real world", Bottelier added,

---

214 *Id.*
215 Van Putten (2008), p. 90. *Note*, the author quotes from an interview conducted with former World Bank Group President, Jim Wolfensohn.
216 *Id.* (emphasis added).
217 *See* section 2.3.
218 Bottelier (2001), p. 11. *Also see* Miller-Adams's remarks *at* note 17, Ch. 1.
219 *Id. Also see, China: Western Poverty Reduction* (Qinghai) (1999), MRIR, p. 6.

and they have to work within a budget. It would have cost the Bank (i.e. its Part II shareholders) more than ten times the original cost of project preparation and appraisal if all panel recommendations had been implemented.[220]

Or, as Mallaby commented with regard to the Panel's *China: Qinghai*- investigation report, "[a]ll in all, the panel was quibbling with details"

> but not asking the big questions. Would this project reduce poverty? The answer was yes, but the panel seemed indifferent. Would it cause environmental damage? The bottom line was no, and yet the panel insisted on poking holes in the Bank's methods and procedures.[221]

Yet, Wolfensohn also underscored that the Bank's "desire was to keep the panel out of the substance" and "leave the decision making to the bank".[222] In other words, Wolfensohn explained, the Panel had "to make sure" that the Bank "had fulfilled our responsibility"; which meant, in concrete terms, that the panel had to check, for example,

> [t]hat [the Bank] did in fact notify at due time. And that we appeared to section 3 [sic] and that we gave them x number of times [sic] and did whatever it was we had to do. That is the function of the panel. The panel is not to say whether we did right or wrong. The panel was to look at whether we adhered to the rules.[223]

However, "if you take the [*China: Qinghai case*]," Wolfensohn added, "it got down to the issues of"

> whether we did or did not meet the letter of the law.[224] In terms of counting the rodents or looking at the grains of sand or doing what we had to do. The

---

220 *Id.* For similar remarks, *also see* Wade's comments *at* note 231, Ch. 7.
221 Mallaby (2004), p. 280. *Also see e.g.*, section 6.3.
222 Van Putten (2008), pp. 349-350. *Note*, the author quotes from an interview conducted with former World Bank Group President, Jim Wolfensohn.
223 *Id. Note*, compare Wolfensohn's comments to the Panel's approach that emphasize compliance with procedural and substantive policy components – as discussed *in* section 6.3.4.
224 *Note*, Wolfensohn's comments should also be viewed in the context of a remark made by Van Putten during her interview. Van Putten explained (*id.*, at p. 349), that, as Inspection Panel member, she often "noticed a certain US culture in the bank and in the panel that is more used to look rather legalistic when judging on projects and problems. The US style in judging to the letter of the law instead of the principle of the law, the more European style." In this regard, *also see* Mallaby (2004), p. 279, describing the Panel's investigative style during the *China: Qinghai* case, as follows: "The Bank's staff described MacNeill [Inspection Panel chair] as a 'know-all', 'patronizing', 'nonlistener', 'curmudgeonly'; he was prone to phrases like 'only an idiot

real issue was whether we were disadvantaging the Tibetans. And whether in fact it was Tibet, and whether people were less well off or better off. And that was the case that was being "cried". So we were trying the case but on the wrong basis. The thing that I was legally concerned about was: how are we dealing fairly with the people that are affected, and what are the ramifications of doing that in terms of the impact on the Tibetan culture? The people were not the least bit interested in whether or not we gave a 120 days notice or whatever time schedule. They were concerned about the political aspects about the projects. And you in the panel are not supposed to be involved in the political aspects. But in fact MacNeill, Jim,[225] was deeply moved from the NGO point of views about the politics. It didn't come out as that but it was very clear that the case that the panel was trying was not the case that the public was trying. What they were concerned about was to block the project – that was what the Tibetans wanted. [The Bank] took a somewhat different view. We thought this people would be a hell of a lot better off physically, emotionally, and in terms of the sustenance. Because we had done 1,300 project like this.[226]

Furthermore, in responding to Van Putten's question "whether the existence of the Inspection Panel was leading to a weakening of the Bank's policies," Wolfensohn emphasized that he did "not see any connection"; in fact:

---

could say that'. It felt [...] like a court-martial – with the slight difference that in most courts-martial you have a right to an attorney." *Also note,* on the negative connotations associated with the formalist paradigm, *also see* note 150, Ch. 2; and on the Inspection Panel's insistence on emphasizing its non-judicial nature, *see* section 6.2.4.

225 *Note,* Wolfensohn refers to Jim MacNeill, Inspection Panel member and chair between 1997-2002. For a criticism of Mallaby's highly critical depiction of the Inspection Panel's role cases such as *China: Qinghai* (as depicted *e.g., in* Mallaby (2004), pp. 270-285), *also see* MacNeill's retort *in* J. MacNeill, S. Mallaby, B. Rich & P. Bosshard, 'Dammed Project', *Foreign Policy*, Issue: 145, November-December 2004, p. 4: "Safeguard policies, on issues such as resettlement and indigenous peoples, are designed to ensure that those affected by a project are not harmed and, also, that they are helped in their efforts to rise out of poverty. If we abandon these policies, as Mallaby suggests we should, we would neither improve the quality of life for locals, nor reduce costs. Mallaby cites a 2001 bank study to claim that "environmental and social safeguards" inflate the overall cost of bank projects by over $200 million annually. Wrong on two counts. First, environmental and social safeguards make up only a small fraction of the $200 million. Second, Mallaby omits the costs of not implementing these policies. The bank itself has concluded that a majority of its projects fail to reach their objectives, suggesting that the costs would be enormous."

226 Van Putten (2008), pp. 349-350. *But also see* Wolfensohn's comments on the Bank's political neutrality *at* p. 351: "I have always thought the suggestion that we be nonpolitical is complete nonsense. I think everything is political. It is the nature of the institution. If you get involved in food or education projects, or a housing project, or an environmental project, every one of these things has political implications. If you do not think that the Western China Poverty Project was a political investigation, you are probably crazy."

I do no think there is the slightest consideration given to the will of the Inspection Panel. [...] It would really amaze me if Jim Adams or Shengman [Zhang] thought at any time about the panel. *They think about doing what is right, pragmatic.*[227]

"Behind the media glare of" controversial Inspection Panel investigations such as *China: Qinghai*, as Woods remarks, there is often a sense of unease, if not dissatisfaction, within the institution about "the role and implications of such inspections" and their implications for the strengthening of institutional governance.[228] These concerns, moreover, stem from the fact that such matters "touch on the core question of how widely or narrowly 'accountability' should be defined, and what kind of breach should trigger an enforcement action."[229] If, for example, "the 'triggering mechanism' for inspection is unlawfulness," as Woods elaborates, "this not only presumes that actions that are legal must also be legitimate in the eyes of the citizenry, but opens up the risk that minor 'legal' infractions can be used as a weapon for much larger political purposes."[230]

Or, as Wade argues, given that the Panel's "image of success is to find projects out of compliance" – combined with the consideration that "almost any project can be found to be out of compliance if one pushes hard enough" – there is arguably "no limit to the cases that affected groups can bring".[231] "[A]ssisted by Washington-based NGOs", as Wade predicted in the aftermath of the *Qinghai* case, "the Bank is likely to be deluged with Inspection Panel investigations."[232]

Ultimately, the diverse interests, demands, expectations and conceptions surrounding the Inspection Panel mean it is "constantly walking a tightrope" in practice

> between the Board (its nominal boss), the staff of the Bank (at various levels, from task manager to vice-president to the President), the Requesters, the NGO community, and the borrower government of the country where the project is

---

227 Van Putten (2008), p. 355 (emphasis added). *Note*, on the positive/negative connotations related (respectively) to the instrumentalist and formalist paradigms, *also see* note 150, Ch. 2. *Also note*, Jim Adams is currently Vice President of the East Asia and Pacific Region, at the World Bank; previously, Vice President and Head of Network, Operations Policy and Country Services, at the World Bank; Shengman Zhang was Vice President Corporate Secretary, at the World Bank between 1995 and 1997; Head of the World Bank's corporate and support functions between 1997-2001, and Managing Director of the World Bank between 2001 and 2005.
228 Woods (2001), pp. 93-94.
229 R. Wade, 'A Defeat for Development and Multilateralism: The World Bank has been Unfairly Criticised over the Qinghai Resettlement Project', *Financial Times*, 4 July 2000, available at www.ft.com; quoted in Woods (2001), pp. 93-94.
230 *Id.*
231 *Id. Note*, Wade's prediction about a 'deluge' of cases has not since been realized; that being said, the factors driving the absolute number of Inspection Panel cases filed are, as argued earlier, also more complex than mere NGO-involvement – *see* section 1.2.1.
232 *Id.*

located. It cannot function without their cooperation, yet must call things as
it sees them and stand up for its judgments.[233]

In other words, the Panel's 'balancing act' means that it has to deal with the underlying
tensions between the 'institutional' and 'public' sides of its mandate – which, in practice,
also means it is often concerned with achieving equilibrium among the Bank's wide range
of institutional aims.[234]

And while the Inspection Panel may not be the only internal accountability mechanism
dealing with such challenges, since it is a citizen-driven mechanism, it has to execute its
dual accountability mandate of *restraining* and *enabling* World Bank activities under much
closer public scrutiny. Indeed, as Brown Weiss comments, executing such a mandate
"demands a reputation for scrupulous fairness and careful technical work,"[235] and requires
that the Panel gain (and constantly retain) "the trust of all parties" – including the trust
of "Requesters (who are not used to trusting anyone), borrower governments, World Bank
management and staff, and […] civil society."[236]

As to how this might be achieved, the Inspection Panel mechanism "institutionalizes
discourse into a quasi-legal process", as Hale argues, through which "[c]ompeting infor-
mational claims"

> are explicitly formulated by all the concerned parties in the form of briefs,
> counter-statements, and, ultimately, the investigation reports. By initiating a
> complaint the affected parties force the Bank into an information-rich environ-
> ment.[237]

As "the Panel adjudicates between competing truth claims," its "published findings replace
inaccurate or deceitful discourse with an official record of 'what really happened' – which
rules were broken, which not."[238] Hence, Hale adds, "[t]he arguments of Bank management
and the complainants that are validated by the investigative process gain significant credibility," which is significant "because, as Keohane and Nye note, "[c]redibility is a crucial
resource, and asymmetrical credibility is a key source of power."[239] And by "provid[ing]

---

233 Brown Weiss (2010), pp. 488-489.
234 *Also see* the Panel's comments *at* notes 113 & 114, Ch. 4.
235 Brown Weiss (2010), pp. 488-489.
236 *Id.*
237 Hale (2008), p. 8.
238 *Id.*
239 *Id. Note,* Hale is quoting R.O. Keohane & J.S. Nye (2001), 'Democracy, Accountability, and Global Governance', Politics Research Group Working Papers on International Relations, Kennedy School of Government,
   Harvard University. On the importance of information in the standard accountability model, and of the
   need for strengthening this aspect through models of surrogate accountability, *also see* Rubenstein's comments
   in section 2.2.

information about the Bank's compliance with its own principles," to internal and external accountability holders, Inspection Panel practice "connect[s]"

> the discursive, external information processes to the normative internal ones. By giving the Bank information about its compliance with its own norms, the Panel empowers Bank management to regulate itself via self-reflection. But by connecting that reflection to dialogue with outside actors – the complainants – the Panel links internal and external critique in the reflexive law process Teubner imagines.[240]

****

"Ensuring accountability is not easy," Brown Weiss once remarked – and, as a former Inspection Panel chair that has overseen some of the Panel's most prominent investigations to date, the complexity underlying this understated remark would not have escaped her attention.[241]

Ensuring the accountability of an international financial institution such as the World Bank is profoundly challenging because it requires, in effect, the continuous alignment of all the dimensions of accountability. Such alignment, in turn, requires a deep understanding of the complementary and contradictory relationships between multiple variables, which cut across all the accountability dimensions discussed in Part I of this book. And the development of such an understanding, furthermore, relies on a continuous analysis of the diverse, dynamic and complex interests, demands, expectations and conceptions that characterize the "kaleidoscopic" transnational regulatory governance context in which World Bank development-lending operations are situated.[242]

For an international financial institution such as the World Bank "to be accountable," as Brown Weiss elaborates, "it is essential," that it should "listen" to external constituency groups – notably "to the people who are affected by projects and programs designed to

---

240 Hale (2008), p. 8. Hale argues (*id.*, at p. 7) that Teubner's work synthesizes "Habermasian [external] discourse theory" of the "ideal speech situation", with Luhmann's [internal] notion of autonomous, self-regulating social spheres", where "[a]ctors consider their behavior in light of their own values and react accordingly." [...] Teubner's contribution, in my reading, is to link these internal and external exchanges into a theory of regulation. In this account actor's behavior is governed both by dialogue with others and by internal reflection vis-à-vis their own values. Teubner terms this complex process "reflexive law." In this regard, *see* G. Teubner (1983), 'Substantive and Reflexive Elements in Modern Law', 17 *Law and Society Review* 2; *and see* T. Risse, 'Global Governance and Communicative Action', *in* D. Held & M. Koenig-Archibugi (Eds.) (2003), *Global Governance and Public Accountability*, Oxford: Blackwell, at p. 170.
241 Brown Weiss (2010), pp. 489-490. *Note*, Edith Brown Weiss was a member of the World Bank Inspection Panel between 2002-2003, and Inspection Panel Chair between 2003-2007.
242 *See* Brown Weiss's remarks *at* note 87, Ch. 2.

help them."[243] Furthermore, "[a] process for holding management and staff accountable is essential if an institution is to be viewed as legitimate," by its internal and external constituency groups, "and if economic development is to be effective."[244] Accountability is also "dynamic process," "with important feedback loops" that should occur throughout the entire project cycle and which "must engage those who are being held accountable at all times."[245] The notion of accountability should encompass both prospective and retrospective aspects,[246] whereas institutional "learning from accountability should be an inherent part of the process."[247] Moreover, the "consequences ensuing as part of accountability," Brown Weiss concludes, "must be tailored to the situation and may change over time."[248]

Moreover, as this chapter demonstrated, accountability outcomes have to be realized and enforced, which present considerable challenges – especially given the existence of multiple interdependencies. Meeting these challenges, however, is critical for the realization of 'output legitimacy' – both of the World Bank, and of the normative system at the core of the Bank's development-lending operations, which involves the processes of norm creation and norm application of the operational policy framework, as well as norm enforcement by means of internal accountability mechanisms such as the Inspection Panel. In this regard, it should also be noted that the Bank's internal and external constituency groups have to be convinced that there *is* "congruence" between the Bank's words and its actions – between World Bank accountability *in theory* and *in practice.*[249]

While we might question whether or not the notion of 'accountability' should have been extended so as to incorporate "all manner of analytical and rhetorical tasks and carr[y] most of the burdens of democratic 'governance'",[250] it *has* come to encompass multiple, interdependent dimensions – as discussed in Part I of this book. To be sure, addressing each of these dimensions in isolation would have proven to be challenging enough.

However, when considering the continuous alignment of all the dimensions of accountability – which involves, for example: achieving equilibrium among multiple variables that function in terms of competing or contradictory relationships, managing the intricacies following from various interdependencies, and realizing the potential for

---

243 Brown Weiss (2010), pp. 489-490.
244 *Id.*
245 *Id.*
246 *Id.*
247 *Id.*
248 *Id.*
249 *See e.g.,* Clark (2002), p. 206 (arguing that there are "troublesome" "gap[s] between" the Bank's "rhetoric" and the "implementation of the policy framework" in development reality); *and see* Brunnée & Toope (2010), p. 35 (arguing that "fidelity to law" is "damaged" when norms are "seen to have no possibility of effect"; and, "[w]hen explicit rules are unrelated to how states and other international actors actually behave, [such] fidelity is destroyed."). In this regard, *also see* the discussion *in* section 2.3.
250 *See* Mulgan's remarks *at* note 67, Ch. 2.

integration underlying several complementary or reinforcing relationships – it becomes clear why there often are significant differences between what has been conceptualized *on paper* and operationalized *in the field*.[251]

The window onto World Bank development-lending operations offered by Inspection Panel practice presents a significant opportunity to gain a deeper understanding as to what the operationalization of accountability entails and how theory and practice might be better aligned.

---

251 In this regard, *also see* the Panel's comments *at* note 3, Part II.

Part II
Operationalizing World Bank Accountability

"Cases that come before IAMs commonly center on conflicts over control of scarce natural resources, disputes about the distribution of project risks and benefits, and socioeconomic impacts like the loss of livelihoods or threats to cultural identity. The rights of vulnerable people, including indigenous peoples, and the protection of forests and other unique ecosystems are, in a sense, "trademark" IAM issues. Their scope is far broader, however, extending over a host of issues that arise from the myriad trade-offs and competing interests that are invariably part and parcel of large, complex development projects and programs. When asymmetries of power, historical enmity among stakeholders, lack of capacity and/or due diligence, insufficient information, or a breakdown of trust make local-level resolution impossible, IAMs offer people affected by IFI-financed projects a way forward."[1]

"The Panel recognizes the challenges faced by the Bank in its operations. Compliance with policies is not just black or white. In its reports, the Panel gives credit to the institution where due, highlights the challenges it faces, and puts on record statements of appreciation by affected people and communities for positive efforts and engagement of the Bank. The Panel also recognizes that both the Bank and its borrowers have changed since the creation of the Panel in 1993. A possible causal relation between the Bank's application of its policies and adverse impacts on people or the environment, which is the underlying premise of a Panel investigation, is less obvious in the emerging context of more programmatic loans, more co-financing with other donors, and a greater share of financing from the client country. Risks for affected people and the environment, however, remain. The Panel is one of the main pillars of accountability for the Bank in the context of such risks. How to ensure the continued role of citizen-driven accountability in light of evolving operational models built on enhanced partnerships and leveraging of resources is an important part of the risk management discourse."[2]

"What looked reasonable on paper turned out not to be realistic."[3]

"The key is that the significant can only be revealed through practice."[4]

---

1   Independent Accountability Mechanisms Network (2012), p. 1.
2   Inspection Panel (2013), p. 1.
3   Cambodia: Land Management and Administration (2009), IR, § 290.
4   Taleb (2012), e-Book.

SEGMENT A
SYSTEMIC ISSUES – CUTTING ACROSS
POLICY AREAS

8   WORLD BANK AND BORROWER OBLIGATIONS – IN DEVELOPMENT PRACTICE

The formal division between World Bank and Borrower obligations has been set out earlier; however, as the analysis in Chapter 4 illustrated, this division is marked by complexity that can make it difficult to discern between Bank and Borrower obligations.[1] Chapter 8 considers a number of factors that can further add to this complexity in practice – namely: instances where there are *disagreement, misunderstanding or ambiguity concerning the division of Bank and Borrower obligations*; project scenarios involving particular *interfaces with borrowers' constitutional systems* (thus, involving domestic legislative, executive and/or judicial functions); and situations where borrowers and/or their project implementing agencies have *institutional and/or professional capacity constraints.*[2]

These factors have the potential to add to the complexity surrounding the division between Bank and Borrower obligations especially since they tend to strengthen underlying interdependencies, obscure the lines delineating World Bank (primary) obligations and Borrower (primary) obligations, and, finally, often require the Bank to 'step-in' so as to ensure that the Borrower meets its (primary) obligations in terms of the credit/loan agreement.

8.1   DISAGREEMENT, MISUNDERSTANDING OR AMBIGUITY CONCERNING POLICY OBLIGATIONS

The World Bank and its borrowers are not always in agreement about all aspects of their respective obligations in terms of the operational policies. In some instances, such disagreements are well-known and the Inspection Panel investigation merely serves to highlight – and subsequently, raise public awareness – these issues. Often, however, such disagreements – but also misunderstandings and ambiguities about specific policy obligations – come to the fore over the course of an Inspection Panel investigation.

In *Nepal: Arun III*, for example, the Inspection Panel noted that the project implementing agency ('NEA') was "fully responsible for implementation of the Environmental

---

1   *See* section 4.3.

2   *Note*, additional factors that can add to the complexity surrounding the delineation of Bank and Borrower obligations include: the involvement of multiple actors in various (and varying) capacities; and, (the often associated issue of) complexity of project design. While these two factors are not specifically discussed here, they often contribute to the complex project scenarios sketched in this chapter. For examples of how these factors manifest in Inspection Panel practice, *see e.g.,* sections 3.1.2 & 3.1.3.

Management Plan", but that "no specific mention [was] made" about "the responsibility for RAP [regional action plan] implementation."[3] Project documentation only stipulated that the RAP would be "implemented independently but in coordination with the EMP."[4] What this statement seemed to have meant was that "direct mitigation measures [were] to be undertaken by the NEA", while "indirect and induced ones [were] to be undertaken by the National Planning Commission [established] under the RAP." However, the Panel emphasized, this arrangement implied that there was "no single chain of command to oversee implementation."[5]

Hence, the Panel concluded, "[a] heavy burden has been placed on the Regional Action Plan" "to deal with a variety of complex issues."[6] This, in turn, was cause for "serious concern due to the lack of experience on the part of IDA [at the time of this project] to oversee such a plan" and also because of "the widely recognized lack of institutional experience in the borrowing government."[7] Moreover, the Inspection Panel observed that the implementation of the RAP "relies almost exclusively on resources provided by other donors."[8] This meant, "[i]n effect," that "a major burden of compliance with IDA policies falls on project components not financed by IDA."[9] And "unless closer coordination is achieved quickly", the Panel warned,

> it is quite likely that critical pre-emptive and remedial measures of the RAP will fail to see the light of day. Therefore, questions related to donor coordina-tion and collaboration take on even greater relevance. The Panel believes that these measures have not been given adequate attention on the part of Manage-ment and [the Borrower].[10]

In *India: Ecodevelopment*, the Inspection Panel observed that there was "a profound differ-ence" between the "expectations of Management and those of state officials" with regard to the "role and scope of microplanning and the investments which are to follow the approval of microplans".[11] On the one hand, Bank management stipulated

---

3   *Nepal: Arun III* (1994), IR, § 95, 99.

4   *Id.*

5   *Id.*

6   *Id.*

7   *Id. Note*, this example also illustrates issues related to borrower/project implementing agency capacity con-straints – as discussed *in* section 8.3.

8   *Id.* For an overview of the *Nepal: Arun* case, *see e.g.*, Bissell *in* Clark et al. (Eds.) (2003), pp. 25-44; Bradlow (1996); Undall (1994); Shihata (2002), pp. 102-104; Schlemmer-Schulte (1998), pp. 359-361; Schlemmer-Schulte *in* Alfredsson & Ring (Eds.) (2001), pp. 87-106; *and see* Naudé Fourie (2014), pp. 11-20.

9   *Nepal: Arun III* (1994), IR, § 95, 99.

10   *Id.*

11   *India: Ecodevelopment* (1998), ER, § 82. For an overview of *India: Ecodevelopment*, *see e.g.*, Schlemmer-Schulte (1998), p. 372; Shihata (2000), pp. 133-136; *and* Naudé Fourie (2014), pp. 79-85.

that microplans are required prior to each set of investments at the village level. (They) must be prepared by, and be agreeable to, the involved people [...] and (they) [...] would ultimately cover 100 percent of interested villages [...].[12]

On the other hand, Borrower "[s]tate officials were equally unequivocal in telling the Panel that microplans will not be undertaken for any of the 58 haadi (villages) within the park."[13] If the Borrower's view "were to prevail in practice," the Panel emphasized, "it would of course vitiate the stay option"; hence, "the only way that the adivassi [tribal] peoples could benefit from project investments would be to relocate."[14]

Concerning compliance with the Bank's policy on Involuntary Resettlement in *Nigeria/Ghana: West African Gas Pipeline*, the Panel concluded that it was "highly improbable that the displaced persons could have made an informed decision as to their resettlement options, within the Bank guidelines," because "there was disagreement or, at least, ambiguity, in April 2004 (after the Sponsor claimed the consultation had closed) between the Sponsor and the Bank over the process and the applicable standard."[15] This situation, in turn, was indicative "of Management's failure"

to adequately convey the objectives and methods of the Involuntary Resettlement Policy, particularly their relationship to national legal frameworks, before consultation with the displaced people.[16]

In this instance, the Panel emphasized, "[t]he lack of meaningful and timely consultation prevented participation and informed negotiation of resettlement options by the displaced

---

12 *India: Ecodevelopment* (1998), ER, § 82.
13 *Id. Note,* the formulation of 'microplans' formed part of Bank's 'process design' approach – in this regard, *also see India: Ecodevelopment* (1998), ER, § 45 (emphases omitted): "Management claims that its past experience with conservation projects in areas with human pressures pointed towards '[...] a process design project, which after a period of indicative planning to establish the framework and define appropriate processes, proceeded to get things done on the ground.' This basically involves '[...] a two phase three-step process. Indicative planning to establish the main areas of conflict, appropriate participatory mechanisms, eligible types of investment, and effective institutional arrangements was undertaken during project preparation. The more detailed consultative microplanning and Protected Area management planning, during which individual families and groups express their needs and resolve conflicts in a context with funding available, will be carried out during project implementation'." On the 'process design approach' and related compliance issues resulting from the postponement of consultation to later stages of the project, *see* section 11.2.
14 *India: Ecodevelopment* (1998), ER, § 73. On the role of 'real choice' in matters concerning (in-) voluntary resettlement, *also see* section 12.1.
15 *Nigeria/Ghana: West African Gas Pipeline* (2006), IR, §§ 283 & 285. For a definition of the term 'sponsor', *see* the list of explanations/definitions of acronyms, abbreviations and other terminology used in World Bank development-lending operations *in* the Appendix.
16 *Id.* For an overview of *Nigeria/Ghana: West African Gas Pipeline, see e.g.,* Naudé Fourie (2014), pp. 311-321.

persons as called for in OP 4.12."[17] Hence, the Panel concluded, "Management did not provide adequate guidance and instructions to the Project Sponsor to carry out meaningful consultation with the displaced people."[18]

Whereas in *Cambodia: Land Management and Administration*, concerning claims of non-compliance regarding the Resettlement Policy Framework (RPF), Bank management acknowledged that the Borrower was "obligated to apply the RPF in this case" but added that the Borrower "[did] not share that view."[19] Management also "acknowledge[d] that"

> a lack of specificity in the Project documents and the apparent absence of detailed discussions about the reach of the RPF may have contributed to the Government's understanding of its obligations.[20]

Moreover, with regard to compensation paid for forced evictions that occurred within (as well as adjacent to) the project area – a matter that will be discussed in more detail in section 8.2.2 – Bank management asserted that it was its "insistence on [the resolution of] this issue [that] precipitated [the Borrower] Government's decision to close the Project prematurely."[21] Management expressed its "regre[t] that further dialogue was cut short by an inability to find common ground between the Bank, Development Partners, the Government and civil society groups advocating on land issues", but added that it "has not had an opportunity to review actual compensation, offered or paid, or the standard of resettlement sites due to the Government's decision to prematurely close the Project."[22]

In *Kenya: Lake Victoria Environmental Management*, disagreement on Bank versus Borrower obligations seemed to stem from a misunderstanding about the underlying project objectives. Bank management acknowledged in this instance that it had not been "sufficiently proactive in explaining the purpose of the water hyacinth tender."[23] The Inspection Panel, however, questioned Management explanation, and noted that was difficult to "understand how the Borrower, as Management alleges,"

> could have misunderstood the objective of the tender and believed that shredding and sinking was a lakewide solution to water hyacinth control. It was the

---

17 *Id.*

18 *Id.* For a discussion of compliance issues related to consultation in the context of this project as well as in others, *see* section 11.2.

19 *Cambodia: Land Management and Administration* (2009), MR, p. vii. For an overview of *Cambodia: Land Management and Administration*, see e.g., Naudé Fourie (2014), pp. 329-340.

20 *Id.*

21 *Cambodia: Land Management and Administration* (2009), MRIR, Annex 1, §§ 20, 23.

22 *Id. Note*, this example also illustrates the challenges involved in realizing and enforcing Borrower remedial actions (which could also result in redress for project-affected people), *as discussed e.g., in* sections 7.1.2, 7.1.3 & 15.1.

23 *Kenya: Lake Victoria Environmental Management* (1999), IR, § 167.

Borrower that initiated the shredding and sinking operation. And it seems evident that the Bank agreed to finance the operation only as one of the trial pilots, and one not to be applied lakewide unless subsequently found to be environmentally, socially and economically feasible.[24]

Nevertheless, the Panel concluded that it was "disturbing"

> that the Bank did not ensure that the Borrower and local stakeholders possessed a full understanding of the purpose and scope of the operation.[25]

During its 1996 investigation of *Argentina/Paraguay: Yacyretá Hydroelectric Project*, the Panel found that there was a discrepancy between the Bank's policy on Involuntary Resettlement, which stipulated that "new housing has to be provided at no cost and consequently property titles issued to relocatees should not be encumbered by mortgages" and the reality on the ground.[26] This discrepancy, moreover, was the result of an on-going disagreement between the Bank and the project implementing agency ('EBY'). The Panel acknowledged that that both "EBY and the Bank" were, at the time, "exchanging views in an effort to resolve this disagreement;" nevertheless, the Panel concluded, "until this issue is resolved, the Bank is not in compliance with its policies."[27]

The Panel's 2002 investigation of the *Yacyretá* project, finally, highlighted disagreements concerning "the sewer system [intended] to serve [the] Encarnación [community]".[28] Although the sewer system was "under construction" during the Panel's investigation, the Panel emphasized that it "could not elicit a definite answer as to who will be responsible for connecting domestic users to the new sewer network."[29]

"EBY staff informed the Panel that the residents of Encarnación will themselves be responsible for connecting their houses to the system"; but the Panel pointed out that such an arrangement "is likely to negate the purpose of the sewerage reticulation scheme"

> as few of the residents of the poorer neighborhoods will have the capital, or disposable income, to pay for their connection to the network. They are thus

---

24   *Id.*
25   *Id.*
26   *Argentina/Paraguay: Yacyretá Hydroelectric Project* (1996), Inspection Panel Review & Assessment, § 239(a)(i). For a discussion of both *Yacyretá* investigations (1996 and 2002), *see e.g.,* Treakle & Díaz Peña *in* Clark et al. (Eds.) (2003), pp. 69-92; Bissell *in* Alfredsson & Ring (Eds.) (2001), pp. 107-125; Clark & Hunter, *in* Alfredsson & Ring (Eds.) (2001), pp. 167-189; Umaña *in* Alfredsson & Ring (Eds.) (2001), pp. 127-141; *and see* Naudé Fourie (2014), pp. 45-54 & pp. 195-207.
27   *Id.*
28   *Paraguay/Argentina: Yacyretá Hydroelectric Project* (2002), IR, § 217.
29   *Id.*

likely to continue to discharge sewage to open drains or to septic tanks. Bank staff are also of this opinion. One Bank staff member noted that if the connection of houses to sewers must be paid for by the owners, it will never happen.[30]

"[R]esponsibility for the cost of connection to the sewer system", the Inspection Panel cautioned, therefore had the potential to

> become a significant source of conflict in the not too distant future. If the matter is not resolved in a way that will enable the vast majority of households to be connected to the sewer lines, the entire exercise of providing a sewer network will be largely negated. The Panel finds that this issue needs the urgent attention of Bank Management and that an effective means of financing the connection of houses to the sewer, plant and network is required, especially for poor communities.[31]

8.2   INTERFACES WITH THE BORROWER'S CONSTITUTIONAL SYSTEM

As an international agreement, the loan/credit agreement (as well as those policies that have been incorporated into the agreement) supersedes national law; however, as discussed earlier, several aspects of the Borrower's constitutional system might be entirely relevant for the design and preparation, appraisal and implementation of World Bank-financed development projects.[32]

However, dealing with the interfaces between the Bank's development lending operations and borrowers' constitutional systems presents several challenges for the Bank, especially since it might concern issues of state sovereignty, as well as the Bank's need to maintain its own 'political neutrality'.[33] Certain project scenarios involving distinct interfaces with the Borrower's constitutional system might also have significant implications for the manner in which the formal division between Bank and Borrower obligations play out in practice. This section considers two of these scenarios, namely: those involving the *adoption, amendment and/or application of specific national legislation* associated with the realization of a project's development objectives; and those where *Bank-financed projects are implemented alongside or concurrent with development projects in borrower territories that have*

---

30   *Id.*
31   *Paraguay/Argentina: Yacyretá Hydroelectric Project* (2002), IR, § 218. *Note*, this example, also illustrates compliance issues related to replacement housing, sites and facilities, in the context of projects involving involuntary resettlement – as discussed *in* section 12.4
32   *See* sections 5.1 & 5.2.
33   On these matters, *see e.g.,* sections 3.1.1 & 3.1.2.

the same or similar goals, involve the same or similar activities, but are not financed by the Bank.

8.2.1   *Project interfaces with the adoption, amendment and/or application of national legislation*

Some projects – often those financed by development policy lending instruments – require the adoption or amendment of national legislation in order to realize specific development objectives. In other situations, the adoption or amendment of national legislation might not be specifically related to the realization of development objectives but might nevertheless affect it. Such scenarios often present challenges for the Bank in meeting is (secondary) obligations – not only in light of considerations of state sovereignty and Bank 'political neutrality', but also because domestic legislative processes tend to inject an additional degree of complexity – related, for instance, to the time required to adopt/amend legislation, or the legislative content to which legislatures might ultimately agree to.

In *Honduras: Land Administration*, for example, several claims in the Request related to the "2004 Honduran Property Law".[34] Bank management argued that these claims were indicative of the Requesters' 'disagreement' with the particular legislation and were therefore "beyond matters related to the Project" since the content of national laws and regulations is the responsibility of the Government of Honduras," and also because the Borrower "has put in place mechanisms, such as the Project's consultation framework [the 'Mesa Regional'], for civil society to raise their concerns on such matters."[35] Management added that the project was compliant with the Bank's policy on Indigenous Peoples since the "IPDP contain[ed] an assessment of the legal framework in the country, including legal status of affected groups, as reflected in the constitution, laws and regulations," which paid "[p]articular attention"

> to the rights of indigenous peoples to use and develop the lands that they
> occupy, to be protected against illegal intruders, and to have access to natural

---

34   *Honduras: Land Administration* (2006), IR, §§ 214-215. *Also see Honduras: Land Administration* (2006), IR p. x: "A major claim of the Request is that the Project has failed properly to consult with and identify the needs and interests of the affected communities, and has failed to consult adequately with people who are the legitimate representatives of the affected communities. The Requesters claim that this failure occurred both in the preparation and implementation of the Project and express concerns about the consequences of certain provisions of Honduras' new [2004] Property Law." For an overview of *Honduras: Land Administration, also see* Naudé Fourie (2014), pp. 291-303.

35   *Honduras: Land Administration* (2006), IR, §§ 214-215. On issues related to the *Mesa Regional, also see* the discussion *in* section 13.3.

resources (such as forests, wildlife, and water) vital to their subsistence and reproduction.[36]

"In short," Bank management concluded, "the business of development often takes place within complex and suboptimal legal and institutional settings," which means that a "country's legal system [...] need not be ideal"

> before the Bank can support an operation, provided that the Bank's applicable policies are met. [...] Bank safeguard policies are equally realistic: it is Bank policies that prevail for particular projects instead of local rules that may fall short of the standards represented by those policies.[37]

In the present case, Management added, it "intends to enforce policy-consistent 'Project rules' embodied in the [loan agreement]"

> while simultaneously engaging the local authorities to refine the 'law of Honduras', but without [...] jeopardizing the Project which already contains relevant protections for the interests of Project-affected indigenous or Afro-Honduran peoples. To act otherwise would be to allow OFRANEH [the Requesters] to interject the Inspection Panel process into its arguments for obtaining legal reforms at a national level. This result could lead to a review beyond the scope of the Project and adversely affect Project implementation.[38]

The Inspection Panel found the project to be compliant to the extent that it incorporated "measures to protect indigenous peoples' land rights," including:

> mechanisms of conflict resolution including conciliation and arbitration, the provision of legal advice and training for indigenous peoples and a covenant in the [Development Credit Agreement] that requires that "no titling and physical demarcation of lands adjacent to Ethnic Lands will take place unless procedures that adequately protect the rights of the indigenous and Afro-Honduran peoples, duly consulted with affected parties in a manner satisfactory to the Association and set forth in the Operational Manual, have been followed.[39]

---

36 *Id. Note*, Management is referring to OD 4.20, § 15.
37 *Honduras: Land Administration* (2006), MRIR, § 41.
38 *Id.*
39 *Honduras: Land Administration* (2006), IR, §§ 214-215.

Nevertheless, "given the relative weakness of indigenous peoples" (a matter that had been "acknowledged in the Project documents"), as well as "the fact that the [2004] Property Law"

> gives specific rights to non-indigenous occupants of Ethnic Lands that cannot be amended or limited by regulations to the Law or by the provisions of the Project Operational Manual[,][40]

the Panel concluded "that [the above-mentioned] measures are not sufficient to protect indigenous people land rights that may be affected by Project implementation, as required by OD 4.20."[41]

The Panel also observed that "the Project files show" very similar concerns about the new Property Law than those voiced by the Requesters.[42] Indeed, the Panel noted, "Bank staff were also concerned about the Property Law, as it was under discussion in [the Borrower's legislative body] during Project preparation and approval."[43] In this regard, the project's "Legal Analysis states that"

> if the bill of law is approved, as it stands in the draft reviewed, it will entail a significant change to the existing legal and institutional framework since, in addition to creating new legal mechanisms ("figuras"), it eliminates or repeals existing legal institutions and norms [...].[44]

However, "[i]n spite of these warnings to Management before and after the enactment of the Law – which occurred during Project preparation and after Credit approval" – "the Panel did not find any record that these changed circumstances,"

> which are potentially directly relevant for the land rights of indigenous people, were acted upon by Management, aside from a[n] inconclusive exchange of communications between the Region and the Legal Department. To the contrary, Management states in its Response to the Request for Inspection that during Project design it "anticipated the possibility of a new law by providing mechanisms [...] for the continuous flexible adaptation of the Project to the new Law" and that after the Law was enacted, it "found the law acceptable."[45]

---

40   *Honduras: Land Administration* (2006), IR, § 223.
41   *Id.*
42   *Honduras: Land Administration* (2006), IR, §§ 220-221.
43   *Id.*
44   *Id.*
45   *Id. Note*, these examples also demonstrate the value of fact-fining in terms of strengthening institutional governance – *see* section 7.1.4.

In *Panama: Land Administration*, several claims, filed by members of the Naso and Ngäbe tribes,[46] concerned Panama's 'Law No. 72 on Collective Lands', which, among other things, "established collective land property in indigenous territories and specifically prohibited the creation of new 'áreas anexas' [annex areas]."[47] The Naso-Requesters argued, for instance, that Law No. 72 had "limit[ed] the prospects of a future Naso Comarca",[48] whereas the Ngäbe-Requesters asserted that the Bank-financed Project's support of the new law was "contrary to the creation of a juridical framework for the Ngäbe people."[49]

These concerns, the Panel observed, "seem[ed] to depend in part on the legal interpretation of [Law No. 72's] controversial Article 17," which "was inserted into the bill without prior consultation with key stakeholders, including the Project and Management."[50] Management contended "that it only *'became aware'* of Article 17 five days after the approval of the law"

> and that it did not have any information about it before it was included in the law. However, Management also states that as soon as it learned about Article 17 it promptly took up the issue with the Government to express concerns about the implications of the Law for the Naso people [...].[51]

The Inspection Panel affirmed that it was "not within [its] purview [...] to interpret domestic law" but only "to determine whether the Bank's policies" – which "require the Bank to analyze the legal framework within which a Project is implemented" – "were complied with by Bank Management."[52]

---

46 *Panama: Land Administration* (2009), ER, § 1. *Note*, these two groups filed two separate Requests, which were subsequently consolidated, as per the usual Inspection Panel practice; the Panel's practice of consolidating claims (which it typically does for efficiency reasons) is another reason why the absolute 'count' of Inspection Panel Requests can be misleading.

47 *Panama: Land Administration* (2009), IR, § 16. For an overview of *Panama: Land Administration, see* Naudé Fourie (2014), pp. 403-412. *Note*, 'Annex areas' refers to "territories outside the core area of [the tribal group's specific] comarca"; a 'comarca' refers to "a territory over which indigenous groups have collective land rights and considerable administrative authority, as established by specific law". *See Panama: Land Administration* (2009), IR p. iv.

48 *Panama: Land Administration* (2009), IR, § 172.

49 *Panama: Land Administration* (2009), IR, xi.

50 *Panama: Land Administration* (2009), IR, § 172.

51 *Panama: Land Administration* (2009), IR, p. xii (emphasis in original).

52 *Panama: Land Administration* (2009), IR, § 172. *Also compare* this argument with the Panel's comments in *Brazil: Land Reform* (1998), ER, § 19, where the Panel noted that the "Requesters raise a number of political and pragmatic issues that do not relate directly to Bank policies and procedures", such as "[t]he role of expropriation and the legality of alternative methods to carry out the constitutionally mandated agrarian reform program." The Inspection Panel concluded (at *id.*) that these issues were "clearly outside the purview of the Panel" since they did not relate to World Bank operational policy obligations, although they "provide[d] a useful context to understand the concerns of the Requesters about the Bank's role in the Project."

The Panel conceded that "Management cannot be held responsible for the legislative actions of a sovereign country, as acknowledged in the Management Response," however, it added that "OD 4.20 [Indigenous People] and OP/BP 13.05 provide guidance on how to follow up on this kind of situation."[53] After assessing Management's actions against these guidelines, the Panel concluded that "the Project's support for the preparation of a comarca bill in the early years of Project implementation"

> was directly supportive of the territorial and administrative aspirations of the Naso, and consistent with OD 4.20 on Indigenous Peoples and OP 13.05 on Supervision. The failure of the bill to pass National Assembly in 2004 and again in 2005 does not alter this assessment.[54]

However, the Panel also found that Bank management "did not follow up"

> on several inconclusive and, at times contradictory legal opinions and reports on legal and regulatory developments directly affecting the Requesters' rights and aspirations; this failure to follow up had a negative impact on the execution of the Project and the attainment of its objectives regarding indigenous people.[55]

Hence, the Panel concluded,

> Management's decision to support the process of establishing Law No. 72 was a good faith measure that seemed reasonable under the prevailing political situation. The Panel has determined that the decision cannot be viewed as deliberately backing off from the commitment enshrined in the PAD to support the aspirations of the Naso people. The Panel finds, however, that this decision, consistent with the policy on Project Supervision, should have been followed by stronger efforts to seek clarity on the legal ambiguities of Law No. 72 with respect to the territorial aspirations of the Naso.[56]

In *Nigeria/Ghana: West African Gas Pipeline*, which concerned the application of Nigerian property law in the context of compensation paid to project-affected people along the pipeline's 'right of way' (ROW), the Inspection Panel noted that the Board "was told" –

---

53   *Panama: Land Administration* (2009), IR, § 190.
54   *Panama: Land Administration* (2009), IR, § 134. *Also see*, IR, §§ 130-133.
55   *Panama: Land Administration* (2009), IR, § 191. *Note*, these examples also demonstrate the nature of the Bank's secondary obligations, here manifested as 'follow up' activities – as discussed *in* section 15.2.
56   *Panama: Land Administration* (2009), IR, § 192. *Note*, this example also demonstrates that Inspection Panel findings are often a mixture of compliance/non-compliance/partial-compliance – *see* section 1.2.1.

"both in the PAD and RAP" – "that there were 1,557 landowners" qualifying for compensation.[57] However, based on the Panel's "in-country interviews" and review of the project's "supervision reports," the Panel found that the project Sponsor ('WAPCo') had "informed what the RAP calls 'land owners' along the ROW that they were not legal owners of the land under the Land Use Act."[58] Furthermore, "[d]uring compensation negotiations,"

> the same "land owners" were told by WAPCo that they are not land owners under Nigerian law. At best, this undermines meaningful land-for-land negotiations, basically arguing that you must first establish your rights in order to exercise the option.[59]

These "conflicting views," the Panel added, "persisted throughout the Project planning and implementation until today."[60] For example, as the Inspection Panel elaborated on this ambiguity and some of its implications, "extended household heads in Igbesa notified Chevron during the RAP preparation that the extended family heads, are the land owners."[61] Although "[t]hey recognized "individual persons" as owning crops," the family heads "insisted that the land belonged to the extended family."[62] The "RAP survey," on the contrary, "claimed to substantiate the notion"

> that individual ownership is the most common form of land ownership on the ROW. However, the RAP then modified this position by stating that the landowners do not necessarily "own" the land in the Western sense. WAPCo agents reported to the Panel that they had told the displaced persons during negotiations for compensation that they were not land owners – a position consistent with parts of the RAP. The Panel examined receipts for payments and found that the displaced were not compensated for land ownership, but for 'all my building, land and other improvements and satisfaction for the

---

57 *Nigeria/Ghana: West African Gas Pipeline* (2006), IR, § 169. On issues related to the identification and quantification of PAP, *see* section 10.3; on issues related to compensation in involuntary resettlement scenarios, *see* section 12.3.

58 *Id. Also see* IR, § 166: "Pursuant to Nigerian law [in reflection of the Land Use Act], for land held under the customary right of occupancy for agricultural purposes, the local government can allocate alternative lands for the same purpose."

59 *Nigeria/Ghana: West African Gas Pipeline* (2006), IR, § 169. On what constitutes 'meaningful consultation', *see e.g.*, section 11.2.

60 *Nigeria/Ghana: West African Gas Pipeline* (2006), IR, § 135. *Note*, this example also demonstrates disagreement and/or ambiguity about Bank and Borrower obligations – as discussed in section 8.1.

61 *Id.*

62 *Id.*

deprivation of use of land [...] and for all inconveniences suffered.' No evidence was apparent of an official governmental transfer of land ownership.[63]

Furthermore, "[t]he plots that were acquired by the Project" along the pipeline ROW "appear to be portions of extended family holdings that were not subject to the requisite socio-economic analysis."[64] The Panel noted that its "interviews with WAPCo community agents" had affirmed "that the number of people who lined up along the ROW claiming ownership was a function of the family head's decision as to who should go to the line that day" – which "brings into doubt calculations of the size of the project affected population in the Nigerian segment of the WAGP."[65]

In other words, the Panel concluded, the "complexities of the traditional land tenure system,"

> wherein large extended families control land and the heads of the extended families distribute user rights among members of the extended family, were not adequately taken into account. This does not comply with the OP 4.12 requiring studies on land tenure and transfer systems.

"Such an analysis", the Panel emphasized, "would have helped to prevent the lack of transparency in the way compensation payments were made."[66]

8.2.2   Project interfaces with similar Borrower activities, not financed by the Bank

It can be decidedly challenging to extricate Bank from Borrower obligations – especially from the perspective of project-affected people – in scenarios where, in addition to the World Bank-financed project, another project is being implemented in the territory of the Borrower that does not involve any World Bank financing but has the same development objectives and involve the same or similar activities.[67] This situation might be further complicated if, for example, the 'respective project areas' are in relatively close proximity

---

63   *Nigeria/Ghana: West African Gas Pipeline* (2006), IR, § 135.

64   *Nigeria/Ghana: West African Gas Pipeline* (2006), IR, 128.

65   *Nigeria/Ghana: West African Gas Pipeline* (2006), IR, 128. *Note*, these examples also illustrate the effect of the identification and quantification of project-affected people on project content and scope – as discussed in 10.3.

66   *Nigeria/Ghana: West African Gas Pipeline* (2006), IR, § 136. For a similar discussion, *see e.g.*, *India: Coal Sector* (2001), at IR, §§ 166 & 174. *Note*, these examples also illustrate the impact of the interpretation of key phrases in project documentation on a project's content and scope – as discussed in section 10.4.

67   *Also see* the Panel's comments in the *India: Mumbai Urban Transport* case, *at* note 19, Ch. 7.

from each other;[68] where multiple actors (such as co-financiers and their respective project implementing agencies) are involved; or where there are notable complexity in the project designs.

Cambodia: Land Management and Administration (LMAP) provides a prominent example in this regard. The LMAP involved, as mentioned earlier, several "Development Partners" and served as the "major vehicle [...] for [obtaining] donor support to the Government's overarching LAMDP."[69] The Requesters claims centred on "events surrounding the denial of BKL residents' land claims and their forced resettlement from the BKL area located in central Phnom Penh."[70]

The Inspection Panel noted "that there is a fundamental disagreement between Bank Management and the Government on the linkage between events in the BKL area and LMAP."[71] The Borrower – as well as other "Development Partners of LMAP" did "not recognize a link between the Project and BKL events"; whereas Bank management contended that the BKL area [was] within the adjudication area declared under the Project [LMAP].[72] The Panel found, however, that this disagreement was exacerbated by various ambiguities in project design documents.

For instance, the Project Appraisal Document included the term "disputed lands," but failed to include "any definition of the term and the process to be followed" to resolve such disputes, which, subsequently "led to significant confusion among different stakeholders during Project implementation."[73] "Furthermore", the Panel added, "even though it was known that the boundaries of State public land were undefined,"

> the Project design excluded informal settlers/squatters from receiving land titles, unless approved by the Government, and left the issue to be addressed by the UNCHS [United Nations Human Settlements Programme/Centre for Human Settlements (UN HABITAT)].[74]

These "ambiguities in the Project design in part contributed to the harm that Requesters are facing", the Panel argued; hence, the Panel found that "although risks associated with

---

68 Indeed, this situation might cause some difficulties to delineate the 'project area', to which the Bank's operational policy framework will be applicable. On issues related to the delineation of 'project area' and 'project area of interest', and how it affects project scope, *see* section 10.2.

69 *See* notes 103, 104 & 105, Ch. 3.

70 *Cambodia: Land Management and Administration* (2009), MRIR, p. iv. *Note*, 'BKL area' refers to the 'Boeung Kak lake' area – *see* ER (1), § 1.

71 *Cambodia: Land Management and Administration* (2009), IR, p. xvii.

72 *Id.*

73 *Cambodia: Land Management and Administration* (2009), IR, § 170.

74 *Id.*

the Project were properly *identified*, Management did not comply with OMS 2.20 on Project Appraisal with respect to *addressing* these risks."[75]

Furthermore, the Panel found that Management "failed to acknowledge that terms like 'squatter' and 'informal settlements' are subjective until determined in fact through the process of adjudication," whereas "in Cambodia and other countries,"

> these often represent the poorest and most vulnerable groups in terms of exposure to eviction and other forms of abuse. These design flaws made it difficult for Bank Management to achieve stated objectives of the Project related to poverty reduction and providing tenure security for the poor, and thus did not comply with OMS 2.20.[76]

The Inspection Panel took note that Bank Management had subsequently ordered a "limited field research" 'review' – albeit only after the filing of the Request – "to understand whether there were any overlaps between reported evictions by NGOs and the media and systematic titling areas under LMAP [project]."[77] The outcomes of this review caused the Bank to conclude that, "in addition to the evictions at BKL which are affecting around 4,250 families,"

> about 20 villages were identified that fall within declared adjudication areas, and where evictions have occurred or are threatened, potentially affecting about 2,600 families. The review's initial findings note that there were no public displays in half of the 23 cases examined, and most of the cases do not appear to have gone through the envisaged systematic titling procedure. According to the review, while several of the evictions seem to involve people living on State land claimed by the Government, the RPF appears not to have been applied and in most cases affected people either did not receive any compensation or received compensation not in accordance with OD 4.30 Bank Policy on Involuntary Resettlement.[78]

In other words, the Panel concluded, "although there are several documents indicating that a significant number of families were adversely affected,"

---

75   *Id.* (emphases added). *Note*, this example also demonstrates the Panel's approach towards emphasizing the procedural and substantive elements in the policies – *see* section 6.3.4.
76   *Cambodia: Land Management and Administration* (2009), IR, § 265.
77   *Cambodia: Land Management and Administration* (2009), IR, § 293. *Note*, this example also demonstrates that the mere filing of a Request can trigger corrective Bank actions – as discussed *e.g., in* section 7.1.1.
78   *Id.*

the [full] extent of the negative impact on families living in adjudication areas is unknown. The Panel is extremely concerned about the large number of people who were forcibly evicted, displaced, or are under threat of eviction in Project areas.[79]

The Panel concluded – in what it considered to be reflecting Management's position – that "the BKL area"

is within a Project Province and was declared for adjudication under LMAP; hence, activities relating to verification of land tenure and ownership subsequent to the notice of adjudication are directly linked to the Project.[80]

But the Panel also pointed out that it was only "in the period leading to the presentation of the Request for Inspection" that the Bank "underst[oo]d and acknowledge[d]"

that the evictions in the BKL area were linked to LMAP implementation activities and that the RPF was to be applied to the displacement of BKL residents. However, once the Bank brought this to the attention of the Government and proposed a joint suspension of disbursements, the Government cancelled the undisbursed balance of the Credit on September 7, 2009.[81]

Nevertheless, the Panel found "that the failure of Management to ensure the application of the Resettlement Policy Framework was not in compliance with OD 4.30 and with OP/BP 13.05 on Project Supervision."[82]

Responding to the Inspection Panel's findings, however, Bank management commented that, although it agreed "with the Panel regarding a number of significant Project shortcomings," it also "consider[ed] it essential to characterize these shortcomings properly in terms of their relationship to the harm suffered by the residents of BKL."[83] "The cause of the harm or risk of harm suffered by the Requesters," Management asserted,

is eviction or threatened eviction from the BKL area. These evictions were carried out, and continue to be carried out, by the Municipality of Phnom Penh and the BKL area developer (neither of which is the Project implementing

---

79 *Id. But see* Management's comment in light of this finding *at* note 84, Ch. 8.
80 *Cambodia: Land Management and Administration* (2009), IR, p. xvii.
81 *Cambodia: Land Management and Administration* (2009), IR, §§ 216-217. On the Borrower's cancellation of the undisbursed balance, *also see* Management's comments *at* note 21, Ch. 8.
82 *Cambodia: Land Management and Administration* (2009), IR, §§ 216-217.
83 *Cambodia: Land Management and Administration* (2009), MRIR, p. v.

agency), based on the Government's assertion that the land in question is State land that has legitimately been leased to the developer and that the Requesters do not have possession rights. LMAP was not used by the Government as an instrument to assert or confirm ownership over the area. Instead, the Government maintains that its actions were outside the scope of the Project.[84]

The core concern in *Albania: Integrated Coastal Zone Management* centred around the actions of "the Construction Police of the Municipality of Vlora, under the supervision of the Ministry of Public Works and 'in line with the Southern Coastal Development Plan [SCDP] of the World Bank'," which "demolished either totally or partially [Requesters'] permanent residences."[85]

In its initial response to the Request, Management stated "categorically" that there was "no direct or indirect linkage between the Project."[86] Instead, Management asserted, the demolitions that formed the basis of the Request "were part of an ongoing Government program."[87] The Inspection Panel's interviews conduced with project-affected people, however, revealed a different picture. "The demolition process," the Panel emphasized,

> caused wrenching and painful scenes of opposition and resistance to demolition, but to no avail. People screamed and cried. According to the people present at the time in Jale, an official of the Construction Police said, 'you are crying now, but don't worry, you will be eating with a silver spoon soon, *as this is a part of a big World Bank project. They will invest here and will take care of you.*'[88]

But "what the Panel found on the ground after the intervention of the Construction Police," instead, "was a totally ruined social community and a physically destroyed village":

> Several piles of ruins abutted the row of plots on which the buildings existed. The debris still left consisted of big chunks of destroyed concrete and bricks, a clear testimony that destroyed houses were solid buildings and not commercial kiosks or other facilities built overnight for speculative purposes. Virtually all plots were in the possession of, and were claimed to be owned, by their users. The Panel observed that the destroyed houses do not seem to fit the description of what the Bank's PAD defined as "unauthorized encroachments in public

---

84   *Id.* On the 'causal relationship' between harm and Bank non-compliance (which is a recurring point of contention between Management and the Inspection Panel), *also see* sections 4.3.2 & 6.2.4.

85   *Albania: Integrated Coastal Zone Management* (2007), ER, § 11. For an overview of *Albania: Integrated Coastal Zone Management, see e.g.,* Naudé Fourie (2014), pp. 355-363.

86   *Albania: Integrated Coastal Zone Management* (2007), IR (ES), p. ix.

87   *Id.*

88   *Albania: Integrated Coastal Zone Management,* IR, § 78 (emphases added).

space". They were mostly located within seemingly privately-built boundaries (fences, pillars, etc.) which are still left standing, while the ruins of the demolished structures are inside these private boundaries. This indicates that, even according to the definition used in the PAD, those buildings could not be treated prima facie as "encroachments in public space" that are subject to demolition. Furthermore, the Panel observed that the buildings were not blocking "public access to beaches" one of the main reasons cited by Management to justify the demolition drive, in view of the "impending tourist season".[89]

While the Project Appraisal Document indeed "identified '[d]emolitions of illegal buildings" as among the "[c]ritical risks and possible controversial aspects" of the Project'",[90] the PAD also stipulated that "the Government had made an important commitment to suspend demolitions until criteria and procedures were developed to assist the vulnerable affected people."[91] "In the absence of applying the Bank Policy on Involuntary Resettlement" to the Project (which the Panel also criticized, as will be discussed later on),[92] the Panel pointed out that "this claimed 'agreement' gave the impression that a safeguard was in place to protect potentially affected people and the Bank against the critical Project risk of demolitions."[93]

In this regard, however, the Panel "uncover[ed] an unexpected yet very serious finding" – namely, that the "Government had not made such a commitment and had not agreed with what the PAD was stating."[94] In other words, this "crucial statement […] turned out to be unfounded and incorrect."[95] Instead, the Panel affirmed, its investigation team "was told" that a statement "was read to the Board", which contained the following paragraph:

> We want to clarify that the Bank does not have a blanket agreement with the Government to put a moratorium on the application of the Urban Planning Law, which calls for removal of unauthorized encroachments in public space

---

89 *Albania: Integrated Coastal Zone Management* (2007), IR, §§ 83-84. *Note*, this example also demonstrates the value of the Panel's fact-finding function – and the Panel's contribution towards making the harm 'real' (which, in turn, increases the probability of the realization of redress for project-affected people); in this regard, *also see* sections 7.1.1 & 7.1.3.

90 *Albania: Integrated Coastal Zone Management* (2007), IR, §§ 142-144.

91 *Id. Note*, the PAD stated: "The Government has agreed that further encroachment removal will take place only after the criteria and procedures for identifying and assisting such vulnerable affected people are in place." (*Id.*)

92 *See* section 12.1.

93 *Albania: Integrated Coastal Zone Management* (2007), IR, §§ 142-144.

94 *Id.*

95 *Id.*

in general. We will take another look at the PAD to remove any possible confusion in the public document.[96]

On reviewing the transcript of the relevant Board meeting, however, the Panel found such
a statement "was not read to the Board", and was "not in compliance with OMS 2.20 and
Annex D of BP 10.00 on Investment Lending: Identification to Board Presentation."[97]

Had such a statement been read, the Inspection Panel emphasized, it "would have
provided to the Board crucial factual information"

> on the status of a critical risk mitigation measure in the PAD, and which was
> welcomed and relied upon by the Board members while approving the Project.[98]

8.3   BORROWER AND/OR PROJECT IMPLEMENTING AGENCY CAPACITY
CONSTRAINTS

Institutional and/or professional capacity constraints – both of borrowers and their contracted project implementing agencies – can put the realization of development objectives
significantly at risk.

Clearly, as an international *public* development institution, the World Bank cannot
choose to operate only in contexts where there are no capacity constraints – in fact, those
contexts might be where the Bank's development assistance is required the most. Instead,
the Bank has to manage the risks associated with Borrower and project implementing
agency capacity constraints, throughout the project cycle. Indeed, several of the Bank's
operational policies have provisions that have this aim in mind. For example, OP 4.01
(Environmental Assessment) stipulates:

> When the borrower has inadequate legal or technical capacity to carry out key
> EA-related functions (such as review of EA, environmental monitoring,
> inspections, or management of mitigatory measures) for a proposed project,
> the project includes components to strengthen that capacity.[99]

---

96 *Albania: Integrated Coastal Zone Management* (2007), IR, §§ 259, 267-268.
97 *Id. Note*, this example also illustrates the value of the increased transparency brought about by the Bank's
    decision to publish the *minutes* of Board meetings – since the 2010 update of the Bank's policy on Access
    to Information; the example also demonstrates the 'transparency-effect' of the Panel, *as discussed e.g., in*
    section 7.2.2.
98 *Id. Note*, these examples also demonstrate the value of the Inspection Panel's fact-finding function in
    strengthening the Bank's governance structure – *see* sections 6.2.4 & 7.2.
99 OP 4.01, § 13.

In Inspection Panel practice, however, activities related to the management of capacity-risks are often identified as significant root causes of non-compliance with the Bank's operational policy framework.[100]

8.3.1   Managing risks associated with Borrower capacity constraints

In *Brazil: Rondônia Natural Resources Management* ('PLANAFLORO'), the Panel noted that the OED (now, IEG) had identified institutional capacity constraints as a major shortcoming of POLONOROESTE (the predecessor project of PLANAFLORO. The OED's review identified "[a]n obvious lesson for the future" – namely, "the need to give particular attention"

> to the judicious selection of the coordinating agency, as well as to the design of inter-institutional and implementing arrangements, in programs of similar complexity. More generally, this implies the need for the Bank to give much greater attention to institutional analysis and assessment during project appraisal and to institutional strengthening and development in project design and supervision.[101]

In its review of the current (successor) project, however, the Panel found that "[s]ufficient institutional capacity building to handle the ambitious, complicated PLANAFLORO program was not incorporated in the design phase."[102] The Panel noted that the project design reflected "[h]igh standards, tight timetables/deadlines, and multiple tasks spread among a large number of State level implementing agencies were built into the program."[103] However, the Panel commented, "[i]n view of past experience,"

> the Bank's expectations of the borrower were unrealistic given the then existing or foreseeable capacity for implementation. Basic implementation problems

---

100 For an example where the Panel found the Bank to be compliant with respect to identifying and managing risks associated with borrower capacity, *see Ecuador: Mining Development* (1999), IR, §§ 76-77: "The Project included a specific sector policy management component that included US$2.8 million equivalent for institutional strengthening and modernization of the regulatory framework, including technical assistance to build capacity and strengthen sector oversight institutions (MEM), especially those responsible for environmental protection (DINAMI), land management (DINAMA), geological information infrastructure and small scale mining matters (CODIGEM/DINAGE). [...] The Panel finds that the EA Report's analysis of the institutional, policy and legal framework, although not comprehensive, was in compliance with relevant Bank policies as set forth in OD 4.01."

101 *Brazil: Rondônia Natural Resources Management* (1995), Additional Review, §§ 41-42. For similar findings, *also see Nepal: Arun III* (1994), IR, § 21.

102 *Id.*

103 *Id.*

and delays stem from this fundamental flaw in the design of the institutional infrastructure.[104]

The Inspection Panel observed in *Peru: Lima Urban Transport* that "[s]everal" of its "investigations of other projects" had identified "important shortcomings" concerning compliance with operational policies that require the Bank "to properly assess and support the capacity of the borrower and the implementing body, in support of project objectives."[105] With regard to the *Lima Urban Transport* project, the Panel pointed out that Bus Rapid Transit (BRT) "systems are complex technical and social systems"

> that need to be planned and managed carefully, and require effective urban transport institutions with skilled staff. Importantly, the skills required for the design and execution of BRT systems include those needed not only to address technical issues of engineering design but also to deal with social and environmental matters, such as stakeholder analysis, consultation with affected parties, and analysis of potential adverse social and environmental impacts.[106]

During its investigation, however, the Panel "was informed by a range of stakeholders that professional and institutional capacity in urban transport management remains a challenge in Peru."[107] There was, in particular,

> limited capacity for detailed implementation of complex systems such as the BRT and for attention to broader issues of environmental, social and historical/cultural aspects of sustainable urban transportation management. The Management Response also acknowledges that implementation and coordination capacity of Project agencies, especially in the environmental social management areas, needed significant strengthening at the time of Project initiation.[108]

---

104 *Id.*
105 *Peru: Lima Urban Transport* (2009), IR, § 213. For an overview of *Peru: Lima Urban Transport, see* Naudé Fourie (2014), pp. 441-449. *Note,* this example also demonstrates the Inspection Panel's practice of referencing previous findings – *see* section 1.2.1.
106 *Peru: Lima Urban Transport* (2009), IR, § 213.
107 *Peru: Lima Urban Transport* (2009), IR, § 214.
108 *Id. Also see Peru: Lima Urban Transport* (2009), ER, § 28: "Management also states 'institutional capacity for environmental and social management was insufficiently developed at the time of Project approval' and 'the Bank team could have intervened more forcefully' to promote institutional strengthening."

"Under these conditions," the Panel noted, "it was a challenge simply to get the technical job done. Not surprisingly, compliance with Bank safeguard policies proved problematic."[109]

In *Colombia: Cartagena Water & Environmental Management*, the Panel observed that the Bank's assessment of borrower capacity seemed to focus "on ensur[ing] that the District [of Cartagena] had the funding required to finance its share of Project costs and to repay the Bank loan."[110] However, the Panel noted, there was "little evidence that the Bank made efforts"

> to improve the District's financial management and finances in general, beyond seeking agreements on certain performance monitoring targets with the District.[111]

Although it may be concluded that the Bank had "carried out its due diligence in accordance with its policies and procedures" – "from a strict Project point of view" – the Bank had also "misjudged the importance to the Project"

> of improving the borrower's capacity to collect the IPU [property] taxes. Pledging a percentage of IPU revenues was not enough to guarantee that the District would be able to meet its financial obligations to the Project.[112]

"By failing to take full advantage of Project supervision work," the Panel concluded, "the Bank missed an opportunity to strengthen the District's financial capacity."[113]

Whereas in its 1996 investigation of the *Argentina/Paraguay: Yacyretá Hydroelectric Project*, the Panel was critical of the project's "reliance on weak government conservation agencies," which received "little funding in both countries (in the case of Argentina, a Provincial government)" "to carry out the protection of large expanses of territory."[114] This decision, the Panel pointed out, was "made with little analysis of the institutional capacities of these agencies to take on the responsibility of purchasing and managing these areas."[115]

---

109 *Id.*
110 *Colombia: Cartagena Water & Environmental Management* (2004), IR, § 386. For an overview of *Colombia: Cartagena, see* Naudé Fourie (2014), pp. 233-243.
111 *Colombia: Cartagena Water & Environmental Management* (2004), IR, § 386.
112 *Id.*
113 *Id.*
114 *Argentina/Paraguay: Yacyretá Hydroelectric Project* (1996), Inspection Panel Review & Assessment, § 160. *Note,* this example also illustrates how Inspection Panel practice can be seen as implicit criticism of borrowers or of the prevailing conditions in borrower countries – as discussed *e.g., in* section 4.3.2.
115 *Argentina/Paraguay: Yacyretá Hydroelectric Project* (1996), Inspection Panel Review & Assessment, § 160.

The Inspection Panel concluded in *India: NTPC Power* that the project's "Resettlement Action Plans appear to have complied, at least on paper," with the operational policy, however, the "loan was processed so rapidly" ("the RAPs [were] completed immediately before the project was presented to the Bank's Board") that there simply was

> no time to ensure that essential mechanisms and preconditions, such as State Government commitment, capacity of implementing agency, etc. were in place or adequate.[116]

Although the Bank had therefore "introduced a project component dealing with the implementation of Resettlement and Rehabilitation and Environmental Action Plans", "[i]n line with its policies," the Bank failed to "assure itself that the Borrower had the necessary initial capacity to carry out these tasks."[117]

Indeed, the Panel added, "the Bank did not have the necessary capacity to support the Borrower in carrying out these tasks."[118] These findings, the Panel concluded, constituted "a serious violation of Bank policies on Environmental Assessment (Operational Directive 4.01) and Involuntary Resettlement (Operational Directive 4.30)."[119]

Finally, the analysis of borrower capacity also plays a critical role in projects to which OP/BP 4.00 (Use of Borrower Systems to Address Environmental and Social Safeguard Issues) is applicable. "OP 4.00 contains requirements to identify and fill 'gaps' that may be present, in order to meet the objectives and principles of the Policy with respect to issues of equivalence and acceptability," as the Panel noted in *South Africa: Eskom Investment Support*, and "[t]hese requirements include the need for the borrower"

> to undertake measures to strengthen implementation practices and capacity and '[...] may include Bank-supported efforts to strengthen relevant capacity, incentives, and methods for implementation' (OP 4.00: para. 3).[120]

---

116 *India: NTPC Power* (1997), IR, § 19. For a discussion of *India: NTPC Power, see e.g.,* Clark *in* Clark *et al.* (Eds.) (2003), pp. 167-190; Umaña *in* Alfredsson & Ring (Eds.) (2001), pp. 127-141; *and see* Naudé Fourie (2014), pp. 69-78. *Note,* this example also demonstrates the Panel's approach to compliance review, which emphasizes the necessity of compliance with procedural and substantive policy components – as discussed *in* section 6.3.4; it also demonstrates an imbalance between project components as a result of the tension between competing institutional aims – as discussed *in* Ch. 9.

117 *India: NTPC Power* (1997), IR, §§ 16-17.

118 *Id.* On the effects of *World Bank* resource capacity constraints in the area of project supervision, *also see* section 15.3.

119 *Id.*

120 *South Africa: Eskom Investment Support,* IR, §§ 222-223.

In this instance, the Panel's investigation pointed to various "shortcomings" in the Bank's "analysis of institutional capacity and implementation practices."[121] Hence, the Panel concluded that "Management did not have an adequate basis"

> to properly identify gap-filling measures to help address issues of capacity within competent environmental authorities at certain tiers of government to, inter alia, review EIAs, draft robust authorizations, and monitor and enforce compliance. This is not consistent with OP 4.00. The Panel considers that relying mostly on the institutional strength of Eskom [project implementing agency] was not a sufficient response to address these important and well-documented concerns relating to institutional capacity related to environmental authorization and enforcement.[122]

8.3.2 Managing risks associated with project implementing agency capacity constraints

Nigeria/Ghana: West African Gas Pipeline was implemented by 'WAPCo', which shareholders, at the time, included Shell, Chevron, Nigerian National Petroleum Corporation (NNPC), Volta River Authority (VRA) of Ghana, BenGaz o Benin and SotoGaz of Togo ([collectively known as] the Sponsors)."[123] The Panel's investigation of this project highlighted several compliance issues, which the Panel attributed partly to the fact that Bank management had "assumed, rather than evaluated"

> the Sponsor's capacity in dealing with the social safeguard issues. The Panel was informed that the Sponsor's partners have a strong reputation for physical environmental work, as was evident in the quality reports of the Project's environmental assessment. However, the Panel did not obtain evidence that this technical capacity implied that the Sponsor's had commensurate capacity in dealing with social issues, particularly those related to land acquisition. It seems that Management did not take into account some signs regarding the Sponsor's limited capacity to meet the Bank's Policies.[124]

---

121 *Id.*
122 *Id.*
123 *Nigeria/Ghana: West African Gas Pipeline* (2006), IR, p. ix. On the project's financing arrangements, *also see* note 86, Ch. 3. *Note*, this project had no separate capacity development component (compared to *e.g.*, the *Chad* and *Cameroon* oil pipeline projects) – *see* MR, § 10.
124 *Nigeria/Ghana: West African Gas Pipeline* (2006), IR, § 301.

"Full awareness of the Sponsor's limited capacity to deal with social issues, in a manner expected by the safeguard policies," the Panel emphasized, "should have led to action, including increased training, intensified supervision,[125] and urgency to field an international Expert Panel."[126]

Furthermore, the Panel found that Management had failed "to provide complete information to the Board" with regard to "the Sponsor's limited capacity to acquire land in accordance with the standard set in OP 4.12," as well as "the Project's lack of sufficient baseline data and the lack of a sustainable benefit plan for the displaced people."[127]

In *Papua New Guinea: Smallholder Agriculture*, where the project implementing agency was the Oil Palm Industry Corporation ('OPIC'), Management acknowledged "that the PAD failed to identify the risk of slow implementation start-up including the time needed to establish OPIC's project management capacity," which, in practice, meant that, "two years after Board approval,"

> key Project activities including road reconstruction and maintenance, infill planting and provision of local services and infrastructure through CDD [Community Driven Development] [had] not commenced [...].[128]

Furthermore, the Panel noted that "neither OPIC nor the Bank" could provide "any information"

> on [financial] returns to company estates and mills. Considering the decades of work supported by the Bank in the oil palm sector in Papua New Guinea, in partnership with oil palm companies, and the companies' important role in implementing the Project and their direct impact on smallholder income, the Panel finds that Management did not conduct appropriate due diligence of the companies' institutional and financial viability. The Panel finds this not to be in compliance with OMS 2.20 and OP/BP 10.04.[129]

---

125 On project scenarios requiring higher standards of project supervision, *see* section 15.2.2.

126 *Nigeria/Ghana: West African Gas Pipeline* (2006), IR, § 301.

127 *Nigeria/Ghana: West African Gas Pipeline* (2006), IR, § 317. *Note*, this example also demonstrates the value of the Panel's fact-finding function in terms of strengthening institutional governance – *see* section 7.1.4.

128 *Papua New Guinea: Smallholder Agriculture* (2009), ER, § 26. *Note*, the project's primary objective was to "increase the income and improve livelihoods of smallholders already involved in oil palm production by enabling them to plant additional oil palm through 'in-filling' [*i.e.*, 'new blocks of oil palm being planted between established blocks of oil palm along existing access roads'], rehabilitating and maintaining rural access roads, and improving local-level service provision and infrastructure through community participation." *See* ER, § 4. For an overview of *Papua New Guinea: Smallholder Agriculture*, *see e.g.*, Naudé Fourie (2014), pp. 451-462.

129 *Papua New Guinea: Smallholder Agriculture* (2009), IR, § 318. On the other hand, the Panel found (at IR, § 440) that "Management has recognized the capacity gaps in OPIC and has put in place institutional mecha-

"An important lesson from this investigation," the Panel concluded, "is that the implemen-tation capacity of borrower institutions and the capacity of the Bank to carry out adequate implementation support" are conclusive factors in "determin[ing] whether the Project is implemented as designed and adequately prevents adverse social and environmental impacts," especially when "strong economic incentives [are] being super imposed on a weak governance framework."[130]

In *India: Mumbai Urban Transport*, which was implemented by the Mumbai Metropolitan Region Development Authority ('MMRDA'), the Panel found that the project implementing agency "was not prepared to deal with a resettlement Project of that magni-tude."[131] In fact, the Panel noted, MMRDA's capacity constraints "was one of the reasons why" it had "delegated substantial parts of its responsibilities" with respect to resettlement and rehabilitation ('R&R') to local "outside NGOs."[132] The Panel acknowledged "the effort to involve local NGOs in the Project" but expressed concern

> about the transfer of the main implementation responsibilities from the State Government and municipal agencies to NGOs with insufficient institutional capacity and knowledge to deal with the overwhelming magnitude of the responsibilities transferred.[133]

Among these responsibilities, for instance, the NGOs were tasked with the collection of social baseline data by surveying various categories of affected people – data that would serve as key input, for instance, in the quantification of project-affected people and in calculating their compensation. The Panel found, however, that the NGOs "were not given adequate training about the Bank's R&R requirements concerning the tenure of structures and land and how these link with population characteristics;" nor did the Panel found any "evidence that the NGOs have developed skills in displacement planning or engineering

---

nisms to address the gaps and build the capacity of OPIC extension staff to perform the tasks necessary to ensure that oil palm operations are carried out in conformance with defined environmental and social standards. The Panel finds that the Project's approach in its design to building the capacity of OPIC extension staff conforms to the requirements of OP 4.04 on Natural Habitats."

130 *Papua New Guinea: Smallholder Agriculture* (2009), IR, § 543. *Note*, this example also demonstrates the Inspection Panel's contribution towards facilitating institutional learning – *see* section 7.1.5.

131 *India: Mumbai Urban Transport* (2004), IR, § 250. For an overview of *India: Mumbai Urban Transport, see e.g.*, Nurmukhametova (2006), pp. 405-408; *and see* Naudé Fourie (2014), pp. 245-258. *Note*, NGOs that are contracted by borrowers or project implementing agencies to assist with specific project implementation activities are often referred to as 'implementing NGOs' – in this regard, *also see* section 3.1.4.

132 *India: Mumbai Urban Transport* (2004), IR, § 250.

133 *Id.*

interface work."[134] In fact, the Panel's examination of the "survey forms" affirmed that "their low quality and sometimes prima facie inaccuracy was apparent."[135]

The implementing NGOs' capacity constraints were a root cause of several significant compliance issues identified by the Panel during its *Mumbai: Urban Transport investigation*.[136] And these constraints were also aggravated, the Panel highlighted, "by MMRDA staff's problems in supervising because of their own lack of capacity;" for instance, the Panel noted that it appeared that none of "the MMRDA staff interacting with the NGOs were familiar with census methodology or with the population dynamics and asset acquisition questions that needed to be asked."[137]

By transferring part of the project implementation responsibilities to two local NGOs, the Panel commented, they

> became in effect two small [project implementing] agencies contractually employed by the government, with insufficient capacity, decreasing status, and declining abilities to act as exponents of the local civil society.[138]

8.3.3   Projects or project components related to strengthening Borrower institutional capacity

The enhancement of Borrower institutional capacity might be a specific development objective; or, identified Borrower institutional capacity constraints might be considered as a significant impediment to the realization of development objectives. In such scenarios, the Bank might decide to fund a related project or a distinct project component specifically aimed at strengthening institutional capacity. The realization of these development objectives, however, often prove to be challenging – often, unsurprisingly, as a result of the issues emanating from the capacity constrains the objectives are aimed at addressing.

Cameroon: Petroleum, for instance, concerned two closely related Bank-financed projects: the Petroleum Development and Pipeline Project (the Pipeline construction Project) and the Petroleum Environment Capacity Enhancement Project ('CAPECE').[139] CAPECE was specifically aimed at "strengthening" the "local institutional, regulatory and

---

134 *India: Mumbai Urban Transport* (2004), IR, §§ 263-264.
135 *Id.*
136 *See e.g.*, sections 10.3, 12.2 & 12.3.
137 *India: Mumbai Urban Transport* (2004), IR, §§ 263-264.
138 *India: Mumbai Urban Transport* (2004), IR, § 245.
139 For an overview of *Cameroon: Petroleum*, *see e.g.*, Naudé Fourie (2014), pp. 209-220. *Note*, the "Pipeline Project is partially financed by (i) a loan from the [International Bank for Reconstruction and Development or IBRD] [...] and (ii) a loan from the [IFC]. The Pipeline Project is principally financed by three private sector petroleum companies (ExxonMobil, Chevron and Petronas or the 'Consortium'). The CAPECE Project is financed by the [IDA]." *See Cameroon: Petroleum* (2002), IR, p. vi.

legal framework"; enhancing the "coordination of capacities for environmental management"; and developing the Borrower's "public intervention capacity for environmental
management".[140] The Inspection Panel's investigation (which covered both of these
projects), noted that the CAPECE project suffered significant implementation delays particularly in comparison with the Pipeline Project.

In this regard, the Panel pointed to "the fragility of the local institutional framework
which, ultimately, is in charge of monitoring the Pipeline Project on behalf of the GOC
[Borrower]."[141] Furthermore, "[t]he delays associated with the implementation of the
CAPECE Project" – which "was specifically designed to mitigate this fragility" – "affected
the GOC's performance during the entire [oil pipeline] construction period."[142] Hence,
the Panel concluded, "the purpose of OD 4.01, paragraph 12"

> regarding the strengthening of environmental capabilities to adequately assess
> construction impacts during the Implementation and Monitoring Phase of the
> project has not been achieved.[143]

The Panel emphasized that it was "not in the mandate, or is it the purpose of the Panel to
evaluate the capabilities of the GOC in implementing the CAPECE project" – instead, the
Panel affirmed that it "seeks to evaluate the role of the Bank in its supervision and assistance
to the GOC to ensure effective project implementation."[144] Nevertheless, the Panel noted
that it "could not confirm" whether the Pipeline Steering and Monitoring Committee
('CPSP', appointed by the Borrower)[145]

> indeed had an effective field monitoring presence during pipeline construction
> activities. In fact, it was reported from independent sources that the CPSP often
> lacked adequate training, equipment and transport in the field and therefore
> relied heavily on logistical support provided by COTCO [the project imple-
> menting agency].[146]

Pointing to the negative effects of the delays in establishing 'FEDEC' – an "Environmental
Foundation" that would be established as part of the CAPECE project in order "to provide

---

140 *Cameroon: Petroleum* (2002), IR, § 5.
141 *Cameroon: Petroleum* (2002), IR, § 68.
142 *Id.*
143 *Id. Note*, this example demonstrates the Panel's practice of emphasizing the underlying policy objective –
as discussed *in* section 6.3.3.
144 *Cameroon: Petroleum* (2002), IR, p. xi. On the Panel's mandate and its relationship with the formal division
between Bank and Borrower obligations, *see* section 4.3.1.
145 *I.e.*, the 'Pipeline Steering and Monitoring Committee' of the Borrower's project implementing agency.
146 *Cameroon: Petroleum* (2002), IR, p. xi.

defined long-term financial support for defined IPP-related projects/programs", and, ultimately, that would be charged with implementing the project's Indigenous Peoples Plan[147] – the Panel acknowledged that, while "very unfortunate," it "may have been unavoidable given the capacity predicament of the GOC and the undefined and in-process nature of the specific IPP."[148]

While the Inspection Panel therefore accepted the "reasoning behind Bank Management's decision to support the creation of FEDEC to implement the IPP", especially in light of the "fact that the GOC did not have an adequate institutional framework in place at the time to deal with the needs of the Indigenous Peoples," the Panel also highlighted the fact "that the delays in implementing the programs of the IPP were related to both their lack of specificity and to delays in constituting FEDEC's Board."[149] The Panel added "that the Bank could have taken"

> a more direct role in constituting the Board instead of leaving the responsibility to COTCO only. Similarly, the Bank could ensure that FEDEC implements the IPP effectively and that its Board members are adequately compensated and have the necessary logistical support to function effectively.[150]

Chad: Petroleum, the 'sister project' of *Cameroon: Petroleum*, involved the "development of the oil fields in the Doba Basin (Chad) and the transportation of the oil through Cameroon,"[151] and was therefore similarly organized in terms of a 'Pipeline Project' and 'Capacity Building Project'.[152]

The Inspection Panel noted that the "Requesters and NGOs alike have questioned the ability of the Capacity Building Project to produce timely results."[153] They argued, therefore, that "adequate institutional capacity should have been put in place before the construction of the pipeline."[154] On the other hand, interviews with Bank staff conducted by the Inspection Panel illustrated some of the difficulties with such arguments. For example, the Panel explained, "Bank staff recalled that for several years there was no certainty whether the Pipeline Project would materialize or not", whereas borrower governments tend to be

---

147 *See Cameroon: Petroleum* (2002), IR (ES), § 65.
148 *Cameroon: Petroleum* (2002), IR, § 221.
149 *Cameroon: Petroleum* (2002), IR, § 211-212. On issues concerning the adequacy of IPPs or IPDPs, *also see* section 13.2.
150 *Cameroon: Petroleum* (2002), IR, § 211-212. *Also see* the discussion in section 8.3.4.
151 *Chad: Petroleum* (2001), ER, § 2-3 & 8. For an overview of *Chad: Petroleum, see* Naudé Fourie (2014), pp. 153-166.
152 *Chad: Petroleum* (2001), ER, § 2-3 & 8.
153 *Chad: Petroleum* (2001), IR, § 76.
154 *Id.*

"reluctant to borrow funds to reinforce their institutional capacity 'in a vacuum'."[155] "[T]here is no way", as Bank staff told the Panel,

> that we would have ever gotten the Government of Chad (or the Government of Cameroon) to agree to a project to sit for several years to develop a capacity for a project which might happen or might not.[156]

In other words, as the Panel commented, "[d]etermining when a country can be expected to be ready to cope with a Project's impacts represents a challenging dilemma."[157] "On the one hand,"

> institutions in developing countries have technical and operational limitations, and Chad is no exception. On the other hand, the Bank has the obligation to ensure that systems are in place to avoid or mitigate adverse impacts.[158]

Democratic Republic of Congo: Transitional Support for Economic Recovery provides a prominent example of many of the challenges surrounding the operationalization of the division between Bank and Borrower obligations – but also of the ensuing difficulties it presents an accountability mechanism such as the Inspection Panel that is mandated to 'assess *World Bank* compliance' (only).

The *Transitional Support* project had multiple development objectives that would be realized by several project components – including a component aimed at strengthening borrower institutional capacity, which also formed the focus of the Requesters' claims.[159] The Requesters' concerns related to a specific objective of the 'institutional strengthening' component, which aim was "to help restore effective institutions in the forestry sector"

> in those provinces that have been reunified. It is intended to help improve local governance over natural resources, and in particular to help bring the [Bor-

---

155 *Chad: Petroleum* (2001), IR, § 76. For controversies about the Bank's financing of this project, *see e.g.*, Van Putten (2008), pp. 351-354; *and* Mallaby (2004), pp. 354-573. *Also see*: 'Chad Threatens Oil Cutoff Over World Bank Dispute: African Nation Seeks Release of $125 Million', *USA Today*, 15 April 2006, available at: http://usatoday30.usatoday.com/news/world/2006-04-15-chad-oil-pipeline_x.htm; *and* D. White, 'Why a World Bank Oil Project has Run into the Sand', *Financial Times*, 22 January 2006, available at: www.ft.com.
156 *Chad: Petroleum* (2001), IR, § 76.
157 *Id.*
158 *Id.*
159 *Democratic Republic of Congo: Transitional Support* (2005), ER, §§ 3-4. The project's five components included: "(a) balance of payment support; (b) institutional strengthening; (c) infrastructure rehabilitation; (d) urban rehabilitation; and (e) community empowerment." (*Id.*) For an overview of *DRC: Transitional Support*, *see e.g.*, Naudé Fourie (2014), pp. 281-290.

rower's] new Forestry Code into practice and to address the problem of illegal logging.[160]

Throughout its investigation report, the Inspection Panel acknowledged that, during the time of the project's design and appraisal, the "DRC was emerging"

> from a devastating period of conflict and turmoil that cost millions of lives, ravaged large sections of the country, and caused the effective collapse of Government services.[161]

The Panel repeatedly recognized "the difficulties and even risks facing Bank staff and others working in this environment," as well as "the quick nature of their response in offering assistance to DRC in this uncertain post-conflict environment."[162] The Panel also elaborated on the significant institutional capacity constraints which the project had to deal with. For example, the Panel observed, "an adequate institutional framework to ensure sustainable management and active participation of local people"

> does not yet exist at the national, provincial and local levels. There is no com-prehensive forestry plan. The social and environmental assessments of forests under commercial use are absent or inadequate. The forests set aside for forest dwellers are non-existent or seriously inadequate. The Panel observed during its visit, as confirmed by information from other sources, that the institutional capacity to implement and enforce any rules or regulations in the remote forest areas is minimal.[163]

Furthermore, the Inspection Panel emphasized that it did "not hold the Bank responsible for these regrettable realities," – on the contrary, "[t]he Bank and the new Government [...] are working in a post-conflict situation where government institutions have been destroyed;"[164] whereas it was "reasonable to conclude that the Bank was 'seeking' those kinds of commitments when [the project] was designed, and has continued to seek them, under very difficult circumstances."[165]

---

160 *Democratic Republic of Congo: Transitional Support* (2005), ER, § 5. *Note*, the Requesters were concerned about the "possible negative effects of a forest zoning plan under preparation with IDA support"; and "fear[ed] the implementation of a new commercial forest concession system [would] cause irreversible harm to the forests where they live and on which they depend for their subsistence." *See* ER, § 4.
161 *Democratic Republic of Congo: Transitional Support* (2005), IR, § 214.
162 *Id.*
163 *Democratic Republic of Congo: Transitional Support* (2005), IR, §§ 381-382 (emphasis in original).
164 *Id.*
165 *Id.*

That being said, the Panel concluded that Management had "paid insufficient attention" during the project design stage "to the potential social consequences of this new Project affecting the management and use of the DRC forests" – "[e]ven taking into account the absence of information and the post-conflict nature of the Bank's interventions."[166] This issue, the Panel added, was "at the core of many problems of non-compliance with Bank policies" highlighted by the Panel (and which are included throughout Part II of this book) and "was a major shortcoming"

> of the concepts underlying the Bank's good intentions to deal with the difficult issues of bringing order into the forest concession system.[167]

In addition, given the "widespread awareness" that the Borrower "lacks basic institutional, technical and field capacity to address social, environmental and other issues relating to logging in its forests," the Panel voiced its concern with the "potential impact" of the project's support for "actions to validate long-term concession contracts when the capacity to ensure sustainable forest concession operations does not exist."[168]

For example, the Panel observed that "Bank staff have attached high importance to getting the appropriate legal framework in place for forests" and have also "contributed significantly to this process."[169] While "the importance of a solid legal framework and the difficulty of developing and establishing it" cannot be denied, the Panel added that "the lack of institutional capacity to implement and enforce [these] laws and regulations" is "an almost overwhelming problem in the forest sector in DRC," particularly "at the provincial and local levels."[170]

"Until [such institutional capacity] is developed," the Panel concluded, "the [enhanced] legal framework,"

> although an essential step, cannot be relied upon to ensure sustainable devel-
> opment in the forest sector or to ensure that the people benefit from the
> forests.[171]

---

166 *Democratic Republic of Congo: Transitional Support* (2005), IR, § 167.
167 *Id.*
168 *Democratic Republic of Congo: Transitional Support* (2005), IR, §§ 207-208.
169 *Democratic Republic of Congo: Transitional Support* (2005), IR, § 540.
170 *Id.*
171 *Id.*

8.3.4   *'Stepping in' to mitigate risks related to Borrower capacity constraints*

Project scenarios involving Borrower capacity constraints also present another challenge for the Bank – that is, when to 'step in' in order to mitigate capacity-related risks and, even more challenging, what actions to take.[172]

In *Cameroon: Petroleum*, for instance, concerning FEDEC's delay in implementing the Indigenous Peoples Plan, the Panel identified an additional "reason for [this] delay (that is, in addition to factors related to the delay in establishing FEDEC and in constituting its Board),[173] namely: FEDEC's "budgetary problems."[174] In this regard, the Panel observed, "Bank staff voiced two lines of thinking [that] were prevalent during the decision-making process."[175] The first point of view argued "that the Bank, through the CAPECE Project should make a financial contribution to FEDEC"; whereas the second point of view argued "that it was not for the Bank to pay for the social and environmental mitigation required for the Project."[176]

"In the end," the Panel noted, "the first view prevailed."[177] The Panel subsequently "recognize[d] that as a result of Bank intervention and oversight,"

> FEDEC is now up and running and that it is moving ahead with its programs, including the anti-tuberculosis campaign, the issuing of national identification cards, and contributing to school supplies and medicines.[178]

Hence, the Panel concluded that the Bank was 'in compliance'

> with OD 4.20 in regards to paragraph 15 (c) "the institutions responsible for government interaction with indigenous peoples should possess the social, technical, and legal skills needed for carrying out the proposed development activities."[179]

Whereas in *Cambodia: Forest Concession Management*, the Inspection Panel found that "the Bank took on some of the responsibility of the borrower with respect to [information] disclosure and related consultations," particularly in the light of insufficient Borrower

---

172 *Note*, this discussion is also closely related to the Bank's so-called 'step in obligation (as discussed *in* section 4.3.2) as well as to issues concerning the adequacy of corrective supervision activities (as discussed *in* section 15.2).

173 As discussed *in* section 8.3.3.

174 *Cameroon: Petroleum* (2002), IR, § 211-212.

175 *Id.*

176 *Id.*

177 *Id.*

178 *Cameroon: Petroleum* (2002), IR, § 221.

179 *Id.*

capacity to meet these obligations.[180] While recognizing that this was done "with the best of intentions", the Panel pointed out that the Bank's mitigating actions eventually resulted in a situation where "the responsibilities of the Bank and the Government became conflated in the minds of many people" – including the Requesters – which "subsequently perceived the Bank as being complicit"

> in restricting access to full documentation of the SFMPs and in being a party to a faulty consultation process, which included the imposition of unrealistically short periods for the review. The Bank was also increasingly seen as an apologist for the concession system, and was perceived to be going out of its way to push for the legitimization of the concession system at all costs.[181]

However, it should also be noted that borrower capacity constraints might present similar challenges for project implementing agencies. In its 2002 investigation of the *Paraguay: Yacyretá Hydroelectric Project*, for instance, the Inspection Panel noted that the project implementing agency ('EBY')[182] "[i]ncreasingly has had to assume public responsibilities that usually would be taken on by local and national governments" and which were "well beyond its original tasks as project implementing agency."[183] Notably, "EBY has been entrusted"

> with providing basic services to the local population as well as with responsibil-ities ranging from health, sanitation, and safety to flood mitigation and river basin protection.[184]

In other words, it had "gradually turned into 'a government authority without parallel in the local region'."[185] Conversely, EBY's "shortfalls" had resulted in a "profound distrust from affected people, community leaders, and NGOs, particularly in Paraguay."[186] Conse-quently, the Inspection Panel concluded, EBY's "institutional weakness,"

---

180 *Cambodia: Forest Concession Management* (2005), IR, § 352. For similar comments, *also see Peru: Lima Urban Transport* (2009), IR, §§ 213-214. For examples where borrowers have taken up Bank responsibilities in the context of supervision activities, *see* section 15.3.

181 *Cambodia: Forest Concession Management* (2005), IR, § 352.

182 *Note,* "[t]o implement the project, a semi-autonomous bi-national entity, Entidad Binacional Yacyretá (EBY), was created in 1976, with equal representation of the two 5 countries in EBY's governance structures." *See Paraguay/Argentina: Yacyretá Hydroelectric Project* (2002), ER, § 2.

183 *Paraguay/Argentina: Yacyretá Hydroelectric Project* (2002), IR, §§ 39-40.

184 *Id.*

185 *Id.* On the diminishing functional value of existing systems of categorization employed in transnational governance and regulatory contexts (here concerning the division between public and private sectors), *also see* section 2.1.

186 *Paraguay/Argentina: Yacyretá Hydroelectric Project* (2002), IR, §§ 39-40.

the excessively broad range of its activities, and the mistrust of the area's affected people are considered by many to be key factors that have adversely affected Project execution and have created a situation that seems very difficult to solve.[187]

****

The discussion in Part I of this book demonstrated that there is significant complexity underlying the formal division between World Bank and Borrower obligations. This chapter illustrated that challenging project scenarios – such as those involving disagreement and ambiguities about Bank and Borrower obligations, various interfaces with Borrowers' constitutional systems, or institutional and/or professional capacity constraints on the part of Borrowers or their contracted project implementing agencies – can further complicate the operationalization of this division, especially since it tends to intensify existing interdependencies and create additional ones.

The manner in which the delineation between Bank and Borrower obligations play out in development practice, moreover, holds significant implications for the manner in which internal and external constituency groups view the content and scope of World Bank accountability – an issue that is illustrated prominently in scenarios where the Bank 'steps in' to mitigate some of the risks associated with capacity deficiencies. It is these types of scenarios, in particular, that seem to push the contours of World Bank obligations out even further – and, in some instances, to the point where questions about the limits of World Bank accountability become a legitimate concern.

Several of the examples from Inspection Panel practice included in this chapter, furthermore, illustrate the complex nature of the relationship between the Bank and Borrowers. As Boisson de Chazournes comments, "the distinction to be made between the World Bank's behaviour and that of the borrower," "is likely" to continue affecting the content and scope of World Bank accountability "because of the permeable nature of the relationship that prevails between the World Bank and its borrowers."[188]

Inspection Panel practice demonstrates some of the challenges involved in balancing the requirements to respect state sovereignty, uphold the institution's political neutrality, ensure the realization of development project objectives – while facilitating borrower ownership for development, maintaining client satisfaction, and managing economic, social and environmental risks involved in particular Bank (co-) financed development projects. The next chapter will consider these matters in more detail.

---

187 *Id.*
188 Boisson de Chazournes *in* Treves et al. (Eds.) (2005), p. 193.

9 Achieving Equilibrium Among Institutional Aims: 'Technical/Commercial' versus 'Non-technical/Non-commercial' Project Components

Reflecting the interests, demands, expectations and underlying conceptions of internal and external constituency groups, the World Bank has, over time, adopted a wide range of institutional aims. These institutional aims, in turn, came to be reflected in the Bank's operational policy framework, as well as in its performance areas and indicators. However, as discussed in Chapter 4,[1] while these aims might be complementary (and the underlying assumption often seems to be that they are), there is also potential for tension. In development practice, moreover, such tensions would often require efforts to reconcile competing aims or – when such reconciliation is not possible (or, perhaps, not desirable) – efforts to achieve institutional equilibrium could involve challenging prioritization and trade-off decisions.

Chapter 9 focuses on these matters – and particularly, how they manifest in Inspection Panel practice, namely: as concerns about the balance between 'technical' or 'commercial' project aspects *versus* those with a 'non-technical' or 'non-commercial' focus. Early on in its institutional history, the Inspection Panel had described these as "two important types of systemic problems that are interrelated and have other critical links to project performance."[2] The first problem, as Umaña described it, concerns "the persistent imbalance that develops in projects that have infrastructure as well as social and environmental components."[3] Whereas the second problem relates to "the unequal status"

> that social and environmental operational policies still seem to have vis-à-vis other directives in the execution of projects. This is related to other problems such as the 'approval culture' and the incentive/punishment system for task

---

1   *See* section 4.2.
2   Umaña (1998), p. 326.
3   *Id. Note*, this issue had also been identified in OED (now IEG) post-implementation reviews – *see e.g., India: NTPC Power* (1997), ER, §§ 38-39.

managers, where due attention to environmental and resettlement problems may delay project approval.[4]

Subsequent Inspection Panel practice has also identified these types of issues as significant root causes of policy non-compliance. However, as the examples included in this chapter demonstrate, imbalances between technical and/or commercial *versus* non-technical and/or non-commercial project elements occur not only in the context of large scale infrastructure projects (financed by investment loans), but also in development projects with institutional (governance) aims (financed by development policy loans) – although these issues tend to manifest in slightly different ways in DPL contexts.[5]

Chapter 9 considers three broad categories of issues related to the matter of *equilibrium* between project components, as highlighted in the course of Inspection Panel investigations – although several examples included here illustrate more than one issue, which also indicate how tightly interwoven these issues can be. The chapter focuses, firstly, on the influence of *project modality* (referring to the type of project), *project design* and *project organization*; secondly, on the impact of *project financing* (referring to 'which entity finances which project component'), *project expenditure* (that is, 'on what is the money actually spent'), and the focus of *project implementation* and *supervision* activities; and, thirdly, on the effect of *diversity within project areas*, as well as the *transparency surrounding project prioritizing and trade-off decisions*.

9.1   PROJECT MODALITY, PROJECT DESIGN AND PROJECT ORGANIZATION

Project modality – or, underlying perceptions about project modality – can have a significant (if implicit) impact on a project's design focus, as well as Management's focus during the project implementation stage. In *Brazil: Itaparica Resettlement and Irrigation*, for example, the Inspection Panel observed that, in "hindsight," Bank "Management viewed this primarily as an irrigation project" – which, in practice, meant that the "broader issues raised in OMS 2.33 with regard to resettlement compliance appear to have taken a back seat."[6]

For instance, the Panel questioned whether Bank management "could have maintained compliance with all covenants and aspects of resettlement policies without" having a

---

4   *Id.* On the 'approval culture', *also see e.g.,* Shihata's comments *at* note 70, Ch. 4.
5   On the Bank's two primary lending instruments, *see* section 4.1.1.
6   *Brazil: Itaparica Resettlement and Irrigation* (1997), ER, § 39. On issues related to project modality, *also see* section 10.1.

"resettlement specialist" on project "supervision missions."[7] Although the Panel commended the Bank's supervision efforts regarding "the irrigation work", the Panel emphasized that "the original impetus for the Project was supposed to be successful resettlement."[8]

In *Pakistan: National Drainage Program*, the Inspection Panel commented that "the Project's balance between irrigation and drainage interventions, on the one hand,"

> and measures to protect and restore the environment and natural habitat on the other hand needs to be re-considered, in order to be compliant with the Bank's policy on Natural Habitats.[9]

For example, while "[l]ow-cost measures, such as biological re-vegetation, exist," the Panel explained, in this project, however, "biological components have been absent."[10]

Argentina: Santa Fe Road Infrastructure "involved," among other things, "upgrading a road going through a very flat area that was constantly being flooded."[11] This upgrade "entailed adding two lanes and elevating them slightly so that traffic could flow even if there were heavy rains."[12] The "local farmers", however, "were concerned that the elevated roads would act like a small dam, flooding their fields during heavy rains;" whereas the project's "social and environmental assessment concluded"

> that the structural measures planned to ensure that the road did not flood would in themselves guarantee that the impact of the project on local flooding would be minimal,

the Panel pointed out that these measures did not "provide specific information on the project's additional flood impacts."[13] In this instance, the Inspection Panel concluded that Bank management "seemed to focus principally on ensuring that the road did not get flooded, rather than on the impacts of the project on the additional flood risks faced by local residents."[14]

---

7   *Id.* For a discussion of *Brazil: Itaparica, see e.g.*, Vianna *in* Clark *et al.* (Eds.) (2003), pp. 145-165; *and see* Naudé Fourie (2014), pp. 61-67. On issues related to the resourcing of World Bank supervision missions, *also see* section 15.3.

8   *Brazil: Itaparica Resettlement and Irrigation* (1997), ER, § 39.

9   *Pakistan: National Drainage Program* (2004), IR, § 368.

10 *Id.*

11 *Argentina: Santa Fe Road Infrastructure* (2007), IR, §§ 602-603.

12 *Argentina: Santa Fe Road Infrastructure* (2007), IR, §§ 602-603. For an overview of *Argentina: Santa Fe, see e.g.*, Naudé Fourie (2014), pp. 387-395.

13 *Id.*

14 *Id.*

The Inspection Panel made similar comments in *South Africa: Eskom Investment Support.*[15] In this instance, the Panel observed that Management's focus "appears to have been on ensuring that the Medupi power plant had a reliable source of water supply," while "insufficient attention was given in Project documents"

> to the potential impacts that the use of water by the plant might have on other users and to the evaluation of the potential significance of Project impacts on quantity and quality of surface and groundwater resources. The evaluation of the potential significance of impacts on water quality, on maintenance of "the reserve," on the affected freshwater systems and the services they provide, and on non-strategic and downstream water users (some of whom may be particularly vulnerable) is, in the view of the Panel, inadequate.[16]

The Panel also noted that it had identified comparable issues during its earlier investigation of *Argentina: Santa Fe Road Infrastructure.* "In both these cases," the Panel pointed out, "Management's focus was on the engineering design issue of ensuring that the project was "water secure" (i.e., that it had a reliable source of water supply or was adequately protected against floods),"

> rather than on the environmental impact issue of assessing the Project's impacts on local water regimes. In other words, Management seemed to focus on examining the water related risks to the Project, with less attention to the risks to project affected people.[17]

The environmental risks, the Panel added, were likely "to become even more relevant in future with increasing water variability and concerns about water security," which "suggested the need for the Bank's highly qualified water resource professionals"

---

15 *Eskom Investment Support* consisted of three project components: "(a) 4,800 megawatt Medupi Power Plant and associated transmission system; (b) investments in renewable energy projects; (c) low carbon energy efficiency investment and technical assistance." *See South Africa: Eskom Investment Support* (2010) ER, § 6.

16 *South Africa: Eskom Investment Support* (2010), IR, § 342. For an overview of *Eskom: Investment Support*, see e.g., Naudé Fourie (2014), pp. 471-483.

17 *South Africa: Eskom Investment Support* (2010), IR, §§ 602-603. *Note*, this example also demonstrates the Inspection Panel's practice of referencing previous findings (*see* section 1.2.1.) as well as the Panel's contribution towards institutional learning by identifying recurring systemic or structural issues that come to the fore in the course of its investigations (*see* section 7.1.5.).

to give specialized attention to projects in transport, energy, agriculture and other 'non-water' sectors that have the potential to have negative impacts on water resources.[18]

The design focus on technical infrastructure aspects was also prevalent in *Albania: Power Sector*. In this case, the Requesters were specifically concerned with the selected site of a new thermal power plant, arguing that it would "irreparably destroy"

> environment, tourism, safe fisheries, natural habitat, ecosystem, coral colonies as well as the unique historical and cultural significance of the entire Vlora Bay and Narta lagoon. In short, it will destroy our past, present and future.[19]

In its examination of project design documents, the Inspection Panel concluded that "socio-economic impacts on Vlora's population were not properly considered in the weighting methodology" that had been employed in "selecting the most adequate site" of the power plant.[20] Notably, only "one of the ten criteria"

> used in the ranking of alternatives was "socio-economic concerns." This crite-rion, given 8% of the total weighting, included "the location of residential areas, religious buildings, cemeteries, schools, wet-lands, environmentally protected areas etc. relative to the proposed site, as well as the generation facility's potential impact on these items."[21]

Since "the social assessment" for the project "was not carried out," furthermore, "no actual data"

> could be included for this criterion. The project's file makes in this respect only a passing reference to "social development" which, in this case, was reduced narrowly to "consumer satisfaction" about power supply. It did not consider any community reaction to the selected site.[22]

---

18 *South Africa: Eskom Investment Support* (2010), IR, §§ 603-604.
19 *Albania: Power Sector* (2007), MR, Annex 1, § 1.
20 *Albania: Power Sector* (2007), IR, § 280. For and overview of *Albania: Power Sector, see e.g.*, Naudé Fourie (2014), pp. 355-363.
21 *Id.*
22 *Id.*

The Panel attributed this oversight, in part, to the deficiencies of the consultation process. The Panel noted that, during its own meetings with project-affected people in the Vlora area, they explained "that the installation of the thermal oil plant adjacent to Vlora beach,"

and of its oil terminal in the Bay's waters close to the shore, will considerably detract from the area's attractiveness for tourism, causing them substantial opportunity costs and losses.[23]

However, the Panel added, "[t]hese opportunity costs were not factored into the project's social impact analysis or economic feasibility analysis."[24] A meaningful "consultation process," (as will be discussed later on) "should have revealed these strong concerns and addressed them, most obviously by addressing them in the economic analysis" – "even", the Panel asserted, "if only to reveal that the impact would have been less than anticipated."[25]

Whereas in *Nigeria: Lagos Drainage*, the Panel concluded that "most of the Operational policies and particularly the OD 10.04 on Economic Evaluation of Investment Operations" appeared "to have been followed during the preparation of the Project."[26] However, the Panel highlighted that "the sociological considerations did not appear fully integrated into the project design."[27] Notably, there seemed to be a "lack of appropriate measures which should have been introduced in the project design to ensure the effective maintenance of the drainage channels constructed under the Project."[28] The Panel also pointed to "[a] typical example of the socio-cultural dimension" of this project – namely, "the refusal of the people who have been provided with built-in flush toilets to use such hygienic facilities instead of using the banks of the drainage channels and any empty space they see."[29]

On the other hand, the Inspection Panel acknowledged, "enormous measures"

would be required to enlighten the entire slum communities in Lagos to practice hygienic disposal of human waste and other refuse. This, the Panel believes, is outside the scope of this particular Project.[30]

---

23 *Albania: Power Sector* (2007), IR, § 305.
24 *Id.*
25 *Id.* On what constitutes 'meaningful consultation', *see* section 11.2. *Note*, this example also demonstrates the importance of transparency regarding project prioritization and trade-off decisions (*see* section 9.3) and issues related to the scope and content of Environmental Assessments (*see* sections 14.2.2 & 14.2.3).
26 *Nigeria: Lagos Drainage (1998)*, ER, §§ 42, 44.
27 *Id.* For an overview of *Nigeria: Lagos Drainage, see e.g.*, Naudé Fourie (2014), pp. 95-99.
28 *Id.*
29 *Id.*
30 *Id. Note*, this example also pertains to the 'limits' of World Bank accountability – as *e.g.*, reflected in the discussion *in* section 6.3.

In *Panama: Land Administration* the Inspection Panel observed that the project design "appears to have led to the potential for conflict"

> between the "left-hand" of the Project (titling activities) and the "right-hand" of the Project (protection of indigenous land areas), which were exacerbated by the scale and pace of titling activities under the Project.[31]

In this instance, the Panel commended Bank management for the 'prompt' corrective actions it undertook as soon as it was identified "during implementation."[32] Nevertheless, "[b]ased on its experience with this investigation and others, and in line with suggestions made during staff interviews," the Panel commented that "the inclusion of relevant covenants in Project documents can help safeguard against the possibility"

> that activities under one project component could come into conflict with project objectives and related policy requirements under other components. This is particularly important for projects in which one component deals with the protection of the rights of indigenous people.[33]

The development objectives of *India: Ecodevelopment* also had a dual nature. The project would provide "support" for the "management of protected areas of significant global biodiversity" by means of an 'Ecodevelopment strategy', while also "protect[ing] local people living in and around these areas."[34] The Inspection Panel recognized that these were both "important goals" but also pointed out that there were "inherent conflicts as well as potential complementarities between them."[35]

The potential for conflict materialized, furthermore, as a result of "the paucity of information and research at the appraisal stage" – a situation, the Panel added, which Bank management "appears to have been aware of."[36] Indeed, the Panel concluded, by "simply accepting the fact that objective data and scientific studies were very limited," Bank man-

---

31   *Panama: Land Administration* (2009), IR, § 353. *Note, Panama: Land Administration* consisted of four components: "(a) land policy, legal and institutional framework; (b) land regularization services; (c) consolidation of protected areas and indigenous territories; and (d) project administration, monitoring and evaluation." *See Panama: Land Administration* (2009), ER, § 6.

32   *Panama: Land Administration* (2009), IR, § 353. On compliance issues related to the identification of problems and corrective actions taken as part of the Bank's supervision activities, *also see* sections 15.1 & 15.2.

33   *Id. Note,* the example also demonstrates the Inspection Panel's practice of referencing previous findings (*see* section 1.2.1.) as well as the Panel's contribution towards institutional learning by identifying recurring systemic or structural issues that come to the fore in the course of its investigations (*see* section 7.1.5.).

34   *See India: Ecodevelopment* (1998), MR, § 4 and ER, § i.

35   *India: Ecodevelopment* (1998), ER, § i.

36   *India: Ecodevelopment* (1998), ER, § 36.

agement "appears to have allowed much of the debate about the potential conflict between the two main thrusts of the project to be conducted on the basis of predetermined views and unsubstantiated claims."[37]

In *Cambodia: Land Administration Project* the Inspection Panel underlined the fact that "the Bank has an important development role in financing high risk operations," however, the Panel's investigation demonstrated "the danger of responding to risks by creating an excessively complicated project".[38] Specifically, the Panel commented, "new components were added during the preparation process"

> at the expense of clarity in how the different parts were supposed to be func-
> tionally interconnected, and without due consideration of the feasibility of the
> total approach.[39]

"[I]n hindsight," the Panel concluded, "it [was] evident" "that there was not full ownership among the stakeholders" of such a "multi-pronged approach."[40]

Although the project's design "acknowledges these challenges by way of an integrated approach that involves systematic land titling, conflict resolution and State land classification and management", the Panel found that it "does not adequately reflect the appreciation of the risks involved."[41] One such example concerned the "risks associated with overlapping claims to land by public agencies and individuals" – which also formed a core concern of the Requesters.[42] While "this problem was clearly noted in the PAD," the Panel pointed out, it "does not clearly identify the process by which to handle these risks."[43] "To the contrary," the Panel concluded, "the Project design is not clear what will be the Project's strategy"

> both with respect to determining areas for systematic land titling (i.e. adjudica-
> tion areas) and dealing with disputes between State entities and private individ-
> uals during the adjudication process.[44]

---

37 *Id.*
38 *Cambodia: Land Management and Administration* (2009), IR, p. xxx. On the place of 'risk' in the competing conceptions of what the Bank should be accountable 'for' ('performance' *versus* 'harm'), *see* section 4.2.2.
39 *Cambodia: Land Management and Administration* (2009), IR, p. xxx.
40 *Cambodia: Land Management and Administration* (2009), IR, § 290.
41 *Cambodia: Land Management and Administration* (2009), IR, § 169.
42 *Id.* On this matter, *also see* the discussion in section 8.2.2.
43 *Cambodia: Land Management and Administration* (2009), IR, § 169. *Note*, this example demonstrates the Panel's emphasis on the procedural and substantive elements of compliance (*see* section 6.3.4) – but it also demonstrates how closely interlinked these elements can be within a particular operational policy provision.
44 *Cambodia: Land Management and Administration* (2009), IR, § 169.

The Panel made similar observations in its *Papua New Guinea: Smallholder Agriculture* investigation. The Panel cited a key recommendation of the World Bank's Quality Assurance Group's 2008 Quality Enhancement Review of projects in the Pacific region, with respect to the improvement of lending quality – which was to "Keep it simple!"[45] The review emphasized that "[t]here is a clear correlation between project complexity and implementation problems"; whereas "the simple, focused projects,"

> regardless of size have tended to achieve satisfactory outcomes and there is evidence that these can have a strategic impact if designed in the context of good advisory work.[46]

On the other hand, the Panel added, "'[k]eeping it simple and focused'," "should not mean that risks should not be taken."[47] "Indeed," in this instance, the Panel "applauded Management for trying to set up a permanent and sustainable mechanism for road maintenance, which is critical for sustaining oil palm cultivation."[48] That being said, "a key issue for risk management under the Project" was also to ensure "that the burden of risk does not fall on the poor," which was "a major concern raised in the Request."[49] In this regard, however, the Inspection Panel concluded that "the financial burden and risk" associated with establishment of the Road Maintenance Trust Fund were indeed placed "disproportionately on the smallholders"

> as there is no guarantee in funding from the other two sources of financing – the provincial governments and the mill companies – even though the companies have a clear vested interest in road maintenance.[50]

In its investigation of *Cambodia: Forest Concession Management*, the Inspection Panel acknowledged that the project "operated within a difficult and dynamic political and social environment in Cambodia," in which "[t]he reform process in the forest sector"

---

45 *Papua New Guinea: Smallholder Agriculture* (2009), IR, § 536; *also see* MR, p. 34. *Note*, this example also demonstrates the complementary nature of the Inspection Panel's mandate vis-à-vis other internal accountability mechanisms – *see* section 6.2.

46 *Papua New Guinea: Smallholder Agriculture* (2009), IR, § 536. For a discussion of the relationship between design complexity and issues regarding the delineation of Bank and Borrower obligations, *also see* Ch. 8.

47 *Papua New Guinea: Smallholder Agriculture* (2009), IR, § 537.

48 *Id.*

49 *Id.*

50 *Papua New Guinea: Smallholder Agriculture* (2009), IR, § 537. On the need for balance between "the need for risk-taking in development work" and the proportionate distribution of such risk, *see* note 240, Ch. 6.

requires change to take place in many aspects of the way in which forests are perceived and managed to ensure that national policy objectives (not least being poverty alleviation) are achieved.[51]

Nevertheless, the Panel observed that its investigation revealed "a consistent picture" – namely, "that Project management was perceived"

> as having a narrow focus on concession management (and particularly the technical aspects), as not seeing the big picture, and as being confrontational and divisive with civil society.[52]

This situation, in turn, "led to the unraveling of relationships, with the Bank perceived as being an apologist for the concession system", and "as a result", the Panel explained, the project – and the Bank – "became a target for wide spread dissatisfaction."[53]

By placing a greater emphasis on concession management, the Panel elaborated, "other aspects that were important to the Bank program in Cambodia and [for] the Government"

> were largely ignored or at least marginalized throughout the planning phase of the Project. In particular, the Project did not seem to take on the key objective of using the potential of forests to reduce poverty.[54]

The Inspection Panel was also critical of the "decision not to prioritize assessment of social issues," which the Panel considered to be "a further reflection of the lack of attention given under the Project to social and poverty reduction issues."[55] As a result, "insufficient focus on social and poverty reduction issues," the Panel emphasized,

> (i) biased the collection of information needed to design the Project towards technical and financial aspects, and (ii) ignored the important role of forests in Cambodia as livelihood and cultural assets for local and indigenous communities.[56]

Moreover, the Panel argued, the Bank's "nearly exclusive focus on reforming forestry concessions," combined with the "view that this could be done effectively on a technical

---

51 *Cambodia: Forest Concession Management* (2005), IR, §§ 389, 391.
52 *Id.*
53 *Id.*
54 *Cambodia: Forest Concession Management* (2005), IR (ES), p. xvi.
55 *Cambodia: Forest Concession Management* (2005), IR, §§ 119, 123.
56 *Cambodia: Forest Concession Management* (2005), IR, § 128.

basis," had the effect of "a reduced emphasis on compliance with safeguard policies."[57] Hence, the Panel concluded that there was "merit in the contention" raised in the Request "that the Project's association with concession management to some degree served to legitimize the concessions"[58] – although, the Panel emphasized, this did not "contradict" its "finding that working on sustainable forestry in some way, was well justified," nor was it negating the Panel's acknowledgement of the Bank's "risk-taking" required to do so.[59] In fact, the Inspection Panel specifically commended the World Bank for its "willingness to become involved in the forestry sector at a time when others would not," and it also "recognize[d] the dedication of Staff and the risks that they took."[60]

Instead, the Panel argued, what its findings indicated – and "reemphasize[d]" – was "the need for a meticulous application of the appropriate safeguard policies."[61] In other words, while "what may be referred to as 'technical-level' work is important," the Panel concluded, it is "often not sufficient to cause fundamental change, "

> particularly in a forest-rich, post-conflict country such as Cambodia. Issues involving timber, illegal logging, the rights and welfare of rural communities and indigenous peoples, and biodiversity conservation go well beyond technical considerations. In line with relevant policies, they require well-informed, high-level and wide-spread political and strategic consultations and negotiations. The skill sets and seniority level for technical forestry and strategic political dialogue are quite different. Operating on one level without the other will often prove futile and lead to problems as in the present case.[62]

And the World Bank, the Inspection Panel emphasized, "is one of few institutions that can operate in an effective way on these two levels."[63]

The Panel, finally, acknowledged that its investigation might contribute to the "danger" that the Bank, "in the future", steers clear of financing "projects dealing with natural forests"

---

57 *Cambodia: Forest Concession Management* (2005), IR, § 409. For a discussion of the Bank's decisions to limit the application of safeguard policies in DPL contexts, *see* section 10.1.
58 *Cambodia: Forest Concession Management* (2005), IR, § 127.
59 *Id.*
60 *Cambodia: Forest Concession Management* (2005), IR, § 409.
61 *Cambodia: Forest Concession Management* (2005), IR, § 127.
62 *Cambodia: Forest Concession Management* (2005), IR, § 129.
63 *Id. Note*, The Inspection Panel also referred to the findings of an Asian Development Bank-funded study of the forestry sector, which "warned of the consequences of focusing on industrial logging to the exclusion of other aspects" and emphasized that the forestry sector's "primary focus" had "for too long" been "the sustained supply of wood products for forest processing facilities" – to the detriment of "the needs of forest dependent communities" as well as "the broad hydrological and soil conservation functions of forests, their conservation value and their broader significance in cultural and other term." *See Cambodia: Forest Concession Management* (2005), IR, §§ 119, 123.

"simply to avoid controversy and criticism."[64] The Panel accentuated, however, that "compliance with safeguard policies" in such project contexts is particularly "essential" – "even though transaction costs may be higher."[65] "It is precisely because of the strong economic incentives for unsustainable timber exploitation," the Panel argued,

> that the Bank has an important role to play and a comparative advantage in its effort to support sustainable forestry. And in this regard donor partnership and cooperation is equally important.[66]

9.2 PROJECT FINANCING STRUCTURE, EXPENDITURE, IMPLEMENTATION PROGRESS AND FOCUS OF SUPERVISION ACTIVITIES

In its 1996 investigation of *Argentina/Paraguay: Yacyretá*, the Inspection Panel pointed to "one of the basic problems" it had identified – which "was the imbalance that developed, and persists until today,"

> between the completion of the civil and electro-mechanical works vis-à-vis the "complementary works" which include environment and resettlement plans. While the former are 99.8% complete, less than a third of environmental and resettlement plans have been completed.[67]

The Inspection Panel reiterated this finding and elaborated on the consequences of the 'imbalance' during its 2002 investigation of the *Yacyretá* project. The "imbalance" between "electro-mechanical" and "complementary" R&R activities, the Panel explained, "led to increasing social and environmental 'liabilities' with mounting financial costs," which were further "exacerbated by the Bank's usual practice of financing mostly civil works and leaving resettlement and environmental measures for counterpart funding."[68]

"[A]s the Yacyretá Project proceeded, the resettlement issues became progressively more important and difficult to address"; yet, the Panel noted, "Management's supervision of the Yacyretá Project's resettlement and rehabilitation activities"

---

64 *Cambodia: Forest Concession Management* (2005), IR, § 108. For criticisms concerning this effect of the Inspection Panel process, *see e.g.*, sections 4.2.2 & 7.2.2.
65 *Id.*
66 *Id.*
67 *Argentina/Paraguay: Yacyretá Hydroelectric Project* (1996), Inspection Panel Review & Assessment, § 253.
68 *Paraguay/Argentina: Yacyretá Hydroelectric Project* (2002), IR, § 78.

did not adapt effectively to this change by using more technical and social expertise to address problems of technical and social nature, as required to carry out by OD 13.05, paragraph 1 (b).[69]

Instead, the Bank's "supervision missions appear to have been locked into formats established early in the project's life and to have not adapted to changing project needs."[70] For example, "project supervision initially focused on plants, animals and biodiversity issues," and subsequent supervision activity "appears to have continued to concentrate on them even though the project's central problems changed from biophysical concerns to problems of a social nature."[71]

These failures, the Panel concluded, had multiple consequences. For example, project-affected people were "dissatisfied with the Bank's resettlement schemes," whereas the "resettlement schemes" contributed to "problems of storm-water run-off, overloading of sewerage lines, and the limited resources of the local municipal authorities being taxed."[72]

In other words, it resulted in "a situation, which neither Bank staff, project proponents, or affected persons desire or with which they are satisfied" – "[i]nstead of a Bank-supported project reflecting positively on the Bank and its borrowers," the Inspection Panel emphasized, "the opposite has occurred."[73] Indeed, the Inspection Panel commented, "[t]his Project demonstrates that taking short-cuts with the Bank's safeguard policies is counter-productive for all concerned."[74]

As discussed earlier, in *Nigeria/Ghana: West African Gas Pipeline* the Inspection Panel identified certain capacity constraints of the project implementing agency, related to the implementation the project's social components.[75] One significant implication of these capacity issues, as the Inspection Panel pointed out, was that the Resettlement Action Plan's "livelihood restoration objectives [were] yet to be completed despite the physical completion of the infrastructure."[76] "Without the measures to mitigate project related impoverishment risks," the Panel underscored, whether these measures be "adequate baseline data, compensation, land-for-land, in-kind, permanent employment etc. the involuntary resettlement component of the Project is not finished."[77]

---

69   *Paraguay/Argentina: Yacyretá Hydroelectric Project* (2002), IR, §§ 405, 408.
70   *Id.* For compliance issues related to supervision missions, *also see* section 15.1.
71   *Id. Note,* this example also demonstrates issues related to the content of supervision missions, as discussed *in* section 15.3.3.
72   *Paraguay/Argentina: Yacyretá Hydroelectric Project* (2002), IR, § 160.
73   *Id.*
74   *Id.*
75   *See* section 8.3.2.
76   *Nigeria/Ghana: West African Gas Pipeline* (2006), IR, § 210.
77   *Id.*

The Panel added that it "recognize[d] the importance of public-private partnerships," as well as "the benefits and challenges involved."[78] The Panel also "note[d] the Bank's efforts to broaden its portfolio through support of public-private partnerships of the kind funded under this Project."[79] However, the Panel commented, its investigation illustrated that "private partners are often chosen"

> for their strong technical competence in a particular field, but may not be well equipped to address the range of Bank Policy requirements absent effective guidance, engagement and project supervision.[80]

The Inspection Panel's investigation *Chad: Petroleum* (which, as noted in the previous chapter, consisted of two related projects that were respectively dedicated to infrastructure construction and institutional capacity building) revealed that the capacity-building project did not enjoy the same degree of focus as was placed on the infrastructure construction project.[81] This was reflected, for example, in the fact that "some of the key implementing agencies for the [institutional capacity-building] Project [were] not yet properly in place" or functioning effectively.[82] The CTNSC, for example, had no "operating budget, central office or regional personnel" and neither did the 'Collège du Pétrole'; whereas FACIL was "not yet in place although it has been discussed since 1998."[83]

In other words, the Inspection Panel observed, "the development of the oil production capacity [was] moving faster than the development of the social capacity needed to manage it."[84] "This 'two speed' pace of advance," the Panel noted, "with the infrastructure component well in advance of the social component," "illustrates the relevance of attaching as much importance to Project implementation as to assessment, and formulation."[85] "Unfortunately", the Panel concluded, "this situation raises serious questions about the ability of the Project to realize several of its more crucial social objectives."[86]

"A related concern that arose" during the Panel's investigation of *Panama: Land Administration* concerned the fact "that the co-financing arrangements for the Project"

---

78 *Nigeria/Ghana: West African Gas Pipeline* (2006), IR, § 484.
79 *Id.*
80 *Id.*
81 See section 8.3.3.
82 *Chad: Petroleum* (2001), IR, § 42.
83 *Id.* For more information on the role of the CTNSC, *see* IR, § 76.
84 *Chad: Petroleum* (2001), IR, § 42.
85 *Id.*
86 *Id.*

provided additional financing for those components of the Project that related to titling, but not to the component that related to protection of indigenous territories.[87]

"While these co-financing arrangements undoubtedly played an important role in increasing the overall impact of the Project, particularly in relation to its important land titling objectives," the Panel commented, it "may have heightened the possibility that titling activities could take place within indigenous land areas intended for protection under Component 3 of the Project."[88]

The Panel added that its "[i]nterviews with staff responsible for the Project in its early days" also indicated "that considerable time and effort"

> was involved in securing Project co-financing, which may have contributed to delays in implementation of crucial aspects of Project Component 3.[89]

Whereas in its *DRC: Transitional Support for Economic Recovery* investigation, the Inspection Panel underscored "the importance of implementing regulations and measures that firmly establish the institutional reforms, and put them into practice for the benefits of forest peoples and in line with Bank policies."[90] "Key elements" in this regard, "include"

> free, prior and informed consultation and participation at different levels and in various aspects of current institutional reforms, respect for customary rights to the forest, equitable benefits, and in particular empowerment of their representation system.[91]

However, the Panel found that "that there has been little progress on these types of measures as compared with progress in reforms relating to logging concessions" – which seemed to indicate that the Requesters had good reason "to fear negative impacts of the current reforms."[92] There was indeed "a possibility," the Panel concluded, "that the Project [...] may not contribute much to alleviating poverty of the forest people", but "instead contribute to adverse impacts on poverty to the extent that unsustainable logging-related practices

---

87 *Panama: Land Administration* (2009), IR, § 354. *Note*, Component 3 concerned the "Consolidation of Protected Areas and Indigenous Territories" – *see* MR, § 29. *Also see* the discussion *in* section 8.2.1.
88 *Panama: Land Administration* (2009), IR, § 354.
89 *Id.*
90 *Democratic Republic of Congo: Transitional Support* (2005), IR, § 320.
91 *Id.*
92 *Id.*

are encouraged."[93] The Inspection Panel particularly expressed its concern "about the delay"

> in developing implementing regulations concerning customary forest rights, including for "community forests," and in supporting small-scale forest-based enterprise.[94]

The Panel also observed "that when the Bank initially became engaged in the DRC and decided to support work in the forest sector, it provided estimates of export revenue from logging concession that turned out to be much too high."[95] This over-estimation of commercial potential "had a significant effect," the Panel noted, "for it encouraged a focus on reform of the forest concession system"

> at the expense of pursuing sustainable use of forests, the potential for community forests, and conservation. For the most part, foreign companies or local companies controlled by foreigners have been the beneficiaries of this focus. Those whose concessions are confirmed in the concession review process will be the beneficiaries of the new 25 year leases.[96]

Furthermore, another "central focus of the Bank's early efforts in the forestry sector,"

> was to increase tax and revenue streams through increased industrial logging in the country, supported by the controlled granting of forest concessions.[97]

This focus, which the Panel also found to be reflected in the *DRC: Transitional Support* project, resulted in an emphasis "on developing a Project that would facilitate increased levels of industrial forest exploitation."[98]

These approaches, the Panel concluded, resulted in a project scenario in which "there was inadequate consideration of the many important socio-economic and environmental issues of forest use" – as "embedded within Bank safeguard policies" – which "distorted the actual economic value of the country's forests."[99] "This, in turn," the Panel commented,

---

93 *Democratic Republic of Congo: Transitional Support* (2005), IR, § 312.
94 *Id.*
95 *Democratic Republic of Congo: Transitional Support* (2005), IR, p. xxxiv.
96 *Id.*
97 *Democratic Republic of Congo: Transitional Support* (2005), IR, §§ 165-166.
98 *Id.*
99 *Id.*

distorted the design and the implementation of the Bank's important engagement in this vital sector, and appeared to contribute to major issues and problems of Bank compliance with its social and environmental policies at the stage of Project design and appraisal.[100]

9.3   Diverse interests within project areas, transparency about project prioritization and trade-off decisions

It is a significant challenge, as Bank management commented in *Brazil: Paraná Biodiversity*, to "promot[e] conservation in intensively developed areas" where there are "strong potential for agriculture and other highly profitable economic activities."[101] Indeed, as Management added, "[d]ifferences among stakeholders" with regard to "conservation policy approaches, priorities, and trade-offs and uneven speed of project implementation are unavoidable constraints."[102]

Such constraints, moreover, complicate the achievement of equilibrium among various development aims. In this case, "as in any society," the Inspection Panel acknowledged, "the potential for economic gains, and the natural feeling of rural landowners that they should make decisions on their own land would lead to difficulties in enforcing such [conservation] regulations" as those involving the project.[103] For example, the Panel explained, "[i]n Paraná, the "Araucária, and other protected hardwood trees, may be removed if they are dead;" but

> across extensive rural areas it is very difficult to tell if single trees were dead, although large movements of logs would certainly be questionable. Also the delineation in the field of the boundaries of the forest covered areas is a massive undertaking which has not been done, so that 'chipping away' at forest areas would be very difficult to detect.[104]

"The Requesters", moreover, "have emphasized"

---

100 *Id.*
101 *Brazil: Paraná Biodiversity* (2006), MR, § 75. For an overview of *Brazil: Paraná, see* Naudé Fourie (2014), pp. 323-329.
102 *Id.*
103 *Brazil: Paraná Biodiversity* (2006), Final ER, § 41.
104 *Id.*

that many actions supported by the Project, such as farmer training sessions or tree planting on bare land, are positive, but should not have utilized scarce funds that could have been used for valuable natural area protection.[105]

On the other hand, the Panel pointed out, "an overwhelming majority of biodiversity experts would agree that the latter should be the highest program priority."[106] The Panel commented, therefore, "that there may be debate, and even trial and error,

in many forest eco-system biodiversity conservation programs regarding the extent to which, and how, a program should work with local communities living within or near eco-systems with important biodiversity. The situation varies according to local circumstances. Often natural eco-systems provide very important benefits for local communities, especially indigenous people, and should be protected from "outsiders" seeking quick profit opportunities. Contrarily, there are also many cases where very poor people need to utilize eco-systems for immediate needs in a way that lowers the level of biodiversity. An important point is that poor local communities are often closely involved with high biodiversity value ecosystems. Projects, if they are to be effective, need to consider the needs of those communities while working toward conserving biodiversity.[107]

In other words, the Panel concluded, "almost every project explores strategies to find win-win situations"

where local communities benefit through poverty reduction, while biodiversity is protected. These strategies may take myriad forms according to local situations.[108]

Indeed, the achievement of equilibrium among disparate development aims would often require the employment of differentiated approaches, but this, in turn, could also lead to complications – especially when there is insufficient transparency or inadequate consultation surrounding prioritization and trade-off decisions.[109] While differentiation might be the desirable approach in specific circumstances, it can also add significant complexity

---

105 *Brazil: Paraná Biodiversity* (2006), Final ER, § 47.
106 *Id.*
107 *Id.*
108 *Id.*
109 On opposing approaches towards policy application and compliance review with respect to the employment of differentiated approaches, *also see* section 6.3.1.

– and cost – that could have a negative impact on effective and efficient project implementation.

In *India: NTPC Power*, for example, the Inspection Panel observed that, "[w]hile in the field," it had "observed the very real practical complications" – "both in terms of understanding and acceptance by PAPs and management of the process" – "of implementing Bank R&R policies introduced during a later phase of an ongoing project."[110] "The substance of R&R issues raised by various local NGOs, activists, or community leaders", the Panel commented, "appeared to reflect the difference between treatment of PAPs from Vindhyachal Stages I and II, differences in pre displacement standards of living, occupations, etc. [...]."[111]

But what these issues reflected in particular, the Panel added, was "differences in expectations based on alleged promises" – and this situation, the Panel concluded, was caused by "the fact that the 1993 RAPs contained elements, or held promises to PAPs, that Management admits were unrealistic."[112]

Whereas in *Papua New Guinea: Smallholder Agriculture*, the Inspection Panel highlighted "the significant differences in terms of the recent history of the oil palm sector within the project area" as an issue "which calls for adjustments during implementation".[113] These differences, the Panel explained,

> is reflected in different levels of smallholder productivity, which has led to the decision by the same mill company to support infilling in one province, but to give it less priority in the other and instead place greater emphasis on replanting.[114]

However, the Project Implementation Manual "does not respond to such differences in the field realities of the two provinces."[115] Therefore, the Panel concluded,

> it becomes even more incumbent during the implementation stage for the Project to apply a differentiated rather than a cookie-cutter approach in making progress toward achieving the Project objective.[116]

---

110 *India: NTPC Power* (1997), ER, §§ 38-39. *Note*, the Panel tends to be critical of decisions to postpone project activities intended for the design stage (as required by the operational policies) to the implementation stage of the project cycle – in this regard, *see e.g.*, the Panel's comments on the postponement of consultation *at* section 11.2.
111 *India: NTPC Power* (1997), ER, §§ 38-39.
112 *Id.*
113 *Papua New Guinea: Smallholder Agriculture* (2009), IR, § 539.
114 *Id.*
115 *Id.*
116 *Id.*

The Inspection Panel concluded in *Colombia: Cartagena Water & Environmental Management* that "the underlying economic evaluation may have been carried out competently and broadly in line with OP 10.04," nevertheless, "parts of the material in Annex 4" were "not presented and explained in the PAD with sufficient clarity, transparency and consistency to demonstrate this compliance."[117] "This matters," the Panel explained

> because partial or confusing explanations in the PAD risk failing successfully to communicate and confirm to stakeholders the nature and robustness of the appraisal processes that the Bank's operational procedures like OP 10.04 promote and require. This could be important for a Project that is acknowledged to have controversial aspects.[118]

Finally, the Inspection Panel's investigation of *India: Mumbai Urban Transport* highlights several of the issues discussed in this chapter, and also illustrates the intricate relationships between these issues.

The *India: Mumbai Urban Transport* project had initially been set up as two related projects – a rail and road infrastructure project and a project aimed at managing the resettlement and rehabilitation (R&R) activities – however, a decision was taken to merge these two projects before project appraisal.[119] The Inspection Panel identified the decision to merge the two project to be at the root of several serious non-compliance issues that surfaced over the course of its investigation – essentially, because the merger led to an imbalanced focus on the rail and road infrastructure component, to the detriment of the R&R component.

For example, the Panel noted that while "the R&R component was critical for the success of the Project," it "was not ready for implementation when the Project was launched."[120] The decision "to merge the Twin Projects set them on a radically uneven path" since the separate projects "were very unequal in their preparation and readiness for Bank appraisal at the time of the merger, and remained so subsequently," but the merger "obscured this unevenness."[121] In the aftermath of the merger, however, it became "apparent [...] that on several key matters

> the Borrower had advanced the preparation of the [road and rail infrastructure] Engineering Project much faster than that for the Resettlement Project. Many of the policy requirements for preparation had not been met. For example, no

---

117 *Colombia: Cartagena Water & Environmental Management* (2004), IR, p. xxiv.
118 *Id.*
119 *India: Mumbai Urban Transport* (2004), ER, §§ 6-7.
120 *India: Mumbai Urban Transport* (2004), IR (ES), p. xix & § 185.
121 *Id.*

reliable population count or baseline income assessment for the to-be-displaced inhabitants had been done, and the shopkeeper issues identified earlier by the Bank had not advanced towards a solution tailored to their situation.[122]

In addition, as will be discussed later on,[123] "the estimate of the number of people to be resettled was reduced dramatically, as was the cost estimate for resettlement."[124] When this estimate was later increased again, it was surrounding with significant ambiguity and, as the Inspection Panel uncovered during its investigation, errors in the underlying methodology.[125]

Furthermore, the Panel pointed out that issues related to the compensation of a group of middle-income shopkeepers (which ultimately resulted in their filing of a "Request for Inspection") were "initially present in the separate Project", but appeared "to have been dropped from consideration after the merger."[126] The merger also "diverted attention away from the institutional capacity required for effective resettlement, which had been correctly identified and initially provided for when the projects were separate."[127]

The original "resettlement Project was intended to ensure that the people to be resettled would have a comparable standard of living after resettlement;" however, the Panel commented, in terms of the merged "MUTP the resettlement component evolved into one focused primarily on the restoration of housing."[128] This meant, for instance, that the "social aspects" of the project – "particularly of R&R" – were "conspicuous by their near-absence in the Consolidated EA."[129] In their interviews with the Inspection Panel, "Bank staff noted that they had the impression that MUTP is driven by need for infrastructure and not by social concerns" and also that the "social aspects were dealt with almost separately from the environmental aspects."[130] Hence, the Panel concluded, "consideration of natural and social aspects of the environment in an integrated way has not occurred, which [was] not consistent with the intent and spirit of OP 4.01."[131]

This imbalance was also reflected in the project's finances. Where the "cost of the engineering components ha[d] continuously increased during preparation to over US $800 million," the Panel observed, "the cost of the resettlement operation stayed the same at

---

122 *India: Mumbai Urban Transport* (2004), IR, § 151.
123 On issues related to the delineation of 'project area' and 'project area of interest' *see* section 10.2.
124 *India: Mumbai Urban Transport* (2004), IR (ES), p. xix & § 185.
125 *See* sections 10.3 & 12.2.
126 *India: Mumbai Urban Transport* (2004), IR (ES), p. xix & § 185.
127 *Id.* For a discussion of the issues related to the project implement agency and 'implementing NGO' capacity constraints, *see* section 8.3.2.
128 *India: Mumbai Urban Transport* (2004), IR (ES), p. xix & § 185.
129 *India: Mumbai Urban Transport* (2004), IR, §§ 639-640.
130 *Id.*
131 *Id.*

US $100 million, despite the substantial increase in the number of people affected."[132] "Only after the Requests" for Inspection were filed, the Panel pointed out, "were the figures updated for the R&R component" – and even so, the Panel noted, this update

> appears to be mostly an accounting change in the way items long included in costs, but not monetized previously, are now reflected, and does not appear to represent an increase in financing for resettlement.[133]

In addition, the Panel noted that "the IDA resources allocated for resettlement have not been fully spent."[134] The Inspection Panel expressed its concern that this situation "may lead to the shifting of funds away from other resettlement needs, which would compound issues of compliance with the relevant policies," and therefore "urge[d]" Bank management to provide "further clarification on this point."[135]

"While the Panel is not the appropriate body to undertake a financial audit of the R&R budget and expenditures," it concluded, "the apparent incongruence"

> between the changes in the magnitude of the Project component and the non-commensurate changes in the budget allocations may warrant a specialized re-examination by the Bank of these aspects.[136]

****

The World Bank's approach to providing development assistance to its borrowers is influenced by several factors, which have, in turn, resulted in a situation in which the World Bank has to operationalize a wide range of institutional aims that might function in terms of complimentary or contradictory relationships.[137]

This chapter focused on the manner in which these tensions manifest in Inspection Panel practice – namely, as issues concerning the imbalance between project elements described as technical or commercial *versus* those that are considered to be non-technical or non-commercial.

This imbalance or disequilibrium, as the examples from Inspection Panel practice included in this chapter demonstrated, can be reflected in the manner in which the project modality is described (or, more implicitly, perceived to be), the focus of project design and

---

132 *India: Mumbai Urban Transport* (2004), IR, §§ 307-308.
133 *Id.*
134 *India: Mumbai Urban Transport* (2004), IR, § 692.
135 *Id.*
136 *Id.*
137 *See* section 4.2.2.

organization, project financing and expenditure, progress during the implementation phase, and management attention as reflected in supervision activities.

Moreover, several of the examples pointed to the existence of diverse interests – also among the interests of project-affected people. Such scenarios often require differentiated approaches, as well as involve difficult prioritization and trade-off decisions. However, Inspection Panel practice also suggests that there is an opportunity for enhancing the transparency surrounding these decisions – which, in turn, could strengthen the Bank's legitimacy among its external constituency groups, and could also contribute to improved institutional performance.

As for the reasons behind the imbalance between technical and/or commercial versus non-technical and/or non-commercial project elements, one explanation relates to the Bank's institutional culture, which, as noted earlier, is marked by a pronounced technical focus.[138] While the strong technical capabilities of World Bank staff are part of the Bank's competitive edge, it can also skew the balance in favour of technical/commercial components. For example, Cernea points to "three conceptual biases in the Bank's approach to development", which have arguably been grounded in the Bank's "technocratic culture", namely:

> the *econocentric model* that regards economic and financial variables as the only ones that matter; the *technocentric model* that addresses the technological variables of development apart from their contextual social fabric; and the *commodocentric model* that emphasizes the "thing" more than the social actors that produce it, highlighting, for example, the Bank's tendency to focus on coffee production but not coffee growers, or water provision but not water users [...].[139]

That being said, "[e]nvironmental considerations have come to occupy a central place in the Bank's activities in part," as Miller-Adams argues, "because they can be addressed technically."[140] "Once the Bank had signed on to the environmental agenda," moreover,

> it was able to extend its traditional analytic approaches to this new area. The Bank has pushed accounting reform so that natural resources can be treated as economic assets. It has extended its work on the negative externalities of subsidies to the environmental field, showing, for example, how government-subsidized pesticides entail hidden costs. It has developed complex and inno-

---

138 For a discussion of core aspects of institutional culture, *see* section 3.1.1.
139 Miller-Adams (1999), p. 6, quoting Cernea (1996), pp. 15-16 (emphases added).
140 Miller-Adams (1999), p. 140.

vative financial instruments, such as debt-for-nature swaps, that contribute to environmental preservation. In all these endeavors, the Bank's emphasis on development as a technical and apolitical process has been preserved."[141]

Integrating social issues in its development-lending operations, however, has proved to be more challenging. Influenced by "the growing number of calls for [the World Bank] to recognize the centrality of social issues in its work,"

the number of social, as opposed to economic, issues on the Bank's agenda has proliferated. The range of social concerns addressed by the Bank includes poverty reduction, gender, indigenous people, resettlement, participation, and governance.[142]

However, Miller-Adams adds, this proliferation presents a challenge to "the Bank's identity," which is strongly grounded in a "technical orientation".[143] In practice, it has meant that social issues are often "treated as "add-ons" to Bank projects"

that are concerned chiefly with economic impact and financial rate of return. (One NGO advocate calls this the "Christmas tree model," where Bank loans are given "an ornamental poverty component, a gender bauble, and a partici-pation star on top.")[144]

While "advocates within and outside the Bank have attempted to raise the profile of social issues" in order to address the "lack of connection between social issues and the Bank's core mission of poverty reduction and sustainable development," the examples from Inspection Panel practice included in this chapter suggest that there remains significant room for improvement in this regard.[145]

Improving the integration of social and environmental issues into project design and implementation, however, also requires a recognition of the significant role played by diverse interests, demands, expectations and underlying conceptions (notably, the compet-ing paradigms of accountability for performance *versus* accountability for harm)[146] – which, in turn, remains a function of a transnational development context marked by pluralism and dynamic complexity.[147]

---

141 *Id.*
142 Miller-Adams (1999), p. 148.
143 Miller-Adams (1999), pp. 148-149.
144 *Id.*
145 *Id.*
146 *See* section 4.2.2.
147 *See* section 2.1.

While the Inspection Panel and World Bank management often find themselves on opposing ends of arguments concerning perceived project imbalances, Inspection Panel practice points to the multiple challenges involved in achieving equilibrium among the Bank's diverse institutional aims. But it also provides examples of how some of these underlying tensions can be reconciled – as, for instance, when the Panel points to the negative effects that the materialization of social, economic and/or environmental risks (*harm*) has on the realization of development objectives (*performance*).

10 Decisions Determining Project Content and Scope – Affecting the Content and Scope of World Bank Accountability

There are several decisions, made over the course of the project cycle, that determine the content and scope of a World Bank-financed development project. Chapter 10 considers four broad categories of such decisions, namely: *choice of lending instrument* and *description of project modality*; the *delineation of 'project area'* and *'project area of influence'*; the *identification* and *quantification of project-affected people*; and, the *interpretation of 'key phrases' in operational policy provisions and project documentation*.

Decisions related to these areas influence the content and scope of World Bank accountability because they determine, for instance, which of the Bank's operational policies would be applicable to a specific project, and can also influence the approach followed in applying operational policies to the particular project context.[1]

10.1 Description of project 'modality' and choice of lending vehicle

Decisions about project modality (thus, determining what type of project it is) can affect the choice of lending vehicle (thus, with what type of lending instrument to finance the project), which, in turn, can influence decisions about the applicability of certain operational policies – notably, of the safeguard policies.[2]

Generally speaking, the World Bank has limited the application of its safeguard policies in projects financed by development policy lending ('DPL') instruments (formerly known as 'structural adjustment lending' instruments).[3] For example, Di Leva notes that, especially "since 2004", the safeguard policies "have not been applied to loans that are provided for development policy support."[4]

The Bank's policy on Development Policy Lending (OP/BP 8.60) explains, on its part that "[a] development policy operation draws on relevant analytic work on the country"

---

1   On different approaches to operational policy application and compliance review, *see* section 6.3.
2   On the Bank's primary lending instruments, *see* section 4.1.1; on the safeguard policies, *see* section 5.1; on the effect of project modality on the achievement of equilibrium among multiple institutional aims, *also see* section 9.1.
3   *Also note*, the Panel has constituently argued that its mandate extends to all Bank-financed projects, irrespective of project modality and the underlying lending vehicle – as discussed *in* section 6.2.4.
4   Di Leva *in* Bradlow & Hunter (Eds.) (2010), pp. 350-351.

– whether "undertaken by the Bank, the country, and third parties."[5] "Drawing on a consultative process," OP 8.60 elaborates,

> the CAS assesses the adequacy of analytic work on the country and indicates
> how gaps will be addressed. The Program Document describes the main pieces
> of analytic work used in the preparation of the operation and shows how they
> are linked to the proposed development policy program. *As appropriate, prior*
> *analytic work includes analyses of the country's economywide or sectoral policies*
> *and institutions aimed at stimulating investment, creating employment, acceler-*
> *ating and sustaining growth, as well as analyses of the poverty and social impacts*
> *of proposed policies, environment and natural resource management, governance*
> *and public expenditure management, procurement, and financial accountability*
> *systems.*[6]

The policy on Development Policy Lending also has various provisions that relate to critical areas covered by the safeguard policies,[7] although they typically refer staff to 'Good Practice Notes',[8] which fall outside the Inspection Panel's mandate since they do not contain mandatory provisions.[9]

The Inspection Panel typically questions the Bank's decision not to apply particular safeguard policies in the context of development policy lending projects. In a recent publication, for example, the Panel commented about the Bank's limited application of its safeguard policies in the context of land administration and management projects. The Panel noted that its investigations of such projects have "revealed a policy lacunae" – namely, it is "not clear within the Bank's safeguards framework" how "to address consequences for people's livelihoods from changes in rights to land and land based resources," especially since Bank management "has issued a Guidance Note on Land Use Planning noting that the Involuntary Resettlement Policy does not apply to such projects."[10] This

---

5   OP 8.60, § 9.
6   *Id.* (emphasis added).
7   *See e.g.*, OP 8.60, § 6 (on "Consultations and Participation"); § 10 (on "Poverty and Social Impacts"); *and* § 11 (on "Environmental, Forests, and other Natural Resource Aspects"); *and see* OP 8.60, fn. 40, which "sets out a requirement for environmental and social review of potential impacts due to policy lending, but does not require an environmental social impact assessment with its attendant requirements related to multiple public consultations and participation."
8   *See e.g.*, OP 8.60 fn. 5 (referring to "Good Practice Note in Supporting Participation in Development Policy Operations"); fn. 9 (referring to Good Practice Note on Poverty and Social Impact Analysis and Development Policy Lending"); *and* fn. 10 (referring to "Good Practice Note on Environmental and Natural Resource Aspects in Development Policy Lending").
9   *See* section 5.1.
10   Inspection Panel (2012), p. 3.

decision, the Panel emphasizes, results in the "[i]nadequate assessment of social, political, institutional and legal risks during project preparation [...]."[11]

For example, in *Papua New Guinea: Governance Promotion*, which was financed by means of a structural adjustment loan,[12] the Requesters questioned, among other things, why OP 4.36 (Forestry) was not applied to the project and also listed several claims related to OP 4.36.[13] In its initial response to the Request, however, Bank management argued that there had been no violations of OP 4.36 since "this particular policy [was] inapplicable to Structural Adjustment Loans."[14] The Inspection Panel, on its part, rejected Management's argument and pointed out that it "could not find any provision in the [policy on Forestry] supporting such assertion."[15] The Panel subsequently reviewed the Bank's activities in light of the requirements in OP 4.36.[16]

Because of the close relationships between certain lending vehicles and the application of particular operational policies, therefore, the Panel has also been known to question the choice of lending instruments in specific project contexts.

In *Democratic Republic of Congo: Transitional Support*, for instance, which was financed by means of a Development Policy Lending (DPL) instrument, the Inspection Panel reviewed the Bank's "experience with DPLs'" across its development-lending portfolio "in order to gain a better understanding of the Bank's choice in this instance."[17] The Panel's review highlighted what "appear[ed] to be a trend in the Bank" – namely, an assertion that "DPLs rarely have significant impact on the environment."[18] "[V]arious Bank documents," the Panel noted, appeared to emphasize that the effects of DPLs "on the environment"

---

11 *Id. see e.g.*, the discussion of compliance issues related to *Honduras: Land Administration* (2006) and *Panama: Land Administration* (2009) *in* Ch. 13; and on the compliance issues related to *Cambodia: Land Administration Project, see e.g.*, sections 8.2.2 & 9.1. *Also note*, this example demonstrates the Panel's contribution towards institutional strengthening by providing 'policy advice' – as discussed *in* section 7.1.5.

12 *See Papua New Guinea: Governance Promotion* (2001), ER, § 17. For an overview of *Papua New Guinea: Governance Promotion, see e.g.*, Naudé Fourie (2014), pp. 189-194.

13 *See e.g., Papua New Guinea: Governance Promotion* (2001), ER, § 12.

14 *Papua New Guinea: Governance Promotion* (2001), ER, § 29.

15 *Id.*

16 *See e.g., Papua New Guinea: Governance Promotion* (2001), ER, §§ 42-43. *Note*, while the Panel acknowledged (at *id.*) that "the customary landowners have suffered tremendously due to environmental destruction to their natural forests and rivers; non-payment of premium and royalty entitlements, and emerging social problems within village communities", it also concluded that "this was not caused by Bank (non)-action, but rather a consequence of the fact that the "national Government through the PNGFA [Papua New Guinea Forest Authority] seems to have been incapable of protecting the landowners and the rights to their land and from being deprived of their forest resources." Hence, the Panel concluded (at ER, § 55) that, as Management argued, the Request was not eligible for inspection, since "the evident harm suffered by the Requesters is not related to an act or omission of the Bank, as required by paragraph 12 of the Resolution." *Also see* the discussion about the 'causal link' between harm and World Bank actions or omissions, *at* sections 4.3.2 & 6.2.4.

17 *Democratic Republic of Congo: Transitional Support* (2005), IR, §§ 408-409.

18 *Id.*

– "if any" – would be "felt only indirectly."[19] "[B]est practice guidance describing incorporation of environmental concerns into development policy lending," furthermore, "reaches
the same conclusion on the basis that the majority of DPLs are solely focused on areas
such as the public sector, financial, health, and education sectors, which are not directly
linked to the environment."[20] "Despite this trend," however, the Panel observed, "a large
number" of projects financed through DPLs – including *Democratic Republic of Congo:
Transitional Support* – "include components supporting policies or reforms that may significantly affect environment, forests or other natural resources."[21]

The Panel also suggested that the Bank-wide conclusion that DPLs had no or limited
"environmental impact may be the result of Management's lack of sufficient analytical
resources" – "such as" Country Environmental Assessments and Sectoral Social and
Environmental Assessments – that could "properly measure the impact of policy reforms
on environment, forests and other natural resources."[22] In fact, the Panel added, "Bank
documents acknowledge that in most cases there" had been "a paucity of environment-
related analytical work," whereas "projections for completed CEAs and SEAs are 'below
the level anticipated in 2004 when the new policy was introduced'."[23]

"The lower than anticipated number of completed" CEAs and SEAs was "especially
problematic", the Panel emphasized, "because the lack of analytical work may prevent
Management from reaching an informed decision on whether a specific DPL will have
significant environmental effects."[24] It also increased the probability "that for DPLs with
environment, forest and other natural resource sector related components," the Bank
might fail to identify project components that might potentially cause significant adverse
environmental effects.[25]

With regard to the *DRC: Transitional Support* project, the Inspection Panel concluded
that it was "questionable whether the choice of a DPL under its present guidelines was the
right instrument for achieving the agreed-upon goals of reforming this sector with its
many social and environmental complexities," although the Panel "recognize[d] that the
DPL is an instrument that can engage high-level attention of the Finance or other influential
Ministry, which in the specific country context can be important."[26]

---

19   *Id.*
20   *Id.*
21   *Id.*
22   *Id.* On the necessity of reflecting 'cumulative impacts' in the content and scope of EAs, *also see* the discussion
     in section 14.2.2.
23   *Democratic Republic of Congo: Transitional Support* (2005), IR, §§ 410-412. *Also note*, these examples
     demonstrate the Panel's contribution towards institutional strengthening by providing 'policy advice' – as
     discussed *in* section 7.1.5.
24   *Democratic Republic of Congo: Transitional Support* (2005), IR, §§ 410-412.
25   *Id.*
26   *Democratic Republic of Congo: Transitional Support* (2005), IR, §§ 426-427.

In this instance, however, the choice of the DPL as lending vehicle influenced the decision not to conduct a comprehensive "[e]nvironmental assessment," "even as [it] may have [had] added importance in a post-conflict environment like in DRC,"

> where there is a lack not only of institutional capacity but also of basic informa-
> tion about the affected lands and about people who have an interest in these
> reforms, and might be affected by the regulated activities. The failure to carry
> out this analysis may mean that even the best-intentioned "reform" initiatives
> can fall out of line with Bank social and environmental policy objectives, and
> indeed lay the basis for significant harms.[27]

The choice of a DPL also meant that the Bank's Policy on Indigenous Peoples was not applied to the project, and, because no Indigenous Peoples Development Plan "was pre-pared," the Panel concluded, "potentially critical interests and needs of the indigenous Pygmy People in relation to these Project activities have been left unaddressed."[28]

In its response to the Inspection Panel's comments, however, Bank management emphasized "that development policy lending and investment lending cannot be used interchangeably."[29] "DPL operations", Management explained, "support implementation of institutional and policy actions, whereas investment operations finance specific invest-ment expenditures."[30] "The appropriate use of instruments is determined by the nature and content of Bank support", Management asserted, while emphasizing "that the actions supported by TSERO [project]"

> fall clearly in the domain of policy and institutional actions, and that the use
> of DPL was therefore appropriate and could not have been substituted by
> investment lending. In fact, DPL support for a limited set of policy actions was
> used to complement and enhance the impact of existing and planned investment
> lending.[31]

On the other hand, as the Inspection Panel pointed out, "from the perspective of the people who depend on the forest environment," the "difference between so-called 'investment' actions and 'policy and institutional reform' actions does not exist."[32]

---

27 *Democratic Republic of Congo: Transitional Support* (2005), IR, § 359.
28 *Democratic Republic of Congo: Transitional Support* (2005), IR, §§ 242-243. *Also see* the discussion in section
    13.1.
29 *Democratic Republic of Congo: Transitional Support* (2005), MRIR, Annex 1, § 10.
30 *Id.*
31 *Id.*
32 *Democratic Republic of Congo: Transitional Support* (2005), IR, §§ 242-243.

In *Cambodia: Forest Concession Management*, which was financed by a Learning and Innovation Loan ('LIL'), the Requesters claimed that "Bank staff associated with the FCMCPP [the project] are evidently keen to push the idea that because the FCMCPP was backed by a learning and innovation loan, it was therefore not bound by Bank operational policies."[33] The Panel affirmed that "the Bank document defining LILs as financing instruments" clearly stipulated that "LILs would conform to the Bank's *basic* operational policies."[34] However, the Inspection Panel also questioned whether an LIL was the appropriate lending instrument for the specific project context.

"LILs were established in 1997," the Panel explained, "in part to pilot operations in untested areas before scaling up, and to test new approaches that are attractive but risky."[35] But when Bank management and staff were asked to elaborate "about the way in which learning was made explicit within the Project, and how this led to innovation," the Panel's questions "were generally met with puzzlement."[36] "Staff referred to the Project as a "technical assistance project," the Panel noted, whereas "the LIL was evidently seen as a relatively quick and easy mechanism to mobilize a loan," which primary objective "was to support a legal and regulatory program on the basis of which long-term concessions were to be granted."[37]

"[T]he elements conditioning the use of the LIL instrument do not apply convincingly to the Project," the Panel concluded,[38] especially since "the Bank document defining LILs as financing instruments" clearly states that an "LIL may not be appropriate when the policy framework is poor and the borrower commitment and ownership are especially weak" – "two conditions [that] were present at the time of the design of the Project."[39] Although "the use of the LIL" made it possible for "the funds to be disbursed quickly," the Panel emphasized that it "was not designed for the kind of forestry project for which it was used in Cambodia," and also played a significant role in the project's "classification as [environmental and social risk] Category B" – which the Panel criticized[40] – "and resulted in lesser attention to Bank safeguard policies and procedures, which in the long run proved costly."[41]

---

33 *Cambodia: Forest Concession Management* (2005), IR, § 141.
34 *Cambodia: Forest Concession Management* (2005), IR, § 151 (emphasis added).
35 *Cambodia: Forest Concession Management* (2005), IR, § 142. *Also see* Miller-Adams's comments about the need to adapt project cycle to new lending vehicles *in* section 4.1.2.
36 *Cambodia: Forest Concession Management* (2005), IR, §§ 143, 145.
37 *Id.*
38 *Id.*
39 *Cambodia: Forest Concession Management* (2005), IR, § 146.
40 *See e.g.*, *Cambodia: Forest Concession Management* (2005), IR, p. xx. On issues related to project risk categorization for EA purposes, *also see* section 14.1.
41 *Cambodia: Forest Concession Management* (2005), IR, § 410. *Note*, this example also demonstrates the Panel's attempts to relate an identified incidence of non-compliance to the (non-)realization of specific development objectives – as discussed *in* section 4.2.2.

Whereas in *Liberia: Development Forestry*, which was "carried out by the United Nations Development Programme (UNDP) for the benefit of Liberia, under a Trust Fund administered by" the Bank,[42] the Panel was critical about the manner in which project modality influenced the project risk categorization. In it is initial response to the Request, Bank management argued that it did "not believe that technical assistance projects like this one"

> should be classified as Category A simply because they concern complex and risky sectors like forestry. Rather, Management believes that risks should be appropriately evaluated and managed in each project (as is the case in this project).[43]

The Inspection Panel, on the other hand, rejected the use of "the modality of the Project, in this case technical assistance" as "a determinant factor for environmental categorization."[44] Reiterating its findings "in previous reports involving sensitive sectors like forestry," the Panel emphasized that "technical assistance to support or establish a policy environment, management framework, and institution building"

> could have a significant influence, positive or otherwise, on activities such as large-scale logging that in turn may have highly significant social and environmental implications.[45]

Moreover, with regard to the Requesters' claim that the project favoured commercial logging, the Inspection Panel observed that there "was total convergence among all the stakeholders that the Panel [had] met" during its field visit that "there was an emphasis," during "the first years" of the project,

> on commercial forestry to the detriment of the other components of the '3Cs' (community forestry and Conservation).[46]

---

42 See *Liberia: Development Forestry* (2010), MR, § 1; *also see* fn. 1: "Two grants also mentioned in the request FLEG (TF096154-LR) and PROFOR (TF096170-LR) constituting the Liberia Chain of Custody System Project are being carried out by the Government of Liberia."

43 *Liberia: Development Forestry* (2010), ER, § 39. For an overview of *Liberia: Development Forestry*, *see e.g.*, Naudé Fourie (2014), pp. 499-506.

44 *Liberia: Development Forestry* (2010), ER, § 93.

45 *Id. But note*, while the Panel found the Request to have met all the 'technical' eligibility criteria, it did not recommend a full investigation in this instance since the Panel considered Management's action steps (filed at the same time as its formal response to the Request) to "constitute a meaningful platform for dialogue to address issues raised in this Request that pertain to the Project and possibly to influence the design of future Bank- financed operations in the sector." *See Liberia: Development Forestry* (2010), ER, § 113; on management's corrective actions, *see* ER, §§ 30, 43 & 44; *and see* MR, p. 25.

46 *Liberia: Development Forestry* (2010), ER, § 74.

"The reason given" for this focus, however, "was to attain the lifting of the United Nations Security Council Sanctions, and to start generating revenue and creating jobs to rebuild the devastated society and economy."[47]

10.2 DELINEATING THE 'PROJECT AREA' AND 'PROJECT AREA OF INFLUENCE'

'Project area' and 'project area of influence' are two closely related terms used throughout the Bank's development lending operations that can significantly affect the content and scope of a project.[48]

'Project area' generally refers to the physical location, in the territory of a (member state) Borrower, where a project is situated – where, in other words, a project (as designed, prepared, appraised and approved) is being implemented. A project's 'area of influence', on the other hand, encompasses a broader notion, as defined, for instance, in the Bank's policy on Environmental Assessment, which describes it as the "area likely to be affected by the project, including all its ancillary aspects [...] as well as unplanned developments induced by the project."[49] In a hydroelectric infrastructure construction project, for example, the physical location where the hydroelectric facility is situated would typically comprise the 'project area', whereas the areas further downstream from the hydroelectric facility would usually be considered as the 'project area of influence'.

The delineation of the project area and/or project area of influence could have several potential consequences for the content and scope of a project – including, for instance, the identification and quantification of project-affected people,[50] and the content and scope of Environmental Assessments.[51] Generally speaking, Inspection Panel practice tends to highlight instances where a narrow delineation of project area and/or project area of influence have narrowed project scope – often to the detriment of managing social, environmental and economic risks and of realizing specific development objectives.

In a recent publication, for example, the Panel notes that it has "encountered several cases" over the course of its investigations where "the definition of the project's area of influence [were] restrictive and narrow," and where narrow delineation subsequently resulted in an

---

47 *Id. Note,* this example also demonstrates issues related to the balance between project components, as discussed *in* Ch. 9.

48 *Also note,* these two terms are also sometimes used interchangeably.

49 *See* OP 4.01 (Environmental Assessment), Annex A, § 5. On compliance issues related to 'project areas of influence', *also see* the Inspection Panel's 'Submission to the World Bank's Safeguard Review and Update Process', p. 10, available at: http://go.worldbank.org/QHT9YU3820.

50 *See* section 10.3.

51 *See* section 14.2.

inadequate assessment of potential environmental and social risks and impacts, and hence inadequate identification of ways to prevent, minimize, mitigate or compensate for adverse impacts.[52]

The "determination of a project's area of influence", as the Panel emphasizes, "must 'follow' impacts in the short-, medium- and long-term," and should "not be guided by a limited geographical understanding of 'physical footprint'."[53] On the other hand, as Inspection Panel practice also demonstrates, the delineation of a project's 'physical footprint' can be quite challenging in certain project scenarios.

In *Cambodia: Land Management and Administration*, for example, it proved to be particularly complex due to related activities that were implemented by the Borrower, as discussed earlier, and which had resulted in disagreement between the Bank and the Borrower as to whether a particular area (the 'BKL') was part of the Bank-financed LMAP project area.[54] The Inspection Panel demonstrated this complexity when it set out its own understanding of the situation, as follows:

> The Panel notes that LMAP, according to the Development Credit Agreement and the PAD, was designed to be implemented in 11 provinces and municipalities, defined as "Project Provinces", including the Municipality of Phnom Penh, subject to amendment from time to time by agreement between the Borrower and the Bank. The BKL area is within the Municipality of Phnom Penh. The Panel further notes that there is no reference or criteria developed in the PAD or the DCA to exclude any areas from the definition of "Project Provinces". In principle, therefore, LMAP, envisaged as a first phase in a national land titling program, could work in any part of Phnom Penh. The PAD stipulated a target of 198,000 parcels to be surveyed and adjudicated in Phnom Penh from 2002 to 2007. [...] Based on the above, the Panel finds that the BKL area is within a Project Province and was declared for adjudication under LMAP, hence activities relating to verification of land tenure and ownership subsequent to the notice of adjudication are directly linked to the Project.[55]

---

52   Inspection Panel (2012), p. 2.
53   *Id.*
54   *See* section 8.2.2.
55   *Cambodia: Land Management and Administration* (2009), IR, §§ 114 & 116. *Also note*, this example demonstrates the impact of the definition of key terms in operational policies and project documentation on project content and scope (here, "project provinces") – as discussed *in* section 10.4.

However, the Panel was also critical of the Bank's decision to focus "only on the areas covered by the concessions to define the Project Area" since "this led to an overly restrictive definition of the Project Area."[56] Because "[e]ach concession was considered separately without looking at multiplier effects and interactions between the concessions," the Panel argued, "the Project's social impacts were significantly understated and the Bank social and environmental safeguards not applied to the proper area and population", which, the Panel concluded, was "not consistent with the applicable Bank policies, OP 4.01 and OD 4.20."[57]

Whereas in *China: Western Poverty Reduction*, the Inspection Panel found that there was "confusion" about "what is and what is not included in the definition of the 'project area'."[58] This confusion, the Panel added, was "compounded by the fact that the [project] documentation"

> is very poorly supported by maps. Those maps that were in the documentation were of a very small scale. Most lacked scale lines and all omitted latitude and longitude or other co-ordinates. Even detailed 1:50000 maps of the irrigated areas that were provided to the Inspection Team on the day it visited the main irrigation area of Xiangride-Balong did not provide grid references or latitude and longitude, so that exact positions on the map could be determined. It is thus very difficult, if not impossible, for anyone reading the Environmental Assessment to gain a clear and unambiguous view of the locational aspects of the Project from the information provided. This applies to both the Move-out and Move-in areas.[59]

Hence, the Panel concluded that "the spatial boundaries of the Project" were "extremely narrow" and "deeply flawed," which held several consequences for policy compliance.[60] For instance, the Panel observed, if the project area were to be "corrected to include all the population directly impacted by the Project, rather than restricting them largely to the proposed irrigation site,"

---

56 *Cambodia: Forest Concession Management* (2005), IR, § 215.
57 *Id.*
58 *China: Western Poverty Reduction (Qinghai)* (1999), IR, § 53. Over the adequacy of existing maps used in the Project, *also see* §§ 54 & 58.
59 *China: Western Poverty Reduction (Qinghai)* (1999), IR, § 53. For a discussion of *China: Qinghai, see e.g.,* Clark *in* Clark et al. (Eds.) (2003), pp. 211-246; Gowlland-Gualtieri (2001), pp. 238-242; Ricarda Roos (2001); Shihata (2000), pp. 150-154; *and see* Naudé Fourie (2014), pp. 113-128. *But also compare* the Panel's findings with Wolfensohn's comments *in* section 7.2.2.
60 *China: Western Poverty Reduction (Qinghai)* (1999), IR, § 278.

the overall figures for impacted populations would shift towards the population in the Move-in area. And, among this larger population, it would increase the overall percentage of those who have the status of "indigenous people" as well as the number of those who could be considered adversely impacted by the Project.[61]

The Panel acknowledged that the delineation of the 'project area' is a matter that falls within the purview of Bank Management's discretion or professional judgement, but the Panel also argued that the exercise of such managerial discretion needs to be considered against the underlying objective of safeguard policies, such as the policy on indigenous people, which aims

> to ensure that indigenous peoples do not suffer adverse effects during the development process, particularly from Bank-financed projects, and that they receive culturally compatible social and economic benefits.[62]

Hence, the Panel concluded, "it is simply not within Management's prerogative"

> to define the Project in a very limited way (the 'immediate project area') for purposes of fulfilling this OD, since that does not ensure against adverse impacts on indigenous populations who live and work beyond the "immediate project area."[63]

The Panel also noted that there was significant potential to manipulate the application of World Bank policies if the project area could be "defined in a way that effectively determines the balance between those who benefit and those who are adversely affected by a project."[64] In this instance, "Management's narrow definition of the Project's boundaries"

> potentially subsumes the rights and cultural uniqueness of the most vulnerable ethnic minorities, in favor of other ethnic minorities who outnumber them as a direct result of the way in which the boundaries are defined.[65]

---

61 *Id.*
62 See *China: Western Poverty Reduction (Qinghai)* (1999), IR, § 79; *and see* OD 4.20, § 6. On the approaches emphasizing the underlying policy objectives, *see* section 6.3.3; *and* on the issue of the 'margins' of managerial 'discretion', *see* section 6.3.2.
63 *China: Western Poverty Reduction (Qinghai)* (1999), IR, § 79. *Note,* this example also demonstrates the Panel limiting/restricting the exercise of Managerial discretion – here, allowing Management a narrower 'margin of appreciation' – *see* section 6.3.2.
64 *China: Western Poverty Reduction (Qinghai)* (1999), IR, §§ 277-278.
65 *Id.* On issues related to the definition and identification of indigenous people, *see* section 13.1.

In its 2007 investigation of *Uganda: Power Projects*, the Panel found that the narrow delineation of a particular part of the project area affected the proper implementation of the Bank's policy on Physical Cultural Resources.[66] Management incorrectly "assumed that what they called the 'Bujagali spirits'," the Panel argued, "were restricted to the Project construction and flooding area,"

> in contravention to the BP 4.11 requirement that they work with and assist the Borrower to identify the spatial and temporal boundaries of the cultural resources affected by the project.[67]

By "[n]arrowing its size, location, and scale," the Panel elaborated,

> Management discounted the significance of what should have been identified as the Bujagali Falls spiritual site to all of the Busoga, not just to those living in close proximity to the Project area.[68]

Consequently, "Management defined the project-affected-people under OP 4.11 on Physical Cultural Resources as those covered under OP/BP 4.12 on Involuntary Resettlement".[69] However, the Panel noted, "[i]n the case of the Bujagali project, the[se] groups are distinct;" hence, the Panel concluded, "the culturally and spiritually affected people were not adequately identified as required by Bank policy."[70]

In addition, the Panel commented, "Management publicly injected the Bank into a religious misunderstanding"

> without competence in the cultural spiritual context of its position, including passing judgment on legitimacy and credibility of a spiritual medium's performance. Management unnecessarily and inappropriately took sides in a spiritual

---

66 OP/BP 4.11 (Physical Cultural Resources). The policy "addresses physical cultural resources, which are defined as movable or immovable objects, sites, structures, groups of structures, and natural features and landscapes that have archaeological, paleontological, historical, architectural, religious, aesthetic, or other cultural significance. Physical cultural resources may be located in urban or rural settings, and may be above or below ground, or under water. Their cultural interest may be at the local, provincial or national level, or within the international community." (*See* OP 4.11, § 1.)

67 *Uganda: Power Projects* (2007), IR, §§ 596-597. For a discussion of both *Uganda: Power* investigations (2001 and 2007), *see* Mallaby (2004), pp. 7-9; *and see* Naudé Fourie (2014), pp. 179-188 & pp. 337-348.

68 *Uganda: Power Projects* (2007), IR, §§ 596-597.

69 *Id.*

70 *Id.*

controversy of a religion in which millions of Ugandans believe. The Panel
finds this action by Management to be non-compliant with the OP 4.11.[71]

In *Ghana: Second Urban Environment Sanitation*, the Inspection Panel found that the
Environmental and Social Assessment[72] did not "adequately identify the full extent of the
'area of influence' of the proposed landfill" (a sub-component of the Project) and, as a
result, failed to identify "potential impacts on nearby people and residents."[73] The ESA
included "no formal and scientifically justified determination of the area of influence of
the future landfill," the Panel elaborated, which "does not comply with OP 4.01."[74]

"This instance of non-compliance," the Panel explained, "has made it difficult for the
affected people and decision-makers" alike "to understand the various types of impacts of
the landfill and whether adequate measures would be taken to prevent, minimize, mitigate
or compensate for these impacts."[75]

And in *Peru: Lima Urban Transport*, the Panel observed that an overly narrow delineation of the project's area of influence was a "recurrent finding from other Panel investigations."[76] The Panel pointed out that such narrow delineations often meant that project-
effected people "fall off the radar screen,"

> with the result that the negative impacts of the Project on those communities
> were overlooked and not properly addressed as part of the Project's harm
> avoidance and mitigation elements.[77]

---

71 *Uganda: Power Projects* (2007), IR, § 591. *Note*, here the Inspection Panel points to the consequences of the
Bank's actions for the preservation of its political neutrality – as discussed *in* section 3.1.1.

72 *Note*, the EA process "considers natural and social aspects in an integrated way. It also takes into account
the variations in project and country conditions; the findings of country environmental studies; national
environmental action plans; the country's overall policy framework, national legislation, and institutional
capabilities related to the environment and social aspects; and obligations of the country, pertaining to
project activities, under relevant international environmental treaties and agreements. The Bank does not
finance project activities that would contravene such country obligations, as identified during the EA. EA
is initiated as early as possible in project processing and is integrated closely with the economic, financial,
institutional, social, and technical analyses of a proposed project." (*See* OP 4.01 (Environmental Assessment),
§ 3.) For compliance issues related to the EA process, *also see* Ch. 14.

73 *Ghana: Second Urban Environment Sanitation* (2007), IR, § 143. For an overview of *Ghana: Second Urban
Environment Sanitation, see* Naudé Fourie (2014), pp. 377-386.

74 *Ghana: Second Urban Environment Sanitation* (2007), IR, § 143. *Also see* the discussion of the project's
environmental screening process *in* section 14.1.

75 *Id.*

76 *Peru: Lima Urban Transport* (2009), IR, § 215. *Note*, this example demonstrates the Inspection Panel's contribution towards identifying structural or systemic issues in order to facilitate institutional learning – *see*
section 7.1.5. For more on the identification of project affected people that are not related to the definition
of the project area or project area of influence, *also see* section 10.4.

77 *Peru: Lima Urban Transport* (2009), IR, § 215.

In this instance, while the Inspection Panel's investigation "was limited only to the one segment of the bus corridor in the District of Barranco," the Panel noted that its "findings suggest[ed] that an overly narrow delineation appears to have been a factor in this Project too."[78] For example, the Panel found that "little attention was paid"

> to assessing impacts and identifying harm that might take place beyond the bus corridor itself as a result of changes in traffic patterns, a shortcoming that had particular implications for the Barranco District, given its difficult geography and the fact that the Project would cause significant traffic rerouting.[79]

"Had the Barrando community been 'on the radar screen' from the outset," the Panel concluded, "later tension and conflict about this project could have been avoided and there would have been greater opportunities to avoid or mitigate harms."[80]

Similar compliance issues arise in the context of the Bank's policy on the Use of Borrower Systems (OP/BP 4.00), which requires an analysis of 'associated impacts'.[81]

For example, in *South Africa: Eskom Investment Support*, the first Inspection Panel Request that concerned OP/BP 4.00, the Inspection Panel acknowledged that "achieving policy compliance in the context of 'associated impacts' (and associated activities and facilities giving rise to these impacts) [was] not straightforward."[82] The Panel's investigation, however, "raise[d] questions about the Bank's understanding of what constitutes an "associated impact", "associated facility", and/or "associated activity"."[83] "The Bank", the Panel concluded, "does not seem to have a clear definition of these terms" – "[y]et,"

> it is of the utmost importance when undertaking an EIA to define the area of influence and potentially significant impact of the project. For this reason, clarity on the inclusion or exclusion of activities or facilities that could qualify as "associated" is needed. Only by achieving this clarity will the Bank be in a position to exercise sound judgment on the need for, and scope of, studies proportional to potential risks and impacts.[84]

The Panel subsequently commented about the types of project scenarios that would require an analysis of 'associated impacts' – for instance, in situations

---

78 *Id.*
79 *Id.*
80 *Id.*
81 *See* OP 4.00 (Piloting the Use of Borrower Systems to Address Environmental and Social Safeguard Issues in Bank-Supported Projects), Table A1.
82 *South Africa: Eskom Investment Support* (2010), IR, § 597.
83 *Id.*
84 *Id.*

where new activities/facilities are developed specifically to support the Project
(i.e. the Project depends on these activities/facilities), and/or where existing
activities/facilities are expanded expressly to meet the needs of the Project and
represent a significant increase in the scale, capacity, or size of those facili-
ties/activities in relation to the "without project" conditions, they should be
regarded as "associated" with the Project, regardless of the source of financing.
That is, their potentially significant effects should be assessed or more simply
regarded as potential impacts of the Project, and in either case included in the
scope of the Bank's appraisal and evaluation.[85]

On the other hand, the Inspection Panel emphasized that it was "mindful that the scope
of 'associated impacts' is potentially large, and needs appropriate limitations."[86] For
example, "[i]t would clearly be impractical and inappropriate

to define each and every facility and activity linked to the project as an "associated impact"; inputs likely to have insignificant impacts would best be addressed
through procurement and supply chains.[87]

"However," the Panel added, "where the associated facilities and/or activities could result
in significant individual or cumulative effects,"

it is important to bring them into the scope of the Project and related appraisal
and supervision; the objective being to ensure that the impacts, risks and
externalities would comply with the Bank's policies.[88]

Finally, the definition of 'project area' can also be a significant factor in determining the
eligibility of a Request, since the Resolution requires the Requesters to be residing 'in the
territory of the borrower'.

In *Lebanon: Greater Beirut Water Supply,* for example, the Inspection Panel specifically
considered Bank management's "definition of Project area," as included "in the Management
Response" to the Request.[89] Management had defined the 'project area' as being comprised
of the "areas where land will be expropriated and infrastructure works will be carried out

---

85   *South Africa: Eskom Investment Support* (2010), IR, § 285.
86   *South Africa: Eskom Investment Support* (2010), IR, § 297. *Note,* this example also demonstrates the Inspection
Panel acknowledgement of the 'limits' to World Bank accountability – on the content and scope of World
Bank accountability, *see* Ch. 4.
87   *South Africa: Eskom Investment Support* (2010), IR, § 297.
88   *Id.*
89   *Lebanon: Greater Beirut Water Supply* (2010), First ER, §§ 42-43. For an overview of *Lebanon: Greater Beirut
Water Supply, see* Naudé Fourie (2014), pp. 515-523.

(such as upgrading the water distribution network in parts of southern Beirut)."[90] On the basis of this definition, moreover, Bank management had objected to the eligibility of this particular Request. "[N]one of the Requesters is shown to be an 'affected party'" as required by the Inspection Panel Resolution, Management argued, because of the Requesters' "inability to demonstrate any right or interest that is or will be harmed" and also because the Request is essentially a "disagreement over the water source and project design chosen by the Borrower and a procurement decision of the Borrower."[91] Specifically, "45 of the 51 Requesters do not live in the Project area and thus cannot demonstrate any valid link with the Project"; whereas "the six Requesters who live within the Project area," Management concluded, "are likewise not able to demonstrate"

> a nexus to harm or likelihood of harm with the Project as they will not have their land expropriated, will not suffer from delivery of polluted water and will not pay higher tariffs under the Project.[92]

The Panel, however, was critical of the fact that Management's definition excluded "all areas where drinking water will be delivered."[93] The inclusion of this aspect, the Panel argued, was necessary since there could be "no definite distinction between areas that will be supplied by the new water source to be provided under the Project and those supplied by the existing one."[94] Hence, the Panel concluded, "all inhabitants of the Greater Beirut, including the Requesters, may be affected by the potential harm alleged in the Request."[95]

A similar situation arose in *Uzbekistan: Energy Loss Reduction*, where World Bank management questioned the eligibility of the Request, arguing that the Requesters were not "in the Borrower's territory" (as the project had a 'transboundary element') and could not have suffered any harm "from the Assessment Studies that the Bank intends to

---

90 *Lebanon: Greater Beirut Water Supply* (2010), First ER, §§ 42-43.

91 *Lebanon: Greater Beirut Water Supply* (2010), First ER, § 22.

92 *Id.*

93 *Lebanon: Greater Beirut Water Supply* (2010), First ER, §§ 42-43.

94 *Id.*

95 *Id. Also note*, the Panel found the Request to have met the eligibility criteria, and had initially recommended a full investigation; however, the Board "invited the Inspection Panel to return by July [2011] after considering and taking into account the analysis of the study commissioned by Management on the water quality, availability, and cost, in order to inform the Board on whether or not subsequent investigation is warranted, and if so, on its precise focus." *See* Final ER, §§ 13-14. *But note*, after completing these actions, the Panel noted in its final ER, that it was "pleased to note Management's commitment in the course of the Panel process to ensure that the issues raised in the Request and identified by the Panel as warranting further consideration were seriously taken into account to ensure that the Project is in compliance with Bank policies. As a result, important steps are being taken to address potential harm to the Requesters and other Project affected people. [...] [T]he Panel concludes that subsequent investigation of whether the Bank has complied with its operational policies and procedures, with respect to the allegations contained in the Requests for Inspection, is not warranted." *See* Final ER, §§ 55-57.

finance."[96] The Inspection Panel noted that "this is not the first Project with transboundary effects about which the Panel has received complaints."[97] The Panel emphasized that it had "considered the literal and legalistic reading of the eligibility criterion" before registering the Request", and "also took into account the relevant precedents" from Inspection Panel practice.[98] "These precedents", the Panel concluded, "adopted an interpretation"

> which calls for a focus on *where* the material adverse effect of the Bank-financed Project occurs, even if it is in a territory that happens not to be that of the Borrower.

"This interpretation" – employed in the past by both "Management and the Panel", the Inspection Panel underscored, "was previously accepted by the Board."[99]

10.3   IDENTIFYING AND QUANTIFYING PROJECT-AFFECTED PEOPLE

The accurate and timely identification and quantification of project-affected people involve critical decisions that determine project content and scope, and which are underlying the proper functioning of the Bank's operational policy framework, but are often dependent on other decisions such as the delineation of the 'project area' and 'project area of influence' or the interpretation of specific phrases in the operational policies, as discussed elsewhere in this chapter.[100] Identification and quantification activities also depend on the effective deployment of various scientific methods (such as conducting social surveys and statistical analyses), which, in turn, depends on sufficient institutional and/or professional capacity of borrowers and/or project implementing agencies.[101]

Yet, the "[u]nderestimation" of the number of project-affected people has long been a recurring occurrence across the Bank's development-lending operations, as the Panel

---

96   *Uzbekistan: Energy Loss Reduction* (2010), MR, § 51.
97   *Uzbekistan: Energy Loss Reduction* (2010), IP Chair's Statement to the Board, 3 February 2011, pp. 1-2. For an overview of *Uzbekistan: Energy Loss Reduction, see* Naudé Fourie (2014), pp. 507-513. For other cases with a transboundary element, *see Argentina/Paraguay: Yacyretá Hydroelectric Project* (1996); *Paraguay/- Argentina: Yacyretá Hydroelectric Project* (2002); *Nigeria/Ghana: West African Gas Pipeline* (2006); *and Lesotho/South Africa: Highlands Water* (1998).
98   *Uzbekistan: Energy Loss Reduction* (2010), IP Chair's Statement to the Board, 3 February 2011, pp. 1-2.
99   *Id. Note,* this example also demonstrates the Inspection Panel's practice of referencing previous findings – *see* section 1.2.1. *Also see* the discussion about the institutional scope of the Inspection Panel's mandate *at* section 6.2.4.
100 *Note,* issues surrounding the identification and definition of *indigenous peoples* are discussed in section 13.1.
101 On issues related to surveying methodology, *also see* section 12.2; on issues related to borrower and/or project implement agency institutional and/or professional capacity, *also see* section 8.3.

observed at the time of its first investigation of *Nepal: Arun III.*[102] "As pointed out in one Bank study," the Panel elaborated,

> [s]urveys carried out in the early stages of the project usually covers only those who are directly affected by loss of property or who are "displaced" and it is only much later [that] other forms of impact is recognized.[103]

In its investigation of *Nepal: Arun III*, the Panel found a similar scenario, which it contributed in part to the Bank's decision to focus only on those people who were "seriously-affected" by the project because they had lost land.[104] The Panel stressed that "the loss of jobs and traditional markets will be wide-scale with thousands of families 'seriously-affected' without losing any land at all, since the land is only one source of income."[105] Yet, in this instance, the Board had specifically instructed the Panel to limit its investigation into "losses due to the taking of land."[106] In doing so, the Panel commented, "the Board has created a category that does not exist in OD 4.30,"

> and indeed, is not addressed in the current principal Bank guide to the subject, Resettlement and Development (1994). The policy, on the other hand, appears to state that all losses are to be taken seriously; the construct of "seriously-affected" families as one category in the road projects seems to be a compromise with the borrower to limit the application of the extensive provisions for resettlement to a minority of those losing land.[107]

Moreover, the Panel also pointed out that the project had only included project-affected people along the new 'Valley' access route – while excluding people that had already been affected by the (at that point, abandoned) 'Hill' access route. "[T]he comparison between the number of families affected by the Hill and Valley Routes", the Panel urged, "must clarify the fact that over 1,600 families have already been affected in the Hill Route, while an additional 1,146 families will also be affected by the (right of way) of the Valley route."[108]

---

102 *Nepal: Arun III* (1994), IR, § 19. *Note,* this example also demonstrates the complementary nature of the Inspection Panel's mandate, as discussed *e.g., in* section 6.2.4.
103 *Nepal: Arun III* (1994), IR, § 19.
104 *Id.*
105 *Id.*
106 *Id.*
107 *Id.*
108 *Nepal: Arun III* (1994), ER, § 83.

The Panel also warned against an extensive reliance on subjective phrases such as "seriously affected" or "large-scale" since it could result in or contribute to an inaccurate quantification of project-affected people.[109]

For instance, the Panel noted that "[s]ome observers ha[d] dismissed the scale of the resettlement problem in the Arun case" and, indeed, "[r]elative to the Narmada experience,"

> or most other South Asian projects, the number can seem trivial. But that is not the test for IDA policy. In OD 4.30, the question of scale is addressed in paragraph 4, where reference is made to "large-scale population displacement." The number used is a negative reference "[...] a few people (e.g., about 100-200 individuals)". This is substantially less individuals than the approximately thousand families losing land in the Arun III project which means the issue has to be seen as a serious compliance challenge.[110]

For its part, however, the Panel asserted (contrary to Bank management's position) that "a very large number of families" was being relocated.[111]

On the other hand, the Inspection Panel tends to be critical of insufficient differentiation among potential project-affected people to the extent that it affects their proper identification and quantification.[112]

In *Colombia: Cartagena Water & Environmental Management*, for example, the Panel found that "the poverty impact analysis" in the Project Appraisal Document was "limited to the highly aggregated 'poor'/'non-poor' columns of Table 6 in Annex 4 and eight lines of text."[113] This issue, the Panel argued, was "of great importance to the Project," since "the first of the Project development objectives" was "to improve water and sewerage services and sanitary conditions of the city's poorest population."[114]

Furthermore, "as with many projects that may benefit poor people," it was likely "that some of the poor may gain while others lose" – and the Panel found it therefore "disturbing"

---

109 *Nepal: Arun III* (1994), IR, § 18.
110 *Id.* On the 'Narmada experience', *also see* note 187, Ch. 3.
111 *Nepal: Arun III* (1994), ER, § 78. *But see Nepal: Arun III* (1994), MR § 22: "Arun III does not involve the resettlement of communities or of very large numbers of people. A total of 1,097 project affected families (PAFs) have been identified in the project area. Of these, 140 have been identified as seriously project-affected families (SPAFs)." *Also see* the Panel's comments in *Uganda: Power Projects* (2001), IR, § 253: "While the numbers of those relocated are small [ca 8700 people] relative to most Category A dam projects, dislocation is just as significant to those directly affected by it and calls into play the full force of OD 4.30."
112 On the need to employ differentiated approaches in project areas with diverse interests among project-affected people, *also see* section 9.3.
113 *Colombia: Cartagena Water & Environmental Management* (2004), IR, §§ 348-349.
114 *Id.*

that more effort was not put in during the Project preparation and appraisal to enable sufficient income and/or other data to be assembled to assess the Project's impacts on the poor "with any accuracy." [...] It might have been possible, for example, to augment the analysis by introducing other related evidence, such as that in the social assessment, which the PAD (p. 20) states, "proved that the project will benefit the poorest communities in Cartagena which currently lack sanitary services."[115]

Similarly, in *Ghana: Second Urban Environment Sanitation*, the Inspection Panel was critical of the "Entitlements Matrix" included in the project's Resettlement Policy Framework, since it had "failed to include quarriers as a category of affected or entitled persons."[116] "The issues of livelihoods," the Panel emphasized, "were particularly pertinent for women and migrants who made up a large number of the quarriers."[117] However, the Panel concluded,

the RPF pays insufficient attention to the needs of vulnerable groups including women and other displaced persons who are not protected through national land compensation legislation.[118]

The accurate quantification of impacted people can prove to be highly challenging in some project scenarios, however; notably, in instances where there have been significant implementation delays and where a 'successor' project has to address a 'legacy' aspect, related to a 'predecessor' project.

The *Paraguay/Argentina: Yacyretá Hydroelectric Project*, for instance, suffered significant implementation delays. Among the numerous challenges the project faced as a result of these delays, the Panel specifically noted "the lack of adequate identification of vulnerable groups who required special assistance."[119] Whereas "the number of people to be involuntarily resettled" had "originally [been] estimated to be 50,000", it had subsequently "increased to at least 70,000 people."[120] However, as the Panel pointed out, this issue was exacerbated by the constant "inflow of people from new areas" that were not consistently included in the revised planning.[121]

Both the Bank and the Borrower acknowledged that previous censuses (conducted to "identify people affected by the project and to determine the benefits or compensation

---

115 *Id.*
116 *Ghana: Second Urban Environment Sanitation* (2007), IR, § 270.
117 *Id.*
118 *Id.* On compliance issues related to income and livelihood restoration, *see* section 12.5.
119 *Paraguay/Argentina: Yacyretá Hydroelectric Project* (2002), IR, § 84.
120 *Id.*
121 *Id.*

that they should receive under the project") were deficient and therefore undertook additional surveying efforts rectify these deficiencies.[122] The Panel, however, found that these supplemental activities were "at best ad hoc arrangements that allowed some corrections to the census."[123] "Most people who felt excluded," the Panel concluded, "did not have a clear and objective method to bring their concerns to" the project implementing agency, and there was also not "a standard and transparent appeals procedure available to affected people;" this did "not comply with OD 4.30.[124]

For example, the Inspection Panel pointed to a "large number of informal workers who worked in large, mechanized industries as well as in small-scale brick-making facilities" – "for whom employers did not keep official employment records or pay social security taxes."[125] The Panel found that this category of project-affect people "[was] in practice excluded from the compensation system that the Bank approved, even though they suffered the adverse impacts of the project,"[126] and subsequently "had to rely on their employer complying with the law and/or the court recognizing their status and rights."[127] This, in turn, highlighted "a matter of considerable concern," the Panel commented, namely: "that the Bank would accept, in a notoriously weak institutional setting,"

> a compensation system that is based on the "assumption that Paraguayan labor laws would be applied effectively" by employers. The system essentially penalizes the workers because, if the employer has not complied with all legal and social securities obligations, it does not provide any compensation to the workers.[128]

During its 2007 investigation of *Uganda: Power Projects*, the Panel highlighted several complications brought about by "legacy issues" related to the predecessor projects.[129] For example, the Panel noted that it had "encountered a situation of adverse effects on people", which were the result of "a failure to assess, correct and complete resettlement actions initiated in the previous effort to develop the Bujagali dam."[130] "When the implementation

---

122 *Paraguay/Argentina: Yacyretá Hydroelectric Project* (2002), IR, §§ 248-249.
123 *Id.*
124 *Paraguay/Argentina: Yacyretá Hydroelectric Project* (2002), IR, §§ 248-249. On issues related to project-level grievance mechanisms, *see* section 12.6; on project-level grievance mechanisms as a form of 'recourse', *also see* section 7.1.1.
125 *Paraguay/Argentina: Yacyretá Hydroelectric Project* (2002), IR, §§ 328 & 330.
126 *Id.*
127 *Id.*
128 *Paraguay/Argentina: Yacyretá Hydroelectric Project* (2002), IR, §§ 332 & 334. *Note*, this example also demonstrates the interfaces with borrowers' constitutional systems – *see* sections 5.2 & 8.2; *and* it also provides an example of Inspection Panel comments that can be construed as implicit (negative) comments pertaining to the Borrowers – as discussed *e.g., in* section 4.3.2.
129 *Uganda: Power Projects* (2007), IR, p. lvii.
130 *Id.*

of this earlier project was halted, following withdrawal of the sponsor," the Panel explained, "many of these people were essentially left in limbo, and they did not receive key elements of the resettlement process to which they were entitled under Bank policy."[131]

In addition, the project's 'Assessment of Past Resettlement Activities' and 'Action Plan' failed to adequately "assess and update the previous 2001 RAP" and, subsequently, "disenfranchised any stakeholders not previously identified in 2001, including vulnerable people who slipped through the flawed sampling."[132] As a result, the current project's "[l]ivelihood restoration was mainly limited to the people identified in 2001 [at the time of predecessor projects] and the terms and conditions set forth in 2001."[133]

Finally, *India: Mumbai Urban Transport* provides several examples of issues related to the identification and quantification of project-affected people, as well as the broader implications of these issues.

The Inspection Panel's investigation illustrated, for example, how one category of affected people – 'middle-income shopkeepers' – can be "subsumed" into a larger category, resulting in a situation where their specific compensatory needs are not identified, quantified or, ultimately, provided for.[134] In terms of the project's resettlement and rehabilitation (R&R) policy, for instance, "displaced wage workers [were] fully included in the impact categories"; however, "in the table of entitlements in the [R&R] policy annex," the shopkeepers' "entitlement is subsumed under the right of all employees to receive an allowance to meet extra transportation costs if merited."[135] However, as the Panel further explained, because middle-income shopkeepers "will not have an address within the Project after [their] shops are demolished,"

> it is extremely unlikely they could make any claim. Nor is it likely they will ever learn they may be entitled to make a claim. The Panel is not aware that any of the employees have been informed about their rights or that they have received any financial or other support.[136]

With regard to the number of affected shopkeepers, the Panel noted that significant adjustments were made over the course of the project cycle. "When this issue was [first] identified in 1995," the Panel observed, "the exact numbers of shopkeepers were not yet available,"

---

131 *Id.*
132 *Uganda: Power Projects* (2007), IR, § 452.
133 *Id.* On compliance issues related to income and livelihood restoration, *see* section 12.5.
134 *India: Mumbai Urban Transport* (2009), §§ 465-466.
135 *Id.*
136 *Id.*

but it was obvious to the Bank's specialist staff that they were a large group. This was confirmed when the shopkeepers, at a much later date, were counted. The Panel found the first report on this number to come up only in the end of 2003, when the Bank claimed a requirement of 2,500 units for shops and in April 2004, when the Bank's supervision mission indicates no less than 3,800 shopkeepers (with additional significant sets of uncounted employees).[137]

"Nevertheless," the Panel concluded, the project failed to "make adequate arrangements to respect their entitlements and restore their livelihoods and status."[138] The Panel also pointed out that "[t]he large group of shopkeepers is well organized socially" – as illustrated by the fact that "[i]ts several professional organizations have now become Requesters in the present investigation."[139]

The Inspection Panel also identified several significant compliance issues related to the total number of people that would be displaced as a result of the project. The Panel noted, for example, that "the Bank supervision mission [of] April 2004," which took place "[d]uring implementation, and shortly before the Requesters submitted their complaints to the Panel,"

> reported that the number of people displaced and to be resettled under MUTP was in fact larger, by about 40,000 persons. This brought the total number of PAPs to about 120,000, an increase of about 50%.[140]

That "increase alone [was] larger than entire resettlement components in many other Bank projects in India", the Panel noted, and it meant a significant change in the scope of the Project resettlement component."[141] Yet, "the Bank did not re-assess the Project"

> to confirm that the Project, as modified, was still justified, that the requirements of the Bank's policies were met, and that the implementing arrangements were still satisfactory, as required by BP 13.05.[142]

---

137 *Id.*
138 *India: Mumbai Urban Transport* (2004), IR, §§ 117-118.
139 *Id.* Note, *India: Mumbai Urban Transport* involved four Requests – one which was filed by the "United Shop Owners Association (USOA), local NGO acting on its own behalf and on behalf of 118 Mumbai residents, medium-sized shop owners in Kismat Nagar." (*See* IR, §§ 3-4).
140 *Id.*
141 *Id.*
142 *Id.*

"To [the Panel's] surprise", however, it also found "that the Bank's October 2005 Aide Memoire on its Mid Term Review and Supervision Mission" stipulated "that there has been only a 'marginal increase'"

> of 4% in the number of Project Affected Households (PAHs), raising the figure from 19,200 households to 20,000 households affected by the Project. This differs significantly from the previous figures noted in the Bank's earlier documents, particularly the figures in April 2004, which indicated a 50% increase in the number of PAPs.[143]

"Clarification in this regard is urgently needed," the Panel emphasized, "especially since the numbers are sometimes given for Project affected *people* and other times for Project affected *households*, or *families* without consistent correlation between the two."[144]

The Panel underlined, moreover, that several of these compliance issues were "compounded by incorrect understatements made by some Bank staff in positions of influence."[145] Indeed, many of the Panel's findings did not merely involve instances where "staff work might have simply failed to identify risks;" instead, the Panel found "that advanced project documents testif[ied] that major specific risks had been identified, had been known and recorded in writing," but had subsequently been "left out from the most decisive project document – the PAD – that was submitted to the Bank's Board of Directors for project approval."[146]

10.4 INTERPRETATION OF KEY PHRASES IN OPERATIONAL POLICIES AND PROJECT DESIGN DOCUMENTS

The interpretation of key phrases in the Bank's operational policies and in key project design documents can influence the decision not to apply a particular policy to a project, or influence the manner in which specific policy provisions are applied in a particular project context.[147]

---

143 *India: Mumbai Urban Transport* (2004), IR (ES), p. xxii.

144 *Id.* (emphases added); for a detailed analysis of the methodological inconsistencies between calculating 'PAPs' and PAHs', *also see* IR, §§ 267-268. *Note*, this example also illustrates issues related to surveying methodologies – as discussed *in* section 12.2.

145 *India: Mumbai Urban Transport Project* (2004), IR, § 297.

146 *India: Mumbai Urban Transport Project* (2004), IR, § 202. *Note*, this example also demonstrates the Panel's contribution with regard to the strengthening of the Bank's governance structure, by means of its fact-finding function – as discussed *in* section 7.1.4.

147 *Note*, the definition of 'involuntary resettlement' and 'indigenous people' – which both affect the Bank's application of the policies on Involuntary Resettlement and Indigenous People – will be discussed in sections 12.1 & 13.1, respectively.

For example, part of the Panel's 2007 investigation of *Uganda: Power Projects* concerned the Bank's application of OP/BP 4.04 (Natural Habitats). The Inspection Panel observed that "project documents recognize[d] that the inundation of the Bujagali Falls [would] destroy a *natural habitat of significance* to the people of Uganda," whereas Bank Management affirmed that "specific actions" had been "identif[ied]" "to offset this impact."[148]

However, Management also contended that "the Project [was] not significantly converting or degrading a *"critical natural habitat"* as defined in OP 4.04,"[149] which stipulates that "the Bank does not support projects that, *in the Bank's opinion*, involve the significant conversion or degradation of critical natural habitats."[150] The Inspection Panel specifically focused on this "aspect of the text" ('in the Bank's opinion'), arguing that there was a decided "need" to assess "the considered judgment of the Bank on this crucial question" as part of the Panel's compliance review.[151] "This phrasing," the Panel emphasized, "does not imply or give Management a blank check"

> to apply or not certain policy provisions to a specific project but rather requires Management to form and provide expressly an opinion on the issue in question, which must be consistent with the objectives of the applicable policy. This is particularly relevant in view of the controversy surrounding these issues in the present Project.[152]

On reviewing Management's exercise of discretion in this regard, the Panel commented that it "did not find sufficient documentation that would have permitted Management to make such a considered judgment," especially since Management failed to clearly set out "the reasons behind an opinion of not declaring the [Bujagali] Falls a critical natural habitat" – which, the Panel concluded, was "not consistent with the objectives of OP/BP 4.04."[153]

---

148 *Uganda: Power Projects* (2007), IR § 699 (emphasis added). On the debate between the Panel and Management about the legally binding nature of the agreement between the Bank and Borrower to conserve Kalagala Falls as an environmental offset in terms of OP 4.04 Natural Habitats, *also see Uganda: Power Projects* (2001) IR, §§ 152-153; *and* Legal Opinion § 22-24.

149 *Uganda: Power Projects* (2007), IR § 799 (emphasis added).

150 *See* OP 4.04 (Natural Habitats), § 4 (emphasis added).

151 *Uganda: Power Projects* (2007), IR, §§ 605-606.

152 *Uganda: Power Projects* (2007), IR, § 607.

153 *Id.* (emphasis added). *Note*, this example also demonstrates the Panel limiting/restricting the exercise of Managerial discretion – here, allowing Management a narrower 'margin of appreciation' (*see* section 6.3.2.); on the Panel's emphasis on the policy underlying objective, *see* section 6.3.3. *Also note*, for an example, where the Panel found the Bank to be in compliance with respect to its definition of 'natural habitat' (which resulted in the Bank's decision that OP/BP 4.04 would not be applicable to the project), *see Chad: Petroleum Development and Pipeline* (2001), IR §§ 109-114.

The Panel also added that, "in contrast to this apparently narrow application" of OP 4.04, "there [has been] a strong and increasing recognition over the years," "of the importance of sacred places both for their spiritual and cultural values, and for and as part of broad conservation objectives, both individually and collectively."[154] The Panel specifically cited the World Conservation Union's process ('IUCN'), as an example – where "[a]n IUCN Category III Protected Area", for instance, is specifically defined "as an "[a]rea containing one, or more, specific natural or natural/cultural feature which is of outstanding or unique value because of its inherent rarity, representative or aesthetic qualities or cultural significance"[...].[155] The Bujagali Falls, the Panel concluded, qualified in terms of this category as it was "a sacred place, like a sacred grove,"

> recognized by the Basoga, a traditional local community, for its high cultural and spiritual significance and inter-related ecological features and values. In this context and for the reasons described above, the Panel finds that the Bujagali Falls area may be regarded as a critical natural habitat for purposes of OP 4.04. The Project entails flooding of the Bujagali Falls area. Bank policy regards inundation as a form of significant conversion or degradation.[156]

Furthermore, the Inspection Panel highlighted a discrepancy between the content of OP 4.04 – which "defines critical natural habitats" as including "existing and proposed protected areas," "areas initially recognized as protected by traditional local communities (e.g., sacred groves)" and "sites that maintain conditions vital for the viability of these protected areas" – and "[i]nternal guidance [issued] to staff for the application of the Natural Habitats policy."[157] The internal guidelines, "by comparison," define 'critical natural habitats' as "those Natural Habitats which are either legally protected, officially proposed for protection, or unprotected but of known high conservation value."[158] In other words, the Panel concluded, the internal guidelines "see[m] to suggest a more limited interpretation and application of the policy than a plain reading of its terms would warrant."[159] "As a result,"

---

154 *Uganda: Power Projects* (2007), IR, § 636.
155 *Id. Note*, this example also demonstrates the Panel's practice of referencing normative standards contained in other normative systems – here, the international legal system – as discussed *e.g., in* sections 5.1.1 & 5.3.
156 *Uganda: Power Projects* (2007), IR, §§ 605-606 (emphasis added).
157 *Uganda: Power Projects* (2007), IR, §§ 634-635. *Note*, this example also demonstrates the Panel's contribution towards institutional strengthening by providing policy advice – as discussed *in* section 7.1.5. *Also note* that best practice and comparable operational 'guideline' documents fall outside the Panel's institutional mandate – as discussed *e.g., in* section 5.1.
158 *Uganda: Power Projects* (2007), IR, §§ 634-635.
159 *Id. Note*, on expansive *versus* restrictive interpretative approaches, *also see* section 6.3.3.

areas recognized as sacred and protected by traditional local communities, but considered to be lacking a unique biodiversity and/or official protection, may not have been regarded as "critical natural habitats."[160]

In *Pakistan: National Drainage Program Project* (NDP), another example of a 'successor' project with a 'legacy' component inherited from a 'predecessor' project, Bank management argued that OP 4.04 (Natural Habitats) was "not applicable to the Project" since it was "being implemented in a manner that [did] not add to or exacerbate the environmental problems of the already degraded Indus River Delta or the Coastal Zone."[161] Moreover, Management added, the 'Left Bank Outfall Drain/National Surface Drainage System' ('LBOD'), which construction was a primary objective of the (at the time, closed) predecessor project, would "not be extended under the [successor] NDP Project."[162]

The Inspection Panel, however, disagreed with this assessment, arguing that it was "difficult to judge the extent of negative impacts resulting from the NDP as distinct from the [predecessor project]," especially since "the NDP Project supported substantial actions to complete the LBOD system."[163] The Panel also pointed out that the NDP project "focused on ensuring the evacuation of LBOD effluents, and paid little attention to impacts on, or means to rehabilitate, the dhands[164] as a habitat and ecosystem," which "was not consistent with OP 4.04."[165] For example, the Panel elaborated, "[t]he Jubho Lagoon and the dhands system more generally in the southern reaches of Sindh Province"

> are under severe threat. The visual data show a decrease in the size of the dhands. According to the Panel expert, the hyper-salinity readings in the Rann of Kutch are "remarkable" and the Pateji Dhand, inter-connected with the Ramsar-listed dhands, is biologically dead.[166]

The "negative effects on the dhands," the Panel concluded, "amount[ed] to a 'significant conversion or degradation' within the meaning of OP 4.04.[167]

Whereas in *Ecuador: Mining Development*, the Inspection Panel considered the Bank's decision not to apply OPN 11.02 (Wildlands) to the project. Bank management did "not

---

160 *Id.*
161 *Pakistan: National Drainage Program Project* (2004), IR, § 339. For a discussion of *Pakistan: NDP, see e.g.,* Nurmukhametova (2006), pp. 408-412; *and see* Naudé Fourie (2014), pp. 259-268.
162 *Id.*
163 *Pakistan: National Drainage Program Project* (2004), IR, § 346.
164 *Note,* 'dhands' refers to a "shallow lake, depression, or wetland" – *see Pakistan: National Drainage Program Project* (2004), ER, p. 5, fn. 38.
165 *Pakistan: National Drainage Program Project* (2004), IR, § 346.
166 *Pakistan: National Drainage Program Project* (2004), IR, § 354.
167 *Id.*

dispute the fact that the [project] area contain[ed] unique biodiversity," but it argued that OPN 11.02 was "not applicable" since "the objectives of the Project was not to convert wildlands into intensive land and water uses" – in fact, Management emphasized, "[t]he Project is primarily a technical assistance Project."[168]

The Inspection Panel disagreed with this argument and described the interpretation on which this decision was based, "on its face," as "a narrow interpretation of the Bank's policy on wildlands" that "fails to take into account the overall aim of the Project"

> which is to increase the amount of mining in the country, and which, if success-
> ful, will lead to an increase of the area of land (and any vegetation cover and
> biodiversity contained in it) that is converted, modified, damaged or contami-
> nated.[169]

The Bank's policy on Involuntary Resettlement was not deemed to be applicable to *Albania: Integrated Coastal Zone Management*, based on a specific agreement between the Bank and the Borrower to "develop certain criteria and procedures" to provide assistance to project-affected people as a result of "encroachment removal" that would take place under the project.[170]

The Panel pointed out, however, that terms such as "encroaching buildings" and "illegal buildings" had not been "defined and used clearly in the Project documents."[171] Instead, "[t]hese terms were basically 'imported' from the terminology and vernacular used in Albania, where they are employed liberally, yet without precise definitions."[172] For example, the Project Appraisal Document, as the Panel elaborated,

> refers to "unauthorized encroachments in public space". This is one of the few
> correct usages of the term "encroachment," because, in Bank practice,
> encroachment is the appropriation and usage of public or someone else's space
> by an unauthorized private user. By the same token, however, land owners
> cannot be held to be "encroachers" if they use their own private land for
> building their house. Even in situations of delays in getting a permit for building

---

168 *Ecuador: Mining Development* (1999), IR, § 113. *Note*, this example also illustrates the effect of project modality on project content and scope – *see* section 10.1.

169 *Ecuador: Mining Development* (1999), IR, § 113. For an overview of *Ecuador: Mining*, *see* Naudé Fourie (2014), pp. 147-152. *Note*, this example also illustrates restrictive *versus* expansive interpretative approaches, as well as the Panel's practice to employ underlying project objectives as an interpretative scheme – as discussed *in* section 6.3.3.

170 *Albania: Integrated Coastal Zone Management* (2007), IR, § 165. On issues pertaining to this 'agreement', *also see* the discussion *in* section 8.2.2.

171 *Albania: Integrated Coastal Zone Management* (2007), IR, §§ 168-170.

172 *Id.*

a house, the construction could be seen as illegal due to the lack of permit. However, a building on one's own private land without permit cannot be regarded as an "encroaching" building.[173]

Clarifications about these terms were extremely "important for understanding correctly the Bank's Policy and the Project's policy framework in this case," the Panel explained.[174] Indeed, "[w]ith some possible exceptions of improvised seasonal facilities on the sandy part of the beach," the Panel's field visit revealed that "almost all the houses"

> which were demolished and were labeled by the [Borrower's] Construction Police as 'encroaching', were in fact built on land long regarded as owned legally by, or at least in peaceful possession of, the villagers who built them.[175]

Hence, the Inspection Panel emphasized "the need for clarification of the terminologies used, because Bank staff has to make judgments on practical issues."[176]

Whereas the Bank's policy on Involuntary Resettlement was clearly applicable to the *India: Mumbai Urban Transport Project*, the Inspection Panel's investigation highlighted an issue with regard to the manner in which a particular provision in the policy had been applied – that is, related to the specification that "particular attention should be paid to the poorest among the PAPs."[177]

Although the RAP had reflected this requirement, the Panel observed that there appeared "to have been some difficulty," to determine "which PAPs" should be considered "vulnerable."[178] For example, the Panel elaborated,

> the RIP for the SCLR lists four categories of vulnerable households: (1) below poverty line (BPL) households; (2) women-headed households without a male over 21 years of age; (3) woman-headed households with an income up to Rs. 5.000; and (4) physically handicapped.[179]

On the other hand, the Panel commented, it did "not seem to be entirely clear" from the project's Baseline Socio-Economic Surveys "which households or persons"

---

173 *Id.*
174 *Id.*
175 *Id.*
176 *Id. Also see* the discussion *in* section 12.1.
177 *India: Mumbai Urban Transport* (2004), IR, §§ 541-542.
178 *Id.*
179 *Id. But also see* the discussion *in* section 10.3, about the employment of subjective phrases.

are thought to merit classification as "economically vulnerable." In India to speak of vulnerable households could indicate that they are below the state's poverty line and thus entitled to buy basic commodities in public distribution shops and at special prices. These households are usually thought of as BPL card holders. It is unclear to the Panel whether the BPL status in fact may be the main measure of vulnerability in MUTP operations.[180]

In *Cambodia: Land Management and Administration*, which, as discussed earlier, involved forcible evictions and a fundamental disagreement between the Bank, the Borrower and other 'development partners' about the definition of the 'project area',[181] the Inspection Panel commented that this unfortunate situation was, in part, caused by "an unclear and confusing reference to 'lands in areas where disputes are likely'" included in the PAD.[182] The PAD stipulated, as the Panel explained "that the Project [would] not title such lands"

> until agreements are reached on the status of the land. Although recognizing the difficulty of classifying land and demarcating the boundaries between public and private domains, the Project design expected this important contro-versial aspect of the Project to be resolved through public consultations.[183]

"[D]uring Project implementation," however, "this PAD statement over time" came to be interpreted so as "to exclude lands under dispute."[184] "This issue became more acute", the Panel added,

> when land in question was claimed to be State land and characterized as dis-puted land and its residents were denied the opportunity to claim their posses-sory rights due to exclusion of such land from the adjudication process under the Project.[185]

In other words, the Panel concluded, "[i]n an environment where there is no land classifi-cation and no mapping to determine the boundaries of different type of land" – and, "most importantly between the State public land and State private land" – "this Project design"

---

180 *Id.*
181 *See* section 8.2.2.
182 *Cambodia: Land Management and Administration* (2009), IR, § 261.
183 *Id.*
184 *Id.*
185 *Id.*

led to the determination of land arbitrarily and de facto as State public land. As a result, residents of such lands were declared as informal settlers/squatters and excluded from titling process under the Project.[186]

A final example mentioned here concerns the Bank's decision not to apply OPN 11.03 (Management of Cultural Property, effective at the time) to *Albania: Power Sector*. Management based this decision based on the argument that the selected project site (where a new thermal power plant would be constructed) was "not of archaeological significance."[187]

The Panel noted that OPN 11.3 required that Bank staff, "before proceeding with a project that includes large-scale excavations," had to ensure that the borrower had undertaken "the following steps:"

> (i) determine what is known about the cultural property aspects of the proposed project site; (ii) draw the government's attention specifically to impacts on those aspects; (iii) consult relevant agencies, NGO's or university departments; (iv) if there is any question of cultural property in the area, a brief reconnaissance survey should be undertaken in the field by a specialist.[188]

The Panel's investigation revealed, however, that the "feasibility study for the Project omitted"

> to take into account the above-the-surface cultural endowments of the Vlora area, which are well known even without any archaeological reconnaissance survey. Their existence and location vis-à-vis thermal plant site and its ancillary structures, as well as their current and future contribution to the area's economic and tourist development of the area, were not considered in the EIA. Rather, it focused on technical and physical-environmental factors.[189]

The Inspection Panel added that it did not find any "reference to Vlora Bay's [the selected project site] cultural endowments during Project preparation", whereas other project documentation failed to "reflect any of the [above-mentioned] due-diligence steps specifically listed in OPN 11.03 […].[190]

In fact, since "the historical importance of the Treport's ancient port and location is widely known and its archaeological remains are easily visible 2.5km northwest of the

---

186 *Cambodia: Land Management and Administration* (2009), IR, § 262.
187 *Albania: Power Sector* (2007), IR, § 204.
188 *Albania: Power Sector* (2007), IR, § 214.
189 *Albania: Power Sector* (2007), IR, § 218.
190 *Albania: Power Sector* (2007), IR §§ 221 & 226.

project's selected site" (something which "a brief reconnaissance survey" "undertaken in the field by a specialist", as required by the policy, would have revealed), the Panel questioned the validity of Bank management's statement in the PAD that "the Project did not trigger the Bank's Safeguard Policy on Cultural Property (OPN 11.03)."[191]

****

Decisions – such as those concerning the description of project modality, the choice of lending vehicle, the delineation of the project area (of influence), the identification and quantification of project-affected people, and the interpretation of key phrases in operational policies and project documentation – affect the content and scope or reach of World Bank-financed development projects and, therefore, hold implications for the content and scope of World Bank accountability.

Indeed, because of the significance of these decisions, they are often identified as root causes of non-compliance in Inspection Panel practice, as several of the examples included throughout Part II of this book illustrate. In fact, the complex relationships that exist between many of the prominent compliance issues in Part II will become more pronounced with the discussion of each successive chapter.

Finally, the issues discussed in this chapter also constitute an area of Inspection Panel practice that prominently illustrates opposing approaches to policy application and policy compliance review. Generally speaking, as several of the examples included in this chapter demonstrate, Bank management tends to limit the application of the operational policy framework so as to limit project content and scope, whereas the Inspection Panel's findings often point to the need for expansion.[192] As such, the issues discussed here also illustrate the tension between the competing paradigms of accountability *for performance versus* accountability *for harm* – and, ultimately, also of instrumentalist *versus* formalist conceptions on the role of normative systems.[193]

---

191 *Id.*
192 *See* section 6.3.
193 *See*, respectively, sections 4.2.2 & 2.3.

11 ACCESS TO INFORMATION AND PARTICIPATION IN DECISION-MAKING – AT THE PROJECT LEVEL

The Rio Declaration principles of access to information, access to justice and participation in decision-making reflect the "[...] possible integrative nature"

> of development efforts and environmental protection and highlights the close interrelationships between the fields of development, environment, and human rights in promoting sustainable development.[1]

For example, as the Inspection Panel observed in *Nepal: Arun III*, access to project information is "not an end in itself", "but rather a means of enhancing the ability of affected people to participate in the design and consideration of project alternatives."[2]

The focus of Chapter 11 falls on the operationalization of *access to project-related information* and *participation in decision-making processes* – at the project level. The chapter specifically considers what constitutes 'compliance' with respect to these principles, as highlighted by Inspection Panel practice.

In analyzing what constitutes *adequate project-information disclosure*, the chapter provides examples that reflect the importance of the *timing* and *frequency*; *form* or *format*; specific *content*; as well as the *context* of project-information disclosure activities. Next, the chapter considers what constitutes *meaningful participation or consultation with project-affected people*, reflecting on the importance of *timing* and *frequency*, the *form* or *format*, specific *content* and *context*, as well as the *participants* of consultation activities.[3]

11.1 'ADEQUATE' PROJECT-INFORMATION DISCLOSURE

"The World Bank recognizes that transparency and accountability are of fundamental importance to the development process and to achieving its mission to alleviate poverty",

---

1   Boisson de Chazournes *in* Shelton (Ed.) (2000), p. 301. For the extent to which the operational policies reflect the Rio Declaration principles, *see e.g.*, section 5.1; on the operationalization of the principle of 'access to justice', *see in particular* sections 7.1.1 & 12.6.
2   *Nepal: Arun III* (1994), ER, §§ 69-70. *Note,* for compliance issues related to the consideration of design alternatives, *see* section 14.3.
3   *Note,* compliance issues concerning consultation with *indigenous peoples* are discussed *in* section 13.3.

as the Bank notes in its policy on Access to Information.[4] "Transparency is essential," the Bank elaborates,

> to building and maintaining public dialogue and increasing public awareness about the Bank's development role and mission. It is also critical for enhancing good governance, accountability, and development effectiveness. Openness promotes engagement with stakeholders, which, in turn, improves the design and implementation of projects and policies, and strengthens development outcomes. It facilitates public oversight of Bank-supported operations during their preparation and implementation, which not only assists in exposing potential wrongdoing and corruption, but also enhances the possibility that problems will be identified and addressed early on.[5]

Achieving transparency, however, and realizing the benefits derived therefrom, requires 'adequate' project-information disclosure, which, in turn, is influenced by several variables – such as the ones discussed in this section.[6]

11.1.1   Timing and frequency of project-information disclosure

In *Argentina: Santa Fe Road Infrastructure*, the Inspection Panel found that there was an "extensive delay in hiring an individual with special skills to manage the program of communication and consultation with the target population."[7] Furthermore, "community information points envisaged in the RAP were only opened [...] during the Project implementation stage, while they had been envisaged to operate since the early preparation phase."[8]

Consequently, "community members wishing to raise their concerns directly had to seek an appointment with the" Project Implementation Unit based "in Santa Fe," or "go directly to" the Provincial Road Directorate, which, the Panel pointed out, "made Project authorities less accessible to rural communities."[9] These delays also meant "that the critical

---

4   World Bank Policy on Access to Information, July 2010, § 1.
5   *Id.*
6   *Note*, for examples where the Inspection Panel found *compliance* in the areas of information disclosure and consultation, *see Honduras: Land Administration* (2006), IR, § 149; *Chad: Petroleum Development and Pipeline* (2001), IR, §§ 140-141; *and Uganda: Power Projects* (2001), IR, §§ 336-337. For examples where Management acknowledged non-compliance with respect to information disclosure, *see Lebanon: Greater Beirut Water Supply* (2010), ER, § 31; *Papua New Guinea: Smallholder Agriculture* (2009), ER, § 41; *Peru: Lima Urban Transport* (2009), ER, §§ 28 & 30; *Nepal: Power Development Project* (2013), ER, § 42.
7   *Argentina: Santa Fe Road Infrastructure* (2007), IR, §§ 131 & 136.
8   *Id.*
9   *Id.*

communication and consultation components of the Project" – notably, "disclosure of timely and complete information" – "were managed by engineering staff largely without experience or skills in community consultation;" indeed, the Panel concluded "the delays in hiring the communication expert," which further resulted in "delays" to "adequately implementing the communication and consultation program," may well be "at the root of some of the complaints of the Requesters and other affected people."[10]

In *Nigeria/Ghana: West African Gas Pipeline*, the Inspection Panel was critical of "[a]n eight-page Yoruba translation of the Executive Summary [of the EMP and RAP]" since it "was prepared about 24 months following the last compensation payment," which "effectively render[ed] its information useless to the displaced persons who needed to make choices among the alternatives it discusses."[11] Furthermore, because "the RAP was not timely disclosed," the "description of locally affected people as owners" contained in the RAP "was unavailable to those who were displaced during negotiation" and could therefore not enable the "displaced persons to make meaningful, informed choices about livelihood restoration."[12] These failures, the Panel concluded, do "not comply with OP 4.12 on Involuntary Resettlement, or with the World Bank Policy on Disclosure of Information."[13]

In reviewing the project's "emergency response plans," the Panel found these documents to be "[s]ound and wide ranging"; yet "as of July 2007," the Panel commented, they "had not been communicated to communities along" the pipeline's ROW.[14] "Such emergency response plans," the Panel emphasized, "will not be effective"

> unless communities in Nigeria, Togo, Benin and Ghana are properly informed of emergency procedures, both orally and via clear, understandable written text in a form that can be retained and readily accessed, before the pipeline becomes operational.[15]

Furthermore, while the "March 2007 [Supervision] BTO notes that WAPCo translated and distributed several documents" such as the "Safety Booklet in Egun Language (Nigeria); Grievance Procedure in Yoruba Language (Nigeria); WAPCo RAP Executive Summary in Yoruba Language (Nigeria)," the Panel pointed out that "the adaptation and distribution of these essential documents took over three years – "despite early problem identification."[16]

---

10   *Id.*
11   *Nigeria/Ghana: West African Gas Pipeline* (2006), IR, §§ 261-263.
12   *Id.* On compliance issues related to income and livelihood restoration, *see* section 12.5.
13   *Id.*
14   *Nigeria/Ghana: West African Gas Pipeline* (2006), IR, § 382.
15   *Id.*
16   *Nigeria/Ghana: West African Gas Pipeline* (2006), IR, §§ 470 & 476.

Concerning the decision to merge the resettlement and infrastructure projects into one overarching project in *India: Mumbai Urban Transport*, discussed earlier,[17] the Inspection Panel noted that the "previous Bank Twin Project approach had been widely announced and known to the public in Mumbai," whereas the decision to "combine the two Projects should have been brought to public attention as well, and primarily to the affected population."[18]

That said, the Panel was critical of the Bank's failure to "consult the Project area affected population before considering or deciding on a major departure from a previous policy position it had announced."[19] Furthermore, "[a]fter this decision was made," the Panel noted, "the Bank did not inform and explain it publicly to those affected."[20] "[B]y not consulting with and informing the very large number of PAPs of its change in approach," the Panel concluded, "the Bank did not comply with the provisions on disclosure of information in Bank Policies."[21]

And in *Albania: Power Sector*, in reviewing "[t]he Meeting Notes of the September 3, 2003" consultation meeting, the Inspection Panel noted that the "draft EIA was disseminated on July 20, 2003, in three different places in Vlora (Prefecture, Municipality and District)", whereas "over 20 copies of the EIA summary, translated into Albanian, were distributed in different local government institutions and [to] NGOs," and was also made "available for public comments until September 20, 2003."[22] Nevertheless, the Panel pointed out, these activities constituted "the only reported instance of timely provision of information" – and "this single instance of public notification", the Panel concluded, "is insufficient to meet the requirements of OP 4.01 [Environmental Assessment]."[23]

11.1.2 *Format and content of project-information material*

"In spite of all clear recommendations in support of a transparent consultation process, with adequate representation of residents' and other stakeholders' concerns," as the Panel commented in *Peru: Lima Urban Transport*, "it seems clear that efforts in this direction were not taken as very important in the preparation and a significant part of implementation phases of the Project."[24] "An early signal of this", the Panel elaborated, was "the fact that when environmental studies were published on the Web,"

---

17 *See* section 9.3.
18 *India: Mumbai Urban Transport* (2004), IR, §§ 190-191.
19 *Id.*
20 *Id.*
21 *Id.*
22 *Albania: Power Sector* (2007), IR, §§ 355, 308.
23 *Id.*
24 *Peru: Lima Urban Transport* (2009), IR, §§ 110-111.

only abstracts were included and the full versions were released much later, under pressure. Although many reports were made available online, they were frequently insufficient for careful scrutiny by the affected parties, and the additional information requested was not promptly (if at all) provided.[25]

In *Panama: Land Administration*, the Panel found that the "dissemination of project information of particular relevance to the indigenous people in the Project areas did not comply with OD 4.20," since "[n]either the SA nor the IPS" had been "disclosed in Spanish in Panama or in English at the [Bank's] Infoshop", whereas "[t]he content of the IPS was not disseminated in the Ngäbe language."[26] Moreover, the Panel added, "[a] *summary* of both documents became public only with the publication of the PAD following Project approval by the World Bank Board of Executive Directors."[27]

Whereas in *Papua New Guinea: Smallholder Agriculture*, the Inspection Panel observed that "none of the documentation associated with the Environmental Assessment"

> indicates whether any relevant material was provided in a timely manner prior
> to consultation and in a form and language understandable and accessible to
> the groups being consulted, as required by OP 4.01.[28]

On further investigation, the Panel found that "the EA and related documentation were publicly disclosed in Port Moresby and Washington [D.C.] on February 22, 2007," while the "formal notification to the public announcing where the documents were disclosed was published by OPIC [project implementing agency] in the press on the same day."[29] However, the Panel pointed out, these "documents were made available only in English, and not in a form and language understandable and accessible to the groups being consulted."[30]

The Panel also noted that a "report on the EA workshop [conducted] with Project-affected groups in Port Moresby" was "silent on this issue, but a reading of the report suggests"

> that no material was distributed before the event. The same conclusion applies
> in relation to consultations carried out in West New Britain and Oro provinces

---

25   *Id.*
26   *Panama: Land Administration* (2009), IR, § 252.
27   *Id.* (emphasis added).
28   *Papua New Guinea: Smallholder Agriculture* (2009), IR, §§ 212-213.
29   *Id.*
30   *Id.* For similar comments, *also see India: Coal Sector* (2001), IR, §§ 408-409.

during the subsequent field visits (i.e., no material in any language was distributed prior to the consultations).[31]

Indeed, Management had acknowledged "that the only information shared with stakeholders during consultations for the EA was done verbally."[32]

Information disclosure typically involves considerations of cost,[33] as the Inspection Panel acknowledged in *Colombia: Cartagena Water & Environmental Management*. In this instance, however, the Panel was critical of a decision taken by the project implementing agency to contract "a local company" to "implement the [project's] communication strategy" since this company "produce[d] documentaries, videos and glossy brochures."[34]

Such an "expensive strategy," the Panel commented, "may have worked well for the urban Cartagena beneficiaries, but has scarcely penetrated to the affected communities who submitted the Request to the Panel."[35] "The main brochure costs about US$15 each," the Panel explained, which meant that "so few copies were printed" that "allegedly not one was seen in the affected villages."[36] On the other hand, the Panel pointed out, "[t]he strategy of producing many simple leaflets, posters and cartoons may have been overlooked."[37]

The Inspection Panel was particularly critical of the *India: Mumbai Urban Transport* project's reliance on disseminating project-information via "the use of Internet."[38] "Communication through the Internet has been helpful to a small section of the middle income PAHs along the SCLR and the JVLR", the Panel commented; yet, "according to the RAP,"

> nearly all PAHs are squatters and nearly half of them are below the poverty
> line. PAPs from the above mentioned socio-economic background are not
> computer literate. Therefore, disclosure of information via executive summaries
> posted on MMRDA's website is not accessible to them.[39]

The Panel proceeded by pointing to "additional efficient means of informing the PAPs", such as "advertisements on local radio and/or TV,"

---

31   *Id.*
32   *Id.*
33   *See e.g.,* Woods's comments *at* note, 69, Ch. 11.
34   *Colombia: Cartagena Water & Environmental Management* (2004), IR, § 236.
35   *Id. Note,* the Request was submitted by "Corporación Cartagena Honesta, a local NGO, acting on its own behalf and on behalf of 125 residents of Punta Canoa, 139 residents of Arroyo de Piedra, 41 residents of Manzanillo and 119 residents of Cartagena." (*See* ER, § 2.)
36   *Colombia: Cartagena Water & Environmental Management* (2004), IR, § 236.
37   *Id.*
38   *India: Mumbai Urban Transport* (2004), IR, §§, 353-354.
39   *Id.*

announcements on loudspeakers in slum areas or areas marked for vacating prior to the start of the BSES or widely circulated newspapers in English and vernacular media. Newspapers could have been particularly useful for circulating details, like areas marked for demolition. Furthermore, information would have been more genuine and meaningful if disclosure to PAPs had included the specifics on road alignments and copies of the BSES.[40]

In *Nigeria/Ghana: West African Gas Pipeline*, the Inspection found that the "EA documentation" to be "all of good quality", but it was "written in sound technical English" that "require[ed] a high degree of education to be fully comprehended."[41] Hence, while the "EIA reports were made available to the public and to stakeholders as required by the OP 4.01," the Panel concluded that "no documentation has been seen that would meet the OP 4.01 paragraph 15 requirement," which stipulates that "the borrower provides relevant material in a timely manner prior to consultation and in a form and language *that are understandable and accessible to the groups being consulted.*"[42]

Indeed, the accessible format of project documentation can also be of importance to the Bank's own decision-makers, especially during the project appraisal and approval stages. In its 2001 investigation of *Uganda: Power Projects*, for example, the Panel acknowledged that the "economic and financial appraisal contain[ed] much analysis that ha[d] been carried out with considerable technical skill."[43] However, the Panel explained, "questions that have arisen" in the course of the Panel investigation

relate mainly to whether the analysis and its presentation have been carried far enough, and whether the appraisal gave sufficient consideration to the Project alternatives and downside risks of the Project and their mitigation.[44]

In this regard, the Panel concluded that the Summary of Economic Due Diligence, "although achieving much"

---

40   *Id.* In this regard, *also see* Naudé Fourie (2014), commenting on the public availability of Inspection Panel practice material via the Internet: "It might appear to some as though I am stating the obvious (while others might have difficulty to comprehend the continuing significance of this challenge), but it has to be emphasized: merely stating that 'documents are available on the Internet' does not necessarily mean the material is accessible in practice – in particularly not by those who might have the most urgent need of such access. And even where Internet access is available, downloading only a few documents can be a painstakingly slow and expensive process in many countries [...]."

41   *Nigeria/Ghana: West African Gas Pipeline* (2006), IR, § 344.

42   *Id.* (emphasis added).

43   *Uganda: Power Projects* (2001), IR, §§ 210-211.

44   *Id.* On compliance issues related to the consideration of design alternatives, *also see* section 14.3.

in summarizing the results of many substantial, complex documents, does not always succeed in conveying transparently the essence of the analysis in areas that are clearly controversial.[45]

"[S]uch a lack of transparency", the Panel commented,

is inappropriate when dealing with areas of high sensitivity: to reach an informed judgment, concerned stakeholders need to be able to appreciate both the complexity of the appraisal problem and the sophistication with which the Bank has addressed it. In addition, the SEDD does not always make clear the documentary origin of the analysis that it summarizing.[46]

With regard to 'content' – or, 'what' is disclosed – project-affected people require access to a variety of different information, including information that the Bank, borrowers and project implementing agencies might deem (politically or commercially) 'sensitive'.[47]

During the Panel's 2001 investigation of *Uganda: Power Projects*, it also considered the disclosure of information related to the project's economic risks. In this regard, the Panel was critical of a decision to exclude the Acres Group's Report on "Economic Review of the Bujagali Hydropower Project" (the 'Acres Report') from public disclosure. This report, the Panel contended, was prepared by an external "consultancy firm for the benefit of IFC and IDA" and should therefore

be regarded as a "feasibility study, including cost-benefit analyses", which is listed in the OM [on Disclosure][48] as an example of the documents for a public disclosure. Furthermore, because [the] Acres Report was prepared for IFC and IDA as the basis for their involvement in the financing of the Project, the restrictions on the "confidential material that could compromise govern-ment/Bank interactions" seem not to be applicable to it.[49]

---

45 *Uganda: Power Projects* (2001), IR, §§ 210-211.
46 *Id. Note*, this example also demonstrates the Panel's contribution to strengthening institutional governance, as discussed *in* section 7.1.4. On the Panel's 'editing function', *also see* Hale's comments *at* 188, Ch. 7.
47 *Note*, with the Bank's adoption of the 2010-version of its policy on Access to Information, the Bank's approach changed to one where *all* documents were, in principle, publically accessible, while all types of information specifically *exempted* from this requirement had to be clearly listed. For the types of information that is currently exempt from the Bank's requirements on information disclosure, *see*: http://go.world-bank.org/OJ15TX6G00. *Also note* that the new version of the policy instituted an appeals procedure – *see* note 21, Ch. 5.
48 The Panel is referring to 'OM: Disclosure of Factual Technical Documents', dated 20 June 1994.
49 *Uganda: Power Projects* (2001), IR, §§ 331-332.

"Given the increase in private-public partnerships and issues relating to access to information in this context," as the Panel commented during its 2007 investigation of *Uganda: Power Projects*, the Bank "might incur reputational risks that are thus far not adequately handled."[50] Hence, the Panel reiterated "the importance"

> of clarifying Bank policy concerning the disclosure of all project-related documents. This is of particular relevance in public-private partnership projects where some of the documents may be concluded among private parties relying on Bank financial support.[51]

While in *Ghana: Second Urban Environment Sanitation*, the Panel was critical of the fact that information concerning the planned location of the Kwabenya landfill – which was a highly controversial issue and also a primary concern of the Requesters – was not included in several official announcements.[52] Neither "the World Bank Press Release of April 2004, a key document announcing the proposed funding" for the project nor "the first official document on the project following the Community's direct protest", as the Panel explained, "made [any] mention" of it.[53] Indeed, the Panel commented, "[i]t was not until June 2004 that the Minister announced [...] that the Bank had agreed in late 2003 to fund the building of a landfill at Kwabenya."[54]

"Accurate information," the Panel emphasized, "is the key for effective consultation, and such inaccuracies in Bank documents may have generated more mistrust and pushed the parties apart."[55]

Inspection Panel practice also illustrates that access to information not only facilitates the informed participation of project-affected people – as discussed in the next section – but can also shape the perceptions and expectations of project-affected people about issues such as a project's modality and development objectives, the nature and extent of project benefits that will be realized, and the nature and extent of compensation that will be provided to mitigate the project's adverse effects.

---

50   *Uganda: Power Projects* (2007), IR, § 632.
51   *Id. Note*, this example also illustrates the Panel's contribution towards institutional strengthening by providing policy advice – as discussed *in* section 7.1.5.
52   *Note*, the location of the Kwabenya sanitary landfill was a core concern of the Requesters, as they feared that it would cause "the possible pollution of their water supply [and thus] will result in an involuntary displacement of much of the community and leave many of the remainder of the community living in conditions detrimental to their health." (*See Ghana: Second Urban Environment Sanitation* (2007), ER, § 8.)
53   *Ghana: Second Urban Environment Sanitation* (2007), IR, § 174.
54   *Id.*
55   *Id. Note*, the Panel recognized (at IR, § 171) "that attempts were made by the Government to consult with the affected population. However, [...] the level of tension between the local community and project authorities increased, and this affected the ability to have a structured consultation process in accordance with Bank Policy."

In *India: Coal Sector*, for instance, the Panel observed that "nearly half the [project-affected people] wanted and expected jobs in the mine," which was a highly unrealistic expectation.[56] Hence, the Panel noted, it was "surprise[ing] to observe that, in 1994, the PAPs were allowed to express a preference"

> for a job in CCL ['the mine'], regardless of the size of their land holding, considering that, during Project Preparation, Management itself made the point that CCL was the only subsidiary that was "unlikely to be able to offer any jobs to affected people."[57]

"Management had 'failed to notice'," the Panel elaborated, "that 223 EPAPs in Parej East wanted a job in the mine, "

> while the RAP stated clearly that only 15 of them qualified for one. [...] Management also failed to notice that the PAPs who wanted jobs expressed no alternative if a job was not available. The Panel believes that if Parej East had been a stand-alone Bank project, instead of one of fourteen subprojects, the Bank appraisal review of the RAPs would have picked up this very misleading message being given to the PAPs.[58]

It is "quite understandable," the Panel commented, "that PAPs who opted for jobs in June 1994"

> should naturally expect to receive those jobs. Nor is it surprising that those who owned less than two acres continued to demand and expect jobs for land. It must have been a shock for them to discover otherwise when finally presented with the reality of their situation in early 1997.

Hence, the Panel concluded, "Management was not in compliance with paragraph 30(e) of OD 4.30 during preparation and appraisal of the Parej East RAP.[59]

In *Colombia: Cartagena Water & Environmental Management*, the Panel found that the project's "compensatory measures" had been "inadequately disseminated to the villages" of the "North zone communities."[60] Hence, these communities "have been suffering from

---

56 *India: Coal Sector* (2001), IR, §§ 223-224, 227. For an overview of *India: Coal Sector, see* Nurmukhametova (2006), pp. 402-405; *and* Naudé Fourie (2014), pp. 167-178.

57 *Id.*

58 *Id.* For similar comments related to the merger of the infrastructure and resettlement projects in *India: Mumbai Urban Transport, see* section 9.3.

59 *India: Coal Sector* (2001), IR, §§ 223-224, 227.

60 *Colombia: Cartagena Water & Environmental Management* (2004), IR, § 224.

fears of low benefits and potentially big costs as a result of this Project."[61] There was a "real fear of major potential negative impacts of the project," the Panel emphasized, whereas the "Requesters feel resentment that this compensation has not been agreed on and clarified."[62] The Panel also pointed out that "[m]any people seem not to be aware about the details of the benefits they are supposed to receive, including their timing."[63]

The "Afro-Colombian communities" (from where the Request had originated) "seem[ed] to have been considered less important than the major beneficiaries of Cartagena", the Inspection Panel included, since "[t]hey are relatively small in numbers, quiet, weak in political power, and lack voice in decisions that affect them severely."[64] These communities "may be exposed to significant risks under the project", and although "[s]ome compensation for the potential impacts is provided under the Project, e.g. water and sanitation services, in accord with OD 4.01," the Panel also found "that details about some of the compensation measures are not specific," whereas it was also "unclear"

> whether appropriate financial arrangements have been made to implement benefits, such as sanitation services and maintenance and operation of community centers. The Panel also finds that implementation of these measures seems to be lagging behind.[65]

The Inspection Panel observed in *Cameroon: Petroleum Development* that many of the Requesters' concerns regarding compensation were not related to "the amount of compensation offered or the procedure for its implementation," but were rather a reflection of their "unfulfilled hopes of obtaining more benefits from the project than was offered."[66] As a "COTCO representative" told the Panel:

> when we surveyed villages and mapped the location of water sources, people mistakenly assumed we would come back and build them permanent wells. When we did not do this, they were angry and disappointed with us.[67]

---

61   *Id.*
62   *Id.*
63   *Id.*
64   *Colombia: Cartagena Water & Environmental Management* (2004), IR, § 223. *Note*, this example also demonstrates the Panel's contribution towards giving project-affected people 'voice' by making the adverse effects they are suffering 'real' – as discussed *in* section 7.1.1.
65   *Colombia: Cartagena Water & Environmental Management* (2004), IR, § 223. *Note*, this example also demonstrates an imbalance between 'technical' and 'non-technical' project components, as discussed *in* section 9.2. On compliance issues related to compensation and livelihood restoration involving involuntary resettlement contexts, *also see* sections 12.3 & 12.5.
66   *Cameroon: Petroleum* (2002), IR, §§ 178-179.
67   *Id.*

While the Panel found "the design and implementation of the compensation policy and the grievance mechanism to be orderly, transparent, and fair," it nevertheless emphasized that "communication among the parties could have been more effective" to manage unrealistic expectations held by project-affected people.[68]

As Woods comments, "transparency of selected data, policy or considerations – and not of others – can distort decision-making or perceptions of it"; hence, "[c]areful consideration and balance in what is made available is essential."[69]

11.1.3   The context of project-information disclosure activities

The context or physical setting in which information is provided to affected people can be a considerable obstacle to the providing adequate access to information at the project level.

"[E]nforcing [the] release of information in borrowing countries" was a "serious problem," as the Inspection Panel commented in *Nepal: Arun III*, since there was often "a gap in the availability of information in Washington," at World Bank Head Quarters, "and in the country where the project is located" – "in particular in the actual project area."[70] The establishment of country-based 'Public Information Centres' (PICs) was therefore an important mechanism through which project information could be locally disseminated to project-affected people. However, Inspection Panel practice often points to factors that affect the effectiveness of these PICs – especially from the perspective of vulnerable groups within the project area.

In *India: Mumbai Urban Transport*, for example, the Inspection Panel recognized that PICs were located at the project implementing agency's offices and at "the resettlement site", but pointed out that both PICs were "distant from affected communities."[71] Moreover, "even when other PICs closer to the affected areas were established," the Panel noted that its subsequent field visit "found them either to be closed or not containing usable information."[72] While the Panel acknowledged the importance of "recent efforts to improve the situation by putting trained attendants in the PICs" as well as to "improve PIC opening hours and accessibility", the Panel cautioned that "problems remain."[73]

---

68   *Id.*
69   Woods (2001), pp. 90-91.
70   *Nepal: Arun III* (1994), ER, § 67.
71   *India: Mumbai Urban Transport* (2004), IR, §§ 348-349.
72   *Id.*
73   *Id. Note*, this example also demonstrates that the mere filing of Inspection Panel Requests can trigger Bank and/or Borrower corrective/remedial actions – as discussed *in* section 7.1.1.

As a result of these issues, the Panel underscored, "the PICs did not operate effectively during the crucial period when people needed to be informed about the Project."[74] Subsequently, the "dissemination of substantive information about the Project was neither timely nor effective."[75]

In *India: Coal Sector*, the Inspection Panel noted that Bank "Management [had] ensured that the SEIA and the Parej East EAP and RAP were placed in the Bank's PICs in Washington and New Delhi before [project] appraisal."[76] However, the Panel added, it had "failed to ensure that the reports were available in Parej East"

> at a public place accessible to affected groups and local NGOs for their review
> and comment, [while] not even a Summary of their conclusions [was provided]
> 'in a form and language meaningful to the groups being consulted,' as required
> by OD 4.01/BP 17.50.[77]

Furthermore, the Panel noted that the country-based PIC was located in the project implementing agency's "gated" "Headquarters' compound" – a situation that did not "facilitate information being provided "[…] in a timely manner and in a form that is meaningful for, and accessible to, the groups being consulted," as required by paragraph 21 of OD 4.01."[78] "On the contrary," the Inspection Panel underscored, "for poor, vulnerable and now dependent people,"

> it is clearly intimidating to approach an office in that location, let alone walk
> in and freely request information, register complaints and engage in dialogue.[79]

While there are often significant logistical complexities involved in operationalizing the principle of access to information, the Inspection Panel generally emphasizes that the challenges presented by different operational realities do not diminish the need for access to information – and might, in fact, intensify its significance.

In *Democratic Republic of Congo: Transitional Support*, for instance, the Inspection Panel acknowledged that there were "high logistical challenges"

---

74 *India: Mumbai Urban Transport* (2004), IR, § 355. On issues specifically related to the disclosure of information about project-level grievance mechanisms, *see* section 12.6.

75 *India: Mumbai Urban Transport* (2004), IR, § 355.

76 *India: Coal Sector* (2001), IR, § 394.

77 *Id.*

78 *India: Coal Sector* (2001), IR, §§ 408-409.

79 *Id.*

to disclosure and distribution of information in DRC, due to its sheer size and scale, as well as enormous constraints relating to transportation, communication and, in many cases, security.[80]

"Bearing [these challenges] in mind," however, the Inspection Panel "expresse[ed] its concern that information relating to the Forest Code, a foundation for actions under the [project], has not yet reached many of the indigenous Pygmy people living in the forest."[81]

In its response to the Requested filed concerning *Pakistan: National Drainage Program*, Bank management acknowledged that the project "was not in compliance with BP 17.50, Disclosure of Operational Information," because the "DSEA was not disclosed prior to appraisal at the Infoshop and no records of disclosure in country could be located."[82] The Inspection Panel, while taking note of this statement, elaborated "that Management actively ensured that Project information was provided to farmer beneficiaries," but failed to make the same efforts for other affected people in southern Sindh."[83] "The Panel recognize[ed]"

> that information disclosure in the region involves significant logistical difficul-
> ties. At the same time, local people affected by the Project face major obstacles
> in gaining access to Project-related information that is of vital significance to
> them.[84]

The World Bank "policy on disclosure requires that most Bank documents be made available to the public upon request;"[85] however, the Panel elaborated, "[t]his does not mean that Management distributes these documents widely or always free of charge."[86] Indeed, "[t]hose who want to obtain documents need to make their request to the Bank," which implies that they must be aware of the existence of particular documents, and "indicate the specific documents they would like."[87]

On the other hand, the operationalization of the principle of access to information also places an 'active' (as opposed to an entirely 'passive') obligation on the Bank. In *Lesotho/South Africa: Highlands Water*, for instance, Management argued that the "disclosure requirements stipulated under BP 17.50" did "not require"

---

80 *Democratic Republic of Congo: Transitional Support* (2005), IR, § 325.
81 *Id. Also see* the Panel's comments about the *DRC* case *in* section 9.2.
82 *Pakistan: National Drainage Program* (2004), IR, §§ 552-553.
83 *Id.*
84 *Id. Note*, this example also demonstrates the need for differentiated approaches in project scenarios involving diverse interests among project-affected people – as discussed *in* section 9.3.
85 *Pakistan: National Drainage Program* (2004), IR, § 544.
86 *Id.*
87 *Id.* This example also demonstrates the Inspection Panel acknowledgement of the 'limits' to World Bank accountability – on the content and scope of World Bank accountability, *see* Ch. 4.

the Bank to provide open and full access to the Bank's project files to the public
or to the Requesters, as they had claimed. In keeping with the letter and spirit
of BP 17.50, the staff advised the Requesters to contact the Public Information
Center (now the Infoshop) to obtain all information pertaining to the Project
that was available for release to the public in accordance with the provisions
of BP 17.50.[88]

The Inspection Panel, however, was "not satisfied" that Management has complied in full
with the provisions of this paragraph" by merely referring project-affected people to the
Infoshop.[89]

11.2   'MEANINGFUL' PARTICIPATION OR CONSULTATION

"The concept of participatory development", as Miller-Adams comments, "is based on the
simple idea"

that development agencies should pay closer attention to the individuals and
groups affected by a development project and involve them in its design and
implementation. While participation is ultimately something done by individuals, much of the Bank's work along these lines involves communities of individuals and the NGOs that represent them. The Bank's rationale for this new
approach is largely pragmatic: "[to] improve the quality, effectiveness and
sustainability of projects, and strengthen ownership and commitment of governments and stakeholders" [...]. In other words, by ensuring that its projects
are not imposed from above but are responsive to the needs of the communities
they affect, the Bank improves their prospects for success, and hence its own.[90]

---

88   *Lesotho/South Africa: Highlands Water* (1999), MR, § 9.
89   *Lesotho/South Africa: Highlands Water* (1999), ER, § 25.
90   Miller-Adams (1999), p. 70. On different forms of participation, *see e.g.*, Ebbesson *in* Bodansky et al. (Eds.)
     (2007), pp. 682-683: "[...] individuals and groups can increase their general awareness; express their views;
     influence and engage themselves in law- and policy-making; affect decision-making concerning specific
     activities, plans, and programmes; trigger reviews of administrative decisions; and/or have existing laws
     enforced." *Also see* Ebrahim (2003), p. 818: "At one level, participation refers to information about a planned
     project being made available to the public, and can include public meetings or hearings, surveys, or a formal
     dialogue on project options. [...] A second level of participation includes public involvement in actual
     project-related activities, and it may be in the form of community contribution toward labor and funds for
     project implementation, and possibly in the maintenance of services or facilities. At a third level, citizens
     are able to negotiate and bargain over decisions with NGOs or state agencies, or even hold veto power over
     decisions. At this level, citizens are able to exercise greater control over local resources and development
     activities. Finally, at a fourth tier of participation, are people's own initiatives which occur independently of
     NGO- and state-sponsored projects."

Operationalizing the principle of participation, however, requires 'meaningful' consultation with project-affected people and NGOs, which, in turn, is dependent on similar variables than those discussed in the context of information disclosure.[91]

11.2.1   Timing and frequency of consultation

As with information disclosure, consultation processes need to be initiated 'timely', and, as Inspection Panel practice indicates, 'the sooner the better'. As noted in the previous chapter, the Inspection Panel is generally critical of approaches that might increase the risk of (certain categories of) project-affected people 'falling off the project's radar screen.'[92]

In *India: Ecodevelopment*, for instance, Bank Management asserted that it was in compliance with respect to consultation requirements since "the intention [was] to comply during implementation," which had "not yet started" at the project site from which the Request had originated.[93] Management added that there was "a history of mistrust between tribals and government at Nagarhole" and that the "Project [was] being condemned for the problems it [had been] designed to address."[94] In following such a 'process' or "phased approach," Management elaborated, "[c]onsultation programs have been carried out only in areas identified to be affected, and where there are identifiable legitimate stakeholders."[95]

However, as noted earlier, the Inspection Panel found "a profound difference"

> between the expectations of Management and those of state officials concerning the role and scope of microplanning and the investments which are to follow the approval of microplans. Management states that "microplans are required prior to each set of investments at the village level. (They) must be prepared by, and be agreeable to, the involved people [...] and (they) [...] would ultimately cover 100 percent of interested villages [...]." State officials were equally unequivocal in telling the Panel that microplans will not be undertaken for any of the 58 haadi (villages) within the park.[96]

---

91 Note, compliance issues concerning consultation with *indigenous peoples* are discussed *in* section 13.3. *Also note,* for examples where the Panel found the Bank to be in compliance with regards to consultation *see Uganda: Power Projects* (2001), IR, § 323; *Ecuador: Mining Development* (1999), MRIR, § 8; *and Brazil: Land Reform* (1998), ER, § 20(c). For examples where Management acknowledged non-compliance with regards to consultation, *see Kazakhstan: South-West-Roads* (2010), ER, § 42; *Papua New Guinea: Smallholder Agriculture* (2009), ER, § 41; *Peru: Lima Urban Transport* (2009), ER, §§ 27 & 30.

92 *See* especially section 10.3.

93 *India: Ecodevelopment* (1998), MR § 32.

94 *Id.*

95 *India: Ecodevelopment* (1998), MR, § 5.

96 *India: Ecodevelopment* (1998), ER, ix. *And see* section 8.1.

The Panel concluded that the decision to postpone consultation had denied "most of the long-resident adivasi or tribal peoples of the park" of the opportunity to provide "any significant input"

> on the basic assumptions and concepts underlying the indicative plan, including the traditional rights of the adivasi to use the resources of the park, the nature of future microplanning processes, and their role in the future management of the park.[97]

"[P]ast experience may well indicate that a step-by-step 'process design project' is the best way to proceed," the Panel added, but "in this case," "it does appear that" the Bank

> preempted participation in decisions on a number of basic questions, decisions which establish at least a part of the framework within which the second phase microplanning will take place [...]. Instead, Management chose to keep the project design phase at a level of generality that did not allow the real problems to appear, in particular the inherent conflicts at Nagarahole.[98]

Similarly, in *Ghana: Second Urban Environment Sanitation*, the Panel was critical of the project's decision to postpone the development of the Resettlement Action Panel since it "would have helped"

> bring to the surface the crucial and difficult questions involving resettlement planning prior to the time of Project appraisal, rather than leaving these to Project implementation.[99]

The Bank's policy on Involuntary Resettlement, for instance, "envisages a form of negotiated compensation" that is "achieved through fully informed and participatory consultation and demands an iterative and ongoing, rather than one-off, engagement."[100]

Moreover, the Panel added, "[t]he achievement of genuine participation and consultation in sensitive development situations that involve the loss of assets and livelihoods, and potentially relocation,"

---

97   *India: Ecodevelopment* (1998), ER, § 78.
98   *India: Ecodevelopment* (1998), ER, §§ 43, 45. *Note*, this example also demonstrates the different approaches towards employing differentiated approaches between borrowers and projects – as discussed *in* section 6.3.1.
99   *Ghana: Second Urban Environment Sanitation* (2007), IR, § 234.
100 *Ghana: Second Urban Environment Sanitation* (2007), IR, § 290.

raises a series of challenges that need to be considered and addressed in the preparation of a RAP. Such challenges are greatest where the individuals involved are vulnerable and where power imbalances between the state and the citizen are amplified.[101]

Whereas the Requesters in *Bangladesh: Jamuna Bridge* claimed, among other things, that 'the char people'[102] "were forgotten" – that is, the Bank "failed to include [the] char people in the process of planning, designing and implementing resettlement and environmental measures", which "has resulted in specific damages in some chars for which they have not been appropriately compensated."[103] Management affirmed that the char people had, at the time, not been consulted yet because, until "a clear erosion policy was approved, the design and location of the bridge finalized, and information available about impacts, consultation with large numbers of people would have caused confusion, [and] raised unrealistic expectations."[104] "To do otherwise," Management cautioned, "would cause confusion, unrealistic expectations and exaggerated or false claims for compensation, as was experienced on a large scale in the second phase of the RRAP [Revised Resettlement Action Plan]."[105]

The Inspection Panel observed, however, that the project documents "seem[ed] to indicate that"

> IDA did not single out char people as a separate and distinct particularly vulnerable group of potentially affected people during project and EIA preparation. The Panel has not received satisfactory evidence that the potential threat to char people was taken into account early in the project cycle, as required under OD 4.00 and Annexes, and OD 4.30.[106]

Another justification for employing a 'process approach' in this instance was the argument that the final location of the multipurpose bridge still had to be finalized. In this regard, however, the Panel pointed out that "the general location of the bridge project had been established [...] and the precise location fixed within a range of 5 kms", [b]y the time the

---

101 *Id.*
102 People living on "chars which are sand bars, or temporary islands" in the Jamuna river, "created by seasonal flooding and unstable river paths." (*See Bangladesh: Jamuna Bridge* (1996), MR, § ii.).
103 *Bangladesh: Jamuna Bridge* (1996), ER, § 11 & 35. For a discussion of *Bangladesh: Jamuna Bridge*, see e.g., Huq Dulu *in* Clark et al. (Eds.) (2003), pp. 93-114; Bissell *in* Alfredsson & Ring (Eds.) (2001), pp. 107-125; *and see* Naudé Fourie (2014), pp. 55-60.
104 *Bangladesh: Jamuna Bridge* (1996), ER, § 24.
105 *Bangladesh: Jamuna Bridge* (1996), MR, p. v. *Also compare* Management's comments with the issues of unrealistic expectations about project benefits and/or compensatory measures, noted *in* section 11.1.3.
106 *Bangladesh: Jamuna Bridge* (1996), ER, § 35.

EIA was completed in 1989.[107] "At this time," the Panel concluded, "the nature of the impacts"

> could also [have been] established in general terms and morphological models, such as those commissioned in 1995, could have been utilized to estimate the area of influence. Independent of the final location, if commissioned earlier in the assessment process, the models would have shown that the impacted area of more than 10 km where erosion could take place and where populations could be at risk. *Char* people should have been identified *ex-ante* as a particularly vulnerable group.[108]

In fact, the Panel commented, "the very filing of the Request and its contents"

> in large part must be attributed to the fact that char people were not included in the planning process, nor informed about what was being considered for their benefit. Paragraph 41 of the Request, for example, shows that these people had no information on the possible adverse effects on them. Lack of information appears to have led char people to believe that everything adverse to their land is caused by the project.[109]

And in *Democratic Republic of Congo: Transitional Support*, the Panel determined that it was "not sufficient under the relevant policies to defer consideration" of the "issues and impacts" on forests or to postpone "consultations with local indigenous people"

> more generally, to later stages of Project implementation, e.g., at such time that the zoning proposal is implemented, and/or after the conversion of concessions during the development of concession management plans.[110]

Although "consultation and appropriate action at these later stages would be critical," the Panel concluded, "a safeguard postponed in the design and appraisal stages"

> may become a safeguard denied, due to the central importance, as described above, of assessing and planning for social and environmental issues during Project design and preparation.[111]

---

107 *Bangladesh: Jamuna Bridge* (1996), ER, § 50.
108 *Id.*
109 *Bangladesh: Jamuna Bridge* (1996), ER, § 48.
110 *Democratic Republic of Congo: Transitional Support* (2005), IR, § 293.
111 *Id.*

While there is a need for consistent interaction with affected communities throughout the project cycle, it is critical for 'meaningful consultation' to have occurred before key project design documents are finalized. In *India: Mumbai Urban Transport*, for instance, the Inspection Panel concluded that the Bank had failed to "demonstrat[e] to the Panel"

> that there has been any significant stakeholder consultation before the RAP was endorsed. Though the Panel acknowledges that there have been some instances in which PAP concerns have been reflected [in the RAP], such as the height of the shops, the Panel found that meaningful consultation with PAPs on issues related to resettlement and rehabilitation did not take place. Interviews with the Requesters and other PAHs reveal that PAPs were not systematically informed and consulted about their rights and options. Bank staff interviewed by the Panel also confirmed that the affected persons did not have a chance to be consulted properly.[112]

The Panel also found that "neither the PAPs nor the shopkeepers"

> were consulted in advance about resettlement sites. The shopkeepers were not consulted about any possible alternatives to the resettlement sites for these shops. This does not comply with OD 4.30 and OP 4.01.[113]

While in *Ecuador: Mining Development*, the Inspection Panel emphasized that "a program of consultation undertaken shortly after a draft EA has been prepared, as required by the OD" – and which did not occur in this instance – "could have addressed"

> the legitimate needs of potentially affected people for information about the Project. Conducted in the spirit of the OD, it could have led to a better under-standing about what was intended, allayed latent fears, and provided feedback that would have improved the Project and increased community cooperation in implementing it.[114]

Bank management had agreed with a decision in *Cambodia: Forest Concession* "to postpone an active social assessment and consultation procedure until the preparation of the ESIAs

---

112 *India: Mumbai Urban Transport* (2004), IR, §§ 370-371. On issues related to compensation, *also see* section 12.3.

113 *India: Mumbai Urban Transport* (2004), IR, §§ 370-371. On issues related to the adequacy of resettlement sites, facilities and replacement housing, *see* section 12.4.

114 *Ecuador: Mining Development* (1999), IR, §§ 106-107. *Note*, this example also illustrates the Inspection Panel's attempts at reconciling institutional aims focused primarily on 'harm' versus those focused on 'per-formance' – *see* section 4.2.2.

by concessionaires."[115] However, Inspection Panel found this to have been a 'flawed' decision that was "not consistent with Bank policies, including OP 4.01, OP 4.04 and OD 4.20, which require early consultations and/or surveys in the preparation phase."[116]

While the Panel "recognize[d] the challenges in carrying out consultations in this early phase, taking into consideration the political and social context in Cambodia at the time," it also added that these challenges did not "diminish the importance and need for doing so."[117] In fact, the Panel underscored, "failure to meet the provisions of Bank policies on consultations"

> had significant effects on the path of this Project. Consultation with those affected by an action is critical to understanding potential impacts and identi-fying alternatives during Project design and implementation to reduce and avoid such impacts. In the present situation, the Panel finds that the lack of early consultation greatly reduced Management's capacity to be informed of critical concerns relating to indigenous peoples, resin tapping, local community ownership of trees, community forestry initiatives, and other matters of central importance to the affected communities.[118]

11.2.2   Format and content of consultation

In addition, meetings conducted with project-affected people *after* key project decisions had been taken do not constitute 'meaningful consultation,' as intended by the Bank's policies.

For example, in *Albania: Power Sector*, the Inspection Panel noted that two meetings held in April and September of 2003 (which Management considered to be "the two EA consultations required by the Bank for a Category A project") had, in fact, occurred "after the [borrower government] had approved the siting for the Project."[119] "This form of EA consultation created the appearance of consultation and of consistency with the OP," the Panel concluded, "but in reality was a 'pro-forma move,' not a genuine consultation" since "[i]t contributed nothing to improving project selection, siting, planning or design of the Project, and was not consistent with timing required by the OP."[120]

---

115 *Cambodia: Forest Concession Management* (2005), IR, § 253 & 255.
116 *Id.*
117 *Id.*
118 *Cambodia: Forest Concession Management* (2005), IR, §§ 253 & 255. On consultation with indigenous people in the context of this project, *also see* section 13.3.
119 *Albania: Power Sector* (2007), IR, §§ 343-344.
120 *Id. Note*, the Panel also noted (at *id.*) that the "Aarhus Committee has commented on these meeting in its decision and concluded that these meetings 'cannot be considered as events contributing to the involvement of the public in that decision'." On the 'IAM Network', which extends to the Aarhus Convention's Compliance

The mere statement, furthermore, that consultation meetings 'were held', even if substantiated with proof that such meetings had actually occurred, is not enough by itself to constitute compliance with the Bank's policies – the form and content of interactions with project-affected people matter.

For example, in *Colombia: Cartagena Water & Environmental Management*, the Inspection Panel concluded that "the Afro-Colombians living in the area of the proposed outfall" "were not consulted about the location of the outfall but rather only *informed* about its construction and operation."[121]

Similarly, in *India: Mumbai Urban Transport*, the Panel acknowledged that "meetings with PAPs took place" but concluded that the Bank was not in compliance since such

> "consultation" with [PAPs] seemed to be more in the nature of *telling them what was to occur* than engaging them in meaningful discussion on alternative options that might better meet their needs.[122]

Whereas Bank management asserted in *India: Coal Sector* that "Coal India" (the project implementing agency) "ha[d] made an effort to consult with all project-affected people, their representatives and local NGOs."[123] Moreover, Management added, "[a]t each of the mines included under the project,"

> mine managers held meetings with project-affected people in which they explained the program of mitigating actions that would be undertaken in the course of implementation of Environmental Action Plans.[124]

The Inspection Panel concluded, however, that these were information meetings, which "may be a preliminary to 'informed' consultations," but they did not qualify as "consultations."[125]

And in *Nigeria/Ghana: West African Gas Pipeline*, the Inspection Panel recognized that several "meetings were held with communities and stakeholders", but it "questioned" "the adequacy with which [these meetings] were prepared to engage meaningfully in the consultation process," in order to meet "[t]he requirement of OP 4.01 paragraph 15 that

---

Committee, *see* section 3.1.3. *Also see* the discussion *in* section 5.3.1. *Also note*, this example demonstrates the Inspection Panel's compliance review approach that emphasizes 'process' *and* 'substance' as necessary components of 'compliance' – *see* section 6.3.4.

121 *Colombia: Cartagena Water & Environmental Management* (2004), IR, § 233 (emphasis added).
122 *India: Mumbai Urban Transport* (2004), IR, § 372 (emphasis added).
123 *India: Coal Sector* (2001), IR, § 421.
124 *Id.*
125 *Id.*

disclosure be in a form and language that is understandable to the groups being consulted [...]."[126]

"[I]nteraction with PAPs," the Panel elaborated, "does not automatically mean that their opinions were consulted and taken into account."[127] Indeed, while Bank supervision reports described "WAPCo's communication approach overall as 'fairly open and pro-active'," the reports were also critical of "WAPCo for being 'too focused on education and public relations activities that try to sell the project rather than listening to stakeholders'".[128] WAPCo's "communication team", Management noted, "relies too heavily on its own perceptions of success rather than empirical reviews."[129] Hence, as a result of the Bank's supervision findings, the "Consultation Appraisal Mission BTO of October 2004 recom-mended"

> that the information in the RAPs, EIA s, and EMPs be concisely presented, perhaps in the form of an information sharing workshop conducted in the local language(s) between then and the final investment decision and land acquisi-tion.[130]

Whereas "Annex 2 of the Management Response lists numerous consultations on the RAP and EIA prior to May 2004."[131] However, the Panel noted, "from this list it is unclear whether the recommended presentations took place before land acquisition that began in early 2005."[132]

As to the matter of taking the 'issues, perspectives concerns, suggestions and/or opinions' of project-affected people, raised during consultation meetings, *'into account'*, Inspection Panel practice points to various complexities involved that might impede the development of consistent approaches in this area.

For instance, in its 1998 investigation of *Lesotho/South Africa: Highlands Water*, the Inspection Panel noted (concerning the incorporation of NGO views) that it was "evident" from its investigation that, "beginning in September 1995,"

---

126 *Nigeria/Ghana: West African Gas Pipeline* (2006), IR, § 347.
127 *Nigeria/Ghana: West African Gas Pipeline* (2006), IR, §§ 470 & 476.
128 *Id.*
129 *Id.*
130 *Id.*
131 *Id.*
132 *Id.*

consultations did take place between project authorities in South Africa and local NGOs, which the Bank is supposed to encourage according to paragraph 9 of the above-mentioned OD 4.00.[133]

Nevertheless, the Panel noted that "[s]ome NGOs appear[ed] to consider the results" of these consultations "disappointing, since the South African Government did not accept their 'perspective' that Phase 1B [of the project] should be delayed."[134] However, the Panel emphasized,

> 'consultation' means just that: it does not necessarily mean that the parties must agree on the issues in question, nor that the decision-makers must adopt any particular NGO's "perspective".[135]

On the other hand, evidence that such input had simply been gathered only to be ignored or summarily dismissed might be indicative of non-compliance – and might also not be in the project's best interest, since project-affected people are likely to have relevant opinions and perspectives, borne out of experience, that appointed 'experts' might not have. As the Panel noted in *Kenya: Lake Victoria Environmental Management*, "some consultations should have been undertaken not only with experts"

> but also with potentially affected people, as required in paragraph 19 of OD 4.01. Indeed, involving them in the design of the shredding pilot could have avoided a lot of unnecessary misunderstanding. And it may also have had a positive influence on the design and implementation of the pilot project.[136]

Or, as the Inspection Panel observed in *Bangladesh: Jute Sector*, "[t]he reluctant agreement of the private mill owners" with the Borrower's "decision to carry out the JSAC program" "appears to be" the product of "a participation process in which they were present but where their views were not incorporated into the final design."[137] "Whether or not" the private mill owners' "prediction" "that their difficulties have been instrumental in the

---

133 *Lesotho/South Africa: Highlands Water* (1998), ER, p. 12. For an overview of both *Lesotho/South Africa: Highlands Water* investigations (1998 and 1999), *see* Shihata (2000), pp. 147-150; *and see* Naudé Fourie (2014), pp. 87-93 & 107-111.

134 *Lesotho/South Africa: Highlands Water* (1998), ER, p. 12.

135 *Id.*

136 *Kenya: Lake Victoria Environmental Management* (1999), IR, § 46. For an overview of *Kenya: Lake Victoria*, *see* Naudé Fourie (2014), pp. 141-146.

137 *Bangladesh: Jute Sector* (1996), ER, § 77. For an overview of *Bangladesh: Jute Sector, see* Clark *in* Alfredsson & Ring (Eds.) (2001), pp. 167-189; *and see* Naudé Fourie (2014), pp. 39-44.

breakdown of the project" turned out to be "true", the Panel commented, "it is at least clear that their prediction of the areas of potential damage to their interests was accurate."[138]

And in *Argentina: Santa Fe Road Infrastructure*, the Panel's investigation affirmed "that the Requesters"

> were able to meet at various occasions with Project and local authorities and Bank staff, that they could express their worries and, as they state, were always treated with respect.[139]

This being said, "during its visits to the Project area and discussions with Project technicians," the also Panel observed that "several of the Requesters' concerns were swiftly dismissed"

> because affected people were sometimes characterized as non experts and not competent to discuss hydrological issues. While the Management Response to the Request for Inspection noted that the Requesters' concerns over the drainage design "include no engineering or other evidence to support their assertion," the Panel notes that the Requesters were likewise not provided initially with all relevant information about impact analyses to support the assertion that the project would not worsen the Requesters' flood risks.[140]

Hence, the Panel concluded that "Bank staff did not sufficiently emphasize"

> with the [Project Implementation Unit] the importance of communicating and consulting affected people on flood risks and taking the Requesters' many years of field-based experience more seriously.[141]

In its 2002 investigation of *Paraguay/Argentina: Yacyretá Hydroelectric Project*, the Inspection Panel considered the Requesters' claim that the project implementing agency "offered only two options (resettlement within a developed resettlement site and payment of compensation) and did not consider the affected people's alternative proposals."[142] As evidence, several affected people "showed the Panel copies of letters"

---

138 *Bangladesh: Jute Sector* (1996), ER, § 77.
139 *Argentina: Santa Fe Road Infrastructure* (2007), IR, § 129.
140 *Id.*
141 *Id.*
142 *Paraguay/Argentina: Yacyretá Hydroelectric Project* (2002), IR, §§ 285-286.

they had sent EBY proposing that they be allowed to purchase a site near their existing properties. They claim that this solution would be cheaper for EBY than the cost of the resettlement site houses, and would let them stay near their church and community. Some of these families could have relocated under the PDA [Urban Creeks] program but refused to move in the hope of negotiating a better solution with EBY. However, according to the affected people, EBY responded that only the resettlement sites of Itá Paso and Arroyo Porá were available at that moment and that alternative sites could be considered if and when the water rises.[143]

The Panel concluded that this evidence constituted a "failure to consider acceptable resettlement alternatives," which was "not consistent with OD 4.30."[144]

Finally, in *Peru: Lima Urban Transport*, the Inspection Panel found that "consultation was often unsubstantial," because, while "many meetings have been held," they were "consistently" lacking "adequate explanations" and also displayed no "willingness to listen to claims and suggestions."[145] Indeed, Bank staff acknowledged in interviews with the Panel that "consultations with residents were not carried out, rather meetings were held with organizations and local authorities," particularly "in the early phases of the Project."[146]

This meant, the Panel concluded, that "[i]nterested citizens,"

> did not seem to be provided sufficient information about the Project and their views did not seem to have been taken into account in Project decision-making process.[147]

11.2.3 Context in which consultation activities take place

The context in which consultation activities occur has to be conducive to ensure 'meaningful consultation'. In *China: Western Poverty Reduction*, for example, the Panel found that affected people could not "talk freely" – also not during the Panel's field visit as part of its investigation.[148] "[M]any people were clearly afraid to talk about the Project", while "those who were willing to talk about the Project"

---

143 *Id.*
144 *Id.* On issues related to the consideration of design alternatives, *see* section 14.3.
145 *Peru: Lima Urban Transport* (2009), IR, § 110.
146 *Id.*
147 *Id.*
148 *China: Western Poverty Reduction (Qinghai)* (1999), IR, §§ 119-123.

were strongly opposed to it. During these interviews, those who opposed the
Project clearly felt threatened and asked that their identity be kept secret.[149]

Hence, based on the "opinions it [had] found, and the incidents it [had] witnessed," the
Panel concluded that there was a need "for far greater efforts"

> to obtain public consultation under adequate conditions before Management
> can be said to have met the requirements for public consultation in the Opera-
> tional Directives.[150]

"The mere fact that opinions expressed were so strikingly different," the Panel commented,
"and especially the fact"

> that there was a strong perception of risk from those expressing opposition to
> the Project during the Inspection Team's visit, indicates that methods of public
> consultation used for this Project have so far been inadequate.[151]

And in *Chad: Petroleum Development and Pipeline*, the Inspection Panel noted that it was
"evident" that, "at least prior to 1997", consultations with affected people "were conducted
in the presence of security forces, which is incompatible with the Bank's policy requirements."[152] Indeed, the Panel emphasized, "full and informed consultation is impossible"
– as the Panel "has said on previous occasions" – where "those consulted perceive that
they could be penalized for expressing their opposition to, or honest opinions about, a
Bank financed project."[153]

'Meaningful consultation' might also be difficult to realize where there is a significant
level of distrust between the project-affected people and those entities charged with conducting consultation activities. Moreover, the involvement of 'independent third parties'
acting as mediators might not be effective either and could even aggravate the situation –
as occurred in *Ghana: Second Urban Environment Sanitation,* for instance. The Panel
noted that the Requesters "perceived a lack of transparency and genuine consultation"
regarding "the preparation of the RPF" and, therefore, "lost trust in the process of
preparing the RAP."[154] Moreover, the Panel commented, since "the same consultants were

---

149 *Id.* For more on the Panel's criticism of the surveying methodology employed in this project, *also see China:
Western Poverty Reduction (Qinghai)* (1999), IR, § 115; *and see* section 12.2. On issues related to the intimidation of (potential) Requesters, *also see* section 3.1.5.
150 *China: Western Poverty Reduction (Qinghai)* (1999), IR, §§ 119-123.
151 *Id.* For criticism of the Panel's *China: Qinghai* investigation, *also see* section 7.2.2.
152 *Chad: Petroleum* (2001), IR, § 135.
153 *Id.*
154 *Ghana: Second Urban Environment Sanitation* (2007), IR, § 288.

contracted to prepare both the RPF and the RAP," they "may not have been ideally positioned to gain the trust of the affected population and to ensure genuine participation and
consultation in the critical RAP process."[155]

In addition, the Inspection Panel expressed its concern with some of the practices
employed by these consultants – such as "gain[ing] access to the community through
individuals who were variously described as 'agents,' 'spies,' or 'informants'."[156] As a result
of this practice, the Panel explained, "the affected population was not provided"

> with clear information on the objectives of the survey and the eventual use of
> the collected data [...]. While these actions might have been undertaken with
> good intentions to secure potential resettlement benefits for affected families,
> they are not consistent with the implicit requirements of informed consulta-
> tion.[157]

While in *Cambodia: Forest Concession Management*, the Inspection Panel was critical of
the project implementing agency's practice of delegating some of the consultation
responsibility to 'concessionaires'. The Panel specifically questioned whether "concession
holders would [adequately] manage community consultations or resource assessments,"
especially since it was a "known fact"

> that the forest concessions were exploiting a resource which rural poor people
> (including indigenous peoples) relied upon for an important part of their
> livelihoods.[158]

Hence, the Panel concluded, "the Project's design created a structure likely to lead to
inadequate levels of local involvement, community consultations, and social and environmental assessments", which "does not comply with OP 4.36 [Forests]."[159] It was also "highly
unlikely," the Inspection Panel added, "that the concessionaires can impartially carry out
the "meaningful consultations" required under OP 4.01 [Environmental Assessment]"

> when they so clearly have a conflict of interest in the outcome of the consulta-
> tions and negotiations. It is also unlikely that such a procedure can meet the

---

155 *Id.*
156 *Ghana: Second Urban Environment Sanitation* (2007), IR, § 293.
157 *Id.* For more compliance issues related to surveying methodology, *see* section 12.2.
158 *Cambodia: Forest Concession Management*, IR, § 169. *Note*, this example demonstrates the power imbalance
between various constituency groups, which affects the proper functioning of the 'standard model' of
accountability – as noted *in* section 2.2; the example also demonstrates the effect of conflicting interests and
the tension between various institutional aims – *see* section 4.2.
159 *Cambodia: Forest Concession Management*, IR, § 169.

requirements of OD 4.20 [Indigenous People] to ensure the "informed participation" of the indigenous peoples in addressing issues pertaining to them, and
the "identification of local preferences through direct consultation, incorporation of indigenous knowledge into project approaches, and appropriate early
use of experienced specialists are core activities for any project that affects
indigenous peoples and their rights to natural and economic resources." (OD
4.20 par. 8.)[160]

Indeed, the Panel commented, "unequal power relationships between the concession
companies and the affected people"

> make this type of consultation an inequitable situation. Within the context of
> recent Cambodian history and conditions, it also makes it very difficult for
> individuals or local communities to defend their rights.[161]

11.2.4   Participants of consultation activities

Inspection Panel practice generally reflects a preference for direct consultation with project-
affected people, as opposed to consultation solely or primarily through their political or
NGO representatives.[162]

In *Nigeria/Ghana: West African Gas Pipeline,* for example, the Panel acknowledged
that there was sufficient "evidence of community participation" but emphasized that there
was "no evidence that the 2,485 households of displaced persons directly participated in
the planning and preparation of the RAP."[163] Instead, the Panel commented, "both the
Sponsor's and Management's methodologies assumed that the political representatives of
the displaced peoples would listen, speak, and make decisions for them."[164]

---

160 *Cambodia: Forest Concession Management* (2005), IR, § 344. *Also see* IR, § 346: "The Panel finds that
assignment of the responsibility for consulting with the indigenous peoples to the concessionaires, who are
planning to log the forests used by the indigenous peoples, led to a flawed and inadequate consultation
process that was inconsistent with OD 4.20." For more on issues related to consultation with indigenous
peoples, *see* section 13.3.

161 *Cambodia: Forest Concession Management* (2005), IR, § 345. For similar comments, *see Uganda: Power
Projects* (2001), IR, § 286.

162 *Note,* the World Bank's engagement with NGOs is regulated by GP 14.70 (Involving Nongovernmental
Organizations in Bank-Supported Activities) (formerly OD 14.70), which states, *e.g.,* that the Bank
"encourages borrowers and staff members to consult with NGOs and to involve them, as appropriate, in
Bank-supported activities, including economic and sector work and all stages of project processing – identification, design, implementation, and monitoring and evaluation." (*See* GP 14.70, § 1.)

163 *Nigeria/Ghana: West African Gas Pipeline* (2006), IR, §§ 275-276.

164 *Id.*

Similarly, in *India: Ecodevelopment*, the Panel concluded that the "consultation required by OD 4.20" was "clearly meant"

> to involve the "[...] informed participation of the potential affected peoples themselves." It is not meant to be restricted mainly to institute-type NGOs, as valuable as their views may be, as a result of their surveys of potentially affected peoples. In fact, consultation with NGOs is the subject of another OD entirely, namely OD 14.70.[165]

Concerning requirements to consult with NGOs, moreover, Inspection Panel practice emphasizes the necessity to involve *local* NGOs. However, there are additional complexities in scenarios where NGOs are actively involved in project implementation activities (thus, where the NGO is an 'implementing NGO').[166]

In *India: Coal Sector*, for example, the Inspection Panel was critical of the fact that "Management did not consider that it was the Bank's responsibility to listen directly to local NGOs or PAPs, while it "did respond to the international NGOs, which had actually taken up and raised the complaints made by CASS and other Indian NGOs."[167] "In its response to a letter from a group of international NGOs in 1996," the Panel added, "Management admitted that it had ignored CASS's suggestions during Project Preparation" based on the argument

> that "[i]t is Coal India's [project implementing agency] concern to consult with the project-affected people, their representative and NGOs directly. Coal India informed us that they consulted extensively with the St. Xavier Institute ['XISS', a local NGO, involved in implementation activities]."[168]

Referring to the situation in 'Parej East' (the part of the project area from which the Request originated), the Inspection Panel noted that "the implementing NGO, XISS (employed only in March 1997)"

> was located in Ranchi, and could not be considered a local NGO until it set up an office in Parej East only in July 1997. It is evident therefore that, prior to

---

165 *India: Ecodevelopment* (1998), ER, § 41.

166 On the distinction between 'local' and 'international' NGOs, as well as potential issues involving 'implementing NGOs', *see* section 3.1.4. On the complexity involving actors fulfilling multiple roles within transnational regulatory governance contexts, *also see* section 2.1.

167 *India: Coal Sector* (2001), IR, §§ 444 & 446. On the cooperation between 'local' and 'international' NGOs with respect to the filing of Inspection Panel cases, *see in general* Clark et al. (Eds.) (2003).

168 *India: Coal Sector* (2001), IR, §§ 444 & 446.

mid 1997, any consultation the borrower may have had with XISS did not constitute consultation with a local Parej East NGO.[169]

"It is also worth noting," the Panel added, that "XISS was contracted by CCL" and was therefore "accountable to the subsidiary that employed it."[170] Therefore, the Panel concluded, "it is at best"

> not clear how this arrangement could serve to discharge Management's obligation to ensure consultation with local NGOs acting on behalf of the PAPs, rather than on behalf of CCL. At worst, it places the implementing NGO in a serious conflict of interest, the results of which the Panel itself had an opportunity to witness.[171]

As to *who* must be consulted, among the project-affected people in the project area, the Inspection Panel generally acknowledges that there are limits to this obligation. For instance, the Panel accepted Management's argument in *Lesotho/South Africa: Highlands Water* that the Bank's policy on Environmental Assessment "cannot intend"

> that all consumers' of a commodity to be produced as a result of a Bank-financed project, and particularly those residing in a third country, be included in the consultation process.[172]

"After all," the Panel concluded, "tests of reasonableness and common sense must be applied. And they are not usually hard to find."[173]

Similarly, the Panel acknowledged in *Pakistan: National Drainage Program*, that, "[a]s a national-level project, covering most of the two most populous provinces of Pakistan, it cannot be expected"

> that everyone who is possibly affected by the [Project] could be informed or consulted prior to implementation. It is reasonable to expect, however, an effort to reach as many people as possible through intermediaries, especially NGOs that work with the communities in the project area, in particular where project activities are planned.[174]

---

169 *India: Coal Sector* (2001), IR, § 446.
170 *Id.*
171 *Id.*
172 *Lesotho/South Africa: Highlands Water* (1998), ER, p. 13.
173 *Id.*
174 *Pakistan: National Drainage Program* (2004), IR, § 532.

Finally, as Bank management observed in *Honduras: Land Administration*, "World Bank safeguard policies as well as the disclosure policy require the Borrower"

> to undertake consultations with key affected groups, beneficiaries, and other relevant stakeholder groups before a project can be appraised, and for both the Bank and the Borrower to disclose information to the public. These require-ments may give rise to contested views of consultation and participation, or confusion about the nature of representation. Nevertheless, the essence of the Bank's policy in this regard rests on the need for transparent information dis-closure to the public and a process of meaningful consultation. Key stakeholder groups should be involved systematically in project planning and implementa-tion, through a process of informed participation.[175]

However, Management added, "achieving consensus among all stakeholders is unrealistic. To the contrary,"

> a good social assessment process with transparent and systematic stakeholder involvement probes beyond superficial claims of uniform opinion and is more likely to highlight different views and perspectives.[176]

****

In assessing whether project-information disclosure was adequate or whether consultation with project-affected people was meaningful – whether, in other words, project activities aimed at operationalizing the principles of *access to information* and *public participation in decision-making* constituted *compliance* with the relevant operational policies – the Inspection Panel considers variables such as the timing, frequency, form, content, context and the participants of these activities.

Given the foundational nature of these principles, non-compliance with respect to access to information and participation in decision-making are often identified as the root causes of non-compliance in other policy areas – which, importantly, might not only result in *harm*, but might also serve as impediments to *performance*. For example, as the Panel explained in *Albania: Power Sector*:

> The root of many of the problems that surfaced in the Project lie in the manner in which the Bank's Policy on public consultation and transparent information

---

175 *Honduras: Land Administration* (2006), MRIR, §§ 30-32.
176 *Id.*

disclosure has or has not been complied with, both during Project preparation and also later, in its implementation.[177]

Or, as the Panel commented in *Papua New Guinea: Smallholder Agriculture*, "adequate consultation, respecting customary structures and languages and allowing prior access to Project information,"

> would have had a significant impact on the design and implementation of the SADP [project]. With such consultation at each stage of the Project, indigenous smallholders would have had the opportunity to express their concerns about the Project components and their views on alternative approaches. This process would have yielded constructive improvements in Project design and imple-mentation. In particular, inadequate consultation may have undermined the potential benefits that smallholders were expecting from the Project with regard to improving livelihoods and design of the road maintenance mechanism.[178]

"Despite the fairly narrow construction of participation at the Bank," as Miller-Adams argues, it should be recognized that it remains "a radical concept"

> in light of the [World Bank's] history and organizational culture. The paradigm that has guided Bank lending from the beginning emphasizes economic signals and technological development, the econocentric, technocentric, and commod-ocentric biases […]. Participatory approaches that require the Bank to focus on the people affected by its projects call into question this paradigm.[179]

However, it can also be argued that "[t]he participation agenda has come as far as it has because its advocates have shaped it to fit the Bank's organizational culture."[180] In other words, "[r]ather than framing participation as an end in itself,"

> supporters have cast it as a means to more sustainable – hence, more successful – Bank projects. Participation thus fits well with current efforts to improve the Bank's portfolio and shift its culture to greater concern with results.[181]

---

177 *Albania: Power Sector* (2007), IR, § 308. *Also see India: NTPC Power* (1997), ER, § 24(i); *and see India: Coal Sector* (2001), IR, §§ 56-57.
178 *Papua New Guinea: Smallholder Agriculture* (2009), IR, § 220. *Also see Albania: Power Sector* (2007), IR, § 347.
179 Miller-Adams (1999), pp. 70-71. On core aspects of the World Bank's institutional culture, *see* section 3.1.1.
180 Miller-Adams (1999), pp. 137-138.
181 *Id.*

Nevertheless, Miller-Adams adds, "[e]ven in its narrower conception, participation violates key tenets of the Bank's organizational culture:"

> its emphasis on learning from beneficiaries challenges the Bank's top-down, expert stance; participatory approaches require a different kind of project cycle; and the skills needed for working effectively with beneficiaries and NGOs are not those possessed by the majority of Bank staff.[182]

These factors, Miller-Adams concludes, "have hindered the full incorporation of participatory approaches into Bank operations."[183]

Another factor that plays a crucial role in the operationalization of access to information and participation in decision making is *cost*. Woods points out, for instance, that there are "high costs" associated with "collecting, editing and publishing information," which are often under-estimated by major shareholders pushing for greater transparency.[184] "Such costs," Woods adds, "are borne in large part by borrowing members of the institutions, since they add to the running costs of the institutions and thereby to their loan charges."[185]

However, Inspection Panel practice often illustrates that considerations of cost should not only be limited to the net present value sense of the term. As the Inspection Panel commented in *Colombia: Cartagena Water & Environmental Management*, "[c]alming down a stressed community will be far more difficult than maintaining good relationships with a neutral pre-project community."[186] While "[s]tarting a communications strategy"

> for the affected communities five years after appraisal is more expensive and less effective than starting it during project preparation, the time as it was done for the citizens of Cartagena.[187]

"[I]t would have been better to prevent Afro-Colombian consternation and stress beforehand," the Panel concluded, "by building effective and permanent channels of communication in 1998 or earlier and by agreeing on unambiguous net benefits in compensation"

> for the significant impacts threatening the Afro-Colombian communities. The compensation for tolerating the impacts should have been negotiated at the same time Cartagena citizens were negotiating their net benefits, and in any

---

182 *Id.*
183 *Id.*
184 Woods (2001), pp. 90-91.
185 *Id.*
186 *Colombia: Cartagena Water & Environmental Management* (2004), IR, §§ 239, 241.
187 *Id.*

event long before the Afro-Colombian minorities became hostile to the project. The communities voiced their concern long ago about water and dust. Provision of low-cost plastic tanks to catch roof rainwater for those households lacking capacity for storage would have been an instantaneous benefit. Sealing the two main streets in Punta Canoa from the end of the blacktop would prevent the main complaint of dust, could have boosted tourist revenues, and decreased fish handling costs.[188]

As Brett argues, "greater participation" might be "central to social development," but "it will only work in practice where it can be reconciled with expertise, low cost decision making, and discipline in organisational systems."[189] Indeed, several of the examples discussed in this chapter demonstrate that the broader discourse on World Bank accountability stands to benefit from "challeng[ing] some rather simplistic assumptions" that some of the "proponents" of participation "make about the nature of the relationships that should prevail between agencies and their users."[190]

Finally, several examples from Inspection Panel practice presented in this chapter illustrate how the Panel develop the normative content contained in the operational policies – notably, by sharpening their degree of "precision", which refers to the extent to which normative "rules unambiguously define the conduct they require, authorize, or proscribe".[191] Moreover, the significance of such normative development is increased by the Inspection Panel's approach to compliance review, which often emphasizes both the procedural and substantive elements contained in specific policy provisions.[192]

And, given the foundational character of the principles of access to information and participation in decision-making processes, normative development in these areas holds significance beyond the transnational development context. "There is no doubt," as Boisson de Chazournes argues, that the inclusion of these principles in the Bank's operational policy framework, "which are operationalized in the Bank's activities" – including those of its internal accountability mechanisms – "contribute to a large extent to the development of international rules and standards."[193]

---

188 *Id.* For similar comments, *also see South Africa: Eskom Investment Support* (2010), IR, § 228.

189 Brett (2003), p. 3.

190 *Id.*

191 *See* Abbot et al. *in* Goldstein et al. (Eds.) (2001), pp. 17-34.

192 *See* section 6.3.4.

193 Boisson de Chazournes *in* Shelton (Ed.) (2000), pp. 289 & 301. On the "development of international norms concerning public participation in environmental decision-making", *also see in general* Ebbesson *in* Bodansky et al. (Eds.) (2007). *And see* Bradlow & Naudé Fourie (2013), p. 45, arguing that "[...] the IAMs contribute to the 'legalizing' or 'hardening' of the operational policies by strengthening the obligatory nature of the policies and by adding to the precision of particular policy provisions. However, the IAMs have to balance the need for hardening with their institutions' needs for pragmatism."

SEGMENT B
COMPLIANCE ISSUES IN CRITICAL OPERATIONAL POLICY AREAS

12   INVOLUNTARY RESETTLEMENT

Involuntary resettlement continues to be one of the most contentious aspects of World Bank-financed development projects; yet, it remains an inevitable part of the transnational development context, especially in projects involving large-scale infrastructure development.[1] On the other hand, as Boisson de Chazournes observes, it is "a basic policy objective" of the Bank that "involuntary resettlement should be avoided or minimized where feasible and all viable alternative project designs should be reviewed."[2] This means, for instance, that projects "involv[ing] involuntary land acquisition is reviewed for potential resettlement requirements early in the project cycle."[3]

"Bank experience indicates", as the Bank's policy on Involuntary Resettlement reflects, "that involuntary resettlement under development projects, if unmitigated,"

> often gives rise to severe economic, social, and environmental risks: production systems are dismantled; people face impoverishment when their productive assets or income sources are lost; people are relocated to environments where their productive skills may be less applicable and the competition for resources greater; community institutions and social networks are weakened; kin groups are dispersed; and cultural identity, traditional authority, and the potential for mutual help are diminished or lost.[4]

The primary aim of the World Bank's policy on Involuntary Resettlement is, therefore, "to assist displaced people who have lost their land, houses, or both, or their means of livelihood,"

> in their efforts to restore or improve former living standards and earning capacity. Where displacement is unavoidable, the borrower country is required to prepare and carry out resettlement plans or development programs indicating the compensatory measures to be carried out, and implementation scheme,

---

1   On the 'four stages' of development lending' (which began with an emphasis on large-scale infrastructure development and appears to be heading in the same direction again) – see section 4.1. *Also see* S. Donnan, 'World Bank Chief Warns of Surge in People Facing Resettlement', *Financial Times*, 4 March 201, available at: www.ft.com: "The head of the World Bank expects a surge in the number of people forced to relocate from their homes as a result of projects it funds, as the organisation ramps up lending for new infrastructure in the developing world."
2   Boisson de Chazournes *in* Alfredsson & Ring (Eds.) (2001), p. 76. On issues related to the consideration of design alternatives, *see* section 14.3.
3   *Id.*
4   OP 4.12 (Involuntary Resettlement), § 1.

including a reference to a grievance mechanism permitting affected peoples to bring complaints, as well as a time-time and a table.[5]

However, these issues – which form the focus of Chapter 12 – are also the most prominent compliance issues highlighted by Inspection Panel practice in the area of involuntary resettlement.[6]

The chapter sets off by considering the matter of the *definition of involuntary resettlement* employed in different project contexts, which typically affects the application of the policy on Involuntary Resettlement to the particular project. Next, the chapter considers compliance issues pertaining to the *surveying of affected communities;*[7] the determination and provision of *compensation*; the adequacy of *resettlement sites, facilities and housing*; activities related to *income and livelihood restoration*; as well as the effective functioning of *project-level grievance mechanisms* aimed at resolving disputes, related to the issues discussed in this chapter.

12.1 DEFINING 'INVOLUNTARY RESETTLEMENT'

Most examples from Inspection Panel practice concern the 'voluntary' versus 'involuntary' aspect of the term – whether or not, in other words, project-affected people have a 'choice' to resettle and, furthermore, whether this constitutes a 'real choice'. In addition, projects involving involuntary (and voluntary) resettlement typically have pronounced 'move out' and 'move in' (or 'host') areas. In defining involuntary resettlement, the focus often falls on project-affected people in the move-out area, whereas considerations of the choice of project-affected people in the move-in area might be less pronounced and perhaps even ignored.[8]

In *China: Western Poverty Reduction*, for example, Bank management contended that "the nearly 60,000 migrants from the Move-out area [were] 'voluntary' resettlers and [were] therefore not covered by OD 4.30."[9] "In Management's view," the policy on Involuntary

---

5   Boisson de Chazournes *in* Alfredsson & Ring (Eds.) (2001), p. 76.
6   As also reflected, *e.g.*, in the Bank's latest internal review of the application of its policy on Involuntary Resettlement – *see* World Bank Press Release, 4 March 2015, 'World Bank Acknowledges Shortcomings in Resettlement Projects, Announces Action Plan to Fix Problems', available at: http://www.world-bank.org/en/news/press-release/2015/03/04/world-bank-shortcomings-resettlement-projects-plan-fix-problems. *Note*: this 'Action Plan' "is aligned with the World Bank's ongoing safeguards review process, and is largely based on recommendations from three reports: a 2014 Internal Audit Department (IAD) Advisory Review of the Bank's Environmental and Social Risk Management; and two internal draft working papers – Involuntary Resettlement Portfolio Review Phase l and Phase ll." (*Id.*)
7   For other examples where definitions of key terms affect project and scope, *see* sections 10.4 & 13.1.
8   On tension between the needs of 'move-in' ('host') communities versus those of 'move-out' ('resettlement') communities, *also see* section 12.4.
9   *China: Western Poverty Reduction (Qinghai)* (1999), IR, §§ 353-354.

Resettlement would therefore "appl[y] only to the 4,000 individuals in the Move-in area considered to be 'involuntarily' affected."[10]

Noting that "it is difficult to say whether the choice was an informed one in many instances," since "OD 4.30 does not give clear guidance on the quality of full and informed choice that is needed to consider a resettlement as 'voluntary'",[11] the Inspection Panel interviewed various "people in the Move-out area," and was subsequently "able to confirm that they felt they had a choice whether they could move or not, and most interviewed wanted to move to Haixi Prefecture."[12]

However, the Panel also pointed out that, when asked "to describe the Move-in area,"

> many described it as fertile with irrigation water, and having schools, hospitals, electricity, and other improvements. Most were not informed, however, of the desert climate, poor soils, danger of salinization, and the long start-up time needed before farms would be functioning in the new irrigation areas. Also, when asked, most did not recall being offered any other alternative to improve their condition except for the chance to become a migrant to Haixi. Yet, when pressed on whether they had the choice of staying or leaving, they agreed they had the choice.[13]

In addition, "[m]ost of the farmers interviewed by the [Inspection Panel] Team understood that they could move back within the first two years."[14] Yet, the project's Voluntary Settlement Implementation Plan "appears to raise an obstacle to their return" since it stipulated

> that those who do return would have to repay their government subsidy of 850 yuan, and this might be difficult for a poor migrant. The "Notice to Resettlers" clarifies the VSIP in this regard, however. It states that these direct subsidies may be repaid "in cost or in kind." If the resettler decides to move back, the subsidy will be repaid from the added value of the housing constructed in the Move-in area, which will be distributed to others.[15]

Hence, the Inspection Panel accepted Management's limited application of OD 4.30 to the 'move-in' area only.[16]

---

10 *Id.*
11 *China: Western Poverty Reduction (Qinghai)* (1999), IR, p. xxviii.
12 *China: Western Poverty Reduction (Qinghai)* (1999), IR, §§ 353-354.
13 *Id.*
14 *China: Western Poverty Reduction (Qinghai)* (1999), IR, § 356.
15 *Id.*
16 *Id.*

In *India: Ecodevelopment*, Bank management argued that the policy on Involuntary Resettlement was not applicable since the project did not "require anyone to move" – in fact, Management pointed out, the loan covenant "contain[ed] provisions which prevent[ed] [the borrower] government from requiring this in sites receiving [World Bank] assistance."[17]

The Panel accepted the veracity of the statement, but added that its "[d]iscussions with Management reveal[ed]

> that the fundamental premise underlying the Ecodevelopment Project is that the population resident in the park, including all the adivasi ['tribal' peoples], have a choice to stay or leave. They can choose to stay in their communities within the park, or they can choose to voluntarily resettle in communities adjacent to but outside the park.[18]

Moreover, the Panel emphasized, the project was based "on the further premise that these two options are true options," meaning,

> they have equal weight and value in terms of the support they are to receive from project resources. Indeed, Management informed the Panel that budgetary allocations for investments to support either option would be driven entirely by the choices made.[19]

"While the intent of the above seems clear enough," the Inspection Panel concluded,

> the reality on the ground, as witnessed by the Inspector, does not appear to support it. The two options do not in fact appear to have the same weight and value. The voluntary relocation option is very real. For historical and other reasons, however, the stay option appears to be very tenuous, to the point perhaps of not being a real option at all.[20]

---

17 *India: Ecodevelopment* (1998), ER, §§ 68 & 71. *Note*, this example demonstrates the type of conditionalities related to the safeguard policies that the Bank can attach to its loan/credit agreements – as discussed *in* section 5.1.

18 *India: Ecodevelopment* (1998), ER, §§ 53 & 58.

19 *Id.*

20 *Id.* For a similar situation, *also see India: Coal Sector* (2001), IR (ES), at § 20. For an example illustrating similar issues, but related to the policy on Indigenous Peoples, *see Honduras: Land Administration* (2006), IR (ES), pp. xxx-xxxi: "[...] Management claims that communities are free to choose whether they want to participate in the Project and 'individual communities can avoid the potential harm alleged by the Requesters by choosing not to participate in the Project.' The Panel doubts, however, whether there is a meaningful option for most communities not to participate in the demarcation and titling activities provided under the Project. The new Property Law, enacted after the Credit was approved by the Board, grants specific rights to non-indigenous peoples who occupy and hold a 'valid title' within Ethnic Lands. As a result, these non-

The 'resettlement' aspect of the definition can also prove to be a contentious issue, especially when the policy on Involuntary Resettlement is not applied consistently throughout the project area (of influence).

For example, in *Albania: Integrated Coastal Zone Management*, the Inspection Panel took note of the decision "not to apply the Bank's Policy on Involuntary Resettlement to on-going demolitions in the Project area" that were not financed by the Bank (as discussed earlier).[21] The Panel also took note of Management's decision "not to apply the policy to demolitions that might take place as a result of the implementation of the" Bank-financed project ('SCDP').[22] The Panel noted further that Bank management and the Borrower had agreed that the Borrower "would develop certain criteria and procedures"

> to assist "affected people who lose their primary residence or main source of livelihood due to encroachment removal." The Panel notes, however, that this promise becomes effective only once the SCDP is prepared. As a result, this Project design has not enabled the provision of assistance to people who lost their homes or sources of livelihood in Jale. As far as the Panel can ascertain, as of the date of this Report, no assistance has been provided to these people."[23]

However, the Panel also registered its "surprise" at reading the following statement made by Bank management in the Project Appraisal Document:

> *While some of the affected people would lose their structures and access to land as a result of encroachment removal, this neither 'result directly from the Bank-supported project' nor is such removal tantamount to 'taking the land'.*[24]

The Panel noted that the policy clearly "state[d] that 'land' includes anything growing on or permanently affixed to land, such as buildings and crops."[25] The Panel, therefore, concluded that "the kind of encroachment removal that the Government intends to carry out in the area covered by the Bank assisted Project"

---

indigenous title holders may trigger title regularization activities in Ethnic Lands. Communities may face a choice of participating in a Project which, as currently structured, they believe does not represent their interests, or attempt to opt out of the Project and face significant challenges from non-indigenous people occupying and claiming rights over their Ethnic Lands. Given the relative economic and political vulnerability of the indigenous peoples, the Panel finds that the safeguards provided under the Project are not adequate to protect the Garífuna rights over their Ethnic Lands in the context of Project implementation." On issues related to the protection of indigenous peoples rights and interests, *also see* section 13.2.

21   *See* section 8.2.2.
22   *Albania: Integrated Coastal Zone Management* (2007), IR, § 165.
23   *Id.* On issues pertaining to this agreement between Bank and Borrower, *also see* section 8.2.2.
24   *Albania: Integrated Coastal Zone Management* (2007), IR, p. xv (emphasis in original).
25   *Id.*

clearly falls within the three categories stated in paragraph 4 of the Bank's Policy. These activities are directly and significantly related to the Bank-assisted Project, even if they are not included as such among the activities to be directly financed under the Project and a demolition program [that] predates the Project's approval. In particular, they aim to achieve objectives which are declared to be the same as the objectives pursued by the Project itself – the sustainable development and proper use of the coastal zone. As such, the activities are necessarily part of actions to achieve these objectives.[26]

The Inspection Panel also pointed to the potential consequences of the Bank's decision to apply the policy on Involuntary Resettlement to "specific infrastructure investments that will eventually occur as a result of the implementation of the SCDP", but "not to ongoing demolitions in the Project area", "nor to the rezoning and possible removal of buildings that will likely result from the implementation of the SCDP."[27] Such a "differentiated approach to the application" of the policy, the Panel warned, "could lead to different treatment of the affected people with similar situations under different phases of the Project."[28] For example, the Panel elaborated,

> consider the situation of three vulnerable households, whose livelihoods depend on the houses they have in the coast, which they have built on their own land without a construction permit. The first might receive nothing if his house is demolished by the Construction Police prior to the finalization of the SCDP. If the second house is demolished, due to zoning restrictions based on the implementation of the SCDP, this household might receive a package of assistance if determined by the Government to fit into the criteria and procedures to be developed under the SCDP. Such a package may not be at the level of the assistance provided for under OP/BP 4.12. And finally, the third household might receive a full package of assistance provided for under OP/BP 4.12 if that house is demolished due to road construction or other investment financed under the SCDP.[29]

The Inspection Panel affirmed "the importance of [borrower state] regulation to protect natural resources", and also "recognize[d] that there [were] limits to the application of the

---

26 *Albania: Integrated Coastal Zone Management* (2007), IR, §§ 137-138. On the definition of 'encroachments' *also see* the discussion *in* section 10.4.

27 *Albania: Integrated Coastal Zone Management* (2007), IR, § 163.

28 *Albania: Integrated Coastal Zone Management* (2007), IR, § 164.

29 *Id. Note*, on differentiated versus consistent approaches to policy application – within project areas and among borrowers, *also see* the discussion *in* sections 6.3.1 & 9.3.

Policy on Involuntary Resettlement;" the Panel nevertheless concluded that the "objectives and content of the Project [...] go well beyond the regulations of natural resources and therefore" the policy should have been applied consistently throughout he project area.[30] "Doing so," the Panel emphasized "would have served the key objectives of the Bank Policy to safeguard the Project, the potentially affected people, and the reputation of the Bank."[31]

12.2   SURVEYING PROJECT-AFFECTED COMMUNITIES

The effective implementation of the policy on Involuntary Resettlement relies on the collection of a wide range of data about project-affected communities, which serve as critical input for implementing various other aspects of the policy, discussed later on in this chapter. The quality of this data, in turn, depends on the deployment of sound surveying designs, data collection processes, and data processing and analysis methodologies. Inspection Panel practice highlights various issues concerning these matters, and also demonstrates the often far-reaching consequences thereof.[32]

In the Panel's 2001 investigation of *Uganda: Power Projects*, it concluded that

> the socio-economic survey requirement may have been met in the formal sense that surveys are mentioned and ultimately carried out, but there is no real evidence of their use or utility in planning. Thus, the requirements of OD 4.30 have been met in respect of process but not in respect of substance.[33]

While during its 2007 investigation of *Uganda: Power Projects*, the Inspection Panel noted that survey participants "had difficulty focusing their responses to a question that simultaneously asked for opinions on changes to their lives on at least two issues over a six year period."[34] Moreover, "[t]he methodology used to assess livelihood restoration:

> did not compare the 2006 livelihood status of the resettlers to their previous conditions. Nor did it set a new 2006 baseline for future actions. This methodology was ambiguous as to what was and was not being measured and,

---

30 *Albania: Integrated Coastal Zone Management* (2007), IR, § 154.

31 *Id.*

32 For an example where the Panel found to the Bank to be in compliance with respect to surveying activities, see e.g., *Chad: Petroleum* (2001), IR, § 62.

33 *Uganda: Power Projects* (2001), IR, § 259. *Note*, this example also demonstrates the Inspection Panel's compliance review approach that emphasizes 'process' *and* 'substance' as necessary components of 'compliance' – *see* section 6.3.4.

34 *Uganda: Power Projects* (2007), IR, § 473; *also see* IR, § 259, on the Panel's criticism of the data methodology underlying the RAP.

as a result, it produced only a list of unfulfilled promises left over by the [pre-decessor] project.[35]

Hence, the Panel concluded, "[t]he methodology used to assess livelihood restoration in the context of this Project, while suggestive of issues, cannot substitute for an economic analysis of the livelihood risks and restoration."[36] "Livelihood restoration economics", the Panel emphasized, "encompasses many dimensions that cannot be evaluated using an opinion survey due to inter-respondent variation in interpretation of such a general question."[37]

Whereas in *Nigeria/Ghana: West African Gas Pipeline*, the Inspection Panel was critical about the adequacy of surveys used in preparation of the Resettlement Action Plan. "[T]wo surveys provided the only data on the displaced persons available for preparation of the RAP," the Panel noted.[38] The first data source concerned the "household and community surveys" that were subsequently incorporated into an Environmental and Social Impact Assessment (ESIA)," which covered "[o]nly 6 percent of the 2,485 households who were losing assets."[39] The EISA, the Panel underscored, "was a broad social impact analysis" that "did not specifically target the households whose lands and other assets were to be acquired for the Project."[40]

The second data source was a "survey distinct from the ESIA," which "surveyed the proposed" pipeline 'right of way' by "making a list of the names of landowners and tenants, measuring their plots, and classifying land use."[41] This "Estate Survey", the Panel noted, clearly "did not collect any socio-economic information on the land owners or tenants or their productive activities outside the ROW."[42]

Furthermore, Inspection Panel found that Bank management had "relied on analytical shortcuts to align available yet insufficient information and knowledge with the pressing needs to complete the RAP."[43] The Panel's criticism pertained specifically to a decision that was made "to use the 510 household ESIA survey" (which, as noted above, covered only '6%' of the affected households) "and draw from it a *subset of 167 households* that were losing assets to the Project."[44] "This subset," was subsequently "used to estimate the

---

35 *Uganda: Power Projects* (2007), IR, § 473.
36 *Id.*
37 *Id.*
38 *Nigeria/Ghana: West African Gas Pipeline* (2006), IR, §§ 119, 121, 123 & 125.
39 *Id.*
40 *Id.*
41 *Id.*
42 *Id.*
43 *Nigeria/Ghana: West African Gas Pipeline* (2006), IR, § 126.
44 *Id.* (emphasis added).

Project impact on the displaced households that were to lose assets because of the pipeline and related facilities."[45]

The Panel noted that WAPCo (project implementing agency) "recognized the ESIA survey fell short"

> of meeting socio-economic data requirements in OP 4.12, but claimed that this sample of a sample met the socio-economic data requirements specified in OP 4.12 with respect to the 'project-affected populations.'[46]

However, the Inspection Panel pointed out, OP 4.12 "calls for a socio-economic study of the displaced persons" and "Policy requirements cannot be met by general data on the project affected area or populations nor by extrapolation from a sample."[47]

In addition, the Panel also highlighted that WAPCo had "discovered an inconsistency" when they compared "the directly-impacted subset with the overall ESIA survey," which indicated that "the average household size of the project affected communities is surprisingly low: 3.48 persons."[48] "According to the RAP," for instance, "Nigeria's average household is 5.4 persons based on data collected between 1985 and 1990."[49] WAPCo nevertheless failed to "resolv[e] this inconsistency," deciding instead "to use the lower estimate of the directly affected number of people to calculate the number of displaced persons" – which is "fundamental involuntary resettlement information that is routinely reported to the Board."[50] Indeed, the Panel concluded that "the size of the displaced population seems to be underestimated as a result of the methodology used for their identification."[51]

"Project documents presented to the Board," moreover, stated that "owners lose *less than 6 percent of their total land holdings*."[52] "This figure," the Panel argued, "was meaningless in terms of identifying the actual risks of any individual household."[53] Moreover, "[t]he same defective methodology was used to report estimated household income losses, resulting from the loss of land, as being *less than 2 percent of total household income*."[54] "These major methodological flaws," the Panel concluded,

---

45 *Id.*

46 *Id.*

47 *Id.*

48 *Nigeria/Ghana: West African Gas Pipeline* (2006), IR, §§ 129-131.

49 *Id.*

50 *Id.*

51 *Id.* On errors made related to the calculation of compensation in this case, *also see* section 12.3. *Note,* this example also demonstrates the effects of the identification and quantification of project-affected people on the content and scope of a project – as discussed *in* section 10.3.

52 *Nigeria/Ghana: West African Gas Pipeline* (2006), IR, §§ 140-141 (emphasis added).

53 *Id.*

54 *Id.* (emphasis added). *Note,* these examples also demonstrate the value of Inspection Panel fact-finding with respect to the strengthening of the Bank's governance structure, as discussed *in* sections 6.2.4 & 7.1.4.

make substantiating compliance with the Bank Policies impossible and pre-vented Management from making a data-based counter-response to the Requesters' complaint. The Panel finds that Management did not ensure that Project planners used reliable and specific data on individuals or households affected by the ROW, rather than assumptions and averages.[55]

Consequently, the Inspection Panel elaborated, the RAP"did not contain adequate infor-mation on the needs of vulnerable groups that were to be affected by the Project in Nigeria, which includes women, the elderly, the poor and tenants."[56] For instance, "[a]fter noting that higher incomes were associated with larger land holdings,

> the RAP's perfunctory impoverishment analysis concluded that the impacts will be more adverse for the higher income people with larger parcels. The brief analysis of the vulnerability of women concludes that since 'female landowners constitute a smaller portion of the affected people, and they also lose less land than the men. This may be due to women owning smaller amounts of land. Male landowners, on average, lose twice as much land as female landowners. Women do not lose more than proportionate to their holdings and thus will not be vulnerable.'[57]

This "'analysis',," the Panel emphasized, "cannot be deemed adequate or defensible for an analysis of impoverishment or female vulnerability."[58] Hence, the Panel concluded "that Bank Management failed to ensure"

> the Sponsor performed an adequate analysis of the socioeconomic risks to vulnerable peoples. This does not comply with Bank Policy on Involuntary Resettlement, and denied these peoples the protections provided under the Policy.[59]

Finally, the Inspection Panel underscored that the "lack of adequate socio-economic data gathered as a foundation for actions relating to resettlement" was an important root cause

---

55   *Nigeria/Ghana: West African Gas Pipeline* (2006), IR, §§ 140-141. *Note,* this example also illustrates the dis-tinction – as well as the interdependencies – between primary (Borrower) and secondary (Bank) obligations, as discussed *in* section 4.3.2.

56   *Nigeria/Ghana: West African Gas Pipeline* (2006), IR, § 138.

57   *Id.*

58   *Id.*

59   *Id. Note,* this example also illustrates the distinction – as well as the interdependencies – between primary (Borrower) and secondary (Bank) obligations, as discussed *in* section 4.3.2.

for several "of the problems raised in the Request."[60] "In line with Bank Policy, effective poverty reduction, resettlement and compensation need to be based on reliable and thoroughly gathered numbers;" without this, "resettlement planning mitigation measures"

> risk falling short of what is required by Bank Policies to safeguard affected-people against risks of impoverishment, particularly if Bank Policy targets specific at-risk segments of the displaced persons (defined in OP 4.12).[61]

The Inspection Panel identified several concerns with regard to the surveying methodology employed in *China: Western Poverty Reduction*. For example, the Panel found that "[a]ll four surveys" conducted in "the Move-out area" failed to guarantee anonymity since they "required the respondent to put his name on the survey."[62] Furthermore, based on "the internal evidence of the questionnaires themselves," the Panel found that "they must have been filled out by someone other than by the individual respondents."[63] "More than 25% of the respondents in the Move-out area indicated they were 'illiterate or semiliterate'," the Panel noted, and it was "unlikely that non-literate villagers had their surveys filled out by their literate friends or family members."[64] Usually, where "1,458 respondents fill out a standardized survey individually,"

> at least one of them would normally be expected to have skipped at least one question (accidentally or intentionally), or contradicted himself within a series of related questions. This did not occur.[65]

Additionally, the specific "questions asked and the context in which they were asked" suggested "that opinions and information gathered are likely not reliable because respondents – "[i]mpoverished farmers, who are being offered no other poverty alleviation program" aside of what was offered in terms of this project – "will probably think that this questionnaire could directly influence whether they get selected for the resettlement project."[66] "Those who want to keep open the option of migrating," however,

---

60 *Nigeria/Ghana: West African Gas Pipeline* (2006), IR, § 114.
61 *Id.*
62 *China: Western Poverty Reduction (Qinghai)* (1999), §§ 109, 110 & 113; *also see* IR, §§ 91, 94 & 95. *Note*, these issues were closely related to concerns about the consultation in the Qinghai project – as discussed *in* section 11.2. On issues related to the intimidation of (potential) Requesters, *also see* section 3.1.5.
63 *China: Western Poverty Reduction (Qinghai)* (1999), §§ 109, 110 & 113.
64 *Id.*
65 *Id.*
66 *Id.*

or whose application is pending, cannot answer this survey with information that states they might wish to stay, or with information that reduces their chance of being selected.[67]

Therefore, the Panel concluded, "a respondent's indication of willingness to (conditionally) participate in the resettlement project,"

> marked on this survey form filled out by or in the presence of officials, may only be evidence of the respondent's practical good judgement in how official survey forms should publicly be filled out. It is not necessarily direct evidence of his desperate poverty. It may serve only as indirect evidence of his desire to resettle.[68]

Regarding the surveying methodology employed with respect to the "Move-in areas," the Inspection Panel noted that "the hazards" were "even greater, because respondents are being asked" – again, "without guarantee of confidentiality" – "whether they would welcome the influx of settlers."[69] "Management must bear in mind," the Panel cautioned, "that if there is even a perception"

> of potential adverse effects that could result from a truthful statement of opposition to this Bank-financed project, then Bank staff has a responsibility to guarantee confidentiality of the respondent.[70]

The Inspection Panel also commented on the project's failure to "consider weighting the surveys by ethnicity, or to assure adequate representation in the survey sample of affected minority groups."[71] For example, "in the entire Move-in area"

> only three Tibetan households were included in the survey (used here as a proxy measure of public consultation). This is in spite of the fact that the Project occurs in a Tibetan and Mongolian Autonomous Region, and the physical infrastructure for the Project (its supply-canal) passes through Tibetan villages that were not included within Management's definition of the 'project area.'[72]

---

67 *Id.*
68 *Id. Also see* the Panel's comments about the voluntary nature of the activities in the move-out area, *in* section 12.1.
69 *China: Western Poverty Reduction (Qinghai)* (1999), IR, § 115.
70 *China: Western Poverty Reduction (Qinghai)* (1999), IR, § 116; *also see* IR §§ 119-123.
71 *China: Western Poverty Reduction (Qinghai)* (1999), IR, § 95; *also see* §§ 91 & 94.
72 *China: Western Poverty Reduction (Qinghai)* (1999), IR, § 95.

Furthermore, concerning the independence of the entity tasked by the Bank with conducting "an opinion survey about the Project," the Inspection Panel noted that this was apparently "a government institute directly involved in the Project."[73] "In eliciting opinions about the Project," the Panel observed, "the Bank should be very cautious since"

> (a) respondent confidentiality was not being guaranteed and (b) there is an obvious potential conflict of interest when an institute that will directly benefit from a project is asked to carry out an open-ended opinion survey about the project from which it will benefit.[74]

And, finally, the Inspection Panel also found that the necessary baseline data required to determine the compensation of affected people were not collected. "Without the results of this work," the Panel emphasized, "it is difficult to assess the adequacy of the compensation offered,"

> not only for the Panel but also, in the first instance, for Management. Indeed, it is difficult to understand how the OD's policy objectives can be achieved without this information.[75]

In *India: Mumbai Urban Transport*, the Inspection Panel expressed its concern about the independence of the 'implementing NGOs'. The Resettlement Implementation Plans (RIP) of the road construction component, the Panel noted, were "undertaken by the same NGOs that were already involved in the Project" (on the project's railway component).[76] "These NGOs were selected," the Panel noted, specifically

> because they had been contracted to facilitate slum-dweller acceptance of the need for resettlement (initially from railway tracks to temporary resettlement sites, and later extended to the road component of the MUTP).[77]

---

73 *China: Western Poverty Reduction (Qinghai)* (1999), IR, § 100.

74 *Id.*

75 *China: Western Poverty Reduction (Qinghai)* (1999), § 373. On issues related to social and environmental baseline data collection, *also see* section 14.2.

76 *India: Mumbai Urban Transport* (2004), IR, § 642. *Also see Albania: Power Sector* (2007), where the Panel criticized Management (at IR, § 129) for "allowing the Borrower to employ the same consultant that conducted the siting and feasibility studies for also undertaking the Project's Environmental Assessment." On the potential issues involving 'implementing NGOs', *see* section 3.1.4; on actors fulfilling multiple roles within transnational regulatory governance contexts, *also see* section 2.1.

77 *India: Mumbai Urban Transport* (2004), IR, § 642.

However, the Inspection Panel's investigation revealed several critical errors made with respect to the quantification of affected people (discussed earlier), and the surveying process (as will be discussed next), which the Panel specifically attributed to capacity constrains on the part of the implementing NGOs ('SPARC' and 'SRS').[78]

For example, concerning the residential structures that had to be demolished as a result of the widening of the road, the Panel found significant "discrepancies between the information that was gathered during surveys regarding [these] structures and the actual situation."[79] Official project documents stated "that only a very small number of the structures are made of brick walls," whereas the Panel estimated during a field visit "that about 90 % or even more structures are made out of brick."[80] Affected people "interviewed during field visits" told the Panel that they

> believed that the data in the RIP would describe their structures as "temporary" structures (no brick walls, plastic or temporary walls etc.) to declare them as slums.[81]

In addition, the Panel noted, "[d]ata were collected over several years"

> without adjustment for the time lapses between different blocks of information and without a consistent definition of the household, the survey's unit of measurement.[82]

The Inspection Panel was also critical of the "participatory method" employed by the NGOs "for demarcating structures."[83] While acknowledging that these "methodologies [...] were designed to stimulate community involvement," it "made the process more subjective and less predictable" and also "substituted the population census with some form of self-reporting improvised by the affected groups themselves."[84] For instance, the Panel noted, affected people were

---

78   *See* sections 8.3.2 & 10.3.
79   *India: Mumbai Urban Transport* (2004), IR, § 288.
80   *Id.*
81   *Id.*
82   *India: Mumbai Urban Transport* (2004), IR, § 266.
83   *Id.*
84   *Id.*

asked by the NGOs to "report" numbers of families to the best of their own subjective understanding on what there was to report, how and whom to count, what is a "family", what is a "household" or what is a house structure, etc.[85]

Crucially, "[w]hen NGOs staffers counted house structures,"

> they failed to record the presence of second floors. Thus, many social and physical "units" to be counted were mis-measured, reducing the entitlement of those displaced to a measure based only on floor-space. The Panel finds that this resulted inevitably in inexact physical data and in highly conflicting demographic estimates, with negative consequences for Project planning.[86]

In this regard, the Inspection Panel also identified an additional factor to the NGOs' capacity constraints – namely, the focus "on [physical] structures and not so much on socio-economic issues."[87] The NGOs told the Panel that "their instruction was"

> to "treat income data as non-essential" and that they were only concerned about the enumeration of structures on the land. The NGOs had been instructed that the main aim of the [Baseline Socio-Economic Survey] was to record project affected structures and to list the occupants of these so that correct housing entitlements could be allocated. [...] Differences in levels of income among the affected population were therefore not given any priority. Moreover, the survey did not cover land status. Instead the NGOs used the assumption that the land was public unless proven otherwise through documents, etc., and treated everyone as a slum-dweller.[88]

Indeed, "[t]he lack of attention shown to income variation and levels in the baseline survey," the Panel concluded, "tends to confirm the 'tenement supply' emphasis in the Project's design and operation"

---

85   India: Mumbai Urban Transport (2004), IR, § 277. Also see IR, § 437: "[...] the Panel found different estimates in different documents of the number of commercial units that need to be constructed, without recognition or explanation of the discrepancy in estimates."
86   India: Mumbai Urban Transport (2004), IR, § 277.
87   India: Mumbai Urban Transport (2004), IR, §§ 282-284. On issues related to the perceived imbalance between 'technical'/'commercial' and 'non-technical'/'non-commercial' project components, see Ch. 9. On the potential for tension between different institutional aims, see section 4.2.
88   India: Mumbai Urban Transport (2004), IR, §§ 282-284.

and the parallel lack of attention paid to the affordability of houses and building facilities after PAP relocation. It also reflects the inequitable "one-size-fits-all" approach to entitlements, contrary to what is required by Bank policy.[89]

12.3 DETERMINING COMPENSATION

Compensation for project-affected people, as a result of losses suffered due to involuntary resettlement project activities, is a fundamental tenet of the Bank's policy on Involuntary Resettlement. In development practice, however, this area can be fraught with difficulty and often lead to much controversy and dissatisfaction among project-affected people.[90] This section focuses specifically on issues regarding the *definition and differentiation of 'loss'*; *cash versus in-kind replacement approaches*; and the *calculation of property replacement values*.

12.3.1 Defining and differentiating 'loss'

Compensation for the loss of assets concerns a distinct policy obligation, which cannot be obviated by the realization of project benefits. In *Nigeria/Ghana: West African Gas Pipeline*, for example, Bank management underscored the expected "macro-economic benefits, in the context of OP 10.04 on Economic Evaluation of Investment Operations," both in its Response to the Request for Inspection and in its "approval of the RAP."[91]

"Evidence of general national or sector benefits is laudable and expected for the overall project's success," the Panel acknowledged, "but does not satisfy the Policy requirements that the displaced persons share in benefits."[92] Instead, the Panel commented, Bank management "confuses compensation with ensuring sustainable development" by making "arguments that the displaced did not lose *that much land*," for instance, or "that employment is *'not an issue'* for the displaced," which "are unsubstantiated by either baseline surveys or consultation records."[93]

---

89   *Id.* On issues related to the affordability of replacement housing, *see* section 12.4. On the need for differentiated approaches in light of diverse interests among project-affected people, *also see* section 9.3.

90   For an example where the Panel found the Bank to be in compliance with respect to compensation, *see e.g.*, *Chad: Petroleum* (2001), IR, §§ 161-162.

91   *Nigeria/Ghana: West African Gas Pipeline* (2006), IR, §§ 228-229.

92   *Id.*

93   *Id.* (emphasis added). On issues related to the collection of socio-economic data in this case, *also see* the discussion *in* section 12.2. *Also see* the Panel's comments on the reliance on subjective phrases in making key project decisions *in* section 10.3.

The policy obligation to provide compensation is not limited "to people physically displaced by projects," as the Inspection Panel emphasized in its 2001 investigation of *Uganda: Power Projects*, but extends "to those who suffer other kinds of losses such as"

> the dismantling of production systems, the loss of productive assets or income sources, as well as any increased difficulties accessing, among other things, public services, customers and fishing and grazing. Paragraph 2 of OD 4.30, for example, describes the severe social, economic, cultural and environmental problems which people may face as a consequence of development projects, and paragraphs 11, 14 (c) and 15 address several factors that may disturb the resource base used by affected people: partial loss of assets that render households economically unviable, and loss of access to, among other things, public services, customers and fishing and grazing.[94]

"The Panel agrees with this view of Bank policy," it emphasized, but pointed out that it "was not applied in this case."[95] "In failing to ensure that compensation was paid, and/or rehabilitation was provided, to people who will loose [sic] their primary sources of income as a result of the Project's impacts on the tourist industry," the Inspection Panel concluded, "Management [was] not in compliance with OD 4.30."[96]

Both the Panel's investigations of *Paraguay/Argentina: Yacyretá Hydroelectric Project* highlighted the harm suffered by a specific group of project-affected people working in the informal brick- and tile-making sector (the '*oleros*').[97] During its 2002 investigation, the Inspection Panel pointed out that "[l]oss of access to natural resources that must be compensated in this Project includes access to clay deposits."[98] Hence, the Panel concluded, "to the extent that the resettlement plan provides for compensation for loss of access to these resources,"

> the Bank is in compliance with the requirements of OD 4.30. However, as detailed in this report the procedures set forth by EBY for compensation may have resulted, in practical terms, in a denial of compensation to some affected people.[99]

---

94   *Uganda: Power Projects* (2001), IR § 306.
95   *Uganda: Power Projects* (2001), IR § 307.
96   *Id.*
97   See e.g., *Paraguay/Argentina: Yacyretá Hydroelectric Project* (2002), IR, § xxi.
98   *Paraguay/Argentina: Yacyretá Hydroelectric Project* (2002), IR, § 270.
99   *Id.*

As the Panel noted in its 1996 investigation, while it is understandable "that there may be other factors" that need to be taken into consideration in matters of compensation, from an "equity" perspective, "it is difficult to regard as equivalent the compensations"

> received by the different groups of oleros, when the one in kind (housing, lot, etc.) is equivalent on the average to almost double the highest value of the cash compensation.[100]

Whereas in *Pakistan: National Drainage Program* the Panel found that there was "a sharp asymmetry in the costs and benefits" of the entire program, which comprised an "extensive and large-scale irrigation and drainage system of the Indus River Basin".[101] "In general," the Panel noted,

> the upstream abstracters of the waters using it for irrigation receive the benefits, while downstream people in southern Badin and Thatta districts incur the costs, with little or no compensation.[102]

12.3.2   Cash versus in-kind replacement

The Bank's resettlement policy encourages 'in-kind replacement' over 'cash compensation' since experience has generally proven cash compensation to be less conducive to realizing sustainable development. Yet, Inspection Panel practice reflects a tendency to revert to cash compensation, whereas in-kind replacement also involve notable challenges.

For instance, as Management acknowledged in *India: NTPC Power*, it had "underestimated the practicability"

> of implementing the land for land options and difficulties in carrying out income generating schemes. Accordingly, in the implementation of these RAPs by NTPC significant problems and delays have arisen, reflecting certain shortcomings in design.[103]

---

100 *Paraguay/Argentina: Yacyretá Hydroelectric Project* (1996), Inspection Panel Review & Assessment, § 240(b)(ii).
101 *Pakistan: National Drainage Program* (2004), IR, § 37.
102 *Pakistan: National Drainage Program* (2004), IR, § 41.
103 *India: NTPC Power* (1997), ER, § 34.

Or, as the Inspection Panel explained in *Nepal: Arun III*, "[d]elays in payment of [cash] compensation," "leads to erosion of the value of the moneys received."[104] "In fact," the Panel elaborated, "the norm in Nepal is government taking possession of land"

> prior to the completion of the valuation process, thus removing any incentive for government officials to promptly pay compensation due [...].[105]

"On the other hand," the Panel added, "experience has shown that compensation payments received too far in advance of the actual physical move are either squandered or snatched up by money lenders."[106]

However, the Panel concluded, the "need for forms of compensation other than cash is most apparent in the case of tribal or other minority populations whose ancestral lands are expropriated by the State;" in this case, however, "when the land was acquired" for the "Hill [access] route" (which was later abandoned), "the only compensation identified so far"

> was cash – no land, no jobs, and no training. The risk is that the same tragedy could emerge in the valley route [which replaced the Hill route] as well.[107]

The preference for 'in-kind replacement' contained in the policy means, as the Panel explained in *Nigeria/Ghana: West African Gas Pipeline*, that "neither cash compensation nor in-kind replacement of lost assets is a policy objective" *per se*,[108] although "in-kind compensation is generally considered a more reliable means for assuring sustainability of incomes for people who rely on these lost assets."[109] In other words, the Panel elaborated, both can be "strategies"

> to achieve compliance with the Bank's Involuntary Resettlement Policy to avoid impoverishment of displaced people as a result of the Project. Selecting and effectively implementing the appropriate "means" begins with an impoverishment risk assessment, the elements of which are well defined. Management

---

104 *Nepal: Arun III* (1994), IR, § 25.
105 *Id.*
106 *Id.*
107 *Id.*
108 *Nigeria/Ghana: West African Gas Pipeline* (2006), IR, § 157.
109 *Nigeria/Ghana: West African Gas Pipeline* (2006), IR, §§ 172-173.

has to assess the RAP in terms of meeting the three policy objectives.[110] The approved RAP is implemented, monitored, and evaluated.[111]

In this instance, however, the Panel noted that the RAP reflected "a case in favor of a cash-compensation option, as found in OP 4.12, paragraph 12, which states:"

> Cash compensation for lost assets is acceptable where "(a) livelihoods are land-based but the land taken for the project is a small fraction of the affected asset and the residual is economically viable." To determine whether condition (a) is applicable, the Policy may apply if the land taken constitutes less than 20 percent of the total productive area.[112]

Whereas the "RAP argues that all three conditions are largely met 'in Nigeria'."[113]

The Panel expressed its concern with this decision since "so little was done to inform the displaced of the land-for-land option."[114] "In the case of housing," for example,

> 38 households received cash payments, mostly in one community. The Panel interviewed neighbors who stated the families had moved on, however, there is no evidence of the Project following-up in order to determine whether or not they were actually impoverished. No resettlement assistance, apart from cash compensation, was evident. Land was available, some of it nearby this community, but it appears that no efforts were taken to educate the displaced on this option. The Project has neither verified whether the compensation provided to the displaced peoples was sufficient enough for them to purchase alternate housing, nor have the additional risks involved in transferring cash to displaced peoples been assessed, including by the monitoring units.[115]

---

110 Which are: "(a) Involuntary Resettlement should be avoided where feasible, or minimized, exploring all viable alternative Project designs; (b) where it is not feasible to avoid resettlement, resettlement activities should be conceived and executed as sustainable development programs, providing sufficient investment resources to enable the persons displaced by the Project to share in Project benefits. Displaced persons should be meaningfully consulted and should have opportunities to participate in planning and implementing resettlement programs; and (c) displaced persons should be assisted in their efforts to improve their livelihoods and standards of living or at least to restore them, in real terms, to pre-displacement levels or to levels prevailing prior to the beginning of Project implementation, whichever is higher." (See OP 4.12, § 2.)

111 *Nigeria/Ghana: West African Gas Pipeline* (2006), IR, § 157.

112 *Nigeria/Ghana: West African Gas Pipeline* (2006), IR, §§ 172-173.

113 *Id.*

114 *Id.*

115 *Id.*

In fact, the Panel concluded that it was "unclear" "who if anyone, was actually offered the land-for-land option."[116]

Moreover, the Panel commented, the cash-compensation approach favoured in the RAP "undermine[d] the land-for-land resettlement option preferred by OP 4.12 for people who derive their income from the land," as potentially applicable to "an area in Abeokuta along the Ogun/Lagos boundary, some distance from the bulk of those being displaced."[117]

Instead, the "land-for-land option appears to have been applied or made available to urban house plots, not agricultural land," whereas "Management supervision showed"

> no record of visiting or even mentioning the proposed land-for-land resettle-
> ment area in Abeokuta. No reference is made to the land-for-land resettlement
> options or the set-aside area of Abeokuta in the 455 pages of Regional Stake-
> holder Consultation. This view is reinforced by the absence of a land-for-land
> provision in the resettlement budget or the lack of a land-for-land component
> in the RAP implementation timeline. Nor were provisions made to increase
> organizational capacity for resettlement within WAPCo for land-for-land
> resettlement implementation. Management should have quickly identified
> these shortcomings.[118]

It might also be questioned, in some instances, whether project-affected people had 'freely opted' for cash compensation over alternative forms of compensation.[119]

For example, in its 1996 investigation of *Argentina/Paraguay: Yacyretá Hydroelectric Project*, the Panel took note of Bank management's firm position "that no further compensation [was] required for those" *oleros*, which had previously "opted for cash compensation" – in particular, Management argued, since EBY "has assisted some of them after they invaded public lands."[120] "Once compensation was paid," Management reiterated,

> owners of the olerías were free to exercise their discretion as to whether or not
> to continue with their manufacturing activity. Many of them opted to continue
> [...] [while] others in exercise of their entrepreneurial rights decided not to
> continue with the olería and shifted to new economic activities [...].[121]

---

116 *Nigeria/Ghana: West African Gas Pipeline* (2006), IR, § 168.
117 *Nigeria/Ghana: West African Gas Pipeline* (2006), IR, § 170.
118 *Nigeria/Ghana: West African Gas Pipeline* (2006), IR, § 170. On issues related to the identification of issues arising during implementation as part of the Bank's supervision activities, *also see* section 15.1.
119 In this regard, *also see* section 12.1.
120 *Argentina/Paraguay: Yacyretá Hydroelectric Project* (1996), Inspection Panel Review & Assessment, § 240(b)(v).
121 *Id.*

The Inspection Panel, however, was critical of this position and commented that "Management argues from a mere legalistic point of view," based on the "assumption that the oleros freely opted for cash compensation" and therefore "may have given up all other rights to rehabilitation."[122] "From a policy point of view, however," the Panel argued, "Management should carry out an independent assessment on"

> whether the requirements of OD 4.30 that "the population displaced by a project receives benefits from it" and that people should be "assisted in their efforts to improve their former living standards, income earning capacity, and production levels, or at least to restore them" are being met with regard to the oleros in Argentina and Paraguay.[123]

Finally, as the Inspection Panel commented in *India: Coal Sector*, it should be recognized that the act of "[p]resenting a poor oustee, whose previous source of survival included a small patch of land, with a check" – containing "probably more money than he or she has ever seen or expected to see in a lump sum" – "may be a legal way of getting them to move on, *but it should not be confused with development.*"[124]

12.3.3   Calculation of property replacement values

The calculation of property replacement values, including the degrees of transparency and consultation that surround valuation activities, can be a prominent source of controversy – also between the Bank and Borrowers.

In *Nepal: Arun III*, for example, the Panel noted that resettlement compensation "became a sticking issue" on the Project, thereby "affirming what the Bank-wide reviews of resettlement in all projects had stated" – namely,

> that landholders rarely received compensation sufficient to restore their standard of living, and that governments tend to rely on outdated, understated estimates of land value.[125]

---

122 *Argentina/Paraguay: Yacyretá Hydroelectric Project* (1996), Inspection Panel Review & Assessment, § 240(b)(v). *Note,* this example also demonstrates the negative connotations surrounding the formalist paradigm – as discussed *in* section 2.3.

123 *Id.*

124 *India: Coal Sector* (2001), IR, § 88 (emphasis added).

125 *Nepal: Arun III* (1994), IR, § 37. On the recent internal Bank review of the application of its policy on Involuntary Resettlement, *see* note 6, Ch. 12.

The Panel also noted that the Bank and the Borrower were not in agreement about the basis for property replacement value calculations – with the Borrower arguing it should be changed from "fair value" to "replacement value" because the employment of a 'fair value' approach "would cause financial difficulties for all the other road projects in Nepal, whether locally-funded or donor-funded."[126]

The Bank and Borrower held "extended discussions over compensation to tenants (particularly informal), and with regard to families seriously affected by land loss," however, the Panel noted, "a clear split developed."[127] "The initial proposal from the IDA staff to the borrower"

> was that seriously affected families would be "those losing more than 25% of their main source of income" – a fairly standard practice at that time in Bank projects, and a standard that has been strengthened since then.[128]

Yet, the Panel noted, "[t]he borrower never accepted that proposal. IDA also argued that the provision of land should be included as part of the rehabilitation measure."[129]

The Panel's 2002 investigation of *Paraguay/Argentina: Yacyretá Hydroelectric Project* highlighted project-affected people's objection to the employment of an "estimated appraisal" of property value.[130] This complaint, the Inspection Panel commented, was "very understandable", given the excessive implementation delays suffered by the project,[131] which resulted in a situation where "the movement of some of the people ha[d] been postponed or extended indefinitely pending the raising of the water level," while "the values of [their] homes and property [were] changing."[132]

"In the absence of a final estimate for their properties," as the Panel explained this dilemma, "local people cannot seriously assess"

> whether it would be better to take monetary compensation, take the house in the new settlement, or propose an alternative solution for an entire neighborhood of houses. Yet it is practically impossible for EBY to provide detailed appraisals until it is known when a group of houses will be moved.[133]

---

126 *Nepal: Arun III* (1994), IR, § 37.
127 *Id.*
128 *Id.*
129 *Id. Note*, this example also demonstrates disagreements between Bank and Borrowers about the content and/or scope of their respective obligations, as discussed *in* section 8.1.
130 *See e.g., Paraguay/Argentina: Yacyretá Hydroelectric Project* (2002), IR, § 85.
131 *Id.*
132 *Paraguay/Argentina: Yacyretá Hydroelectric Project* (2002), IR, §§ 267-268.
133 *Id.*

Nevertheless, since "the terms of OD 4.30 clearly 'require' a 'valuation procedure' [to be] applicable to the assets and the type of land tenure enjoyed by affected persons," the Panel concluded, "the use of provisional appraisals is not inconsistent with Bank policies."[134] Additionally, "because affected people were not consulted and did not receive adequate information about the purpose and use of the provisional appraisals there has been considerable confusion"; yet, "OD 4.30 calls for the Bank to monitor the actual appraisal values that will be paid when these properties are expropriated if the water level is raised."[135]

The implementation delays also placed severe constraints on financial resources, which affected the payment of compensation to project-affected people. Both the Bank and EBY "staff told the Panel that, because the limited financing did not allow EBY to attend to all affected families,"

> EBY tried to give priority to hardship cases, such as those who are elderly or infirm and need to sell their property in order to obtain money to treat their illnesses.[136]

However, the Panel pointed out, because of the delays, "[i]n the area that is scheduled for flooding, it is impossible to sell property other than to EBY."[137]

The Panel also commented that "OD 4.30 does not provide guidance regarding "fairness" in selecting a "proper" sequence of houses to be compensated,"

> as long as all are adequately compensated in the course of the move. OD 4.30 does establish that the resettlement plan must be "time-bound," and the presumption seems to be that, in whatever sequence the compensation and resettlement occurs, it will be done [at a] time-bound fashion and in consultation with those eligible for resettlement.[138]

"When the presumption that resettlement will happen relatively quickly fails," however, "Bank Management needs to ensure, consistent with the purpose of OD 4.30, that there is a rationale for resettlement sequencing and that the sequencing process is transparent and fair."[139]

---

134 *Id.*

135 *Id. Note,* this example also demonstrates issues related to information disclosure and consultation, as discussed *in* Ch. 11.

136 *Paraguay/Argentina: Yacyretá Hydroelectric Project* (2002), IR, §§ 279-281.

137 *Id.*

138 *Id.*

139 *Id. Note,* this example demonstrates the Panel's emphasis on the underlying policy objective, as discussed *in* section 6.3.3.; *and also* reflects the Panel's contribution towards institutional strengthening by providing policy advice, as discussed *in* section 7.1.5.

In *Nigeria/Ghana: West African Gas Pipeline*, the Inspection Panel's investigation uncovered "a major flaw" in compensation calculations.[140] "[S]omehow, someone forgot the 10x multiplier in providing compensation," the Panel noted, with the significant consequence that "the displaced people were paid one-tenth of what was planned in the RAP."[141] This constituted "a major failure to comply with Bank Policy on Involuntary Resettlement," the Panel concluded, "and to ensure that the displaced people are at least as well-off as they were before the displacement as required by this Policy."[142]

The Panel took note that both "Management and WAPCo recognized that under-compensation occurred and are preparing for another compensation disbursal" – based, however, on "a uniform rate for the entire ROW adjusted into three zones based in type of land use."[143] But the Inspection Panel was critical of the employment of a uniform rate, since it "continues to ignore"

> not only the valuator's findings, but endangers again the application of the principle of full replacement value. It is a decision that structurally may lead to over-compensation for some and under-compensation for others.[144]

Furthermore, the Panel commented, this additional 'compensation disbursal' was "being done without consultation with the displaced peoples,"[145] without

> identifying or preparing mitigation for at-risk populations, without setting clear eligibility requirements based on local land tenure, without correction for the transition cost error discussed above, without benefit-sharing provisions for the displaced population, and without determining whether cash compensation is or is not the appropriate instrument to be used to avoid project-induced impoverishment.[146]

"A basic principle" of the policy on Involuntary Resettlement, as the Panel observed in *India: Coal Sector*, is that "'[d]isplaced persons should be [...] compensated for their losses at full replacement cost prior to the actual move'."[147] In this instance, however, the Panel found that "many of the displaced PAPs" "in Parej East had not been compensated at full

---

140 *Nigeria/Ghana: West African Gas Pipeline* (2006), IR, § 184.
141 *Id.*
142 *Id.*
143 *Nigeria/Ghana: West African Gas Pipeline* (2006), IR, § 207.
144 *Nigeria/Ghana: West African Gas Pipeline* (2006), IR, § 208.
145 On issues related to consultation, *also see* section 11.2.
146 *Nigeria/Ghana: West African Gas Pipeline* (2006), IR, § 208. On issues related to cash compensation, *see* section 12.3.2.
147 *India: Coal Sector* (2001), IR, §§ 72-73.

replacement cost, with the result that many of them have suffered and are still suffering harm."[148] The Panel noted that the Borrower's "Land Acquisition Act reflects the principle in OD 4.30 that PAPs should be compensated for their land at its 'market value,'" but "in practice," the Borrower "defines 'market value' to be the registered value of plots in official land records."[149] However, the Panel pointed out, because "these values are substantially under-reported," "as a rule,"

> the principle is effectively disregarded and the PAPs are usually compensated at considerably less than replacement cost, even with the customary 30 percent 'solatium' paid in addition to 'market value.'[150]

Moreover, the Panel added, "Bank staff preparing the Project were aware that compensation paid for land is usually inadequate."[151] "The Task Manager decided, however,"

> that the issue should be dealt within each of the mine specific RAPs, stating that the 'ultimate test of whether compensation is adequate in light of OD 4.30 will be the provisions contained in the RAPs.'[152]

The Inspection Panel concluded, nevertheless, that "the Parej East RAP is not tailored to the situation at that mine and merely provides the usual Land Acquisition Act formula that is described in the Management Response."[153]

The Inspection Panel was also critical of the degree of transparency surrounding the compensation process. The Panel pointed to a specific incident that had occurred in "late December 1999" (which was the "subject of conflicting reports"), during which project-affected people "from Borwa Tola were" allegedly "shifted under suspicious circum-stances."[154] In the aftermath of this controversial incident, the Panel noted,

> the supervision team felt that in the future relations between CCL [implement-ing agency] and the PAPs would be better and transparency would be promoted if PAPs were to have access 'to the house measurement report with information on compensation valuation at the Public Information Center.'[155]

---

148 *Id.*
149 *Id.*
150 *Id.*
151 *India: Coal Sector* (2001), IR, § 65.
152 *Id.*
153 *Id.*
154 *India: Coal Sector* (2001), IR, §§ 75-78.
155 *Id.*

During its field visit to the PIC, however, the Inspection Panel could find only "a specimen of a house compensation assessment."[156]

As noted earlier, an additional purpose of information disclosure and consultation activities is also to ensure that project-affected people do not hold unrealistic expectations regarding compensation, since the non-realization of these expectations is bound to add further tension to an area that is often fraught with contention.[157] The situation might be exacerbated, however, if the payment of compensation is delayed. As the Panel noted in *India: Coal Sector*, "[t]he process of compensation payment should be quick," whereas "[c]ompensation packages should be consistent, transparent and fair."[158]

In *Cameroon: Petroleum Development and Pipeline*, for instance, the Inspection Panel considered "the compensation packages" offered to be "fair and equitable," but also observed that there was a "large disparity between expectations of local people about the rewards and consequences of the project and what the project was in fact able to offer."[159] Project-affected people "had expectations that they would receive goods or services that had not in fact been promised," which, the Panel noted, constituted "a major problem" for the Project.[160]

For instance, the Panel explained, "COTCO's Regional Compensation plan for the Bakola/Bagyeli"

> was to assist each affected village by building a demonstration house and pro-viding materials and training for other members of the village to construct their own houses. However, when interviewed by the Panel, villagers said that 'COTCO will build everyone a new house in the village,' something for which there was no evidence of having been ever promised.[161]

The Panel added, however, that "local villagers often felt frustrated with the length of time it took between the centerline surveys (1997-1999) and the payment of compensation (2001-2002)."[162]

---

156 *Id*. On issues related to PICs, *also see* section 11.1.3.
157 *See* section 11.1.2.
158 *India: Coal Sector* (2001), IR, §§ 75-78.
159 *Cameroon: Petroleum* (2002), IR, § 128.
160 *Id*.
161 *Id*.
162 *Id*.

12.4 RESETTLEMENT SITES, FACILITIES AND REPLACEMENT HOUSING

Project-affected people who are 'involuntarily' removed have to be 'resettled' elsewhere; hence, the adequacy of resettlement sites, facilities and housing is crucial to ensure that the affected people are not left 'worse off' than before the project.[163] In practice, however, realizing this policy objective can prove to be challenging.

For example, in *India: Mumbai Urban Transport*, "[d]espite the fact that access to individual water and toilet facilities have been determined as one of two key resettlement performance indicators," the Panel observed that "adequate water supply ha[d] not been established."[164] The Panel also noted that this matter had been "raised as a concern"

> during the May 2005 Bank supervision mission where the Bank acknowledged the water problem and expressed its concern over the inadequate supply.[165]

However, MMRDA (the project implementing agency) "informed the Panel that the Bombay Municipal Corporation (BMC) is responsible"

> for supplying water and expects to have water supply fully set up in Mankhurd by 2007. The Panel is concerned about the severe lack of water and concerned that PAPs have already been moved despite the problematic situation and despite the plans to set up adequate water supply only by 2007.[166]

The Panel also found "that sewerage and water connections are not working properly and there are no collections for garbage and waste", which did "not comply with OD 4.30."[167]

Replacement housing should also be affordable for project-affected people in the long term. In this regard, estimates conducted by independent experts (appointed by the Inspection Panel)[168] with regard to "Mankhurd C, of the few housing cooperatives in place" at the time, found that "each cooperative"

---

163 For an example where the Panel found the Bank to be compliant with respect to resettlement housing and facilities, *see e.g., Nigeria: Lagos Drainage* (1998), ER, § 43.

164 *India: Mumbai Urban Transport* (2004), IR, §§ 578 & 580.

165 *Id.*

166 *Id. Note*, this example also demonstrates potential issues related to the involvement of different types of (public and private) actors, as well as different levels of governance in transnational regulatory governance contexts – as discussed *in* section 2.1.

167 *India: Mumbai Urban Transport* (2004), IR, §§ 578 & 580.

168 On the role of independent subject-matter experts contracted by the Panel in support of its fact-finding and compliance review functions, *see e.g.*, section 5.4.

has a remaining average liability of more than Rs. 6,000 on behalf of individual households after the interest income from the Rs. 20.000 lump sum has been disbursed to meet the charges. The remaining average individual debt thus equals two to three months of gross income for the average resettled household and is not a liability that households can plausibly discharge.[169]

"During the Panel's site visits, several PAPs told the Panel"

that due to their severe economic situation and because they would no longer be able to fund their children's education, they seriously considered moving out of the new flat. In discussion with the Panel, PAPs in a building in Anik-Rockline estimated that about forty to fifty residents of the building (nearly a third to half) have sold their ornaments and even their marriage necklaces (*mangal sutra*) to pay the charges they are facing.[170]

Hence, the Panel concluded, "OD 4.30's most basic requirement that PAPs must be assisted in their efforts to improve their living standards or at least to restore them"

has not been achieved with regard to the affordability of housing maintenance. Housing standards may be better at the resettlement sites but basic living and maintenance costs are not affordable for many of the PAPs.[171]

Emphasizing the importance of the underlying policy objectives, the Panel also found that the project's Resettlement Action Plan was "conceived very narrowly," "as if mostly for a re-housing component"

and not as one where the fundamental policy objective is an improvement in standards of living that will necessarily include the need for income restoration. Housing is integral to livelihood and to standards of living, but without an income with which to buy food, basic expenses, health and education, and to pay the costs of modern housing, the flat cannot be afforded and PAPs are likely to be worse off than before. The Panel observes that the PAPs' standards

---

169 *India: Mumbai Urban Transport* (2004), IR, §§ 535 & 540.
170 *Id. Note*, this example also demonstrates the value of recourse to the Inspection Panel mechanism in terms of making the harm suffered by project-affected people concrete or 'real' – as discussed *in* section 7.1.1.
171 *India: Mumbai Urban Transport* (2004), IR, §§ 535 & 540.

of living are falling, even though the flats and their sanitation provisions are much improved and much appreciated.[172]

After having visited the "resettlement site where some people from the BKL area have relocated" as part of its investigation in *Cambodia: Land Management and Administration*, the Inspection Panel observed that "the conditions of the site are well below the standards provided for in the Bank Policy on Involuntary Resettlement."[173]

"While there is a school, a hospital, electricity, and water," the Panel acknowledged, "there were complaints about access;" but the "primary complaint" related to the fact "that the resettlement site" was

> too far away from their previous sources of income and no adequate alternative income generation opportunities are available at or near the site. A market provides basic services and livelihoods, though incomes are generally much lower because the majority is forced to spend considerable time and scarce resources on commuting to their jobs in the city.[174]

Whereas in *India: Coal Sector*, the Inspection Panel was particularly critical of temporary resettlement housing provided for certain project-affected people, describing these facilities "hardly fit for human habitation, especially [for] families."[175] Moreover, the Panel observed, several affected people considered "remaining there" since it was thought to be "a better alternative than building a house in Pindra because of the proximity of the barracks to causal labor opportunities and the informal economy at the mine site."[176] "The Parej East RAP", the Panel explained, "limited its discussion of causal labor opportunities for resettlers at Pindra"

> to mentioning some future nearby industrial development. The Panel could not find any record of a professional analysis of the pre- and post- relocation causal labor market.[177]

In other words, the Panel concluded, "[t]hose who have moved to Pindra thus have superior physical accommodation but lack access to formal and informal labor opportunities at

---

172 *India: Mumbai Urban Transport* (2004), IR, § 557. *Note, also see* the Panel's comments related to this case *in* section 12.2.
173 *Cambodia: Land Management and Administration* (2009), IR, § 227.
174 *Id.*
175 *India: Coal Sector* (2001), IR, § 102. On issues related to income and livelihood restoration, *see* section 12.5.
176 *Id. But also see* the Panel's comments about the unrealistic expectations about future employment prospects – as discussed *in* section 11.1.2.
177 *India: Coal Sector* (2001), IR, § 102.

[the] mine site" – but, "in neither case have these PAPs regained their former standard of living."[178]

Concerning the adequacy of the facilities at replacement housing, furthermore, the Panel emphasized that this was "a situation where most of the PAPs are poor and illiterate" and where "parents would need every incentive to continue with their children's education."[179] However, "the PAPs from Borwa Tola were involuntarily relocated some distance away to Pindra" where

> they found a school building with no teachers, despite OD 4.30 and promises to the contrary. The Panel therefore finds that Management was not in compliance with paragraph 19 of OD 4.30.[180]

Obligations regarding the provision of adequate resettlement facilities also extend to the 'move-in' or 'host populations'. Indeed, inadequate attention to this aspect of involuntary resettlement activities can lead to significant tension between 'move-out' and 'move-in' or 'host' communities.

For instance, concerning the "nine families from Borwa Tola [that] were moved to Pindra," the Inspection Panel commented that these families "needed to use a host community well,"

> but they were prevented from doing so because the host community fenced it in. As a result, the women had to walk about a kilometer to fetch potable water.[181]

"Management does not dispute this," the Panel noted, but argued "that the host community was resentful because they were of a higher caste."[182] The Inspection Panel's "[i]nterviews at the site", however, "revealed that the host community withdrew its objections to the sharing of the well when it realized that only about 20 families were expected, rather than around 200."[183]

In other words, the Panel concluded, "the host community's initial opposition to allowing the PAPs to have access to their well" was indicative of

---

178 *Id.*
179 *India: Coal Sector* (2001), IR, § 126.
180 *Id.*
181 *India: Coal Sector* (2001), IR, § 114.
182 *Id.*
183 *Id.*

a failure to consult with the host community as required by paragraph 8 of OD 4.30. By failing to ensure access to potable water before the PAPs were moved to the Pindra resettlement site, the Panel finds that Management was not in compliance with paragraph 19 of OD 4.30.[184]

During its 2002 investigation of the *Paraguay/Argentina: Yacyretá Hydroelectric Project* the Inspection Panel highlighted the "school at San Cosme y Damian" as "another example of a host population adversely affected by the project."[185]

The Requesters claimed that "the school ha[d] become very crowded and is operating beyond its capacity" due to the "large influx of resettled families with children," which had "caused the quality of schooling services and education to decline."[186] During its field visit, the Inspection Panel indeed found "evidence that host populations near resettlement sites"

> are in some cases adversely affected by the design and construction of the resettlement sites, or by added burdens on local infrastructure due to the influx of resettled population.[187]

Such "impacts [should] be assessed and mitigated" in accordance with the Bank's policy framework, the Panel commented, whereas "an appropriate consultation process" – that specifically included the "host population" – as well as the "timely design of mitigation measures might have prevented such negative impact."[188]

12.5 INCOME AND LIVELIHOOD RESTORATION

The Bank's policy on Involuntary Resettlement is aimed at ensuring that people who are moved involuntarily can both 'resettle' and 'rehabilitate'. In addition to receiving compensation for losses, and gaining access to adequate replacement housing and facilities, the 'rehabilitation of involuntarily resettled people' also requires the restoration of their ability to earn income – whether through employment or other forms of 'livelihood restoration activities'. However, the realization of these policy objectives are also dependent on multiple variables.

In *Chad: Petroleum Development and Pipeline*, the Inspection Panel acknowledged that "project-related expenditures can bring benefits in the form of incremental incomes" but

---

184 *India: Coal Sector* (2001), IR, § 117. On issues related to consultation, *also see* section 11.2.
185 *Paraguay/Argentina: Yacyretá Hydroelectric Project* (2002), IR, §§ 255-257.
186 *Id.*
187 *Id.*
188 *Id.* On issues related to consultation, *also see* section 11.2.

added that "they may also impose costs" on project-affected people.[189] For instance, the Panel pointed to "evidence of price rises for some commodities, such as food and housing, in the project region."[190] "On the one hand," the Panel commented,

> this 'excess demand' can be a positive force, since it signals potential opportunities for people to earn incomes through supplying goods and services for which demand currently outstrips supply. On the other hand, for poorer consumers competing with those who have money to spend, there can now be an affordability problem if the prices of the products on which they depend have risen.[191]

"The poor are often not in a position to compensate through exploiting increased earning opportunities," the Panel emphasized,

> because they have little human, physical or financial capital with which to do so. In such circumstances it is important that the conditions are rapidly created in which output can increase, incomes can rise and prices fall or be stabilized, and if necessary a safety-net be provided.[192]

As noted earlier, adequate data, gathered by employing sound methodologies, is a critical input for the development of plans aimed at restoring income and livelihood.[193]

In *China: Western Poverty Reduction (Qinghai)*, for example, the Inspection Panel was critical of the lack of "[a]dequate baseline data on pastoralism, including the data on land use and inheritance".[194] "[I]t is difficult to understand how the OD's policy objectives can be achieved without this information," the Panel commented, since the policy stipulates, for instance, that "Displaced persons should be (iii) assisted in their efforts to improve their former living standards, income earning capacity, and production levels, or at least restore them."[195] Clearly, "[t]o achieve this [objective], one requires a clear understanding of their 'former living standards, income earning capacity, and production levels'."[196]

In its 2002 investigation of *Paraguay/Argentina: Yacyretá Hydroelectric Project*, the Inspection Panel concluded that certain categories of project-affected people "were moved

---

189 *Chad: Petroleum* (2001), IR, § 291.
190 *Id.*
191 *Id.*
192 *Id.*
193 On issues related to surveying methodologies, *see* section 12.2; on issues related to the collection of environmental and social baseline data, *also see* section 14.2.
194 *China: Western Poverty Reduction (Qinghai)* (1999), IR, §§ 372-373.
195 *Id.*
196 *Id.*

far from the market for their products and services, while others have found transportation to their place of work difficult and costly."[197] "Few of those who lost their livelihood," furthermore, "have been offered adequate training to replace their lost source of income."[198]

The Panel acknowledged "that a severe economic crisis has occurred in the area" at the time but added that this fact "did not negate the importance of restoring pre-resettlement income earning capacity"

> with long-term measures rather than temporary solutions such as a temporary free transportation or five-year access to clay deposits. Thus the Panel finds that to the extent the measures are inadequate the Bank is not in compliance with OD 4.30[199]

Similarly, in *Brazil: Itaparica Resettlement and Irrigation*, concerning "maintenance payments to resettled farmers" ('VMT'), Bank management argued that these temporary payments, originally intended to be "palliative", had actually been "sufficient to maintain a level of living substantially higher than previous levels for a large majority of cases."[200]

Management's assertion was "undoubtedly correct" from a "household income" perspective, the Panel acknowledged, however, "temporary income is not the test of the Bank's resettlement policy" – the test, the Inspection Panel asserted, is whether "sustainable income" is "greater than, or at least equal to,"

> the family's income before resettlement, and on that score, welfare payments do not count, and the variability of income from highly perishable crops such as tomatoes should be understood. The general experience has been that income is only temporarily higher for a number of reasons. In surveys of resettlement areas currently irrigated, crop yields have fallen substantially year to year, normally by 10-20 percent each year.

"Indeed," the Panel concluded, "the long-term impact of VMT can be damaging for the work ethic where people are given a choice, whereas "[t]he impact of such welfare payments over so many years [...] would then need to be considered."[201]

Project planning activities aimed at ensuring income and livelihood restoration rely, in addition to accurate data, on certain assumptions. However, as the Inspection Panel

---

197 *Paraguay/Argentina: Yacyretá Hydroelectric Project* (2002), IR, § 294. For an example where the Panel found the Bank to be compliant with respect to income and livelihood restoration, *see e.g., Nigeria: Lagos Drainage* (1998), ER, § 43.
198 *Paraguay/Argentina: Yacyretá Hydroelectric Project* (2002), IR, § 294.
199 *Id.*
200 *Brazil: Itaparica Resettlement and Irrigation* (1997), ER, § 27(4).
201 *Id.*

commented in *India: Coal Sector*, such planning assumptions have to be verified once plans are put to practice, whereas project planning should also not rely excessively on specific assumptions.

In this instance, for example, the Panel pointed out that Management had "relied almost entirely on non-farm self-employment"

> as the strategy to regain standards of living, without assessing its feasibility for income restoration in Parej East. As a result, many PAPs in Parej East have failed to restore their living standard and incomes to their previous levels and consequently have suffered and continue to suffer harm.[202]

In addition, the Panel argued, it "was unrealistic to assume that, in the space of five short years,"

> people affected by the project in Parej East, many of them poor tribals lacking social mobility, education, or an entrepreneurial culture, can be uprooted from their communities, transferred to a new one, provided with training for self employment, and some level of monetary compensation and then expected to improve, or at least restore, their former living standards, income earning capacity and production levels.[203]

These assumptions were "[d]oubly unrealistic," the Panel added,

> when it is understood that, before this can commence, the implementing agency, CCL, must undergo a significant change in institutional culture and build new capacity to undertake environmental, social and resettlement work.[204]

While it was "absolutely essential for the Bank to support" the Borrower in overcoming the "difficult challenges" involved in restoring project-affected people's income and livelihood, the Panel commented, unless the Bank's supportive actions were

> matched by time, the early planning required by OD 4.30 and the resources and realism needed to achieve them, the poorest and most vulnerable of the

---

202 *India: Coal Sector* (2001), IR, § 258.
203 *India: Coal Sector* (2001), IR, §§ 266-267.
204 *Id.*

people affected by the project may end up carrying a disproportionately heavy burden.[205]

The flawed surveying methodology employed in *India: Mumbai Urban Transport*, discussed earlier, resulted, among other things, in erroneous data about the number (and square footage) of shops that would have to be replaced.[206] Consequently, in addition to not having received adequate compensation for their loss of property, the Panel explained that "many of the new shops will be much smaller than the shops" affected shop-keepers "had before," which, in turn, "may make it impossible for some to carry on their businesses."[207] For instance, the Panel elaborated, "the poor location of the [replacement] shops,"

> which previously had a major road-facing position, will likely reduce the number of customers for many of the businesses and thus significantly decrease the income of the shopkeepers. The new location also presents other conditions that could have severely negative effects on the ability of the shopkeepers to achieve their former income earning capacity and production levels, as required by the Bank Policy. The site lacks adequate water supply, has major sewerage and pollution problems, and the customer base appears to be much less than at the existing locations of the shopkeepers.[208]

Indeed, the Panel noted that it was "very concerned that unless further actions are taken, the shopkeepers will be put in significantly worse conditions as a result of the relocation. This would not comply with Bank Policy."[209]

Furthermore, with respect to the income restoration of other categories affected people, the Panel found that "Bank Management assumed" incorrectly "that jobs would not be a problem in Mumbai and thus did not anticipate major income losses" nor did Management pay sufficient "attention to income restoration."[210] In interviewing these people at the relocation sites, however, the Inspection Panel found that "[a] high proportion were without conventional jobs" and worked "mainly in casual daily employment and in petty trade and services" since "[t]hey needed to be close to their jobs."[211]

---

205 *India: Coal Sector* (2001), IR, §§ 211-212. On the need for balance between "the need for risk-taking in development work" and the proportionate distribution of such risk, *also see* the Panel's comments *at* note 240, Ch. 6.

206 *India: Mumbai Urban Transport* (2004), IR, § 474. On issues related to the surveying methodology employed in this case, *also see* section 12.2.

207 *India: Mumbai Urban Transport* (2004), IR, § 474.

208 *Id.*

209 *Id.*

210 *India: Mumbai Urban Transport* (2004), IR, § 494; *also see* IR, § 514.

211 *India: Mumbai Urban Transport* (2004), IR, § 491. On issues related to the adequacy of resettlement sites, housing and facilities, *also see* section 12.4.

The Panel also noted that is findings in this regard were corroborated "by the TISS Report" (an impact assessment pertaining to the 'Initial Phase of R&R Implementation'), which noted that project planning was based on the assumption that "being from very poor family backgrounds – such vulnerable groups would feel very secure after getting permanent residence 'free of cost'."[212] However, the TISS Report added, "the harsh reality of survival for the poor"

> in a competitive informal market like Mumbai is that the place of stay is only one factor positively affecting their life. Better job prospects need equal attention for them.[213]

Moreover, concerning the provision of income-related compensation in the form of a lump sum equivalent to one year's income, the Panel acknowledged that this arrangement was included in the RAP but noted that there "were little mention in subsequent documents of this provision actually being implemented."[214]

As "of the date of [the Panel's investigation] report," the Panel pointed out, there has been no "evidence that a year's wages for permanently lost jobs has been paid to the PAPs."[215] "Furthermore, because of the difficulty of finding jobs at or near the resettlement sites," the Panel expressed its concern "that the payment of a cash supplement equivalent to one year of income will not sufficiently address PAPs' lack of income at the resettlement sites."[216]

The Resettlement Action Plan developed as part of *Nigeria/Ghana: West African Gas Pipeline* stipulated that "landowners 'are expected to be able to restore income streams without further assistance once they have received compensation for their land and assets'."[217] The Panel argued, however, that this provision in the RAP "transferred the burden for the restoration of livelihood onto the displaced persons,"

> once they had obtained cash compensation, without providing additional assistance as called for in Bank Policy. The Panel finds that issues of livelihood restoration, resettlement assistance beyond compensation, and benefit-sharing, were not properly negotiated with the displaced persons. This does not comply with Bank Policy on Involuntary Resettlement.[218]

---

212 *India: Mumbai Urban Transport* (2004), IR, § 494; *also see* IR, § 514.
213 *Id.*
214 *India: Mumbai Urban Transport* (2004), IR, § 550.
215 *Id.*
216 *Id.*
217 *Nigeria/Ghana: West African Gas Pipeline* (2006), IR, § 180.
218 *Id.*

Moreover, "[t]he RAP livelihood restoration objectives are yet to be completed despite the physical completion of the infrastructure."[219] "Without the measures to mitigate project related impoverishment risks" – "be they adequate baseline data, compensation, land-for-land, in-kind, permanent employment etc." – the Inspection Panel emphasized,

> the involuntary resettlement component of the Project is not finished. The Policy makes it clear that this must be done. What is an appropriate replacement depends, to some extent, on the situation of the displaced person. The Policy also makes this clear when it calls for vulnerability tests among the project-affected-people.[220]

In its 2007 investigation of *Uganda: Power Projects*, the Inspection Panel was critical of the fact that "[l]ivelihood restoration", under the successor project, "was mainly limited to the people identified in 2001 [as part of the predecessor project] and the terms and conditions set forth in 2001."[221]

As an example of the consequences of this decision, the Inspection Panel highlighted the situation of a particular "group of vulnerable people, the landless tenants and share-croppers."[222] "Ineligible for replacement land," these people "were compensated only for their lost crops."[223] When AESNP, the project implementing agency of the predecessor project, "announced compensation rates, including prices for young seedlings (known as '1-4' for their months of age)," some tenants and shareholders purchased and planted seedlings" in anticipation of receiving compensation.[224] However, the 'Sponsor' or the project implementing agency of the successor project ('BEL'), "believing they were observing fraudulent attempts to maximize compensation through the planting of young seedlings,"

> reneged on their compensation commitment and did not pay for the "1-4" crops. AESNP requested and got the support of the GoU on their non-compen-sation decision. This left landless peoples worse off, with new debt, no crops, and no harvest. Heated disputes arose, some of which are still in court, repre-senting half the current court docket on the resettlement issues of the Project. They were frequently mentioned in consultations. From the perspective of a

---

219 *Nigeria/Ghana: West African Gas Pipeline* (2006), IR, § 210. *Also see* section 9.2.
220 *Id. Note*, this example also illustrates how interrelated the issues discussed in this chapter are.
221 *Uganda: Power Projects* (2007), IR, § 452. On issues related to the identification and quantification of PAP, *see* section 10.3.
222 *Uganda: Power Projects* (2007), IR, §§ 500-501.
223 *Id.*
224 *Id. Note*, "[d]ue to [financial] difficulties encountered by the former project sponsor [AESNP], the first Project was terminated in September 2003." (*See Uganda: Power Projects* (2007), IR, p. xvi.)

sharecropper or a tenant position, this represents a substantial loss of income – an issue that after five years is still fresh on people's minds, surfacing repeatedly during the consultations.[225]

But while the successor project's Assessment of Past Resettlement Activities and Action Plan noted that "the situation of tenants and sharecroppers (who were compensated only for crops as they did not own land) appears to be worse in this respect than that of landowners)", it also recommended "not paying the claims" – a recommendation, furthermore, that was subsequently "approved by the Bank."[226] "In light of Management's failure to pay particular attention to the needs of vulnerable people," the Panel concluded, "this on-going dispute could constitute a reputational risk for the Bank and the new Sponsor."[227]

12.6   PROJECT-LEVEL GRIEVANCE MECHANISMS

Project-level grievance mechanisms operating in the context of involuntary resettlement activities are, as noted earlier, an example where the Bank's operational policy framework 'interfaces' with the Borrower's national legal system.[228] Furthermore, project-level grievance mechanisms' also constitute an example of the operationalization of the Rio Declaration Principle, 'access to justice'.[229]

Whereas the Panel's findings with regard to project-level grievance mechanisms have the potential to strengthen the avenues of recourse and redress for affected people in the project area, the Inspection Panel process is not a supplement for a fully functional project-level grievance mechanism.

For instance, as the Inspection Panel commented in *Kazakhstan: South-West Roads*, the mere act of filing a Request for Inspection "cannot be viewed" – neither by the Bank nor the Borrower – as having "the effect of escalating" the issues mentioned in the Request.[230] "Rather, it is a legitimate exercise of their rights"

---

225 *Uganda: Power Projects* (2007), IR, §§ 500-501. *Note*, this example also demonstrates the interfaces with borrowers' (national) constitutional systems – as discussed *e.g., in* sections 5.2 & 8.2.

226 *Id.*

227 *Id.*

228 *See* section 5.2. For an example where the Panel found the Bank to be in compliance with regards to the area of project-level grievance mechanisms, *see e.g., Cameroon: Petroleum Development and Pipeline* (2002), IR, §§ 174-176. For an example where Management acknowledged non-compliance in this policy area, *see Peru: Lima Urban Transport* (2009), ER, § 28. For examples of deficiencies concerning project-level grievance mechanisms in a context different from involuntary resettlement, *see Cambodia: Forest Concession Management* (2005), IR, § 135; *and see Honduras: Land Administration* (2006), IR § 375.

229 *See* note 66, Ch. 5; *and see* section 7.1.1. *Also see* Di Leva *in* Bradlow & Hunter (Eds.) (2010), pp. 355-356.

230 *Kazakhstan: South-West Roads* (2011), ER, § 59. For an overview of *Kazakhstan: South-West Roads*, *see* Naudé Fourie (2014), pp. 537-543.

– granted by the Bank's Board of Executive Directors under the Panel Resolution and its Clarifications – to approach the Panel for an independent review of Management actions or omissions. The Panel would like to add that the Panel process is not, and cannot be regarded as, an appeals instance for Project level grievance mechanisms.[231]

On the other hand, the Panel pointed out, "the fact that there is a grievance mechanism in a project"

does not necessarily mean that this mechanism has been established and is operating in full compliance with Bank operational policies and procedures. Affected people have the right to ask for an independent review of Management's actions with regard to such a mechanism.[232]

The Inspection Panel identified several deficiencies regarding the project-level 'grievance office' in *Peru: Lima Urban Transport*. While each of these deficiencies, when considered separately, may not seem appear to be a 'material' instance of non-compliance; their combined effect, nevertheless, had a significant impact on the mechanism's functional effectiveness. The Panel commented, for example, that "[i]t was not easy"

for the Panel team to identify the grievance office since no sign was posted outside. In meetings with Bank staff the Panel was told that the grievance officer is usually not in the office but generally visits houses in the District and can be reached by cell phone. Bank staff also informed the Panel that the office is not advertised and the person in charge usually not present because of strong opposition from local authorities who have become forceful opponents of the Metropolitano in Barranco.[233]

Although "this project level grievances system has the potential to be an important avenue for residents to present their grievances and have their issues addressed," the Panel concluded, "to do so effectively requires a functioning office" – which had not been the case on this project.[234]

---

231 *Kazakhstan: South-West Roads* (2011), ER, § 59.
232 *Id. Note*, this example also illustrates the ambiguity with which terms such as 'rights' and 'interests' are used in the transnational development context – *compare, e.g.*, Schlemmer-Schulte' argument *in* note 52, Ch. 5, with the Inspection Panel's statement *in* note 115, Ch. 13.
233 *Peru: Lima Urban Transport* (2009), IR, § 124.
234 *Id.*

In *Nigeria/Ghana: West African Gas Pipeline*, the Panel expressed its concern that "the displaced persons could not have understood grievance avenues available to them," due to a lack of "meaningful consultation" and insufficient access to project information, as discussed earlier.[235]

Bank management, on the other hand, cited the "low incidence of grievance[s]" filed as justification for its argument that the project was in compliance in this regard.[236] The Panel argued, however, that the low number of grievances filed might actually be "indicative of a lack of awareness by the displaced persons of their rights" and Panel concluded, therefore, that Management "failed to ensure that the Sponsor had in place an effective grievance process to identify and redress resettlement issues, as required by OP 4.12."[237]

In *India: Mumbai Urban Transport*, the Panel found that the project information centres "offered no information about the grievance process."[238] It would also "have been important," the Panel commented, "to provide PAPs with copies of the lists of eligible PAPs early in the Project, thus to enable them to verify their status and be able to ask for corrections."[239] Yet, "[i]n interviews with the Panel," the MMRDA (project implementing agency) stated "that the [grievance] system and the procedures were sufficiently explained in the existing MUTP brochure".[240] On closer investigation, however, the Panel found that this "brochure only briefly mentions that there is such procedure" and fails to "provide any details."[241] In its initial response to the Request, Management acknowledged this oversight, and "stated that MMRDA and SPARC"

> would prepare and distribute a "due process brochure" for PAPs with information on the grievance process by September 30, 2004. However, as of its last field visit in May 2005, the Panel observed that PICs still did not provide any information about the system.[242]

Hence, the Panel concluded that it had "found no evidence"

> that the Requesters have been adequately informed about the grievance system and its procedures. Though Requesters and PAPS interviewed by the Panel

---

235 *Nigeria/Ghana: West African Gas Pipeline* (2006), IR, § 296. On issues related to access to information and consultation, *see* Ch. 11.
236 *Nigeria/Ghana: West African Gas Pipeline* (2006), IR, § 296.
237 *Id.*
238 *India: Mumbai Urban Transport* (2004), IR, §§ 352 & 406-407. On issues related to PICs, *see* section 11.1
239 *India: Mumbai Urban Transport* (2004), IR, §§ 352 & 406-407.
240 *Id.*
241 *Id.*
242 *Id.*

seemed to be aware of the general existence of the grievance mechanism, they are not aware of its procedures and thus cannot use the system appropriately.[243]

The Inspection Panel also found that the project-level "grievance system lacked clear responsibilities, procedures and rules"

> and has not been independent. Moreover, many PAPs have learned only recently about the existence of a grievance system and were not aware of the details of the process. In other cases, they have been frustrated with the alleged lack of objectivity and independence of the grievance mechanisms.[244]

Moreover, the Panel's interviews with MMRDA staff "revealed a lack of common understanding"

> of how the mechanism works and what its major duties are. MMRDA stated that the procedures are to be addressed in the IM [implementation manual] to be drafted. However, when reviewing the Draft IM, the Panel found that clear procedures and timeframes were still not included.[245]

While in *Cambodia: Forest Concession Management*, as noted earlier, the Inspection Panel was critical of the fact that the project's consultation obligations were delegated to concessionaires.[246] In its review of the guidelines provided to concessionaires – which were aimed to ensure that consultation activities complied with Bank policy guidelines – the Panel found that, while compliant in some respects, the guidelines did not "set up a method of confirming that local people have been informed of the concessionaires' plans,"

> nor do they set up a transparently monitored grievance procedure that allows affected people to dispute the characterization of their lands, their cultural properties, and the value that should be placed on, or recognized for, their traditional uses of forest products.[247]

The "absence of an effective grievance procedure and monitoring mechanism," the Panel emphasized, "can be an open license for the suppression of the poorest and most vulnerable

---

243 *Id.*
244 *India: Mumbai Urban Transport* (2004), IR, § 415.
245 *India: Mumbai Urban Transport* (2004), IR, § 405. *Note*, this example also demonstrates disagreements between the Bank and its borrowers about their respective obligations – as discussed *in* section 8.1.
246 *See* section 11.2.
247 *Cambodia: Forest Concession Management* (2005), IR, § 135

populations' rights, whom Bank policies were developed to protect" – and this was certainly applicable to situations such as those existing in "remote parts of Cambodia" (and many other countries) where the power relationship between local forest dependent communities and industrial logging concessionaires is so unequal [...]."[248]

Finally, the Inspection Panel's 2002 investigation of *Paraguay/Argentina: Yacyretá Hydroelectric Project* provides a prominent example of how compliance issues in the area of project-level grievance mechanisms can prevent their effective functioning, which, in turn, can exacerbate the adverse effects of involuntary resettlement.

The Inspection Panel noted that Bank's policy on Involuntary Resettlement "requires that full compensation be paid to displaced persons prior to their actual move"; yet, as the Panel found during its 1995 investigation of this project, "[n]ot all persons flooded out of their property when the reservoir was raised in 1994 to the 76 masl level were properly compensated beforehand."[249] Indeed, the Panel noted, "[i]n 1997, Management assisted EBY in developing the so-called Plan A in part to compensate for this violation of OD 4.30."[250]

However, over the course of the 2002 *Yacyretá*-investigation, the Panel "found many instances in which people whose homes were flooded when the water level was raised in 1994, after Plan A was in effect, still feel inadequately compensated."[251] The Panel concluded that this situation was caused, "[i]n part," by the inadequacy of the "grievance procedure in place at that time for people to object to the valuations offered for their property was inadequate.[252]

What concerned the Panel specifically, was the fact that "[p]eople without adequate resources to live when denied access to their property"

> were asked either to accept the amount offered by EBY and in doing so agree to forego any further claim to additional funds, or to take the matter to court.[253]

"If they took the matter to court," the Panel explained, "they would have no access to the funds until after a court decision", whereas "by accepting the payment offered and thus having access to the funds, a person had to sign that this was full valuation for the property lost."[254] "It is unreasonable," the Panel concluded, "for a person losing access"

---

248 *Cambodia: Forest Concession Management* (2005), IR, § 136.
249 *Paraguay/Argentina: Yacyretá Hydroelectric Project* (2002), IR, §§ 271-273.
250 *Id.* The Panel refers to the 'Action Plans' agreed between the Bank and Borrower in light of the 1995 *Yacyretá* Inspection Panel Request. For a discussion of the adoption and implementation of such 'Action Plans', *see* section 7.1.2.
251 *Paraguay/Argentina: Yacyretá Hydroelectric Project* (2002), IR, §§ 271-273.
252 *Id.*
253 *Id.*
254 *Id.*

to his/her home or livelihood resources by flooding to be given no better grievance procedure than taking the matter to court and to have no means of livelihood during the potentially protracted court battle.[255]

In addition, concerning compensation of another group of adversely affected people, the Panel was critical that the "Bank approved compensation procedures whereby workers must go to court to enforce their rights if their employer does not follow the law"

and have no effective recourse against EBY. In this respect, the Panel observes that the law firm, which prepared the legal opinion upon Management's request acknowledges that even though it is legally possible for the employees to sub-rogate a passive owner and sue EBY, that option is not a simple lawsuit but one with a restricted scope and an ample range of defenses available to EBY.[256]

Moreover, the Panel pointed out, "based on the Treaty" between Argentina and Paraguay underlying the *Yacyretá* project, these "workers would also have to travel from Encarnación to Asunción, Paraguay – five hours away – to file and follow such a lawsuit."[257]

It was "matter of considerable concern," the Inspection Panel emphasized, "that the Bank would accept, in a notoriously weak institutional setting,"

a compensation system that is based on the "assumption that Paraguayan labor laws would be applied effectively" by employers. The system essentially penalizes the workers because, if the employer has not complied with all legal and social securities obligations, it does not provide any compensation to the workers.[258]

Therefore, the Panel concluded, "the compensation program approved by the Bank was not consistent with OD 4.30"

because it excluded in practice compensation for a specific category of economic losses that affected one of the poorest segments of the area population – that is, the informal workers of the brick- and tile-making industries.[259]

---

255 *Id. Note*, this example also demonstrates the interface between the Bank's operational policy framework and the Borrower' constitutional system (here, specifically the judiciary) – as discussed *in* sections 5.2 & 8.2. For an additional example, *also see Paraguay/Argentina: Yacyretá Hydroelectric Project* (2002), IR, § 274.

256 *Paraguay/Argentina: Yacyretá Hydroelectric Project* (2002), IR, § 333.

257 *Id.*

258 *Paraguay/Argentina: Yacyretá Hydroelectric Project* (2002), IR, §§ 332 & 334. For issues related to borrower and/or project implement agency institutional and/or professional capacity, *see* section 8.3.

259 *Paraguay/Argentina: Yacyretá Hydroelectric Project* (2002), IR, §§ 332 & 334.

****

The examples from Inspection Panel practice presented in this chapter demonstrate why involuntary resettlement has been – and remains – such a controversial part of the World Bank's development-lending operations. Indeed, all of the issues discussed in this chapter – the definition of involuntary resettlement; surveying project-affected communities; determining compensation; adequate resettlement housing and facilities; income and livelihood restoration; as well as effective project-level grievance mechanisms – have the potential to result in serious adverse affects for project-affected people and also impede the realization of development objectives.

In fact, if any one policy area were to provide justification for the argument that the World Bank should be accountable not only for performance but also for harm since these two aspects are inextricably linked – or, for that matter, that normative systems have to enable and restrain action – involuntary resettlement would be it.[260]

To be sure, while several examples from Inspection Panel practice included in this chapter point to significant opportunities for improvement (notably, in the areas of surveying, identifying and quantifying project-affected people), other examples illustrate the significant challenges involved in getting involuntary resettlement 'right' (notably, in the areas of property valuation and income/livelihood restoration).

On the other hand, recurring compliance issues in the area of involuntary resettlement – identified not only in Inspection Panel practice but also in various internal reviews conducted by other World Bank internal accountability mechanisms – leave an undeniable impression that the World Bank, indeed, fails to learn from its mistakes.[261]

And the importance of strengthening institutional learning in the area of involuntary resettlement, furthermore, gains additional significance in light of the Bank's recent announcement of its intention to refocus its lending operations on large-scale infrastructure projects (in which involuntary resettlement activities are typically more prevalent), and also in light of the Bank's recent acknowledgement that the realization of the policy on Involuntary Resettlement's underlying objectives remains a systemic problem across the Bank's development-lending operations.[262]

Indeed, the ability to convincingly strengthen performance while effectively mitigating the adverse effects of involuntary resettlement has arguably become critical as the World Bank re-positions itself – vis-à-vis a growing number of competitors in the field of multi-lateral development finance – as having a "unique link between its lending function and

---

260 On the competing paradigms of accountability for performance *versus* harm, *see* section 4.2.2; on the instrumentalist and formalist paradigms, as well as arguments that 'neither' paradigm's logic is 'mutually conclusive', *see* section 2.3.
261 In this regard, *see* the discussion *in* section 7.1.5.
262 *See* note 6, Ch. 12.

its expertise"[263] or, as the Inspection Panel put it, as having the unique ability to "operate in an effective way" at both the "technical" and "strategic political dialogue" levels.[264]

As noted in the Introduction, this book does not aim to form an overall conclusion as to the 'state of World Bank accountability', based on a 'general compliance track-record' with respect to its operational policy framework.[265] If anything, the analysis presented in this book points to the complexity involved in forming such conclusions.

It is important to note, however, that for many of the Bank's accountability holders – external constituent groups in particular – the Bank's application of safeguard policies such as Involuntary Resettlement, Environmental Assessment and Indigenous Peoples, as well as the policy on Project Supervision, constitutes the litmus test of World Bank accountability. Moreover, the perceptions of many of these stakeholders are strongly influenced by what is reflected in Inspection Panel practice.

It is therefore significant that Inspection Panel practice reflects a recurring approach to policy application that has the effect of narrowing the content and scope of obligations. There may indeed be many valid arguments to justify such an approach in particular circumstances, for example, or that point to the limitations of Inspection Panel practice as a window onto World Bank development-lending operations, or that argue that the Bank's other internal accountability mechanisms are better positioned to provide input that can be based to form an overall conclusion on the state of World Bank accountability, or, for that matter, that the Inspection Panel is biased to finding non-compliance in order to justify its existence.[266]

Nevertheless, because the Panel has, over time, proven to be functionally independent from Bank management – and, in particular, because the Panel's agenda is citizen-driven – for many, Inspection Panel practice remains the only legitimate window onto the World Bank's development lending-operations.

---

263 *See* S. Donnan, 'World Bank: Stress Test', *Financial Times*, April 16, 2015, available at www.ft.com: "These new dynamics, Mr Morris says, mean that the bank should be moving out of its traditional lending function and focusing more on deploying expertise, or as a hub for discussions on big issues such as climate change. "[The World Bank] is losing salience if it sticks with that core model and doesn't go in another direction," he says. [Current World Bank President] Kim disputes that. He argues *that the bank's competitive advantage comes from the unique link between its lending function and its expertise.*" (Emphasis added.)

264 *See* the Panel's comments *in Cambodia: Forest Concession Management*, as noted *in* section 9.1.

265 *See* section 1.2.

266 *See e.g.*, Wade's comments *at* note 231, Ch. 7.

13   INDIGENOUS PEOPLES

Indigenous peoples are considered to be a special category of project-affected people due to their significant and distinct vulnerability. "Over a very short period, the few decades since the early 1970s," as Kingsbury observes, the notion of "'indigenous peoples' has been transformed from a prosaic description without much significance in international law and politics,"

> into a concept with considerable power as a basis for group mobilization, international standard setting, transnational networks and programmatic activity of intergovernmental and nongovernmental organizations.[1]

The World Bank's development efforts aimed at indigenous peoples have been facilitated by a safeguard policy dedicated specifically to ensure that "these social groups benefit from development projects and that potentially adverse effects of Bank projects on indigenous people are avoided or mitigated."[2] The application of the policy on Indigenous Peoples – which is the focus of Chapter 13 – "contributes to the Bank's mission of poverty reduction and sustainable development

> by ensuring that the development process fully respects the dignity, human rights, economies, and cultures of Indigenous Peoples.[3]

"For all projects that are proposed for Bank financing and affect Indigenous Peoples," the policy elaborates, "the Bank requires the borrower"

> to engage in a process of free, prior, and informed consultation. The Bank provides project financing only where free, prior, and informed consultation results in broad community support to the project by the affected Indigenous Peoples. Such Bank-financed projects include measures to (a) avoid potentially adverse effects on the Indigenous Peoples' communities; or (b) when avoidance is not feasible, minimize, mitigate, or compensate for such effects. Bank-financed projects are also designed to ensure that the Indigenous Peoples receive social

---

1   Kingsbury (1998), p. 414.
2   Boisson de Chazournes *in* Alfredsson & Ring (Eds.) (2001), p. 75. For more on the development of the Bank's policy on Indigenous People, *see* Sarfaty (2005), pp. 1801-1802; MacKay (2005); *and see* MacKay *in* Bradlow & Hunter (Eds.) (2010).
3   OP 4.10 (Indigenous Peoples), § 1. On the notion of 'intergenerational equity in international law', *see e.g.*, Brown Weiss (1987).

and economic benefits that are culturally appropriate and gender and intergenerationally inclusive.[4]

Chapter 13 reflects on the manner in which the Bank operationalizes these matters, as viewed through the window offered by Inspection Panel practice.

The chapter sets off by considering the *definition of indigenous peoples* in particular project contexts, as well as their *identification* within project areas, which, in turn, affect the application of the Bank's policy on Indigenous Peoples to the projects in question.[5] Next, the chapter highlights compliance issues related to project activities aimed specifically at safeguarding indigenous peoples' rights and interests, and at meeting their development needs, as reflected, for instance, in the *adequacy of development of Indigenous Peoples (Development) Plans* (IPDPs or IPPs) or *Social Assessments*. Chapter 13 concludes with a discussion of compliance issues related to *consultation with indigenous peoples*, as stipulated in the policy on Indigenous Peoples.

13.1   DEFINING AND IDENTIFYING 'INDIGENOUS PEOPLES'

The "development [of] 'indigenous peoples' as a significant concept in international practice," as Kingsbury observes, had "not been accompanied by any general agreement as to its meaning, or even by agreement on a process by which its meaning might be established."[6] Indeed, Inspection Panel practice reflects the ambiguity and political sensitivity surrounding the concept – although the examples include in this chapter also demonstrate how an interactional process such as those provided by the Inspection Panel mechanism might serve as a platform from which a 'general agreement' can be developed.

As a point of departure, the "notion of indigenous peoples" typically extends to "'indigenous ethnic groups', 'tribal groups' and 'scheduled tribes'," as Boisson de Chazournes comments, "but is not restricted to these groups".[7] Hence, it is broadly "defined as"

> social groups whose social and cultural identity is distinct from that of the dominant society and makes them vulnerable to being disadvantaged in the development process.[8]

---

4   OP 4.10 (Indigenous Peoples), § 1.
5   On other types of decisions affecting project scope, *see* Ch. 10.
6   Kingsbury (1998), p. 414.
7   Boisson de Chazournes *in* Alfredsson & Ring (Eds.) (2001), p. 75.
8   *Id.*

In other words, "although other criteria have a role to play," for instance, as set out in the Bank's policy on Indigenous Peoples, "definitional criteria" typically centre "on the issue of vulnerability and distinctiveness [...]."[9]

Reaching "an agreed understanding" on the definition of 'indigenous peoples' "in any given situation" is "not always easy or clear-cut," as the Inspection Panel acknowledged in *China: Western Poverty Reduction (Qinghai)*, which is also why the policy "allows Management some flexibility in deciding what groups will be considered 'indigenous' in any given project and [...] provides a number of guidelines to assist them."[10]

Indeed, Sarfaty comments, there is "no particular formula"

> for the relative importance of each criterion. While national constitutions and relevant legislation provide 'a preliminary basis,' identification ultimately relies on the judgment of Bank staff with regional technical expertise. Due to the diversity of perspectives within the Bank – along disciplinary and geographic lines, among others – many views need to be reconciled or rejected before the Bank can reach a final decision.[11]

For these reasons, Inspection Panel practice also reflects significant variation in the manner in which the Bank defines the concept – and how the Panel reviews the exercise of managerial discretion in this policy area.[12]

In *Nepal: Arun III*, for example, the Inspection Panel observed that "some observers have sought to dismiss the applicability of the [policy on Indigenous Peoples]" "[b]ecause the ethnic groups of the area being impacted" by the project did "not fit the classic expectations associated" with the policy.[13] This particular instance did not involve "the kind of isolated tribal group untouched by modernity that some would argue is foreseen in the OD," the Panel acknowledged, but to limit the application of the policy to such groups would also be an "unsustainable" situation.[14] In fact, the Panel argued, "other observers on the ground and in Bank Management have recognized the larger purposes of the OD" – which are,

---

9   *Id.*
10 *China: Western Poverty Reduction (Qinghai)* (1999), IR, § 256.
11 Sarfaty (2005), p. 1804.
12 In other words, it is an area with a significant degree of managerial discretion, for which the Inspection Panel has allowed for broader and narrower 'margins' of appreciation in its respective reviews of this area. *Note*, on the issue of managerial discretion with regard to the application of operational policies, *see* section 6.3.2.
13 *Nepal: Arun III* (1994), IR, § 110.
14 *Id.*

to ensure that groups in the population chronically vulnerable to damage from the development process, who can be identified by their ethnic affiliation, need special monitoring and programs.

"The fact that some of any given ethnic group have achieved some degree of integration into mainstream society", the Panel concluded, "does not discount the concerns of the majority of a given ethnic group, whether labeled 'indigenous people' or not.[15]

Whereas in its 2007 investigation of *Uganda: Power Projects*, the Panel commented that the fact that an ethnic group meets "some of the criteria necessary to be regarded as indigenous peoples in the context of Bank-financed projects," does not automatically mean that they will be classified as 'indigenous people'.[16] In this instance, for example, the Panel noted that the Basoga people were "a large and influential group with political, social and economic standing in Uganda's society," and "did not find any indication that they are regarded as a 'marginalized and vulnerable segment' of the population that is unable to participate in and benefit from development'."[17] Therefore, the Panel concluded, it "did not find any evidence that Management violated the provisions of the Bank's policy on Indigenous Peoples, with regard to the Basoga people."[18]

In *Colombia: Cartagena Water & Environmental Management*, the Panel reviewed the Bank's decision not to apply the policy on Indigenous Peoples to "the communities living in the North zone of Cartagena" – that is, 'Afro-Colombian communities' living in the project area.[19]

The Inspection Panel noted that these communities were "not recognized as indigenous peoples" in terms of "Colombian legislation;" however, the Panel underscored, "the issue under investigation is whether the Bank followed OD 4.20 on Indigenous Peoples"

---

15 *Id. Also see* Kingsbury (1999), p. 337, who argues that the Inspection Panel has adopted a "purposive approach to the scope of application of OD 4.20 on indigenous peoples," thereby "eschewing debate about the exact meaning of the term in favour of the view that identifiable ethnic groups chronically vulnerable to damage from the development process were encompassed." On the employment of expansive interpretative approaches, *see* section 6.3.3.

16 *Uganda: Power Projects* (2007), IR, § 535.

17 *Id.*

18 *Id.* For an additional example where the Panel found the Bank to be compliance with respect to the definition of the phrase and the identification of Indigenous Peoples in the project area, *see Chad: Petroleum Development and Pipeline* (2001), IR, § 199: "[...] OD 4.20 was not applicable, since "[t]he population affected by the Oil Pipeline Project in southern Chad does not constitute an *'indigenous people'* because it forms a majority found throughout the region. [...] These people share similar cultures, speak related Chadic languages, and practice similar religious customs. They share a common social structure including egalitarian and non-chiefdom polities, patrilineal kinship, and autonomous village organization. They hold similar land tenure rules and production regimes including the practice of 'shifting agriculture', growing millet, sorghum, and cotton. This population makes up a majority group in southern Chad and shares a larger identity with southern Chad as a whole, and do not constitute a minority or indigenous population."

19 *Colombia: Cartagena Water & Environmental Management* (2004), IR, § 185.

during the design, appraisal and execution stages of the Project with regards to the Afro-Colombian communities living in the area of the proposed [marine] outfall. The classification of certain groups as indigenous peoples under Bank policy OD 4.20 is not necessarily consistent with, or subject to, local legislation, but is still binding on the Bank.[20]

The policy defined "indigenous peoples," the Panel noted,

> as 'social groups with a social and cultural identity distinct from the dominant society that makes them vulnerable to being disadvantaged in the development process.' The policy recognizes that no single definition is available to embrace all indigenous peoples and their 'diversity'. Thus, it provides for a number of criteria, whose 'presence in varying degrees' is useful to identify indigenous peoples [...].[21]

However, the Panel added, "the policy does not say that all the criteria have to be met in order for the policy to be triggered" and "neither are these criteria ranked in any hierarchy of importance."[22] The policy merely specified that the decision to classify an ethnic group as 'indigenous people' ultimately lies with the project's Task Managers (TMs), who had to "exercise" their "judgment" in this regard.[23]

Concerning the Afro-Colombian communities, the Inspection Panel observed that they were "vulnerable to being disadvantaged by economic development"

> as the policy specifies. They suffer disproportionately from social exclusion. They are closely attached to their natural resources of the ocean and some practice subsistence-oriented production. The Afro-Colombians living in the North Zone of Cartagena identify themselves as a distinct society different from the dominant society and they are treated in Cartagena as being a separate group. The main OD 4.20 criterion they lack is an indigenous language. After all these years, their language has been largely lost during 400 years of slavery, although it has been reported to linger on elsewhere in the Palenque community. The Panel finds that in the case of the Afro-Colombians who submitted the Request, the affected community meets most of the OD's criteria, except for

---

20 *Id.* On the interfaces with the Borrower's constitutional system, *see* sections 5.2 & 8.2.
21 *Colombia: Cartagena Water & Environmental Management* (2004), IR, §§ 186-187.
22 *Colombia: Cartagena Water & Environmental Management* (2004), IR, § 188.
23 *Colombia: Cartagena Water & Environmental Management* (2004), IR, §§ 186-187.

an "indigenous language" and arguably a predominant "primarily-oriented subsistence production."[24]

Furthermore, while the policy instructs Task Managers to "make use of specialized anthropological and sociological experts throughout the project cycle" in order to assist them with the application of the policy on the project, the Panel noted that

> no "specialized anthropological and sociological experts" were consulted in this decision, contrary to the intention of OD 4.20. The Panel could [also] find no discussion during project preparation as to whether the presence of Afro-Colombian communities should trigger application of the Indigenous Peoples Policy.[25]

On the other hand, while the "Afro-Colombians *could reasonably have been regarded as indigenous peoples under Bank policies*,"[26] the also Panel took note of the fact "that the World Bank's Quality Assurance Team approved the decision reflected in the Project's Social Assessment that no indigenous people would be affected by the Project."[27] Hence, the Panel accepted that the specific decision not to apply the policy on Indigenous Peoples to the Afro-Columbian community "may not be deemed as noncompliance with the 'judgment' called for in OD 4.20, paragraph 5," due to "the absence of" one and, arguably, "two of the policy [definitional] criteria."[28]

Yet, the Inspection Panel also emphasized the particular vulnerability of the Afro-Columbian communities, noting that they "seem to have been considered less important"

> than the major beneficiaries of Cartagena. They are relatively small in numbers, quiet, weak in political power, and lack voice in decisions that affect them severely. The Panel notes that these communities may be exposed to significant risks under the project.[29]

The Panel was also critical of the project's Social Impact Assessment, since it "focuse[d] on the major social benefits to the target population in the city of Cartagena," but did "adequately address compensation for the affected Afro-Colombian communities in the

---

24 *Colombia: Cartagena Water & Environmental Management* (2004), IR, § 191.
25 *Colombia: Cartagena Water & Environmental Management* (2004), IR, §§ 186-187. In this regard, *also see* Cernea's comments *at* note 223, Ch. 13.
26 *Colombia: Cartagena Water & Environmental Management* (2004), IR, § 191 (emphasis added).
27 *Colombia: Cartagena Water & Environmental Management* (2004), IR, §§ 186-187.
28 *Colombia: Cartagena Water & Environmental Management* (2004), IR, § 191. *Note*, this example demonstrates the Panel allowing Management a broader 'margin of discretion' – *see* section 6.3.2.
29 *Colombia: Cartagena Water & Environmental Management* (2004), IR, § 223.

North Zone for bearing most of the risk of negative impacts of the sewerage component for the Project."[30]

"Irrespective of whether Afro-Colombians are classified as indigenous peoples or not," the Panel concluded, "they are affected by the Project because they will be exposed to a wide range of risks as a result of the construction and operation of the Project."[31] Hence, the Panel commented, "the Bank would have been well advised"

> to require an Indigenous Peoples Development Plan (IPDP) or a similar document identifying impacts of the Project on these people and providing mitigation measures for risks and potential harm, particularly in light of the inadequacies of the Social Impact Assessment.[32]

The policy on Indigenous Peoples requires that an "appropriate screening research" should be carried out "in the early stage of the Project to determine the possible presence of indigenous peoples."[33]

In *Democratic Republic of Congo: Transitional Support*, the Inspection Panel found that Bank management failed to conduct such a screening and, as a result, "lacked sensitivity to the presence of the Indigenous People in the Project area."[34] Although "most of the Bantu- and Sudanic-speaking agricultural peoples living in the forests" did not form the dominant group in DRC's political process," the Panel noted, "they still occupy the dominant position over the Pygmy people"

> in the local political and economic contexts. The Panel, therefore, finds it necessary to take into consideration the unequal social relationships among the co-existent local peoples, in order to consider the Indigenous People with respect to the OD 4.20 of the Bank policy. Namely, most Pygmy people in the Project area are more or less marginalized and underprivileged, paid less for their service, have less access to modern health and education facilities, and are much less represented in a wider political arena than their agricultural neighbors.[35]

---

30 *Colombia: Cartagena Water & Environmental Management* (2004), IR, §§ 205-206. On issues of compensation, *also see* section 12.3.

31 *Id. Note*, this example also illustrates the need for balance between "the need for risk-taking in development work" and the proportionate distribution of such risk, as the Panel commented *at* note 240, Ch. 6.

32 *Colombia: Cartagena Water & Environmental Management*, IR, § 196.

33 *Democratic Republic of Congo: Transitional Support* (2005), IR, §§ 227-228.

34 *Id.* On the influence of project modality and the lending vehicle on the (non-)application of the policy on Indigenous People, *also see* the discussion *in* section 10.1.

35 *Democratic Republic of Congo: Transitional Support* (2005), IR, § 237.

"In this sense," the Panel concluded, "they conform to the definition of Indigenous People in its "modern analytic form," and in the narrow sense – and, therefore, "the Pygmy People in DRC should [have been] considered to be Indigenous People under OD 4.20."[36]

However, because the policy on Indigenous Peoples "was not triggered during Project design" and "has to this date not been triggered in relation to the Component of the Project relating to the logging concessions," the Panel pointed out, "no IPDP was prepared."[37] Consequently, "potentially critical interests and needs of the indigenous Pygmy People in relation to these Project activities have been left unaddressed."[38]

The Panel also questioned how "Management could arrive at such an underestimation of the distribution and population of the Mbuti Pygmies in the Project area."[39] Even "at the time of [Management's formal] Response to this Request," the Inspection Panel emphasized, "some Pygmy groups" remained unidentified, although they were adversely "affected by the Project [...]".[40]

Whereas in *Pakistan: National Drainage Program*, the Panel noted the presence of several "nomadic groups" in the project area, which would have "made it appropriate," at least, "to assess whether these groups [...] fit within the criteria of indigenous peoples under OD 4.20."[41] Specifically, the Panel commented, an "assessment of the Bhil and Kohli, sharecroppers and agricultural laborers"

> who would be directly affected by any changes in the distribution of agricultural resources and in agricultural production, would have been appropriate not just as sharecroppers or laborers but also as members of distinct cultural and ethnic groups who are especially vulnerable and poor.[42]

Therefore, the Panel concluded that the Bank was not in compliance with the policy since "Management did not initiate a process to determine whether the NDP Project would affect any group of people which would qualify as indigenous peoples under OD 4.20."[43] The Panel also concluded that the Bank failed to "consult with local anthropological and/or sociological experts"

---

36 *Id.*
37 *Democratic Republic of Congo: Transitional Support* (2005), IR, § 243.
38 *Id. Also see* the discussion *in* section 10.1.
39 *Democratic Republic of Congo: Transitional Support* (2005), IR, § 231.
40 *Id.* For a critical analysis of the Bank's decision not to apply the policy on Indigenous Peoples to a project in Morocco – and which reflects similar issues as noted in this chapter – *see in general Sarfaty* (2005).
41 *Pakistan: National Drainage Program* (2004), IR, §§ 412-413.
42 *Id.*
43 *Id.*

to determine whether or not any of the ethnic groups living within or near the Project area would qualify as indigenous peoples under OD 4.20. The failure to do so does not comply with OD 4.20.[44]

"[A]t least some of these groups," the Panel emphasized, "may have required an Indigenous Peoples Development Plan (IPDP) under OD 4.20"

> during Project preparation. Such a document, or a similar document, could have identified potential Project impacts on these people and set forth measures to mitigate risks and potential harm.[45]

Finally, in *China: Western Poverty Reduction (Qinghai)*, Bank management had decided that the Bank's policy on Indigenous Peoples would "appl[y] to anyone who is a member of an officially recognized "national minority."[46] "In all such Chinese documents," Management pointed out, "the national minorities are recognized as peoples distinct from the 'Han' majority (92 percent of the population),"

> enjoying special legal and administrative protections. In the context of this Project, it is important to note that following this approach, not only Mongols and Tibetans come under the safeguard umbrella of the OD, but also the Hui, Salar, and Tu peoples. A judgement as to the degree of adherence to the OD must include the impacts of the Project on all such indigenous peoples.[47]

The Inspection Panel noted that it had "inquired in detail about the status of officially recognized minority group members"

> who no longer speak their indigenous language or practice their indigenous religion. This includes many households in the Move-out area that are officially registered as "Tibetan." During its visit to the Move-out area, the Team met some of these families and found that they had effectively been assimilated in the culture and society of their Han neighbors in the same villages.[48]

"Treating fully assimilated minorities as "Tibetans," or as other national minorities, might be questioned by some," the Panel admitted; yet, it accepted Management's explanations

---

44   *Pakistan: National Drainage Program* (2004), IR, §§ 412-413.
45   *Pakistan: National Drainage Program* (2004), IR, §§ 412-413. *Also see* the discussion *in* section 13.2.
46   *China: Western Poverty Reduction (Qinghai)* (1999), IR, § 261.
47   *Id.*
48   *China: Western Poverty Reduction (Qinghai)* (1999), IR, § 265.

"why these "assimilated" households might maintain their official registration as minority ethnic group members."[49]

The Panel also took note of the Bank's statement that, "[f]or Bank-financed projects,"

> the 55 national minorities officially recognised by the Chinese government are considered 'indigenous peoples' for purposes of application of OD 4.20.[50]

"It would appear," the Inspection Panel concluded, "that there is effectively no better method for judging "indigenous" status for purposes of OD 4.20"

> than to equate 'indigenous peoples' with 'national minority' status as enshrined in the constitution of the People's Republic of China.[51]

13.2 PROTECTING INDIGENOUS PEOPLES' 'RIGHTS AND INTERESTS': SOCIAL ASSESSMENTS AND DEVELOPMENT PLANS

Indigenous people have specific vulnerabilities and development needs, for example, as the Inspection Panel highlighted in *Democratic Republic of Congo: Transitional Support*, "one of the most frequent complaints about logging operations made by the Indigenous People" over the course of the Panel's "field investigation"

> was that logging destroys the sources of edible fruit, honey and caterpillars, and seriously affects their livelihood in the forest. Other adverse impacts of logging include over-hunting of animals by outside poachers who come to the interior forest using logging roads, rapid infiltration of cash economy and consumerism, alcoholism accelerated by the sale of bushmeat, disappearing of game animals from the forest frightened by the noise, and other indirect influences of logging operations.[52]

Furthermore, the Inspection Panel noted, "Pygmy people in some areas [were] denied access to forest areas which they traditionally have used for cultivation."[53]

---

49 *China: Western Poverty Reduction (Qinghai)* (1999), IR, § 264.
50 *China: Western Poverty Reduction (Qinghai)* (1999), IR, § 265, fn. 173.
51 *China: Western Poverty Reduction (Qinghai)* (1999), IR, § 265. But for the Panel's criticism of employing 'past country experience' as the conclusive factor in determining the project's environmental and social risk category, *see* section 14.1; *and also* compare with the discussion *in* section 6.3.1.
52 *Democratic Republic of Congo: Transitional Support*, IR, §§ 259-260.
53 *Id.*

If all "these negative influences are taken into consideration," the Panel concluded, it is clear "that active logging operations"

> impose adverse impacts and are mostly incompatible with the customary use of the forest by local and Indigenous Peoples if they take place simultaneously in the same area.[54]

This made the Bank's failure to apply its policy on Indigenous Peoples to the project area all the more troubling, the Panel commented, since the development of an IPDP would have identified and mitigated such risks.[55]

For example, as the Panel elaborated, issues regarding "overlapping territorial claims by the Pygmy People and the Bantu villagers did not result in much trouble"

> when the forest areas were large enough for the people to use them, or when the economic opportunity for exploiting forest resources was limited. When the forests are allocated to logging concessions, however, the overlapping rights over the forests often develop into extremely severe conflicts, as in the case reported from the Panel's visit to a village in Equateur Province. In most cases, Pygmy people are placed in disadvantageous position by the more powerful agriculturalists who try to monopolize the benefits from such an opportunity.[56]

Furthermore, "[t]he lack of disclosure to the local people,"

> in particular the Pygmy people, of information regarding forest reform and their legal rights – to the extent this has occurred – means that legal reforms and policy initiatives supported by the Bank may not as a practical matter be applied in the many remote areas where these people live.[57]

The Panel conceded that the "2002 Forest Code," which was aimed at "address[ing] the problem of illegal logging" (and which implementation of the Bank-funded project aimed to facilitate),[58] "contains certain innovations on the customary rights of forest residents and local communities," which might ensure that the Pygmy People's "traditional use of

---

54   *Id.*
55   In this regard, *see* the discussion *in* sections 10.1 & 13.1.
56   *Democratic Republic of Congo: Transitional Support* (2005), IR, § 332. On recourse as a mechanism to address power imbalances, *also see* the discussion *in* section 7.1.1.
57   *Democratic Republic of Congo: Transitional Support* (2005), IR, § 332. On issues related to information disclosure, *see* the discussion *in* section 11.1.
58   *Democratic Republic of Congo: Transitional Support* (2005), ER, § 5.

forest resources can be secured to some extent."[59] However, the Panel pointed out, "these innovations"

> would need to be implemented, for example through additional decrees and arêtes, in which the rights of particularly vulnerable Indigenous People need to be clearly established.[60]

Furthermore, "[t]he effective implementation of these provisions [...]"

> as well as the effective regulation of logging concession activities that might, in the near future, be validated and confirmed, depends to a crucial extent on the existence of adequate institutional capacity to ensure enforcement of laws within the country, both at the national and local levels.[61]

And, as noted earlier, the Panel found that "there is a stark lack of capacity to implement such measures and enforce the law in favor of the rights of local communities within DRC."[62]

The remainder of this section considers two aspects that affect the protection of indigenous peoples' rights and interests, as well as the realization of their specific development needs, namely: the *development of 'stand-alone' IP(D)Ps*; and the *content and scope ('reach') of IP(D)Ps*.

13.2.1   'Stand-alone' IP(D)Ps

A long-standing debate between the Inspection Panel and Bank management concerns the need for the development of separate or 'stand-alone' IP(D)Ps where indigenous people constitute the majority or 'bulk' of the project-affected people.[63]

China: Western Poverty Reduction (Qinghai) provides a prime example of this issue. Bank management argued that the development of a separate IPDP was unnecessary in this instance, and pointed to OD 4.20, paragraph 13, which stated: "When the bulk of the direct project beneficiaries are indigenous people, the Bank's concerns would be addressed

---

59 *Democratic Republic of Congo: Transitional Support* (2005), IR, §§ 252-256; *and see* IR, §§ 207-208 & 540.
60 *Id.*
61 *Id.*
62 *Id.* On issues related to borrower capacity constraints, *also see* the discussion *in* section 8.3.
63 *Note*, the difference in terminology is due to the conversion of the policy on Indigenous Peoples from the operational directive (OD) format to the current OP/BP structure – as discussed *in* section 5.1. The OD referred to 'Indigenous Peoples Development Plans', whereas the OP/BP refers to 'Indigenous Peoples Plans'.

by the project itself and the provisions of this OD would thus apply to the project in its entirety."[64]

The Panel, on the other hand, argued that "Management's interpretation of this one sentence of paragraph 13 of OD 4.20 cannot be accepted" since, "[in the case of this Project,] it is inconsistent with other parts of the OD"

> and especially inconsistent with the objective of Bank policy towards indigenous people, which is '[...] to ensure that the development process fosters full respect for their dignity, human rights, and cultural uniqueness [...]' and to 'ensure that indigenous peoples do not suffer adverse effects during the development process [...], and that they receive culturally compatible social and economic benefits'.[65]

The "danger in [Management's] approach," the Panel elaborated, lay specifically therein "that a Bank-financed project"

> could legitimately overwhelm the hopes and aspirations of an indigenous population, so long as the project benefits a larger population of some other indigenous people.[66]

Indeed, the Inspection Panel argued, Bank management should have developed separate IPDPs for each of the ethnic groups present in the project area since the "Bank's overall intent"

> in giving special attention to 'indigenous peoples', derives from the fact that they have a cultural identity and social status that make 'them vulnerable to being disadvantaged in the development process.'[67]

In fact, the Panel added, "the 'indigenous peoples,' or national minorities, in the Move-in area" – "the Hui, Mongol, Tibetan, Tu and Salar" – "are very different from each other, in their 'cultural uniqueness' as well as in their 'local patterns of social organization, religious beliefs, and resource use.'"[68] "In the Qinghai Project, however," the Panel emphasized,

---

64   See *China: Western Poverty Reduction (Qinghai)* (1999), IR, pp. xxvi-xxvii. In this regard, *see* the discussion *in* section 13.1.

65   See *China: Western Poverty Reduction (Qinghai)* (1999), IR, pp. xxvi-xxvii. *Note*, this example also demonstrates the Panel's emphasis on the underlying policy objective to support expansive ('purposive') interpretation – *as* discussed *in* section 6.3.3.

66   *China: Western Poverty Reduction (Qinghai)* (1999), IR, §§ 281-287.

67   *Id.*

68   *Id.*

"Management has effectively and retroactively lumped together these very different cultures into a single 'one-plan-fits-all' IPDP; that is, the 'project in its entirety.'"[69] "The application of" Management's "interpretation of the OD", the Panel emphasized, "can easily serve to increase the vulnerability"

> of the most vulnerable cultural and ethnic groups, and increase their chances of "[...] being disadvantaged in the development process." [...] Bundling these groups together in a single IPDP, whether that is the "project in its entirety," or a single IPDP for the whole of the Move-in area, effectively denies these very different ethnic groups, especially the numerically weakest and most vulnerable, an opportunity to participate in a process that would ensure that their minority cultural traditions are taken into account in the overall design of the Project.[70]

Furthermore, "Management's interpretation of [OD 4.20, paragraph 13] requires that careful attention be paid to exactly how the 'bulk of the direct project beneficiaries' [is] counted," the Panel commented.[71] Management's argument that "the majority of intended beneficiaries (58 percent of those in the Move-out area and 78 percent of those in the Move-in area)" in "the overall 'project area'" "are indigenous peoples,"[72] is based on the assumption "that the displaced pastoralists in the Move-in area are all 'beneficiaries' of the Project," which, the Panel emphasized,

> they are not. Rather, they are adversely affected by the Project. Their so-called 'benefits' are merely mitigating compensation for their involuntary displace-ment.[73]

The Inspection Panel had been critical of the lack of integration between the different project components in *India: Ecodevelopment*, as noted earlier.[74] In this instance, Management had also argued that a "separate IPDP was [not] prepared because indigenous people form the bulk of those of are affected by the project".[75] Furthermore, responding to the

---

69 *Id.*
70 *Id. Note*, these examples also illustrate the potential for conflict between multiple interests – here among project affected people (*see* section 3.1.5) – which reflects the pluralism and dynamic complexity of the transnational development context (*see* section 2.1). The examples also demonstrate the need for differentiated approaches in diverse project areas, *as* discussed *in* section 9.3.
71 *China: Western Poverty Reduction (Qinghai)* (1999), IR, §§ 273 & 276.
72 *Id.*
73 *Id. Note*, for more examples of issues related to the identification and quantification of project-affected people, *see* section 10.3. *And* for an example where the Panel found the Bank in compliance with respect to its decision not to develop a stand-alone IPDP, *see Nepal: Arun III* (1994) IR, § 14 (p. 34).
74 *See* the discussion *in* section 9.1.
75 *India: Ecodevelopment* (1998), MR, § 28.

claim that 'local people' was used in an ambiguous way in project documents in order to support this conclusion, and, therefore, justify 'involuntary resettlement', Management asserted that "[t]he language of the SAR and the legal agreements is very clear," namely that the Borrower "shall, in pursuing the objectives of the Project, not carry out any involuntary resettlement for any people resident within the [Project Areas]'."[76]

The Inspection Panel, however, argued that a separate IPDP should have been "prepared for the Nagarahole site during the years 1995 and 1996," particularly since "it would have further exposed the tension between biodiversity protection objectives "

> and the condition and aspirations of the indigenous people at Rajiv Gandhi National Park. It would have enabled significant input on the basic assumptions and concepts underlying the Ecodevelopment Project. And it might well have exposed the weakness of some of the premises under which the Project was conceived, at least for this particular park.[77]

In *Panama: Land Administration,* Bank management argued that a separate "IPDP was not prepared during Project preparation" since "a comprehensive" Social Assessment and Indigenous Peoples Strategy "were undertaken" instead.[78]

In this instance, the Inspection Panel agreed that "the absence of a stand-alone IPDP at appraisal"

> did not prevent the Bank from taking important actions in support of the *aspiration of the Naso* [the first group of Requesters] to have their own comarca.[79]

The Panel also agreed that the "Social Assessment and PAD prepared for the Project"

> properly highlighted the core need to give high priority to the work to develop a comarca, in light of risks faced *by the Naso people*. The Panel finds that this is consistent with the objectives of OD 4.20.[80]

Nevertheless, the Inspection Panel was critical of the Bank's "decision not to prepare a stand-alone IPDP for the Project" since it constituted an important root cause of the issues

---

76   *Id. But also see* the discussion *in* section 12.1.
77   *India: Ecodevelopment* (1998), ER, § 48.
78   *Panama: Land Administration* (2009), IR, §§ 249-250; *also see* IR, § 127.
79   *Panama: Land Administration,* IR, § 129 (emphasis added). *Also see* notes 46 & 47, Ch. 8.
80   *Id.*

the Panel's investigation highlighted with respect to the Ngäbe people (the second group of Requesters).[81]

For example, the Panel commented, the lack of a stand-alone IPDP "may partly explain" why the "consultation activities related to the consolidation of the Ngäbe-Buglé Comarca did not include residents and local leaders of the Annex Areas."[82] "[A]n IPDP with adequate consultations and studies that inform an IPDP," moreover, "could have identified the Annex Areas in Bocas del Toro as a critical issue requiring timely attention."[83] The preparation of an IPDP would also have provided "baseline data on the areas inhabited by the Ngäbe,"

> including adequate and up-to-date maps, and an assessment of the relevant
> legal framework of the country, giving particular attention to the rights of
> indigenous peoples 'to use and develop the lands that they occupy, to be pro-
> tected against illegal intruders, and to have access to natural resources (such
> as forests, wildlife, and water) vital to their subsistence and reproduction.'[84]

Furthermore, the development of a stand-alone IPDP would also have "analyzed relevant international instruments and whether the Project would be supportive of the borrower's international obligations with regard to indigenous peoples," as required by the Bank's operational policy framework.[85] In this regard, the Inspection Panel cited a 2001 case of the International Court of the Organization of American States, which affirmed that "indigenous people have a 'right' to the lands they historically occupy by virtue of being indigenous."[86] This "right," the Panel emphasized, was "reaffirmed by the Inter-American Court of Human Rights" in another 2001 case, which "establish[ed] a historical precedent"

---

81 *Panama: Land Administration*, IR, § 61. *Note*, "the Ngäbe people are Panama's largest indigenous group. They are neither highly organized, nor well placed politically. They were granted a comarca in 1997 together with the Buglé, a smaller related group. According to the PAD: 'consolidation of indigenous peoples' territories includes not only technical actions related to demarcation' but also a number of complementary activities, including conflict resolution and 'support to design or complete the Cartas Orgánicas [organic charters] and other regulations and norms dealing with the administration of indigenous territories'." (*See Panama: Land Administration*, IR, §§ 61 & 73.)

82 *Panama: Land Administration*, IR, § 61. On issues related to consultation with indigenous peoples, *see* section 13.3.

83 *Panama: Land Administration* (2009), IR, §§ 249-250; on issues pertaining to the Bocas del Toro-Annex Area, *see* IR, § 127.

84 *Panama: Land Administration*, IR, § 254. *Note*, on the importance of baseline data, obtained through sound surveying processes, *also see* the discussion *in* sections 12.2 & 14.2. On the importance of accurate maps in delineating the project area, *also see* the discussion *in* section 10.2.

85 *Panama: Land Administration* (2009), IR, § 254. In this regard, *see* the discussion *in* 5.3.1. *Also note*, these examples also demonstrate the tight relationships between the underlying objectives of several of the Bank's operational policies – as discussed *e.g.*, *in* section 4.2.

86 *Panama: Land Administration* (2009), IR, § 68.

at the international level in the struggle of indigenous peoples for their communal rights. This decision represents extremely important progress in the protection of the human rights of indigenous peoples in the Americas.[87]

"While the Panel understands why Bank staff may have adopted this approach," the Panel concluded, "our investigation has shown that this lack of a stand-alone IPDP prepared through a participatory process led to adverse consequences,"

> especially for the Ngäbe people of the Annex Areas. As this case suggests, safeguard policies, particularly in land projects involving indigenous people, play a crucial role in anticipating and preventing harm and thereby avoiding possible future grievances.[88]

"This reinforces the need," the Panel emphasized, "to ensure that not only the *content*, but the *purpose* of safeguard policies and the *potential consequences* of policy noncompliance, are properly understood by staff."[89]

Whereas in *Papua New Guinea: Smallholder Agriculture*, the Inspection Panel took note of Management's decision "not to prepare an Indigenous Peoples Plan (IPP) for the Project" based on the argument that "the Project in its entirety would benefit indigenous communities."[90] The Panel also noted that "Management made a similar judgment" with regard to the *Panama: Land Administration Project*.[91] However, the Panel concluded, "[i]n both the Panama investigation and this investigation," Management's interpretation did not constitute "compliance with OP 4.10" and, in both cases, was a root cause of several issues pertaining to indigenous people, such as "most serious concern" regarding "consultations with indigenous communities."[92] The lack of a stand-alone IPP also meant that the

---

87   *Id.*

88   *Panama: Land Administration* (2009), IR, § 347 (emphases omitted).

89   *Id. Note*, this example also demonstrates the Inspection Panel's emphasis on 'process' *and* 'substance' as necessary components of 'compliance' (*see* section 6.3.4), as well as the Panel's emphasis on the underlying policy objective to support expansive ('purposive') interpretation (*see* section 6.3.3). The example also serves to demonstrate the Panel's contribution towards institutional strengthening through institutional learning – as discussed *in* section 7.1.5.

90   *Papua New Guinea: Smallholder Agriculture* (2009), IR, § 523. *Note*, OP 4.10 was applicable to this project. *And compare* the language of OP 4.10, § 12 (which states: "The IPP is prepared in a flexible and pragmatic manner, its level of detail varies depending on the specific project and the nature of effects to be addressed. The borrower integrates the IPP into the project design. When Indigenous Peoples are the sole or the overwhelming majority of direct project beneficiaries, the elements of an IPP should be included in the overall project design, and a separate IPP is not required.") with the language contained in OD 4.20, § 13 (*see* note 64, Ch. 13).

91   *Id.*

92   *Id. Note*, the example also demonstrates the Inspection Panel's practice of referencing previous findings (*see* section 1.2.1.), as well as the Panel's contribution towards strengthening institutional performance by means of institutional learning – as discussed *in* section 7.1.5.

"significant economic, financial, and institutional differences" among the three "different Project areas" were not properly accounted for, which meant, in turn, that the smallholders could not "receive appropriate economic, social, and cultural benefits from the Project, as required both by "OMS 2.20 and OP/BP 4.10."[93]

Other project documents, the Panel asserted, could not adequately reflect and address the diversity among the different project areas. For example, the Panel explained, "the Social Assessment and Beneficiaries Assessment contain[ed] a wealth of information on social and economic issues affecting oil palm growers in the various Project areas," but it did "not include sufficient 'social, cultural, and political characteristics of the affected Indigenous Peoples,' as required by Annex A of OP 4.10," so as "to complete an ethnographic baseline."[94]

Furthermore, while the Beneficiaries Assessment "identifie[d] the major ethnolinguistic groups in the two Project provinces", it concluded that "the indigenous ethnic/language groups" in both these areas "are relatively homogenous in terms of culture, social organization, and land tenure systems."[95] Although "[t]he indigenous inhabitants of the Project area in Oro province [...] are from one large ethnic and cultural group," the Inspection Panel commented, "the Orokaiva, [is] comprised of seven tribes – each with several patrilineal clans and sub-clans – with a high degree of cultural uniformity," while their language – Orokaiva – "has several dialects."[96] "The population of West New Britain [WNB] province is far more diverse," the Panel added, "with seven major ethnic/tribal groups speaking some 25 languages,

> about whom the Beneficiaries Assessment notes that 'whilst there are minor differences in the subsistence and agricultural systems of the various ethnic and language groups, they share similar social and cultural systems.'[97]

In addition, the Social and Beneficiaries Assessment contained "little further discussion or information"

> on the identification of customary leadership, decision-making structures, and dispute-mediation and conflict-resolution processes applicable to Project-affected Indigenous Peoples, nor of how they might differ across various ethnic groups. Such information is likely to be key, for example, in addressing the question of who decides, how, when, and whether specific families choose to

---

93 *Papua New Guinea: Smallholder Agriculture* (2009), IR, § 314.
94 *Papua New Guinea: Smallholder Agriculture* (2009), IR, §§ 171-172.
95 *Id.*
96 *Id.*
97 *Id.*

cultivate more oil palm, either to re-plant, or to go for the infilling option; on which piece of customary land; and which land can be made available to other clans/sub-clans, settlers or mini-estates for oil palm cultivation.[98]

"This absence of analysis in the Social Assessment," the Panel concluded, "does not correspond to the terms of reference of the Social Assessment," which specifies that

> it should "Gather anthropological information (primarily socio-political) on significant variations (if any) between or among the various indigenous groups in the project areas of West New Britain and Oro regarding the local political economy leadership, political competition, decision making, representation, and relations/linkages with LLGs [Local Level Governments]."[99]

It "might be useful," therefore, the Panel commented, "to formulate clearer guidelines"

> for the application of OP 4.10 to projects where a self-standing IPP is not warranted. The emphasis is on the appropriateness of benefits intended under the project and community support for the project as a whole.[100]

Such guidelines are particularly important given the "unique challenge" that "projects in Papua New Guinea" generally "pose for the Bank," since "the population is almost entirely composed of indigenous peoples from over eight hundred distinct ethnic groups" – which means that "the Bank's policy on Indigenous Peoples is "trigger[ed] [...] for every project."[101] And since "particular attention to the Indigenous Peoples Policy during implementation is critical," given this 'ethnic complexity', the Panel added, this "may call for clearer guidelines for staff in making OP 4.10 operational in Papua New Guinea."[102]

In its formal response to the Panel's investigation report, however, Bank Management affirmed that it "does not see the need for such guidelines, as it believes that the current provisions of the policy adequately address this situation."[103]

---

98 *Papua New Guinea: Smallholder Agriculture* (2009), IR, §§ 167-169. *Note,* such issues can also play a considerate role in consultation – *as* discussed *in* section 13.3. For an example of a how a poor understanding of customary property rights affected project content and scope, *also see* the issue of 'land ownership' in *Nigeria/Ghana: West African Gas Pipeline, as* discussed *in* section 8.2.1.

99 *Papua New Guinea: Smallholder Agriculture* (2009), IR, §§ 167-169.

100 *Papua New Guinea: Smallholder Agriculture* (2009), IR, §§ 527-528.

101 *Papua New Guinea: Smallholder Agriculture* (2009), IR, § 531. *Note,* this example also demonstrates the Panel's contribution towards strengthening institutional performance through learning and policy advice – *as* discussed *in* section 7.1.5.

102 *Id.*

103 *Papua New Guinea: Smallholder Agriculture* (2009), MRIR, p. ix.

13.2.2   Content and scope of IP(D)Ps and associated project documentation

The Inspection Panel also reviews the content and scope of IP(D)Ps and, as the examples from *Smallholder Agriculture* illustrate, of associated project documentation such as Social Assessments.

In *India: Coal Sector*, for example, the Panel was critical of the "IPDP activities in Parej East," noting that the actions included in the plan appeared to be "disconnected, have little depth, are just marginal and, on the whole, do not reflect a real 'felt' need."[104]

For instance, the Panel elaborated, the activities contained in the IPDP "have focused largely on projects for physical development of villages"

> such as the construction of village roads, repair of wells, making of ponds for irrigation and the repair of a community hall. CCL informed the Panel that its plan was gradually to reduce expenditure on infrastructure and to raise it on skill development and capacity building. [...] The Panel is concerned that there has been no concentration on long-term projects such as literacy and numeracy classes, maternal and child health, and self help groups.[105]

"Although very late," the Panel commented, it was "encouraging to note that the 2002 IPDP implementation plans consists exclusively "

> of self-help group capacity building and income generation. The Panel would urge that Management take steps to ensure that this does in fact materialize.[106]

The Inspection Panel also expressed its concern that the IPDP failed to reflect the diversity that existed among indigenous communities. "In Parej East," the Panel explained, "the population in each of the eleven hamlets"

> ranges from 14 to 123 families. Each has its own unique composition (some hamlets are fully tribal, some only partly, some follow one faith, others another). The IPDP ignores this. The descriptions of each of the hamlets begin and end with the same qualitative paragraph, and each of the plans end with very similar recommendations and the same total budget.

---

104 *India: Coal Sector* (2001), IR, §§ 346-348.
105 *Id. Note*, this example also illustrates the issue of 'balance' between 'technical/commercial' and 'non-technical/non-commercial' project components, *as* discussed *in* Ch. 9.
106 *India: Coal Sector* (2001), IR, §§ 348-349.

"This approach," the Panel concluded, "flies in the face of [...] the Bank's OD 4.20 requirement that location-specific IPDPs should address the specific needs of each community."[107]

The Inspection Panel's investigation also highlighted that the Resettlement Action Plan for Parej East was "silent in terms of data and process for tribal's cultivation land under traditional rights."[108] The RAP "simply does not say," the Panel explained, "what a project affected tribal cultivating land under customary right"

> is supposed to do, or when, or how he is supposed to do it. In addition, while the RAP describes the need for "authentication" of GMK ['tribal'] land, the Panel finds it difficult to understand how this can be achieved when neither the Baseline Survey, nor the 1994 RAP (nor subsequent annual updates of the RAP, nor the later database) provided the CCL with any list of tribals cultivating, or claiming to cultivate, land under customary rights. It is not possible to discern who owns what types of land, or to isolate those who "cultivate land under traditional rights" [...].[109]

Furthermore, while World Bank "Management expected" that the Borrower and its project implementing agency would treat 'tribal' communities "in accordance with Bank ODs 4.30 and 4.20", "it appears that the laws of the State of Bihar precluded" 'land authentication' "without documentation."[110] The Inspection Panel questioned "how, at the time of preparation, Management could be unaware of this"

> when the Bank had been involved in resettlement projects in India for some years. Furthermore, based on the foregoing, it seems clear that, during preparation, Management did not raise any questions about the possible lack of legal recognition or the process required to ensure compensation for tribals cultivating traditional land without title or documentation.[111]

---

107 *India: Coal Sector* (2001), IR, § 313. *Note*, on the need to employ differentiated approaches in light of diversity among project-affected people, *also see* the discussion *in* section 9.3.
108 *India: Coal Sector* (2001), IR, §§ 166 & 174.
109 *Id. Note*, on the importance of social and environmental baseline data, *also see* the discussion *in* section 14.2.
110 *Id.* This example also demonstrates the interfaces with the Borrower's domestic legal and regulatory system – *see* section 5.2.
111 *Id. Note*, this example also demonstrates the interfaces with the Borrower's constitutional system, also at the 'sub-national' level – *as* discussed *in* section 5.2. On issues related to property valuation and compensation for 'loss', *also see* section 12.3.

"These findings," the Panel concluded, constituted "a serious failure to comply with the" Bank's policies on Indigenous Peoples and Involuntary Resettlement.[112]

Whereas in *Honduras: Land Administration*, the Panel commended the project for having incorporated several "important positive features in the IPDP," such as "budget allocations for capacity building and training of local community leaders on national laws, and for training of conciliators and arbitrators," which were "consistent with the stated intent of the IPDP to protect indigenous peoples from the results of depredations and invasions of their territory."[113]

However, the Panel also drew attention to "the potential impact of power and/or class divisions in the resolution of conflicts both in the past and perhaps more recently."[114] While the policy "require[d] that the IPDP contain an assessment of the ability of the indigenous peoples 'to obtain access to and effectively use the legal system to defend their rights'," the Panel expressed its "concer[n]" that "the IPDP does not adequately reflect"

> or address the risks posed to the Garífuna people by its proposed means of resolving conflicts. These include, in particular, risks posed by disparities of power in the process.[115]

Concerning the adequacy of the Indigenous Peoples Development Plan in the context of Honduras's proposed 'Property Law' (discussed earlier),[116] the Panel found that the IPDP did not "adequately assess the potential implications for indigenous peoples of the special expedited judicial procedure that is contained in the draft Property Law."[117] The Panel specifically highlighted "the complexity of the conflict resolution procedures" in the new Law, which exacerbated "the concerns of Requesters"

> that the existence of multiple conflict resolution procedures including those in the IPDP, in the new Property Law and others generates confusion in the communities.[118]

Indeed, the Panel affirmed, the "IPDP envisions arbitration, conciliation" as well as the establishment of "*mesas*" ('boards') for conflict resolution," whereas the "new Property Law"

---

112 *Id.*
113 *Honduras: Land Administration* (2006), IR, §§ 371-372.
114 *Id.*
115 *Id. Also see* the discussion *in* section 13.3.
116 *See* section 8.2.1.
117 *Honduras: Land Administration* (2006), IR, §§ 374-375. For additional examples of project-interfaces with borrowers' judicial systems in the context of project-level grievances mechanisms, *also see* section 12.6.
118 *Honduras: Land Administration* (2006), IR, §§ 374-375. *Also see* the discussion *in* section 13.3.

sets forth its own judicial abbreviated procedure, and, alternatively, provides for conciliation (for which the Property Institute would be the competent authority to initiate or support), arbitration or mediation. It should also be noted that the Project's Operational Manual describes the instances of extrajudicial conflict resolution as included in the Project IPDP, but also states that every conflict between indigenous peoples and third parties with respect to communal land will be subject to the special procedure created in the Property Law. In addition, during Project implementation, the Mesa Regional was created with a role in conflict resolution.[119]

"Understandably," the Panel concluded, "these many instances and options"

> have created confusion and anxiety among the affected communities. The Panel finds that there is a need for clarification and consultation with the affected communities as to which procedures apply, and a need for better dissemination of this information.[120]

Responding to several claims concerning the adequacy of the IPP in *Cameroon: Petroleum Development and Pipeline*,[121] Bank management argued it was a "work-in-progress."[122] Management affirmed its "commitment to help the Bakola/Bagyeli to secure a better stature in the Cameroonian social structure", but emphasized that this was "a process"

> for empowering the people to make decisions for themselves, and that's going to mean some negotiation. While delay in the IPP was a problem, this is a long-term commitment. The ID cards are a big jump forward, as they give Bagyeli personhood. FEDEC's plans for Agriculture, health, and education are going in the right direction. Pygmy participation in FEDEC is not precluded; it is a 30-year process. Moreover, land security is do-able, we have to work with civil authorities, and it has to work between *préfet* and local *chef de terres*, between Bantu and Bakola.[123]

"Although under normal circumstances such 'work' would not be in compliance with the provisions of OD 4.20," the Inspection Panel nevertheless recognized "the practicality of

---

119 *Id. Also see* the discussion *in* section 13.3.
120 *Honduras: Land Administration* (2006), IR, §§ 374-375. *Note,* this discussion also demonstrates issues related to the content of project-information, *as* discussed *in* section 11.1.2.
121 Such as inadequate consultation regarding the IPDP's adoption, incomplete baseline studies and delays regarding the IPDP's implementation – *see e.g., Cameroon: Petroleum* (2002), IR, §§ 195, 199 & 207.
122 *Cameroon: Petroleum* (2002), IR, § 223.
123 *Cameroon: Petroleum* (2002), IR, § 215.

Management's strategy because of the conditions and practices of the Bakola/Bagyeli/Bantu community within the wider Cameroonian society."[124] In addition, the Panel noted "that Bank Management and COTCO have corrected the shortcomings in the intervening years since the EMP was written."[125] Moreover, the Panel acknowledged, these shortcomings "did not produce harm to the Bakola/Bagyeli community" – on the contrary, "[t]he Project has created a positive environment"

> for the Bakola/Bagyeli through its procedures on consultation, compensation, and development programs, where the Bakola/Bagyeli community now is in a stronger position to assert their rights as full citizens of Cameroon.[126]

This particular IPP, the Panel concluded, was "a long-term endeavor expected to be carried out over the 25 years of the Pipeline operation. Of necessity it must be fine-tuned in the process of implementation."[127]

However, the Inspection Panel was critical of the scope of the IPP since it considered "only those Bakola/Bagyeli communities within 2 km of the pipeline".[128] "By limiting the IPP to this narrow band of settlements along the road," the Panel commented, "the EMP (and IPP) lack a wider regional assessment of the potential risks posed by the pipeline project in the larger area utilized by the Bakola/Bagyeli."[129] Although it was an accepted practice on pipeline projects "to designate project-affected people among agricultural populations as those individuals and communities whose fields and property have been traversed by the pipeline right-of-way," the Panel pointed out that "the impact of the pipeline may indeed be greater for the Bakola/Bagyeli,"

> whose subsistence still include, to a large extent, hunting areas covering a larger segment of the littoral forest in addition to their agricultural settlements along the pipeline route. Narrowing the impact area that affects the Bakola/Bagyeli in the semi-sedentary agricultural communities close to the pipeline route, ignores the wider social, economic and ecological dimensions of Bakola/Bagyeli subsistence patterns.[130]

---

124 *Id.*

125 *Cameroon: Petroleum* (2002), § 222. For examples of the corrective/remedial actions undertaking with regard to strengthening the IPP, *see Cameroon: Petroleum* (2002), § 216.

126 *Id.*

127 *Cameroon: Petroleum* (2002), IR, § 223.

128 *Cameroon: Petroleum Development and Pipeline* (2002), IR, § 202.

129 *Id. Note*, for issues related to the content and scope of EAs, *see* section 14.2; *and* on the concept of a project's 'area of influence' *also see* the discussion *in* section 10.2.

130 *Cameroon: Petroleum Development and Pipeline* (2002), IR, § 202. On industry and professional best practices and standards as a source of normativity, *also see* the discussion in section 5.4.

And, "[a]lthough it does not appear that the Project directly impacts on the hunting and gathering resources in the wider forest region," the Panel commented, "the narrowness of the baseline survey's geographical range precludes a comprehensive impact assessment."[131]

Finally, in *Cambodia: Forest Concession Management*, the Requesters "claim[ed] that, since the [logging] concessions threaten the livelihood and culture" of indigenous communities, "the Bank should have required the preparation of an Indigenous Peoples Development Plan (IPDP) to address these social impacts", whereas the Bank's failure to "take into account the impacts of the concessions on the indigenous peoples" has subsequently "allowed the concession companies 'to ignore these issues completely'."[132]

Bank management, on its part, "acknowledge[d] that the Bank was not in full compliance with OD 4.20 and that, in hindsight,"

> screening studies and a framework IPDP, along with more discussion of the issue would have been more appropriate during project design.[133]

Management added that the Bank had since "decided to assist the Government in preparing community consultation guidelines which would include a step-by-step manual with provisions specifically related to indigenous peoples."[134]

The Inspection Panel agreed that, "in line with OD 4.20, an IPDP should have been prepared for this Project,"[135] while adding that the project showed "a serious lack of information about baseline social structure," "traditional land and resource use" and also had "no information about the inheritance of traditional land and passageway rights across generations."[136] "This lack of adequate baseline data," the Panel elaborated, "even for the area within the overly restricted boundaries of the 'Project area' as designated by Management,"

> severely hampers any attempt to determine potential adverse impacts of the Project on the indigenous peoples affected by it.[137]

---

131 *Id.*
132 *Cambodia: Forest Concession Management* (2005), IR, § 256.
133 *Cambodia: Forest Concession Management* (2005), IR, § 257.
134 *Id.*
135 *Cambodia: Forest Concession Management* (2005), IR, § 260.
136 *Cambodia: Forest Concession Management* (2005), IR, § 261.
137 *Id. Note*, on issues related to the delineation of project area and project areas of influence, *see* section 10.2; on issues related to baseline data, *see* section 14.2. *Also note*, this example also demonstrates the tight relationships between the underlying objectives of several of the Bank's operational policies – *as* discussed *e.g.*, *in* section 4.2.

The Inspection Panel also questioned why "no attempt was made to develop social, technical, and legal capacity within the institutions responsible for Government interaction with indigenous peoples as required by OD 4.20."[138] The Panel noted, furthermore, that "no provision was made for early handover of project management," nor "for the education and training in management skills for indigenous people" – although the Panel added that its investigation team had "observed such skills at work in villages where indigenous people had formed committees to protect forests from illegal logging."[139]

Hence, the Inspection Panel concluded, "even many of the prerequisites for" the development of "an IPDP are lacking."[140] "Had they been developed," the Panel emphasized, "many of the problems that have afflicted the Project would have been recognized and might have been corrected."[141]

13.3 CONSULTATION WITH INDIGENOUS PEOPLES

Compliance concerns relating to consultation with indigenous peoples reflect many of the same issues, as discussed earlier.[142] But it also involves specific issues – such as the meaning of core phrases included in the policy on Indigenous Peoples (notably, "*free, prior, informed consultation*" and "*broad community support*"), as well as issues related to *consultation in ethnically complex communities*. The final section of Chapter 13 considers these matters.[143]

13.3.1 *The meaning of 'free, prior, informed consultation' and 'broad community support'*

The inclusion of the phrase, 'free, prior, informed *consultation*' – as opposed to free, prior, informed *consent*' – has been a longstanding subject of criticism, with some advocacy groups arguing that this aspect of OP 4.10 "does not meet the requirements of international law because it does not provide indigenous peoples with a veto right over projects that take place within their territories," whereas "such a veto right", they add, "has become

---

138 *Cambodia: Forest Concession Management* (2005), IR, § 262. *Note*, on issues related to borrower capacity constraints, and project activities aimed at strengthening borrowers' institutional capacity, *also see* the discussion *in* section 8.3.

139 *Cambodia: Forest Concession Management* (2005), IR, § 262.

140 *Id.*

141 *Id.*

142 *See* section 11.2.

143 *Note*, for an example where the Panel found the Bank to be compliance regarding consultation with indigenous people, *see e.g., Mexico: Indigenous and Community Biodiversity Project* (2003), ER § 44; *and* for an example where Bank management acknowledged non-compliance in the area of consultation with indigenous people, *see Panama: Land Administration* (2009) IR, § 270.

customary [international] law."[144] On the other hand, as Di Leva comments, "a comprehensive study by the Environmental Law Institute"

> related to prior informed consent in the context of mining operations concluded that there is *no universally accepted definition of the term 'consent'*.[145]

Inspection Panel practice reflects similar issues with regard to the meaning of 'free, prior, informed consultation' – whereas narrow interpretations of this phrase tend to affect the operationalization of the Bank's policy on Indigenous Peoples.

"[S]hortcomings in consultations with the affected [indigenous] populations, and in particular, failure to adequately account for local structures of representation" are significant compliance issues that have been identified in several Inspection Panel cases, as the Panel observed in *Papua New Guinea: Smallholder Agriculture*.[146]

With respect to the *Smallholder Agriculture* case, Bank management emphasized that it "strongly believe[d]"

> that broad community support for the Project exists in the three oil palm growing areas targeted under the Project and that the Project design reflects the concerns of the beneficiaries.[147]

Moreover, Management added, "requirements regarding 'broad community support' and 'free, prior and informed consultations'" in OP 4.10 (Indigenous Peoples) are "not meant to require unanimity of views or to condition a Bank project on the receipt of consent from all affected individuals or groups."[148]

By contrast, the Inspection Panel concluded that "the widespread community *interest* in growing oil palm cannot be equated with broad community *support* for the Project."[149] "Broad Community Support," the Panel underscored, "can only be confirmed on the basis

---

144 Di Leva *in* Bradlow & Hunter (Eds.) (2010), p. 359. *Note*, for arguments regarding the relationships between the Bank's operational policy framework and the international legal system, *see* the discussion *in* section 5.1.1.

145 *Id.* (emphasis added). *Note*, Di Leva quotes S. Bass (2004), *Prior Confirmed Consent and Mining, Promoting Sustainable Development of Local Communities*, Washington, D.C: Environmental Law Institute, p. 41.

146 *Papua New Guinea: Smallholder Agriculture* (2009), IR, § 527. *Note*, the Panel referred specifically to its investigations of *Democratic Republic of Congo: Transitional Support* (2005) and *Honduras: Land Administration* (2006). *Also note*, this example demonstrates the Panel's practice of referring to recurring findings in order to contribute towards strengthening institutional performance through institutional learning – as discussed *in* section 7.1.5.

147 *Papua New Guinea: Smallholder Agriculture* (2009), ER, § 35.

148 *Papua New Guinea: Smallholder Agriculture* (2009), IR, § 142.

149 *Papua New Guinea: Smallholder Agriculture* (2009), IR, § 219 (emphases added).

of free, prior, and informed consultation, as noted by OP 4.10," whereas in this instance, the Panel "was unable to find"

> in Project documents, including the Social and Beneficiaries Assessments, any information documenting how broad community support was reached. The Panel finds that this is not in compliance with OP 4.10.[150]

In fact, the Panel concluded that consultation with indigenous people was inadequate in terms of "scope, extent, and form in addition to not taking adequate account of customary decision-making structures."[151] For instance, the "identification of the legal and institutional framework, including customary leadership and decision-making processes," the Panel elaborated, "is critical for consultation and for gaining community support"; yet, the project's analysis of these aspects, as well as "the variations (if any) of these practices among different ethnic groups, fell short of the requirements of Annex A of OP 4.10, and thus did not comply with Bank Policy."[152]

Moreover, the Panel commented, "OP 4.10 requires that consultation of communities"

> takes place not only at the project design stage, but throughout implementation, and the continuous involvement of appropriately trained staff is critical.[153]

While "Management had been attentive to OP 4.10 requirements at the early planning stage (i.e., the Social Assessment and Beneficiaries Assessment)," the Panel noted, "references to this Policy gradually diminished as the Project moved into the concrete design phase and subsequently into implementation and supervision."[154]

The Inspection Panel also emphasized the requirement contained in the policy on Indigenous Peoples that projects should be designed so as "*to ensure that the Indigenous Peoples receive social and economic benefits that are culturally appropriate and gender and intergenerationally inclusive.*"[155] The Panel pointed out that World Bank "staff may become less focused" on this requirement, particularly "in projects where 'adverse effects' are not obvious" and where there is a general conclusion that "there is no need to develop an IPP",

---

150 *Id. Note*, since obligations related to information-disclosure and consultation with project-affected people are active in nature, the Inspection Panel typically looks for evidence of concrete actions taken in line with these obligations – as reflected, *e.g.*, *in* notes 88 & 89, Ch. 11.

151 *Papua New Guinea: Smallholder Agriculture* (2009), IR, § 526.

152 *Papua New Guinea: Smallholder Agriculture* (2009), IR, § 170.

153 *Papua New Guinea: Smallholder Agriculture* (2009), IR, 529.

154 *Id.*

155 *Papua New Guinea: Smallholder Agriculture* (2009), IR, 525 (emphasis in original).

as in the present case.[156] Furthermore, the Panel added, with the policy also specifying that an IPP should ensure that "potential adverse effects on Indigenous Peoples are identified," and that "those adverse effects are avoided, minimized, mitigated, or compensated for", Management attention "may [be] divert[ed] [...] away from a focus"

> on how to ensure culturally appropriate benefits. A key concern in this regard appears to be the consultation process; whether it adequately meets the standards of *free, prior and informed consultation*, whether *broad community support* by indigenous communities has been obtained, and whether consultations also focus properly on *benefits*.[157]

Indigenous people are at a distinct disadvantage when it comes to the consultation process – a fact that needs to be recognized and compensated for in order to ensure that there is, indeed, 'free and prior consultation' that result in 'broad community support'.

For example, in *Democratic Republic of Congo: Transitional Support*, "[w]ith regard to outreach to Indigenous People," Management argued that it "understood the importance of reaching out to Pygmy groups" but asserted that "its efforts were restricted to policy dialogue and to contacts with stakeholders in Kinshasa because the forest areas were still inaccessible" due to the prior political conflict in the project area.[158]

The Inspection Panel "recognize[d] the many difficulties that Bank staff and their partners encounter when they have to develop initiatives in a post-conflict situation," and also affirmed that it was "fully aware of the lack of political stability that existed in DRC during the implementation of the activities that have become subject to the Request for this inspection."[159] Nevertheless, the Panel also pointed out "that indigenous Pygmy peoples generally have a disadvantage in relation to information and systems of 'consultation'" since "they have been keeping inter-dependent but unequal relationship[s] with their particular Bantu-speaking agricultural neighbors,"

> who are called "kpala" among the Mbuti in Ituri, and "nkolo" among the Batswa in Equateur Province; both words have a connotation of "patron" or "boss." While this relationship may have changed recently, particularly during the last few decades with social and economic changes in DRC, the long-term influences

---

156 *Id.* On the Panel's criticism of the decision not to develop a stand-alone IP(D)P in this instance, *see* section 13.2.1.
157 *Id.*
158 *Democratic Republic of Congo: Transitional Support* (2005), § 323.
159 *Democratic Republic of Congo: Transitional Support* (2005), § 442.

of this relationship still remain in the political structure of a regional community.[160]

"This social dynamic with their neighbors," the Panel elaborated, "coupled with overlapping customary rights to the same forest areas,"

> makes the situation more difficult for the Pygmy people to express their interest. These factors also underline the importance of a proper IPDP analysis and social assessment, as discussed above, to ensure that such characteristics are taken into account in actions to achieve consultation and participation by the Pygmy people in accordance with the relevant Bank policies.[161]

Whereas in *Cambodia: Forest Concession Management*, the Panel was found that the Project had "failed to identify the population affected by and to develop an IPDP for the affected indigenous peoples during the planning phase."[162] Instead, the Panel commented, the "Project left the development of this information to the concessionaires [logging concession companies]," to be completed as part of their Environmental and Social Impact Assessments.[163] Therefore, the Panel concluded "a safeguard postponed is a safeguard denied,"

> because by failing to identify beforehand the affected population, the Bank policies requiring consultation and participation of that population could not be properly followed.[164]

Moreover, with respect to consultation with the indigenous communities, the Panel emphasized that it was "unlikely that such a procedure can meet the requirements of OD 4.20 to ensure the 'informed participation' of the indigenous peoples in addressing issues pertaining to them [...]."[165] Indeed, the Panel concluded, the "unequal power relationships between the concession companies and the affected people"

> make this type of consultation an inequitable situation. Within the context of recent Cambodian history and conditions, it also makes it very difficult for individuals or local communities to defend their rights.[166]

---

160 *Democratic Republic of Congo: Transitional Support* (2005), § 328.
161 *Democratic Republic of Congo: Transitional Support* (2005), IR, § 330.
162 *Cambodia: Forest Concession Management* (2005), IR, § 212.
163 *Id.*
164 *Id. Also see* the Panel's criticisms about the postponement of consultation with project-affected people to later stages of the project cycle, as discussed *in* section 11.2.1.
165 *Cambodia: Forest Concession Management* (2005), IR, §§ 344-345.
166 *Id.*

In addition, "this kind of arrangement", the Panel commented, "missed the opportunity to fulfill an objective of Bank policies, which is to develop local governmental and non-governmental capacity within this sector."[167] "OD 4.20, para 14(c), for example,"

> indicates that the 'institutions responsible for government interaction with indigenous peoples should possess the social, technical, and legal skills needed for carrying out the proposed development activities [...].' It adds that they 'should normally involve appropriate existing institutions, local organizations, and nongovernmental organizations (NGOs) with expertise in matters relating to indigenous peoples.'[168]

Finally, as to the meaning of '*free*, prior, informed consultation', the Inspection Panel emphasizes that such activities have to involve 'real choice' – as it does in other project contexts.[169] In *Honduras: Land Administration*, for example, Bank management contented that "communities are free to choose whether they want to participate in the Project" and that "individual communities can avoid the potential harm alleged by the Requesters by choosing not to participate in the Project."[170] However, the Inspection Panel questioned "whether there is a meaningful option for most communities not to participate in the demarcation and titling activities provided under the Project."[171] "The new Property Law, enacted after the Credit was approved by the Board," the Panel elaborated,

> grants specific rights to non-indigenous peoples who occupy and hold a 'valid title' within Ethnic Lands. As a result, these non-indigenous title holders may trigger title regularization activities in Ethnic Lands. Communities may face a choice of participating in a Project which, as currently structured, they believe does not represent their interests, or attempt to opt out of the Project and face significant challenges from non-indigenous people occupying and claiming rights over their Ethnic Lands.[172]

Hence, "[g]iven the relative economic and political vulnerability of the indigenous peoples," the Panel concluded, "the safeguards provided under the Project are not adequate to protect the Garífuna rights over their Ethnic Lands in the context of Project implementation."[173]

---

167 *Cambodia: Forest Concession Management* (2005), IR, § 347.
168 *Id. Also see* the discussion on the participants of consultation activities, *in* section 11.2.4.
169 *See e.g.,* the discussion *in* section 12.1.
170 *Honduras: Land Administration* (2006), IR, pp. xxx-xxxi.
171 *Id.*
172 *Id. Note,* on the 2004 Honduran Property Law,' *also see* the discussion *in* section 8.2.1.
173 *Id.*

13.3.2   Consultation in ethnically complex communities

Consultation in ethnically complex communities typically requires differentiated consultation approaches – not only due to differences caused by related factors such as ethnicity, language or religion, but also because different indigenous groups might have very different (and potentially competing) needs and interests.

For example, in *China: Western Poverty Reduction (Qinghai)*, the Inspection Panel contrasted the differences between the needs and interests of the various 'ethnic minorities' in the project area. "Ethnic minorities in the Move-in area (as well as those from the Move-out area)", the Panel noted, "will have major changes to their subsistence systems:"

> the resettled farmers will shift from dryland to irrigated agriculture; pastoralists in the Move-in area will switch to mixed agriculture and pastoralism. OD 4.20 requires that 'Development activities [...] support production systems that are well adapted to the needs and environment of indigenous peoples, and [...] help production systems under stress to attain sustainable levels.'[174]

"This is not something that can be imposed," the Panel pointed out; rather, it "requires an open-ended process of extensive consultation with and full participation by the people concerned."[175] However, the Panel concluded, "[t]he form of 'consultation' which Management employed" in this instance, "essentially treated"

> each of the different ethnic communities in the Move-out area in the same way. In no case did 'consultation' involve bringing people from the same ethnic group together to help envision a development plan for their own minority group.[176]

Inspection Panel practice also reflects different types of issues related to representation during the consultation process. The Inspection Panel's investigation in *Panama: Land Administration*, for example, highlighted competing claims as to who could claim to be the 'true' representatives of specific indigenous communities. This became a significant issue, in particular with respect to consultation about the controversial 'Law No. 72'.[177]

The Panel noted, for instance, that in its interview with "Tito Santana," (the king of the Naso who was subsequently removed from power during project implementation), "he freely states that he was consulted on Law No. 72 and claims broad community support"

---

174 *China: Western Poverty Reduction (Qinghai)* (1999), IR, §§ 284-285.
175 *Id.*
176 *Id.*
177 *Note*, on 'Law No. 72', *also see* the discussion *in* section 8.2.1.

for the new law, from the community he represented at the time.[178] "Valentín Santana's group," however, "denies having been consulted on this issue", while "also claim[ing] broad community support" for their position.[179] In other words, the Panel summarized, "Valentín Santana's supporters"

> have made no secret of their adamant opposition to that law, while Tito Santana has made no secret of his approval of same, while insisting that he acted with the full support of village leaders in Naso territory.[180]

"Whether the majority of the Naso opposes or supports the law is difficult for the Panel to ascertain," the Panel commented, "but there certainly has been strong opposition, as reflected by the Request for Inspection."[181] However, the Panel also acknowledged "that the evidence before it regarding the consultation process [was] mixed" – over the course of its field visit, the Panel

> heard various claims regarding Law No. 72 that appeared to demonstrate both disagreement and misunderstanding of the law by the Naso, as well as poor information about its content. Many of the Naso the Panel met with, nevertheless, were aware of this law and, as noted, had serious concerns about its implications.[182]

On the other hand, Bank management also affirmed "that, in an effort to maintain momentum in the protection of indigenous lands,"

> it decided to support the consultation process related to the new bill of law (eventually Law No. 72) being proposed to regulate land under collective management outside established comarcas.[183]

But Management also recognized "that there were inadequate consultations with the Naso on the inclusion of Article 17 of Law No. 72 and the preparation of the draft organic charter" – an "assessment" with which the Inspection Panel "concur[red]".[184]

Furthermore, the Inspection Panel acknowledged "the difficulty of identifying and addressing an issue that official leaders representing an indigenous group did not bring

---

178 *Panama: Land Administration* (2009), IR, § 159.
179 *Id.*
180 *Id.*
181 *Id.*
182 *Panama: Land Administration* (2009), IR, §§ 161-162.
183 *Id.*
184 *Id.*

to the attention of Project officials" – referring specifically to the "unsuccessful attempt in 1998–99 [*i.e.*, "[b]efore the Project began"] to "delimit ['measure and map'] the Annex Areas."[185] Nevertheless, the Panel commented, "more-inclusive consultations should have been carried out," which "would likely"

> have brought the Annex Area issue to light. This in turn could have called for greater attention to these critical issues early in the Project cycle. It is the Panel's view that failing to identify the Annex Area as an issue during Project design had adverse consequences for the indigenous population as tourism and other development activities started to take place in Bocas del Toro province.[186]

The Inspection Panel was also critical of the "methodology used for determining the boundaries of the Annex Areas" during the project design stage particularly because it had the effect of limiting consultation to "only the main leaders of the Ngäbe people," which meant that "the interested communities" were "not involve[d]."[187] "These communities, which in some cases had views different from those of the main leaders," the Panel commented, "were the last to be involved, as supervision reports note;" hence, the Panel concluded, "this methodology was not adequately participatory as required by OD 4.20."[188]

Furthermore, the Inspection Panel's investigation also highlighted different expectations about "the role of the Bank" in situations where there are "conflict between indigenous peoples and their governments," as there had been, in this instance, "over the question of leadership of the Naso people."[189]

"While the Bank sees the Government as its primary client and partner," the Panel emphasized, the policy on Indigenous Peoples "also requires the Bank to take a proactive role to ensure that its provisions are applied,"

> including provisions on the informed participation of and representation of indigenous communities. The proper application of these policies is intended to provide crucial safeguards for the affected indigenous peoples, and is of special significance in light of the risks and vulnerabilities that they may face.[190]

---

185 See *Panama: Land Administration* (2009), IR, §§ 243-244; *and see* IR xii. *Note*, 'Annex areas' refers to "territories outside the core area of [the tribal group's specific] comarca"; 'comarca' refers to "a territory over which indigenous groups have collective land rights and considerable administrative authority, as established by specific law". *See Panama: Land Administration* (2009), IR p. iv.
186 *Panama: Land Administration* (2009), IR, § 248.
187 *Panama: Land Administration* (2009), IR, § 288.
188 *Id. Note*, this example also demonstrates the effect of the demarcation of the project area on the project's content and scope – as discussed *in* section 10.2.
189 *Panama: Land Administration* (2009), IR, § 350.
190 *Id.*

"This," in turn, "has important implications for other Bank-supported projects," the Panel commented,

> including those related to financing for the sustainable use of forest resources and biodiversity conservation under Reducing Emissions from Deforestation and Forest Degradation (REDD) activities.[191]

Whereas in *Democratic Republic of Congo: Transitional Support*, concerning a planned consultation event (the 'Inter-Ministerial Commission'), the Inspection Panel observed that "there are significant issues and problems"

> regarding how to choose only one representative properly from Indigenous People who have been living in a number of scattered groups without much contact with one another.[192]

The Panel also underscored that "the Pygmy people"

> have little experience with a political system of representation, and special issues and difficulties arise in seeking their participation in a decision-making process.[193]

However, the Panel commented, "the selection of representatives to attend the Inter-Ministerial Commission from each of the 156 contract areas" had been "made even more difficult given the extremely limited time and resources" involved in this consultation event.[194] The Panel expressed its concern that an approach, such as the one employed with regard to the Inter-Ministerial Commission, "may produce [a] rough and hasty consultation process[s]"

> that fall out of line with basic Bank policy objectives and requirements described in other sections of this report. This is a concern especially given the time and resources as compared with the size of the country, lack of information, extremely inconvenient access to the concession areas, and difficulty in proper

---

191 *Id. Note*, this example also demonstrates the Inspection Panel's contribution towards strengthening institutional performance by identifying structural issues in order to facilitate institutional learning – *as* discussed *in* section 7.1.5.

192 *Democratic Republic of Congo: Transitional Support* (2005), IR, § 493.

193 *Id. Also see* the discussion *in* section 13.3.1.

194 *Democratic Republic of Congo: Transitional Support* (2005), IR, § 495.

information disclosure to the people who are not familiar with such a representation system.[195]

"In most cases," the Panel elaborated, "the NGOs must have started"

> with explanations of the forest code, concessions, and what the 'representation'
> means, before facilitating for the local community to select their representative
> in three weeks' time.[196]

The Panel also expressed its concern "that those who are selected" to attend the Inter-
Ministerial Commission "may find themselves in a situation of weak political capacity"

> as they arrive in the capital city and join other permanent Commission members
> who may have had additional opportunities to become familiar with the process
> and the file.[197]

Unless these concerns are addressed, the Inspection emphasized, "the inclusion of an
indigenous representative"

> might somehow legitimize a process under which the more powerful members
> of the Commission would take decisions that could run contrary to the interests
> of locally-affected people.[198]

Finally, in *Honduras: Land Administration*, a new representative body – the 'Mesa Regional'
– was specifically established to facilitate consultation with indigenous communities that
would be affected by the project, as well as resolve project-related disputes, as noted earlier.[199]

The Requesters claimed, among other things that "consultations did not include people
that are legitimate representatives of the Garífuna communities,"[200] and objected specifically
"to the establishment of the Mesa Regional," arguing that this institution had not been
recognized by the OFRANEH (the Requesters).[201] The Mesa Regional, the Requesters
contented, had "been created in spite of the disagreement of the communities, was not

---

195 *Democratic Republic of Congo: Transitional Support* (2005), IR, §§ 496-497.
196 *Id.*
197 *Id.*
198 *Id.*
199 *See* section 13.2.2. *Note,* for issues related to project-level grievance mechanisms, *also see* section 12.6.
200 *Honduras: Land Administration* (2006), IR, § 15.
201 *Id.*

elected by the communities", was "alien to their own institutions" and was therefore "not an organization that represent[ed] them."[202]

The Inspection Panel noted that, over the course of its field visits to "various Garífuna communities," it was "told by Garífuna people who are not part of any organization or group"

> that little or no PATH ['project'] information had been made generally available in the communities, that notice of informational meetings had not been made widely available, and that those Garífuna consulted were not chosen by the people themselves, but, many believed, by leaders and organizations selected by the PATH [project] personnel.[203]

The Panel also commented that it had not found any "evidence"

> of written materials such as brochures, announcements for posting having been sent directly to the communities so as to let the ordinary people know what to expect.[204]

The Panel's investigation also highlighted starkly contrasting views as to the adequacy of the consultation with indigenous peoples. For instance, concerning a specific consultation meeting that took place between project officials and members of the Garífuna communities about the project's objectives (generally) and the Indigenous Peoples Development Plan (specifically), the Panel noted that the outcome of this meeting had been documented in the so-called 'Sambo Creek document'. "While the Requesters state that this document is a firm rejection of the Project," the Panel observed, "Management objects to this characterization"

> claiming that the document rather 'praises the diagnosis of Garífuna land tenure issues presented in the IPDP.' In support of its interpretation of the Sambo Creek document, Management reports a quotation from page 18 concerning the IPDP: 'The excellent analysis of the issues that affect ethnic communities [...] in general give hope to the indigenous and Garífuna communities of Honduras that these will be translated into a concrete application of the design by Government and the World Bank, with regards to the territorial planning issue [...].'[205]

---

202 *Id.*
203 *Honduras: Land Administration* (2006), IR, § 148.
204 *Id.* On issues related to the adequacy of information disclosure, *see* section 11.1.
205 *Honduras: Land Administration* (2006), IR, §§ 145-147.

However, on completing its own review of this document, the Inspection Panel added that "page 18 of the Sambo Creek document immediately continues as follows:"

> However, said hope is frustrated by a detailed analysis of the plan in which the following is to be emphasized: 1. the relevant legal framework in which the PATH is moving embraces laws and norms (Land Use Law etc.) which created, more than once, prejudices to the ethnic populations [...] 2. In no part of the Plan there is a reference to the obligation of the State of Honduras to recognize at normative level the collective rights of the ethnic populations, in the absence of which the decent protection of the indigenous peoples and garifúnas of Honduras can never be obtained [...].[206]

Furthermore, the "subsequent pages of the 2003 Sambo Creek's document raise the same issues presented in the 2006 Request for Inspection."[207] Hence, the Panel expressed its 'concern' "that the description by Management of the minutes of this important meeting"

> omits reference to the major concerns being expressed by the participants, which are similar to those contained in the present Request for Inspection.[208]

With respect to the Mesa Regional, the Inspection Panel observed that such a representative body, which "involves any members of a community,"

> can have the effect of marginalizing the existing representative bodies of the community as a whole and at the local level who have worked on the issues for many years.[209]

Indeed, the Panel commented, "[t]he fact that OFRANEH and ODECO – leaders of the communities in land rights issues – have chosen not to be part of the Mesa Regional"

> is a serious concern. Despite their different views on many issues, both organizations claim that the Mesa was formed without properly consulting the communities at large. The Panel considers that a consultation framework for Garífuna people in which their leading representative body or bodies are not

---

206 *Id.*
207 *Id.*
208 *Id. Note*, this example also demonstrates the value of the Panel's 'editing function', as discussed *in* section 7.2.2.
209 *Honduras: Land Administration* (2006), IR, §§ 182-183.

part and do not give their support and guidance cannot ensure genuine representation of the Garífuna people, as required by OD 4.20.[210]

The Panel emphasized that it appreciated the "difficult situation faced by Bank Management in this regard" and also "acknowledge[d] the extensive efforts made by Management to seek the engagement of OFRANEH and ODECO in the consultation process."[211] Nevertheless, the Panel pointed out, "[t]hese efforts do not"

> alter the risks created by the present situation. The Panel finds that the Mesa system has divided the community and could potentially undercut the ability of its leading representatives to work on behalf of the community to achieve its objectives for collective title to ancestral land.[212]

This "dual-system of representation, and the conflicts that it is engendering," the Panel concluded, "has the potential to contribute to larger rifts and vulnerabilities for the people as a whole."[213]

****

"Among the various areas in which the Bank has shaped domestic law," as Sarfaty comments, "one of the most overlooked is indigenous peoples' rights."[214] "Given its day-to-day experience carrying out development projects that directly or indirectly affect indigenous peoples,"

> the Bank has become a critical international player in the formulation of indigenous rights norms. Its projects have the potential to have a significant impact on the social and economic welfare of these peoples. Therefore, how the Bank approaches indigenous rights can have serious consequences.[215]

The World Bank's operationalization of its policy on Indigenous Peoples – as discussed in this chapter – would seem to corroborate these arguments. Yet, the examples from

---

210 *Id.*
211 *Honduras: Land Administration* (2006), IR, §§ 189-190.
212 *Id.*
213 *Id.*
214 Sarfaty (2005), p. 1801. On the interfaces between the operational policy framework and borrowers' constitutional systems, *see* section 5.2.
215 *Id.* On arguments that the Bank's operationalization of its policy framework is shaping its own international legal obligations, *see* sections 5.1.1 & 5.3.2.

Inspection Panel practice presented here also reflect a 2003 OED (now IEG) report, which "found that only 55 of the 89 projects (or about 62% of the projects)"

> that could have potentially affected indigenous peoples (as determined by the OED's application of the policy's stated criteria) actually applied OD 4.20. Of the 55 projects that applied the policy, only 32 (or 58% of the 55) were assessed to have done so in a satisfactory or highly satisfactory way.[216]

These findings indicate, as Sarfaty argues, that "[t]here is a disjuncture between the Bank's articulation of its indigenous peoples policy and its day-to-day application" – whereas "[b]ridging this gap requires an analysis of the Bank's difficulties in operationalizing the policy."[217] In this regard, Inspection Panel practice offers a few perspectives.

One such difficulty pertains to the close interfaces between the policy area of indigenous peoples and borrowers' constitutional systems – juxtaposed against the requirement to respect (member) state sovereignty and, for the Bank, to retain its political neutrality. Clearly, the Bank's formal recognition of indigenous peoples in a project area constitutes a prominent demonstration of the manner in which the Bank's operational policy framework, incorporated in the credit/loan agreement, supersedes a Borrower's constitutional system – particularly, where the Borrower does not extend the same recognition to an indigenous group or groups, or provide such groups with the same level of protection.

It should be recognized, therefore, that the application of the policy on Indigenous Peoples in a project area has the potential of placing a significant strain on the relationship between the Bank and borrowers. And in scenarios where the Bank's emphasis is placed on performance areas such as ensuring client satisfaction and growing the Bank's lending portfolio, the application of an operational policy that is viewed as not only increasing financial but also political cost, is more likely to be applied as narrowly as possible. In fact, the challenges involving the operationalization of the policy on Indigenous Peoples provide prominent examples of tensions surrounding various institutional aims, as discussed earlier in this book.[218]

In other words, as Sarfaty explains, "[w]hen attempting to operationalize the indigenous peoples policy," Bank management and staff "are often influenced by a country's political stance with respect to indigenous peoples" – especially when the borrower "do not recognize ethnic minorities within their borders as indigenous or provide only limited rights for these minorities in their legal systems".[219] "Approving a loan in these countries"

---

216 Sarfaty (2005), p. 1802.
217 *Id.*
218 *See* in particular section 4.2.
219 Sarfaty (2005), pp. 1802-1803.

becomes more problematic when there are disagreements within the Bank about whether these peoples are in fact indigenous and thus require special protections that countries do not want to institute.[220]

Moreover, when a Borrower "contests the Bank's recognition of an ethnic group as indigenous, the Bank faces two undesirable options," namely:

(1) canceling the loan on the ground that the country is refusing to comply with the indigenous peoples policy or (2) proceeding with the loan without implementing the special provisions required by the policy, thereby conceding the country's position that there are no indigenous peoples within its borders.

"This dilemma is exacerbated," Sarfaty points out, "when the country is in dire need of funding due to high poverty rates. Should the Bank's poverty-reduction strategy supersede its indigenous rights strategy?"[221]

In practice, it would seem, the Bank often elects to limit the application of its policy on Indigenous Peoples – whether in the definition or identification of indigenous people (which, in turn, affects its decision to apply the policy in the first place), in the content and scope of project activities aimed at mitigating harm specific to indigenous groups or attending to their specific developmental needs, or in the process of consultation.

While a narrower application of the policy on Indigenous Peoples might therefore be understandable from the perspective of preserving a long-term relationship with a Borrower; on the other hand, it can also be argued that the Bank aggravates what is an undeniably challenging situation with its own practices.

For example, reflecting the Bank's focus on technical and commercial skills once again, commentators have noted that Bank staff "who deal with indigenous peoples and related issues (like the environment and resettlement) have historically occupied a subordinated position within the Bank."[222] And while there may have been "substantive changes in the

---

220 *Id.*
221 *Id.*
222 Sarfaty (2005), p. 1806. *Note*, on the Bank's focus on technical and commercial skills as a core aspect of institutional culture, *see* Miller-Adams's remarks *in* section 3.1.1; on issues related to the balance between 'technical/commercial' and 'non-technical/non-commercial' project components, *see* Ch. 9. *Also note*, Sarfaty identifies other factors (*i.e.*, in addition to the "borrower country's political and legal climate") that play a role in the narrower application of the policy on Indigenous Peoples in some project contexts – *notably*: the level of "civil society activism within borrower countries"; and "[d]ifferent perspectives on social issues" among World Bank staff (especially noting the differences in opinion between economists and social scientists employed by the Bank) – *see* Sarfaty (2005), pp. 1806-1809. *However*, Sarfaty adds (*at* p. 1817) that it should be recognized that the World Bank is not "an institution with uniform interests and a single voice, represented by official policies and documents," but rather an institution in which there are a "multiplicity of perspectives"

institution's culture spurred by a 'critical mass' of social scientists," the Bank arguably "still [has] a long way to go in mainstreaming and generalizing social analysis in World Bank activities."[223]

Indeed, Inspection Panel practice is illustrative of these matters, and also demonstrates that key project decisions concerning indigenous people are not always made based on a comprehensive understanding of their specific vulnerabilities and needs, for instance, their social and cultural practices, or of the rich diversity among – and within – indigenous groups.

Perhaps it could be concluded that the Bank's uneven application of its policy on Indigenous Peoples is indicative, as some have argued, that the World Bank, *in practice*, does not consider "indigenous rights" to be norms "of high value," "as opposed to others" – irrespective of what it may profess *in theory*.[224] However, as Sarfaty points out, "[t]he World Bank's approach to indigenous rights is but one case study of [a] broader theme" – namely: "[u]nderstanding how the line between economic and political issues is drawn both inside and outside the Bank;" the operationalization of a policy such as Indigenous Peoples, "reveals how seemingly depoliticized power is exerted by an institution that is itself the product of competing internal interests."[225]

– including about the manner in which the operational policy framework should be applied to particular development projects.
223 Sarfaty (2005), p. 1806. *Note*, Sarfaty quotes "Michael Cernea, the first non-economist social scientist hired by the Bank (in 1974)." *Also note*, on related issues with respect to the staffing of project supervision missions, *see* section 15.3.
224 Sarfaty (2005), fn. 88.
225 Sarfaty (2005), p. 1817.

14   ENVIRONMENTAL ASSESSMENT

The primary objective of the World Bank's policy on Environmental Assessment is "to ensure that the project options are environmentally sound and sustainable, and thus to improve decision-making."[1] The main vehicle for realizing this objective is the environmental assessment process, which "identif[ies] ways for improving project environmentally" as well as analysing risks in order to ensure "minimizing, mitigating or compensating for adverse impacts."[2]

The World Bank describes its policy on Environmental Assessment as the "cornerstone" of its operational policy framework,[3] and it is also considered to be "the umbrella policy for the Bank's environmental safeguard policies, which include natural habitats, forests, pest management, physical cultural resources, and safety of dams."[4]

Chapter 14 considers a number of prominent compliance issues related to the Bank's application of its policy on Environmental Assessment, as highlighted by Inspection Panel practice, namely: the *environmental screening* of projects, which involves the *classification of environmental* as well as *social risks*; various aspects of the *environmental assessment process*; and, the *consideration of design alternatives*.

14.1   ENVIRONMENTAL SCREENING (RISK CATEGORIZATION)

Environmental screening of projects, which results in the designation of an environmental and social risk category, "is an essential component of the environmental assessment (EA) process," as the Panel observed in *Peru: Lima Urban Transport*, because it "determines 'the appropriate extent and type of EA'" that would be "applicable to a given project" – a matter that will be discussed later on.[5]

"Screening assigns a project to one of three categories," the Panel explained:

> "Category A": a full EA is required. "Category B": an environmental analysis is required but not a full EA. "Category C": beyond screening, no further EA action is required.[6]

---

1   Boisson de Chazournes *in* Alfredsson & Ring (Eds.) (2001), p. 74.
2   *Id.*
3   *Id.*; *and see* World Bank (2011), e-Book.
4   *Id.*
5   *See* section 14.2.
6   *Peru: Lima Urban Transport* (2009), IR, §§ 67-68. *Note*, in this case, the Panel ultimately agreed with the Bank's risk categorization of the project as 'B', despite "some shortcomings in the environmental studies,

"The classification of the proposed project", the Panel added, "depends in general on the type, location, scale, sensitivity, magnitude and nature of the proposed project's potential environmental impacts."[7] Generally speaking, therefore,

> Projects are categorized as A when their likely adverse environmental impacts are unprecedented, diverse or sensitive, that is, impacts that may be irreversible. Projects may be classified as Category B if it is judged that their potentially adverse environmental impacts on human populations or environmentally important areas 'including wetlands' do not warrant a Category A, as they are less adverse, site-specific, and few, if any, of them are irreversible. Nevertheless, even in a Category B project, the environmental assessment is required to examine the project's potential environmental impacts and recommend any measures needed to mitigate or to compensate for adverse impacts and to improve environmental performance. The findings and results of a Category B environmental assessment must be described in the project documentation (Project Appraisal Document and Project Information Document). However, when the screening process determines, or national legislation requires, that any of the environmental issues identified warrant special attention, the findings and results of a Category B environmental assessment may also be set out in a separate report.[8]

In other words, the environmental screening process involves the exercise of a significant degree of 'professional judgment' or 'managerial discretion' – the exercise of which, the Inspection Panel typically includes in its compliance review.[9]

Indeed, this was one of the issues the Inspection Panel's investigation highlighted in *China: Western Poverty Reduction (Qinghai)*. The project had been classified as 'Category B' by the project task team leader.[10] The Panel noted, however, that it had been "informed" that it was "common practice" at the time "for a project task team leader to decide on an environmental classification more or less on his/her own," and also to postpone this decision "until later – perhaps as late as the Project Concept Document (PCD) stage [...]."[11]

---

especially with respect to the analysis of alternatives and the depth of analysis of the Project's impacts on Physical Cultural Resources and its impacts on the traffic rerouting in Barranco [...]." (*See* IR, § 74.) *Also note*, for other examples where the Panel found the Bank to be compliance with regards to environmental screening, see *Argentina: Santa Fe Road Infrastructure* (2007), IR, § 74; *Ecuador: Mining Development* (1999), IR, § 57; *and Kenya: Lake Victoria Environmental Management* (1999), IR, §§ 22-23.

7   *Peru: Lima Urban Transport* (2009), IR, §§ 67-68.
8   *Id.*
9   *Note*, on the Panel's review of the exercise of managerial discretion, *also see* section 6.3.2.
10 *Note*, for a statistical overview of the risk categories of projects that had been the subjects of Inspection Panel cases, *see* Naudé Fourie (2014), p. 584.
11 *China: Western Poverty Reduction (Qinghai)* (1999), IR, § 184.

"If this is indeed common practice," the Panel commented, "it leaves much to be desired" since "[t]he official who must manage a project and ensure that it goes ahead on schedule"

> is often not in the best position to judge whether or not serious questions relating to project safeguards should be allowed to 'interfere' with schedules and consume 'precious' time and resources. Some form of mandatory third-party review would seem desirable, at the very least.[12]

Another practice that seemed to play an important role in the environmental risk classification decision was 'past experience' in a country or region. The Panel acknowledged that "Management's past experience in a country [was] obviously important" since it could "provide the basis for a certain level of comfort that the work that is required by the policies will be undertaken successfully."[13] It was "an entirely different matter, however," the Panel commented, "to suggest that experience and precedent can determine what is required by the policies."[14]

Instead, the Panel asserted, "a straightforward reading of Annex E [of the policy]"

> would lead an environmental professional to classify the project an "A" if it included more than two of the components listed in Annex E, and if one or two of the descriptors in the preamble were found to apply. The Annex does not provide for exceptions on the basis of "past experience" or "precedent" in the country in question. Nor does it allow for exceptions on the basis of the area of the project relative to the area of the geographic or political jurisdiction involved. Yet, both arguments were advanced by Management in its July 18, 1999 Response.[15]

Hence, the Inspection Panel concluded, the project's overall risk classification (at least of the 'Qinghai' component) should have been an 'A' instead of 'B'.

In its initial response to the Request in *Pakistan: National Drainage Program*, Bank management explained the "rationale for assigning the NDP project to Category B" by relating it to the project's "primary objective" – which "was to address environmental

---

12   *Id. Note,* this example also demonstrates the potential for tension among the Bank's institutional aims – *as* discussed *in* section 4.2.

13   *China: Western Poverty Reduction (Qinghai)* (1999), IR, § 42.

14   *Id. Note,* this example demonstrates an approach to compliance review emphasizing the need for consistent policy application across the Bank's development-lending portfolio – *as* discussed *in* section 6.3.1.

15   *China: Western Poverty Reduction (Qinghai)* (1999), IR, § 152. *Note,* in this instance, the Inspection Panel employed a restrictive interpretative scheme – *as* discussed *in* section 6.3.3.

issues associated with *irrigation*."[16] "Significant, *beneficial* environmental effects were anticipated," Management noted, "i.e., the project would address problems such as waterlogging and salinity and mitigate the effects of sedimentation, soil erosion and water contamination."[17] Reflecting its arguments made in the *Qinghai* case, Management also explained that the Bank's "Asia environment department" had, over the course of the 1990s, "placed some relatively large projects"

> in Category B ("the big Bs"). Such categorization appears to have reflected a premature (pre-EIA) balancing of possible adverse effects with positive effects, and a focus on individual infrastructure activities, without regard to their potential cumulative effects. Thus, a Category B for the NDP project was consistent with the Region's practice at the time – it had potential environmental benefits and the investments were individually small – to medium-sized subprojects that had not yet been designed but would be subject to environmental and social screening.[18]

The Inspection Panel, however, registered its "surprise" with this decision – and particularly that the 'Drainage Master Plan' (DMP), "one of the most significant activities" of the project, "was designated as a Category 'B' project under Bank policies."[19] This "assignment was made," the Panel noted, "notwithstanding the fact that it contemplated not only multiple projects over years, but also" covered the 'Trans-Basin Outfall Drain' (TBOD), which was "a major new drainage infrastructure investment and northward extension of the LBOD."[20]

The Panel concluded, therefore, "that the development of the DMP merited a Category 'A' designation under OD 4.01, and that the designation of it as Category 'B' did not comply with Bank policy."[21] Whereas "[t]he proposed TBOD, among other elements of the draft DMP," the Panel added, "had the potential to lead to high adverse environmental consequences that may be sensitive, irreversible and diverse within the meaning of OD 4.01."[22]

---

16 *Pakistan: National Drainage Program* (2004), MR §§ 40-41 (emphasis added). *Note*, on the Panel's comments regarding the project's balance between irrigation and drainage interventions, *see* section 9.1.
17 *Id.* (emphasis added).
18 *Id. Note*, the project was co-financed by the ADB (which had also classified the project as a category B in terms of its policy on Environmental Assessment) and the Japan Bank for International Cooperation – *see* *Pakistan: National Drainage Program* (2004), IR, § 59.
19 *Pakistan: National Drainage Program* (2004), IR, §§ 314, 316 & 318.
20 *Id.*
21 *Id.*
22 *Id.*

"A proper and timely Category 'A' Environmental Assessment for the NDP", the Panel underscored, "would have provided the necessary opportunity for the Bank to fully analyze risks and issues presented by the Project,"

> and to identify alternative approaches that would minimize adverse impacts and maximize possibilities to restore and improve the environment. It might also have assisted the Project in giving closer attention to the specific impacts upon the environment and non-Project beneficiaries in southern Sindh during both the design and implementation phases of the Project.[23]

"[A]s a result of shortcomings in the Environmental Assessment," however, "decision-making on environmentally-crucial elements under the Project"

> became less systematic, less informed, and more ad hoc. As a consequence, the Bank and the Project missed important opportunities to address concerns raised by Requesters, and to consider providing compensation for harms that could not otherwise be mitigated. This did not comply with OD 4.01.[24]

Significantly, for the first time in the Inspection Panel's institutional history, Management "acknowledge[d]" in its formal response to the Panel's investigation report that it would have been more "appropriate to categorize [the Project] as an EA Category 'A' project."[25]

As noted earlier, the Inspection Panel generally argues that "the modality of [a] Project" should not be "a determinant factor for environmental categorization" – as had been the case in *Liberia: Development Forestry*.[26] The Panel made similar comments in *Democratic Republic of Congo: Transitional Support*. It "should have been anticipated," the Panel commented, that "forest land-use planning" would "have a potentially fundamental impact on land, forests, and people."[27] Therefore, the Panel concluded, "the potential impacts of land use planning in DRC should have been analyzed as part of a 'Category A' EA", whereas "[t]he failure to develop an environmental (and social) assessment which addressed these issues, at the time when the forest zoning plan was part of the Project, [did] not comply with OP 4.01."[28]

---

23 *Pakistan: National Drainage Program* (2004), IR, § 332. *Note*, on issues related to the consideration of design alternatives, *see* section 14.3.
24 *Pakistan: National Drainage Program* (2004), IR, § 333.
25 *Pakistan: National Drainage Program* (2004), MR §§ 40-41.
26 *Liberia: Development Forestry* (2010), ER, § 93; *and see* the discussion *in* section 10.1.
27 *Democratic Republic of Congo: Transitional Support* (2005), IR, § 346.
28 *Id.*

In fact, the Panel added, an extensive "[e]nvironmental assessment" process, as required for a Category A project, "may have added importance in a post-conflict environment like in DRC,"

> where there is a lack not only of institutional capacity but also of basic informa-tion about the affected lands and about people who have an interest in these reforms, and might be affected by the regulated activities. The failure to carry out this analysis may mean that even the best-intentioned 'reform' initiatives can fall out of line with Bank social and environmental policy objectives, and indeed lay the basis for significant harms.[29]

Comparably, in *Cambodia: Forest Concession Management*, the Panel pointed to the "very serious potential impacts, and the close association of the Project with these impacts," and concluded "that the Project should have been placed in Category A and a full Environmental Assessment carried out. By failing to do this, the Bank did not comply with OP 4.01."[30]

"[C]areful study and debate by multiple parties, as required for a Category A project under OP 4.01," the Panel emphasized, "could have helped avoid serious errors"

> in the design and implementation of the Project. This type of assessment might have led, for example, to a greater focus on alternative approaches to industrial scale logging, such as various types of community and partnership forestry.[31]

As a 'repeater project',[32] *Ghana: Second Urban Environment Sanitation Project* ('UESP II') had a 'legacy component', which, as noted earlier, involved the location of the planned 'Kwabenya landfill'.[33] "The mechanism of Repeater Projects," as the Panel observed, "is intended"

> to make full use of [...] existing knowledge and work, avoid duplication of effort and enable a more streamlined processing of projects for approval.[34]

---

29 *Democratic Republic of Congo: Transitional Support* (2005), IR, § 359. For examples of the negative conse-quences following from the environmental screening decision, *see e.g.*, the discussion *in* sections 10.1 & 13.1.
30 *Cambodia: Forest Concession Management* (2005), IR, § 205.
31 *Id. Note*, on issues related to the consideration of design alternatives, *see* section 14.3.
32 *Note*, 'repeater projects' "are defined as 'projects whose basic design and effectiveness have been proven, and which a borrower proposes to augment and scale up.' The Bank can scale up the impact of its assistance by allowing for rapid replication and expansion of successful projects." (*See Ghana: Second Urban Environment Sanitation* (2007), IR, § 79 *and see* fn. 58.)
33 *See* the discussion *in* section 11.1.2.
34 *Ghana: Second Urban Environment Sanitation* (2007), IR, § 81.

However, "[o]ne of the key elements in determining whether a project is eligible to be a 'repeater'," the Panel noted, "is that the project does not have any environmental, social, or other safeguard problems."[35] In order to make this determination, furthermore, "the Team Leader (TL) is required to carry out an initial assessment on the existing project's suitability for a repeater", and upon his or her positive recommendation a "specialist review" is conducted by a "Regional Review Panel," which is "composed of legal, quality, safeguard and fiduciary specialists, as well as sector and country specialists."[36]

Hence, in accordance with the Bank's guidelines, the Panel noted, "a safeguard policy review [...] must be carried out at the very outset, and a new ISDS must be prepared *regardless of the category of the Project*."[37] However, the Panel "note[d] with concern that, in this case, it seems that the safeguards specialists were absent from the decision meeting held on December 15, 2003," whereas

> the safeguards issues [were] not even mentioned at that meeting. In a communication dated June 16, 2003, the Regional Review Panel, set up in March 2003, looked at the viability of the executing the Project as a repeater project. In assessing whether there were environmental, social or other safeguard problems, the Review Panel *"indicated some issues, not considered major by the specialists."*[38]

In other words, "a formal safeguard review meeting did not take place for UESP II", although "Management informed the Panel that a separate safeguard review" had been conducted "prior to appraisal," and also "describes additional safeguards actions that will be taken during the process of project implementation."[39]

Nevertheless, the Panel concluded, at the time of the Special Review – mid 2003 – and the subsequent Project appraisal at the end of 2003, there was a highly contentious environment and strong voices of local opposition to the landfill", that was not identified by the screening process.[40] This, the Panel pointed out, in spite of the fact that the Project Appraisal document "itself indicates that resettlement at the Kwabenya sanitary landfill

---

35 *Id.*
36 *Ghana: Second Urban Environment Sanitation* (2007), IR, §§ 82-85. *Note*, the Panel is referring to the Bank's 'Guidelines for Processing of Repeater Projects'; *also note* that the Panel's formal mandate does not extend to World Bank 'Best Practices' and other forms of operational guidelines – *as* discussed *in* section 5.1.
37 *Ghana: Second Urban Environment Sanitation* (2007), IR, § 89 (emphasis added). *Note*, on the 'integrated safeguards data sheet' (ISDS), *also see* Freestone's comments *at* note 46, Ch. 6.
38 *Ghana: Second Urban Environment Sanitation* (2007), IR, § 90 (emphasis in original). *Note*, this example also demonstrates the value of the Panel's fact-finding function with respect to strengthening institutional governance – *as* discussed *in* section 7.1.4.
39 *Ghana: Second Urban Environment Sanitation* (2007), IR, §§ 92-93.
40 *Id.*

could cause considerable controversy, and lists it as a 'high' Project risk" – which "complies with OMS 2.20 on Project Appraisal."[41] "The PAD states elsewhere, however,"

> that the safeguards screening category indicates that one or more safeguard policies are triggered "[...] *but the effects are limited to their impact and are technically and institutionally manageable.*" This corresponds to Category S2 in the safeguards classification system.[42]

"This latter assessment," the Panel commented, "seems to have downplayed the foreseeable problems in achieving compliance with Bank safeguard policies associated with the proposal to construct a landfill at Kwabenya."[43] "By comparison," the Panel added,

> Category S1 applies to "significant, cumulative and/or irreversible impacts; or significant technical and institutional risks in management of one or more safeguard areas." The Panel considers that this category (S1) corresponds to the situation at Kwabenya, which is also reflected in some of the statements of the ISDS.[44]

"Close screening of key social and environmental issues by the Bank," the Panel emphasized,

> would have made clear, from the outset, the imminent problems and the high risks in managing safeguards that would be caused by including Kwabenya as a subcomponent of the Repeater Project.[45]

14.2   THE ENVIRONMENTAL ASSESSMENT PROCESS

This section considers three aspects of the environmental assessment process: firstly, the collection of *environmental and social baseline data*, which is intended to provide a clear picture of the 'before project' situation and therefore also serves as important input both for the estimation of project benefits as well as for the assessment of potential risks. Baseline data can also form the basis of several key assumptions on which project designs and plans are based.[46] Secondly, the section focuses on the *'spatio-temporal' scope of EAs*, as well as

---

41   *Ghana: Second Urban Environment Sanitation* (2007), IR, § 94.
42   *Id.* (emphasis in original).
43   *Ghana: Second Urban Environment Sanitation* (2007), IR, § 95.
44   *Id.*
45   *Id.*
46   *Note*, on issues related to the collection of social data in the context of involuntary resettlement, *see* section 12.2.

cumulative impact assessments; and, thirdly, on the *content of EAs*, referring to the substantive areas covered by the environmental assessment process. Note, the scope and content of EAs are also closely related to the delineation of the project 'area' and – in particular – project 'area of influence', discussed in an earlier chapter.[47]

14.2.1   Environmental and social baseline data collection

Inspection Panel investigations typically highlight instances where baseline data had not been collected within the required timeframe; where certain types of baseline data had not been collected; and, where certain deficiencies with respect to underlying collection methodology had a negative impact on the quality and/or the credibility of the data.[48] Inspection Panel practice also points to the negative consequences of baseline data deficiencies for the effective management of environmental and social risks.

Given the nature of the project cycle, there is typically a limited window for collecting baseline data. In *Brazil: Itaparica Resettlement and Irrigation,* for example, the Requesters claimed that "[t]he delay in the installation and commissioning of the irrigation projects ha[d] contributed to an increase of violence in the communities, to alcoholism, and to family breakdown."[49] Responding to these claims, Bank management confirmed that it was 'aware' of these issues but argued that "such occurrences also occur[ed] in many populations in this region including those unaffected by [the] Itaparica [project].'"[50] Moreover, Management added, "it would need baseline data to determine the effect of the lack of jobs in causing these social crises."[51] The Inspection Panel, on its part, pointed out that such "baseline data [had] never [been] collected," and that "it [was] now too late to obtain it."[52]

Whereas in *Brazil: Rondônia Natural Resources Management,* the Panel noted that, at a later stage of the project, "1994 was substituted as the year to be used as baseline data to measure project progress".[53] "This choice of year is disturbing," the Panel commented, "given the fact that the Loan was approved in March 1992."[54] And because "no baseline had been chosen prior to this," the Panel added, "no deforestation rates have been calculated since 1992."[55] Moreover, the Panel pointed out, such baseline data deficiencies occurred

---

47   *See* section 10.2.
48   For an example where the Panel found the Bank to be compliant with regards to the collection of baseline data, *see Colombia: Cartagena Water & Environmental Management* (2004), IR, §§ 65-55, § 105 & § 176.
49   *Brazil: Itaparica Resettlement and Irrigation* (1997), ER, § 27(3).
50   *Id.*
51   *Id.*
52   *Id.*
53   *Brazil: Rondônia Natural Resources Management* (1995), Additional Review, § 70.
54   *Id.*
55   *Id.*

despite the OED's review of the predecessor project, which specifically recommended "that much better and more extensive data gathering"

> had to occur before launching follow-on efforts, with particular criticism leveled at the state of knowledge about agro-ecological and socio-economic realities in Rondonia.[56]

And in *Cameroon: Petroleum Development and Pipeline*, the Panel noted that "the existence of conflicts over damage to water resources [including] fisheries" could be contributed to "an inadequate collection of baseline data that did not unequivocally establish conditions prior to [the pipeline's] construction."[57]

For instance, the Panel elaborated, "the environmental baseline assessment conducted by COTCO did not provide a full year's data" at the project appraisal and approval stage, which would have allowed "for comparisons" to be drawn "between the wet and dry seasons," as required by "paragraph 7 of Annex D of OD 4.01."[58]

In fact, the Panel concluded, there was an "[o]verall" "lack of baseline data upon which approval of the Project could be made."[59] While the Panel took note of "COTCO's extensive commitment to an ongoing collection of baseline data," it emphasized, nevertheless, "that this has occurred only since the start of project implementation."[60] "Such an effort should provide more data on seasonal and annual differences in environmental conditions over the life of the Project," the Panel acknowledged,

> and may eventually accomplish the intent of OD 4.01 on collection of baseline data. However, there is still a limited amount of information available on pre-project conditions.[61]

"Many of the resource conflicts that have arisen during project construction," the Panel reiterated, "could have been avoided by having a full year's availability of baseline information prior to project approval.[62] Hence, the Panel underscored the "importance of collecting sufficient baseline data"

---

56 *Brazil: Rondônia Natural Resources Management* (1995), Additional Review, § 46. On the complementary nature of the Inspection Panel's mandate – specifically in relation to other internal accountability mechanisms – *see* sections 6.2 & 7.2.

57 *Cameroon: Petroleum Development and Pipeline* (2002), IR, §§ 36-37.

58 *Id.*

59 *Id.*

60 *Id.*

61 *Id. Note,* this example also demonstrates the Panel's practice of emphasizing the underlying objective of policy provisions – *as* discussed *in* section 6.3.3

62 *Cameroon: Petroleum Development and Pipeline* (2002), IR, §§ 36-37.

prior to project approval to ensure that the best information is at hand for informed decision-making and to provide an adequate background for the project to proceed if it is approved.[63]

World Bank management, in its response to the Panel's investigation report, noted that, "[i]n conducting EAs, the question of *how much data is enough* frequently arises,"

> given the need to make case-by-case judgments on the type and amount of data to be collected. The problem is exacerbated in situations where [project implementation] agencies have not routinely collected baseline environmental data. Original field data collection, however detailed, cannot replace historical, multi-year data that would show trends and the extent of 'normal' variation.[64]

"In the early years of EA practice," Management added, "EAs often presented voluminous data"

> but lacked sufficient attention to impact analyses, design of mitigative measures and monitoring. OD 4.01, Annex D (para. 7) recognizes that *trade-offs have to be made between the amount of data collected and the need to provide estimates of environmental impact, while not delaying project decisions.*[65]

In this instance, Management emphasized, it had "considered the trade-offs, because the data collected did provide a sufficient basis for mitigative measures through the EASs and for monitoring."[66] However, management added, it "would welcome an occasion to exchange views with the Inspection Panel on what should constitute adequate data collection" in project contexts involving petroleum infrastructure construction.[67]

In *China: Western Poverty Reduction,* the Inspection Panel noted that "[a]n exhaustive inventory of biodiversity would not be expected in an EA"; yet, the Panel added, "[i]t would have been appropriate [...] to search the literature and to reference studies

---

63 *Id.*
64 *Cameroon: Petroleum Development and Pipeline* (2002), MRIR, § 28 (emphasis added).
65 *Id. Note*, this example also demonstrates the tension underlying many of the Bank's institutional aims – and the necessity to prioritize or make trade-off decisions, *as discussed in* section 4.2.2. On cost considerations affecting the operationalization of the Bank's policy on Environmental Assessment, *also see* Sarfaty's comments *at* note, 251, Ch. 14.
66 *Cameroon: Petroleum Development and Pipeline* (2002), MRIR, § 28.
67 *Id. Note*, on institutional learning as an outcome of accountability processes, *also see* section 7.1.5.

that have already been undertaken, including lists (or at least a reference to them) so that reasonable assessment of the extent, importance and uniqueness (endemism) of the biodiversity, and risks to it, could be made.[68]

In this regard, the Panel questioned "Management's acceptance of the total absence of data on the biodiversity of the Move-out areas and the inadequate level of data on the Move-in area," noting that this constituted "a major failing in the EA."[69]

The Inspection Panel also noted the absence of any "sources of scientific data" in the project's Environmental and Social Assessments.[70] "Sound scientific practice [...] requires that sources of scientific data be acknowledged and referenced," the Panel observed, whereas "[t]he absence of such references can call the reliability of an entire assessment into question" and "lead to enormous confusion" – indeed, "as the Inspection Team found"

in trying to source lists of plant and animal species in the Project areas. The Inspection Team was provided with different lists at different times with no explanation as to why they varied and no indication of the sources of the original data, or whether there were any endangered species involved.[71]

The Panel's investigation in *India: Ecodevelopment* highlighted "Management's apparent failure to require objective data and scientific studies to support many of the critical assumptions underlying the project."[72] Instead, the Panel found, Management relied on what was "apparently considerable anecdotal evidence of the recovery of wildlife populations during the past decades since the national park was established."[73] Moreover, the Panel added, "no baseline studies exist" whereas "integrated studies of evolution of wildlife populations are lacking."[74]

"Management appears to have been aware of the paucity of information and research at the appraisal stage," the Panel noted, and by "simply accepting the fact that objective data and scientific studies were very limited," the Bank appears

to have allowed much of the debate about the potential conflict between the two main thrusts of the project to be conducted on the basis of predetermined views and unsubstantiated claims.[75]

---

68 *China: Western Poverty Reduction (Qinghai)* (1999), IR, § 210.
69 *Id.*
70 *China: Western Poverty Reduction (Qinghai)*, IR, § 198.
71 *Id.*
72 *India: Ecodevelopment* (1998), ER, §§ 31, 35 & 36.
73 *Id.*
74 *Id.*
75 *Id. Note,* on the tension between the project's 'two main thrusts', *see* section 9.1.

Kenya: Lake Victoria Environmental Management was "a mechanical shredding pilot project, in which the method of shredding and sinking of [water hyacinths] was tested," with the aim of controlling these plans in parts of Lake Victoria.[76] Hence, the successful outcome of this pilot depended heavily on the collection of reliable baseline data.[77] Yet, over the course of its investigation, the Panel found that there had "been a serious lack of attention to the scientific underpinnings of the water hyacinth shredding pilot."[78]

For instance, the Panel noted, "[a]n adequate water sampling and analysis program"

> was not put in place. A before-shredding baseline was not established. No samples were collected during the shredding operation. The laboratory and other required scientific infrastructure was not, and is not yet, in place. Much relevant data on related factors have simply not been collected and that which has is largely inadequate, inappropriate, or useless. Data with which to compare shredding and other forms of control are simply inadequate.[79]

In other words, the Panel concluded, "from the perspective of research and experimental design,"

> as well as the adequacy of equipment and facilities to undertake appropriate sampling and monitoring, the Water Hyacinth shredding pilot, at this point in time, must be deemed a failure.[80]

In *Cambodia: Forest Concession Management*, the Inspection Panel was critical of the Bank's failure to "carry out a careful assessment or inventory that might quantify resin-trees,"

> other timber and non-timber forest products traditionally used by indigenous peoples and others. The Panel finds that such an assessment or inventory should have been part of a proper environmental assessment, and should have been the subject of a participatory survey and inventory at an early stage of the Project. The failure to do so does not comply with OP 4.01.[81]

---

76 *Kenya: Lake Victoria Environmental Management* (1999), ER, §§ 2 & 6.
77 *Kenya: Lake Victoria Environmental Management* (1999), IR, § 186.
78 *Id.*
79 *Id.*
80 *Id.*
81 *Cambodia: Forest Concession Management* (2005), IR, § 242. *Note*, on the Panel's criticism of the risk category assigned to this project, *see* section 14.1.

The Panel was also highly critical of the project's Strategic Forest Management Plans and Environmental and Social Impact Assessments, describing these documents to be "deficient in almost all regards *from process to content.*"[82] The Inspection Panel recognized that "carrying out forest cover surveys and comparing the results with earlier surveys"

> is almost always fraught with uncertainties and difficulties because of numerous variables, such as different photo scales, different standards for categorizing forest and other land use cover and uncertainties with defining boundaries between different land use and vegetation types. Such exercises are generally open to various interpretations and frequently give rise to debate and contention. The present study is no exception [...].[83]

Nevertheless, the Panel concluded, there was "sufficient evidence" in this instance "to suggest that the work was not carried out to the standards that should be expected for such an exercise."[84] For instance, the Panel elaborated, "[a]pplying arbitrary factors to the raw data"

> to align them with values that are perceived to be 'more correct' constitutes an arbitrary correction that provides an inadequate estimate of this critical data.[85]

Finally, in *Nigeria/Ghana: West African Gas Pipeline*, the Inspection Panel explained some of the consequences of inadequate baseline data. "In the absence of an adequate baseline survey, and without an adequate baseline to measure against," the Panel elaborated, "it is difficult to measure the impact of the Project"

> and to conduct impact monitoring in the future. This problem was also mentioned by the Environmental and Social Advisory Panel (ESAP), which stated that "ideally a household baseline survey of compensated households would have been done just prior to compensation payment, and before land-take. That did not happen. The first impact monitoring survey will provide a less than ideal but still useful base for establishing change."[86]

Hence, the Panel concluded, "the absence of adequate baseline information"

---

82 *Cambodia: Forest Concession Management* (2005), IR, § 336 (emphasis added). *Note*, this example also demonstrates the Inspection Panel's compliance review approach that emphasizes 'process' *and* 'substance' as necessary components of 'compliance' – *as* discussed *in* section 6.3.4.
83 *Cambodia: Forest Concession Management* (2005), IR, §§ 356 & 361.
84 *Id.*
85 *Id.* For more detail on the issues to which the Panel is referring, *see* IR, §§ 357-360.
86 *Nigeria/Ghana: West African Gas Pipeline* (2006), IR, § 127.

makes it impossible to ensure that the impacts and potential impoverishment risks facing local people are properly addressed, as required under Bank Resettlement Policy.[87]

14.2.2   Spatio-temporal scope of EAs and cumulative impact assessments

In *Nepal: Arun III*, the Inspection Panel concluded that the project's environmental assessment did not constitute "a comprehensive approach to the Arun basin," since it failed to "include a long term perspective"

> that also considered the Upper and Lower Arun Projects, access roads (including the Valley Route and additional spurs), as well as transmission lines.[88]

"Environmental assessments should be integrated into project design from its inception," the Panel added, and "must go beyond descriptive studies,"

> focusing on the interaction of all project components and decisions that affect the natural and social environment, including mitigation plans and the institutional capacity to develop, implement and monitor them.[89]

The Requesters in *Ecuador: Mining Development* "claim[ed] that the development of mining activities in the Intag and surrounding areas,"

> especially the Cotacachi-Cayapas Ecological Reserve, would, in general, threaten biodiversity in the area where they live, and have a destructive impact on protected areas and their buffer zones, which constitute critical natural habitats.[90]

The Inspection Panel found that the environmental assessment had indeed failed to mention "the north of Ecuador, and more particularly the biologically rich Cotacachi-Cayapas

---

87   *Id. Note,* on deficiencies regarding the surveying of project-affected people in this case, *also see* the discussion *in* section 12.2.

88   *Nepal: Arun III* (1994), ER, § 51. *Note,* for examples where the Panel found the Bank to be in compliance with regards to the scope of the environmental assessment, *see Uganda: Power Projects* (2007), IR, § 159; *and Brazil: Land Reform* (1998), ER, § 20(c). For examples where Management acknowledged deficiencies with regards to this area, *see Papua New Guinea: Smallholder Agriculture* (2009), ER, § 42; *Peru: Lima Urban Transport* (2009), ER, § 27; *and Ecuador: Mining Development* (1999), MRIR, § 8.

89   *Id. Note,* on issues related to the integration of various project elements, *also see* Ch. 9.

90   *Ecuador: Mining Development* (1999), IR § 14.

Ecological Reserve."[91] Instead, the "scope of the EA" had appeared to "cover only the south of the country,"

> focussing on the environmental and social impacts of existing small scale gold mining activities.[92]

"[I]n limiting the spatial/geographical scope of the Environmental Assessment in the manner described above," the Panel concluded, "the Bank was not in compliance with the relevant provisions of OD 4.01 (and OD 4.00, Annex A)."[93]

And in *South Africa: Eskom Investment Support,* here in the context of assessing the "equivalence of borrower/country systems with those of the Bank," the Inspection Panel pointed "to the importance of being specific about the timeline" of the environmental impact assessment.[94] This meant, in particular, that Management had to "identify any discrepancies"

> between the [country] systems in place *at the time* the project's environmental impact assessment is carried out and the systems in place [*at the time*] when the Bank is approached for financial assistance and the [Safeguards Diagnostics Review] is carried out.[95]

In this instance, the Panel concluded, "the equivalence analysis in the SDR did not adequately make this distinction", which meant that "gaps that were in the system at the time of the Medupi EIA were not properly addressed."[96]

Importantly, environmental assessments that are sufficiently broad in terms of their 'spatio-temporal' scope also enable the adequate assessment of a project's 'cumulative impacts', which, as the Panel explained in the *Eskom* case,

> comprises the sum of impacts from the past, present, and reasonably foreseeable future projects that would compound the impacts of the project under consideration.[97]

Although the Inspection Panel "acknowledge[d] the challenges of" identifying "'reasonably foreseeable" future developments in a dynamic project context – noting specifically the

---

91 *Ecuador: Mining Development* (1999), IR, §§ 63 & 66.
92 *Id.*
93 *Id.*
94 *South Africa: Eskom Investment Support* (2010), IR, § 594.
95 *Id.* (emphasis added).
96 *Id.*
97 *South Africa: Eskom Investment Support* (2010), IR, § 266.

challenges of determining "cumulative impacts on air quality" – the Panel added that "due consideration should have been taken"

> of other probable projects in the area (e.g. additional coal mines and coal-fired power stations), in determining an appropriate level of mitigation measures for the project.[98]

In addition, the Panel also commented on "the way that impacts on water resources have been addressed in the project," noting that it "may not be consistent with" the operational principle in paragraph A1 of Table A1 of OP 4.00 relating to the assessment of indirect, cumulative and associated impacts.[99] The Panel concluded that "the potential cumulative impacts of both the expanded mine and the power station"

> on groundwater quality/resources (together with other issues such as an increase in labor force and public services infrastructure) should have been identified early on in the EIA process, taking into account the likely increase in coal mining and coal-fired power plants in the area.[100]

"Early recognition of potentially significant cumulative, indirect and associated impacts," the Panel emphasized, "would enable collaboration"

> between proponents, competent authorities, and other stakeholder groups. Moreover, it would allow for potential synergies and more effective and efficient joint options for mitigation and adaptive management, and the optimum allocation of associated responsibilities at least between the Grootegeluk Mine and the Medupi plant.[101]

During its 2001 investigation of *Uganda: Power Projects*, the Inspection Panel was critical of the project's inadequate analysis of cumulative impacts. The Panel noted that the "safeguard policies or directives" applicable to the project at the time did not explicitly "require a cumulative effects analysis."[102] "Good professional practice in environmental impact assessment has in recent years stressed the need for project-specific cumulative

---

98   *South Africa: Eskom Investment Support* (2010), IR, § 403.
99   *South Africa: Eskom Investment Support* (2010), IR, § 348.
100 *Id.*
101 *Id.* Note, this example also demonstrates the Panel emphasizing both the mitigation of harm and the enhancement of performance – *as* discussed *in* section 4.2.2. For similar issues, *also see Argentina: Santa Fe Road Infrastructure* (2007), IR, §§ 87-88.
102 *Uganda: Power Projects* (2001), IR, §§ 87-88.

effects analysis," the Panel commented; however, this "thinking" had "not been incorporated in Bank directives" at the time.[103]

"Although each hydroproject on the Victoria Nile would require an individual project-specific EA," the Inspection Panel argued,

> a series of hydro projects would give rise to cumulative effects which should be formally evaluated. Moreover, at the time that the environmental assessments for Power III and Power IV were being undertaken, it was common knowledge that other hydropower schemes were being proposed and investigated by sponsors. It would thus have been prudent to have assessed the potentially cumulative effects of these schemes and their various possible combinations.[104]

The "issue of cumulative effects" was "of real significance" and was "deserving of greater attention", the Panel observed.[105] Hence, the Panel recommended,

> a further assessment of the cumulative effects of existing and potential hydropower developments on the Victoria Nile as a freestanding Sectoral Environmental Assessment, or as an important component of the Regional Management Plan for the Upper Nile Basin, may need to be undertaken.[106]

On the other hand, the Panel also pointed out that World Bank management, in the Staff Appraisal Report, "not only recommended" that "a Sectoral Environmental Assessment of hydro power be undertaken," but "also produced draft terms of reference for an SEA."[107] Bank management also "conceded that its failure to ensure that an SEA was carried out reflected inadequate supervision," which caused the Panel to conclude that Management was "not in compliance with OD 13.05 on Project Supervision" in this regard.[108]

And in its 2007 investigation of *Uganda: Power Projects*, the Inspection Panel was critical about the Sectoral Environmental Assessment (SEA), in particular, because it excluded areas both upstream and downstream of the project area "based on the assumption that the Project's upstream area of influence ends downstream of Kiira-Nalubaale dams."[109]

---

103 *Uganda: Power Projects* (2001), IR, §§ 84-85. On the relationships between the Bank's operational policy framework and international industry and/or professional standards and best practices, *see* section 5.4.
104 *Uganda: Power Projects* (2001), IR, §§ 84-85.
105 *Uganda: Power Projects* (2001), IR, § 136, 138.
106 *Id.*
107 *Uganda: Power Projects* (2001), IR, §§ 87-88.
108 *Id.*
109 *Uganda: Power Projects* (2007), IR, §§ 224, 229.

As a result, the Panel concluded, the SEA did "not take into account the Project's potential impacts" on Lake Victoria's water levels.[110]

The Panel also questioned the Project's failure "to address the cumulative effects of transmission lines or to propose mitigation to reduce additive effects."[111] Management's statement that "several transmission lines already come in/out of the Nalubaale switchyard," the Panel argued, was

> used to dismiss the possible aesthetic effect of yet another transmission line rather than to examine the cumulative effect of numerous lines emanating from the same switchyard.[112]

In *Chad: Petroleum*, while the Panel was "satisfied that the EA cover[d] the life of the Project and that the temporal context ha[d] been clearly defined," it also pointed out that the EA "did not explicitly consider" the "spatio-temporal context of the Project" – and it was therefore unclear how the specific spatio-temporal delineation had been made.[113] The documentation included "neither a discussion on how the boundary of the study area was defined," the Panel commented,

> nor any mention of the potential area that could be affected by project development. In the light of this, the Panel finds Management not in compliance with OD 4.01 in this respect.[114]

The Inspection Panel also observed that World Bank staff had initially recommended that the project's environmental assessment (as well as the EA of the related project, *Cameroon: Petroleum*) should include an assessment of the "cumulative effects of all project components (pipeline routes, infrastructure upgrades etc.)."[115] However, in reviewing the final versions of project documents, the Panel noted it could not "find any indication"

> that any cumulative effects assessment was completed. This is surprising since the evidence clearly indicates that the Consortium[116] recognized the need for cumulative effects analysis in the review of the Draft 1997 EA. Moreover [...]

---

110 *Id.*
111 *Uganda: Power Projects* (2007), IR, § 145.
112 *Id.*
113 *Chad: Petroleum* (2001), IR (ES), § 7; *also see* IR, §§ 27 & 29.
114 *Id.*
115 *Chad: Petroleum* (2001), IR, §§ 36-37.
116 *I.e.*, ExxonMobil, Petronas and Chevron – the pipeline project's co-financiers. On co-financiers, *see* section 3.1.3. *Also see* note 118, Ch. 14.

Bank staff also drew attention to the need to assess the cumulative effects of other energy and industrial developments.[117]

The Inspection Panel considered this to be "a serious omission," especially "when one of the objectives of the Petroleum Sector Capacity Management Project"[118]

> is to assist the Government of Chad to manage the development of its petroleum resources in an environmentally and socially sound manner, "including the need for cumulative/regional/sectoral environmental assessments." The Panel finds that in failing to require a cumulative effects assessment, Management is not in compliance with OD 4.01.[119]

Bank management, however, explicitly rejected this finding and emphasized that the policy did "not 'require' the use of the tool of Regional EA"; instead, Management asserted, it stipulated that

> Regional EAs *may* be used where a number of similar but significant development activities with potentially cumulative impacts are planned for a reasonably localized area.[120]

In any event, Management added, "the absence of a formal Regional EA is largely a semantic issue,"

> because, in the manner in which the Project is proceeding, the appropriate elements of a Regional EA will be part of the RDP [regional development plan].[121]

The Inspection Panel, in turn, objected to Management's "narrow interpretation of the word 'may'," arguing that the inclusion of this word did "not necessarily confer immunity

---

117 *Chad: Petroleum* (2001), IR, §§ 36-37.
118 *Note, Chad: Petroleum* consisted of three projects – (1) The Petroleum Development and Pipeline Project (primarily financed by the 'Consortium', but also partly by the IFC and IDA); (2) The Management of the Petroleum Economy Project (IDA financed); and The Petroleum Sector Management Capacity-Building Project (IDA financed), which were aimed at the "(a) management and monitoring of social and environmental impacts; and (b) strengthening of the Borrower's capacity to manage the petroleum sector." (*See Chad: Petroleum* (2001), ER, §§ 4-8.)
119 *Chad: Petroleum* (2001), IR, §§ 36-37.
120 *Chad: Petroleum* (2001), MR to IR § 19 (emphasis in original).
121 *Id. Note*, on the employment of expansive versus restrictive interpretive schemes, *see* the discussion *in* section 6.3.3.

from the need for a Regional Assessment in all situations."[122] In some instances, the Panel elaborated, "the use of a Regional EA may only be partially indicated," whereas in other circumstances, "the situation on the ground makes its use essential."[123] In this particular instance, the Panel reiterated, "the potential for cumulative and wide-ranging socio-economic and environmental impacts indicates that the use of a Regional EA is essential to proper evaluation of the Project."[124]

Similarly, in *Cameroon: Petroleum* (where a Request for Inspection was filed roughly a year after the conclusion of the Inspection Panel's *Chad* investigation), the Panel noted that it was

> troubled by Management's narrow interpretation of cumulative impacts of the project in that it is restricted to the narrow imprint of the pipeline right-of-way through Cameroon.[125]

"It is clear," the Panel pointed out, "that this project will be a stimulus to the development of additional oil resources in Cameroon"

> and that the development of project infrastructure such as roads and other associated offsite developments will lead to further development within the Pipeline area. Additionally, the Panel sees no basis for [Management's] comment that 'the cumulative impacts of the Pipeline project are expected to be below the threshold that would warrant further analysis or a "formal" cumulative impact assessment.'[126]

The Panel questioned "under what criteria regarding project impacts was the threshold determined that would warrant further analysis or a formal cumulative impact assessment", and also noted "that a formal cumulative impact assessment was not in fact completed even though it had been identified as a requirement by Management of the revision of the 1997 EA."[127]

Hence, the Panel concluded, an "assessment of cumulative effects should have been conducted during the early scoping of the project's environmental effects prior to project approval"

---

122 *Chad: Petroleum* (2001), Inspection Panel Chair address to Board, p. 1.
123 *Id.*
124 *Id. Note*, this example also demonstrates the Panel's review of the exercise of Managerial discretion (here allowing for a narrower margin of discretion), *as* discussed *in* section 6.3.2.
125 *Cameroon: Petroleum* (2002), IR, §§ 53-54.
126 *Id.*
127 *Id.*

and included as part of the original project environmental assessment and subsequent EMP. The Panel finds, therefore, that Management is not in compliance with OD 4.01 as regards the need for an adequate assessment of the Project's cumulative effects.[128]

Whereas in *Albania: Power Sector*, the Requesters claimed that the cumulative impacts of the construction of "large oil storage deposits just 1 km" from the planned Vlora TPP had not been properly assessed.[129] The Inspection Panel concurred with this claim, and noted "that failure to give consideration"

> in both the Final EIA and the Addendum to the medium- and long-term risks associated with the construction phase and the alternative ways of delivering fuel to the Vlora TPP in the operational phase is a serious shortcoming and renders the Final EIA non-compliant with the OP 4.01 requirement that 'EA evaluates a project's potential environmental risks and impacts in area of influence,' where 'area of influence' is defined as the 'area likely to be affected by the project, including all its ancillary aspects, such as power transmission corridors, pipelines [...]'.[130]

Because "the Vlora TPP is a part of the 'Albanian Power Sector Generation and Restructuring Project,' the Panel concluded, "and there is prima facie evidence"

> that more than one energy related project is being undertaken in Vlora, Bank staff should have insisted on a Sectoral EA and the associated cumulative effects analysis in addition to the project-specific Environmental Assessment.[131]

The scope of cumulative impact assessments should, moreover, not be limited to activities related strictly to World Bank-financed projects. For example, in *Chile: Quilleco Hydropower*, the Panel pointed to the existence of other hydropower plants in the project's area of influence as key considerations that had to be taken into account during a cumulative impact assessment. In this instance, the "reduction in water flow caused by the Quilleco Project," the Panel observed, is "compounded by the initial impact caused by the Rucúe

---

128 *Id.*
129 *Albania: Power Sector* (2007), IR, pp. xvii-xviii.
130 *Id.*
131 *Id.*

Project,"[132] which "constitutes a cumulative impact that should have been properly analyzed as part of the social and environmental impact assessment of the Quilleco Project."[133]

Indeed, "the cumulative impacts of a series of relatively small run-of-river hydropower plants, each of which could be potentially beneficial to the global environment,"

> can have a significant impact on the local environment and the lives of people living in and from the areas affected by such projects.[134]

Hence, the Panel concluded, "these cumulative impacts need to be appropriately evaluated in the social and environmental impact assessments of such projects."[135]

"A clear understanding of the spatial and temporal parameters of a project is fundamental to its proper evaluation and assessment, as the Inspection Panel observed in its investigation of *Pakistan: National Drainage Program*.[136] Yet, the Panel's investigation also highlighted a few issues in this regard.

For instance, the Panel found that, "at the time of the preparation of the [predecessor] LBOD project the Bank did not clearly define the area of influence of the project."[137] Moreover, "the Bank assumed" at the time "that there *would be* no adverse effects *if* adequate safeguards were provided in the project design."[138] As a result, the Panel concluded, "[t]he possible impacts on the *people* of south Badin and Thatta, in particular the possible impacts on those residing in the vicinity of the lower outfall structures, were not adequately assessed despite the major physical works undertaken there."[139]

Furthermore, although the 'NDP Project' (the successor project) "spann[ed] four provinces" and therefore "had a broader geographic scope than the LBOD project," the Panel commented, "the focus of [the NDP Project's] social analysis had been "made narrower."[140] For example, "[d]espite certain references in the 1993 DSEA [of the predecessor project], there did not appear to be any further study"

---

132 *Note*, the Inspection Panel refers to the "existing [upstream] Rucúe hydropower plant" – *see Chile: Quilleco Hydropower* (2010), Final ER, § 9. For an overview of *Chile: Quilleco, see* Naudé Fourie (2014), pp. 491-498.
133 *Chile: Quilleco Hydropower* (2010), Final ER, § 56.
134 *Id.*
135 *Id.*
136 *Pakistan: National Drainage Program* (2004), IR, p. xx.
137 *Id.* Note, on the Panel's comments regarding the need to develop clearer guidelines on projects with 'legacy components', *also see* the discussion *in* section 14.2.3.
138 *Pakistan: National Drainage Program* (2004), IR, p. xx (emphases in original).
139 *Id.*
140 *Id.*

of the possible impacts of the drainage program on the people who depended upon the dhands for at least part of their livelihood, nor of any possible impact of increased drainage waters flowing through the Tidal Link.[141]

"The area covered by the Requesters' claim falls within the general area of the LBOD [predecessor] project and within the project area of influence of the NDP [successor] Project," the Panel affirmed, and "under the NDP Project"

> neither the potential environmental nor the potential social impacts of the Project in the area of concern to Requesters were considered in a meaningful way until the submission of the Request.[142]

Finally, in *Nigeria/Ghana: West African Gas Pipeline* (WAPG), the Panel emphasized "the importance of examining impacts linked to the" Project, which "may occur both upstream and downstream of the new pipeline, including those that relate to the development of new areas of production and transport."[143] The Panel noted that these areas "were within the Project area of influence within the meaning of OP 4.01" and that the Regional Environmental Impact Assessment had indeed "properly flag[ed] these issues."[144] However, the Panel added, "an analysis of their nature and scope has not yet been carried out."[145]

The Panel also pointed out that in several "Project documents, Bank Management itself makes a linkage between the WAGP and the upstream reduction of gas flaring, in this case to highlight a projected benefit of the Project."[146] Such arguments, the Panel commented, "reinforc[e] the view that the Project and associated facilities and supply areas"

> should be viewed as an inter-connected system for purposes of environmental assessment, considering both potential benefits and adverse impacts.[147]

However, the Panel concluded, it was "concerned that Project documentation was not consistent in defining the Project's area of influence."[148]

---

141 *Id. Note*, 'dhands' refers to a "shallow lake, depression, or wetland" – *see Pakistan: National Drainage Program Project* (2004), ER, p. 5, fn. 38.

142 *Pakistan: National Drainage Program* (2004), IR, p. xx. *Note*, on the Panel's argument that the legacy issues formed part of the successor project, *also see* the discussion *in* section 10.4.

143 *Nigeria/Ghana: West African Gas Pipeline* (2006), IR, §§ 359-360.

144 *Id.*

145 *Id.*

146 *Id.*

147 *Id.*

148 *Id.*

14.2.3   Substantive content of EAs

Also at issue in *Albania: Power Sector*, was whether "impacts on tourism potential" should have been included in the project's EA.[149] Bank management argued that tourism was "not an issue covered directly by Bank safeguard policies, but only indirectly through related issues such as potential impacts on cultural property and natural habitats."[150] And while "tourism adjoining the immediate [TPP] site could possibly be reduce[d]," Management added that "the benefit of more reliable power in the Vlore area (and generally in the southern part of Albania) for tourism is undeniable."[151]

The Inspection Panel, however, disagreed with this interpretation, arguing instead that the lack of a direct reference to tourism in the policy "is clearly not a reason for omitting real life impacts,"

> since the Bank's projects are subject not only to safeguard policies but to all operational policies. Social impact risks and economic risks are covered in such policies as OMS 2.20 [Project Appraisal] and OP/BP 10.04, both of which apply to the project. It is precisely because OMS 2.20 was not applied in terms of its social analysis requirements that these social risks were not considered in the project's concept, design, and preparation.[152]

In fact, the Panel added, "a large array of social issues and potential economic risks to the area population, resulting from design, siting and impacts"

> were not considered in the Project's preparation and EAs. This is not compliant with Bank policy. There was also no integration between biophysical and social studies or between the Environmental Assessment and economic and technical studies. In all these respects, Management has failed to ensure that the substance of OP 4.01 was complied with in the preparation and appraisal of the Vlora TPP.[153]

---

149 *Albania: Power Sector* (2007), IR, § 245.
150 *Albania: Power Sector* (2007), IR, §§ 210-211.
151 *Id.*
152 *Albania: Power Sector* (2007), IR, § 245 (emphasis added). *Also see* IR, p. xxvi: "The Panel finds that as a result of errors in the incorporation of levelized cost measures and improper accounting for social and environmental impacts in the decision matrix, Management failed to comply with the requirements of OP 10.04 and OMS 2.20 in terms of preparing an economic appraisal that identifies and quantifies all costs, including opportunity costs, associated with the Project."
153 *Albania: Power Sector* (2007), IR, § 147.

Furthermore, the Panel reviewed the analysis of possible cultural resources in the selected TPP site and commented that the "borrower's EIA", despite "its length ([of] some 417 pages)," paid "little attention to cultural resources (only two paragraphs)."[154]

"[T]hese paragraphs," the Panel pointed out, were also "misleading" as "they incorrectly claim[ed]" that "Detailed information and data concerning cultural resources and any potential archaeological sites in the Vlorë area are not available."[155] On the contrary, the Panel noted that its own "[r]esearch […] ha[d] confirmed that detailed information and data [were] readily available about the cultural resources of the Vlora area from multiple sources."[156]

While in *China: Western Poverty Reduction (Qinghai)*, the Panel noted that it could not "escape the conclusion that Management adopted a very limited definition of 'environment' in the Qinghai Project."[157] Consequently, "the full range of project effects [was] not analyzed or placed before those responsible for project related decisions."[158] Indeed, the Panel commented, it was a "well-established principle of Environmental Assessment that the term 'environment'"

> must be broadly interpreted and must include all relevant biophysical and socio-cultural elements. This principle is well set out in OP 4.01, viz. "3. EA takes into account the natural environment (air, water, and land); human health and safety; social aspects (involuntary resettlement, indigenous peoples, and cultural property); and transboundary and global environmental aspects. EA considers natural and social aspects in an integrated way."[159]

"Although not as clearly stated in the main text of OD 4.01," the Panel acknowledged, it was nevertheless "clear from Annex A to OD 4.01" (referring to the 'Checklist of Potential Issues for an EA') "that a limited definition of the term 'environment'" or a "strongly biophysical bias to the environment" was

> neither intended nor possible. Some twenty issues to be covered in an EA are listed, and among these are Biological Diversity; Cultural Properties; Indigenous

---

154 *Albania: Power Sector* (2007), IR §§ 219-220.
155 *Id.*
156 *Id.*
157 *China: Western Poverty Reduction (Qinghai)* (1999), IR, § 195. For other examples where the interpretation of key phrases in operational policies and project documentation affected project content and scope, *see* sections 10.4, 12.1 & 13.1.
158 *China: Western Poverty Reduction (Qinghai)* (1999), IR, § 195.
159 *China: Western Poverty Reduction (Qinghai)* (1999), IR, § 191.

Peoples; Induced Development and Other Socio-Cultural Aspects; Land Settlement; Natural Hazards; Wetlands; and Wildlands.[160]

Yet, the Panel commented, the project's EA reflected "a strongly biophysical bias to the environment, even though biological diversity itself receives no more than passing mention."[161] For instance, the Panel elaborated, "[n]either the Environmental nor the separate Social Assessment addresses the topic of induced development," whereas the "proposed in-migration to Dulan County"

> will more than double its population and the proposed new towns will each have populations five times as large as Xiangride, the nearest established town to the main irrigation site. But the potential impact of this on the regional economy and on existing commercial, social and political sectors and hierarchies has not been considered.[162]

In *Peru: Lima Urban Transport*, the Panel found that the EA "looked exclusively at the issues of air quality and noise" and, based on this analysis, "concluded that the implementation of this Project would bring very clear benefits in both aspects."[163] But while the EA "include[d] a detailed modeling of air quality and noise," the Panel observed, it only covered "a very general description of traffic patterns after implementation" and also failed to "mention the impacts of the re-routed traffic into the local streets of Barranco."[164] In other words, the Panel concluded, the EA provided a "detailed consideration"

> to multiple aspects and impacts in the various sections of the corridor, generally stating that there will be great improvements in the future situation *but negative aspects on traffic and cultural property are given much less consideration.*[165]

And in *Ghana: Second Urban Environment Sanitation*, the Panel found that the successor (repeater) project's designs failed to account for the "effect of changing circumstances on the ground" that had occurred since the original designs had been completed earlier.[166] The repeater project's "2003 ESA relied heavily on a siting study and environmental assessment from many years earlier," the Panel observed, as required by the Bank's

---

160 *China: Western Poverty Reduction (Qinghai)* (1999), IR, §§ 192-193.
161 *China: Western Poverty Reduction (Qinghai)* (1999), IR, §§ 193-194.
162 *Id.*
163 *Peru: Lima Urban Transport* (2009), IR, §§ 81 & 84.
164 *Id.*
165 *Id.* (emphasis added).
166 *Ghana: Second Urban Environment Sanitation* (2007), IR, § 331-332. *Note*, on repeater projects, *also see* the discussion *in* section 14.1.

guidelines on repeater projects.[167] However, the Panel added, the 2003 ESA take not "properly" account for "the new social and environmental reality in the proposed landfill area," which was caused by "an influx of people with corresponding investments in physical structures and commercial activities."[168]

Noting that it had found similar issues in other cases where "legacy issues" were present – irrespective of "whether or not the initial operation was financed by the Bank"[169] – the Inspection Panel concluded that the *Ghana: Sanitation* project "highlighted the need for particular care when addressing environmental and social safeguard issues in projects initiated and later stopped."[170]

Indeed, the Panel pointed out, in Bank management's formal response to the Panel's 2007 *Uganda: Power Projects* investigation report, it had specifically committed to develop "guidance on how to address environmental and social safeguard issues in legacy projects that suffer significant interruptions in implementation."[171] The Panel expressed the hope "that the issues and findings of the present investigation will also be taken into account in developing this guidance."[172]

Finally, in *Kenya: Lake Victoria Environmental Management*, the Inspection Panel commented that the EA was "largely descriptive" and provided "a general overview of issues and concerns based mainly on literature reviews."[173] Although it "provide[d] an overview of the socio-economic system, and touch[ed] on potential costs and benefits", the Panel noted that "[t]he bulk of the study deals with biophysical matters – physical setting, fisheries, biodiversity, water quality, water hyacinth, and wetlands."[174]

In other words, the Panel concluded, the "Environmental Analysis provide[d] no meaningful environmental analysis or discussion of the potential consequences, *positive or negative*,"

> of the effects that water hyacinth control interventions may have on the liveli-
> hoods of different groups of people, e.g. women dependent upon water hyacinth
> for crafts, fisheries, subsistence farmers in eroded areas.[175]

---

167 *Ghana: Second Urban Environment Sanitation* (2007), IR, § 331-332.
168 *Id. Note*, on issues related to the identification and quantification of PAPs, *also see* section 10.3.
169 *Ghana: Second Urban Environment Sanitation* (2007), IR, § 331-332. *Note*, the Panel was referring specifically to its 2001 and 2007 *Uganda: Power Projects* investigations. *Also note*, this example demonstrates the Inspection Panel's practice of referencing previous findings (*see* section 1.2.1.), as well as the Panel's contribution towards institutional learning by identifying structural issues in World Bank development-lending operations – *as discussed in* section 7.1.5.
170 *Ghana: Second Urban Environment Sanitation* (2007), IR, § 331-332.
171 *Id.*
172 *Id. Note*, on institutional learning as an output of accountability processes, *see* section 7.1.5.
173 *Kenya: Lake Victoria Environmental Management* (1999), IR, § 134.
174 *Id.*
175 *Kenya: Lake Victoria Environmental Management* (1999), IR, § 136 (emphasis added).

Furthermore, some issues raised in stakeholder consultations were recorded in the document, but there was no analysis and little commentary on them.[176] The Panel also found that project "stakeholders were not fully consulted during the scoping of the environmental analysis", whereas the Panel could not find any evidence "that the Environmental Analysis was made available to stakeholders either for discussion or review before and after finalization."[177]

14.3   CONSIDERATION OF DESIGN ALTERNATIVES

The consideration of design alternatives is, as the Inspection Panel explained in *Colombia: Cartagena Water & Environmental Management*, a "basic principle of environmental assessment."[178] In essence, "there can be no choice if there is no alternative" – a principle that "was recognized as early as the late 1960s."[179] The very purpose of environmental assessment," therefore, "is to improve decisions by making appropriate choices,"

> so it follows that careful comparison of realistic alternatives is an important feature of environmental assessments. Without systematic consideration of realistic alternatives, any environmental impact assessment is seriously flawed.[180]

Project activities aimed at ensuring the consideration of design alternatives would therefore identify discrete options, and conduct a comparative analysis with regard to variables such as 'technical feasibility', (different forms of) 'cost', 'benefits' and also (different types of) risk.[181] Inspection Panel investigations typically highlight three types of issues related to the consideration of project design alternatives, namely, concerns about: the substance of the comparative analysis – in other words, whether the analysis included all the variables

---

176 *Id.*

177 *Id. Note*, on issues related to consultation, *see* section 11.2; on issues related to access to project-information, *see* section 11.1.

178 *Colombia: Cartagena Water & Environmental Management* (2004), IR, § 60. For examples where the Panel found the Bank to be in compliance with regards to the consideration of design alternatives, *see Kenya: Lake Victoria Environmental Management* (1999), IR, §§ 245-246; *South Africa: Eskom Investment Support* (2010), IR, §§ 444-446; *Paraguay/Argentina: Yacyretá Hydroelectric Project* (2002), IR, §§ 125-126; *Cameroon: Petroleum Development and Pipeline* (2002), IR, §§ 42 & 45; *and Albania: Power Sector* (2007), IR, § 132.

179 *Colombia: Cartagena Water & Environmental Management* (2004), IR, § 60. *Note*, this example also demonstrates the Panel's reference to other sources of normativity – here, a principle of international environmental law – *as* discussed *in* sections 5.3.2 & 5.4.

180 *Colombia: Cartagena Water & Environmental Management* (2004), IR, § 60.

181 *And see, e.g.*, the criteria employed in the analysis of design alternatives in *Nigeria/Ghana: West African Gas Pipeline* (2006), IR, § 334: "[...] effectiveness of bringing Nigerian natural gas to market; effectiveness of providing energy to Benin, Ghana and Togo; regional stakeholder acceptance; technical feasibility; capital and operating costs; reduction in greenhouse gas emissions; biophysical impacts of construction; land take; human displacement; social impacts of construction; health impacts of construction."

called for by the specific project situation;[182] the 'diligence' or 'rigour' with which the analysis was conducted – referring to the argument that it cannot be a 'pro forma' exercise to justify a decision that had already been made;[183] and, the transparency surrounding the comparative analysis – especially where it involves prioritization or trade-off decisions.[184]

In the *Colombia: Cartagena* case, where the location of a planned 'submarine outfall' was a key concern of the Requesters, the Panel pointed out that the project's feasibility study did not "refer to or explain"

> any change of policy during the 1990s regarding the preferred ways of addressing Cartagena's wastewater problems or to any controversy over the most appropriate solution.[185]

Indeed, the Panel emphasized, "the absence of explanation about the apparent change from an earlier policy favoring stabilization ponds may have exacerbated a public sense of unease or suspicion about the choice of a submarine outfall."[186]

The Panel also questioned "the diligence with which alternatives other than the preferred alternative of submarine outfall were studied."[187] "The voluminous feasibility study and the environmental assessment," the Panel argued, "give greater attention to the submarine outfall than to other options" and therefore "do not demonstrate a systematic comparative study of all the alternatives as required by OD 4.01."[188]

The Inspection Panel also noted "that after the Board approved the Project, the environmental license for the submarine outfall issued in 2001 by CARDIQUE" ("the regional environmental authority"),

> required the installation after ten years of primary treatment of the wastes at the preliminary treatment plant at Punta Canoa.[189]

---

182 *Note*, this issue is therefore also related to other considerations of content and scope – as discussed *e.g. in* sections 13.2.2, 14.2 *and* Ch. 10.

183 *Note*, this issue is therefore also related to the matter of opposing approaches to policy application and compliance review – as discussed *in* section 6.3.

184 *Note*, this issue is therefore also related to the matter of the operationalization of the principle of access to information (as discussed *in* section 11.1), and the need for transparency surrounding prioritization and trade-off decisions in diverse project contexts (as discussed *in* section 9.3).

185 *Colombia: Cartagena Water & Environmental Management* (2004), IR, § 67. On the Panel's criticisms regarding project-information disclosure and consultation with project-affected people in this case, *also see* the discussions *in* Ch. 11.

186 *Colombia: Cartagena Water & Environmental Management* (2004), IR, § 67.

187 *Colombia: Cartagena Water & Environmental Management* (2004), IR, § 76.

188 *Id.*

189 *Colombia: Cartagena Water & Environmental Management* (2004), IR, § 333.

This additional requirement, the Inspection Panel elaborated, "significantly raises both the costs of investment and of operation and maintenance of the submarine outfall option, according to the figures given in the feasibility study."[190] While Management affirmed that "[...] the District will be responsible for upgrading the plant to primary treatment," the Inspection Panel nevertheless pointed out that Management "did not place a value on these costs – nor [did Management made it clear] that this was done after the issue of the license in 2001."[191]

Under the circumstances, the Panel concluded, "the Bank should have recalculated the costs of the alternative and reviewed the economic analysis in light of this new licensing requirement, to be consistent with OP 10.04."[192]

"Risk assessment," as the Inspection Panel commented in *Nepal: Arun III Proposed Hydroelectric Project*, "must include all factors that might have a bearing on the project, and compare them with those of the alternatives."[193] While the Bank had "attempted to deal with those issues" on this project, the Panel found that the "environmental and social impacts of the alternative have not been systematically analysed."[194] Consequently, "a realistic comparison of risks associated with the proposed project and its alternatives could not have been carried out."[195]

In its 2007 investigation of *Uganda: Power Projects*, the Inspection Panel found the "approach to assessing alternatives to the project" to have been "insufficiently transparent," which made "it difficult for Bank Management authoritatively to address claims that [the consideration of design alternatives] was inadequate and biased in favor of the Project."[196] This situation was not helped, the Panel added, by indications that "the net benefits of the Project could be substantially less than Bank Management has claimed."[197]

The consideration of design alternatives was "especially relevant" in this project, the Panel emphasized, "in light of the significant cultural and spiritual importance of the Bujagali Falls to the Busoga people."[198] However, the Panel concluded, "Management did not ensure that cultural and spiritual matters were properly considered when comparing the Bujagali and Karuma alternatives, as required by OP 4.01."[199]

This oversight "had important consequences," the Panel explained, in particular, since "it appears to have led to the conclusion that there was little difference"

---

190 *Id.*
191 *Id. Note,* this example also demonstrates the Panel's contribution to strengthening institutional governance, as discussed *in* section 7.1.4. On the Panel's 'editing function', *also see* Hale's comments *at* 188, Ch. 7.
192 *Colombia: Cartagena Water & Environmental Management* (2004), IR, § 335.
193 *Nepal: Arun III Proposed Hydroelectric Project*, ER, § 28.
194 *Id.*
195 *Id.*
196 *Uganda: Power Projects* (2007), IR, § 633.
197 *Id.*
198 *Uganda: Power Projects* (2007), IR, § 365. *Also see* the discussion of these matters *in* sections 10.2 & 10.4.
199 *Uganda: Power Projects* (2007), IR, § 365.

between the Bujagali and Karuma sites and that therefore the economic and financial aspects of the options should become the determining factor in selecting the preferred option.[200]

While the Inspection Panel acknowledged that a "range of alternatives ha[d] been considered in" the SEA, it nonetheless expressed its concern that "the analysis unduly narrowed its consideration of alternatives on the basis of a priori judgements"

> rather than exploring all technically feasible options, including those that would not involve flooding the Bujagali falls and thus have lower social and environmental costs, and laying them out in a systematic way along with their economic, social and environmental benefits and costs, so that judgements on optimal alternatives could be made with a full understanding of the trade-offs involved.[201]

"This is not consistent with OP 4.01's provisions," the Panel concluded, "and may have led to inadequate consideration of alternatives" that could have "met Project objectives while avoiding the social and environmental costs associated with flooding the Bujagali Falls."[202]

The Requesters in *India: NTPC Power* argued that "involuntary resettlement in Vindhyachal and Rihand could have been partly avoided through upgrading of existing ash dykes and backfilling of ash in existing mines."[203] Whereas Management, in its formal Response to the Request, commented "that backfilling of ash in existing open cast mines in the Singrauli were not found to be feasible by Northern Coalfields Ltd. (NCL)."[204] Yet, the Panel pointed out, Management did not clarify "if the [alternative] option was technically or economically non-viable or if the social costs associated with the chosen option were properly accounted for."[205]

In reviewing the chosen "fly ash disposal" option, the Panel expressed its doubt "that all possible or feasible ash disposal technologies were considered seriously until recently."[206] While the "Management Response reported that upgrading of 'existing ash dykes has been considered and new ash dyke management techniques have been introduced'," the Panel

---

200 *Id.*
201 *Uganda: Power Projects* (2007), IR, § 370.
202 *Id. Note,* this example also demonstrates the Panel's efforts to link considerations of harm and performance – as discussed *in* section 4.2.2.
203 *India: NTPC Power* (1997), IR, § 123.
204 *Id.*
205 *Id.*
206 *India: NTPC Power* (1997), IR, § 124.

commented, "a full analysis of alternatives, as required [by the policy], does not appear to have been carried out and the issue was not addressed in the Staff Appraisal Report."[207]

The Panel also noted that "Coal India's rejection of disposal by backfilling or consideration of other ash disposal/utilization was accepted apparently without further discussion of alternative measures."[208] Hence, the Panel concluded, no "serious alternatives" were "considered during" the project's "design phase."[209]

In *Peru: Lima Urban Transport*, the Inspection Panel observed that "the introduction" of a "segregated BRT [Bus Rapid Transit] corridor in Barranco along the Avenida Bolognesi *as the only option available*" was "difficult to accept" for "the residents of Barranco" since it had "major implications"

> both for the use of the [Avenida Bolognesi] and for the pattern of traffic within Barranco. This led to a very low level acceptance of that option by local residents.[210]

"In many documents the Panel has reviewed, and in interviews with residents," the Panel emphasized, "the need for an alternative solution was indicated to be a key point of concern."[211]

In its review of the '2005 Traffic Study', the Panel noted "that the solution [the study] recommended was not implemented" – instead, "a different traffic pattern was actually put in place."[212] The independent subject-matter experts contracted by the Inspection Panel to assist it with its investigation were of the opinion, however, "that the alternative proposed in the 2005 Traffic Study" would likely have "respond[ed] better to the concerns expressed by the Requesters and other Barranco residents than the solution currently implemented."[213] The Inspection Panel added that it could not find any "record indicating when the 2005 Plan was changed to adopt the existing solution, nor did it find any analysis of this new alternative and its impacts" – which was "not in compliance with OP 4.01 on Environmental Assessment."[214]

In addition, the Inspection Panel's "review of the environmental assessments prepared for the Project" led it to conclude that alternatives to a segregated BRT "were not studied *in sufficient depth* to be able to assess their technical feasibility and cost, or their merits for

---

207 *Id.*

208 *India: NTPC Power* (1997), IR, § 134.

209 *Id.*

210 *Peru: Lima Urban Transport* (2009), IR §§ 93-97 (emphasis added).

211 *Id.*

212 *Peru: Lima Urban Transport* (2009), IR, § 170.

213 *Id. Note,* on the role of independent subject-matter experts contracted by World Bank – and also by the Panel in support of its fact-finding and compliance review functions, *see* section 5.4.

214 *Peru: Lima Urban Transport* (2009), IR, § 170.

Barranco as compared to the selected route."[215] "It is not clear," the Panel concluded, "to what extent these options were put forward for consideration in the environmental assessment," whereas "attention to these alternatives"

> as well as adequate consultations with Barranco residents during the decision-making process could have avoided the tensions and strong opposition to the Project that arose later and that resulted in the Request for Inspection to the Panel.[216]

Whereas in *China: Western Poverty Reduction (Qinghai)*, the Inspection Panel commented that a "proper social assessment"[217]

> should ask (or at least set its more restricted focus within a context of other studies that ask) "How can we most effectively and sustainably alleviate poverty in Qinghai, with full social and environmental safeguards, and full and informed participation, with the funds available?"[218]

However, the Panel argued, "[t]his Project's Social Assessment instead effectively just asks":

> How can we make this proposed, already-decided dam-building and engineering project work? How should we select and move many tens of thousands of people from the Move-out counties in Haidong and Xining City Prefectures to the proposed irrigation area in Haixi Prefecture, and involuntarily resettle the pastoralists who are there now?[219]

Irrespective "of how well those responsible carried out the Social Assessment," the Panel concluded, "its effective terms of reference prevent[ed] it from considering alternatives to the Project as already defined."[220]

During its investigation of *Nigeria/Ghana: West African Gas Pipeline*, the Inspection Panel noted the project's comparative analysis of design alternatives indicated that "the

---

215 *Peru: Lima Urban Transport* (2009), IR §§ 93-97 (emphasis added).
216 *Peru: Lima Urban Transport* (2009), IR, § 99.
217 *Note*, social assessment forms part of the environmental assessment process. *See e.g., China: Western Poverty Reduction (Qinghai)*, IR, § 137 and fn. 86: "The requirements for assessment of social issues within OD 4.01 (Environmental Assessments) could have been met either by including them in the Environmental Assessment or, as in this Project, within a separate Social Assessment. These requirements for the analysis of alternatives are in addition to those found in ODs 4.20 and 4.30."
218 *China: Western Poverty Reduction (Qinghai)* (1999), IR, § 137.
219 *Id.*
220 *Id.*

pipeline option outrank[ed] or equal[led] alternative power generation and delivery options across all criteria," and also "equal[led] or outrank[ed] alternative natural gas export options."[221] The Panel also observed that the 'pipeline option' involved "three options for routing a pipeline from Nigeria to Ghana," which were subsequently analyzed as part of the environmental assessment process.[222] The three options included:

> a 750 kilometers overland route traversing west from Nigeria across Benin, Togo and Ghana; an undersea pipeline from the Niger Delta to Ghana with spur lines to Benin and Togo; and a hybrid onshore route through Nigeria and an undersea route to Ghana with spur lines to Benin and Togo.[223]

The Panel found that the "comparison" of these three options was "not as rigorous or convincing as the analysis of other project alternatives."[224] For instance, the Panel commented, "[t]he only clear-cut benefit of the hybrid onshore/offshore route" – the option that was ultimately selected – was "its lower cost of construction."[225] "The environmental and social impacts of the offshore route are shown to be slightly lower than the preferred hybrid route," the Panel elaborated, whereas "no detailed cost-benefit analysis is made to establish that the preferred hybrid route does indeed produce the least-cost alternative."[226]

"This is a significant weakness in the analysis of project alternatives," the Panel concluded – adding that "the Bank [did] not appear to have drawn this shortcoming to the attention" of "the consultants preparing the project EA reports."[227]

The Requesters in *Albania: Power Sector* were specifically concerned about the selected site for a planned "combined-cycle natural power station at Vlora," as well as the rigour with which alternative sites were considered.[228]

The Inspection Panel questioned the "sequence of preparatory studies undertaken for the Vlora TPP" since it "effectively negated the purpose of the Bank's Policy on Environmental Assessment."[229] "A site for a new TPP was first determined on largely technical grounds," the Panel elaborated, while "a study of the feasibility of constructing a TPP on the selected site was done simultaneously."[230] Moreover, after the Environmental Assessment was completed, the Panel noted that "a final addendum" was added "to the EA to supply

---

221 *Nigeria/Ghana: West African Gas Pipeline* (2006), IR, § 334. On the criteria employed in this analysis, *see* note 181, Ch. 14.
222 *Nigeria/Ghana: West African Gas Pipeline* (2006), IR, § 337.
223 *Id.*
224 *Id.*
225 *Id.*
226 *Id.*
227 *Id.*
228 *Albania: Power Sector* (2007), IR, pp. xiv-xv.
229 *Albania: Power Sector* (2007), IR, §§ 133-134.
230 *Id.*

post hoc justification for site selection."[231] Although World Bank staff "recommended against" adding such addendum, the Panel commented, "no firm action appears to have been taken"

> to ensure that the borrower and its consultants understood the fundamental purpose of undertaking an EA as set out in OP 4.01.[232]

In other words, the Panel concluded, the environmental assessment process had "contributed nothing"

> to improving Project selection, siting, planning, or design. The purpose of the Vlora EA was thus reduced to improving Project implementation after decisions to proceed had been taken. This process was not compliant with OP 4.01 paragraphs 1, 2 and 3.[233]

In *Ghana: Second Urban Environment Sanitation* (which, as discussed earlier, was a 'repeater project'), the Panel voiced its concern about the consideration of design alternatives in light of the project's 'legacy aspect'.[234]

"One means to deal with adverse impacts on people from a landfill is to establish an adequate 'buffer zone' around its boundaries," the Panel explained.[235] "In general," the Panel added, "the Bank relies on the due application of relevant safeguard policies,"

> including the Environmental Assessment Policy, on a project by project basis to determine appropriate buffer zone (or setback distance) in a case such as the present one.[236]

The Requesters claimed that, in this project context, there was a "need for a setback distance of 1 km", which, the Panel noted, is also reflected "in the early documentation relating to the possibility of developing a landfill at Kwabenya" – and which form the core of the Requesters' concerns.[237]

---

231 *Id.*
232 *Id.*
233 *Id.*
234 *See e.g.*, section 14.2.3.
235 *Ghana: Second Urban Environment Sanitation* (2007), IR, § 144.
236 *Ghana: Second Urban Environment Sanitation* (2007), IR, § 146.
237 *Ghana: Second Urban Environment Sanitation* (2007), IR, § 147.

However, the Panel questioned the decision to use the analysis of design alternatives, completed as part of the predecessor project, as basis for the analysis in the successor project.[238]

"In comparing possible alternative sites," for example, "the older study gave to Kwabenya"

> the highest possible scores both on the criteria of 'distance to the next settlement' and 'affected people,' and ranked it tops in the assessment on social issues together with a site at Okpoe Gonno.[239]

However, the Panel noted, since "people have moved into the area over the years," it would be questionable to use these "early rankings" in the current analysis.[240] Indeed, the Panel pointed out, "[i]n the present situation, [...] much of the Agyemankata Community appears to lie within [the setback] distance of 800 meters to 1 km set out in the early guidance document."[241]

Hence, the Panel concluded, the current ESA "did not adequately examine alternative sites for the future landfill"

> and failed to assess adequately the implications of the influx of people and changing conditions on the ground in the years since the earlier studies on which it relied. This does not comply with OP/BP 4.01.[242]

"The lack of an adequate analysis of alternatives, which is central to the Request for Inspection and to the present stalling of the solid waste component," the Panel emphasized, "partly explains the present and costly situation."[243]

Similarly, in *Pakistan: National Drainage Program*, the Inspection Panel was critical of the successor project's reliance on the predecessor project's "1993 DSEA analysis of alternatives."[244] The 1993 analysis (which, the Panel pointed out, had to be considered "in

---

238 *Ghana: Second Urban Environment Sanitation* (2007), IR, § 331.

239 *Ghana: Second Urban Environment Sanitation* (2007), IR, § 149. *Note*, the earlier study "describe[ed] the situation at Kwabenya as follows: The nearest village to the south-east is Kwabenya which is approximately 2 km away. In the West and north at approximately 4 km and 2 km are Pokuase and Mayera respectively. However prominent hills separate both villages from the site. It is noted that there are over 20 farmsteads located mainly on the eastern slope with a total sizeable population. These are temporary settlers mainly engaged in farming activities." (*See* IR § 148.)

240 *Ghana: Second Urban Environment Sanitation* (2007), IR, § 149.

241 *Id.*

242 *Ghana: Second Urban Environment Sanitation* (2007), IR, § 138.

243 *Id. Note*, this example also demonstrates the Panel's efforts to link considerations of harm and performance – as discussed *in* section 4.2.2.

244 *Pakistan: National Drainage Program* (2004), IR, §§ 280, 283 & 285.

the context of its time") suggested that "there would be no appreciable environmental effects from the expansion of the LBOD."[245] The analysis added "that none of the other options, which involved 'disposal within the system',"

> seemed environmentally acceptable on a large scale or on a permanent long-term basis. On this basis, the DSEA concluded that the option to extend and enlarge the LBOD system "seems at present to be the only one which, if feasible, could maintain permanently the present – and still developing – irrigation system which is so crucial to Pakistan."[246]

However, the Panel observed, "the 1993 DSEA analysis of alternatives rapidly became out of touch with the situation on the ground."[247] "Most importantly," the Panel emphasized, it "underestimated the potential negative environmental effects in southern Sindh of relying upon and expanding the LBOD."[248]

Therefore, the Panel concluded, the 1993 DSEA analysis of alternatives "did not provide an adequate basis to inform decision-making for the NDP Project on the core question of available alternatives, as required under OD 4.01."[249]

****

When considering the manner in which the World Bank applies the foundational policy on Environmental Assessment throughout its development-lending operations, viewed from the perspective of Inspection Panel practice, similar issues arise than in other policy areas – notably, that there is a tendency to apply the policy on Environmental Assessment so as to limit the obligations it places on the Bank and its borrowers. This tendency, moreover, reflects the underlying tension between the various institutional aims – particularly, those aimed at maximizing performance *versus* those aimed at minimizing harm.[250]

For instance, as Sarfaty comments, "[f]inancial concerns [...] influence the level of compliance with the Bank's environmental assessment policy" since "full compliance is seen as unreasonably expensive by some borrower countries and Bank management," whereas "[l]oans go through more smoothly when compliance is not questioned," thereby "satisfying the Bank's financiers and getting borrowers the money they need more quickly."[251]

---

245 *Id.*
246 *Id.*
247 *Id.*
248 *Id.*
249 *Id.*
250 *See* section 4.2.
251 Sarfaty (2005), fn. 94, quoting Bridgeman (2001), p. 1025.

Because the policy on Environmental Assessment forms such an important foundation for the other safeguard policies, however, non-compliance in this policy area is likely to trigger compliance issues in others – policy areas, which could result in environmental, as well as social and economic adverse effects that might be impossible or very costly to reverse. Importantly, as some of the examples included in this chapter illustrate, the materialization of such risks can also affect the realization of development objectives, which in turn, is related to considerations of performance.

"Critics of the World Bank and other IFIs in the environmental community", as Di Leva notes, maintain "that these institutions have acted ambiguously or against international environmental law objectives," whereas they would often "point to certain findings in the reports of the World Bank Inspection Panel or its Independent Evaluation Group for support" for their arguments.[252] Many have also voiced "the concern"

> that just when the Bank's environmental and social policies have begun to mature, there appears to be an effort to move away from the safeguards per se, and use borrower systems in their place.[253]

Many of the examples from Inspection Panel practice included here could certainly be viewed as corroboration for such arguments.

On the other hand, it is also accurate to say "that the Bank and its developing country counterparts operate under acute pressure to improve the economic growth of the many millions living in poverty."[254] Indeed, although the transnational development context is changing, institutions such as the World Bank remain at the cutting-edge of making sense of what sustainable development should look like in practice. And with the environmental, social and economic considerations reflected in its policy on Environmental Assessment, as well as in other operational policies, the World Bank remains in a prominent position to do so. Going forward, however, the Bank's main challenge might be to convince its Management, Staff – and particularly its Borrowers – of the enduring importance thereof.

Finally, much of the discussion in this chapter (as well as in other areas of Part II) reflected what might be described as a considerable degree of 'technical detail' – which significance might not always be apparent to those unfamiliar with development practice. However, as practitioners know all too well, the devil often lurks in technical detail such as the 'collection of baseline data', or the interpretation of the term 'landowner.' Given the intricate – and often implicit – connections between various policy aspects, even the number of 'rodents' and 'grains of sand' in a project area can prove to be critical.[255]

---

252 Di Leva *in* Bradlow & Hunter (Eds.) (2010), p. 385.
253 *Id.*
254 *Id.*
255 *See* Wolfensohn's comments *at* note 226, Ch. 7.

Such examples from Inspection Panel practice, moreover, illustrate the level of abstraction required in order to operationalize an abstract notion such as *accountability*.

15 PROJECT SUPERVISION

"[A]s a *lending institution*", the World Bank "is required by its Articles of Agreement to ensure"

> that the proceeds of any loan are used only for the purposes for which the loan was granted, with due regard to economy and efficiency. As a *development agency*, the Bank also has an interest in assisting member countries to achieve their development objectives on a sustainable basis. To these ends, recognizing that project implementation is the borrower's responsibility, the Bank supervises the borrower's implementation of Bank-financed projects.[1]

The World Bank's obligations with regard to project supervision involve "monitoring, evaluative review, reporting" and providing "technical assistance,"[2] and are set out mainly in the policy on Project Supervision.[3] These activities – which form the focus of Chapter 15 – are aimed at "ascertain[ing] the extent of [borrowers'] compliance with loan covenants, including those related to environmental and social safeguards" and should therefore also "assess risks to successful implementation, operation, and sustainability of the project."[4]

Or, as Shihata explained, project supervision entails that the "Bank reviews the borrower's progress reports, and Bank staff visit project sites and facilities to review progress, provide advice, and obtain information. *They do not, however, make decisions on behalf of the borrower.*"[5] And although the World Bank has, over time, increased the resources and efforts dedicated to project supervision activities, this "does not mean," Shihata cautioned, "that the Bank"

> replaces the borrower, as the owner of the project, who is solely responsible for any harmful effect it may inflict on private groups or individuals as a result of such implementation.[6]

---

1   OP 13.05 (Project Supervision), § 1 (emphases added). *Note,* on the dual commercial/public nature of the Bank's development mission, *see* Ch. 4.
2   OP 13.05 (Project Supervision), § 2.
3   *Note,* other operational policies also include provisions pertaining to project supervision – *see e.g.,* BP 4.11 (Physical Cultural Resources), § 17: "For projects in which the physical cultural resources management plan incorporates provisions for safeguarding physical cultural resources, supervision missions include relevant expertise to review the implementation of such provisions." *And* for supervision requirements related to development-policy projects, *see e.g.,* BP 8.60 (Development Policy Lending), §§ 15-17.
4   *Ghana: Second Urban Environment Sanitation* (2007), IR, § 298.
5   Shihata (2000), pp. 11-14 (emphasis added).
6   *Id.*

"In fact," Shihata elaborated, "while the Bank's policies aim at the avoidance of such harmful effects,"

> the Bank does not take any action with direct effect on parties other than the borrower, and any effect of its actions vis-à-vis the borrower cannot have any effect on third parties unless the borrower reflects them in its implementation of the project.[7]

In other words, to employ the conceptual framework presented earlier, the Bank's application of the policy on Project Supervision provides a prominent demonstration of the nature of the Bank's 'secondary obligations'[8] – which, as the Inspection Resolution explicitly stipulates, are included within the Inspection Panel's mandate.[9]

Chapter 15 considers prominent compliance issues related to three aspects of project supervision, notably: the *identification of risks* and *issues throughout the project cycle*; the *corrective* and/or *remedial actions taken to address issues*; and, what constitutes a *'robust' system of project supervision*.[10]

15.1 IDENTIFYING RISKS AND POTENTIAL ISSUES THROUGHOUT THE PROJECT CYCLE

The identification of risks and potential issues that can influence the effective realization of a project's development objectives and/or result in harm are closely related to the adequacy of various analytical activities that form part of the project's design, planning and appraisal stages.[11]

---

7 *Id. Note*, Shihata's comments reflect the 'formal' delineation of World Bank and borrower obligations, as discussed *in* section 4.3.1.

8 *See* section 4.3.2.

9 IP Resolution, § 12: "The affected party must demonstrate that its rights or interests have been or are likely to be directly affected by an action or omission of the Bank as a result of a failure of the Bank to follow its operational policies and procedures with respect to the design, appraisal and/or implementation of a project financed by the Bank (*including situations where the Bank is alleged to have failed in its follow-up on the borrower's obligations under loan agreements with respect to such policies and procedures*) provided in all cases that such failure has had, or threatens to have, a material adverse effect." (Emphasis added.)

10 For examples where the Panel found the Bank to be compliant with regards to the area of project supervision, *see Papua New Guinea: Smallholder Agriculture* (2009), IR, § 440; *Cambodia: Forest Concession Management* (2005), IR, § 307; *Chad: Petroleum* (2001), IR, § 308; *and see Peru: Lima Urban Transport* (2009), IR, § 189. For examples where Management acknowledged non-compliance with regards to project supervision, *see India: NTPC Power* (1997), ER, § 53; *Ghana: Second Urban Environment Sanitation* (2007), IR, § 302; *Albania: Power Sector* (2007), IR, § 208; *Uganda: Power Projects* (2001), IR, § 82; *Chile: Quilleco Hydropower* (2010), ER, §§ 37, 41 & 53; *and see Cambodia: Land Management and Administration* (2009), ER, § 45.

11 *Notably*, the adequacy of the EA process (as discussed *in* Ch. 14), as well as the delineation of the project area (of influence) (as discussed *in* section 10.2), the identification and quantification of project-affected

For instance, in *India: Mumbai Urban Transport*, concerning various issues surrounding income and livelihood restoration, the Inspection Panel noted that, "[a]s of November 15, 2005," the Bank had "still not addressed" certain aspects, "such as compensation for permanently lost jobs, shifting costs, job training, and job opportunities at the resettlement sites."[12] This shortcoming, the Panel argued, was caused by the underlying assumption "that PAPs would benefit from the new housing and that '[l]oss of income and livelihood opportunities is not a major issue in this project'."[13] Hence, the Panel concluded, "Management did not regard income restoration"

> as a significant problem for resettlement of PAPs and thus did not provide the supervision required by OP 13.05 and did not take necessary corrective actions.[14]

Furthermore, the Inspection Panel found that Bank management had "failed to identify the special problems of shopkeepers affected by the road widening and alignment and to take corrective action until the Request was filed with the Panel."[15]

The Request related to the *Pakistan: National Drainage Program* was filed against the backdrop of significant devastation "caused by flooding in the summer of 2003,"[16] which the Requesters had partly attributed to the NDP project. The Inspection Panel found that the "effects of the flood were" indeed "compounded by" the project (notably, as a result of "problems of the LBOD and Tidal Link)."[17] But the Panel specifically commented that the 2003 floods and its consequences should have been identified as significant issues over the course of the Bank's supervision activities; however, the Panel found "no evidence"

> that the dozens of deaths caused by flooding in the summer of 2003 were even mentioned in supervision documents. Further, the Panel did not see that the destruction of many houses caused by flooding in the summer of 2003 was taken up in supervision. [...] The Panel finds that the lack of response to the floods is not in compliance with OD 13.05.[18]

---

people (as discussed *in* section 10.3), or the surveying of PAP in involuntary resettlement contexts (as discussed in section 12.2).

12   *India: Mumbai Urban Transport Project* (2004), IR, § 716.

13   *Id. Also see* the discussion *in* section 12.5.

14   *Id.*

15   *India: Mumbai Urban Transport Project* (2004), MRIR, Annex 1, § 44. *Also see* the discussion *in* sections 12.2 & 12.3 & 12.4. *Note*, this example also demonstrates that the filing of a Request can trigger corrective/remedial actions – as noted *in* section 7.1.1.

16   *Pakistan: National Drainage Program* (2004), IR, § 567.

17   *Id.*

18   *Id.*

In addition, from "late 1998 until the Panel received the Request in September 2004," the Panel pointed out, "Management's supervision reports demonstrate[ed] inadequate concern"

> for the socio-economic damage to the people in Badin and Thatta which resulted from the Tidal Link's failure, with the exception of the March 2001 Fact-Finding Mission. However, even [this] Fact-Finding Mission made few recommendations to directly help those affected. Unfortunately, those recommendations that were in the report were not followed-up in subsequent supervision work [...].[19]

Hence, the Panel concluded, Bank management had failed to "identify and take adequate corrective actions with regard to the negative environmental and social impacts of the Projects."[20]

In *Cambodia: Land Management and Administration*, the Inspection Panel found that "Management's supervision of the Project" had "for several years overlooked the critical issue of adjudicating private claims on land claimed by the State," discussed earlier.[21] "This failure of Management," the Panel argued, "contributed to the events in the BKL area and the harm that Requesters are facing" (referring to forcible evictions that occurred without property claims being properly investigated and adjudicated).[22] Moreover, the Inspection Panel attributed this failure to a "lack of a robust monitoring and evaluation system for the Project" – a matter that will be addressed in more detail later on in this chapter.[23]

And in *Nigeria/Ghana: West African Gas Pipeline*, concerning the inadequate "institutional capacity of the Sponsor" to implement the 'non-technical' (safeguards) aspects of the project, the Panel found that Management had not "adequately review[ed]"

> the Sponsor's past experience and capacity with implementing operations involving similar involuntary resettlement activities. Neither did Management ensure appropriate coordination between agencies responsible for implementing the RAP. This oversight in supervision resulted in a failure to identify the need for training the Sponsor in the involuntary resettlement safeguards as per BP 4.12, paragraph 2(f). This is inconsistent with the provisions of OP/BP 4.12.[24]

---

19 *Pakistan: National Drainage Program* (2004), IR, §§ 580-581.
20 *Id.*
21 *Cambodia: Land Management and Administration* (2009), IR, § 177. *See* section 8.2.2.
22 *Id.*
23 *Cambodia: Land Management and Administration* (2009), IR, § 286.
24 *Nigeria/Ghana: West African Gas Pipeline* (2006), IR, § 313. *Also see* the discussions *in* sections 8.3.2. & 9.2.

Instead, Management had "assumed rather than evaluated"

> the Sponsor's capacity in dealing with the social safeguard issues. The Panel
> was informed that the Sponsor's partners have a strong reputation for physical
> environmental work, as was evident in the quality reports of the Project's
> environmental assessment. However, the Panel did not obtain evidence that
> this technical capacity implied that the Sponsor's had commensurate capacity
> in dealing with social issues, particularly those related to land acquisition. It
> seems that Management did not take into account some signs regarding the
> Sponsor's limited capacity to meet the Bank's Policies.[25]

"Full awareness of the Sponsor's limited capacity to deal with social issues, in a manner expected by the safeguard policies," the Panel emphasized, "should have led to action, including increased training, intensified supervision, and urgency to field an international Expert Panel."[26]

Finally, the failure to identify issues might also be caused by inaccurate or ambiguous progress reporting. For example, the Inspection Panel's 2002 investigation of *Paraguay/Argentina: Yacyretá Hydroelectric Project* highlighted several "discrepancies among the different types of" implementation progress documents.[27] "[I]n relation to specific issues," the Panel noted, "the progress reports to the Board ha[d] given a more optimistic account of the situation on the ground," than what was reflected in the "Aide Memoires" of supervision missions.[28] "[N]ot until October 2003," that is, "after several visits by the Panel to the [project] area," the Panel commented, "did an Aide Memoire accurately identify"

> the many widespread and difficult problems in implementing the project and
> set forth in a realistic way the measures that need to be taken to comply with
> Bank safeguard polices.[29]

The Panel identified "at least three ways in which some of the reports Management prepared for the Board presented a more optimistic outlook than the Aide Memoires and the circumstances merited," namely:

---

25 *Nigeria/Ghana: West African Gas Pipeline* (2006), IR, § 301.
26 *Id.*
27 *Paraguay/Argentina: Yacyretá Hydroelectric Project* (2002), IR, §§ 414-415.
28 *Id. Note,* these examples illustrate that the filing of Inspection Panel Requests can serve to trigger corrective/remedial action (as discussed *in* section 7.1.1); the examples also demonstrate the value of Inspection Panel fact-finding (*see* section 6.2.4) with respect to the strengthening of the Bank's governance and management structures (*see* section 7.1.4).
29 *Paraguay/Argentina: Yacyretá Hydroelectric Project* (2002), IR, §§ 414-415.

by continued reference to virtual completion of Plan A,[30] even though it is still not fully complete; by setting forth dates for the completion of the resettlement that were too reassuring; and by describing the construction of the wastewater treatment plant "as soon to be started and completed", even though construction has yet to begin in 2004.[31]

In addition, the Panel commented, "the 2001 [progress] report"

contains a significant amount of material that is taken verbatim from the 2000 report, which raises a question of whether the report adequately reflected conditions a year later.[32]

15.2   ADDRESSING ISSUES THROUGH CORRECTIVE AND/OR REMEDIAL ACTIONS

This section considers examples from Inspection Panel practice with regard to the *initiation of corrective/remedial actions* and/or *follow-up on the implementation of such actions*;[33] as well as project circumstances requiring the Bank to *'go further'* – for instance, by employing *higher standards of supervision*,[34] or by *enforcing the loan/credit agreement*[35] – although these matters also bring up the question of *'how far'* the Bank's obligations extends.[36]

15.2.1   *Initiate actions and/or follow-up on the implementation of actions*

The Bank's project supervision activities should, as the policy on Project Supervision stipulates, "identify problems promptly as they arise during implementation and recommend to the borrower ways to resolve them;"[37] "recommend changes in project concept or design, as appropriate, as the project evolves or circumstances change";[38] and "identify the key risks to project sustainability and recommend appropriate risk management strategies and actions to the borrower."[39]

---

30 *Note*, referring to one of the action plans adopted after the Panel's investigation of the *Yacyretá* project in 1996. *See e.g., Paraguay/Argentina: Yacyretá Hydroelectric Project* (1996), MR to IR, p. 44.
31 *Paraguay/Argentina: Yacyretá Hydroelectric Project* (2002), IR, §§ 414-415.
32 *Id.*
33 *Note, also see* the discussion *in* sections 7.1.2 & 7.1.3.
34 *Note*, on a related issue *see* section 8.3.4.
35 *Note, also see* the discussion *in* section 5.1.
36 *Note, also see* the discussion *in* section 4.3.2.
37 OP 13.05 (Project Supervision) § 2(b).
38 OP 13.05 (Project Supervision) § 2(c).
39 OP 13.05 (Project Supervision) § 2(d).

In other words, project supervision activities require the Bank to take decisive 'corrective' actions, insofar as its primary obligations are concerned (which includes the potential exercise of legal remedies against the Borrower), and facilitate the realization of 'remedial' actions, insofar as the Borrower's primary obligations are concerned.[40]

Argentina: Santa Fe Road Infrastructure provides a good example of how the Bank's supervision actions during implementation can address shortcomings of the project design. In this instance, the Inspection Panel found that the project's "socio-economic analysis" was incomplete since it did not cover "all people affected by land acquisition", as required by OP 4.12.[41]

However, the Panel added, "communication with landowners on this aspect significantly improved during Project implementation," whereas "some measures to address the potential negative impacts of the partial taking were provided for."[42] Hence, the Panel concluded, "although initially there was only partial compliance with OP 4.12 [Involuntary Resettlement], the situation improved as a result of Bank staff's compliance with the policy on supervision (OP 13.05)."[43]

In *Ghana: Second Urban Environment Sanitation*, where Bank management acknowledged certain shortcomings with regard to its "supervision of the Kwabenya subcomponent of the Project,"[44] the Inspection Panel was particularly critical of the fact that, although World Bank "supervision missions were conducted for the other subcomponents, no one went to the Kwabenya site in the early stages of implementation."[45]

The Panel acknowledged "the difficult security situation for such visits" – which was caused by the significant controversy among local people about the planned Kwabenya landfill; however, the Panel added, "Bank documentation indicates that the [Borrower] Government was reluctant to discuss the issues they faced with regards to the Kwabenya subcomponent, and yet"

> little, if anything, seems to have been done on the part of the Bank, in the early stages of Project implementation, to follow up on the Government's progress on settling the outstanding issues related to the Kwabenya subcomponent.[46]

---

40   On the distinction between these types of actions, *see* section 7.1.
41   *Argentina: Santa Fe Road Infrastructure* (2007), IR, § 145. *Note,* this example also demonstrates issues related to the surveying of PAP in involuntary resettlement contexts – as discussed in section 12.2.
42   *Argentina: Santa Fe Road Infrastructure* (2007), IR, § 145.
43   *Id.*
44   *Ghana: Second Urban Environment Sanitation* (2007), IR, § 302.
45   *Id.* On the importance of 'on-site' supervision, *also see* section 15.3.1.
46   *Ghana: Second Urban Environment Sanitation* (2007), IR, § 305. *Note,* on the issues in this case, *see e.g.,* the discussions *in* sections 14.2.3 & 14.3.

Whereas in *Nigeria/Ghana: West African Gas Pipeline*, the Inspection Panel commented that "a number of warning signs that appeared in the design phases of the Project were not properly interpreted and dealt with."[47] "For instance," the Panel elaborated, "Management did not adequately follow up on the warnings relating to the RAP process that were raised and discussed in the Monitoring reports."[48] During the implementation phase, moreover, the Panel noted that the "monitoring reports from the panel of experts" had "sent ample warnings to Management of underlying problems" in the project – several "of which appear in the Requester's subsequent complaints."[49] Notably, "[t]en months after compensation was disbursed, in November 2005, the Monitors reported that"

> the WAGP staff were neither monitoring disbursement of all compensation payments by verifying and documenting payment to appropriate parties; nor was the ROW Access Manual done. The 2005 monitoring notes the lack of a clear definition of eligibility for communities who will be involved in the CDP. They reported that it was unclear who was responsible for monitoring resettlement, inflation, population migration, and local employment. They reported on the lack of baseline data on the displaced peoples and that earlier recommendations for the collection of such data were not implemented. They concluded that no reliable baseline data on the topic of livelihood/standard of living for the displaced persons is available.[50]

In the "Supervision Mission Aide Memoire", Management affirmed "that the preparation of community development plans and emergency response plans are on schedule"; however, in Management's response to the Request, it "acknowledge[d] that the Safeguards Mission"

> raised the following issues: inadequate compensation, need for an emergency response plan, implementation of the CDPs, and employment of local labor and contractors. [However,] Management claims that all of these issues were followed up on.[51]

The formal Management Response to the Request also cited a "December 2005 Independent Monitoring Report", which "claim[ed] that WAPCo developed an "effective" environmental and social management system"

---

47 *Nigeria/Ghana: West African Gas Pipeline* (2006), IR, § 487.
48 *Id.*
49 *Nigeria/Ghana: West African Gas Pipeline* (2006), IR, § 445.
50 *Id. Note*, on these issues, *see e.g.* sections 10.4, 11.2, 12.2, 12.3 & 12.5. *Also note*, this example demonstrates the tight complementary and causal relationships between the underlying objectives of several of the Bank's operational policies – *as* discussed *in* section 4.2.
51 *Nigeria/Ghana: West African Gas Pipeline* (2006), IR, §§ 446-447.

and that no adverse impacts on resources or local communities from violations of environmental safeguards had been identified.[52]

However, the Panel found that these statements were "inconsistent with the substantive social compliance issues" raised in that report.[53] Therefore, "[r]eferences to this conclusion by Management in response to the Requester's complaint do not address the underlying unresolved issues;" hence, the Panel concluded, "Management did not adequately address and follow-up on the warnings relating to the RAP process that were raised and discussed in the monitoring reports."[54]

And in *India: NTPC Power,* the Inspection Panel found that project supervision "of the Resettlement and Rehabilitation component and of the measures to strengthen NTPC's capacity to monitor ha[d] effectively failed."[55] Specifically, "[d]uring the design phase,"

> the Bank misjudged the Borrower's ability to implement the R&R component and the Bank's capacity to supervise it. As a result, mostly negative outcomes were inevitable.[56]

While the Panel commended Management's increased efforts regarding project supervision, it also commented that is was "most unfortunate that Management did not act on the unsatisfactory nature of the supervision consultant's reports on the social aspects of the Project before February 1999."[57]

Similarly, in *India: Coal Sector* the Inspection Panel was critical that "over three years had passed since the local NGOs in Parej East had begun to submit their complaints about lack of consultation" before the Bank had initiated corrective actions.[58] "[T]he ESRP reports should have alerted Management to a number of problems as early as April 1997," the Panel added; that is – "two years before [Management] concluded that its supervision consultant's reports were unsatisfactory."[59]

Therefore, the Panel concluded, "prior to February 1999, Management was not in compliance with OD 13.05 on Bank supervision on Parej East."[60] On the other hand, the

---

52   *Id.*
53   *Id.*
54   *Id. Note,* these examples also demonstrate the Panel's contribution to strengthening institutional governance, as discussed *in* section 7.1.4. On the Panel's 'editing function', *also see* Hale's comments *at* 188, Ch. 7.
55   *India: NTPC Power* (1997), IR, § 21.
56   *Id. Note,* on issues related to Borrower capacity, *see* section 8.3; on the Bank's capacity constraints related to supervision efforts, *see e.g.,* the discussion *in* section 15.3.2.
57   *India: Coal Sector* (2001), IR, §§ 456-457.
58   *Id.*
59   *Id.*
60   *Id.*

Panel noted, "the original RAP and IPDP for Parej East were fundamentally flawed" and "[n]o amount or quality of Bank supervision could reverse these flaws."[61]

Bank management acknowledged in *Kenya: Lake Victoria Environmental Management* that "[p]rocurement and disbursement delays were a major factor in the poor implementation of the LVEMP Water quality-monitoring program."[62] This problem, the Inspection Panel added, was nevertheless "compounded when a whole year was lost in ensuring that corrective action was taken."[63]

"The expressions of optimism and confidence on the status" of the project, as "contained in the 1999 Aide Memoire, and in the transmittal letter," arguably "misl[ed] Project Management" and "lull[ed] it into complacency."[64] Therefore, the Panel concluded, "Management failed to comply"

> with paragraph 42 of OD.13.05 because supervision of the design and data collection systems for the pilot was inadequate and because supervision of the implementation of the monitoring systems was also inadequate.[65]

In *India: Mumbai Urban Transport,* regarding the registration of "housing cooperatives" (related to replacement housing), the Inspection Panel noted that Management had "early on reminded the Borrower on the need to form and register housing cooperatives.[66] However, the Panel found the Bank's supervision of these activities to be inadequate "in two respects":

> First, Management contradicted itself about the state of the registration of housing cooperatives in different reports, claiming first that the cooperatives were mostly registered and then claiming that registration was progressing very slowly. Second, Management's supervision of the cooperatives was incomplete, in that it focused only on their registration and did not consider their operational capacity and effectiveness.[67]

"Under the Project," the Panel elaborated, "resources for the Maintenance Fund can be transferred only after the housing cooperative is registered."[68] "In the Aide Memoire for

---

61   *India: Coal Sector* (2001), IR, § 463. Compare this comment with the scenario in *Argentina: Santa Fe Road Infrastructure,* as noted *at* notes 41-43, Ch. 15. *Also see* the Panel's remarks *at* note 236, Ch. 15.

62   *Kenya: Lake Victoria Environmental Management* (1999), IR, §§ 211-212.

63   *Id.*

64   *Id. Also see* similar issues in *Paraguay/Argentina: Yacyretá Hydroelectric Project,* discussed *in* section 15.1.

65   *Kenya: Lake Victoria Environmental Management* (1999), IR, §§ 211-212.

66   *India: Mumbai Urban Transport* (2004), IR, § 725.

67   *Id. Note,* on these matters, *also see* the discussion *in* section 12.4.

68   *India: Mumbai Urban Transport* (2004), IR, § 726.

the September-October 2003 [supervision] mission, at which point one society had been registered,"

> Management noted little progress in the transfer of maintenance funds to the registered societies, as did the next several reports. Likewise, the recent August 2005 report noted the lack of progress in transferring maintenance funds. Though Management has consistently mentioned the Maintenance Fund, it has done little to ensure that they have been set up and operating properly. The Panel found that as of November 1, 2005, the MMRDA [implementing agency] had not transferred any maintenance funds to the Housing Cooperative Societies.[69]

Furthermore, concerning the institutional capacity constraints of the project implementing agency, as well as those of the 'implementing NGOs', the Panel concluded that Management "did not adequately follow up with the Borrower's commitment to remedy the lack of institutional capacity."[70]

In *Cambodia: Forest Concession Management*, the Inspection Panel recognized "the difficult context within which the Project was operating," but also emphasized that "many of the issues raised by the Requesters might not have arisen if the Project had received better supervision."[71] Adequate supervision, the Panel elaborated, "should have aimed at ensuring that the unraveling of relationships that became apparent during the early years of the Project's implementation"

> was addressed explicitly and quickly. In particular, supervision should have aimed at ensuring that the Project had the capacity throughout its life to develop a broadly based constituency, embracing donors, Government and NGOs, to advance forest sector reform.[72]

While Bank management argued that past illegal logging activities "of concessionaires cannot be considered a failure of Management to comply with Bank policy," because "they were carried out prior to, or at least not as part of or within the scope of," the project;[73] the Panel added, that "in the critical early stages of the Project," the Bank had "failed to consider or investigate complaints"

---

69 *Id.*
70 *India: Mumbai Urban Transport Project* (2004), MRIR, Annex 1, § 45. *Note*, on these matters, *also see* the discussion *in* sections 8.3, 10.3 & 12.2.
71 *Cambodia: Forest Concession Management* (2005), IR, § 394.
72 *Id.*
73 *Cambodia: Forest Concession Management* (2005), IR, §§ 240-241.

about illegal logging of resin trees on the part of concessionaires covered by the Project, and the associated harms to the local people. The Panel finds that the illegal logging of resin trees has had major negative consequences on the Requesters and the local people. The Panel further finds that the Bank's failure to consider and investigate these problems does not comply with OP 4.01 and OP 4.36.[74]

Finally, in *Cambodia: Land Management and Administration*, the Inspection Panel commented that it had found "evidence in the supervision records that Management on several occasions"

> raised issues related to State land management potentially relevant for the application of the [Resettlement Policy Framework]. The Panel commends the Bank for pursuing this difficult policy issue in the Cambodian context, which is both politically sensitive and complex.[75]

However, the Panel added, "the follow-up of these issues was inadequate and contributed to the problems in the BKL area", which was "not in compliance with the provisions of OP/BP 13.05 on Project Supervision.[76] "Although the Panel found that at least 17 different land specialists traveled to Cambodia as part of the Project's various supervision missions," the Panel emphasized that "these issues were never addressed."[77]

Furthermore, while the Inspection Panel took note of the "repeated findings in Management supervision reports indicating the inadequacy of dispute resolution [grievance] mechanisms" at the project level, "especially when powerful parties are involved," the Panel pointed out that "Bank Management did not take concrete measures to address these adverse impacts."[78] Indeed, it was "[o]nly in the period leading to the presentation of the Request for Inspection," the Panel concluded, that the Bank seemed to "understand and acknowledge"

---

74 *Id.*
75 *Cambodia: Land Management and Administration* (2009), IR, § 211.
76 *Id.*
77 *Id. Note*, on the location, timing and frequency of supervision missions, *also see* section 15.3.1. *And see* the Panel's comments in this regard about *Paraguay/Argentina: Yacyretá Hydroelectric Project*, as discussed *in* section 15.2.2.
78 *Cambodia: Land Management and Administration* (2009), IR, § 280. On issues related to project-level grievance mechanisms, *see* section 12.6.

that the evictions in the BKL area were linked to LMAP implementation activities and that the RPF was to be applied to the displacement of BKL residents.[79]

15.2.2   'Going further' – but how far?

As the previous discussion demonstrated, some project scenarios require that the Bank's supervision efforts are intensified in order to be effective. In other words, it might not be enough to simply raise issues – the Bank might need to ensure that the Borrower initiates, and implements, the necessary remedial actions. However, as the Bank is also mindful of maintaining its ongoing relationship with borrowers – and as the Bank's actions to enforce the credit/loan agreement can significantly damage this relationship – this aspect of project supervision can be decidedly challenging.[80]

Project scenarios requiring higher standards of supervision
Arguably, there are project scenarios where a 'higher standard' of supervision is required from the outset – as made clear, for instance, by the types and magnitudes of risks identified during project design, planning and appraisal.

As the Panel commented in *Panama: Land Administration*, "the Bank should be given credit for engaging in this extremely important Project in Panama."[81] But while land administration projects "may [indeed] constitute an important contribution to social and economic development," the Panel added, they also "pose significant operational risks [and] are often politically controversial."[82] In such contexts, in particular, it is essential "for the Bank to systematically assess, both during design and during project implementation,"

> operational risks and risks of a political economy nature, and devote adequate trained staff and resources to the project.[83]

For instance, "[i]n view of the seriousness of the threat to the Naso as a people from encroachments on their still unprotected lands," the Panel emphasized,

---

79 *Cambodia: Land Management and Administration* (2009), IR, §§ 216-217. *Note*, on these matters, *also see* the discussion in section 8.2.2.
80 *Also see* Shihata's comments *at* notes 5-7, Ch. 15.
81 *Panama: Land Administration* (2009), IR, § 351.
82 *Id.*
83 *Id. Note*, on issues related to resourcing of supervision missions, *also see* section 15.3.2.

supervision should have met a higher standard. The Panel has determined that the key emerging problems should have been detected much earlier, and been accompanied by actions and recommendations appropriate to addressing the changing circumstances.[84]

Similarly, in *Cambodia: Forest Concession Management*, the Inspection Panel recognized that "some Project Management and Staff"

> *consistently attempted to press* the [Borrower] Government to improve the planning process and *to press the concessionaires to conform* to the various guidelines for preparing SFMPs.[85]

Nonetheless, the Panel concluded, the Bank's "supervision of the planning and development of the SFMPs/ESIAs was inadequate" in the sense "that the Bank's *level of supervision in general did not match the magnitude of the problems* caused by poor SFMPs and ESIAs."[86]

As a 'repeater project' that involved a highly sensitive issue (the location of the Kwabenya landfill), the Panel commented in *Ghana: Second Urban Environment Sanitation* that "it should have been anticipated,"

> that the Project would be overlaid with intense local political sensitivities and the possibility of strong local resistance. During interviews, the Panel learned that Bank staff was fully aware of this climate following DfID's [Britain's Department for International Development] decision to withdraw from the project in 2000, in light of reputational and operational risks.[87]

"Notwithstanding these warning signs," the Panel added, "the Bank opted for a hands-off approach on the supervision of the Kwabenya subcomponent,"

> without paying sufficient attention to the social and environmental safeguard aspects of the Project. The Panel finds that supervision of the Kwabenya sub-component was lacking until well into the implementation of the Project, in non-compliance with OP/BP 13.05.[88]

---

84 *Panama: Land Administration* (2009), IR, § 337 (emphasis added).
85 *Cambodia: Forest Concession Management* (2005), IR, § 337 (emphases added). *Note*, for the Panel's criticism of involving logging concessionaires in these types of activities, *see e.g.*, the discussion *in* section 11.2.3.
86 *Id.* (emphasis added).
87 *Ghana: Second Urban Environment Sanitation* (2007), IR, §§ 314. *Note*, for more on the issues in this case, *see e.g.*, sections 14.2.3 & 14.3.
88 *Ghana: Second Urban Environment Sanitation* (2007), IR, §§ 314.

Changing circumstances could also indicate the need for intensified supervision efforts. For example, in *India: Mumbai Urban Transport*, a reassessment of the number of affected people led to an "increase of about 50% of PAPs," which, as noted earlier, was "larger than entire resettlement components in many other Bank projects in India."[89] However, as the Inspection Panel commented, [d]espite the increases in affected people, which meant a significant change in the scope of the Project resettlement component,"

> the Bank did not re-assess the Project to confirm that the Project, as modified, was still justified, that the requirements of the Bank's policies were met, and that the implementing arrangements were still satisfactory, as required by BP 13.05. The Bank did not set in place comprehensive measures, as warranted by the Bank's policy, for assessing the implications and the actions necessary to address the very substantial increment in the number of people to be resettled. The Panel regards this as failing to comply with OP/BP 13.05 and the provisions of OD 4.30 on monitoring and supervision of the Project.[90]

The Panel's "analysis of all Bank supervision reports over the first 3 years of project implementation," moreover, "indicate[ed] that issues of inadequate institutional capacity and performance, understaffing, lack of resettlement monitoring, etc." were the "single most frequently reported non-performing component of the MUTP current set-up for resettlement."[91] Yet, the Panel added, "[i]n the context of these institutional/organizational weaknesses,"

> both the Independent Monitoring Panel (IMP) planned for MUTP and the grievance system have been non-functional. In light of the evidence on *both process and outcomes* in carrying out OD 4.30 provisions on "organizational responsibilities," the Panel finds that the Bank has not met the requirements of this OD to develop an organizational framework with adequate resources provided to the responsible institutions.[92]

In other words, the Panel concluded, "non-compliance has occurred"

---

89 *India: Mumbai Urban Transport* (2004), IR, § 687. *Also see* the discussion *in* sections 10.3 & 12.2.
90 *India: Mumbai Urban Transport* (2004), IR, § 687.
91 *India: Mumbai Urban Transport* (2004), IR, §§ 218-220.
92 *Id.* (emphasis added). *Note*, on compliance issues regarding the project-level grievance mechanism, *see the* discussion *in* section 12.6. *Also note*, this example demonstrates the Panel's emphasis on procedural and substantive aspects as components of 'compliance' – as discussed *in* section 6.3.4.

despite good staff analytical work on institutional matters during the initial years of Project preparation. *Serious errors in managerial judgment were compounded by failures to meet both the word and the spirit of OD 4.30.*[93]

Given the significant delays in project implementation of the *Paraguay/Argentina: Yacyretá Hydroelectric Project*, the Bank intensified its supervision efforts, especially after the 1996 Request for Inspection.[94] However, a 'higher standard of supervision' cannot be met simply by increasing the number of supervision missions. The substance of such missions and the manner in which they are conducted remain critical factors.[95]

For example, in its 2002 investigation of the *Yacyretá* project, the Inspection Panel recognized that "a larger than average number of supervision missions, which included three High Level Supervision Meetings, demonstrates more intense supervision than is usual" – as would be appropriate in this project scenario.[96]

However, the Panel added, the higher number of supervisions missions, by itself, did not constitute "an adequate response *to alleviate the perceptions and suspicions of project-affected persons.*"[97] In fact, the Panel elaborated, "[i]nadequate on site reconnaissance and supervision seems to be one of the biggest problems of this Project in terms of complying with Bank policies" – whereas "[t]his kind of finding" had also "been a common thread in other Inspection Panel cases."[98]

In this instance, the Panel concluded, it may well "have contributed to the affected people's apparent hostility towards the Bank staff."[99] "Many" project-affected people, the Panel emphasized, "perceive[d] that the only 'Bank people' the affected people have met and talked with were the Panel and its staff, even though this may not be the case."[100]

Finally, with regard to the controversy surrounding demolitions in *Albania: Integrated Coastal Zone Management*, as discussed earlier,[101] the Inspection Panel noted that news of these activities eventually "reached the Bank's Tirana office as well."[102] Subsequently, "[a] technical specialist employed by the Project

---

93 *India: Mumbai Urban Transport* (2004), IR, §§ 218-220 (emphasis added). *Note*, this example also demonstrates the Panel's emphasis on underlying policy objectives – as discussed *in* section 6.3.3; the example also demonstrates the prominent role of the exercise of sound managerial discretion in policy application – as discussed *in* section 6.3.2.

94 *Note*, "[t]he Bank ha[d] been involved in the design and implementation of Yacyretá since the mid 1970s." (*See Paraguay/Argentina: Yacyretá Hydroelectric Project* (1996), ER, § 1.)

95 In this regard, *also see* the discussion *in* section 15.3.3.

96 *Paraguay/Argentina: Yacyretá Hydroelectric Project* (2002), IR, § 403.

97 *Id.* (emphasis added).

98 *Id. Note*, this example also demonstrates the Panel's practice of referencing previous findings – *see* section 1.2.1.

99 *Paraguay/Argentina: Yacyretá Hydroelectric Project* (2002), IR, § 403.

100 *Id.*

101 *See e.g.*, sections 8.2.2 & 12.1.

102 *Albania: Integrated Coastal Zone Management* (2007), IR, p. xii.

was sent to Jale [part of the project area] to determine what was going on. He observed the demolitions, took some pictures, and talked to some of the villagers. According to the Requesters, he also mentioned the Bank-financed Project, indicated to the affected people that they would be compensated, and asked about the approximate value of their damages.[103]

The Panel noted further that the Bank sent a "subsequent Fact Finding Mission to Jale on May 3, 2007", however, the Panel commented, since none of the Bank staff involved in this Mission communicated with "the Requesters or the other members of the affected community, Bank staff "concluded that the demolitions were not related to the Project."[104]

But the Inspection Panel's investigation of these supervision activities highlighted a "more serious" issue, namely that the May 2007 Fact Finding mission had "also omitted, in its written formal BTO report, an essential fact"

> about the role of the [Project Coordination Unit] in prompting the Construction Police to proceed to demolition and in sending to the Construction Police a formal letter including aerial photos financed by the Project.[105]

"This certainly [was] a most relevant fact," the Panel underscored, "apt to enable the Bank and its Management to understand the causality that led to the demolitions in Jale,"

> and to deal with the Bank's reputation risk in a forthright and constructive manner both in the Project area and in the country at large. To this day, it remains difficult to understand how a fact finding team could not reveal this central fact and others discussed in this Report, which were known first-hand by the head of the Fact Finding Mission who, as the Project's Task Team Leader, had received from the PCU both the letter sent by the PCU to the Construction Police and the response of the Construction Police to the PCU. [...] Another important omission of the Fact Finding Mission was to leave out references to the debate in Parliament and the various publications that linked the Bank-financed Project to the Jale demolitions.[106]

The Panel reiterated its concern that the May 2007 Fact Finding Mission, which "was formally mandated to 'obtain a fuller understanding' did not interview the Requesters, and

---

103 *Id.*
104 *Id.*
105 *Albania: Integrated Coastal Zone Management* (2007), IR, §§ 225-226.
106 *Id.*

based its findings on discussions with the PCU and the Construction Police."[107] Since "crucial facts did not make their way into the Fact Finding Mission report and Aide-Memoire", the Panel argued, "Management would have been better served"

> by sending in staff who were not directly involved in this Project to undertake a 'fact finding' mission in a highly controversial situation.[108]

Ultimately, the Panel concluded, this case constituted "[a] prime example of inadequate supervision" in which serious instances of non-compliance resulted in significant adverse effects for people in the project area – and, crucially, where a "partial Fact Finding Mission, which ended up not 'finding' some of the most important facts that explained the events which led to the present inspection," was also instrumental in the compilation of "a problematic Management Response" to the Request filed at the Inspection Panel.[109]

In its response to the Panel's Investigation Report, Bank management acknowledged that, "[b]y not responding in a timely manner to the April 2007 demolitions," it had "allowed public opinion to link the demolitions to the Project and thus to the World Bank."[110] "In sum," Management concluded, "Country and Sector Management"

> failed to exercise their responsibilities in a consistent manner, failed to appoint a Task Team with adequate expertise and experience, and failed to provide adequate oversight to the Task Team.[111]

Bank management emphasized that it "deeply regret[ted] these events," and that "[a] series of errors was committed throughout the Project cycle,"

> including during Project preparation, Board presentation, and Project supervision, as well as in the preparation of the first Management Response in September 2007 and the issuance of a Corrigendum to the Project Appraisal Document in September 2008. These errors are unacceptable and *point to a*

---

107 *Albania: Integrated Coastal Zone Management* (2007), IR, § 224.
108 *Albania: Integrated Coastal Zone Management* (2007), IR, § 228.
109 *Albania: Integrated Coastal Zone Management* (2007), IR, § 246. *Note*, in its initial response to the Request, Bank management argued that the Request did not meet the eligibility criteria since "the demolition of the houses in the Request 'were not limited to the Project area, not caused by or linked to the Project, and were not done in anticipation of the Project or to achieve the Project objectives'." (*See* ER, § 34.) Management also argued that "[w]hen the Bank received complaints and allegations in late April 2007 that demolitions had occurred as a consequence of the Project, it promptly sent a fact-finding mission to Albania in early May 2007. The mission determined that the demolitions were not related to the Project [...]." (*See* MR, § 49.)
110 *Albania: Integrated Coastal Zone Management* (2007), MRIR, Annex 2, § 10.
111 *Albania: Integrated Coastal Zone Management* (2007), MRIR, §§ 12-13. *Note*, on issues related to the resourcing of supervision missions, *also see* section 15.3.3.

*serious breakdown of Management's accountability, responsibility and oversight
mechanisms for the Project*. Management is appreciative of the Inspection Panel
for having brought these errors to its attention and agrees with the Panel that
OP/BP 10.00 on Investment Lending – Identification to Board Presentation,
and OP/BP 13.05 on Project Supervision were violated.[112]

Enforcing the loan/credit agreement

As noted earlier, one of the aims of the Bank's project supervision activities is to "ascertain
whether the borrower is carrying out the project with due diligence to achieve its development objectives in conformity" with the credit/loan agreement.[113] In other words, should
project supervision activities reveal significant instances of non-conformity with the
credit/loan agreement, another aspect of 'going further' involves the decision to exercise
particular legal remedies against the Borrower (such as suspension of funds) in order to
enforce the credit/loan agreement.[114]

However, this decision lies within Bank management's margin of discretion. In some
of the Inspection Panel's earlier cases, the Panel questioned the exercise of such discretion
– generally arguing that Management should have exercised legal remedies to enforce the
credit/loan agreement. It is noticeable, however, that this issue has not featured as prominently in the Panel's later cases, which seems to suggest that the Panel has come to accept
that the operational policies allow Bank management a broad margin of discretion in this
area.[115]

During its consideration of the eligibility of the Request in *Bangladesh: Jute Sector*, for
example, the Inspection Panel "sought clarification on this issue by asking the Senior Vice-
president and General Counsel for his opinion" on the exercise of legal "remedies" against
the Borrower in order to enforce the credit/loan agreement.[116] This opinion was clear on

---

112 *Albania: Integrated Coastal Zone Management* (2007), MRIR, § 41 (emphasis added). *Note*, these examples
also demonstrate the value of Inspection Panel fact-finding (*see* section 6.2.4) with respect to the strengthening
of the Bank's governance and management structures (*see* section 7.1.4).

113 OP 13.05 (Project Supervision), § 2(a).

114 *E.g.*, "[t]he General Conditions ['Applicable to Loan, Guarantee or Credit Agreements'] authorize the Bank
to suspend, in whole or in part, the right of the borrower to make withdrawals from the loan account when
the events set out or referred to in Sections 6.02 and 7.01(f) and (g)4 occur and are continuing. These events
pertain either to the failure of the borrower or other contracting parties to fulfill obligations unrelated to
payment under a Loan Agreement or to the borrower's failure to make payments as required." (*See* OP 13.40
(Suspension of Disbursements), § 1.) *Furthermore*, "Loan amounts may be canceled by either the borrower
or the Bank." Borrowers have "a right to cancel unilaterally any amount of the loan not yet withdrawn, except
amounts for which the Bank has entered into special commitments", whereas the Bank can only cancel
undisbursed amounts" in specific circumstances, set out in the OP 13.50. (*See* OP 13.50 §§ 1-3.)

115 On the issue of managerial discretion, *see* section 6.3.2.

116 *Bangladesh: Jute Sector* (1996), ER, §§ 4 & 81. *Note*, the Inspection Panel Resolution requires that the Panel
consult with the Bank's Legal Department on matters concerning the Bank's legal obligations – as discussed
e.g., *in* section 5.3.

the point that the Bank had "legal remedies beyond the mere withholding of tranche disbursement in [particular] circumstances" but it also emphasized

> that any responsibility for exercise of these remedies – as in investment operations – lies in Management and is *a matter of judgment that must take into account all the circumstances of each case.*[117]

The Panel took note of this opinion but pointed out "that the option of [loan] cancellation" had "never moved beyond the informal discussion stage."[118]

And in *Brazil: Rondônia Natural Resources Management (PLANAFLORO)*, Bank management – responding to the Requesters' claim "that the Bank ha[d] failed to enforce various covenants under the Loan and Project Agreements which has resulted in direct and material adverse effects on intended project beneficiaries and residents of Rondonia"[119] – argued that "the suspension of disbursements is not an automatic sanction to be applied in all cases regardless of its impact on the project and the Bank's relationship with the borrower."[120] Instead, Management asserted, it was merely "*one of the remedies* available to the Bank"

> as a *discretionary power to be exercised by it* in cases of default taking into account the interest of the Bank, the borrower and the Bank members as a whole.[121]

The Inspection Panel, on the other hand, noted that Management had "acknowledged delays in the project and cited a number of implementation problems."[122] "Indeed," the Panel added, "supervision missions constantly rated project implementation as 'unsatisfactory'" but seemingly "without triggering any urgent measures to enforce applicable loan covenants".[123] Instead, the Panel commented, "the problem was dealt with by repeated informal revision of deadlines."[124]

---

117 *Bangladesh: Jute Sector* (1996), ER, §§ 4 & 81 (emphasis added). *Note*, the Request expresses concern about IDA adherence to policies in the context of "failing to enforce JSAC [the project] agreement conditionalities which would adversely affect implementation of JSAC's key components and attainment of its objectives [...]. Enforcement could imply the application of OD 13.40, Suspension of Disbursements. The Response argues that the tranching of adjustment disbursements makes it impossible to withhold funds except at the time of release, and that Management had done so after release of the first tranche." (*See* ER, § 81.)
118 *Bangladesh: Jute Sector* (1996), ER, §§ 4 & 81.
119 *Brazil: Rondônia Natural Resources Management* (1995), ER, § 2.
120 *Brazil: Rondônia Natural Resources Management* (1995), MR, § 4.
121 *Id.* (emphasis added).
122 *Brazil: Rondônia Natural Resources Management* (1995), Additional Review, § 35.
123 *Id.*
124 *Id.*

Management's approach was problematic, the Panel added, especially in the aftermath of the controversy surrounding the predecessor project (POLONOROESTE). In fact, the Panel pointed out, the OED's review of POLONOROESTE had specifically "recommended early use of this remedy to ensure compliance in any future project of this type in Rondonia."[125] Yet, the Panel concluded, project "records examined by the Panel show that suspension of disbursements was never considered for PLANAFLORO until after the Request for Inspection was filed with the Panel."[126]

In fact, the Panel elaborated, the claims filed by the Requesters are indicative of "a typical problem which inevitably arises"

> when restrictive agro-ecological zoning plans are publicly announced but planning and execution are not synchronized.[127]

The effective realization of the development objective of projects "such as PLANAFLORO," the Panel added, "depended heavily on its timely execution."[128] But if this does not happen, "as ha[d] occurred before, there is a rush to occupy land or extract wood from targeted areas before it becomes prohibited" – which, the Panel emphasized, is why the Bank's "repeated acceptance of expanded time periods for implementation of critical components enabled the inevitable to continue."[129]

"Despite design failures," the Inspection Panel concluded, "Management should have identified implementation problems"

> and moved expeditiously to solve them through adequate supervision and monitoring. *Failure to enforce loan obligations in violation of policies and procedures has undoubtedly contributed to the above-noted material damage.*[130]

At a minimum, the Panel commented, the World Bank obligated to "conside[r] a possible enforcement of the borrower's and the State's obligations under the loan documents, as provided in ODs 13.05 and 13.40," whereas its failure to do so, which "contribute[d] to the material losses suffered by the Requesters", was not in compliance with the relevant policies.[131]

---

125 *Brazil: Rondônia Natural Resources Management* (1995), Additional Review, § 55-56. *Note*, this example also demonstrates the complementary nature of the Panel's mandate, as discussed *e.g.*, *in* section 6.2.4.
126 *Id*. *Note*, this example also demonstrates that the mere filing of Requests can serve to trigger corrective/remedial actions, *as noted in* section 7.1.1.
127 *Brazil: Rondônia Natural Resources Management* (1995), Additional Review, §§ 28 & 54.
128 *Id.*
129 *Id.*
130 *Id.* (emphasis added).
131 *Brazil: Rondônia Natural Resources Management* (1995), Additional Review, § 77.

Similarly, in its formal response to the 1996 Request concerning *Argentina/Paraguay: Yacyretá Hydroelectric Project*, World Bank Management asserted that "the exercise of available legal remedies is not a requirement but a discretionary tool, *to be applied only after other reasonable means of persuasion have failed.*"[132]

While the Inspection Panel recognized "that Management has flexibility in deciding whether to exercise available legal remedies," it also emphasized that the review of the exercise of managerial discretion in this area fell within the Panel's mandate, since the Inspection Panel Resolution's definition of "an instance of failure in the compliance of Bank policies and procedures" explicitly includes "situations where the Bank has failed in its follow-up on the borrower's obligations under loan agreements with respect to such policies or procedures."[133]

"[C]ompliance is not achieved *by merely including* covenants in Loan Agreements," the Panel pointed out, "but rather by ensuring that their provisions are implemented in a timely fashion by the borrower and executing entities."[134] In fact, the Panel added, "the discretionary use of legal remedies" was also addressed by the "excellent OED analysis" contained in the "recent OED Performance Audit Report for two of the loans providing financing for Yacyretá."[135] Indeed, the OED report had found that "the Bank accepted repeated violations of major covenants," while adding that "[c]ovenanted actions [were] a precarious way"

> to ensure the viability of a financing plan in light of the Bank's willingness to 'accommodate' non-compliance and the added difficulty of stopping a large unitary project once it ha[d] reached a certain stage of implementation.[136]

The Panel's investigation corroborated this OED finding. For example, the Panel commented, the Bank's "inability or unwillingness to exercise available legal remedies" was illustrated by a (at the time) recent supervision report, which stated:

---

132 *Argentina/Paraguay: Yacyretá Hydroelectric Project* (1996), ER, § 30 (emphasis added). *Note*, the Requesters claimed "that the environment as well as the standards of living, health and economic well-being of people in the Yacyretá area have been, and may potentially be, directly and adversely affected as a result of the filling of the Yacyretá reservoir to 76 meters above sea level ('masl') and the failure of the Bank to ensue – *through supervision and enforcement of legal covenants* – the adequate execution of the environmental mitigation and resettlement activities included in the Project." (*See Argentina/Paraguay: Yacyretá Hydroelectric Project* (1996), ER, § 2, emphasis added.)

133 *Argentina/Paraguay: Yacyretá Hydroelectric Project* (1996), ER, § 30. *And see*, Inspection Panel Resolution, § 12.

134 *Id.* (emphasis added).

135 *Argentina/Paraguay: Yacyretá Hydroelectric Project* (1996), ER, § 31. *Note*, this example also demonstrates the complementary nature of the Panel's mandate, as discussed *e.g., in* section 6.2.4.

136 *Id.*

No Legal Covenant Report is attached to this form, because we are negotiating and finalizing with the Borrower and [*sic*] amendment, which will change most of the covenants and conditionalities under the existing legal documents. It would make no sense to report now [Borrower] non-compliance, when we are reaching an agreement on new covenants and conditionalities under the loan.[137]

Whereas in *India: NTPC Power*, the Panel's "review of supervision reports" affirmed that the Bank had consistently employed a supervision approach through which "Bank staff" had repeatedly "pointed out delays in implementation and recommended remedial actions," although "[s]everal warnings that the Bank might exercise its available remedies [had also been] issued through a number of Bank Supervision Aides-Mémoire."[138]

In its response to the Request, Bank management noted that it had "recognized non-compliance with loan covenants", but had "decided not to exercise the formal remedy of suspending disbursements" in order to continue "to work with the Borrower towards a resolution and remedy."[139]

However, the Inspection Panel commented, Management's response to the Request seemed to suggest that this "approach perhaps ha[d] not been effective."[140]

On the other hand, Inspection Panel practice provides a few notable examples where the Panel's investigation had resulted in the Bank suspending the disbursement of outstanding loan amounts, in order to bring the projects back into compliance – as had occurred, for instance, in *India: Mumbai Urban Transport*[141] and *Albania: Integrated Coastal Zone Management*.[142]

Perhaps the Bank's 'unwillingness or inability' to exercise legal remedies so as to enforce the credit/loan agreement can be best explained by the fact that the Bank has, as noted

---

137 *Argentina/Paraguay: Yacyretá Hydroelectric Project* (1996), IR, § 250.

138 *India: NTPC Power* (1997), IR, § 139.

139 *India: NTPC Power* (1997), IR, § 141.

140 *Id.*

141 *See* WB Press Release, 29 March 2006, explaining that the Bank "suspended disbursements on the road and resettlement components of the Project" in the aftermath of the Inspection Panel investigation. *Also note*, following the Board's endorsement "of the Action Plan", "[i]t was agreed that Management would submit a progress report to the Board in no later than six months *and the Panel would report on progress to the Board.*" (*Id.*) On the Panel's limited (informal) monitoring function, *also see* the discussion *in* section 7.1.

142 *See* WB Press Release, 17 February 2009, where the Board decided to suspend the project in the aftermath of the Inspection Panel report, and to keep it "suspended until a decision is reached either on project restructuring without the land planning activities, or full cancellation." *Also note*, "[i]n view of the seriousness of the errors identified under the Project, the President of the World Bank asked the Acting General Counsel to undertake a review of the circumstances surrounding the issuance of the Corrigendum in September 2008. Building on this review, the President has asked the World Bank's Department of Institutional Integrity (INT) to lead an Accountability Review into alleged misrepresentation by Bank staff to the Inspection Panel and internal events surrounding the Project preparation, Board presentation, and Project supervision, and will take appropriate corrective action. Contrary to some press reports, no Government officials, members of the Project Coordination Unit, or Bank staff are under investigation by INT for corruption." (*Id.*)

earlier, a marked interest to preserve its long-term relationship with borrowers – and that, it the Bank's normal supervision activities have the potential to cause tension, the exercise of legal remedies against borrowers is clearly bound to have a decidedly negative impact on these relationships.[143]

That being said, the question remains whether the exercise of legal remedies would, in any event, have the 'desired effect' – which is, ultimately, to ensure compliance with the provisions of the agreement, including the relevant aspects of the operational policy framework, in order to realize the project's particular development objectives. Or, to put it differently, the question remains whether it is not in the best interest of project-affected people for the Bank "to exhaust all possible methods of persuasion before resorting to suspension of disbursements"[144] – and certainly, before cancelling any undisbursed amounts, which, it should be pointed out, remains an option open to borrowers at any given moment.[145]

Indeed, Inspection Panel practice also highlights that the exercise of legal remedies can result in a highly unsatisfactory outcomes for project-affected people. However, Inspection Panel investigations generally point out that such outcomes could have been prevented by higher standards of project supervision, throughout the project cycle – and specifically during the earlier stages of the project.

For instance, as the Inspection Panel noted in *Panama: Land Administration*, "Management made the decision to informally suspend disbursements for certain Project activities that affect the Naso;" and while this "suspension [was] consistent with the requirements of OP/BP 13.05", the Panel added, "such a contradictory situation" (as created by the enactment of the controversial Property Law)

> warrants seeking further explanations from the borrower to achieve full compliance with OP/BP 13.05 and the objective of OD 4.20, to address the concerns of intended Project beneficiaries.[146]

"Unfortunately," the Panel commented, "many of the unresolved issues will remain after the closing of the Loan and many may even blame the Project for them."[147]

These matters were demonstrated prominently in *Cambodia: Land Management and Administration*, whereas Management's supervision actions taken with regard to this project also illustrate that the Bank's influence only extends 'up to a point' – although, as

---

143 In this regard, *also see* Boisson de Chazournes's comments *at* note 223, Ch. 15.
144 *India: NTPC Power* (1997), IR, § 139.
145 *See* note 114, Ch. 15.
146 *Panama: Land Administration* (2009), IR, § 191. *Note*, on the issues concerning Panama's Property Law, *see e.g.* the discussion *in* section 8.2.1.
147 *Id.*

noted in various places in this chapter, the Inspection Panel had also been critical of the Bank's supervision activities.[148]

For example, in its response to the Request, Bank management explained that it had "undertaken a series of actions since February 2009" – notably, "[i]n consultations with Development Partners and NGOs in Cambodia,"

> Management has repeatedly raised the issue of evictions with the Government – through letters, meetings, and in public statements. The Bank has asked the Government to put a halt to evictions until it finalizes its national legal and policy framework for resettlement and improves the dispute resolution mechanism. The Bank has also offered its assistance in reviewing the draft laws on resettlement and in upgrading resettlement sites around Phnom Penh based on a social needs assessment.[149]

"On September 7, 2009," however, "the Government of Cambodia cancelled the undisbursed balance of the LMAP Credit", which significantly "constrain[ed] options for Management and the Government to address the development needs of the communities that were evicted."[150]

Management also emphasized that it would "continue to focus its overall dialogue with the Government on the need to develop jointly concrete actions for communities that were evicted and those that face involuntary resettlement," and that such efforts would include:

- *Working with* the Government and Development Partners towards ensuring that the communities who filed the Request will be supported in a way consistent with the Resettlement Policy Framework; and,
- *Continuing to engage* the Government and Development Partners to ensure that communities that need to be resettled in the future benefit from a resettlement policy that meets appropriate standards and from fair and independent dispute resolution mechanisms.
- Management *will also try to engage* the Government in a dialogue on the need to assess other resettlement sites in Phnom Penh and other cities, with the aim of improving their conditions.[151]

---

148 *Cambodia: Land Management and Administration* (2009), IR, §§ 216-217.
149 *Cambodia: Land Management and Administration* (2009), MR, p. vii.
150 *Id.*
151 *Id.* (emphases added). *Note*, this example also demonstrates the intricate interdependencies between World Bank and Borrower obligations with regard to the realization of corrective/remedial actions – *as* discussed *e.g., in* section 7.1.2.

Ultimately, the Inspection Panel concluded, "not all measures specifically designed to support poor and vulnerable people were implemented as planned" "by the time the Credit was closed."[152] And while the Panel commended the Bank for its planned efforts and recognised the limitations caused by the Borrower's cancellation, the Panel nevertheless emphasized that "this [undesirable] situation," which left the poor "vulnerable to claims on their land," could, in part, be attributed to Bank management's failure to "adequately follow up" on the project's "commitments"

> to strengthen public awareness and community participation, ensure legal protection to residents exposed to the risk of eviction, and provide adequate access to dispute resolution mechanisms. This was not in compliance with OP/BP 13.05.[153]

15.3   'ROBUST' PROJECT SUPERVISION SYSTEMS

Inspection Panel practice also elaborates on what constitutes a 'robust' or 'adequate' system of project supervision by considering issues related to the *location, timing and frequency* of supervision activities, the *resourcing of supervision missions*, as well as the *content* of such missions and the *context* in which they take place.

15.3.1   *Location, timing and frequency of supervision activities*

Inspection Panel practice indicates that a robust system of supervision is based on direct verification and first-hand experience of specific conditions in the project area because it ensures that risks and issues are identified and addressed in an effective manner. Therefore, the Inspection Panel typically emphasizes the importance of 'in-country' versus 'head office-based' (or 'external') supervision activities.

For example, as the Panel underscored in *Cameroon: Petroleum*, irrespective of "how well-structured external supervision may be, it cannot serve as a substitute for in-country monitoring."[154] "A large and strategically sensitive Project such as the Pipeline Project requires constant supervision."[155] However, the Panel noted that, at the time, there was "no local supervision team in place to handle the volume and quality of supervision required

---

152 *Cambodia: Land Management and Administration* (2009), IR, § 270.
153 *Id.*
154 *Cameroon: Petroleum Development and Pipeline* (2002), IR, §§ 232-233.
155 *Id.*

by the Project."[156] Moreover, if this shortcoming were to continue, the Panel added, it would "certainly frustrate"

> an important goal of the Bank's policy on Project Supervision: 'as a development agency, the Bank also has an interest in assisting member countries to achieve their development objectives on a sustainable basis.'[157]

The Panel expressed its appreciation for "Management's effort to comply with the Bank's applicable policy requirements" with regard to this project.[158] The Inspection Panel nevertheless recommended that "the Bank should consider,"

> within its larger dialogue framework with the country, an effective incentive to help integrate important sectors, such as environment and public health, in a local monitoring team for the Pipeline Project.[159]

"[A]dequate supervision," as the Panel elaborated in *Ghana: Second Urban Environment Sanitation*, requires "regular visits to the project site and meetings with project beneficiaries and stakeholders."[160] During the Panel's "discussions with staff working on the Project," however, "it was made clear to the Panel"

> that the Government of Ghana had indicated its desire to handle the issues that existed with the community near the proposed landfill site on its own. It was claimed that the Government repeatedly prevented the Task Team from visiting the site, citing safety conditions, leading one of the TTLs to abandon any site visits to Kwabenya during the course of the Project.[161]

While the Panel acknowledged these difficulties, it also pointed out that this "resulted in very limited on-site supervision", which, in turn, contributed to the inadequate identification and follow-up on issues.[162]

The Inspection Panel concluded in *Brazil: Itaparica Resettlement and Irrigation* that the "focus of Bank supervision was not consistent through the life of the Project" since

---

156 *Id.*
157 *Id.*
158 *Id.*
159 *Id.*
160 *Ghana: Second Urban Environment Sanitation* (2007), IR, §§ 298, 303 & 314.
161 *Id.*
162 *Id. Also see* the discussion *in* section 15.2.

"[i]t began in Brazil (1987-90), was then shifted to Washington (1990-96), and as of August 1996, supervision appears to have been moved de facto back to Brazil."[163]

"A project with implementation now over 10 years," the Panel concluded, "suffers from changing personnel and institutions weary of the tasks."[164]

Whereas in *Nigeria/Ghana: West African Gas Pipeline*, the Panel took note of Bank management's statement that "senior Bank safeguard specialists exercised project oversight," but also pointed that "all of these staff members were based in Washington," at World Bank Headquarters.[165] In the Panel's "experience," it added, "safeguard policy oversight and ensuring Borrower adherence to EA and RAP requirements cannot be undertaken 'from a distance' without Bank staff present close to the project site."[166] In this instance, the Panel noted, "[l]ittle field verification of compliance with safeguards took place", whereas "the expert panel was not appointed soon enough to be helpful to the Project."[167]

The Inspection Panel also pointed out that supervision missions had to be to be initiated early on, and that such missions should be conducted at regular intervals throughout the project cycle. For example, the Panel recognized that the "Safeguards Supervision Mission to oversee the RAP implementation took place in June 2005 following the commencement of land acquisition."[168] "However," the Panel added, "the general supervision missions"

> did not begin until 2006 and, of these four missions, two went solely to Accra. The Panel observes that ten months elapsed between the Safeguards Mission and the first general Supervision Mission.[169]

In other words, "[b]y the time the Request [for Inspection] was received in late-April 2006,"

> only these two missions – the Safeguards Mission and the first Supervision Mission (which traveled only to Accra) – had been completed. The Panel notes that there were long gaps between supervision missions prior to the Request.[170]

Indeed, in interviews with the Inspection Panel, Bank staff acknowledged that here had been no visits to the project area "during construction because they trusted the oil compa-

---

163 *Brazil: Itaparica Resettlement and Irrigation* (1997), ER, § 41.
164 *Id.*
165 *Nigeria/Ghana: West African Gas Pipeline* (2006), IR, § 435.
166 *Id. Note*, this example also demonstrates the Panel's contribution towards institutional learning – as discussed *in* section 7.1.5.
167 *Id.*
168 *Nigeria/Ghana: West African Gas Pipeline* (2006), IR, § 437.
169 *Id.*
170 *Id.*

nies sponsoring the Project" and "took WAPCo's assurances on good faith."[171] Hence, the Panel concluded, "Management did not ensure adequate supervision during the construction phase."[172]

While in *Argentina: Santa Fe Road Infrastructure*, the Inspection Panel noted "that the Project team['s]" supervision efforts were "strengthened" by "consultants based in Argentina who could visit the Project area and monitor progress more frequently and regularly than staff coming from Washington."[173] This approach, the Panel concluded, "seems to be a good and cost effective practice to supervise project implementation."[174]

15.3.2 Resourcing of supervision missions

The allocation of adequate financial and staffing resources is an important element of a robust system of project supervision. In *Nigeria/Ghana: West African Gas Pipeline*, for instance, the Panel highlighted "[o]ne important reason" for the compliance issues it had identified, namely, the "apparent lack of available supervision resources in terms of funds and safeguards expertise."[175]

As a result, the Panel explained, "Management essentially put its faith in the Project Sponsor"

> to carry out oversight and supervision during key preparation phases, as a substitute for direct engagement by staff in this critical function.[176]

Similarly, the Inspection Panel concluded in *Nigeria: Lagos Drainage* "that a much closer supervision by IDA should have been provided,"

> notwithstanding the fact that during the Credit negotiations, the primary responsibility for monitoring the project execution was assigned to responsible officials of the Lagos State Government, since they were poised to meet regularly with the community leaders and help resolve difficulties between the community and the contractors.[177]

---

171 *Nigeria/Ghana: West African Gas Pipeline* (2006), IR, § 438.
172 *Id. Note*, on compliance issues related to the application of the safeguard policies in this project *see e.g.*, the discussion *in* section 8.3.2. On the reasons behind these matters, *also see* the discussion *in* section 15.3.2.
173 *Argentina: Santa Fe Road Infrastructure* (2007), IR, § 157.
174 *Id.*
175 *Nigeria/Ghana: West African Gas Pipeline* (2006), IR, § 487.
176 *Nigeria/Ghana: West African Gas Pipeline* (2006), IR, § 482.
177 *Nigeria: Lagos Drainage* (1998), ER, § 41.

Management, on the other hand, emphasized that the Bank "did not have the financial resources to observe every activity related to project execution as part of its normal supervision."[178]

In *Panama: Land Administration*, the Inspection Panel emphasized that the "proper implementation of the Bank's [indigenous peoples] policy hinges"

> on not only strong and clear foundations during Project preparation, but also [on] appropriate allocation of resources for supervision, in particular to engage the services of staff and consultants with specialized training in indigenous peoples' issues and participatory development.[179]

In this instance, however, the Panel found, for instance, that "supervision visits did not include a social specialist until March 2007," which was not in compliance "with OD 4.20 on Indigenous Peoples."[180]

This omission occurred, the Panel emphasized, "[d]espite the sensitive nature of the indigenous land issues," the "broad experience gained by the World Bank in Nicaragua and Honduras," and notwithstanding "the warnings placed in the Social Assessment, and the explicit provisions in the Bank's Indigenous Peoples policy on engaging social (anthropology) specialists [...]."[181] "In line with Bank policy," the Panel elaborated, "a social specialist would have played a key role in assisting the Project"

> to properly assess the evolving situation and could have recommended appropriate responsive actions, particularly in light of the issues emerging during Project implementation.[182]

"The Panel's experience in this investigation and others suggests," as the Panel concluded, "that while the Bank is making progress in ensuring that more projects trigger the [indigenous peoples] policy, especially in Africa,"

---

178 *Id.*
179 *Panama: Land Administration* (2009), IR, § 348.
180 *Panama: Land Administration* (2009), IR, §§ 341-342. For similar issues, *also see Honduras: Land Administration* (2006), IR, § 191.
181 *Panama: Land Administration* (2009), IR, §§ 341-342.
182 *Id.*

it still faces serious challenges in implementation of these policies, as the result, in part, of insufficient attention to supervision and to the deployment of appropriately trained social specialists.[183]

"The Panel's investigation" also highlighted the fact that the project "experienced discontinuity and turnover in personnel, particularly of Task Team Leaders, during its almost decade-long life."[184] While such "discontinuity" was "not unusual in Projects of this duration," the Panel noted that it was of particular "relevance in the case of the PRONAT Project"

> because core Project activities related to indigenous lands took place during a period in which private investment and disputes over land grew swiftly. This affected Project supervision and the effective implementation of safeguard policies.[185]

Similarly, in *Cambodia: Land Management and Administration*, the Inspection Panel found that "Management's attention to social consequences of land titling, including potential evictions, was not systematic" and "suffered from a lack of attention from social safeguard specialists."[186] It was "a matter of concern," the Panel emphasized, "that several supervision missions concluded"

> that there had been no situation requiring application of the Social and Environmental Safeguards, including the RPF, apparently without any careful scrutiny of the matter.[187]

Whereas in *Papua New Guinea: Smallholder Agriculture*, the Inspection Panel concluded "that, *within the limits of Management's staffing structure* in support of this Project, the Bank had "complied with the requirements of OP 13.05."[188] However, the Panel added, the sufficient allocation of "[r]esources for supervision of the [indigenous peoples] policy

---

183 *Panama: Land Administration* (2009), IR, § 348. On the issues related to this case, *also see* the discussion *in* Ch. 13. *Note*, this example also demonstrates the Panel's contribution towards institutional learning – as discussed *in* section 7.1.5.

184 *Panama: Land Administration* (2009), § 352.

185 *Id.*

186 *Cambodia: Land Management and Administration* (2009), IR, § 211.

187 *Id.*

188 *Papua New Guinea: Smallholder Agriculture* (2009), IR, § 515 (emphasis added).

become[s] even more important with the Bank's new emphasis on implementation support."[189]

Although it was "was uniformly impressed by the calibre of individual staff members who were engaged with the Project," the Panel emphasized,

> greater capacity is needed to respond to challenges that are certain to arise during project implementation in complex and challenging settings such as Papua New Guinea.[190]

Whereas in *India: Mumbai Urban Transport*, the Inspection Panel noted that "[t]he World Bank structure for supervising projects in India involves two separate lines of authority: those for the sector and those for the country."[191] With respect to the *Mumbai Urban Transport* project, the Panel explained,

> the social development specialist, environmental specialist, and transport specialists (in India and in Headquarters) and the External Affairs Officer assist the Task Team Leader (TTL) in the supervision of the Project, but they report to different managers.[192]

Although the Panel acknowledged "that this matrix structure is widely applied by the Bank to Projects of this stature," it nevertheless emphasized that "this structure may sometimes delay Bank actions and dilute accountability."[193]

Finally, in *Pakistan: National Drainage Program*, the Panel found that the Bank's supervision efforts regarding "the failure of the weir and embankments" "focused on technical and environmental issues and dealt only marginally with the social consequences and the effects on the livelihoods of the affected people," as reflected in "the 2001 Fact-Finding Mission."[194] For example, the Panel elaborated, "neither the Tidal Link nor the people harmed by its failure"

---

189 *Papua New Guinea: Smallholder Agriculture* (2009), IR, § 530. *Note*, on the Bank's focus on 'implementation support', *see* note 66, Ch. 4.
190 *Papua New Guinea: Smallholder Agriculture* (2009), § 540.
191 *India: Mumbai Urban Transport* (2004), IR, pp. xxxiv-xxxv.
192 *Id.*
193 *Id. Note*, the implementation of a matrix-based' organization structure was one of the institutional reform initiatives spearheaded during the Wolfensohn-presidency – *see* section 4.2.1.
194 *Pakistan: National Drainage Program* (2004), IR, § 577.

were directly mentioned in the supervision documents reviewed by the Panel from the time of the Fact-Finding Mission to the time of the Request – a period of three-and-a-half years.[195]

Furthermore, "during the critical design and construction period from 1988 to 1994," the Inspection Panel pointed out that the predecessor project "was guided only by irrigation engineers"

> who supervised all technical aspects of the Project, occasionally supported by other specific engineering expertise. In the view of the Panel, this may have been sufficient for the review of the upstream drainage works but was not adequate for the review of the design aspects of the outfall system or the environmental and social impact of the project.[196]

For example, the Panel elaborated, "[t]he design aspects of the outfall system would have required"

> specific expertise in coastal morphology and coastal engineering, while the environmental and social impact of the project would have required expertise in environmental and social sciences.[197]

"Competent technical supervision by the Bank, including specialized expertise," the Panel concluded, "would have identified emerging problems and initiated appropriate action", which, in turn, "could have helped to avoid"

> the many troubles and suffering of the local population linked to the failure of the Tidal Link structures. The Panel observes that Management failed to assign the appropriate expertise for the supervision of technical aspects of the design and construction work under the Project. As a result, Management failed to identify serious flaws in the design and implementation of the Project, and to initiate corrective measures in a timely manner. This does not comply with OD 13.05.[198]

---

195 *Id. Note*, on these matters, *also see* the discussion *in* section 15.1.
196 *Pakistan: National Drainage Program* (2004), IR, § 583. *Note*, this example also demonstrates issues related to the balance between project components – as discussed *in* Ch. 9.
197 *Id.*
198 *Pakistan: National Drainage Program* (2004), IR, § 586.

15.3.3 Content and context of supervision activities

During its 2002 investigation of *Paraguay/Argentina: Yacyretá Hydroelectric Project,* the Inspection Panel pointed out that "Bank staff [were] divided as to whether or not they carr[ied] responsibility"

> for problems arising from poor or inappropriate design. One Bank staff member in a responsible position expressed the view that it is not the responsibility of Bank staff to check project designs and that it was certainly not their job to be 'construction inspectors.' This contrasts sharply with the view of another Bank staff member, also in a responsible position, that it is the responsibility of Bank staff to ensure that detailed project designs and standards being applied are appropriate to the circumstances, and further, that it is their duty to make site visits to inspect the quality of work that has been undertaken with Bank funding.[199]

The Panel commented, however, that "OD 13.05 on Project Supervision [was] specific"

> that it is the responsibility of the Bank's technical departments to 'exercise a quality assurance role in the supervision process' but qualifies this statement by adding 'for which detailed procedures and responsibilities are defined by each Region.'[200]

Hence, the Panel concluded, there was a "clear need for a greater level of supervision"

> of technical design and construction in all facets of the Yacyretá resettlement scheme and notes the necessity for adequate supervision of technical design and supervision in resettlement schemes generally.[201]

Supervision missions also provide an opportunity for World Bank staff to engage directly with project-affected people – however, such opportunities are not always effectively utilized.

In *India: NTPC Power,* for example, the Inspection Panel commented that "there were few qualified Bank staff available,"

---

199 *Paraguay/Argentina: Yacyretá Hydroelectric Project* (2002), IR, §§ 389-390.
200 *Paraguay/Argentina: Yacyretá Hydroelectric Project* (2002), IR, §§ 391-392.
201 *Id.*

either at Bank Headquarters or in Delhi or Singrauli to initiate and to supervise implementation of required measures. Monitoring therefore relied basically on secondary source information.[202]

Hence, the Panel concluded, "[t]here was little meaningful direct consultation with PAPs."[203]

Indeed, the Requesters' concerns about this area demonstrated prominently that the manner in which World Bank staff engages with project-affected people during supervision missions can play a crucial role in changing – or further entrenching – negative perspectives about 'the Bank' and/or 'the project'.

For instance, the Requesters claimed that project affected-people "often had no information about World Bank mission visits" and usually heard "through hearsay" "that a WB team was in the project area."[204] "Unless" project-affected people "hijacked" such meetings, the Requesters added, "the WB representatives preferred not to meet PAPs in situations where NTPC representatives did not have a dominating presence."[205] Moreover, "[t]he Bank missions"

> often relied on NTPC officials to translate statements of PAPs and vice versa. [...] To a team of foreign NGOs in February 1995 a Bank official is understood to have stated that the Bank should not even try to meet PAPs without the NTPC officials. This official further suggested to the NGOs that if PAPs felt intimidated by the presence of NTPC officials, they should resort to legal action.[206]

"With such arrogant and uncaring attitude", the Requesters emphasized, "the Bank missions can hardly be trusted to make unbiased and accurate reports" – whereas "[t]he very purpose of missions become meaningless.[207] "The People of Singrauli," the Requesters concluded, *"have the experience of humiliation of cascades of World Bank jeeps cruising through their villages without stopping."*[208]

As the Inspection Panel observed in its 2002 investigation of the *Yacyretá* project, "BP 13.05 makes explicit the principle that"

---

202 *India: NTPC Power* (1997), IR, § 22.
203 *Id. Note*, this example also demonstrates issues related to resourcing – as discussed *in* section 15.3.2.
204 *India: NTPC Power* (1997), Request, § 59.
205 *Id.*
206 *Id.*
207 *Id.*
208 *Id. (emphasis added). Note*, this example also demonstrates the intrinsic value in giving project-affected people 'voice' – as discussed *in* section 7.1.1.

effective supervision necessarily includes consultation with project affected people. This is both to ensure that affected people have a voice as well as to ensure that problems affecting the project are uncovered.[209]

However, the Inspection Panel commented that it "was struck by the large number of people at resettlement sites"

> who insisted that no one from the Bank had ever come to visit, or discuss problems directly with the them, but rather had held meetings with EBY staff and some "leaders" of the affected people only in hotels or offices. The Panel is concerned that the Bank's supervision missions seem not to have interacted meaningfully with affected people or reviewed thoroughly the resettlement sites.[210]

Moreover, the Panel added, "[a] review of supervision mission reports indicates they do not generally include any minutes or records of on-site meetings with affected people."[211] The Inspection Panel also expressed the concern "that in any pre-arranged visit to a resettlement site with Project staff,"

> the Bank may have seen the places where things were proceeding well and neither saw nor sought out the examples of where the project was not proceeding well.[212]

"Effective consultation with affected people, in a setting in which they feel comfortable in providing information," the Panel emphasized, "may reveal project flaws and inadequacies in implementation."[213] Hence, the Panel concluded, "Management must ensure that it consults with and interacts meaningfully with affected people" over the course of its supervision missions, and that such "consultations" take place

> in settings where affected people feel able to convey effectively their concerns to Management. Bank supervision missions should clearly state the places they visited during field inspections and the conditions under which they visited (e.g. with Project staff or accompanied by representatives of NGOs, etc.), in order to better document not only that supervision missions were present in

---

209 *Paraguay/Argentina: Yacyretá Hydroelectric Project* (2002), IR, §§ 397-399.
210 *Id.*
211 *Id.*
212 *Id.*
213 *Id.*

the area, but that the supervision team members actually had contact with affected persons and looked into matters directly dealing with issues of safeguard policies.[214]

****

During the first decade following the Inspection Panel's inception, most of the claims filed by Requesters concerned "substantive polic[ies] such as Environmental Assessment or Involuntary Resettlement."[215] However, this situation has gradually changed over the past years, with claims concerning the policy on Project Supervision now featuring most prominently in Requests filed at the Inspection Panel.[216]

As to the reasons behind this change, the Inspection Panel argues, for instance, that the growing number of Requests claiming non-compliance with the policy on Project Supervision can be explained by the fact that "it is during project implementation" – the stage of the project cycle which forms the focus of the policy – that "issues of harm become real for affected communities."[217] Ninio, on the other hand, argues that this increase is because prospective Requesters have developed a better understanding of the division between Bank and borrower obligations – and, in particular – of the nature of the Inspection Panel's mandate.[218]

In other words, while the Inspection Panel "is authorized only to investigate breaches of the Bank's policy framework *by Bank Staff*,"[219] this explicitly includes "situations where the Bank is alleged to have failed in its follow-up on the borrower's obligations under loan agreements,"[220] whereas the requirements pertaining to these 'follow-up' activities are primarily set out in the policy on Project Supervision. "If it appears therefore that actions have taken place that are in violation of a Bank policy," as Ninio elaborates, "but that" World Bank Management and staff have not "been directly responsible for" those actions,

> it must *ergo* be a violation of the policy of supervision as Bank staff have an obligation to ensure that projects are implemented according to the Bank policy framework.[221]

---

214 *Id.*
215 Ninio *in* Freestone (2013), p. 69.
216 *Id. Also see* Inspection Panel (2012), p. 3; *and see* the statistical overview of the operational policies most often raised in Inspection Panel Requests, *in* Naudé Fourie (2014), p. 579.
217 Inspection Panel (2012), p. 3. *Note*, however, that other policies also contain supervision requirements, as commented *in* note 3, Ch. 15.
218 Ninio *in* Freestone (2013), p. 69.
219 *Id.* (emphasis added).
220 Inspection Panel Resolution, § 12.
221 Ninio *in* Freestone (2013), p. 69.

Nevertheless, the increasing number of claims concerning the policy on Project Supervision also "highlights the tension of the Panel's role," because, as argued earlier in this book, although the Panel "has no authority to investigate the behaviour of the borrowing country," its review of the Bank's supervision activities typically means that borrower actions become an implicit part of the Inspection Panel's investigation – especially where the Panel identify instances of (borrower) non-compliance with the other operational policies.[222]

The area of project supervision also has the potential to create tension between the Bank and a Borrower, as several of the examples included in this chapter illustrate. And while the Bank has legal means available to it to enforce the credit/loan agreement, it also faces several challenges in this regard. For example, as Boisson de Chazournes observes, "[i]f the Bank is not satisfied with the borrower's performance," it has the option to "suspend disbursement of a loan or credit, cancel it, or accelerate its maturity."[223] However, "[t]his kind of action is rather exceptional because," as Sarfaty argues, "dialogue with the borrowing country is usually persuasive, allowing compliance to be readjusted before the extreme stage is reached."[224] "The interruption of a contractual relationship," on the other hand, "is disfavored because"

> it impedes the continuation of a dialogue with the borrowing country that may find ways to correct the non-complying situation and does nothing to foster the environmental and social policies.[225]

The Bank could also "limit its involvement in future projects in the country for fear of further noncompliance with Bank policies," as Sarfaty points out.[226] Such an approach is likely to lose its appeal, however, in light of the increased number of competitors in the international development financing market.

Compliance issues related to the policy area of project supervision also demonstrate the underlying tensions among various institutional aims – that is, in addition to the tension between those activities related to the prevention of harm and those related to the realization of performance.[227] Pressures to reduce operating costs, for example, might affect the Bank's ability to put 'robust' systems of project supervision in place, as several examples from Inspection Panel practice concerning the location, frequency and resourcing of supervision activities illustrate.

---

222 Ninio *in* Freestone (2013), pp. 64 & 69. *Also see* the discussion *in* section 4.3.2.
223 Boisson de Chazournes *in* Shelton (Ed.) (2000), p. 291.
224 Sarfaty (2005), p. 1799.
225 *Id.*
226 *Id.*
227 *See* section 4.2.1.

It can also be argued that the examples from Inspection Panel practice presented in this chapter demonstrate the challenges involved in realizing and enforcing specific accountability outcomes – notably redress for project-affected people[228] – due to the Bank's dependency on Borrower actions, for example, because of the requirement to respect state sovereignty (while also preserving the Bank's own political neutrality), the possibility that the Borrower can withdraw its application for funding during the initial stages of the project cycle,[229] or (unilaterally) cancel the credit/loan agreement (forfeiting any undisbursed amounts).[230] Such factors significantly limit how far the Bank's influence extends and, as such, are indicative of the limits of the Bank's policy obligations – and, arguably, also of its accountability.

"Hardly a project can be completed without facing implementation problems," as Shihata observed.[231] And, as Inspection Panel practice also demonstrates, "[s]ome of these problems cannot be foreseen,"

> such as abrupt changes in the economic or political situation of the country where the project is located, in project management, or even in the weather.[232]

That being said, "[n]o matter how well a project has been prepared and appraised," as Shihata concluded, "its development benefits cannot be fully realized if it is not properly executed."[233]

In other words, in order to turn development *theory* into development *practice*, there is an "absolute need for appropriate implementation, monitoring, surveillance and supervision."[234] But the effective realization of development objectives at the operational level is unlikely to happen without the effective realization of quality design at the conceptual level. Therefore, as the Inspection Panel commented in *Ghana: Second Urban Environment Sanitation*, "[t]he only way of ultimately producing overall quality is to ensure quality at each step of the process."[235] It is indeed "very difficult, if feasible, to ensure that the 'quality chain' is put in place," *in practice*, "if the foundations for this quality chain," have never been laid, *in theory*.[236]

---

228 *Also see* sections 7.1.2 & 7.1.3.
229 *See e.g., Nepal: Arun III* (1994); and *China: Western Poverty Reduction (Qinghai)* (1999).
230 *See e.g., Cambodia: Land Management and Administration* (2009), *as* discussed *in* section 15.2.2.
231 Shihata (2000), pp. 8-9.
232 *Id.*
233 *Id.*
234 *Ghana: Second Urban Environment Sanitation* (2007), IR, § 189.
235 *Id.*
236 *Id.*

CONCLUSION

16 A Shared Commitment, a Shared Goal – and a Shared Surface

The accountability of international financial institutions such as the World Bank remains a topic of significance that requires further elaboration, in theory as well as in practice. The objective of this book has been to contribute towards the *progressive development of a comprehensive shared understanding* of what such accountability means *conceptually* and *operationally*.

Through the window onto World Bank development-lending operations provided by Inspection Panel practice and the perspectives offered by academic literature, the analysis presented in this book expounded the *pluralism* and *dynamic complexity* that characterize the transnational development context in which the World Bank executes its mission of "working for a world free of poverty."[1] These characteristics are reflected, for instance, in the wide range of interests, demands, expectations and conceptions surrounding the interdisciplinary and multidimensional notion of accountability, as well as in the intricate relationships that exist between manifold variables – including the tight interdependencies between various accountability dimensions.

As a citizen-driven independent accountability mechanism that is mandated to investigate claims filed by project-affected people concerning alleged material adverse effects as a result of the World Bank's failure to comply with its operational policy framework, Inspection Panel practice also provides the opportunity to derive *further insights about the normative system that has come to form an essential part of the World Bank's development-lending operations*. The principle components of this normative system – which has distinct interfaces with the national legal systems of borrower states, the normative systems involved in regulating various professions and industries, as well as the international legal system – include: the actors engaged in the processes of norm creation, norm application and norm enforcement involving the Bank's operational policy framework; the methods or approaches employed by these actors; and the outcomes produced by their interactions.

The analysis presented here, facilitated by several conceptual models that integrate theories, methods and observations drawn from practice, demonstrated the *horizontal and interactional characteristics* of this normative system, *its mutually constitutive nature* – which facilitates the interaction between (and, on occasion) the integration of, opposing forces related, respectively, to the need to restrain and to enable the actions of institutional decision-makers – the *constructivist nature of the outcomes* generated by the normative

---

1   *See* http://www.worldbank.org.

system, as well as the *role of a broader transnational development community of interest* (in which the core processes of norm creation, norm application and norm enforcement have come to be embedded) in producing such outcomes. The analysis also illustrated the (often opposing) *methods or interpretative approaches* employed by Bank management and staff (in applying the operational policy framework) and by internal accountability mechanisms such as the Panel (in reviewing compliance with the operational policy framework).

The final chapter of this book considers an important implication of the analysis, namely, that it is indicative of a particular type of problem that needs to be addressed by a specific type of approach. The chapter explains why *the conceptualization and operationalization of World Bank accountability in the broader transnational development context* can be described as a *wicked problem* or a *complex societal issue* and why it is significant to do so.

Notably, complex societal issues cannot be 'solved' in the conventional sense of the word – they can only be 'managed'. And they are most effectively managed through the continuous employment a specific type of approach. That is, an approach that promotes the defragmentation of information; facilitates interaction, negotiation and collaboration; and assists in the integration of complementary variables as well as the reconciliation of competing variables. An approach, in other words, that is based in a shared commitment to remain engaged with the particular complex societal issue while progressively working towards achieving a shared goal: reaching a shared understanding of what the issue entails and how it should be addressed.

This book argues that the *interactional processes of norm creation, norm application and norm enforcement – embedded in a resilient and adaptable community of practice –* constitute such an approach. The book concludes by offering a few suggestions as to *how the 'shared surface' represented by such a normative community of practice might be further strengthened.*

16.1   World Bank Accountability as a Complex Societal Issue –
Requiring an Interactional, Collaborative and Integrative
Approach

"Wicked problems"[2] or "complex societal issues"[3] are characterized by many of the same features that typify transnational regulatory governances contexts – including pluralism, dynamic complexity, ambiguity and a certain 'disorder of orders'.[4]

"Problem wickedness" is also associated with a high degree of 'fragmentation', which, as defined here, describes "a condition in which the people involved see themselves as more separate than united," where the participants to a discourse "are all convinced that their version of the problem is correct," and where "information and knowledge are chaotic and scattered."[5] "The fragmented pieces," in other words, represent the diverse "perspectives, understandings, and intentions of the collaborators."[6] And these fragmented pieces often co-exist in relative isolation since those involved may not be aware of the differences (or, the nature and extent of these differences) among them, which further strengthens the degree of fragmentation.[7]

The core characteristics that mark complex societal issues are reflected in the dynamics arising from multiple *conflicting* and *causal* relationships surrounding World Bank accountability, and also from the *dual* and *mutually constitutive nature of the underlying social structure* in which the issue of accountability is situated.[8]

16.1.1   Conflicting, competing or contradictory relationships

The dynamics arising from conflicting, competing or contradictory relationships are illustrated, for example, by competing paradigms – such as 'instrumentalism' *versus* 'for-

---

2   *See in general* H. Rittel, W.J. Horst & M.M. Webber (1973), 'Dilemmas in a General Theory of Planning', 4
   Policy Sciences 2, 155. For an example that conceptualizes climate change (what it entails and how we should
   respond to the challenges it presents) as a wicked problem, *see in general* Handke & Hey (2013). The authors
   comment (at p. 1) that wicked problems are "characterized by intricate interdependencies and changing
   contexts."

3   *See in general*, Conklin (2005).

4   *See* the discussion *in* section 2.1.

5   Conklin (2005), p. 3. *Note*, in international legal scholarship, the notion of fragmentation has come to be
   associated largely with a phenomenon in which "the various aspects of the international legal regime are
   branching out and gaining some form of quasi-independence" (*see* Klabbers *in* Klabbers et al. (Eds.) (2009),
   p. 11) or achieving "self-containment" (*See e.g.*, B. Simma (1985), 'Self-contained Regimes', 16 *Netherlands
   Yearbook of International Law*, pp. 112-136).

6   Conklin (2005), p. 3.

7   *Id. Compare e.g.*, the various definitions of accountability noted *in* section 2.2 – *and see* specifically Dowdle's
   remarks *at* note 80, Ch. 2.

8   *See e.g.*, note 164, Ch. 2.

malism',[9] or accountability 'for performance' *versus* accountability 'for harm'[10] – and opposing interpretative approaches to determine 'what constitutes compliance' with the Bank's operational policy framework,[11] which, in turn, result in conflicting understandings of the content and scope of Bank *versus* Borrower obligations.[12] It is also demonstrated by opposing views about the relationship between the Bank's operational policy framework and the international legal system;[13] about the non-legal *versus* quasi-legal nature of citizen-driven independent accountability mechanisms such as the Inspection Panel; and the extent to which existing systems of categorization – such as those distinguishing between legal and social normativity, or national and international law – can be employed to describe the reality of the transnational development context.[14]

And it is reflected, finally, in the competition for primacy between the interests, demands, expectations and conceptions of internal *versus* external accountability holders – which, in turn, are echoed in opposing views as to why the Inspection Panel was established, what its primary purpose should be, where the 'real value' of its contribution lies, and whether it is effective in realizing its supposed objectives.[15]

Conflicting relationships can therefore result in significant tension among actors and generally add to the degree of fragmentation.

16.1.2 Causal, complementary or interdependent relationships

Whereas the dynamics resulting from causal, complementary or interdependent relationships are demonstrated, for instance, by the tight relationships between policy aspects – such as the relationship between the delineation of a project area (of influence), the identification or quantification of project affected people and the scope of the environmental assessment process;[16] or the relationships between the processes of surveying affected communities and collecting baseline data, the provision of compensation, and the realization of income and livelihood restoration.[17]

It is also illustrated by the intricate interdependencies between Bank and Borrower obligations[18] – which, in turn, hold significant implications for the achievement of devel-

---

9   *See e.g.,* section 2.3.
10 *See e.g.,* section 4.2.
11 *See e.g.,* section 6.3.
12 *See e.g.,* sections 10.4, 12.1, 13.1 & 14.2.
13 *See e.g.,* section 5.1.1.
14 *See e.g.,* section 6.2.4.
15 *See e.g.,* sections 3.2.3, 7.2.1. & 7.2.2.
16 *See e.g.,* sections 10.2, 10.3 & 14.2.
17 *See e.g.,* sections 12.3, 14.2. & 12.5.
18 *See e.g.,* section 4.3.2.

opment objectives (related both to minimize 'harm' and maximize 'performance'),[19] the realization and enforcement of particular accountability outcomes,[20] and, ultimately how different constituency groups view the content and scope of World Bank accountability.

Causal relationships might be "hard to detect," however; whereas their "nonlinear responses" can be challenging to predict and understand.[21] This is because, in dealing with complex societal issues, "simple causal associations" are often "misplaced".[22] It is, as Taleb puts it, "hard to see how things work by looking at single parts."[23] Or, as Sterman argues, the dynamic complexity of social systems "overwhelms our ability to understand them" and therefore result in situations where "seemingly obvious solutions to problems fail or actually worsen the situation."[24]

16.1.3   A dual and mutually constitutive social structure

But the characteristics of complex societal issues are also reflected in dynamics driven by the dual and mutually constitutive nature of the underlying structure – as demonstrated by the fact that the logic underlying many of the opposing relationships are not "fully constraining."[25] In other words, it is often not a matter of *versus*, but of *and*.

This is reflected, for instance, in the public *and* the commercial facets of the World Bank's mission, and that both these facets form part of the Bank's corporate strategy and translate into a wide range of institutional aims, performance areas and indicators. This, in turn, means that the Bank has to be accountable for realizing performance *and* for avoiding/mitigating the effects of harm;[26] or, that World Bank-financed projects are usually comprised of 'technical/commercial' *and* 'non-technical/non-commercial' components.[27]

It is also reflected in the Inspection Panel's dual accountability mandate – as demonstrated, for instance, by comments describing the Inspection Panel as a 'recourse *and* accountability' mechanism, or underscoring the Panel's contribution towards 'accountability *and* effectiveness';[28] and as illustrated by the fact that the outcomes to which the Inspection

---

19   *See e.g.,* Ch. 8.
20   *See e.g.,* section 7.1.
21   *See* Taleb (2012), e-Book.
22   *Id.*
23   *Id.* Taleb argues, therefore, for simplification: "A complex system, contrary to what people believe, does not require complicated regulations and intricate policies. The simpler, the better. Complications lead to *multiplicative changes of unanticipated effects.*" (*Id.,* emphasis added.) *Also see* Sterman's description of dynamic complexity *at* notes 24-33, Ch. 2.
24   *See* Sterman (2000), p. 22. *Also see* Sterman's description of dynamic complexity *at* notes 24-33, Ch. 2.
25   *See* Koskenniemi *at* note 151, Ch. 2.
26   *See e.g.,* section 4.2.
27   *See e.g.,* Ch. 9.
28   *See e.g.,* section 7.2.2; *and see e.g.,* Baimu & Panou's comments *at* note 236, Ch. 3.

Panel mechanism contribute have the potential to enable *and* restrain World Bank activities.[29]

What this often means in practice, however, is that the actors involved need to find ways to deal with the tensions arising from this wide array of relationships.

In some instances, these tensions can be alleviated by seeking out those aspects that are (or, that could be) complementary – as reflected, for instance, in arguments that policy non-compliance not only result in harm but also affect performance;[30] or that consultation with project-affected people is not only intended to avoid or mitigate adverse effects emanating from the project, but also to obtain input that can be vital to ensure optimal project design and effective implementation of that design, which, in turn, affects the realization of development objectives.[31] The problem with this approach, however, is that while those involved might be supportive of such arguments in theory (and publically affirm their support), they might not be convinced of the logic of such arguments in practice (even though they might not declare so in public).[32]

In other instances, the actors involved might alleviate such tensions – or, achieve equilibrium among conflicting variables – by making decisions that involve prioritization or require trade-off decisions.[33] The influence of this approach is reflected, for instance, in the significant degree of flexibility and 'managerial discretion' allowed for in the operational policy framework.[34] But this approach can also result in ambiguity, especially from the perspective of project-affected people – who, for instance, might have very different expectations as to what 'meaningful consultation'[35] or 'free prior consultation' with indigenous peoples entails;[36] whether a particular activity involves a 'real choice';[37] what constitutes a 'robust' system of project supervision;[38] whether there had been a 'diligent' consideration of design alternatives;[39] or, when the Bank should 'step in' to ensure that borrowers meet their primary obligations, and what the content and scope of the Bank's 'step-in obligation' should entail.[40] These matters, moreover, can result in additional conflict if the transparency surrounding prioritization and trade-off decisions have not been sufficient.[41]

---

29   *See e.g.,* section 7.2.2.
30   *See e.g.,* Figure 8.
31   *See e.g.,* sections 11.2 & 14.3.
32   *Also see* the discussion *in* section 16.2.1.
33   *See e.g.,* Ch. 9 *and see* sections 8.3 & 15.2.
34   *See e.g.,* section 6.3.
35   *See e.g.,* section 11.2.
36   *See e.g.,* section 13.3.
37   *See e.g.,* section 12.1.
38   *See e.g.,* section 15.3.
39   *See e.g.,* section 14.3.
40   *See e.g.,* sections 4.3.2 & 8.3.4; *and see* Ch. 15.
41   *See e.g.,* section 11.1.

16.2   A SHARED SURFACED OFFERED BY NORM CREATION, NORM APPLICATION AND NORM ENFORCEMENT, EMBEDDED IN A COMMUNITY OF PRACTICE

What the analysis presented in this book ultimately demonstrates, in other words, is that complex societal issues may elicit intense debates but there can be no decisive winners and losers because "one's perspective on a wicked problem determines both its definition and solution".[42]

As result, different "approaches to [addressing] the problem are [...] likely to co-exist."[43] However, if the fragmented pieces were to "interact with each other," it might "help [to] address aspects" of the problem – even as it cannot "constitute a comprehensive solution."[44] This, in turn, is why complex societal issues need to be managed on a continuous basis, or, as Handke and Hey put it, "re-solved over and over again" by means of "continued regulatory and institutional adjustments."[45]

Wicked problems, it should be noted, are not rare. On the contrary, as Conklin points out, they "are so commonplace that the chaos and futility that usually attend them are accepted as inevitable."[46] But because we often "[f]ail to recognize the 'wicked dynamics' in problems," we "persist in applying inappropriate methods and tools" to manage them – instead of employing (and strengthening) "collaborative", "interactional" and integrative approaches that are equipped to deal with the effects of pluralism, dynamic complexity and fragmentation, and which are also, as Conklin comments, better "attuned to the fundamentally social and conversational nature of work."[47]

Importantly, collaborative, interactional and integrative approaches do not involve extensive prerequisites before they can be employed. As long as there is a "shared commitment" among those involved to address the issue on a continuous basis, the actors can start to work towards developing a "shared understanding about the problem."[48] However, as Conklin emphasizes, this "shared understanding" does not necessarily entail reaching an "agreem[ent] on the problem," although it clearly "is a good thing when it happens."[49] What it involves, instead, is that the participating actors work towards "understand[ing] each other's positions well enough to have intelligent dialogue about the different interpre-

---

42   Handke & Hey (2013), p. 1.
43   *Id.*
44   Rittel, Horst & Webber (1973), p. 160.
45   Handke & Hey (2013), p. 2. *Also see* Sarfaty (2005), pp. 1809-1810 commenting that a "key factor in the transnational legal process is repeated participation." On transnational legal process theory, *see* note 114, Ch. 2.
46   Conklin (2005), p. 3.
47   Conklin (2005), pp. 3 & 15.
48   Conklin (2005), p. 15.
49   Conklin (2005), pp. 3 & 15. *Also see* Brunnée & Toope *at* note 169, Ch. 2.

tations of the problem" so that they are able, in turn, to "exercise collective intelligence" on what is required to address the issue, on an ongoing basis.[50]

A conception of social and legal normativity that is based in interactional and constructivist thinking – as presented in the Introduction of this book[51] – offers such an approach. Through the mechanism of the *normative community of practice in the transnational development context*, diverse actors – including power wielders or dominant decision-makers, external and internal accountability holders – can interact by means of the "shared surface" or "platform"[52] represented by the processes of norm creation, norm application and norm enforcement that form part of the development-lending operations of the World Bank and of other multilateral development institutions.

By "reason[ing]" *from* and *through* norms, actors can combat the adverse effects of fragmentation by exchanging information about their respective interests, demands, expectations as well as the conceptions in which these are based. This, in turn, enables them to negotiate and also makes it possible to collaborate and forge new agreements, while serving their respective interests.[53] And in the process of engaging in this continuous "purposive enterprise," the procedural ('thin') *and* substantive ('thick') elements of operational policy framework can be further developed.[54] Such normative development strengthens the degree of "legality" and "obligation" of the operational policy framework (which can be measured, for instance, by Fuller's "criteria of legality")[55] and also has the potential to influence normative development in other (intersecting) normative systems.[56]

In fact, the analysis of Inspection Panel practice presented in Part II suggests that the World Bank's operational policy framework has (or, at least, is fast approaching) the 'theoretical threshold' between social and legal normativity[57] – aided by the dispute resolution triad formed by Requesters, Management and Inspection Panel[58] – although it is probably too soon to form conclusive opinions as to whether these norms should resort under the international legal system or whether this instance of normative development is a further indication of, as Krisch suggests, the emergence of a new 'transnational' or 'postnational' politico-legal order.[59]

Moreover, citizen-driven independent accountability mechanisms such as the Inspection Panel have become an important focal point of the norm-based approach underlying the

---

50   *Id.* In this regard, *also see* Sarfaty's remarks *at* note 121, Ch. 2; *and see* Adler's comments *at* note 169, Ch. 2.
51   *See* the discussion *in* section 2.3.
52   *See* Koskenniemi *at* note 174, Ch. 2.
53   Brunnée & Toope (2010), p. 7.
54   Brunnée & Toope (2010), pp. 42-43.
55   Brunnée & Toope (2010), pp. 22-23.
56   *See* the discussion *in* 5.1.1.
57   *See* the discussion *in* 5.1.1.
58   *See* the discussion *in* 7.1.6.
59   *See* the discussion *in* 2.1.

development-lending operations of multilateral development banks, whereas the learning network established by IAMs have, in many respects, become an embodiment of the broader normative community of practice in the transnational development context.[60]

Indeed, the establishment of citizen-driven IAMs, as Boisson de Chazournes argues, "reflects the evermore urgent need to build 'public spaces,' in the meaning attributed to that concept by the philosopher Jürgen Habermas" – public spaces, in other words, which can facilitate the forging of "unusual connections between partners of different stature, who need to exchange information, work together and even negotiate."[61] Citizen-driven IAMs affiliated with multilateral development banks can be viewed as "a formalization of the type of interrelation contemplated by Habermas' model," because their practice "connects individuals with the very core of the international decision-making process within this institution."[62]

16.2.1   Strengthening the resilience and adaptability of the community of practice

"Demands for accountability will only increase", as the Independent Accountability Mechanisms Network argued recently, because the "[n]otions of what development and accountability mean have irrevocably changed."[63] Moreover, "the means by which people themselves can hold IFIs, governments, NGOs, private sector actors, and others accountable" have become "more diverse and potent" – now ranging "from greater access to information through the internet[,] to laws and policies that require meaningful participation[,] to organizing tools like social media."[64] "There's no going back," the IAM Network asserts, "nor should we wish for this."[65]

While these are valid arguments, experience have also taught us that what has been constructed through social interaction can also be destroyed – perhaps not torn down in a single destructive swoop insofar as being systematically dismantled, to the point that the normative system is incapable of effectively restraining *or* enabling social action.

But the normative community of practice also provides the means for the normative system to *withstand* the adverse impact of variables that belong to, what Taleb calls, the "Extended Disorder Family"[66] – and which arise as a result of the pluralism and dynamic

---

60 On the IAM Network, *see e.g.*, section 3.1.3.

61 Boisson de Chazournes *in* Treves et al. (Eds.) (2005), pp. 187-188. *Also see* Brunnée & Toope's remarks *at* note 123, Ch. 2; *and see* Hale's comments *at* 188, Ch. 7.

62 *Id.*

63 Independent Accountability Mechanisms Network (2012), p. 31.

64 *Id.*

65 *Id.*

66 "The Extended Disorder Family (or Cluster)" includes: "(i) uncertainty, (ii) variability, (iii) imperfect, incomplete knowledge, (iv) chance, (v) chaos, (vi) volatility, (vii) disorder, (viii) entropy, (ix) time, (x) the

complexity that characterize the transnational development context – as well as to *learn* and adapt in the light of these 'disorders'.[67] This has been demonstrated, for instance, at pivotal moments throughout the institutional history of IAMs when, as a result of pressure exerted by internal and external accountability holders, their constitutive documents and/or operating procedures had been revised so as to improve their effectiveness;[68] or when, at critical institutional junctures, multilateral development banks revised their operational policy frameworks (notably, their safeguard policies).[69]

It is important, therefore, that we should seek ways in which we might further strengthen the resilience and adaptability of the normative community of practice in the transnational development context – or, to use Taleb's coined phrase, to strengthen its "antifragility".[70] The remainder of this section offers a few suggestions in this regard.

Reaffirm the need for normativity and clarify its place

The first suggestion concerns what might well be the 'most fragile' aspect of the 'shared surface' represented by normativity.[71] As noted earlier, while normativity does not need an extensive basis of consensus before it can start to facilitate interaction, collaboration and integration, it does require the recognition that there is need for normativity and that it has a decisive role to play – even if there has not been an explicit agreement on the *need for* and *place of legal* normativity.[72]

Looking back over the past few decades, it can be argued that this is indeed what has transpired within the transnational development context. Initiated, perhaps, by the efforts of specific "norm entrepreneurs"[73] and spearheaded by the continued efforts of an emerging normative community of interest (which, it should be emphasized, have always included significant contributions made by power wielders or dominant decision-makers),

---

unknown, (xi) randomness, (xii) turmoil, (xiii) stressor, (xiv) error, (xv) dispersion of outcomes, (xvi) unknowledge." (*See* Taleb (2012), e-Book.)

67   *Also see* Adler's comments *at* note 168, Ch. 2.

68   *See e.g.*, Bradlow (2000-2001); M.M. Philips, 'Effort Would Curb Watchdog of World Bank – Big Borrower Nations Seek Limit on Probing Harm to People and Ecology', *The Wall Street Journal*, 12 January 1999; Shihata (2000), p. 190; *and see* Naudé Fourie (2009), pp. 186-193.

69   The recent World Bank safeguards review provides a prominent example – *see e.g.*, note 28, Ch. 5.

70   *See* Taleb (2012), e-Book. "The antifragile", Taleb argues, "benefit from shocks; they thrive and grow when exposed to volatility, randomness, disorder, and stressors, and love adventure, risk, and uncertainty. Yet, in spite of the ubiquity of the phenomenon, there is not word for the exact opposite of fragile. Let's call it antifragile. Antifragility is beyond resilience or robustness. The resilient resists shocks and stays the same; the antifragile gets better. [...] Antifragility has a singular property of allowing us to deal with the unknown, to do things without understanding them – and do them well." Taleb therefore visualizes the following spectrum: "fragile" "robust" (resilient) "antifragile". (*Id.*) In this regard, *also see* Shapiro & Stone Sweet's remarks *at* note 175, Ch. 2.

71   *And see e.g.*, Koskenniemi's comment *at* note 174, Ch. 2.

72   In this regard, *see* Brunnée & Toope arguments *at* note 170, Ch. 2.

73   *See* Brunnée & Toope's comments *at* note 171, Ch. 2; *but also see* Slaughter's remarks *at* note 134, Ch. 2.

the World Bank Group, followed by other development institutions, embarked on a norm-based approach over the course of the late 1980s and early 1990s.

Criticisms related to the 'accountability deficit' of multilateral development institutions, as well as the acceptance of the need to strengthen institutional performance and realize the objectives of sustainable development, triggered a recognition of the need for norma-tivity – although, to be sure, this has never been an explicit recognition of the need for *law*. Multilateral development institutions, aided by the mechanism of an emerging *normative community of practice*, slowly carved out a place for normativity by *adopting norms* (aimed, for instance, at balancing economic, environmental and social interests, and mainstreaming the principles of access to information, participation in decision-making and access to justice), by *applying these norms* (across the Bank's development-operations and among borrowers), and by *enforcing these norms* (by means of internal accountability mechanisms, including citizen-driven bodies that can register claims originating directly from affected-people residing in the borrower's territory).

That being said, the analysis presented here also indicates that the need for normativity has to be reaffirmed, and its place clarified. While this need may have been precipitated by ongoing shifts in global economic and political power – which have strengthened the position of (particular) borrowers *vis-à-vis* the existing multilateral development banks, while introducing new entrants to the development-financing market[74] – the analysis of Inspection Panel practice, in particular, suggests that this issue goes back much further – and runs much deeper.

Consider, for instance, the wide range of expectations about the content and scope of Bank *versus* borrower obligations;[75] the multiple challenges involved in operationalizing the intricate division between Bank and borrower obligations;[76] the lingering dissatisfaction, on the part of the Bank and of its borrowers, with the role of the Inspection Panel and the value of its contribution;[77] the perceived lack of "congruence" between the World Bank's "words and actions," as reflected, for instance, in the inadequate realization of specific accountability outcomes;[78] the Bank's tendency to narrow the application safeguard policies such as the policy on Indigenous Peoples;[79] as well as the negative perceptions associated with the application and enforcement of social, environmental and economic safeguards (specifically, that it has made Bank management and staff 'too risk adverse'; that is has made World Bank development-lending operations 'too expensive, too slow and too

---

74 *See e.g.,* the discussion *in* Ch. 1.
75 *See e.g.,* the discussion *in* Chapters 10 & 11 *and* section 13.2.
76 *See e.g.,* the discussion *in* Ch. 8.
77 *See e.g.,* the discussion *in* section 7.2.
78 *See e.g.,* the discussion *in* sections 7.1 & 15.2.
79 *See e.g.,* the discussion *in* Chapters 13 & 10.

bureaucratic' – especially when compared to obtaining other (new) sources of development finance).[80]

When reflecting on such matters, it seems questionable whether the notion of 'norm-based development' has been internalized – by the Bank and its borrowers. It seems questionable, in other words, whether World Bank management and staff, borrowers and their contracted project implementing agencies have been convinced (or, whether they remain convinced) of the need for and place of normativity with respect to the conceptualization and operationalization of World Bank accountability. And perhaps the same can be said about the need for and place of normativity with regard to realizing the objectives of sustainable development.

What is clear, however, is that the ongoing changes in the transnational development context have placed the World Bank under pressure to employ *commercial responses* in the face of increased competition – responses that typically focus on revenue growth and operating cost reduction; whereas borrower states increasingly seek to assert their sovereignty and (growing) political and economic authority by pursuing their specific development needs without being encumbered by conditionalities. For both the Bank and its borrowers, in other words, the perceived costs associated with a norm-based approach increasingly outweigh its perceived benefits – especially when normativity is viewed predominantly as a means to *restrain* action;[81] or, when normativity's ability to *enable* action is not deemed to be convincing.

However, if we were to agree that accountability remains a topic of considerable importance and that there remains a need for normativity in facilitating the interaction and collaboration among *all* relevant actors, in integrating conflicting or complementary interests, demands, expectations and conceptions in order to develop a comprehensive shared understanding on what such accountability means in theory and in practice – as this book argues – we simply cannot afford to ignore these matters.

If the development of a shared understanding on accountability is to reflect the pluralism of the underlying transnational development context – not only in theory, therefore, but also in practice – the normative community of practice also has to strengthen its ability to withstand the tension and learn from the challenges brought about by such pluralism. For different actors, however, clarifying the need for and place of normativity are bound to mean different things.

For an international financial institution such as the World Bank, for example, it would likely mean having to reaffirm its commitment to norm-based development – publically and continuously. But it might also mean that institutions such as the Bank has to leverage the opportunities a norm based approach represents – by viewing it, for instance, not

---

80 *See e.g.,* the discussion *in* sections 4.2.2 & 7.2.2.
81 In this regard, *also see e.g.,* Freestone's comments *at* note 176, Ch. 5.

predominantly as a cost, but also as a means to differentiate themselves from new competitors.[82]

In order to fully realize this potential, however, an institution such as the World Bank would have to demonstrate that it is serious about learning from the practice generated by internal accountability mechanisms such as the Inspection Panel and the Operations Evaluation Group – instead, for instance, of viewing the predominant effect of such practice as making the institution's management and staff more risk averse. It requires the acknowledgement, furthermore, that the "errors" highlighted by these bodies of practice are "rich in information," and that the lessons they contain have the potential to strengthen the institution's ability to realize aims related both to maximizing performance and to minimizing harm.[83] And it requires the commitment to strengthen the congruence between what is said 'on paper' and what is done 'in the field',[84] by translating these lessons into the concrete reality of the Bank's development-lending operations.[85]

Reaffirming the need for normativity and clarifying its place, would also require institutions such as the World Bank to actively engage their borrowers in a discussion about the costs and – in particular – the benefits associated with a norm-based approach. In this regard, increased transparency about the underlying tensions between institutional aims could provide a meaningful contribution to facilitate such interaction – and so could increased transparency about the assumptions as well as the arguments underlying complementary institutional aims.[86] In other words, for institutions such as the World Bank to convince their borrowers of the 'case for' employing a norm-based approach to development, their arguments would have to be based in concrete evidence that demonstrates

---

82 *See e.g.*, the Inspection Panel's comments *at* note 64, Ch. 9; *and see* current World Bank President Kim's comments *at* note 263, Ch. 12.

83 Taleb (2012), e-Book, arguing that errors falling in the "fragile category" are "large when they occur; [and] hence irreversible"; whereas errors in the "antifragile category" are "small and benign, even reversible and easily overcome. They are also rich in information." On the complementary relationships between 'feedback', 'information' and 'learning', *also see* Sterman *at* note 26, Ch. 2; *and see* notes 60 & 61, Ch. 1. On the Bank's institutional aims, and their relationship to performance and harm, *see* the discussion *in* section 4.2.

84 *See e.g.*, the Inspection Panel's comments *at* note 3, Part II.

85 In this regard, *also see* the panel-discussion convened by the IEG during the Bank's 2015 Annual meeting (on "why the World Bank seems to have a hard time ensuring that its projects and programs are systematically informed by experience from the past and analysis from available data"), *at*: http://ieg.worldbankgroup.org/blog/can-world-bank-kick-habit. Monika Weber-Fahr ('Chief Knowledge Officer and Senior Manager, Independent Evaluation Group') comments: "The challenge is that we are dealing with an 'organizational habit'. And a peculiar one for that matter. A 'looking away' habit. The Independent Evaluation Group has found testament of this habit in several otherwise unrelated evaluations. In fact, the evaluators consider it a conundrum that the World Bank, an organization whose staff and clients pride themselves in the first class knowledge that they help flow into and from their collaboration, would not ensure systematically the informed nature of its choices." (*Id.*)

86 Indeed, information is "antifragile" because, as Taleb points out, "it feeds more on attempts to harm it than it does on efforts to promote it." (*See* Taleb (2012), e-Book.)

not only how – and why – normativity *restrains*, but also how – and why – it *enables* the actions of institutional and borrower decision-making.

For external constituency groups, who tend to rely more on a formalist conception of normativity as a means to restrain but also to influence dominant decision-makers, it would be important to consider, for instance, the intricate relationship between demands and expectations concerning *World Bank and IFI* accountability, and those concerning *borrower state* accountability; and, furthermore, how borrowers can interpret demands and expectations about World Bank and IFI accountability as impediments to state sovereignty, especially when such demands and expectations are viewed predominantly from a formalist perspective.[87] While the discourse on transnational regulatory governance contexts (rightly) emphasizes the progressively prominent role fulfilled by non-state actors, it should also be recognized that state actors remain dominant actors,[88] whereas some of the Bank's borrower states are increasingly occupying positions of influence *vis-à-vis* donor states. When considering, moreover, that "norm internalization" in transnational regulatory governance contexts "cannot be effective if it bypasses the state,"[89] it seems clear that it is not only up to the multilateral development institutions to convince borrower states of the merits of a norm-based approach – it is a shared responsibility within the normative community of practice.

In this regard, it is also important for academic commentators, especially those based in donor countries, to recognize that the reaffirmation of the need for normativity and the clarification of its place in the transnational development context are likely to present a challenge to many of the theoretical conceptions presented in this book – including the constructivist and interactional conception of social and legal normativity that facilitates a significant portion of this analysis. For many actors in the transnational development context, these theories are too 'Northern-American' or 'European-centric' and are, therefore, not considered to be representative of the interests of 'the South', or are simply not accurate reflections of the realities in borrower countries; while others remain suspicious as to the motives behind these theories, and might therefore perceive their 'real' purpose to be the strengthening (or, prolonging) of 'Western' ('Northern') hegemony, just as the balance of power is shifting towards the 'East' ('South').

We cannot strengthen the resilience and adaptability of the normative community of practice without embracing such challenges, however. It therefore remains up to us, as members of this community of practice, to convince each other of our ideas and – even better – to forge new conceptions through our interactions.

---

87 In this regard, *also see* Kingsbury's remarks *at* note 95, Ch. 16.
88 Brunnée & Toope (2010), pp. 3-5.
89 Sarfaty (2005), p. 1813 (commenting on the internalization of the norms contained in the Bank's policy on Indigenous people).

Reframe how we view citizen-driven IAMs and rethink how we evaluate their contributions

"[A]dministrative law-type" accountability mechanisms operating in transnational regulatory governance contexts run the risk, as Krisch argues, of becoming "overburdened by the demands made on them."[90] The analysis presented in this book suggests that risk has indeed materialized (as demonstrated, for example, by contradictory views as to the role of the Inspection Panel and the persistent criticisms, expressed by internal and external constituency groups alike, concerning the Inspection Panel's lack of effectiveness)[91] – and, importantly, that it has weakened the Inspection Panel's ability to facilitate interaction, collaboration and integration.

The purpose of this analysis, as noted earlier, has not been to refute or corroborate criticisms related to the Panel's effectiveness; however, the analysis does point to an important factor underlying such views, namely: conflicting demands and expectations as to *what the Inspection Panel is supposed to be doing* (or, where its primary focus should be) – and, specifically, *to which accountability outcomes* should the Inspection Panel be contributing. It is important to recognize, moreover, that these conflicting demands and expectations are influenced by the particular interests represented by various constituency groups, and that their opposing arguments are typically grounded in competing conceptions – about the primary purpose of normative systems (instrumentalism *versus* formalism), and what the World Bank should principally be accountable 'for' (realizing performance *versus* avoiding/mitigating harm).

For instance, as Gowlland Gualtieri comments, "[c]ompeting conceptions of the scope" of the Inspection Panel's mandate "have been promoted," respectively, "by the text of the [Inspection Panel] Resolution, the practice of the Panel, the decisions of the Bank's Board of Executive Directors, and interpretations on the part of external observers."[92] Accordingly, "[t]he Panel may be viewed as a body"

> with either limited investigatory and/or mediatory competence, undertaken by means of relatively flexible procedures, or as having functions of a quasi-judicial nature accomplished through a formalized process. The Board has

---

90   *See* Krisch (2006), p. 277, who observes that "the role of treaties as 'transmission belts', ensuring accountability to states and through the ratification process also to the public within states, has become weaker and weaker, just as demands for stronger accountability have risen in the face of ever more intrusive global regulation of formerly domestic affairs." (*Id.*) It has become accepted practice to fill this "gap" "by using domestic models of accountability mechanisms" in transnational settings; however, this practice involves "significant obstacles." (*Id.*) Notably, "[i]n domestic settings, standard elements of administrative law, such as procedural participation and judicial review, perform particular, limited functions, and most of the burden of ensuring accountability lies with the electoral processes that check parliamentary law-making as well as governmental action;" whereas at the global level, this "electoral anchor is lost". (*Id.*)

91   *See e.g.*, the discussion *in* section 7.2.2.

92   Gowlland Gualtieri (2001), pp. 252-253.

sought a strictly non-judicial mechanism. During its first five years, the Panel's competencies were restricted to advisory and fact-finding ones, as it was in the majority of cases not authorized to undertake investigations into the merits of requests. [...] On the other hand, NGOs and external commentators, as well as some sections of Bank staff, have leaned towards the 'judicialization' of the Panel. The Resolution indeed grants the Panel quasi-judicial functions during the eligibility and investigation phases, such as to determine its jurisdiction, examine the merits of a request by applying legal norms to facts, and arrive at a determination on the issue of non-compliance after an inquiry conducted in accordance with legal rules and on the basis of principles of fairness and equity.[93]

But while there is a decided need for the Inspection Panel to "remain a flexible and prag-matic dispute resolution mechanism, Gowlland Gualtieri concludes, "strengthening its quasi-judicial functions" also "has the potential to give the mechanism greater teeth."[94]

Whereas Kingsbury argues that the "board's oscillations between encouraging and discouraging a regulatory approach involving the panel" exacerbate "systemic problems" – such as those issues related to the limitation of the Panel's mandate to investigate only World Bank actions/omissions, while Inspection Panel practice cannot avoid brushing against the intricate relationship between Bank and Borrower obligations[95] – and have, at times, resulted in "unsatisfactory case management".[96]

Or, as Van Putten observes (reflecting on the advice she was given before commencing her term as an Inspection Panel member), "[m]any experts with experience with the panel expressed the view to me that the World Bank's policies have to be understood as nearly

---

93 *Id.*
94 *Id.*
95 Kingsbury (1999), p. 334. The author argues that Inspection Panel practice invariably "confronts a structural problem", namely: that "failures in project implementation are often attributable primarily to the borrowing state, whereas the panel's responsibilities relate to conduct of the Bank." Borrowers, however, "may resent being impugned as part of 'situations where the Bank is alleged to have failed in its follow-up on the borrower's obligations under loan agreements with respect to such policies and procedures', and they may be reluctant to cooperate with information or site Visits. Some borrowing states object to the pressure generated by Bank staff and the inspection panel to spend scarce national resources ameliorating the effects of one project, when there are higher priorities or worse problems demanding resources elsewhere." (*Id.*)
96 *Id. Note,* Kingsbury refers specifically to the Panel's 1996 investigation of the *Yacyretá Hydroelectric* project. In this instance, "the panel recommended full inspection, but the board instead invited the panel to review the existing problems and provide an assessment of the adequacy of the action plan agreed between the Bank and the two states involved. In what appears to be a compromise, the board resolution added: 'independent of the above decision, the Inspection Panel is expected to look at the extent to which the Bank staff had fol-lowed Bank procedures with respect to this project'. Apart from calling for something like an inspection while avoiding the terminology that it had itself established, the board here introduced an element of opacity by referring only to 'Bank procedures', rather than the 'Bank operational policies and procedures' that ordinarily define the scope of inspection." (*Id.*) On the Inspection Panel's varying approach with respect to its 1996 and 2002 investigations of the *Yacyretá* project, *also see* Naudé Fourie (2009), pp. 289-292.

binding 'legal' instruments."[97] But while such an approach may be desirable, "on the one hand," because "one wants to have clear procedures and standards to which one can hold the institution accountable", it is not desirable, "on the other hand," for the Inspection Panel to "become a mere 'blame and shame' instrument."[98] Although the Panel's findings "should contribute to a process of learning," Van Putten concludes, "we have to demand full implementation of the policies or performance standards and not allow any weakening of these policies" because "[t]oo much is at stake for future generations."[99]

In other words, as has been argued in this book, citizen-driven independent account-ability mechanisms like the Inspection Panel have to execute a *dual accountability mandate* – that is, a mandate with an *institutional side* (which typically demands and expects the Panel to serve the interests of internal accountability holders primarily; and, foremost, to enable the actions of the institution's dominant decision-makers) and a *public side* (which typically demands and expects the Panel to serve the interests of external accountability holders primarily; and, foremost, to restrain the actions of the institution's dominant decision-makers).

Such theoretical arguments, however, do not clarify how bodies like the Panel are supposed to deal with the "dilemma" this paradoxical situation presents them, in practice;[100] or, how we, as members of the normative community of practice in which citizen-driven IAMs are imbedded, should evaluate their contributions in light of their dual accountability mandates, and how we might aid the IAMs in becoming more effective – in *becoming better*, in other words, *at fulfilling the wide range of functions we demand and expect from them.*

A possible course of action might be to suggest that citizen-driven IAMs should prior-itize – that they should decide which interests, demands, expectations and conceptions to give primacy, and align their operating procedures and actions in accordance with this strategy. This would also mean that the normative community of practice should adjust its demands and expectations to lower (that is, 'more realistic') levels.

Such suggestions, however, are unlikely to strengthen the resilience and adaptability of citizen-driven IAMs. For example, what would constitute 'realistic' demands and expectations? And would a downward adjustment of demands and expectations not also have an adverse effect on the sociological legitimacy of citizen-driven IAMs – which, in turn, are also likely to have a negative impact on their effectiveness?[101] As for prioritization as a principle course of action, I have argued elsewhere that while the Inspection Panel

---

97 *Id.*
98 *Id.*
99 *Id.* On the 'formalist' and 'instrumentalist' paradigms, as well as arguments that neither paradigm's logic is "mutually conclusive", *see* the discussion *in* section 2.3.
100 Van Putten (2008), pp. 320-221.
101 On the notion of sociological legitimacy, as employed in this book, *see* note 11, Ch. 7.

fluctuates between periods of pronounced *restraint* and *activism*, the Panel's *behaviour over time* is driven by several factors that are related to dynamics existing among the Inspection Panel, internal and external constituency groups.[102] To put this argument in perspective of this analysis: while prioritization may constitute a valid short-term tactic, the achievement of balance or equilibrium among conflicting variables, over time, requires that a citizen-driven IAM cannot be *seen* as consistently (or predominantly) employing a strategy favouring particular variables over others.[103]

An alternative course of action would be to reframe how we view citizen-driven IAMs and to rethink how we evaluate their contributions.

For example, do we see citizen-driven interdependent accountability mechanisms as 'hybrid courts', 'insulated fact-finding bodies', 'distrusted quality inspectors' or 'disempowered arbitrators/mediators' – or, do we see them as mechanisms that are in a unique position to facilitate *interaction, collaboration* and the *integration* of conflicting and complementary variables?

When we consider their role and the nature of their contribution, do we recognize the influence of the specific interests we represent (or, associate with more closely) and are we aware of the influence of underlying conceptions (our own as well as those of others)? And, even as we represent specific interests or prefer specific conceptions that lead us to make certain demands and hold certain expectations of citizen-driven IAMs, do we also recognize that these matters form part of a larger complex societal issue to which there are no conclusive solutions? Do we recognize, moreover, that our interaction through the shared surface provided by citizen-driven IAMs forms part of a broader discursive process through which we can work towards developing a comprehensive shared understanding on the accountability of international financial institutions?

For, if we reframe citizen-driven IAMs in this way, we might be in a better position to understand how these mechanisms operate, why they make certain decisions and what the effects of those decisions are. This, in turn, would place us in a better position to evaluate their contributions and rethink what 'effectiveness' means for mechanisms executing a dual accountability mandate.

Furthermore, when we view the role of citizen-driven IAMs as facilitating interaction, collaboration and integration, we might also be able to identify (and subsequently, analyze) contributions that might otherwise have been overlooked. One example of such a contribution concerns the development of a "coherent" interpretative scheme that "integrat[es]," as Kingsbury puts it, "quasi-regulatory and quasi-judicial approaches."[104]

---

102 *See* Naudé Fourie (2009), pp. 305-314; *and* Naudé Fourie (2012), pp. 212-217.

103 This argument is also reflected, *e.g.*, in claims concerning the imbalance between technical/commercial and non-technical/non-commercial project components, *as* discussed *in* Ch. 9.

104 *See* Kingsbury (1999), p. 334. *Also see* Kingsbury's comments *at* note 95, Ch. 16; *and see* Higgins's remarks *at* notes 159-162, Ch. 2.

The analysis of Inspection Panel practice suggests that such a scheme might indeed be emerging, as set out in Figure 14.

Figure 14   An Interpretative Scheme that Enables the Effective Execution of a Dual Accountability Mandate

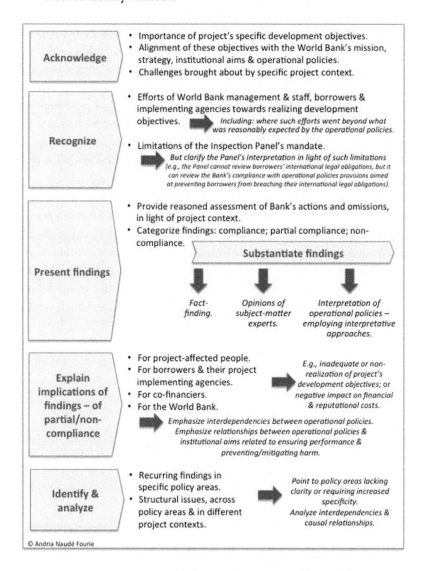

© Andria Naudé Fourie

When a citizen-driven IAM like the Inspection Panel employs such an interpretative scheme in a consistent manner, it is also at its most effective. This is because such a scheme enables the IAM to execute its dual accountability mandate – aimed at restraining and enabling the actions of the multilateral development institution with which it is affiliated – in a manner that asserts and strengthens the IAM's functional independence and authority vis-à-vis institutional power-wielders, while also fostering the IAM's sociological legitimacy with internal and external constituency groups.

The consistent employment of such an interpretative scheme positions the IAM, furthermore, to provide project-affected people with recourse – and this specifically includes the opportunity of giving project-affected people 'voice' by making the harm they are suffering 'real'. It situates the IAM in a position from where it can influence the realization and enforcement of corrective/remedial Bank/Borrower actions – actions, in other words, that could result in the realization of development objectives and in specific measures of redress for project-affected people. Moreover, it facilitates the IAM's contribution towards strengthening the institution's governance structure by providing the Board of Executive Directors with independently verified facts.[105] And it provides the opportunity – at least – for strengthening institutional performance by providing policy advice, by developing the procedural and substantive elements contained in the operational policies, and by highlighting errors that can facilitate institutional learning.

Finally, the consistent employment of an interpretative scheme that integrates "quasi-regulatory and quasi-judicial approaches"[106] demonstrates why the conceptualization and operationalization of the accountability of international financial institutions is a complex societal issue that needs to be addressed on a continuous basis; and, why citizen-driven IAMs – as well as the broader normative community of practice in the transnational development context – can provide a resilient and adaptable mechanism for doing so.

---

105 *Also see* Hale's comments *at* notes 237-240, Ch. 7.
106 *See* note 104, Ch. 16.

Abbreviations, Acronyms and Terminology Commonly Used in World Bank Development-lending Operations

ACRP	(Land) Acquisition, Compensation and Rehabilitation Plan
ACUACAR	Aguas de Cartagena, S.A. E.S.P. (project implementing agency, *Colombia: Cartagena Water & Environmental Management*)
ADB	Asian Development Bank
AESNP	AES Nile Power Corporation (project implementing agency/'Sponsor', *Uganda: Power Projects* [predecessor project])
AfDB	African Development Bank
AG	Associated Gas
AM	[ADB's] Accountability Mechanism *Note*: successor body of the ADB's Inspection Function (IF)
AMR	Annual Monitoring Report
Annex areas	"[T]erritories outside the core area of [the tribal group's specific] comarca" (*Panama: Land Administration*) *See* comarca
APEMU	Arun Project Environmental Monitoring Unit
APL	Adaptable Program Loan
APRAP	Assessment of Past Resettlement Activities and Action Plan
ASOSRP	Area Specific Oil Spill Response Plan
ASTHR	Asia Technical Human Resources Chotanagpur Adivasi Sewa Sami
AT	[WBG's] Administrative Tribunal
BEL	Bujagali Energy Limited (project implementing agency/'Sponsor', *Uganda: Power Projects* [successor project])
BHP	Bujagali Hydropower Project (Uganda)
BIP	Bujagali Interconnection Project (Uganda)
BKL	Boeung Kak Lake
BMC	Bombay Municipal Corporation
Board	[WBG] Board of Executive Directors, which executes "specific duties" delegated to it by the Bank's "ultimate policymaker", the Board of Governors (*see* http://go.worldbank.org/WM8TMERJO0)
Borrower	The term includes "wherever the context requires," the "recipient of an IDA grant, the guarantor of an IBRD loan, and the project imple-

menting agency, if it is different from the borrower" (*see* OP 4.10, fn. 2). In the context of guarantee operations, the term also includes "a private or public project sponsor receiving from another financial institution a loan guaranteed by the Bank." (*see* OP 4.01, fn. 1) *And see* OP 7.00, § 1, which defined 'borrower' as "(a) a member country; (b) a political subdivision of a member; and (c) any business, industrial, and agricultural enter-prise in the territories of a member." *Whereas* OP 7.00, § 3 defines 'guarantor' as follows: "If the member in whose territories the project is located is not itself the borrower, the member must guarantee the payment of the principal and interest and other charges on the loan."

BPL	Below Poverty Line
BRT	Bus Rapid Transit
BSES	Baseline Socio-Economic Surveys
BTO	Back to the Office Report
CAO	[IFC and MIGA's] Compliance/Advisory Ombudsman
CAPECE	Petroleum Environment Capacity Enhancement Project (Cameroon)
CARDIQUE	Corporación Autónoma Regional del Canal del Dique (*Colombia: Cartagena Water & Environmental Management*)
CAS	Country Assistance Strategy
CASS	*Chotanagpur Adivasi Sewa Samiti* (NGO, *India: Coal Sector*)
Case	*See* [Inspection Panel] Request
CCL	Central Coalfields Ltd. (project implementing agency, *India: Coal Sector*)
CD	Concept Document
CDAP	Community Development Action Plan
CDD	Community Driven Development
CDP	Community Development Plan
CEA	Country Environmental Assessment
CELCOR	Center for Environmental Law and Community Rights
CELS	Center for Legal and Social Studies
CEMP	Community Environmental Management Plans
CIS	Cumulative Impact Study
CITES	Convention on International Trade in Endangered Species of Wild Fauna and Flora
CODIGEM	Corporation for Geological - Mining - Metallurgical Research and Development (Ecuador)
COINBIO	Indigenous and Communities Biodiversity Conservation Project (Mexico)

Comarca	"[A] territory over which indigenous groups have collective land rights and considerable administrative authority, as established by specific law." (*Panama: Land Administration*) *See* annex area
COTCO	Cameroon Oil Transportation Company, S.A. (project implementing agency, *Cameroon: Petroleum*)
CPSP	Pipeline Steering and Monitoring Committee
CRA	*Comisión Reguladora de Agua*
CRS	[WBG] Conflict Resolution System
CSO	Civil Society Organization *Also see* NGO *and* NSA
CTNSC	*Comité Technique National de Suivi et de Contrôle* (National Technical Committee for Monitoring and Evaluation of the Pipeline Project – *Chad: Petroleum*)
DCA	Development Credit Agreement
DFI	Development Finance Institutions
DfID	Department for International Development
DINAGE	National Geology Directorate
DINAMA	National Directory of Environment
DINAMI	National Mining Directorate
DMP	Drainage Master Plan
DPL	Development Policy Lending *See* SAL
DPV	Provincial Road Directorate
DRC	Democratic Republic of Congo
DSEA	Drainage Sector Environmental Assessment
EA	Environmental Assessment *Note*: 'EA' "refers to the entire process, as set out in OP/BP 4.01" (*see* OP/BP 4.01, fn. 1)
EAP	Environmental Action Plan; *or* Environmental Advisory Panel
EAS	Environmental Alignment Sheet
[EAP] EASSD	[WBG, East Asia Pacific] Social Development Sector Unit *Note*: part of EASES [EAP Environmental and Social Development Sector Unit] as of January 1999
EBRD	European Bank for Reconstruction and Development
EBC	[WBG] Office of Business Ethics
EBY	*Entidad Binacional Yacyretá* (project implementing agency, *Argentina/Paraguay: Yacyretá Hydroelectric Project*)

EESRSP	Emergency Economic and Social Reunification Support Project (Democratic Republic of Congo)
EFP	Erosion and Flood Policy
EIA	Environmental Impact Assessment
EIB	European Investment Bank
EIR	Environmental Impact Report
EIS	Environmental Impact Statement
EISP	Eskom Investment Support Project (South Africa)
EMAP	Environmental Action Plan
EMMP	Environmental Management and Monitoring Plan
EMPR	Environmental Management Programme Report
EMP	Emergency Management Plan; *or* Environmental Management Plan
EPAP	Project-Affected Person entitled to economic rehabilitation
ER	Eligibility Report (Inspection Panel's 'Report and Recommendation' in which the Panel sets out its finding concerning the eligibility of the case and makes its recommendation regarding the necessity for an investigation)
	Note: in case of multiple ERs (i.e., where the IP defers its recommendation), the citation will be: First ER, Second ER, etc., Final ER
ERM	Enhanced Review Mission
ERP	Emergency Response Plan
E&S	Environmental and Social Assistance
ESA	Environmental and Social Assessment
ESAP	Environmental and Social Advisory Panel
ESIA	Environmental and Social Impact Assessment
ESMAP	Energy Sector Management Assistance Program
ESMP	Environmental and Social Management Plan
ESRP	Environmental and Social Review Procedures/Panel
FA	Forest Administration
FACIL	*Fonds d'Actions Concertées d'Initiative Locale - Local Initiatives Social Fund* ('Local Initiatives Social Fund', put in place to support local groups in the context of the *Chad: Petroleum* project)
FCMCPP	Forest Concession Management Control and Pilot Project (Cambodia)
FEDEC	*La Fondation pour l'Environnement et le Développement au Cameroun*
FS	Feasibility Study
GDP	Gross Domestic Product
GEF	Global Environmental Facility
GFA	GFA Terra Systems
GFM	Global Financial Markets

GHG	Green house gas
GOA	Government of Albania
GOB	Government of Bangladesh
GOC	Government of Cameroon
GOI	Government of India
GOL	Government of Lesotho
GOM	Government of the State of Maharashtra (India)
GOP	Government of Pakistan; *or*
	Government of Paraguay
GOS	Government of Sindh
GOSA	Government of South Africa
	Also see RSA
GOU	Government of Uganda
GPAL	Governance Promotion Adjustment Loan (Papua New Guinea)
Guarantee	Projects where the World Bank acts as guarantee for the loan, provided
Operations	by a private sector actor. "In providing guarantees, the Bank's objective is to mobilize private sector financing for development purposes. The Bank may guarantee private loans with or without an associated Bank loan. The Bank provides guarantees only to the extent necessary. In providing guarantees, the Bank coordinates its approach with IFC and MIGA." (*see* OP 14.25, § 1)
Guarantor	*See* Borrower
HMG/N	Kingdom of Nepal
HPP	Hydropower Plant/Hydroelectric Power Plant
IAD	[WBG] Internal Audit
IAG	International Advisory Group
IAM	Independent Accountability Mechanism
IAM Network	Independent Accountability Mechanisms Network (for the members of the IAM Network, *see* http://ewebapps.world-bank.org/apps/ip/Pages/Related%20Organizations.aspx)
IBRD	International Bank for Reconstruction and Development
	Also see WB *and* WBG
ICESCR	International Covenant on Economic, Social, and Cultural Rights
ICIM/MICI	[IDB's] Independent Consultation and Investigation Mechanism
	Note: successor body of the IDB's Independent Investigation Mechanism (IIM)
ICR	Implementation Completion Report
ICSID	International Center for Settlement of Investment Disputes
	Also see WBG

IDA	International Development Association
	Also see WB *and* WBG
IDB	Inter-American Development Bank
IDU	Institute of Urban Development
IEG	[WBG] Independent Evaluation Group
	See OED
IFC	International Financial Corporation
	Also see WBG
IFI	International Financial Institution
ILA	International Law Association
ILO	International Labour Organization
IM	Implementation Manual
IMC	International Mining Consultants, Group Consulting Ltd.
IMF	International Monetary Fund
IMO	International Maritime Organization
IMP	Independent Monitoring Panel
Infoshop	WBG's "retail bookstore and resource center, offering access to information on World Bank projects and programs to the public", available at: http://go.worldbank.org/EXFM3GNE60
INT	[WBG's] Integrity Vice Presidency, tasked to investigate allegations of "fraud and corruption in Bank-financed projects", available at: http://go.worldbank.org/036LY1EJJ0
IP	Inspection Panel ('Panel')
IPDP	Indigenous Peoples Development Plan
	See IPP
IPP	Indigenous Peoples Plan
	See IPDP
IPS	Indigenous Peoples Strategy
IPU	Unified Property Tax
IR	[Inspection Panel] Investigation Report (issued after the completion of a Board-authorized investigation)
IRM	[AfDB's] Independent Review Mechanism
IRS	Inland Revenue Service
ISDS	Integrated Safeguards Data Sheet
IUCN	International Union for Conservation of Nature
JSAC	Jute Sector Adjustment Credit Project (Bangladesh)
JVLR	Jogeshwari-Vikhroli Link Road
KMTNC	King Mahendra Trust for Nature and Conservation (implementing NGO, *Nepal: Arun III*)

LBOD/NSDS	Left Bank Outfall Drain/National Surface Drainage System
Legacy (project component)	Project component in 'successor project', related to issues in a 'predecessor' project
LHI	Legal Harmonization Initiative ("a joint undertaking of several international financial institutions (IFI), including the World Bank, bilateral aid agencies and United Nations agencies in support of the implementation of commitments expressed in the Paris Declaration to improve aid effectiveness through harmonization and alignment" – *see* http://web.worldbank.org/WBSITE/EXTERNAL/TOPICS/EXTLAWJUS-TICE/0,,content-MDK:22191538~menuPK:6193354~pagePK:148956~piPK:216618~theSitePK:445634,00.html)
LIL	Learning and Innovation Loan
LLG	Local Level Government
LMAP	Land Management and Administration Project (Cambodia)
Loan	"Includes IDA credits and IDA grants" (*see* OP/BP 4.01, fn. 1)
LVEMP	Lake Victoria Environmental Management Project (Uganda)
MAFF	Ministry of Agriculture, Forestry and Fisheries
Management	"World Bank as an institution involved in the design, appraisal and/or implementation of Bank-financed projects, as distinct from the Board of Executive Directors." (*see* IP Operating Procedures (2014), p. 9)
MASL/masl	Metres above sea level
MDB	Multilateral Development Bank
MEM	Ministry of Energy and Mines
MIGA	Multilateral Investment Guarantee Agency *Also see* WBG
MMRDA	Mumbai Metropolitan Region Development Authority (project implementing agency, *India: Mumbai Urban Transport Project*)
MR	[WB] Management Response (initial response to the Request filed at the Inspection Panel)
MRIR	[WB] Management Response to the Inspection Panel's Investigation Report ('Management Report and Recommendation')
MUTP	Mumbai Urban Transport Project (India)
MW	Megawatt
NDP	National Drainage Program Project (Pakistan)
NEA	Nepal Electricity Organization (project implementing agency, *Nepal: Arun III*)

NGO	Non-Governmental Organization
	Note: Implementing NGOs refers to civil society actors directly involved in project design and/or implementation activities
	Also see CSO & NSA
NNPC	Nigerian National Petroleum Corporation
NSA	Non-State Actor
	Also see CSO & NGO
NTPC	National Thermal Power Corporation Project (India)
ODECO	*Organización de Desarrollo Étnico Comunitario* (local NGO representing Garífuna (indigenous peoples group), *Honduras: Land Administration*)
OED	[WBG] Operations Evaluation Department
	See IEG
OFRANEH	*Organización Fraternal Negra Hondoras* (Requesters, *Honduras: Land Administration*, local NGO representing Garífuna (indigenous peoples group))
OM	Operational Manual
OPCS	[WBG] Operations Policy and Country Services
OPIC	Oil Palm Industry Corporation (project implementing agency, *Papua New Guinea: Smallholder Agriculture*)
OP&P	[WB] Operational Policies & Procedures, consisting of:

	OP	Operational Policy
	BP	Bank Procedure
	GP	Good Practice

Note: previous formats include:

	ODO	perational Directive
	OMS	Operational Manual Statement
	OPN	Operational Policy Note
	OP	Memo Operational Memorandum

PA	Project Area (of influence)
PAD	Project Appraisal Document
PAF	Project Affected families
PAH	Project Affected Households
PAP	Project Affected People/Person
PATH	*Programa de Administración de Tierras de Honduras* (*Honduras: Land Administration Project*)
PCD	Project Concept Document
PCM	[EBRD's] Project Complaint Mechanism
	Note: successor body of the EBRD's Independent Recourse Mechanism (IRM)

PCN	Project Concept Note
PCR	Project Completion Reports
PCU	Project Coordination Unit
PDA	*Programa de Desborde de Arroyos*
PIC	Public Information Center; *or*
	Project Information Center
PID	Project Information Document
PIM	Project Implementation Manual
PIU	Project Implementation Unit
PMU	Project Management Unit
PNG	Papua New Guinea
POE/PoE	Panel of Experts
PPA	Power Purchase Agreement
PRG	Partial Risk Guarantee
Project	WB (IDA/IBRD) (co-)financed development project
	Note: the term "includes all components of the project, regardless of the source of financing. The term project also includes projects and components funded under the Global Environment Facility (GEF), but does not include GEF projects executed by organizations identified by the GEF Council as eligible to work with the GEF through expanded opportunities for project preparation and implementation (such organizations include, inter alia, regional development banks and UN agencies such as FAO and UNIDO)." (*See* OP 4.04, fn. 2)
Project implementing agency	Public or private sector entity contracted by the Borrower to implement a Bank-funded development project
	Also see Borrower *and* Sponsor
PRONAT	*Programa Nacional de Administración de Tierras* (*Panama: Land Administration Project*)
QAG	[WBG] Quality Assurance Group
OECD	Organisation for Economic Co-operation and Development (*see* http://www.oecd.org)
RAP	Resettlement Action Plan; *or*
	Regional Action Plan
R&R	Resettlement & Rehabilitation
(R)CDAP	(Resettlement and) Community Development Action Plan
RDP	Regional Development Plan

Request	Request (for Inspection, filed at the Inspection Panel)
	Also see Inspection Panel Case
	Note: "Requests may relate to projects financed by an investment loan or credit; or programs funded through development policy lending (formerly known as structural adjustment operations); or projects financed through a trust fund administered by the Bank (e.g. Global Environmental Facility-funded projects); or projects/programs for which IBRD or IDA has provided only a guarantee (not actual loan/credit); or projects/programs co-financed with other International Financial Institutions; or Program-for-Results operations. This is not a restrictive list and there might be other financing instruments of IBRD/IDA that might be subject to an Inspection Panel process." (*See* IP Operating Procedures (2014), p. 9)
RIP	Resettlement Implementation Plan
RMTF	Road Maintenance Trust Fund
ROW/RoW	Right(s) of Way
RPF	Resettlement Policy Framework
RRAP	Revised Resettlement Action Plan/Resettlement and Rehabilitation Action Plan
RSA	Republic of South Africa
	See GoSA
RSPO	Roundtable on Sustainable Palm Oil
SA	Social Assessment
SADP	Smallholder Agriculture Development Project (*Papua New Guinea*)
SAL	Structural Adjustment Loan
	See DPL
SAR	Staff Appraisal Report
SCDP	Southern Coastal Development Plan
SCLR	Santacruz-Chembur Link Road
SDR	Safeguard Diagnostic Review
	See Operational Policy/Bank Policy 4.00: Piloting the Use of Borrower Systems to Address Environmental and Social Safeguard Issues in Bank Supported Projects
SEDD	Summary of Economic Due Diligence
(S)SEA	Strategic/Sectoral Social and Environmental Assessment
SEIA	Sectoral Environmental Impact Assessment
SFMP	Strategic Forest Management Plan
SIA	Social Impact Assessment

SPARC	Society for Promotion of Area Resources Centers (implementing NGO, *India: Mumbai Urban Transport*)
Sponsor	*See* Borrower
SRS	Slum Rehabilitation Society (implementing NGO, *India: Mumbai Urban Transport*)
SSEA	Strategic/Sectoral Social and Environmental Assessment
TBOD	Trans-Basin Outfall Drain
TDR	Triadic Dispute Resolution
TEP	Thermal Electric Power Plan
	Also see TPP
TISS	Tata Institute of Social Sciences
TM	Task Manager
TOR/ToR	Terms of Reference
TPP	Thermal Electric Power Plant
	Also see TEP
TSERO	Transitional Support for Economic Recovery Credit Operation (Democratic Republic of Congo)
TTL	Task Team Leader
UESP	Urban Environmental Sanitation Project (Uganda)
UETCL	Uganda Electricity Transmission Company Limited
UK	United Kingdom
UN	United Nations
UNCHS	United Nations Centre for Human Settlements; *or* Regional centres of the United Nations Human Settlements Programme (UN-HABITAT)
USA/US	United States of America/United States
US$	United States Dollar
USEPA	United States Environmental Protection Agency
VDP	[WBG] Voluntary Disclosure Program
VRA	Volta River Authority
VSIP	Voluntary Settlement Implementation Plan
WAGP	West African Gas Pipeline Project (Nigeria/Ghana)
WAPCo	West African Gas Pipeline Company Limited (project implementing agency, *Nigeria/Ghana: West African Gas Pipeline*)
WB	World Bank (consisting of IBRD and IDA)
	Also see WBG
WBG	World Bank Group (consisting of IBRD, IDA, IFC, ICSID and MIGA)
	Also see WB

| WNB | West New Britain (Papua New Guinea province) |
| XISS | Xavier Institute of Social Service (implementing NGO, *India: Coal Sector*) |

REFERENCES

BOOKS AND ARTICLES

Abbott, K.W., Keohane, R.O., Moravcsik, A., Slaughter, A. & Snidal, D. (2001). 'The Concept of Legalization', *in* Goldstein, J., Kahler, M., Keohane, R.O. & Slaughter A. (Eds.), *Legalization and World Politics*, Cambridge, Mass.: MIT Press, 17

Ahmad, Q.K. (1996). 'On Sustainable Development and All That', 3 *Brown Journal of World Affairs* 2, 205

Allott, P. (1999). 'The Concept of International Law', 10 *European Journal of International Law* 36

Allott, P. (2001). *Eunomia: New Order for a New World*, 2nd Edn., New York: Oxford University Press

Alston, P. (Ed.) (2005). *Non-State Actors and Human Rights*, Oxford: Oxford University Press

Alvarez, J. (2005). *International Organizations as Law-Makers*, Oxford: Oxford University Press

Alvarez, J. (2007). *International Organizations: Accountability or Responsibility?*, Ottawa: Canadian Council of International Law, 121

Ananthanarayanan, S. (2004). 'A Crippled Inspection Panel', *India Together*, available at: http://www.indiatogether.org/2004/jul/hrt-wbinspect.htm

Anderson, V. & Johnson, L. (1997). *Systems Thinking Basics: From Concepts to Casual Loops*, Waltham: Pegasus Communications Inc.

Arsanjani, H. (1981). 'Claims Against International Organizations: Quis Custodiet Ipsos Custodies', 7 *Yale Journal of World Public Order*, 131

Baimu, E. & Panou, A. (2011). 'Responsibility of International Organizations and the World Bank Inspection Panel: Parallel Tracks Unlikely to Converge?', *in* Cissé, H., Bradlow,

D.D., Kingsbury B. (Eds.), *The World Bank Legal Review: International Financial Institutions and Global Legal Governance*, Washington, D.C.: World Bank, 147

Bass, S. (2004). *Prior Confirmed Consent and Mining, Promoting Sustainable Development of Local Communities*, Washington, D.C.: Environmental Law Institute

Berger, T.R. (1993-1994). 'The World Bank's Independent Review of India's Sardar Sarovar Projects', 9 *American University Journal of International Law & Policy* 1, 33

Beyerlin, U. (2007). 'Different Types of Norms in International Environmental Law: Policies, Principles, and Rules', *in* Bodansky, D., Brunnée, J. & Hey, E. (Eds.), *The Oxford Handbook of International Environmental Law*, Oxford: Oxford University Press, 425

Birnie, P. & Byole, A. (2002). *International Law and the Environment*, 2nd Edn., Oxford: Oxford University Press

Bissell, R.E. (1997). 'Recent Practice of the Inspection Panel of the World Bank', 91 *The American Journal of International Law* 4, 741

Bissell, R.E. (2001). 'Institutional and Procedural Aspects of the Inspection Panel', *in* Alfredsson, G. & Ring, R. (Eds.), *The Inspection Panel of the World Bank: A Different Complaints Procedure*, The Hague: Kluwer Law International, 107

Bissell, R.E. (2002). 'An Inspection Mechanism for the EBRD?', 13 *Newsletter of the CEE Bankwatch Network on International Financial Flows*, 2

Bissell, R.E. & Nanwani, S. (2009). 'Multilateral Development Bank Accountability Mechanisms: Developments and Challenges', 6 *Manchester Journal of International Economic Law* 1, 2

Boisson de Chazournes, L. (2000). 'Policy Guidance and Compliance: The World Bank Operational Standards, *in* Shelton, D. (Ed.), *Commitment and Compliance*, Oxford: Oxford University Press, 281

Boisson de Chazournes, L. (2001). 'Compliance with Operational Standards – The Contribution of the World Bank Inspection Panel', *in* Alfredsson, G. & Ring, R. (Eds.), *The Inspection Panel of the World Bank: A Different Complaints Procedure*, The Hague: Martinus Nijhoff Publishers, 67

Boisson de Chazournes, L. (2005). 'The World Bank Inspection Panel: About Public Participation and Dispute Settlement', *in* Treves, T., Frigessi di Rattalma, M., Tanzi, A., Fodella, A., Pitea, C. & Ragni, C. (Eds.), *Civil Society, International Courts and Compliance Bodies*, The Hague: T.M.C. Asser Press, 187

Boisson de Chazournes, L., Romano, C. & Mackenzie, R. (Eds.) (2002). *International Organizations and International Dispute Settlement: Trends and Prospects*, New York: Transnational Publishers, Inc.

Boix Mansilla, B. (2010). 'Learning to Synthesize: The Development of Interdisciplinary Understanding', *in* Frodeman et al. (Eds.), *The Oxford Handbook of Interdisciplinarity*, Oxford: Oxford University Press, 288

Bosshard, P., Bruil, J., Horta, K., Lawrence, S. & Welch, C. (2003). *Gambling with People's Lives: What the World Bank's New "High Risk/High-Reward" Strategy Means for the Poor and the Environment*, Environmental Defense, Friends of the Earth and International Rivers Network, available at: http://siteresources.worldbank.org/CSO/Resources/EDhigh-risk.pdf

Bottelier, P. (2001). 'Was World Bank Support for the Qinghai Anti-Poverty Project in China Ill-Considered?' 5 *Harvard Asia Quarterly* 1, 1

Bradlow, D.D. (1996). 'A Test Case for the World Bank', 11 *American University Journal of International Law & Policy* 2, 247

Bradlow, D.D. (1999). 'Precedent-Setting NGO Campaign Saves the World Bank's Inspection Panel', 6 *Human Rights Brief* 3, 7

Bradlow, D.D. (2000-2001). 'Lessons from the NGO Campaign against the Second Review of the World Bank Inspection Panel: A Participant's Perspective', 7 *ILSA Journal of International & Comparative Law*, 247

Bradlow, D.D. (2010). 'International Law and the Operations of the International Financial Institutions', *in* Bradlow, D.D. & Hunter, D.B. (Eds.), *International Financial Institutions and International Law*, Alphen aan den Rijn: Kluwer Law International, 1

Bradlow, D.D. (2011). 'The Reform of the Governance of the IFIs: A Critical Assessment', *in* Cissé, H., Bradlow, D.D., Kingsbury B. (Eds.), *The World Bank Legal Review: Interna-*

tional Financial Institutions and Global Legal Governance, Washington, D.C.: World Bank, 37

Bradlow, D.D. & Chapman, M.S. (2011). 'Public Participation and the Private Sector: The Role of Multilateral Development Banks in the Evolution of International Legal Standards', 2 *Erasmus Law Review* 2, 91

Bradlow, D.D. & Grossman, C. (1995). 'Limited Mandates and Intertwined Problems: A New Challenge for the World Bank and the IMF', 17 *Human Rights Quarterly*, 411

Bradlow, D.D. & Hunter, D.B. (2010). 'The Future of International Law and International Financial Institutions', *in* Bradlow, D.D. & Hunter, D.B. (Eds.), *International Financial Institutions and International Law*, Alphen aan den Rijn: Kluwer Law International, 387

Bradlow, D.D. & Naudé Fourie, A. (2011). 'Independent Accountability Mechanisms at Regional Development Banks', *in* Hale, T. & Held, D. (Eds.), *Handbook of Transitional Governance: New Institutions and Innovations*, Cambridge: Polity Press

Bradlow, D.D. & Naudé Fourie, A. (2013). 'The Operational Policies of the World Bank and the International Finance Corporation Creating Law-Making and Law-Governed Institutions?', 10 *International Organizations Law Review*, 3

Brand, O. (2007). 'Conceptual Comparisons: Towards a Coherent Methodology of Comparative Legal Studies', 32 *Brook Journal of International Law* 2, 405

Brett, E.A. (2003). 'Participation and Accountability in Development Management', 40 *The Journal of Development Studies* 2, 1

Brewer, G. (1999). 'The Challenges of Interdisciplinarity', 32 *Policy Sciences*, 327

Bridgeman, N.L. (2001). 'World Bank Reform in the "Post-Policy" Era', 13 *Georgetown International Environmental Law Review*, 1013

Brown Weiss, E. (1987). 'Intergenerational Equity in International Law', 81 *American Society of International Law Proceedings*, 126

Brown Weiss, E. (2010). 'On Being Accountable in a Kaleidoscopic World', 104 *American Society of International Law Proceedings*, 477

Brunnée, J. & Toope, S. (2010). *Legitimacy and Legality in International Law: An Interactional Account*, Cambridge: Cambridge University Press

Carrasco, E.R. & Guernsey, A.K. (2008). 'The World Bank's Inspection Panel: Promoting True Accountability Through Arbitration', 41 *Cornell International Law Journal*, 577

Chesterman, S. (2008)(a). 'An International Rule of Law?', 56 *American Journal of Comparative Law*, 331

Chesterman, S. (2008)(b). 'Globalization Rules: Accountability, Power, and the Prospects for Global Administrative Law', 14 *Global Governance*, 39

Chimni, B.S. (2005). 'Co-option and Resistance: Two Faces of Global Administrative Law', 37 *New York University Journal of International Law and Politics*, 799

Chimni, B.S. (2010). 'International Financial Institutions and International Law: A Third World Perspective', *in* Bradlow, D.D. & Hunter, D.B. (Eds.), *International Financial Institutions and International Law*, Alphen aan den Rijn: Kluwer Law International, 31

Chinkin, C. (2000). 'Normative Development in the International Legal System', *in* Shelton, D. (Ed.), *Commitment and Compliance: The Role of Non-Binding Norms in the International Legal System*, Oxford: Oxford University Press, 21

Circi, M. (2006). 'The World Bank Inspection Panel: Is It Really Effective?', 6 *Global Jurist Advances* 3, 1

Cissé, H., Bradlow, D.D. & Kingsbury B. (Eds.) (2011). *The World Bank Legal Review: International Financial Institutions and Global Legal Governance*, Washington, D.C.: World Bank

Clark, D. (2002). 'The World Bank and Human Rights: The Need for Greater Accountability', 15 *Harvard Human Rights Journal*, 206

Clark, D., Fox, J. & Treakle, K. (Eds.) (2003). *Demanding Accountability: Civil-Society Claims and the World Bank Inspection Panel*, Oxford: Rowman & Littlefield Publishers Inc.

Clark, D. & Treakle, K. (2003). 'The China Western Poverty Reduction Project', *in* Clark, D., Fox, J. & Treakle, K. (Eds.) (2003). *Demanding Accountability: Civil-Society Claims and the World Bank Inspection Panel*, Oxford: Rowman & Littlefield Publishers Inc., 211

Coicaud, J. & Heiskanen, V. (Eds.) (2001). *The Legitimacy of International Organizations*, New York: United Nations University Press

Conklin, J. (2005). *Wicked Problems and Social Complexity*, available at: http://cognexus.org/wpf/wickedproblems.pdf

Crawford, J. (2007). 'Holding International Organisations and Their Members to Account', Fifth Steinkraus-Cohen International Law Lecture', available at: http://www.unawestminster.org.uk/pdf/crawford_lecture.pdf

Cronin, P. (2014). *Herzog on Herzog*, London: Faber & Faber

Curtin, D. & Nollkaemper, A. (2005). 'Conceptualizing Accountability in International and European Law', 36 *Netherlands Yearbook of International Law*, 3

D'Aspremont, J. (2011). *Formalism and the Sources of International Law: A Theory of the Ascertainment of Legal Rules*, Oxford: Oxford University Press

Danaher, K. (Ed.) (1994). *50 Years is Enough: The Case Against the World Bank and the International Monetary Fund*, USA: South End Press

Darrow, M. (2006). *Between Light and Shadow: The World Bank, the International Monetary Fund and International Human Rights Law*, Portland, Oregon: Hart Publishing

Dekker, I. (2010). 'Accountability of International Organisations: An Evolving Legal Concept?', *in* Wouters, J., Brems, E., Smis, S. & Schmitt, P. (Eds.), *Accountability for Human Rights Violations by International Organisations*, Antwerp: Intersentia, 21

De Schutter, O. (2010). 'Human Rights and the Rise of International Organisations: The Logic of Sliding Scales in the Law of International Resonsibility', *in* Wouters, J., Brems, E., Smis, S. & Schmitt, P. (Eds.), *Accountability for Human Rights Violations by International Organisations*, Antwerp: Intersentia, 51

De Wet, E. (2006). 'The International Constitutional Order', 55 *International and Comparative Law Quarterly*, 51

De Wet, E. (2010). 'Holding International Institutions Accountable: The Complementary Role of Non-Judicial Oversight Mechanisms and Judicial Review', *in* Von Bogdandy, A., Wolfrum, R., Von Bernstorff, J., Dann, P. & Goldmann, M. (Eds.), *The Exercise of Public Authority by International Institutions: Advancing International Institutional Law*, Heidelberg: Springer, 855

Di Leva, C.E. (2010). 'International Environmental Law, the World Bank, and International Financial Institutions', *in* Bradlow, D.D. & Hunter, D.B. (Eds.), *International Financial Institutions and International Law*, Alphen aan den Rijn: Kluwer Law International, 343

Dowdle, M.W. (Ed.) (2006). *Public Accountability: Designs, Dilemmas and Experiences*, Cambridge: Cambridge University Press

Dunkerton, K. J. (1995). 'The World Bank Inspection Panel and Its Affect on Lending Accountability to Citizens of Borrowing Nations', 5 *Journal of Environmental Law*, 226

Dunoff, J.L. & Trachtman, J.P. (Eds.) (2009). *Ruling the World? Constitutionalism, International Law, and Global Governance*, Cambridge: Cambridge University Press

Ebbesson, J. (2007). 'Public Participation', *in* Bodansky, D., Brunnée, J. & Hey, E. (Eds.), *The Oxford Handbook of International Environmental Law*, Oxford: Oxford University Press, 681

Ebrahim, A. (2003). 'Accountability In Practice: Mechanisms for NGOs', 31 *World Development* 5, 813

Ebrahim, A. (2007). 'Towards a Reflective Accountability in NGOs', *in* Ebrahim, A. & Weisband, E. (Eds.), *Global Accountabilities: Participation, Pluralism, and Public Ethics*, Cambridge: Cambridge University Press, 193

Fassbender B. (1998). 'The United Nations Charter as Constitution of the International Community', 36 *Columbia Journal of Transnational Law*, 529

Fox, J. (1997). 'Transparency for Accountability: Civil-Society Monitoring of Multilateral Development Bank Anti-Poverty', 7 *Development in Practice* 2, 167

Fox, J. (2000). 'The World Bank Inspection Panel: Lessons from the First Five Years', 6 *Global Governance*, 279

Frank, T.M. (1995). *Fairness in International Law and Institutions*, Oxford: Oxford University Press

Freestone, D. (2003). 'The Environmental and Social Safeguard Policies of the World Bank and the Evolving Role of the Inspection Panel', *in* Bodansky, D. & Freestone, D. (Eds.), *Economic Globalization and Compliance with International Environmental Agreements*, Alphen aan den Rijn: Kluwer Law International, 144

French, H.F. (1994). 'The World Bank: Now Fifty, but How Fit?', 7 *World Watch* 10, 1

Freestone, D. (2013). *The World Bank and Sustainable Development*, Leiden: Martinus Nijhoff Publishers

Fuentes, X. (2002). 'International Law-Making in the Field of Sustainable Development: The Unequal Competition Between Development and the Environment', 2 *International Environmental Agreements: Politics, Law and Economics*, 109

Gerber, D.J. (1998). 'Toward a Language of Comparative Law?', 46 *American Journal of Comparative Law*, 719

Goldmann, M. (2010). 'Inside Relative Normativity: From Sources to Standard Instruments for the Exercise of International Public Authority', *in* Von Bogdandy, A., Wolfrum, R., Von Bernstorff, J., Dann, P. & Goldmann, M. (Eds.), *The Exercise of Public Authority by International Institutions: Advancing International Institutional Law*, Heidelberg: Springer, 661

Gowlland Gualtieri, A. (2001). 'The Environmental Accountability of the World Bank to Non-State Actors: Insights from the Inspection Panel', 72 *British Yearbook of International Law* 1, 213

Grant, R.W. & Keohane, R.O. (2005). 'Accountability and Abuses of Power in World Politics', 99 *American Political Science Review* 1, 29

Graziano, A. & Raulin, M. (2013). *Research Methods: A Process of Inquiry*, 8th Edn., Upper Saddle River, N.J.: Pearson

Guadalope Moog Rodrigues, M. (2003). 'The Planafloro Inspection Panel Claim: Opportunities and Challenges for Civil Society in Rondônia, Brazil', *in* Clark, D., Fox, J. & Treakle,

K. (Eds.) (2003). *Demanding Accountability: Civil-Society Claims and the World Bank Inspection Panel*, Oxford: Rowman & Littlefield Publishers Inc., 45

Habermas, J. (1998). *Die Postnationale Konstellation*, Frankfurt am Main: Suhrkamp Verlag

Hachez, N. & Wouters, J. (2012). 'A Responsible Lender? The European Investment Bank's Environmental, Social and Human Rights Accountability', 49 *Common Market Review*, 47

Hale, T.N. (2008). "Info-Courts' and the Accountability of International Organizations: Evidence from the World Bank Inspection Panel', *From Fragmentation to Unity? IV Global Administrative Law Seminar Viterbo*, June 13-14, 2008, available at: http://www.iilj. org/gal/documents/Hale.pdf

Hale, T.N. & Slaughter, A. (2006). 'Transparency: Possibilities and Limitations', 30 *Fletcher Forum* 1, 153

Handke, S. & Hey, E. (2013). 'Climate Change Negotiations in a Changing Global Energy Landscape: A Wicked Problem', 2 *ESIL Reflections* 7, 1

Handl, G. (1998), 'The Legal Mandate of Multilateral Development Banks as Agents for Change toward Sustainable Development', 92 *American Journal of International Law*, 642

Hansungule, M. (2001). 'Access to Panel – The Notion of Affected Party, Issues of Collective and Material Interest', *in* Alfredsson, G. & Ring, R. (Eds.), *The Inspection Panel of the World Bank: A Different Complaints Procedure*, The Hague: Martinus Nijhoff Publishers, 143

Harlow, C. (2011). 'Accountability as a Value for Global Governance and Global Administrative Law', *in* Anthony, G., Auby, J., Morison, J. & Zwart, T. (Eds.), *Values in Global Administrative Law*, Oxford: Hart Publishing, 173

Head, J.W. (2003-2004). 'For Richer or For Poorer: Assessing the Criticisms Directed at the Multilateral Development Banks', 52 *The University of Kansas Law Review*, 241

Henkin, L. (1979). *How Nations Behave*. New York, NY.: Columbia University Press

Hernández Uriz, G. (2001). 'To Lend or Not To Lend: Oil, Human Rights, and the World Bank's Internal Contradictions', 14 *Harvard Human Rights Journal*, 197

Herz, S. (2010). 'Rethinking International Financial Institution Immunity', *in* Bradlow, D.D. & Hunter, D.B. (Eds.), *International Financial Institutions and International Law*, Alphen aan den Rijn: Kluwer Law International, 137

Hey, E. (1997). 'The World Bank Inspection Panel: Towards the Recognition of a New Legally Relevant Relationship in International Law', 2 *Hofstra Law & Policy Symposium*, 61

Higgins, R. (1994). *Problems and Process: International Law and How We Use It*, Oxford: Oxford University Press

Hirsch Hadorn, G., Pohl, C. & Bammer, G. (2010). 'Solving Problems through Transdisciplinary Research', *in* Frodeman et al. (Eds.), *The Oxford Handbook of Interdisciplinarity*, Oxford: Oxford University Press, 431

Horta, K. (2002). 'Rhetoric and Reality: Human Rights and the World Bank', 15 *Harvard Human Rights Journal*, 227

Hunter, D. (2003). 'Using the World Bank Inspection Panel to Defend the Interests of Project-Affected People', 4 *Chicago Journal of International Law* 1, 201

Hunter D.B. (2010). 'International Law and Public Participation in Policy-Making at the International Financial Institutions', *in* Bradlow D.D. & Hunter D.B. (Eds.), *International Financial Institutions and International Law*, Alphen aan den Rijn: Kluwer Law International, 199

Huq Dulu, M. (2003). 'The Experience of Jamuna Bridge: Issues and Perspectives', *in* Clark, D., Fox, J. & Treakle, K. (Eds.), *Demanding Accountability: Civil-Society Claims and the World Bank Inspection Panel*, Oxford: Rowman & Littlefield Publishers Inc., 93

Josselin, D. & Wallace, W. (Eds.) (2001). *Non-State Actors in World Politics*, New York: Palgrave Publishers Ltd.

Kamminga, M.T. (2005). 'The Evolving Status of NGOs under International Law: A Threat to the Inter-State System?', *in* Alston, P. (Ed.), *Non-State Actors and Human Rights*, Oxford: Oxford University Press, 93

Keohane, R.O. (1997). 'Comment, International Relations and International Law: Two Optics', 38 *Harvard International Law Journal*, 494

Keohane, R.O. (2003). 'Global Governance and Democratic Accountability', *in* Held, D. & Koenig-Archibugi M. (Eds.), *Taming Globalization: Frontiers of Governance*, Cambridge: Polity Press, 130

Kingsbury, B. (1997-1998). 'The Concept of Compliance as a Function of Competing Conceptions of International Law', 19 *Michigan Journal of International Law*, 345

Kingsbury, B. (1999). 'Operational Policies of International Institutions as Part of the Law-Making Process: The World Bank and Indigenous Peoples', *in* Goodwin-Gill, G.S. & Talmon, S. (Eds.), *The Reality of International Law: Essays in Honour of Ian Brownlie*, Oxford: Oxford University Press

Kingsbury, B. (2009). 'The Concept of 'Law' in Global Administrative Law', 20 *The European Journal of International Law* 1, 23

Kingsbury, B. (2011). 'Global Administrative Law in the Institutional Practice of Global Regulatory Governance', *in* Cissé, H., Bradlow, D.D., Kingsbury B. (Eds.), *The World Bank Legal Review: International Financial Institutions and Global Legal Governance*, Washington, D.C.: World Bank, 3

Kingsbury, B., Krisch, N. & Stewart, R.B. (2005). 'The Emergence of Global Administrative Law', 68 *Law and Contemporary Problems*, 15

Klabbers, J. (2009). 'Setting the Scene', *in* Klabbers, J. Peters, A. & Ulfstein G., *The Constitutionalization of International Law*, Oxford: Oxford University Press, 12

Klabbers, J. (2013). *International Law*, Cambridge: Cambridge University Press

Koh, H.H. (1996). 'Transnational Legal Process', 75 *Nebraska Law Review*, 181

Koskenniemi, M. (2006). 'What is International Law For?', *in* Evans, M.D. (Ed.), 2nd Edn., *International Law*, Oxford: Oxford University Press, 57

Kratochwil, F. (1989). *Rules, Norms, and Decisions: On the Conditions of Practical and Legal Reasoning in International Relations and Domestic Affairs*, Cambridge: Cambridge University Press

Krisch, N. (2006). 'The Pluralism of Global Administrative Law', 17 *The European Journal of International Law* 1, 247

Krisch, N. (2010). *Beyond Constitutionalism: The Pluralist Structure of Postnational Law*, Oxford: Oxford University Press

Kumm, M. (2004). 'The Legitimacy of International Law: A Constitutionalist Framework of Analysis', 15 *The European Journal of International Law* 5, 907

Kuo, M. (2008-2009). 'Between Fragmentation and Unity: The Uneasy Relationship Between Global Administrative Law and Global Constitutionalism', 10 *San Diego International Law Journal*, 439

Kuo, M. (2011-2012). 'Taming Governance with Legality? Critical Reflections Upon Global Administrative Law as Small-C Global Constitutionalism', 44 *New York University Journal of International Law & Policy*, 55

MacKay, F. (2005). 'The Draft World Bank Operational Policy 4.10 on Indigenous Peoples: Progress or More of the Same?', 22 *Arizona Journal of International & Comparative Law* 1, 65

MacKay, F. (2010). 'Indigenous Peoples and International Financial Institutions', *in* Bradlow, D.D. & Hunter, D.B. (Eds.), *International Financial Institutions and International Law*, Alphen aan den Rijn: Kluwer Law International, 287

Magraw, D.B. & Hawke, L.D. (2007). 'Sustainable Development', *in* Bodanksy, D., Brunnée, J. & Hey, E., (Eds.), *The Oxford Handbook of International Environmental Law*, Oxford: Oxford University Press, 613

Mallaby, S. (2004)(a). 'NGOs: Fighting Poverty, Hurting the Poor', 144 *Foreign Policy*, 50

Mallaby, S. (2004)(b). *The World's Banker: A Story of Failed States, Financial Crises, and the Wealth and Poverty of Nations*, New York: The Penguin Press

Maxwell, J. (2009). 'Designing a Qualitative Study', *in* Bickman, L. & Rog, D. (Eds.), *The Sage Handbook of Applied Social Research Methods*, 2nd Edn., Thousand Oaks, CA: SAGE Publications Inc., 222

McInerney-Lankford, S. (2010). 'International Financial Institutions and Human Rights: Select Perspectives on Legal Obligations', *in* Bradlow, D.D. & Hunter, D.B. (Eds.), *International Financial Institutions and International Law*, Alphen aan den Rijn: Kluwer Law International, 239

Miller-Adams, M. (1999). *The World Bank: New Agendas in a Changing World*, London: Routledge

Morison, J. & Anthony, G. (2011). 'The Place of Public Interest', *in* Anthony, G., Auby, J., Morison, J. & Zwart, T. (Eds.), *Values in Global Administrative Law*, Oxford: Hart Publishing, 215

Morrison, J. & Roth-Arriaza, N. (2007). 'Private and Quasi-Private Standard Setting', *in* Bodansky, D., Brunnée, J. & Hey, E. (Eds.), *The Oxford Handbook of International Environmental Law*, Oxford: Oxford University Press, 498

Mulgan, R. (2000), "Accountability': An Ever-expanding Concept?', 78 *Public Administration* 3, 555

Nanda, V.P. (2004-2005). 'Accountability of International Organizations: Some Observations', 33 *Denver Journal of International Law & Policy* 3, 379

Nanwani, S. (2008). 'Holding Multilateral Development Banks to Account: Gateways and Barriers', 10 *International Community Law Review*, 199

Nathan, K. (1995). 'The World Bank Inspection Panel: Court or Quango?', 12 *Journal of International Arbitration*, 135

Naudé Fourie, A. (2009). *The World Bank Inspection Panel and Quasi-Judicial Oversight: In Search of the 'Judicial Spirit' in Public International Law*, Utrecht: Eleven International Publishing

Naudé Fourie, A. (2012). 'The World Bank Inspection Panel's Normative Potential: A Critical Assessment, And A Restatement', LIX *Netherlands International Law Review*, 199

Naudé Fourie, A. (2014). *The World Bank Inspection Panel Casebook*, The Hague: Eleven International Publishing

Naudé Fourie, A. (2015). 'Expounding the Place of Legal Doctrinal Methods in Legal-Interdisciplinary Research: Experiences with Studying the Practice of Independent Accountability Mechanisms at Multilateral Development Banks', 8 *Erasmus Law Review* 3, 95

Nurmukhametova, E. (2006). 'Problems in Connection with the Efficiency of the World Bank Inspection Panel', 10 *Max Planck Yearbook of United Nations Law,* 397

Oleschak-Pillai, R. (2010). 'Accountability of International Organisations: An Analysis of the World Bank's Inspection Panel', *in* Wouters, J., Brems, E., Smis, S. & Schmitt, P. (Eds.), *Accountability for Human Rights Violations by International Organisations,* Antwerp: Intersentia, 406

Orakhelashvili, A. (2005). 'The World Bank Inspection Panel in Context: Institutional Aspect of the Accountability of International Organizations', 2 *International Organizations Law Review,* 57

Orford, A. (Ed.) (2006). *International Law and Its Others,* Cambridge: Cambridge University Press

Paul, S. (1994). 'Does Voice Matter? For Public Accountability, Yes', *The World Bank Policy Research Department,* Policy Research Working Paper 1388, available at: http://go.worldbank.org/5JAMY5ZWR0

Phillips, D.A. (2009). *Reforming the World Bank: Twenty Years of Trial – and Error,* Cambridge: Cambridge University Press

Powers, W. (1973). 'Feedback: Beyond Behaviorism', 179 *Science,* 351

Raffer, K. (2004). 'International Financial Institutions and Financial Accountability', 18 *Ethics & International Affairs* 2, 61

Reinisch, A. (2001). 'Securing the Accountability of International Organizations', 7 *Global Governance,* 131

Reinisch, A. (2005). 'The Changing International Legal Framework for Dealing with Non-State Actors', *in* Alston, P. (Ed.), *Non-State Actors and Human Rights,* Oxford: Oxford University Press, 37

Reinisch, A. (2008). *International Organizations Before National Courts*, Cambridge: Cambridge University Press

Reinisch, A. & Wurm, J. (2010). 'International Financial Institutions before National Courts', *in* Bradlow, D.D. & Hunter, D.B. (Eds.), *International Financial Institutions and International Law*, Alphen aan den Rijn: Kluwer Law International, 103

Rittel, H.W.J. & Webber, M.M. (1973). 'Dilemmas in a General Theory of Planning', 4 *Policy Sciences* 2, 155

Röben, V. (2010). 'The Enforcement Authority of International Institutions', *in* Von Bogdandy, A., Wolfrum, R., Von Bernstorff, J., Dann, P. & Goldmann, M. (Eds.), *The Exercise of Public Authority by International Institutions: Advancing International Institutional Law*, Heidelberg: Springer, 819

Romano, C.P.R. (2011). 'A Taxonomy of International Rule of Law Institutions', 2 *Journal of International Dispute Settlement* 1, 241

Roos, S.R. (2001). 'The World Bank Inspection Panel in its Seventh Year: An Analysis of its Process, Mandate, and Desirability with Special Reference to the China (Tibet) Case', 5 *Max Planck Yearbook of United Nations Law*, 473

Rubenstein, J. (2007). 'Accountability in an Unequal World', 69 *The Journal of Politics* 3, 616

Sarfaty, G.A. (2005). 'The World Bank and the Internalization of Indigenous Rights Norms', 114 *Yale Law Journal* 7, 1791

Schermers, H.G. & Blokker, N.M. (2003). *International Institutional Law: Unity Within Diversity*, 4th Edn, Boston/Leiden: Martinus Nijhoff Publishers

Schlemmer-Schulte, S. (1999). 'The World Bank Inspection Panel: A Record of the First International Accountability Mechanism and Its Role for Human Rights', 6 *Human Rights Brief* 2, 1

Schlemmer-Schulte, S. (2001). 'The Inspection Panel's Case Law', *in* Alfredsson, G. & Ring, R. (Eds.), *The Inspection Panel of the World Bank: A Different Complaints Procedure*, The Hague: Martinus Nijhoff Publishers, 87

Scobbie, I. (2006). 'Wicked Heresies or Legitimate Perspectives? Theory and International Law', *in* Evans, M.D. (Ed.), 2nd Edn., *International Law*, Oxford: Oxford University Press, 83

Scott, C. (2000). 'Accountability in the Regulatory State', 27 *Journal of Legal Studies* 1, 38

Shaffer, G. (2012). 'A Transnational Take on Krisch's Pluralist Postnational Law', 23 *European Journal of International Law* 2, 565

Shany, Y. (2010). 'Assessing the Effectiveness of International Courts: Can the Unquantifiable be Quantified?', *University of Jerusalem Law Faculty International Law Forum Research Paper* 03-10, available at: http://papers.ssrn.com/sol3/papers.cfm?abstract_id=1669954

Shapiro, M. & Stone Sweet, A. (2002). *On Law, Politics, and Judicialization*, Oxford: Oxford University Press

Shelton, D. (1997). 'Compliance with International Human Rights Soft Law', 29 *Studies in Transnational Legal Policy*, 119

Shelton, D. (2000). 'Law, Non-Law and the Problem of 'Soft Law'', *in* Shelton, D. (Ed.), *Commitment and Compliance*, Oxford: Oxford University Press, 1

Shelton, D. (2006). 'International Law and 'Relative Normativity'', *in* Evans, M.D. (Ed.), 2nd Edn., *International Law*, Oxford: Oxford University Press, 159

Shields, M. & Rangarajan, N. (2013). *A Playbook for Research Methods: Integrating Conceptual Frameworks and Project Management*, Stillwater, OK: New Forums Press

Shihata, I.F.I (1988-1989). 'The World Bank and Human Rights: An Analysis of the Legal Issues and the Record of Achievements', 17 *Denver Journal of International Law & Policy*, 39

Shihata, I.F.I. (1992-1993). 'Human Rights, Development, and International Financial Institutions', 8 *American University Journal of International Law & Policy*, 27

Shihata, I.F.I. (2000). *The World Bank Inspection Panel: In Practice*, New York: Oxford University Press

Shihata, I.F.I. (2001). 'The World Bank Inspection Panel – Its Historical, Legal and Operational Aspects', *in* Alfredsson, G. & Ring, R. (Eds.), *The Inspection Panel of the World Bank: A Different Complaints Procedure*, The Hague: Martinus Nijhoff Publishers, 7

Siems, M. (2009). 'The Taxonomy of Interdisciplinary Legal Research: Finding a Way Out of the Desert', 7 *Journal of Commonwealth Law and Legal Education* 1

Slaughter, A. (2000). 'International Law and International Relations', 285 *Recueil des Cours* 12, 37

Sterman, J.D. (2000). *Business Dynamics: Systems Thinking and Modeling for a Complex World*, McGraw-Hill Higher Education

Stone Sweet, A. (1999). 'Judicialization and the Construction of Governance', 32 *Comparative Political Studies* 2, 147

Suzuki, E. (2010). 'Responsibility of International Financial Institutions under International Law', *in* Bradlow, D.D. & Hunter, D.B. (Eds.), *International Financial Institutions and International Law*, Alphen aan den Rijn: Kluwer Law International, 63

Suzuki, E. & Nanwani, S. (2005-2006). 'Responsibility of International Organizations: The Accountability Mechanisms of Multilateral Development Banks', *Michigan Journal of International Law* 27, 177

Swepston, L. (2001). 'ILO Supervision and the World Bank Inspection Panel', *in* Alfredsson, G. & Ring, R. (Eds.), *The Inspection Panel of the World Bank: A Different Complaints Procedure*, The Hague: Kluwer Law International, 249

Taleb, N.N. (2014). *Antifragile: Things that Gain from Disorder*, New York: Random House

Teubner, G. (1993). 'Substantive and Reflexive Elements in Modern Law', 17 *Law and Society Review* 2 17, 239

Thompson Klein, J. (2000), 'A Conceptual Vocabulary of Interdisciplinary Science', *in* Weingart, P. & Stehr, N. (Eds.), *Practicing Interdisciplinarity*, Toronto: University of Toronto Press, 3

Toope, S. (2007). 'Formality and Informality', *in* Bodanksy, D., Brunnée, J. & Hey, E., (Eds.), *The Oxford Handbook of International Environmental Law*, Oxford: Oxford University Press, 107

Treakle, K. & Díaz Peña, E. (2003). 'Accountability at the World Bank: What Does It Take? Lessons from the Yacyretá Hydroelectric Project, Argentina/Paraguay', *in* Clark, D., Fox, J. & Treakle, K. (Eds.), *Demanding Accountability: Civil-Society Claims and the World Bank Inspection Panel*, Oxford: Rowman & Littlefield Publishers Inc., 69

Treves, T., Frigessi di Rattalma, M., Tanzi, A., Fodella, A., Pitea, C. & Ragni, C. (Eds.) (2005). *Civil Society, International Courts and Compliance Bodies*, The Hague: T.M.C. Asser Press

Umaña, A. (Ed.) (1998). *The World Bank Inspection Panel: The First Four Years*, Washington, D.C.: The World Bank

Umaña, A. (2001). 'Some Lessons from the Inspection Panel's Experience', *in* Alfredsson, G. & Ring, R. (Eds.), *The Inspection Panel of the World Bank: A Different Complaints Procedure*, The Hague: Kluwer Law International, 127

Undall, L. (1994). 'The Arun III Dam: A Test Case in World Bank Accountability', 26 *Bulletin of Concerned Asian Scholars*, 82

Van Klink, B. & Taekema, S. (Eds.) (2011). *Law and Method: Interdisciplinary Research Into Law*, Tübingen: Mohr Siebeck

Van Putten, M. (2008). *Policing the Banks: Accountability Mechanisms for the Financial Sector*, Montreal: McGill-Queen's University Press

Versi, A. (1994). 'Is the World Bank Deaf?' *African Business* 192, 8

Vianna, A. (2003). 'The Inspection Panel Claims in Brazil', *in* Clark, D., Fox, J. & Treakle, K. (Eds.), *Demanding Accountability: Civil-Society Claims and the World Bank Inspection Panel*, Oxford: Rowman & Littlefield Publishers Inc., 145

Vick, D.W. (2004). 'Interdisciplinarity and the Discipline of Law', 31 *Journal of Law and Society*, 163

Von Bogdandy, A., Dann, P. & Goldmann, M. (2010). 'Developing the Publicness of Public International Law: Towards a Legal Framework for Global Governance Activities', *in* Von Bogdandy, A., Wolfrum, R., Von Bernstorff, J., Dann, P. & Goldmann, M. (Eds.) *The Exercise of Public Authority by International Institutions: Advancing International Institutional Law*, Heidelberg: Springer, 3

Von Bogdandy, A., Wolfrum, R., Von Bernstorff, J., Dann, P. & Goldmann, M. (Eds.) (2010). *The Exercise of Public Authority by International Institutions: Advancing International Institutional Law*, Heidelberg: Springer

Wahi, N. (2005-2006). 'Human Rights Accountability of the IMF and the World Bank: A Critique of Existing Mechanisms and Articulation of a Theory of Horizontal Accountability', 12 *U.C. Davis Journal International Law and Policy*, 333

Weinberg, G.M. (1975). *An Introduction to General Systems Thinking*, New York: Dorset House Publishing

Wellens, K. (2002). *Remedies Against International Organisations*, Cambridge: Cambridge University Press

Winter, G.D. & Price, G. (2006). *Project Finance: A Legal Guide*, 3rd Edn., Sweet & Maxwell

Wirth, D.A. (2000). 'Commentary: Compliance with Non-Binding Norms of Trade and Finance', *in* Shelton, D. (Ed.), *Commitment and Compliance*, Oxford: Oxford University Press, 330

Woods, N. (2001). 'Making the IMF and the World Bank More Accountable', 77 *International Affairs* 1, 83

World Bank (2011). *A Guide to the World Bank*, 3rd Edn., Washington D.C.: World Bank

World Bank (2015). *The World Bank Group: From A to Z*, Washington, D.C.: World Bank

Zürn, M. (1999). 'The State in the Postnational Constellation – Societal Denationalization and Multi-Level Governance', *ARENA Working Papers*, WP 99/35, available at: http://www.arena.uio.no/publications/working-papers1999/papers/wp99_35.htm

Zweifel, T.D. (2006). *International Organizations & Democracy: Accountability, Politics, and Power*, Boulder, CO.: Lynne Rienner Publishers, Inc.

REPORTS, DECLARATIONS, RESOLUTIONS

Independent Accountability Mechanisms Network (2012). *Citizen-driven Accountability for Sustainable Development: Giving Affected People a Greater Voice – 20 Years On*, available at: http://ewebapps.worldbank.org/apps/ip/Pages/Home.aspx

Inspection Panel (1999/2000). *Annual Report*, Washington D.C.: World Bank, available at: http://go.worldbank.org/BKW26CG0V0

Inspection Panel (2011/2012). *Annual Report*, Washington D.C.: World Bank, available at: http://go.worldbank.org/BKW26CG0V0

Inspection Panel (2012). 'Submission to the World Bank's Safeguard Review and Update Process, The Inspection Panel, Lessons from Panel Cases: Inspection Panel Perspectives', available at: http://go.worldbank.org/QHT9YU3820

Inspection Panel (2013).'Risk and Accountability: What Role for the Inspection Panel?', *The Update – The World Bank Inspection Panel Newsletter* 6, April 2013, available at: http://go.worldbank.org/5R0P1T7WL0

Inspection Panel (2013/2014). *Annual Report*, Washington D.C.: World Bank, available at: http://go.worldbank.org/BKW26CG0V0

Inspection Panel (2014). The Inspection Panel at the World Bank, Operating Procedures, April 2014, available at: http://go.worldbank.org/C6MIJ7MIP0

International Law Association (1998). *Report of the Sixty Eighth Conference, Taipei*, available at: http://www.ila-hq.org/en/publications/order-reports.cfm

International Law Association (2004). *Report of the Seventy First Conference, Berlin*, available at: http://www.ila-hq.org/en/publications/order-reports.cfm

OECD (2005). *The Paris Declaration on Aid Effectiveness: Five Principle for Smart Aid*, available at: http://www.oecd.org/dac/effectiveness/45827300.pdf

United Nations (2002). *Human Development Report*, New York: Oxford University Press

World Bank (1992). Wapenhans, W., *Effective Implementation: Key to Development Impact*, (R92-125), available at: http://www-wds.worldbank.org/external/default/WDSContent Server/WDSP/IB/1992/09/22/000009265_3961003221227/Rendered/PDF/multi0page.pdf

World Bank (1993). *Portfolio Management: Next Steps, A Program of Action*, July 22, Washington D.C.: World Bank

World Bank (2014). *World Bank Group and World Bank Corporate Scorecard*, October 2014, Washington, D.C.: World Bank

WORLD BANK POLICIES AND PROCEDURES

OP/BP 3.10	Financial Terms and Conditions of IBRD Loans, IBRD Hedging Products, and IDA Credits
OP/BP 4.00	Piloting the Use of Borrower Systems to Address Environmental and Social Safeguard Issues in Bank- Supported Projects
OP/BP 4.01	Environmental Assessment
	Note: "OP, BP, and GP 4.01 together replace OMS 2.36, Environmental Aspects of Bank Work; OD 4.00, Annex A, Environmental Assessment; OD 4.00, Annex B, Environmental Policy for Dam and Reservoir Projects; OD 4.01, Environmental Assessment" (*See* OP 4.01, p. 1)
OP/BP 4.04	Natural Habitats
OP/BP 4.10	Indigenous Peoples
	Note: "OP and BP 4.10 together replace OD 4.20, *Indigenous Peoples*" (*See* OP 4.10, p. 1)
OP/BP 4.11	Physical Cultural Resources
	Note: OP/BP 4.11 "together replace OPN 11.03, *Management of Cultural Property in Bank-Financed Projects*, dated September 1986." (OP 4.11, p. 1)
OP/BP 4.12	Involuntary Resettlement
	Note: "OP and BP 4.12 together replace OD 4.30, *Involuntary Resettlement*" (*See* OP 4.12, p. 1)
OP/BP 4.36	Forests
	Note: "OP and BP 4.36, *Forests*, replace OP and GP 4.36, *Forestry*, dated September 1993" (*See* OP 4.36, p. 1)
OP/BP 4.37	Safety of Dams

OP/BP 8.60	Development Policy Lending
	Note: "OP and BP 8.60 together replace OD 8.60, *Adjustment Lending Policy*" (*See* OP 8.60, p. 1)
OP/BP 10.00	Investment Lending: Identification to Board Presentation
OP/BP 10.04	Economic Evaluation of Investment Operations
	Note: OP and BP 10.04 are complemented by OP/BP 10.00, *Investment Lending: Identification to Board Presentation*" (*See* OP 10.04, p. 1)
OP/BP 12.00	Disbursement
OP/BP 13.00	Signing of Legal Documents and Effectiveness of Loans and Credits
OP/BP 13.05	Project Supervision
OP/BP 13.40	Suspension of Disbursements
OP/BP 13.50	Cancellations
OP/BP 13.60	Monitoring and Evaluation
OP/BP 14.20	Cofinancing
GP 14.70	Involving Nongovernmental Organizations in Bank- Supported Activities, available at: http://web.worldbank.org/WBSITE/EXTERNAL/PROJECTS/EXTPOLICIES/EXTOPMANUAL/0,,content-MDK:20064711~menuPK:51508119~pagePK:64141683~piPK:4688102~theSitePK:502184,00.html
BP 17.55	Inspection Panel
	Annex A, Inspection Panel Resolution (Inspection Panel Resolution (1993). Resolution No. IBRD 93-10/Resolution No. IDA 93-6, *The World Bank Inspection Panel*, 22 September 1993)
	Annex B, Review of the Resolution Establishing the Inspection Panel: Clarification of Certain Aspects of the Resolution
	Annex C, Conclusions of the Board's Second Review of the Inspection Panel

INSPECTION PANEL REQUESTS

(in alphabetical order)

Albania: Integrated Coastal Zone Management and Clean-Up Project (2007)
Albania: Power Sector (2007)
Argentina: Santa Fe Road Infrastructure (2007)
Argentina: Special Structural Adjustment Loan (1999)

Argentina/Paraguay: Yacyretá Hydroelectric Project (1996)

Bangladesh: Jamuna Bridge (1996)

Bangladesh: Jute Sector (1996)

Brazil: Itaparica Resettlement and Irrigation (1997)

Brazil: Land Reform (1998)

Brazil: Paraná Biodiversity (2006)

Brazil: Rondônia Natural Resources Management (1995)

Cambodia: Forest Concession Management (2005)

Cambodia: Land Management and Administration (2009)

Cameroon: Petroleum Development and Pipeline (2002)

Chad: Petroleum Development (2001)

Chile: Quilleco Hydropower (2010)

China: Western Poverty Reduction (Qinghai) (1999)

Colombia: Cartagena Water & Environmental Management (2004)

Democratic Republic of Congo: Private Sector Development (2009)

Democratic Republic of Congo: Transitional Support (2005)

Ecuador: Mining Development (1999)

Ghana: Second Urban Environment Sanitation (2007)

Honduras: Land Administration (2006)

India: Coal Sector (2001)

India: Ecodevelopment (1998)

India: Madhya Pradesh Water Sector Restructuring (2010/2011)

India: Mumbai Urban Transport Project (2004)

India: NTPC Power (1997)

India: Uttaranchal Watershed Development (2007)

Kazakhstan: South-West Roads (2010)

Kazakhstan: South-West Roads (2011)

Kenya: Lake Victoria Environmental Management (1999)

Lebanon: Greater Beirut Water Supply (2010)

Lesotho/South Africa: Highlands Water (1998)

Liberia: Development Forestry (2010)

Mexico: Indigenous and Community Biodiversity Project (2003)

Nepal: Arun III (1994)

Nepal: Power Development Project (2013)

Nigeria: Lagos Drainage (1998)

Nigeria/Ghana: West African Gas Pipeline (2006)

Pakistan: National Drainage Program (2004)

Pakistan: Tax Administration Reform (2010)

Panama: Land Administration (2009)

Papua New Guinea: Governance Promotion (2001)
Papua New Guinea: Smallholder Agriculture (2009)
Paraguay/Argentina: Yacyretá Hydroelectric Project (2002)
Peru: Lima Urban Transport (2009)
South Africa: Eskom Investment Support (2010)
Tanzania: Emergency Power (1995)
Uganda: Power Projects (2001)
Uganda: Power Projects (2007)
Uzbekistan: Energy Loss Reduction (2010)

Index

A

Aarhus Convention
- Compliance Committee, 65, 154, 155

Accountability
- as interdisciplinary, multidimensional and interdependent concept, 31
- constituency groups,
  - external (stakeholder model), 77, 79, 87. *See also* Accountability, model
  - internal (shareholder model), 77, 87. *See also* Accountability, model
  - primacy of constituency, 82, 87
- deficit, 76, 79, 579
- definition of, 76
- dimensions of, 30
- for harm, 114
- for performance, 114
- holders, 29, 30, 81, 168
- mechanisms
  - independent accountability mechanism. *See* Independent accountability mechanism (IAM)
  - internal accountability mechanisms, World Bank, 168
- model
  - bottom-up, 77, 241-243
  - cosmopolitan, 167
  - horizontal, 77, 82, 241
  - internationalist, 80, 167
  - standard, 30
  - surrogate, 30, 31, 168
  - top-down, 75
  - vertical, 75, 81, 82, 241
- outcomes, 30
- realization, implementation of, 184, 262
- power wielders (dominant decision-makers), 29, 30, 36, 47, 75, 78, 81, 168, 207, 576, 578
- public, 26

Adler, E., 40

African Development Bank (AfDB)
- Independent Review Mechanism, 65

Albania
- Albanian Institute of Archaeology, 148
- Institute of Cultural Monuments, 148
- Integrated Coastal Zone Management Project, 175, 180-182, 223, 233, 245, 283, 357, 404, 545, 549
- Power Sector Project, 65, 148, 154, 308, 359, 364, 382, 392, 508, 512, 522
- Southern Coastal Development Plan (SCDP), 180, 283, 403, 404

Alvarez, J., 42, 139, 143, 153

Anthony, G., 24, 80

Argentina
- (Paraguay) Yacyretá Hydroelectric Project, 60, 123, 199, 272, 288, 300, 315, 349, 386, 416, 420, 422, 430, 432, 442, 532, 542, 549, 560, 563
- Entidad Binacional Yacyretá (EBY), 123, 271, 300, 386, 415, 419, 421, 422, 441, 442, 562
- Santa Fe Road Infrastructure Project, 73, 225, 305, 306, 363, 385, 533, 555

Asian Development Bank (ADB), 62-64, 139, 163

Ayensu, E., 242, 243